ORVILLE SCHELL and DAVID SHAMBAUGH

THE CHINA READER

The Reform Era

Orville Schell is Dean of the Graduate School of Journalism at the University of California, Berkeley, and a longtime observer of China. He has been a regular contributor to magazines such as *Harper's, Newsweek, The New Yorker,* and *The Atlantic Monthly* and has written eleven books on China, most recently *Mandate of Heaven: The Legacy of Tiananmen Square.* His forthcoming book is entitled *Virtual Tibet.*

David Shambaugh is Professor of Political Science and International Affairs at The George Washington University and nonresident Senior Fellow in the Foreign Policy Studies Program at the Brookings Foundation. He is the former editor of *The China Quarterly* and is an authority on Chinese strategic and military affairs, foreign relations, and domestic politics.

THE CHINA READER

The Reform Era

THE
CHINA
READER

The Reform Era

Edited and with an Introduction
by ORVILLE SCHELL
and DAVID SHAMBAUGH

VINTAGE BOOKS
A DIVISION OF RANDOM HOUSE, INC.
NEW YORK

FIRST VINTAGE BOOKS EDITION, JANUARY 1999

Copyright © 1999 by Orville Schell and David Shambaugh

Library of Congress Cataloging-in-Publication Data
The China reader : the reform era / edited by Orville Schell
and David Shambaugh.—First Vintage Books ed.
p.   cm.
Includes index.
ISBN 0-679-76387-2
1. China—History—1949–   2. China—History—1949–   —Sources.
I. Schell, Orville.   II. Shambaugh, David L.
DS777.55. C4477   1999
951.05'8—dc21   98-35842

Book design by Debbie Glasserman

www.randomhouse.com

Printed in the United States of America
10 9 8 7 6 5

Contents

Preface   xv

Introduction: xvii
Orville Schell and David Shambaugh,
Reforming China

POLITICS

I. Inner-Party Politics   3

From Mao to Deng   5

Michel Oksenberg and Richard Bush,
China's Political Evolution, 1972–1982   5

Communiqué of the Third Plenary Session
of the Eleventh Central Committee
of the Communist Party of China   21

Deng Xiaoping,
Answers to the Italian Journalist Oriana Fallaci   29

Resolution on Certain Questions in the History
of Our Party Since the Founding of the People's
Republic of China   37

Radical Reform   50

Zhao Ziyang,
   Advance Along the Road of Socialism
   with Chinese Characteristics   50

The Tiananmen Crisis   78

Chen Xitong,
   Report on Checking the Turmoil and Quelling
   the Counterrevolutionary Rebellion   79

Deng Xiaoping,
   Speech to Officers at the Corps Level and Above
   from the Martial Law Enforcement Troops in
   Beijing   95

Politics in the Nineties   103

Michael D. Swaine,
   China Faces the 1990s: A System in Crisis   103

Anonymous,
   The Ten-Thousand-Character Manifesto   116

China After Deng   136

Ellis Joffe,
   Ruling China After Deng   136

II. *Outer-Party Politics*   155

Democracy Wall   157

Orville Schell,
   The Democracy Wall Movement   157

Wei Jingsheng,
   Democracy: The Fifth Modernization   165

The Student Demonstrations of 1986–87   175

Fang Lizhi,
   Democracy, Reform, and Modernization   175

Deng Xiaoping,
Taking a Clear-Cut Stand Against
Bourgeois Liberalization   182

*The Tiananmen Square Demonstrations
and the Beijing Massacre*   186

Orville Schell,
China's Spring   186

1989 Wall Posters   197

A Hunger Strike Manifesto   199

Yang Jianli,
The Beijing Massacre   204

Ding Zilin,
Who They Were   207

EDUCATION, MEDIA, AND CULTURE

III. Education and Research   215

Deng Xiaoping,
Speech at the National Conference
on Education   215

Geremie Barmé,
A Small Matter of Truth   223

IV. Media   228

Allison Jernow,
The Press in the 1980s: Testing New Ground   229

Seth Faison,
The Press During the 1989 Demonstrations   236

Orville Schell,
The Second Channel   246

The Battle for Cyberspace   256

V. Culture   260

  √ *High Culture*   261

    √ Orville Schell,
        The Reemergence of the Realm of the Private   261

    √ Religion Must Serve the State   267

    ✗ Hong Ying,
        Summer of Betrayal   271

    Low Culture   280

    √ Orville Schell,
        Shake, Rattle, and Roll   280

    √ Sang Ye,
        Computer Insects   291

THE ECONOMY

VI. Building an Economic Superpower   299

    √ Barry Naughton,
        The Pattern and Logic of China's
        Economic Reform   300

    √ Hang-Sheng Cheng,
        A Midcourse Assessment of China's
        Economic Reform   311

    Anthony Y. C. Koo and K. C. Yeh,
        The Impact of Township, Village, and Private
        Enterprises' Growth on State Enterprises
        Reform: Three Regional Case Studies   321

    ✗ Frederick Crook,
        Grain Galore   335

SOCIETY

VII. The Social Consequences of Reform   347

  Rich and Poor   348

  Antoine Kernen,
    Out of Work in the State Sector   348

  Patrick Tyler,
    Rural Poverty   357

  The "Floating Population"   362

  Cheng Li,
    200 Million Mouths Too Many:
    China's Surplus Rural Labor   362

  People's Daily Commentator,
    Strengthening Management over the
    Floating Population   373

  The Environment   376

  Mark Hertsgaard,
    Our Real China Problem   376

  The World Bank,
    China's Environment in the New Century   389

  Crime   394

  Angelina Malhotra,
    Shanghai's Dark Side   394

  Patrick Tyler,
    Crime (and Punishment) Rages Anew in China   401

VIII. The Rule of Law, Rights, and Prisons   406

  Andrew Nathan,
    Getting Human Rights Right   407

Yi Ding,
Opposing Interference in Other Countries'
Internal Affairs Through Human Rights   415

Xu Liangying,
Chinese Officialdom's Miraculous and
Unique Conception of Human Rights   419

Wang Yu, Liu Gang: Stalwart Resistance   422

SECURITY AND FOREIGN RELATIONS

IX. The Military   431

David Shambaugh,
China's Military: Real or Paper Tiger?   432

X. China and the World   448

Samuel S. Kim,
China As a Great Power   448

Liu Huaqiu,
Strive for a Peaceful International Environment   459

David Shambaugh,
The United States and China:
Cooperation or Confrontation?   470

William Jefferson Clinton,
China and the National Interest   479

XI. Greater China   488

The Dalai Lama on China, Hatred,
and Optimism   489

The Joint Declaration of the Government
of the United Kingdom and the
Government of the People's Republic of
China on the Question of Hong Kong   493

Jiang Zemin,
Continue to Promote the Reunification of China   496

WHITHER CHINA?

XII. China Faces the Twenty-first Century 505

  Michel C. Oksenberg, Michael D. Swaine,
  and Daniel C. Lynch,
  The Chinese Future 505

Conclusion: The Legacy of Reform 531

Index 537

Preface

This new edition of *The China Reader* tracks the extensive impact of the reforms that have swept China during the quarter century from 1972 to 1997. Through the compilation of carefully selected documents, articles, offerings from the media, and other representational forms (such as wall posters), we have attempted to cast a wide net in our selections. While we have tried to be representative, we cannot claim to be comprehensive. Because of space limitations and the large volume of pertinent data, important issues have necessarily received short shrift and some phenomena have been omitted altogether. Moreover, many scholarly selections have been edited down from their first publication—and we thus both apologize to the authors and encourage interested readers to refer to the original sources. Nonetheless, the editors have endeavored to collapse twenty-five complex years of contemporary Chinese history into this single volume. This is a longer time span than either of the previous two volumes covering the period of the People's Republic in *The China Reader* series. But no doubt, in retrospect, it will seem but a small part of the continuum of China's modern development.

Orville Schell
Berkeley, California

David Shambaugh
Washington, D.C.

Introduction

Reforming China

No nation in modern history has undergone as total a transformation as has China during the quarter century, from 1972 to 1997, that followed its Maoist revolution. The economy has erupted in unprecedented growth, the polity has pluralized from its former unitary state, and society has spawned much great complexity. Anyone who has visited China annually during this period, as have the editors, cannot but be amazed by the depth and breadth of change unleashed by Deng Xiaoping's reforms. The physical landscape of both cities and countryside has transformed—tall buildings dot the skyline and automobiles have supplanted bicycles on city streets while in rural areas peasants herded into collectives have become farmers of private land, many of whom dwell in comfortable three-story homes. Hundreds of millions of Chinese have experienced dramatic improvements in their standard of living. Dress and personal habits have changed as Chinese seek personal fulfillment (often manifesting itself in crass commercialism, hedonism, and corruption) instead of the socialist collective good of yesteryear.

There are many ways to measure China's social progress and movement toward a market economy. Some selected statistics shall suffice. In 1978 the state sector accounted for more than 90 percent of the economy—by 1997 it was half as much and falling. Concomitantly, the state employed more than 90 percent of the workforce in 1978—by 1997 the figure stood at only 18 percent. Tellingly, those employed in the service sector have risen from less than 5 to nearly 30 percent of the workforce. In 1978 China absorbed no foreign direct investment to speak of—in 1997 it absorbed more than any nation in the world other than the United States ($42 billion in actualized terms). In 1978 China received minimal aid from abroad and had no foreign debt—by 1997 China was the largest borrower from the World Bank and owed approximately $130 billion in foreign debt (most of it long-term). China's foreign exchange reserves climbed from approximately $12 billion to over $140 billion during the same period! Per capita income *quadrupled* between 1978 and 1995![1] Growth in gross domestic product (GDP) *averaged* a world-leading 11.2 percent from 1986 to 1997, while exports grew at an annual rate of approximately 13.5 percent (accounting now for almost 25 percent of GDP).

A variety of quality of life indicators are also telling: daily per capita caloric intake has increased (2600 grams), as has average living floor space (15.5 meters) and life expectancy (70), while infant mortality has declined to 30 per 1,000 births.[2] Access to all levels of education has increased (even if absolute enrollments have declined). Health-care provision has improved in both quality and quantity (although it is still far better for urban than for rural dwellers).

One of the most important aspects of the reforms is that average Chinese are now connected to one another and the modern world in a way that closed and autarkic Maoist China never permitted. As President Clinton noted in 1997 in "China and the National Interest,"

> Today more than a billion Chinese have access to television, up from just 10 million two decades ago. Satellite dishes dot the landscape. They receive dozens of outside channels. . . . Talk radio is increasingly popular and relatively unregulated in China's 1,000 radio stations. . . . China's 2,200 newspapers, up from just 42 three decades ago, and more than 7,000 magazines and journals are open in content. A decade ago [in 1987] there were 50,000 mobile phones in China; now there are more than 7 million. The Internet already has 150,000 accounts in China, with more than a million expected to be on-line by the year 2000.

Economic development has brought many benefits, but it has also bred problems. As China has developed, social expectations and disloca-

---

[1]Whereas it took China only nine years to double its national per capita income, it took the United States forty-seven years.
[2]World Bank, *World Development Report 1996* (Washington, D.C.: World Bank, 1996).

tions have risen. The majority have benefited from the reforms, but many have fallen behind. China's unemployed and downtrodden have increased substantially. In 1995 some 65 million people (7 percent of the population) were still "absolutely poor," according to World Bank definitions. Crime and corruption have spread across the country like cancers. Intellectuals, who have known a long history of repression under Chinese Communist rule, enjoy greater creative freedoms but still ply their professions under tight political restrictions. Human rights of various kinds—civil, political, gender, religious, ethnic, associational—all remain among the most restricted and repressed in the world.

Development has brought industrial growth but, with it, severe pollution and environmental degradation. More than 180,000 deaths per year are now attributable to urban air pollution—a figure due to rise to as many as 600,000 by 2020, given the current rates of increase in particulate matter and sulfur dioxide emissions.[3] Cancer and tuberculosis rates are very high by global standards.[4] Pollution is not limited to the air. A severely contaminated water table affects both drinking water and irrigation supplies. In 1993 about 8 percent of agricultural lands received water so polluted that it was unfit for use—leading to an estimated loss of 1 million tons in grain production.[5] Acid rain is a further detriment to Chinese society's health, as well as that of China's neighbors in Korea and Japan. These pollutants also exact a high economic cost. The World Bank estimates that the effects of air and water pollution cost China between 3 and 8 percent in GDP growth per annum.[6]

Thus China's reforms have brought both benefits and problems to society and the state alike. Occasionally they have caused the two to clash—most notably in the Tiananmen demonstrations of 1989. As Deng Xiaoping himself observed following the military massacre of civilians, "Dictated by both the international climate and domestic climate in China, [this disturbance] was destined to come, and the outbreak of this disturbance is independent of man's will. It was just a question of happening sooner or later, and of how serious the aftermath would be" (see his "Speech to Officers . . . from the Martial Law Enforcement Troops in Beijing").

[3]World Bank, *China 2020: Development Challenges in the New Country* (Washington, D.C.: World Bank, 1997), p. 74.
[4]Nor has China been immune to HIV/AIDS or other infectious diseases. Hepatitis, malaria, cholera, typhoid fever, encephalitis B, and dysentery have yet to be eradicated.
[5]World Bank, *China 2020*, p. 74.
[6]Ibid., p. 71.

It is precisely the paradox of reform—development on the one hand and the Communist Party's attempts to maintain its hegemonic grip on political power on the other characterizing China today—that is the contradictory theme we seek to highlight in this volume. Deng Xiaoping and the CCP *had* to reform in order to stay in power following Chairman Mao's death in 1976, but a quarter century later the dilemma is whether continued reforms will be able to keep them in power or whether the consequences of those reforms will result in the Party's collective downfall. The irony may be that, like those of the Soviet reformer Mikhail Gorbachev, Deng's reforms were necessary to save the system but unleashed forces that undermined the system at the same time. Either way China's society, economy, polity, and role in the world are evolving in unprecedented and unpredictable directions.

There is little doubt that the reforms have spawned centrifugal forces that have substantially eroded the former totalistic power of the CCP and Beijing's control of the far-flung regions of the country. In the process the Party-state and central government have had to renegotiate their respective relationships to society and localities. This is a slippery slope that has led many an authoritarian regime (socialist ones included) to collapse, as they are unable to satiate the citizenry's ever-expanding desires for material well-being, civil society, accountability of government, personal freedoms, and local autonomy. Some of these regimes (e.g., South Korea, Taiwan, Thailand, Brazil, Argentina) have been able to ride the tide of change and remain in power through state-led democratization. Whether the CCP can stay ahead of, and on top of, the revolution of rising expectations, while incrementally democratizing from above, remains an open question.[7] These are issues that, no doubt, the next edition of *The China Reader* will assess.

---

[7]Among the ever-growing "authoritarian transition" literature, see particularly Bruce J. Dickson, *Democratization in China and Taiwan: The Adaptability of Leninist Parties* (Oxford: Clarendon Press, 1997).

POLITICS

I. INNER-PARTY POLITICS

The reform era under Deng Xiaoping and his successors brought a new measure of stability and normalcy to China's leadership politics. The Hobbesian world of elite inner-Party struggle under Mao was replaced by new norms and regulations to govern high-level politics. To be certain, during his lifetime Deng remained the Communist Party patriarch—presiding as a neoemperor over inner-court politics, the institutions of state, and the armed forces. Deng's dictates carried an authoritativeness that his subordinates lacked, yet he was not a dictator. Because of continuing factionalism and a complex bureaucratic environment, Deng had to navigate among competing political and ideological interests—some quarters seeking to accelerate radical reforms, others to limit them. Consequently, inner-Party politics during the reform era displayed a distinct seesaw effect of expansion and contraction—Chinese describe it as the *fang-shou* (expand-contract) cycle—which involved tightening up politically at one moment while loosening up at another.

These cycles were evident from the time Deng returned to power in 1977 until the momentous events of the Beijing Spring of 1989. After the Tiananmen crackdown, the leadership united in the face of the greatest challenge it had faced since the Cultural Revolution. The regime was faced with challenges to its authority not only at home but also abroad. The collapse of Communist regimes across Eastern Europe, Mongolia, and in the Soviet Union paralyzed Chinese leaders. Through a combination of internal repression and economic expansion, the Chinese Communist Party and government were able to weather these challenges, remain in power, and prove wrong the doomsayers who had predicted they would join their erstwhile comrades on the Marxist-Leninist dustbin of history. Yet one imponderable still loomed large: What would happen after Deng Xiaoping died?

The selections in this chapter were chosen to reflect these themes and to reveal five subperiods that punctuate the past quarter century of Chinese politics: the transition from Mao to Deng; the zenith of radical reform under Zhao Ziyang; the Tiananmen crisis; challenges of the early 1990s; and the death of Deng Xiaoping and the immediate post-Deng era.

★ F R O M   M A O   T O   D E N G ★

During the transition from Mao to Deng, China's political system underwent substantial change. No institution or Maoist practice went untouched. While analysts commonly observe that only the economic sphere was reformed under Deng, with the political system remaining largely unchanged, this was not completely the case. Deng clearly saw that Maoist politics had retarded economic growth and social change, and he personally spearheaded efforts to reform the political structure to make it more rational and efficient. This was no small undertaking, as the Communist Party, state structure, and armed forces had all been decimated by the ten-year Cultural Revolution. Like Deng, untold thousands of leaders and cadres had been purged and condemned to hard labor. Some, such as former President Liu Shaoqi, had been killed. Others took their own lives. Still others perished in the bizarre 1971 attempted coup d'état led by Defense Minister Lin Biao.

In such an environment, Deng Xiaoping and his colleagues had their work cut out for them. Not only did they have to resurrect the institutions and personnel of the Party, state, and army but they were also faced with a profoundly alienated and lethargic populace numbed from three decades of unrelenting Maoist political campaigns, persecutions, and catastrophes that had cost tens of millions of lives.

The selections in this section document the scope and pervasiveness of the political challenges that Deng and his colleagues faced when they returned to power in the late 1970s.

MICHEL OKSENBERG AND RICHARD BUSH, CHINA'S POLITICAL EVOLUTION, 1972–1982

This selection examines the Maoist political system at its nadir and reveals it as a decayed totalitarian state. The authors sketch the evolution of the political system — and the country — during the decade 1972–1982, a period of intense political factionalism marked by struggles between "radicals" associated with the "Gang of Four" and "moderates" associated with Deng Xiaoping. They show how Deng and his associates altered the nature of Chinese politics in a relatively short time, setting the stage for further reforms during the 1980s.

This selection was excerpted from an article published in Problems of Communism, *September–October 1982.*

In the past decade, but especially since Mao Zedong's death in 1976, the Chinese political system has experienced a spectacular sequence of events: the arrest of Mao's wife, Jiang Qing, and her associates in the "Gang of Four" one month after his death; the return to political power of Deng Xiaoping in mid-1977, a reversal of fate after his removal but fifteen months earlier; the proclamation by Premier and Party Chairman Hua Guofeng in early 1978 of the ambitious goal of transforming China into a modern state by the year 2000; the quiet abandonment of these unrealistic targets ten months later, although the leaders still remained committed to rapid economic growth and openness to the outside world; the normalization of relations with the United States in late 1978; the incursion into Vietnam in late February 1979; the political experimentation epitomized by the "Democracy Wall" movement in the spring of 1979; the sharpening tension between Hua Guofeng and Deng Xiaoping; the erosion of Hua's position as well as the purge of Politburo members who had advanced during the Cultural Revolution; the proclamation of sharp economic retrenchment and the postponement of several multimillion-dollar import purchases in December 1980; the major reassessment of Mao Zedong in June 1981, which enumerated his many policy errors while reaffirming the essential wisdom of his beliefs; the replacement of Hua as party chairman by Hu Yaobang and as premier by Zhao Ziyang in 1980–81, thereby marking Hu and Zhao as Deng's chosen successors; a major shake-up of personnel in the party and state structure in early 1982; and finally, the Twelfth Congress of the Chinese Communist Party, in September 1982, which consolidated the gains of the previous three years in establishing a more durable political order.

Quieter developments have also occurred. Seven deserve to be specially emphasized:

• The strategy of economic development was changed. The leaders have cut the rate of capital accumulation sharply and allowed the nation's wage bill to increase. Furthermore, they have sought to alter the balance among heavy industry, light industry, and agriculture, moving away from the Stalinist emphasis upon heavy industry toward light industry. Within agriculture, cropping patterns have been changed to boost production of crops used in light industry.

• The methods of organizing agricultural production have undergone sweeping change. The incomes of peasant households in many regions are now based on the crops raised on specific plots of land assigned to the households. The institutions which directed peasant activity (commune, production brigade, and production team) have had their powers significantly curtailed. Changes of equal magnitude are being attempted in industrial management, although the obstacles in this area may be greater.

• The country has been opened to foreign commerce and foreign influence. Special economic zones now exist as a means of encouraging investment in China, and foreign firms enjoy special privileges. Foreign books in translation, classical and popular music, films, and clothing styles—all controlled and in limited scope to be sure—are now available.

• Class labels and other terms of opprobrium (e.g., "landlord," "reactionary," "rightist") are being removed from several million Chinese. The government has promised to restore these people to their previous positions and, in some cases, has offered restitution for the damages they suffered.

• A major corpus of laws and regulations has been enacted which offers some promise of making life for Chinese more just and predictable. This includes criminal, civil, marriage, and tax laws.

• The government has vigorously encouraged family planning. Major programs have been enacted to achieve the goal of the one-child family.

• A growing energy problem has arisen due to a leveling off in coal and petroleum production. Energy shortages now constitute a major brake on rapid industrial expansion.

Without denigrating the importance of these developments, this essay eschews a focus on either the factional power struggles or the specific economic and legal reforms. Instead, we wish to step back and to ask questions about the decade 1972–1982, from the eve of Mao's decline to the arrangement of an initial succession after Deng. How does the Chinese political system today differ from that of a decade ago? What remains the same? More important, why the changes? Has the system reached an equilibrium point? Are aspects of the Maoist system that have been abandoned likely to be restored? Is the political evolution of the past ten years likely to continue?

Our core argument can be summarized succinctly. During the decade under scrutiny, China passed a watershed. In 1972, totalitarian revolutionaries ruled the nation; by 1982, China's rulers had become authoritarian reformers. The totalitarian revolutionaries had acted upon their belief that rapid, violent, and comprehensive transformation of elites and institutions was the most effective mode of change. The leaders had unleashed upon society and themselves a reign of terror. They had constructed a totalitarian regime which sought to deny privacy or cultivation of individuality in society. They expected all citizens, especially those in urban areas, to express their belief in the integrating ideology of the regime, to participate in political life, and to surrender their individuality to a collective identity.

By contrast, in 1982, the top Chinese leadership appears to be committed to gradual and peaceful change within a framework of continuity of elites and institutions. The leaders have shifted their emphasis in implementing policy from mobilization of the populace to action through the bureaucracy. They have also sought to end the terror. While seeking orthodoxy to which all intellectuals and creative artists are expected to adhere, the authoritarians do permit individual silence and a limited withdrawal or distancing from politics. Also, orthodoxy is less well defined and broader in scope.

Being authoritarian, to be sure, China's leaders today maintain extensive surveillance over the population and tolerate no organized opposition or challenges to their rule. They value hierarchy and discipline and are not hesitant to employ force in ordering their realm. Yet, individuals may cultivate personal pursuits and are encouraged to plan their careers. The current leaders no longer measure their own performance by their progress in nurturing a new "socialist man" or in creating a classless society. Instead, they wish their performance to be judged by their ability to improve the material well-being of the populace.

This evolution can be attributed to several interrelated factors. The passing of Mao and the advent of a leadership group who had suffered during the Cultural Revolution is a key factor. More than personnel changes at the top are involved, however. The developments in China bear a great resemblance to trends in other societies after sustained periods of terror and politically induced social change. The case of the post-Stalin Soviet Union and the Khrushchev era comes immediately to mind. Yet societies can manifest different types of Thermidor, and

China's post-Mao moderation reveals the reassertion of certain deeply rooted traditions which the Maoist system had challenged. China's evolution since Mao's death represents the continued adaptation of Communist revolution to the Chinese cultural context.

We note that the process of domesticization has not yet ended. In some respects, the present reforms are not fully congruent with some aspects of the cultural heritage. Furthermore, certain bureaucracies of the Maoist era remain strong and resistant to change, while power is still vested as much in people as in institutions. Finally, China is undergoing massive economic changes, and the exposure to the outside world will also have its impact. For all these reasons, we conclude that the Chinese political system has yet to reach an equilibrium, and further evolution can be anticipated.

The Maoist System Before Its Decay

To understand and trace the changes that have occurred since Mao's death requires a review of the Maoist system. That system, of course, underwent continual change. Therefore, we portray the Maoist order in 1970–1972, the time of Mao's last effective political acts—the elimination of Lin Biao and the opening to the United States. Thereafter, the Chairman was unable to mobilize his resources and impose his will upon the nation in a sustained manner.

In the aftermath of the traumatic Lin Biao affair, the entire population was being told that Mao's designated heir had plotted to assassinate the Chairman. This sordid event and the near anarchy of the Cultural Revolution struggle had seriously eroded the confidence of the populace in the system and its rulers. To the extent that the system retained its ability to elicit compliance from the populace, it was vulnerable to the capricious intervention of one man, Mao Zedong, acting on his idiosyncratic impulses. Indeed, Mao had shaped the system so that it would be responsive to him. To be sure, Mao's power was not totally unconstrained; he had to cajole, threaten, and bargain to attain his ends. On occasion, he was on the defensive and had to acquiesce to the initiatives of others. Still, his was the dominant voice, and opposition to him carried the risk of political oblivion or worse. If the concept of tyrant has any validity, it applied to Mao.

Power was vested more in people than in institutions. Competing factional groupings, some in power, others on the sidelines, and yet others under arrest, sought access to Mao and, if they obtained it, sought to control and manipulate him. Factions struggled to achieve dominance over the four major bureaucratic clusters into which power is organized in China: the personnel system; the apparatus governing allocation of material goods, energy, and capital; the propaganda network; and the coercive apparatus of the military and the public security forces. In Beijing, different factional groupings had bases of power in different organizational hierarchies. Jiang Qing and her associates relied on the propaganda apparatus and a portion of the military (e.g., the Thirty-seventh Army). The emerging cluster of Hua Guofeng, Wang Dong-xing, and Ji Dengkui seems to have had particular strength in the public security forces. Zhou Enlai and the sidelined Deng Xiaoping had supporters in the economic apparatus, among the scientific establishment, and in the organizational apparatus for the administration of personnel. Chen Yun, Bo Yibo, and many others then under arrest had latent but powerful ties within the economic and organizational apparatuses.

Chains or networks of personnel linked leaders in Beijing to provincial, county, and even the primary units (*danwei*) to which each individual in China belongs. Factions in Beijing did not have equally strong links to all parts of the country. Some factions had more intimate connections with certain cities, provinces, and lower levels, while other factions had their strength in different regions. Clearly, Jiang Qing had nourished a strong cluster of support within the Shanghai municipal apparatus and apparently was seeking to root her supporters in Baoding, Zhengzhou, Hangzhou, and Shenyang as well. Hua Guofeng and his associates apparently had strong links with the Hunan, Shanxi, and Hebei provincial party apparatuses. Deng Xiaoping continued to have latent strength in the southwest.

The cement holding these networks together was *guanxi*, a Chinese concept meaning a relationship or interconnection. A sense of loyalty, mutual obligation, and shared vulnerability—given the atmosphere of the times—bound clusters of people together. A high-level official in Beijing was, in effect, the patron or family head of many clients, who in turn were patrons of lower-level clients. This general picture, of course, is overly simplistic. Loyalties at any one moment could be felt toward more than one patron or toward competing clients. An official could move from one network to another. Perhaps it is more accurate, therefore, to speak of shifting constellations of officials in the capital, the provinces, and the lower levels, linked informally through *guanxi* and formally through bureaucratic ties.

Domestic policy choices were not based upon a careful analysis of the alternatives. Factions in Beijing offered documentation on behalf of their preferences from "investigation research" they themselves had sponsored in model units preselected to implement successfully the faction's preferred policy alternative. In addition, reliable statistics on most social and many economic matters were simply not available.

Bureaucracies in the capital and the provinces had been engulfed in relentless campaigns. Few agencies remained untouched not only by the initial terror imposed by marauding Red Guards in 1966–1969 but also by such subsequent campaigns as "Struggle, Criticism, and Transformation" and "One Hit, Three Anti's." A significant portion of cadres in most agencies were undergoing ideological reschooling in May 7 cadre schools. Another portion, while still listed on the table of organization, were living in humiliating circumstances, forced to reside in "cow sheds" and assigned to menial tasks. The latter fate struck the former leaders of units who had been identified as "capitalist roaders" during the Cultural Revolution. Thus, by 1972, most national agencies responsible for identifying issues demanding decision by the leaders, for shaping the choices for the leaders, and for implementing decisions found themselves in varying degrees of chaos and paralysis. The typical unit in the party or government consisted of people who had survived the Cultural Revolution and its aftermath together. Memories of injustices and lost battles were stored away, to be acted upon when the opportunity presented itself. Personal animosities had accumulated, and the malcontents frequently remained in their units since they were unable to transfer elsewhere. Tensions within units were high, and the level of trust among their officials tended to be low. The ability to explore ideas and share information without fear was limited to one's most intimate and reliable friends. Even so, if one's ideas were suspect, one could endanger one's friends. In short, rather than breeding cohesiveness, the external pressures had pulverized bureaucratic units into warring factions and isolated, cautious individuals. Factions within each unit were linked to different external networks of personal ties. . . .

The system of 1972 was not totally irrational, nor was it meant just to suit the power needs of Mao or his factional backers. China's current leaders have wished to convey an image of irrationality partly because this is the perception they have of what they seized and inherited, and partly because—like good politicians anywhere—by darkening the past they enhance their own achievements.

As its principal architect, Mao had designed a system that supported not only his power needs but also his larger goals for China in the late

1960s and his strategy for attaining those goals. Put in its best light, the policy process which Mao shaped through 1972, when for the last time it escaped his control, had this rationale. It was meant to downplay economic interdependence among regions, the national use of material rewards, and the regular, formal promotion system as the best means of preserving China's unity. Instead, Mao relied on coercion and the propagation of a single ideology as his principal instruments for integrating his heterogeneous nation. To be sure, the central economic agencies retained a role in redistributing resources from the more developed to the less developed regions of the country, a process which may have reduced interprovince tensions and promoted unity. Nonetheless, in terms of allocating power among the organizational hierarchies in China, Mao assigned primacy in integrating the society to the propaganda apparatus, the public security forces, and the military. With Mao's proxy, those who presided over these hierarchies wielded great power. . . .

But from the early 1960s until the end of his life, Mao considered the attitudes of Chinese bureaucrats and the populace generally to be the major impediment to China's modernization. Hence he launched a *cultural* revolution. Mao had concluded that a new culture would emerge only through the deliberate fostering of class struggle, pitting portions of the populace against his own bureaucracy. By the mid-1960s, Mao had also decided that many of his associates and their subordinates were beyond salvation and were unworthy of succeeding him. Not only a cultural revolution but a massive purge of the unredeemable was necessary in his view to keep China on his path to modernity.

Similarly, Mao came to view the organizational web of party, government, and armed forces as an inherently conservative repository of the values he was seeking to eradicate. Distrustful of bureaucracy, he sought ways of administration which minimized its role. Hence, his attraction to campaigns (*yundong*) as an alternative mechanism of policy implementation. With the encouragement of his more radical supporters, especially Zhang Chunqiao, Mao deliberately promoted a primitive economy. His demand for maximum local self-sufficiency, the restrictions on the number of commodities that could be traded on the regulated free market, and his simultaneous curtailment of the capacity of planning agencies to allocate goods according to plan—all sought to minimize commerce and the division of labor in society. To bring about such an unstratified social and economic structure, Mao realized, would require enormous change. Thus, instead of the incremental, inherently cautious, fragmented decision making which a bureaucratic policy process tends to yield, Mao sought sweeping, bold, utopian policies that a mobilization system is more likely to engender.

Mao sought a system in perpetual change. According to his dialectic and idealist vision of history, thesis could be turned into antithesis, which in turn would become synthesis. What appeared irreconcilable today could be reconciled tomorrow. To name Mao's three favorite polarities—discipline and freedom, centralism and democracy, a general will and the individual spirit—they were viewed by him as equally desirable but contradictory qualities at this stage in history. However, Mao thought that wise leaders could drive their society forward, raising the material standard of living and altering the consciousness of the populace. Ultimately, the polarities could be reconciled in a classless, abundant society, provided that the greatest threat to the attainment of this vision—the calcification of the social structure—was overcome.

This brings us to the core of Mao and the policy process he structured. As noted earlier, he was to the end of his life a revolutionary and a totalitarian ruler. He believed that the only way to transform China was rapidly, violently, comprehensively; its elites and institutions would have to be subjected to continual change. China's problems were so vast that efforts to attain peaceful, gradual change could not be sustained and would eventually be lost in the morass of bureaucracy. In his view, to transform China required vision and extraordinary confidence that a politically involved Chinese populace—given no respite to cultivate individual pursuits—could overcome its plight of poverty and weakness. To unleash portions of the populace in all their fury required leaders capable of interacting directly with the forces in society without mediation by intervening bureaucracies. Mao saw little intrinsic value in institutions like the party, government, or army. They were to serve as instruments whose credibility and authority could be expended in his larger effort to transform China into a strong, prosperous, socialist nation.

Evolution of the System, 1972–1982

Since early 1972, the Chinese system has evolved through several stages: (1) a concerted effort to restore order and to rebuild institutions based on an amalgam of pre-1966 and Cultural Revolution values, a period lasting until late 1973; (2) an unbridled struggle for political survival and succession to Mao, from late 1973 to October 1976, when the "Gang of

Four" were arrested; (3) a period of uncertainty lasting until mid-1978, with some of the leaders seeking to establish a neo-Maoist system; (4) introduction of broad institutional reforms and a moderation and rationalization of economic goals, a stage that began with the emergence of Deng Xiaoping as the dominant political leader in mid-1978; (5) from late 1980 to mid-1982, the appearance of resistance to reforms and the resultant efforts by Deng and his associates to weaken and remove the points of resistance.

September 1971–August 1973. Mao sought to preserve his rule and surmount the Lin Biao affair by incorporating the two principal factional groupings—led by Zhou Enlai and Jiang Qing respectively—that had supported him in the attack on Lin. Mao turned to Zhou to create order out of the economic chaos, but he gave preeminence to the "radicals" in the cultural domain to preserve his ideological gains of the previous five years. As the military's role in civilian institutions declined, the rebuilding of the state and party apparatuses began, and a number of supposedly chastened "capitalist roaders" returned to help staff them (the most prominent returnee was Deng Xiaoping, who first reappeared in public in April 1973). They began to work with officials who had come to the fore during the Cultural Revolution.

This modus vivendi in personnel was accompanied by an attempt in a range of policy areas to introduce more pragmatic methods while retaining Cultural Revolution values. In industry, for example, limited material incentives were introduced, although mobilization continued to be used to stimulate output. In the educational sphere, examinations were reintroduced to judge the academic competence of students, even though ideological considerations remained important in the admissions process. In design, the policy process remained Mao-centered; in fact, the physically declining Chairman was unable to achieve the coherence he sought or to control the conflict he had built into the system.

September 1973–October 1976. In the wake of the Tenth CCP Congress in August 1973, struggle between the Zhou-Deng and Jiang factions intensified, each side trying to secure advantage for the day that Mao died. (The military and public security factions maneuvered on the sidelines.) Each faction offered competing programs for China's development. Each tried to put through its policy in various sectors. And each seemed to enjoy moments of political ascendancy: the Jiang forces during the first half of 1974 (the "Criticize Confucius—Criticize Lin Biao" campaign); the Deng forces from late 1974 to late 1975 (under the slogan of the "four modernizations"); and the radicals again from late 1975 until Mao's death in September 1976 (a period in which the more pragmatic policies were again set aside). The three years of unabated conflict left behind a weak and largely ineffective political system that had come to rely very heavily on coercion.

October 1976–October 1978. After the euphoria that ensued from the arrest of the "Gang of Four" had somewhat abated, a long list of neglected economic problems came to attention. It became clear that, without major changes in the policy process, the nation would meet with disaster. The disparate groups that had combined to oust the radicals attempted to work together (as had been the case after the Lin Biao affair). Neo-Maoists, led by Hua Guofeng, and the pragmatists who supported the newly rehabilitated Deng Xiaoping could agree on the priority of economic growth and the need for some ideological liberalization in the fields of science, education, and culture. Material incentives and the purchase of foreign technology were again deemed acceptable. A mere eighteen months after Mao's death, this leadership presented an ambitious program in pursuit of the "four modernizations" (in agriculture, industry, national defense, and science and technology).

However, the coalition was inherently unstable. The neo-Maoists were willing to accept modernization, especially when described as "a new leap forward." But they were less prepared to accept dilution of Maoist values or methods of rule. With Hua Guofeng as their principal spokesman, the neo-Maoists essentially advocated continuing the mobilization process, sustaining class struggle, propagating Mao's ideology, and implementing policy through campaigns. The pragmatist camp believed that Maoist values and Mao's style of rule were at the root of China's problems. They also judged that nothing less than an open attack on Mao was necessary to regain popular support. Also, some of Deng's followers came to question whether the leadership had the resources, institutional capacity, and popular support to pursue a policy of forced-draft industrialization. After some fencing over these issues during the spring and summer of 1978, the leadership dispute came to a head in December at the Third Plenum of the CCP Central Committee. In the streets of Beijing, an increasingly bold public began writing posters which attacked the Cultural Revolution and Mao.

November 1978–November 1980. Both in China and abroad, the Third Plenum is now regarded as the crucial watershed of the post-Mao era. It was at that session (and the central work conference preceding it) that Deng Xiaoping unquestionably gained the upper hand in China's leadership. His colleagues living (Chen Yun and Peng Zhen, for example) and dead (Peng Dehuai, Tao Zhu) were rehabilitated. The case of Liu Shaoqi was reopened, and he was rehabilitated in February 1980. The neo-Maoists came under attack, historical verdicts on such issues as the Tiananmen Incident were reversed, and an evaluation of Mao was promised.

Equally important were the new directions charted for the country's institutional life. In law, politics, and economics, liberalization would, it was predicted, have a positive, energizing effect and engender popular support for the regime. In this spirit, the Third Plenum promised that "socialist modernization" was China's long-term priority, and that mass political campaigns and all that came with them were no longer appropriate. In order to promote "socialist legality" and limit police abuses, the criminal justice system was reformed, and economic laws were drafted. To promote "socialist democracy," direct popular vote was mandated for the election of delegates to county-level people's congresses, and plans to end the rubber-stamp nature of the National People's Congress were circulated. Life tenure in office, perceived to be the root of many of the problems of the late-Mao era, came under attack. Even the closing of the Democracy Wall and the later ban on wall posters constrained but did not reverse this democratizing trend.

In addition, a major shift in economic policy became apparent especially after Chen Yun, an economic specialist and a top party official in the 1940s, joined the Politburo Standing Committee in December 1978. This "readjustment" entailed the abandonment of the investment policy stressing high rates of accumulation and development of heavy industry. It also entailed a "restructuring" in the Soviet-style system of central control, in the direction of allowing greater play of market mechanisms.

December 1980–Spring 1982. By late 1982 the institutional reforms and related policies had achieved success in some areas (for example, boosting agricultural production and peasant income) but fostered difficulties on other fronts (for example, generating inflation and a large government deficit). These economic difficulties prompted the declaration of a policy of economic retrenchment in 1980. Perhaps equally unsettling for the leadership, however, were the political and ideological repercussions of reforms. In 1979 elements of the public began to question the necessity for one-party rule and the socialist system itself, while in 1980 the leadership began to perceive a disruptive Western impact upon Chinese thought and behavior.

Indeed, Deng Xiaoping and Chen Yun themselves concluded that reform of institutions without a workable national consensus on ideology would not succeed. The issue was widely discussed during 1981, in the context of an evaluation of the filmscript "Unrequited Love," written by Bai Hua, who worked in the military's large cultural establishment. The film's sympathetic portrayal of a Chinese intellectual victimized during the Maoist era epitomized for the more orthodox party officials the damaging effects of cultural freedom. The leadership tried to disarm the critics with a rebuke of Bai Hua and a general attack on "bourgeois liberalism." In this context, the official verdict on Mao, adopted at the Sixth Plenum in June 1981, was less condemnatory than it might otherwise have been. In the absence of a clear-cut ideological alternative to Mao's thought, the Deng regime had to soft-pedal its criticism of Mao the man in order to be able to espouse elements of his thought.

Writers and artists were not the only group affected by the new stress on values and ideology. Focusing on poor preparation of the party cadres, Chen Yun termed the problem of Party work style a "life-and-death matter," and a drive against economic crimes by officials began in early 1982. Young people were told more and more frequently that a "spiritual civilization" must accompany material progress. Fearing "the corrosive influence of capitalist ideas," the regime tightened restrictions on contacts between Chinese and foreigners.

In short, the parameters of institutional reform were more clearly etched. The Chinese system would remain highly centralized and authoritarian. The Communist Party would retain its monopoly of power and be revitalized in order to perform well its distinctive role. The instruments of totalitarian rule—the public security forces and the propaganda apparatus—would be curbed but not dismantled. The economy would remain largely under state plan; the role of the market would be secondary. Within these constraints, the Maoist system would be significantly altered.

Table 1. Evolution of the Chinese Political System, 1972-1982

Attribute of the System	In 1972	In 1982
Method of change preferred by leader(s)	Revolution	Reform
How leader(s) view process of change	Dialectical	Linear
Preferred method of policy implementation	Mobilization of populace; class struggle	Rule by bureaucracy; regularity
Intrusiveness of state	Total	Pursuit of some private interests and withdrawal tolerated
Main tasks of governance	Restoration of order; attitudinal change; elimination of lingering bourgeois influences	Raising economic production and living standards
Mechanisms for integrating the policy	Networks of personal relations; coercion; ideology	Networks of personal relations; regularized personnel system; planned allocation of material goods and capital; coercion
Techniques for controlling "bureaucratism"	Campaigns	Experimentation with numerous techniques, none successful
Extent of "institutionalization"	Low; rule of men rather than institutions	Low; major efforts under way to rebuild institutions
Nature of politics at top level	Unbridled factionalism below top leader	Struggle among factions and opinion groups governed by unwritten rules
Rule at top	One-man rule	Collective leadership
Empirical bases of decisions	Prior preferences demonstrated in model units	Investigation; statistical compilation; model units
Popular confidence in political system	Low	Somewhat improved
Dominant organizational hierarchies	People's Liberation Army, public security forces, party Propaganda Department	Party committee chain of command, party Organization Department, State Planning Commission, Ministry of Finance, army, public security forces

Causes of Change and Its Durability

Three interrelated factors help to explain the evolution of the system: the change in the top leaders, the course of revolution, and China's specific development problems. The human factor is the passing of Mao and the rise of Deng and Chen. Many of the changes only took place after Mao's death, the arrest of his principal allies in revolution, and the subsequent eclipse of his lingering beneficiaries (e.g., Hua Guofeng). The Chinese system remains one which reflects the aspirations and techniques of rule of the top officials. To that extent, the system will continue to evolve and take on the coloration of Deng's and Chen's successors.

A second, more systemic factor is also at work, namely, the course of any totalitarian revolution. The reform-oriented, institutionalized polity which had begun to emerge by 1982 bears a great resemblance to the

Chinese system which was making its appearance in the mid-1950s and then again in the early 1960s, after the Great Leap Forward campaign (1958–1960). By launching the Cultural Revolution in 1966, Mao sought to postpone in China the inevitable aftermath of revolutions—be they in France, Russia, Germany, Cuba, or Vietnam—that is to say, the strengthened grip of bureaucracy over society. Mao deliberately sought mechanisms to keep society in constant turmoil so as to prevent a bureaucratic domination in China. . . .

To an extraordinary extent, the pressing problems now, even six years after Mao's death, are precisely the ones Mao neglected as he directed the nation's energies elsewhere. The contours of the 1982 political system are, to a considerable degree, a reaction to the Maoist system. The political institutions and process Deng and his associates have called into being have been designed to cope with the particular set of problems Mao had neglected and thus bequeathed to his successors:

- Lagging agricultural production
- An inefficient industrial system
- High unemployment among youth
- A low standard of living
- Widespread apathy and cynicism
- An inadequate scientific and technological manpower base
- Specific bottlenecks in transportation, communications, and energy
- An unacceptably high rate of population increase

So pressing are these problems and so seemingly supportive to their solution is the political system Deng, Chen, and their associates have designed, that the observer might be tempted to assume that rationality has prevailed and an equilibrium may have been reached. Such a conclusion is unwarranted on several grounds.

To begin with, the major instruments of totalitarian rule have been weakened but not eliminated. The military, the public security forces, and the propaganda apparatus have yet to acquire roles in domestic affairs commensurate with the objective resources under their command. They are potentially destabilizing institutions and focal points of resistance to the system which Deng and Chen have forged.

In addition, the current system and set of policies generate their own, new set of problems, and it is not yet clear that the Deng-Chen system is capable of handling these problems. In particular, the system relies heavily on rule through bureaucracy, but it has yet to develop effective mechanisms for ensuring that the bureaucracy will be responsive either to popular will or indeed to orders from above. Over a protracted period, the Deng-Chen system could prove to be one in which tensions accumulate but for which there are no adequate safety valves. To be sure, the new opportunity for individuals to withdraw from politics and the personnel readjustment in the bureaucracies lessen the causes of tension. Furthermore, unlike the Maoist system, the Deng-Chen system does not envision the use of social tensions as an engine of history. Nevertheless, several already apparent cleavages in the system could prove politically troublesome if allowed to become too sharp. These are (1) civil-military relations; (2) generational layering where the experiences and education of age cohorts have differed sharply; (3) urban-rural differences, since living standards and opportunities for social mobility are highly unequal; (4) tensions between coastal and interior provinces, since the benefits of China's opening to the West flow much more rapidly to the coastal provinces; and (5) income differentials within and among localities, with perhaps rising resentment as income differentials grow under the post-1978 remuneration system. The long-term consequences of increased contact with the outside world are also difficult to foresee.

Another potential source of instability stems from the promise the leadership has made to raise the standard of living of the populace. From 1978 to 1982, real income has gone up dramatically for many, particularly in the countryside, and moderately for others, especially in the cities. Not only have wages gone up, but construction of housing has increased significantly as has the production of many consumer durables (watches, bicycles, portable radios, television sets, et cetera). The slightly more affluent urban Chinese populace is beginning to press upon scarce leisure-time facilities, such as theaters, parks, and sports grounds. Therefore, questions remain. Are expectations rising more rapidly than the expansion of consumer goods industries? Is it in fact wise to stimulate support for the regime through such a heavy reliance on material incentives? What might happen if the economic strategy does not succeed, the growth rate falters, and standards of living stagnate? In that case, the fundamental stability of the Chinese regime would not necessarily be at stake, but many of the changes made since 1972 would be threatened, particularly in the relative importance of various bureaucracies and the mechanisms for integrating the society.

Deng and his associates seem to have rekindled the century-old debate over how best to root the quest for modernity in the nation's intellectual heritage. In fact, as Benjamin Schwartz has stressed, it is incorrect to speak of a single or even dominant Chinese intellectual tradition. Rather, aspects of Confucianism, Legalism, Buddhism, and various popular religions offered China's rulers a diversity of traditions upon which to draw. The real question was, which of these diverse strands should be combined with which Western ideas to create an ideological amalgam suited to Chinese needs?

COMMUNIQUÉ OF THE THIRD PLENARY SESSION OF THE ELEVENTH CENTRAL COMMITTEE OF THE COMMUNIST PARTY OF CHINA

No meeting of Chinese leaders was more central to launching China on the path of reform than the Third Plenary Session of the Eleventh Central Committee, convened over a fortnight in December 1978. From this meeting onward Deng Xiaoping and his associates began to dominate the national and government agenda and refocus it on reform — although they still had to contend with Mao's chosen successor, Hua Guofeng, and other neo-Maoists. This meeting (commonly referred to as the Third Plenum) set the stage for economic and political reform and a rollback of Maoism in all spheres, "reversed the verdict" on the 1976 Tiananmen Incident, authorized the normalization of diplomatic relations with the United States, and made the decision to attack Vietnam.

This communiqué was originally published in Beijing Review *in December 1978.*

In the early years after the founding of the People's Republic, especially after the socialist transformation was in the main completed, Comrade Mao Zedong instructed the whole Party time and again to shift the focus of our work to the field of the economy and technical revolution. Under the leadership of Comrade Mao Zedong and Comrade Chou Enlai, our Party did a great deal for socialist modernization and scored important achievements. But the work was later interrupted and sabotaged by Lin Biao and the "Gang of Four." Besides, we had some shortcomings and mistakes in our leading work because we lacked experience in socialist construction, and this also hampered the transition in the focus of our Party's work. Since the nationwide mass movement to expose and criticize Lin Biao and the "Gang of Four" has fundamentally come to a successful conclusion, though in a small number of places and departments the movement is less developed, still needs some time to catch up, and so cannot end simultaneously, on the whole there is every condition needed for that transition. Therefore the plenary session unanimously endorsed the policy decision put forward by Comrade Hua Guofeng on behalf of the Political Bureau of the Central Committee that, to meet the developments at home and abroad, now is an appropriate time to take the decision to close the large-scale nationwide mass movement to expose and criticize Lin Biao and the "Gang of Four" and to shift the emphasis of our Party's work and the attention of the people of the whole country to socialist modernization. This is of major significance for fulfillment of the three-year and eight-year programs for the development of the national economy and the outline for twenty-three years, for the modernization of agriculture, industry, national defense, and science and technology, and for the consolidation of the dictatorship of the proletariat in our country. The general task put forward by our Party for the new period reflects the demands of history and the people's aspirations and represents their fundamental interests. Whether or not we can carry this general task to completion, speed socialist modernization, and on the basis of a rapid growth in production improve the people's living standards significantly and strengthen national defense—this is a major issue which is of paramount concern to all our people and of great significance to the cause of world peace and progress. Carrying out the four modernizations requires great growth in the productive forces, which in turn requires diverse changes in those aspects of the relations of production and the superstructure not in harmony with the growth of the productive forces, and requires changes in all methods of management, actions, and thinking which stand in the way of such growth. Socialist modernization is therefore a profound and extensive revolution. There are still in our country today a small handful of counterrevolutionary elements and criminals who hate our socialist modernization and try to undermine it. We must not relax our class struggle against them, nor can we weaken the dictatorship of the proletariat. But as Comrade Mao Zedong pointed out, the large-scale turbulent class struggles of a mass character have in the main come to an end. Class struggle in socialist society should be carried out on the principle of strictly differentiating the two different types of contradictions and correctly handling them in accordance with the procedures prescribed by the Constitution and the law. It is impermissible to confuse the two different types of contradictions and damage the political stability and unity required for socialist modernization. The plenary session calls on the whole Party, the whole army, and the people of all our nationalities to work with one heart and one mind, enhance political stability and unity, mobilize themselves immediately to go all out, pool their wisdom and efforts, and carry out the new Long March to make China a modern, powerful socialist country before the end of this century.

The plenary session discussed arrangements for the national economic plans for 1979 and 1980 and approved them in principle, and proposed that the State Council submit them after revisions to the Second Session of the National People's Congress to be held next year for discussion and adoption. The session feels that these arrangements are both forward-looking and feasible. The session points out that the restoration and development of our national economy since the downfall of the "Gang of Four" has been very rapid, and that there have been marked increases in total industrial and agricultural output value and revenue in 1978. But it has to be noted that due to sabotage by Lin Biao and the "Gang of Four" over a long period there are still quite a few problems in the national economy, some major imbalances have not been completely changed, and some disorder in production, construction, circulation, and distribution has not been fully eliminated. A series of problems left hanging for years as regards the people's livelihood in town and country must be appropriately solved. We must conscientiously solve these problems step by step in the next few years and effectively achieve a comprehensive balance, so as to lay a solid foundation for rapid development. We must make concentrated efforts within the limits of our capabilities to carry out capital construction actively and steadily and not rush things, wasting manpower and material.

The plenary session holds that the whole Party should concentrate its main energy and efforts on advancing agriculture as fast as possible because agriculture, the foundation of the national economy, has been seriously damaged in recent years and remains very weak on the whole. The rapid development of the national economy as a whole and the steady improvement in the living standards of the people of the whole country depends on the vigorous restoration and speeding up of farm production, on resolutely and fully implementing the policy of simultaneous development of farming, forestry, animal husbandry, side occupations, and fisheries, the policy of taking grain as the key link and ensuring an all-round development, the policy of adaptation to local conditions and appropriate concentration of certain crops in certain areas, and gradual modernization of farm work. This requires first of all releasing the socialist enthusiasm of our country's several hundred million peasants, paying full attention to their material well-being economically, and giving effective protection to their democratic rights politically. Taking this as the guideline, the plenary session set forth a series of policies and economic measures aimed at raising present agricultural production. The most important are as follows: The right of ownership by the people's communes, production brigades, and production teams and their power of decision must be protected effectively by the laws of the state; it is not permitted to commandeer the manpower, funds, products, and material of any production team; the economic organizations at various levels of the people's commune must conscientiously implement the socialist principle of "to each according to his work," work out payment in accordance with the amount and quality of work done, and overcome equalitarianism; small plots of land for private use by commune members, their domestic side occupations, and village fairs are necessary adjuncts of the socialist economy, and must not be interfered with; the people's communes must resolutely implement the system of three levels of ownership with the production team as the basic accounting unit, and this should remain unchanged. Organizations at various levels of the people's commune must firmly carry out democratic management and election of cadres and make public their accounts

The plenary session points out that it is imperative to improve the livelihood of the people in town and country step by step on the basis of the growth of production. The bureaucratic attitude of paying no attention at all to urgent problems in the people's livelihood must be resolutely opposed. On the other hand, since our economy is still very backward at present, it is impossible to improve the people's livelihood very rapidly and it is essential to keep the people informed on the relevant state of affairs and to intensify education in the revolutionary ideas of self-reliance and hard struggle among the youth and other sectors of the people, and leading comrades at all levels must make themselves exemplars in this regard.

.   .   .

The session had a serious discussion on some major political events which occurred during the Great Cultural Revolution and certain historical questions left over from an earlier period. It holds that satisfactory settlement of these questions is very necessary for consolidating stability and unity, facilitating the shift in the focus of the work of the whole Party, and getting the whole Party, the whole army, and the people of all our nationalities to unite as one and to look forward so as to mobilize all positive factors to work for the four modernizations.

The session points out that in 1975, in the period when Comrade Deng Xiaoping was entrusted by Comrade Mao Zedong with the responsibility of presiding over the work of the Central Committee, there were great achievements in all fields of work, with which the whole Party, the whole army, and the people throughout the country were satisfied. In accordance with Comrade Mao Zedong's instructions, Comrade Deng Xiaoping and other leading comrades of the Central Committee waged tit-for-tat struggles against interference and sabotage by the "Gang of Four." The Gang arbitrarily described the political line and the achievements of 1975 as a "Right-deviationist wind to reverse correct verdicts." This reversal of history must be reversed again. The session points out that the Tiananmen events of April 5, 1976, were entirely revolutionary actions. The great revolutionary mass movement, which unfolded around the Tiananmen events and in which millions upon millions of people in all parts of the country expressed deep mourning for Comrade Zhou Enlai and indignantly condemned the "Gang of Four," provided the mass base for our Party's success in smashing the "Gang of Four." The plenary session decided to cancel the erroneous documents issued by the Central Committee in regard to the movement "to oppose the Right-deviationist wind to reverse correct verdicts" and the Tiananmen events.

The session examined and corrected the erroneous conclusions which had been adopted on Peng Dehuai, Tao Zhu, Bo Yibo, Yang Shangkun, and other comrades, and affirmed their contributions to the Party and the people. It points out that historical questions must be settled in accordance with the principle consistently advocated by Comrade Mao Zedong, that is, seeking truth from facts and correcting mistakes whenever discovered. Only by firmly rejecting false charges, correcting wrong sentences, and rehabilitating the victims of frame-ups can the unity of the Party and the people be consolidated and the high prestige of the Party and Comrade Mao Zedong upheld. This task must be fulfilled resolutely without any relaxation after the mass movement to expose and criticize the "Gang of Four" ends. The session unanimously agrees that the adoption of these steps is in itself an example of grasping the scientific system of Mao Zedong Thought comprehensively and accurately and holding high the banner of Chairman Mao.

The session holds that the past practice of setting up special-case groups to examine cadres without Party and mass supervision had great disadvantages and must be abolished once and for all.

The session held a serious discussion on the question of democracy and the legal system. It holds that socialist modernization requires centralized leadership and strict implementation of various rules and regulations and observance of labor discipline. Bourgeois factionalism and anarchism must be firmly opposed. But the correct concentration of ideas is possible only when there is full democracy. Since for a period in the past democratic centralism was not carried out in the true sense, centralism being divorced from democracy and there being too little democracy, it is necessary to lay particular emphasis on democracy at present, and on the dialectical relationship between democracy and centralism, so as to make the mass line the foundation of the Party's centralized leadership and the effective direction of the organizations of production. In ideological and political life among the ranks of the people, only democracy is permissible and not suppression or persecution. It is essential to reiterate the "principle of three nots"; not seizing on others' faults, not putting labels on people, and not using the big stick. Leadership at all levels should be good at concentrating the correct ideas of the masses and making appropriate explanation and persuasion in dealing with incorrect ideas. The constitutional rights of citizens must be resolutely protected and no one has the right to infringe upon them.

In order to safeguard people's democracy, it is imperative to strengthen the socialist legal system so that democracy is systematized and written into law in such a way as to ensure the stability, continuity, and full authority of this democratic system and these laws; there must be laws for people to follow, these laws must be observed, their enforcement must be strict, and lawbreakers must be dealt with. From now on, legislative work should have an important place on the agenda of the National People's Congress and its Standing Committee. Procuratorial and judicial organizations must maintain their independence as is appropriate; they must faithfully abide by the laws, rules, and regulations, serve the people's interests, keep to the facts, guarantee the equality of all people before the people's laws, and deny anyone the privilege of being above the law.

. . .

In the past two years, through the deepening struggle to expose and criticize Lin Biao and the "Gang of Four," many issues of right and wrong in ideology and theory which they turned upside down have been straightened out. However, quite a number of comrades still do not dare to raise questions or deal with them in a straightforward way. This situation came into being under specific historical conditions. The plenary session calls on comrades of the whole Party and the people of the whole country to continue to free themselves from the mental shackles imposed by Lin Biao and the "Gang of Four" and, at the same time, resolutely overcome the bureaucracy caused by the overconcentration of authority, the failure to reward or punish as deserved, and the influence of petty producer mentality so as to help the people emancipate their minds and "start up the machinery."

The session highly evaluated the discussion of whether practice is the sole criterion for testing truth, noting that this is of far-reaching historic significance in encouraging comrades of the whole Party and the people of the whole country to emancipate their thinking and follow the correct ideological line. For a party, a country, or a nation, if everything had to be done according to books and thinking became ossified, progress would become impossible, life itself would stop, and the Party and country would perish.

The session emphatically points out that the great feats performed by Comrade Mao Zedong in protracted revolutionary struggle are indelible. Without his outstanding leadership and without Mao Zedong Thought, it is most likely that the Chinese revolution would not have been victorious up to the present. The Chinese people would still be living under the reactionary rule of imperialism, feudalism, and bureaucrat-capitalism and our Party would still be struggling in the dark. Comrade Mao Zedong was a great Marxist. He always adopted the scientific attitude of "one divides into two" toward everyone, including himself. It would not be Marxist to demand that a revolutionary leader be free of all shortcomings and errors. It also would not conform to Comrade Mao Zedong's consistent evaluation of himself. The lofty task of the Party Central Committee on the theoretical front is to lead and educate the whole Party and the people of the whole country to recognize Comrade Mao Zedong's great feats in a historical and scientific perspective, comprehensively and correctly grasp the scientific system of Mao Zedong Thought, and integrate the universal principles of Marxism-

Leninism–Mao Zedong Thought with the concrete practice of socialist modernization and develop it under the new historical conditions.

The session holds that the Great Cultural Revolution should also be viewed historically, scientifically, and in a down-to-earth way. Comrade Mao Zedong initiated this great revolution primarily in the light of the fact that the Soviet Union had turned revisionist and for the purpose of opposing revisionism and preventing its occurrence. As for the short-comings and mistakes in the actual course of the revolution, they should be summed up at the appropriate time as experience and lessons so as to unify the views of the whole Party and the people of the whole country. However, there should be no haste about this. Shelving this problem will not prevent us from solving all other problems left over from past history in a down-to-earth manner, nor will it affect our concentration of efforts to speed up the four modernizations, the greatest historic task of the time.

Basing itself on the experience and lessons from the history of our Party, the plenary session decided to improve the practice of democratic cen-tralism within the Party, to amplify the Party rules and regulations, and to enforce strict discipline in the Party.

The session holds that just as a country has its laws, the Party should have its rules and regulations. Observance of Party discipline by all Party members and Party cadres is a minimum requirement for restoring nor-mal political life in the Party and the state. Leading Party cadres at all levels should take the lead in strictly observing Party discipline. Disciplin-ary measures should be taken against all violators of Party discipline with no exception, so that there is a clear distinction between merits and faults, awards and punishments, so that honesty prevails and bad tenden-cies are eliminated.

Next year will be the thirtieth anniversary of the founding of the great People's Republic of China. The Third Plenary Session of the Eleventh Central Committee issues the following call to all comrades in the Party, to commanders and fighters throughout the army, to workers, peasants, and intellectuals of all nationalities throughout the country, to people in all political parties, and to non-Party democratic patriots: The best contribution to the thirtieth anniversary of the founding of our Peo-ple's Republic will be to shift the emphasis of our work to socialist mod-ernization and to achieve the expected success next year. Let us rally even more closely under the banner of Mao Zedong Thought, rally round the Party Central Committee headed by Comrade Hua Guofeng, and advance courageously to make a fundamental change in the backward state of our country so that it becomes a great, modern, socialist power.

Deng Xiaoping, Answers to the Italian Journalist Oriana Fallaci

One of the most candid interviews Deng Xiaoping ever gave was to the combative Italian journalist Oriana Fallaci. Deng's direct and blunt style is clear. He provided Fallaci with his assessment of Mao Zedong—telling her that the late Chairman's accomplishments outweighed his mistakes and that "we will not do to Chairman Mao what Khrushchev did to Stalin." Deng also discussed his own relationship to Mao and the "Gang of Four." Deng rated Mao's life as 70 percent good, 30 percent bad, while he opined that he would be pleased to be evaluated fifty/fifty after his death. As for Mao's widow, Jiang Qing, Deng gave her a rating of "a thousand points below zero"!

This interview took place in August 1980 and was included in volume 2 of The Selected Works of Deng Xiaoping (1975–1982), *published in 1984.*

ORIANA FALLACI: Will Chairman Mao's portrait above Tiananmen Gate be kept there?

DENG XIAOPING: It will, forever. In the past there were too many portraits of Chairman Mao. They were hung everywhere. That was not proper and it didn't really show respect for Chairman Mao. It's true that he made mistakes in a certain period, but he was after all a principal founder of the Chinese Communist Party and the People's Republic of China. In evaluating his merits and mistakes, we hold that his mistakes were only secondary. What he did for the Chinese people can never be erased. In our hearts we Chinese will always cherish him as a founder of our Party and our state.

QUESTION: We Westerners find a lot of things hard to understand. The Gang of Four are blamed for all the faults. I'm told that when the Chinese talk about the Gang of Four, many of them hold up five fingers.

ANSWER: We must make a clear distinction between the nature of Chairman Mao's mistakes and the crimes of Lin Biao and the Gang of Four. For most of his life, Chairman Mao did very good things. Many times he saved the Party and the state from crises. Without him the Chinese people would, at the very least, have spent much more time groping in the dark. Chairman Mao's greatest contribution was that he applied the principles of Marxism-Leninism to the concrete practice of the Chinese revolution, pointing the way to victory. It should be said that before the 1960s or the late 1950s many of his ideas brought us victories, and the fundamental principles he advanced were quite correct. He creatively applied Marxism-Leninism to every aspect of the Chinese revolution, and he had creative views on philosophy, political science, military science, literature and art, and so on. Unfortunately, in the evening of his life, particularly during the "Cultural Revolution," he made mistakes—and they were not minor ones—which brought many misfortunes upon our Party, our state, and our people. As you know, during the Yan'an days our Party summed up Chairman Mao's thinking in various fields as Mao Zedong Thought, and we made it our guiding ideology. We won great victories for the revolution precisely because we adhered to Mao Zedong Thought. Of course, Mao Zedong Thought was not created by Comrade Mao alone—other revolutionaries of the older generation played a part in forming and developing it—but primarily it embodies Comrade Mao's thinking. Nevertheless, victory made him less prudent, so that in his later years some unsound features and unsound ideas, chiefly "Left" ones, began to emerge. In quite a number of instances he went counter to his own ideas, counter to the fine and correct propositions he had previously put forward, and counter to the style of work he himself had advocated. At this time he increasingly lost touch with reality. He didn't maintain a good style of work. He did not consistently practice democratic centralism and the mass line, for instance, and he failed to institutionalize them during his lifetime. This was not the fault of Mao Zedong alone. Other revolutionaries of the older generation, including me, should also be held responsible. Some abnormalities appeared in the political life of our Party and state—patriarchal ways or styles of work developed, and glorification of the individual was rife; political life in general wasn't too healthy. Eventually these things led to the "Cultural Revolution," which was a mistake.

QUESTION: You mentioned that in his last years, Chairman Mao was in poor health. But at the time of Liu Shaoqi's arrest and his subsequent death in prison Mao's health wasn't so bad. And there are other mistakes to be accounted for. Wasn't the Great Leap Forward a mistake? Wasn't copying the Soviet model a mistake? How far back should the past mistakes be traced? And what did Chairman Mao really want with the "Cultural Revolution"?

ANSWER: Mistakes began to occur in the 1950s—the Great Leap Forward, for instance. But that wasn't solely Chairman Mao's fault either. The people around him got carried away too. We acted in direct contravention of objective laws, attempting to boost the economy all at once. As our subjective wishes went against objective laws, losses were inevitable. Still, it is Chairman Mao who should be held primarily responsible for the Great Leap Forward. But it didn't take him long— just a few months—to recognize his mistake, and he did so before the rest of us and proposed corrections. And in 1962, when because of some other factors those corrections had not been fully carried out, he made a self-criticism. But the lessons were not fully drawn, and as a result the "Cultural Revolution" erupted. So far as Chairman Mao's own hopes were concerned, he initiated the "Cultural Revolution" in order to avert the restoration of capitalism, but he had made an erroneous assessment of China's actual situation. In the first place, the targets of the revolution were wrongly defined, which led to the effort to ferret out "capitalist roaders in power in the Party." Blows were dealt at leading cadres at all levels who had made contributions to the revolution and had practical experience, including Comrade Liu Shaoqi. In the last couple of years before Chairman Mao's death he said that the "Cultural Revolution" had been wrong on two counts: one was "overthrowing all," and the other was waging a "full-scale civil war." These two counts alone show that the "Cultural Revolution" cannot be called correct. Chairman Mao's mistake was a political mistake, and not a small one. On the other hand, it was taken advantage of by the two counterrevolutionary cliques headed by Lin Biao and the Gang of Four, who schemed to usurp power. Therefore, we should draw a line between Chairman Mao's mistakes and the crimes of Lin Biao and the Gang of Four.

QUESTION: But we all know that it was Chairman Mao himself who chose Lin Biao as his successor, much in the same way as an emperor chooses his heir.

ANSWER: This is what I've just referred to as an incorrect way of doing things. For a leader to pick his own successor is a feudal practice. It is an illustration of the imperfections in our institutions which I referred to a moment ago.

QUESTION: To what extent will Chairman Mao be involved when you hold your next Party congress?

ANSWER: We will make an objective assessment of Chairman Mao's contributions and his mistakes. We will reaffirm that his contributions are primary and his mistakes secondary. We will adopt a realistic approach toward the mistakes he made late in life. We will continue to adhere to Mao Zedong Thought, which represents the correct part of Chairman Mao's life. Not only did Mao Zedong Thought lead us to victory in the revolution in the past; it is—and will continue to be—a treasured possession of the Chinese Communist Party and of our country. That is why we will forever keep Chairman Mao's portrait on Tiananmen Gate as a symbol of our country, and we will always remember him as a founder of our Party and state. Moreover, we will adhere to Mao Zedong Thought. We will not do to Chairman Mao what Khrushchev did to Stalin.

QUESTION: Do you mean to say that the name of Chairman Mao will inevitably come up when the Gang of Four is brought to trial as well as when you have your next Party congress?

ANSWER: His name will be mentioned. Not only at the next Party congress but also on other occasions. But the trial of the Gang of Four will not detract from Chairman Mao's prestige. Of course, he was responsible for putting them in their positions. Nevertheless, the crimes the Gang of Four themselves committed are more than sufficient to justify whatever sentences may be passed on them.

QUESTION: I have heard that Chairman Mao frequently complained that you didn't listen to him enough, and that he didn't like you. Is it true?

ANSWER: Yes, Chairman Mao did say I didn't listen to him. But this wasn't directed only at me. It happened to other leaders as well. It reflects some unhealthy ideas in his twilight years, that is, patriarchal ways which are feudal in nature. He did not readily listen to differing opinions. We can't say that all his criticisms were wrong. But neither was he ready to listen to many correct opinions put forward not only by me but by other comrades. Democratic centralism was impaired, and so was collective leadership. Otherwise, it would be hard to explain how the "Cultural Revolution" broke out.

QUESTION: There was one personage in China who always went unscathed, and that was Premier Zhou Enlai. How do you explain this fact?

ANSWER: Premier Zhou was a man who worked hard and uncomplainingly all his life. He worked twelve hours a day, and sometimes sixteen hours or more, throughout his life. We got to know each other quite early, that is, when we were in France on a work-study program during the 1920s. I have always looked upon him as my elder brother. We took the revolutionary road at about the same time. He was much respected by his comrades and all the people. Fortunately he survived during the "Cultural Revolution" when we were knocked down. He was in an extremely difficult position then, and he said and did many things that he would have wished not to. But the people forgave him because, had he not done and said those things, he himself would not have been able to survive and play the neutralizing role he did, which reduced losses. He succeeded in protecting quite a number of people.

QUESTION: I don't see how terrible things like the "Cultural Revolution" can be avoided or prevented from recurring.

ANSWER: This issue has to be addressed by tackling the problems in our institutions. Some of those we established in the past were, in fact, tainted by feudalism, as manifested in such things as the personality cult, the patriarchal ways or styles of work, and the life tenure of cadres in leading posts. We are now looking into ways to prevent such things from recurring and are preparing to start with the restructuring of our institutions. Our country has a history of thousands of years of feudalism and is still lacking in socialist democracy and socialist legality. We are now working earnestly to cultivate socialist democracy and socialist legality. Only in this way can we solve the problem.

QUESTION: Are you sure that things will proceed more smoothly from now on? Can you attain the goal you have set yourselves? I hear that the so-called Maoists are still around. By "Maoists" I mean those who backed the "Cultural Revolution."

ANSWER: The influence of the Gang of Four should not be underrated, but it should be noted that 97 or 98 percent of the population hate them intensely for their crimes. This was shown by the mass movement against the Gang of Four which erupted at Tiananmen Square on April 5, 1976, when the Gang were still riding high, Chairman Mao was critically ill, and Premier Zhou had passed away. Since the Gang's overthrow [in 1976], and particularly in the past two years, the will and demands of the people have been given expression in the Third, Fourth, and Fifth Plenary Sessions of the Central Committee of the Chinese Communist Party. We are considering ways of resolving our problems by improving our institutions. Many issues have already been raised now. Particular emphasis is being laid on working single-mindedly for the four modernizations, and this is winning the hearts of the people. They want political stability and unity. They are fed up with large-scale movements. Such movements invariably ended up hurting a number—and not a small number—of people. Incessant movements make it practically impossible to concentrate on national construction. Therefore, we can say for sure that given the correctness of our present course, the people will support us and such phenomena as the "Cultural Revolution" will not happen again.

QUESTION: The Gang of Four could only have been arrested after the death of Chairman Mao. Who engineered their arrest? Who initiated the idea?

ANSWER: It was a collective effort. First of all, I think, it had a mass base laid by the April 5 Movement [of 1976]. The term "Gang of Four" was coined by Chairman Mao a couple of years before his death. We waged struggles against the Gang for two years, in 1974 and 1975. By then people clearly saw them for what they were. Although Chairman Mao had designated his successor, the Gang of Four refused to accept this. After Chairman Mao's death, the Gang took the opportunity to try and get all power into their own hands, and the situation demanded action from us. They were rampant at that time, trying to overthrow the new leadership. Under these circumstances, the great majority of the comrades of the Political Bureau were agreed that measures had to be taken to deal with the Gang. The efforts of one or two individuals would not have sufficed for this purpose.

It should be pointed out that some of the things done after the arrest of the Gang of Four were inconsistent with Chairman Mao's wishes, for instance, the construction of the Chairman Mao Memorial Hall. He had proposed in the 1950s that we should all be cremated when we died and that only our ashes be kept, that no remains should be preserved and no tombs built. Chairman Mao was the first to sign his name, and we all followed suit. Nearly all senior cadres at the central level and across the country signed. We still have that book of signatures. What was done in the matter after the smashing of the Gang of Four was prompted by the desire to achieve a relative stability.

QUESTION: Does this mean that the Chairman Mao Memorial Hall will soon be demolished?

ANSWER: I am not in favor of changing it. Now that it is there, it would not be appropriate to remove it. It wasn't appropriate to build it in the first place, but to change it would give rise to all kinds of talk. Many people are now speculating whether we will demolish the Memorial Hall. We have no such idea.

QUESTION: It is said that you are giving up the post of vice premier.

ANSWER: I will not be the only one to resign. All other comrades of the older generation are giving up their concurrent posts. Chairman Hua Guofeng will no longer serve concurrently as Premier of the State Council. The Central Committee of the Party has recommended Comrade Zhao Ziyang as candidate for that post. If we old comrades remain at our posts, newcomers will be inhibited in their work. We face the problem of gradually reducing the average age of leaders at all levels. We have to take the lead.

There were previously no relevant rules. In fact, however, there was life tenure in leading posts. This does not facilitate the renewal of leadership or the promotion of younger people. It is an institutional defect which was not evident in the 1960s because we were then in the prime of life. This issue involves not just individuals but all the relevant institutions. It has an even greater bearing on our general policy and on whether our four modernizations can be achieved. Therefore, we say it would be better for us old comrades to take an enlightened attitude and set an example in this respect.

QUESTION: I have seen other portraits in China. At Tiananmen I've seen portraits of Marx, Engels, and Lenin and particularly of Stalin. Do you intend to keep them there?

ANSWER: Before the "Cultural Revolution" they were put up only on important holidays. The practice was changed during the "Cultural Revolution," when they were displayed permanently. Now we are going back to the former way.

QUESTION: The four modernizations will bring foreign capital into China, and this will inevitably give rise to private investment. Won't this lead to a miniaturized capitalism?

ANSWER: In the final analysis, the general principle for our economic development is still that formulated by Chairman Mao, that is, to rely mainly on our own efforts with external assistance subsidiary. No matter to what degree we open up to the outside world and admit foreign capital, its relative magnitude will be small and it can't affect our system of socialist public ownership of the means of production. Absorbing foreign capital and technology and even allowing foreigners to construct plants in China can only play a complementary role to our effort to develop the socialist productive forces. Of course, this will bring some decadent capitalist influences into China. We are aware of this possibility; it's nothing to be afraid of.

QUESTION: Does it mean that not all in capitalism is so bad?

ANSWER: It depends on how you define capitalism. Any capitalism is superior to feudalism. And we cannot say that everything developed in capitalist countries is of a capitalist nature. For instance, technology, science—even advanced production management is also a sort of science—will be useful in any society or country. We intend to acquire advanced technology, science, and management skills to serve our socialist production. And these things as such have no class character.

QUESTION: I remember that several years ago, when talking about private plots in rural areas, you acknowledged that man needs some personal interest to produce. Doesn't this mean to put in discussion communism itself?

ANSWER: According to Marx, socialism is the first stage of communism and it covers a very long historical period in which we must practice the principle "to each according to his work" and combine the interests of the state, the collective, and the individual, for only thus can we arouse people's enthusiasm for labor and develop socialist production. At the higher stage of communism, when the productive forces will be greatly developed and the principle "from each according to his ability, to each according to his needs" will be practiced, personal interests will be acknowledged still more and more personal needs will be satisfied.

QUESTION: You mentioned that there are others who made contributions to Mao Zedong Thought. Who were they?

ANSWER: Other revolutionaries of the older generation, for example Premier Zhou Enlai, Comrades Liu Shaoqi and Zhu De—and many others. Many senior cadres are creative and original in their thinking.

QUESTION: Why did you leave your own name out?

ANSWER: I am quite insignificant. Of course, I too have done some work. Otherwise, I wouldn't be counted as a revolutionary.

QUESTION: What we did not understand was: If the Gang of Four was, as you said, a minority with all the country against them, how could it happen that they were holding the whole country, including the veteran leaders? Was it because one of the four was the wife of Mao Zedong and the ties between Mao Zedong and her were so profound that no one dared to touch her?

ANSWER: This was one of the factors. As I've said, Chairman Mao made mistakes, one of which was using the Gang, letting them come to power. Also, the Gang had their own factional setup and they built a clique of some size—particularly they made use of ignorant young people as a front, so they had a fair-sized base.

QUESTION: Was Mao Zedong blinded by her so that he wouldn't see what she was doing? And was she an adventuress like the Empress Dowager Yehonala?

ANSWER: Jiang Qing did evil things by flaunting the banner of Chairman Mao. But Chairman Mao and Jiang Qing lived separately for years.

QUESTION: We didn't know that.

ANSWER: Jiang Qing did what she did by flaunting the banner of Chairman Mao, but he failed to intervene effectively. For this he should be held responsible. Jiang Qing is rotten through and through. Whatever sentence is passed on the Gang of Four won't be excessive. They brought harm to millions upon millions of people.

QUESTION: How would you assess Jiang Qing? What score would you give her?

ANSWER: Below zero. A thousand points below zero.

QUESTION: How would you assess yourself?

ANSWER: I would be quite content if I myself could be rated fifty-fifty in merits and demerits. But one thing I can say for myself: I have had a clear conscience all my life. Please mark my words: I have made quite a few mistakes, and I have my own share of responsibility for some of the mistakes made by Comrade Mao Zedong. But it can be said that I made my mistakes with good intentions. There is nobody who doesn't make mistakes. We should not lay all past mistakes on Chairman Mao. So we must be very objective in assessing him. His contributions were primary, his mistakes secondary. We will inherit the many good things in Chairman Mao's thinking while at the same time explaining clearly the mistakes he made.

RESOLUTION ON CERTAIN QUESTIONS IN THE HISTORY OF OUR PARTY SINCE THE FOUNDING OF THE PEOPLE'S REPUBLIC OF CHINA

Crucial to any society's coming to terms with a traumatic past is a public and official reassessment of historical errors. In post-Mao China, this process of reevaluating past policies was partially done in an official resolution adopted by the Communist Party Central Committee in 1981. The Resolution, which passed through multiple drafts and was very carefully edited, took aim at some of the worst transgressions of Maoism: the Anti-Rightist Movement of 1957, the Great Leap Forward of 1958–1960, and the Great Proletarian Cultural Revolution.

This selection was excerpted from the full text of the Resolution, as adopted at the Sixth Plenary Session of the Eleventh Central Committee of the Communist Party of China, and published in 1981.

I n the course of this decade, there were serious faults and errors in the guidelines of the Party's work, which developed through twists and turns.⟩

Nineteen fifty-seven was one of the years that saw the best results in economic work since the founding of the People's Republic owing to the conscientious implementation of the correct line formulated at the Eighth National Congress of the Party. To start a rectification campaign throughout the Party in that year and urge the masses to offer criticisms and suggestions were normal steps in developing socialist democracy. In the rectification campaign a handful of bourgeois Rightists seized the opportunity to advocate what they called "speaking out and airing views in a big way" and to mount a wild attack against the Party and the nascent socialist system in an attempt to replace the leadership of the Communist Party. It was therefore entirely correct and necessary to launch a resolute counterattack. But the scope of this struggle was made far too broad and a number of intellectuals, patriotic people, and Party cadres were unjustifiably labeled "Rightists," with unfortunate consequences.

In 1958 the Second Plenum of the Eighth National Congress of the Party adopted the general line for socialist construction. The line and its fundamental aspects were correct in that it reflected the masses' pressing demand for a change in the economic and cultural backwardness of our country. Its shortcoming was that it overlooked objective economic laws. Both before and after the plenum, all comrades in the Party and people of all nationalities displayed high enthusiasm and initiative for socialism and achieved certain results in production and construction. However, "Left" errors, characterized by excessive targets, the issuing of arbitrary directions, boastfulness, and the stirring up of a "communist wind," spread unchecked throughout the country. This was due to our lack of experience in socialist construction and inadequate understanding of the laws of economic development and of the basic economic conditions in China. More important, it was due to the fact that Comrade Mao Zedong and many leading comrades, both at the center and in the localities, had become smug about their successes, were impatient for quick results, and overestimated the role of man's subjective will and efforts. After the general line was formulated, the Great Leap Forward and the movement for rural people's communes were initiated without careful investigation and study and without prior experimentation. From the end of 1958 to the early stage of the Lushan Meeting of the Political Bureau of the Party's Central Committee in July 1959, Comrade Mao Zedong and the Central Committee led the whole Party in energetically rectifying the errors which had already been recognized. However, in the later part of the meeting, he erred in initiating criticism of Comrade Peng Dehuai and then in launching a Party-wide struggle against "Right opportunism." The resolution passed by the Eighth Plenary Session of the Eighth Central Committee of the Party concerning the so-called anti-Party group of Peng Dehuai, Huang Kecheng, Zhang Wentian, and Zhou Xiaozhou was entirely wrong. Politically, this struggle gravely undermined inner-Party democracy from the central level down to the grass roots; economically, it cut short the process of the rectification of "Left" errors, thus prolonging their influence. It was mainly due to the errors of the Great Leap Forward and of the struggle against "Right opportunism" together with a succession of natural calamities and the perfidious scrapping of contracts by the Soviet government that our economy encountered serious difficulties between 1959 and 1961, which caused serious losses to our country and people.

In the winter of 1960, the Central Committee of the Party and Comrade Mao Zedong set about rectifying the "Left" errors in rural work and decided on the principle of "readjustment, consolidation, filling out, and raising standards" for the economy as a whole. A number of correct policies and resolute measures were worked out and put into effect with Comrades Liu Shaoqi, Zhou Enlai, Chen Yun, and Deng Xiaoping in charge. All this constituted a crucial turning point in that historical phase. In January 1962 the enlarged Central Work Conference attended by 7,000 people made a preliminary summing-up of the positive and negative experience of the Great Leap Forward and unfolded criticism and self-criticism. A majority of the comrades who had been unjustifiably criticized during the campaign against "Right opportunism" were rehabilitated before or after the conference. In addition, most of the "Rightists" had their label removed. Thanks to these economic and political measures, the national economy recovered and developed fairly smoothly between 1962 and 1966.

Nevertheless, "Left" errors in the principles guiding economic work were not only not eradicated but actually grew in the spheres of politics, ideology, and culture. At the Tenth Plenary Session of the Party's Eighth Central Committee in September 1962, Comrade Mao Zedong widened and absolutized the class struggle, which exists only within certain limits in socialist society, and carried forward the viewpoint he had advanced after the anti-Rightist struggle in 1957 that the contradiction between the proletariat and the bourgeoisie remained the principal contradiction in our society. He went a step further and asserted that, throughout the historical period of socialism, the bourgeoisie would continue to exist and would attempt a comeback and become the source of revisionism inside the Party. The socialist education movement unfolded between 1963 and 1965 in some rural areas and at the grassroots level in a small number of cities did help to some extent to improve the cadres' style of work and economic management. But, in the course of the movement, problems differing in nature were all treated as forms of class struggle or its reflections inside the Party. As a result, quite a number of the cadres at the grassroots level were unjustly dealt with in the latter half of 1964, and early in 1965 the erroneous thesis was advanced that the main target of the movement should be "those Party persons in power taking the capitalist road." In the ideological sphere, a number of literary and art works and schools of thought and a number of representative personages in artistic, literary, and academic circles were subjected to unwarranted, inordinate political criticism. And there was an increasingly serious "Left" deviation on the question of intellectuals and on the question of education, science, and culture. These errors eventually culminated in the "Cultural Revolution," but they had not yet become dominant.

Thanks to the fact that the whole Party and people had concentrated on carrying out the correct principle of economic readjustment since the winter of 1960, socialist construction gradually flourished again. The Party and the people were united in sharing weal and woe. They overcame difficulties at home, stood up to the pressure of the Soviet leading clique, and repaid all the debts owed to the Soviet Union, which were chiefly incurred through purchasing Soviet arms during the movement to resist U.S. aggression and aid Korea. In addition, they did what they could to support the revolutionary struggles of the people of many countries and assist them in their economic construction. The Third National People's Congress, which met between the end of 1964 and the first days of 1965, announced that the task of national economic readjustment had in the main been accomplished and that the economy as a whole would soon enter a new stage of development. It called for energetic efforts to build China step by step into a socialist power with modern agriculture, industry, national defense, and science and technology. This call was not fulfilled owing to the "Cultural Revolution."

All the successes in these ten years were achieved under the collective leadership of the Central Committee of the Party headed by Comrade Mao Zedong. Likewise, responsibility for the errors committed in the work of this period rested with the same collective leadership. Although Comrade Mao Zedong must be held chiefly responsible, we cannot lay the blame for all those errors on him alone. During this period, his theoretical and practical mistakes concerning class struggle in a socialist society became increasingly serious, his personal arbitrariness gradually undermined democratic centralism in Party life, and the personality cult grew graver and graver. The Central Committee of the Party failed to rectify these mistakes in good time. Careerists like Lin Biao, Jiang Qing, and Kang Sheng, harboring ulterior motives, made use of these errors and inflated them. This led to the inauguration of the "Cultural Revolution."

The Decade of the "Cultural Revolution"

The "Cultural Revolution," which lasted from May 1966 to October 1976, was responsible for the most severe setback and the heaviest losses suffered by the Party, the state, and the people since the founding of the People's Republic. It was initiated and led by Comrade Mao Zedong. His principal theses were that many representatives of the bourgeoisie and counterrevolutionary revisionists had sneaked into the Party, the government, the army, and cultural circles, and leadership in a fairly large majority of organizations and departments was no longer in the hands of Marxists and the people; that Party persons in power taking the capitalist road had formed a bourgeois headquarters inside the Central Committee which pursued a revisionist political and organizational line and had agents in all provinces, municipalities, and autonomous regions, as well as in all central departments; that since the forms of struggle adopted in the past had not been able to solve this problem, the power usurped by the capitalist roaders could be recaptured only by carrying out a great cultural revolution, by openly and fully mobilizing the broad masses from the bottom up to expose these sinister phenomena; and that the cultural revolution was in fact a great political revolution in which one class would overthrow another, a revolution that would have to be waged time and again. These theses appeared mainly in the May 16 Circular, which served as the programmatic document of the "Cultural Revolution," and in the political report to the Ninth National Congress of the Party in April 1969. They were incorporated into a general theory—the "theory of continued revolution under the dictatorship of the proletariat"—which then took on a specific meaning. These erroneous "Left" theses, upon which Comrade Mao Zedong based himself in initiating the "Cultural Revolution," were obviously inconsistent with the system of Mao Zedong Thought, which is the integration of the universal principles of Marxism-Leninism with the concrete practice of the Chinese revolution. These theses must be clearly distinguished from Mao Zedong Thought. As for Lin Biao, Jiang Qing, and others, who were placed in important positions by Comrade Mao Zedong, the matter is of an entirely different nature. They rigged up two counterrevolutionary cliques in an attempt to seize supreme power and, taking advantage of Comrade Mao Zedong's errors, committed many crimes behind his back, bringing disaster to the country and the people. As their counterrevolutionary crimes have been fully exposed, this resolution will not go into them at any length.

The history of the "Cultural Revolution" has proved that Comrade Mao Zedong's principal theses for initiating this revolution conformed neither to Marxism-Leninism nor to Chinese reality. They represent an entirely erroneous appraisal of the prevailing class relations and political situation in the Party and state.

1. The "Cultural Revolution" was defined as a struggle against the revisionist line or the capitalist road. There were no grounds at all for this definition. It led to the confusing of right and wrong on a series of important theories and policies. Many things denounced as revisionist or capitalist during the "Cultural Revolution" were actually Marxist and socialist principles, many of which had been set forth or supported by Comrade Mao Zedong himself. The "Cultural Revolution" negated many of the correct principles, policies, and achievements of the seventeen years after the founding of the People's Republic. In fact, it negated much of the work of the Central Committee of the Party and the People's Government, including Comrade Mao Zedong's own contribution. It negated the arduous struggles the entire people had conducted in socialist construction.

2. The confusing of right and wrong inevitably led to confusing the people with the enemy. The "capitalist-roaders" overthrown in the "Cultural Revolution" were leading cadres of Party and government organizations at all levels, who formed the core force of the socialist cause. The so-called bourgeois headquarters inside the Party headed by Liu Shaoqi and Deng Xiaoping simply did not exist. Irrefutable facts

have proved that labeling Comrade Liu Shaoqi a "renegade, hidden traitor, and scab" was nothing but a frame-up by Lin Biao, Jiang Qing, and their followers. The political conclusion concerning Comrade Liu Shaoqi drawn by the Twelfth Plenary Session of the Eighth Central Committee of the Party and the disciplinary measure it meted out to him were both utterly wrong. The criticism of the so-called reactionary academic authorities in the "Cultural Revolution" during which many capable and accomplished intellectuals were attacked and persecuted also badly muddled up the distinction between the people and the enemy.

3. Nominally, the "Cultural Revolution" was conducted by directly relying on the masses. In fact, it was divorced both from the Party organizations and from the masses. After the movement started, Party organizations at different levels were attacked and became partially or wholly paralyzed, the Party's leading cadres at various levels were subjected to criticism and struggle, inner-Party life came to a standstill, and many activists and large numbers of the basic masses whom the Party has long relied on were rejected. At the beginning of the "Cultural Revolution," the vast majority of participants in the movement acted out of their faith in Comrade Mao Zedong and the Party. Except for a handful of extremists, however, they did not approve of launching ruthless struggles against leading Party cadres at all levels. With the lapse of time, following their own circuitous paths, they eventually attained a heightened political consciousness and consequently began to adopt a skeptical or wait-and-see attitude toward the "Cultural Revolution," or even resisted and opposed it. Many people were assailed either more or less severely for this very reason. Such a state of affairs could not but provide openings to be exploited by opportunists, careerists, and conspirators, not a few of whom were escalated to high or even key positions.

4. Practice has shown that the "Cultural Revolution" did not in fact constitute a revolution or social progress in any sense, nor could it possibly have done so. It was we and not the enemy at all who were thrown into disorder by the "Cultural Revolution." Therefore, from beginning to end, it did not turn "great disorder under heaven" into "great order under heaven," nor could it conceivably have done so. After the state power in the form of the people's democratic dictatorship was established in China, and especially after socialist transformation was basically completed and the exploiters were eliminated as classes, the socialist revolution represented a fundamental break with the past in both content and method, even though its tasks remained to be com-

pleted. Of course, it was essential to take proper account of certain undesirable phenomena that undoubtedly existed in Party and state organisms and to remove them by correct measures in conformity with the Constitution, the laws, and the Party Constitution. But on no account should the theories and methods of the "Cultural Revolution" have been applied. Under socialist conditions, there is no economic or political basis for carrying out a great political revolution in which "one class overthrows another. It decidedly could not come up with any constructive program, but could only bring grave disorder, damage, and retrogression in its train. History has shown that the "Cultural Revolution," initiated by a leader laboring under a misapprehension and capitalized on by counterrevolutionary cliques, led to domestic turmoil and brought catastrophe to the Party, the state, and the whole people.

The "Cultural Revolution" can be divided into three stages.

1. *From the Initiation of the "Cultural Revolution" to the Ninth National Congress of the Party in April 1969.* The convening of the enlarged Political Bureau meeting of the Central Committee of the Party in May 1966 and the Eleventh Plenary Session of the Eighth Central Committee in August of that year marked the launching of the "Cultural Revolution" on a full scale. These two meetings adopted the May 16 Circular and the Decision of the Central Committee of the Communist Party of China Concerning the Great Proletarian Cultural Revolution respectively. They launched an erroneous struggle against the so-called anti-Party clique of Peng Zhen, Luo Ruiqing, Lu Dingyi, and Yang Shangkun and the so-called headquarters of Liu Shaoqi and Deng Xiaoping. They wrongly reorganized the central leading organs, set up the "Cultural Revolution Group Under the Central Committee of the Chinese Communist Party," and gave it a major part of the power of the Central Committee. In fact, Comrade Mao Zedong's personal leadership characterized by "Left" errors took the place of the collective leadership of the Central Committee, and the cult of Comrade Mao Zedong was frenziedly pushed to an extreme. Lin Biao, Jiang Qing, Kang Sheng, Zhang Chunqiao, and others, acting chiefly in the name of the "Cultural Revolution Group," exploited the situation to incite people to "overthrow everything and wage full-scale civil war." Around February 1967, at various meetings, Tan Zhenlin, Chen Yi, Ye Jianying, Li Fuchun, Li Xiannian, Xu Xiangqian, Nie Rongzhen, and other Political Bureau members and leading comrades of the Military Commis-

sion of the Central Committee sharply criticized the mistakes of the "Cultural Revolution." This was labeled the "February Adverse Current," and they were attacked and repressed. Comrades Zhu De and Chen Yun were also wrongly criticized. Almost all leading Party and government departments in the different spheres and localities were stripped of their power or reorganized. The chaos was such that it was necessary to send in the People's Liberation Army to support the Left, the workers, and the peasants and to institute military control and military training. It played a positive role in stabilizing the situation, but it also produced some negative consequences. The Ninth Congress of the Party legitimatized the erroneous theories and practices of the "Cultural Revolution," and so reinforced the positions of Lin Biao, Jiang Qing, Kang Sheng, and others in the Central Committee of the Party. The guidelines of the Ninth Congress were wrong, ideologically, politically, and organizationally.

2. *From the Ninth National Congress of the Party to Its Tenth National Congress in August 1973.* In 1970–71 the counterrevolutionary Lin Biao clique plotted to capture supreme power and attempted an armed counterrevolutionary coup d'état. Such was the outcome of the "Cultural Revolution," which overturned a series of fundamental Party principles. Objectively, it announced the failure of the theories and practices of the "Cultural Revolution." Comrades Mao Zedong and Zhou Enlai ingeniously thwarted the plotted coup. Supported by Comrade Mao Zedong, Comrade Zhou Enlai took charge of the day-to-day work of the Central Committee and things began to improve in all fields. During the criticism and repudiation of Lin Biao in 1972, he correctly proposed criticism of the ultra-Left trend of thought. In fact, this was an extension of the correct proposals put forward around February 1967 by many leading comrades of the Central Committee who had called for the correction of the errors of the "Cultural Revolution." Comrade Mao Zedong, however, erroneously held that the task was still to oppose the "ultra-Right." The Tenth Congress of the Party perpetuated the "Left" errors of the Ninth Congress and made Wang Hongwen a vice' chairman of the Party. Jiang Qing, Zhang Chunqiao, Yao Wenyuan, and Wang Hongwen formed a Gang of Four inside the Political Bureau of the Central Committee, thus strengthening the influence of the counterrevolutionary Jiang Qing clique.

3. *From the Tenth Congress of the Party to October 1976.* Early in 1974 Jiang Qing, Wang Hongwen, and others launched a campaign to "criticize Lin Biao and Confucius." Jiang Qing and the others directed

the spearhead at Comrade Zhou Enlai, which was different in nature from the campaign conducted in some localities and organizations where individuals involved in and incidents connected with the conspiracies of the counterrevolutionary Lin Biao clique were investigated. Comrade Mao Zedong approved the launching of the movement to "criticize Lin Biao and Confucius." When he found that Jiang Qing and the others were turning it to their advantage in order to seize power, he severely criticized them. He declared that they had formed a "Gang of Four" and pointed out that Jiang Qing harbored the wild ambition of making herself chairman of the Central Committee and "forming a cabinet" by political manipulation. In 1975, when Comrade Zhou Enlai was seriously ill, Comrade Deng Xiaoping, with the support of Comrade Mao Zedong, took charge of the day-to-day work of the Central Committee. He convened an enlarged meeting of the Military Commission of the Central Committee and several other important meetings with a view to solving problems in industry, agriculture, transport, and science and technology, and began to straighten out the work in many fields so that the situation took an obvious turn for the better. However, Comrade Mao Zedong could not bear to accept systematic correction of the errors of the "Cultural Revolution" by Comrade Deng Xiaoping and triggered the movement to "criticize Deng and counter the Right deviationist trend to reverse correct verdicts," once again plunging the nation into turmoil. In January of that year, Comrade Zhou Enlai passed away. Comrade Zhou Enlai was utterly devoted to the Party and the people and stuck to his post till his dying day. He found himself in an extremely difficult situation throughout the "Cultural Revolution." He always kept the general interest in mind, bore the heavy burden of office without complaint, racking his brains and untiringly endeavoring to keep the normal work of the Party and the state going, to minimize the damage caused by the "Cultural Revolution," and to protect many Party and non-Party cadres. He waged all forms of struggle to counter sabotage by the counterrevolutionary Lin Biao and Jiang Qing cliques. His death left the whole Party and people in the most profound grief. In April of the same year, a powerful movement of protest signaled by the Tiananmen Incident swept the whole country, a movement to mourn for the late Premier Zhou Enlai and oppose the Gang of Four. In essence, the movement was a demonstration of support for the Party's correct leadership as represented by Comrade Deng Xiaoping. It laid the ground for massive popular support for the subsequent overthrow of the counterrevolutionary Jiang Qing clique. The

Political Bureau of the Central Committee and Comrade Mao Zedong wrongly assessed the nature of the Tiananmen Incident and dismissed Comrade Deng Xiaoping from all his posts inside and outside the Party. As soon as Comrade Mao Zedong passed away in September 1976, the counterrevolutionary Jiang Qing clique stepped up its plot to seize supreme Party and state leadership. Early in October of the same year, the Political Bureau of the Central Committee, executing the will of the Party and the people, resolutely smashed the clique and brought the catastrophic "Cultural Revolution" to an end. This was a great victory won by the entire Party, army, and people after prolonged struggle. Hua Guofeng, Ye Jianying, Li Xiannian, and other comrades played a vital part in the struggle to crush the clique.

Chief responsibility for the grave "Left" error of the "Cultural Revolution," an error comprehensive in magnitude and protracted in duration, does indeed lie with Comrade Mao Zedong. But after all it was the error of a great proletarian revolutionary. Comrade Mao Zedong paid constant attention to overcoming shortcomings in the life of the Party and state. In his later years, however, far from making a correct analysis of many problems, he confused right and wrong and the people with the enemy during the "Cultural Revolution." While making serious mistakes, he repeatedly urged the whole Party to study the works of Marx, Engels, and Lenin conscientiously and imagined that his theory and practice were Marxist and that they were essential for the consolidation of the dictatorship of the proletariat. Herein lies his tragedy. While persisting in the comprehensive error of the "Cultural Revolution," he checked and rectified some of its specific mistakes, protected some leading Party cadres and non-Party public figures, and enabled some leading cadres to return to important leading posts. He led the struggle to smash the counterrevolutionary Lin Biao clique. He made major criticisms and exposures of Jiang Qing, Zhang Chunqiao, and others, frustrating their sinister ambition to seize supreme leadership. All this was crucial to the subsequent and relatively painless overthrow of the Gang of Four by our Party. In his later years, he still remained alert to safeguarding the security of our country, stood up to the pressure of the social imperialists, pursued a correct foreign policy, firmly supported the just struggles of all peoples, outlined the correct strategy of the three worlds, and advanced the important principle that China could never seek hegemony. During the "Cultural Revolution" our Party was not destroyed but maintained its unity. The State Council and the People's Liberation

Army were still able to do much of their essential work. The Fourth National People's Congress, which was attended by deputies from all nationalities and all walks of life, was convened, and it determined the composition of the State Council with Comrades Zhou Enlai and Deng Xiaoping as the core of its leadership. The foundation of China's socialist system remained intact, and it was possible to continue socialist economic construction. Our country remained united and exerted a significant influence on international affairs. All these important facts are inseparable from the great role played by Comrade Mao Zedong. For these reasons, and particularly for his vital contributions to the cause of the revolution over the years, the Chinese people have always regarded Comrade Mao Zedong as their respected and beloved great leader and teacher.

The struggle waged by the Party and the people against "Left" errors and against the counterrevolutionary Lin Biao and Jiang Qing cliques during the "Cultural Revolution" was arduous and full of twists and turns, and it never ceased. Rigorous tests throughout the "Cultural Revolution" have proved that standing on the correct side in the struggle were the overwhelming majority of the members of the Eighth Central Committee of the Party and the members it elected to its Political Bureau, Standing Committee, and Secretariat. Most of our Party cadres, whether they were wrongly dismissed or remained at their posts, whether they were rehabilitated early or late, are loyal to the Party and people and steadfast in their belief in the cause of socialism and communism. Most of the intellectuals, model workers, patriotic democrats, patriotic overseas Chinese, and cadres and masses of all strata and all nationalities who had been wronged and persecuted did not waver in their love for the motherland and in their support for the Party and socialism. Party and state leaders such as Comrades Liu Shaoqi, Peng Dehuai, He Long, and Tao Zhu and all other Party and non-Party comrades who were persecuted to death in the "Cultural Revolution" will live forever in the memories of the Chinese people. It was through the joint struggles waged by the entire Party and the masses of workers, peasants, PLA officers and men, intellectuals, educated youth, and cadres that the havoc wrought by the "Cultural Revolution" was somewhat mitigated. Some progress was made in our economy despite tremendous losses. Grain output increased relatively steadily. Significant achievements were scored in industry, communications, and capital construction and in science and technology. New railways were built, and the Changjiang River Bridge at Nanjing was completed; a number of large enterprises using advanced technology went into operation; hydrogen bomb tests were successfully undertaken and manmade satellites successfully launched and retrieved; and new hybrid strains of long-grained rice were developed and popularized. Despite the domestic turmoil, the People's Liberation Army bravely defended the security of the motherland. And new prospects were opened up in the sphere of foreign affairs. Needless to say, none of these successes can be attributed in any way to the "Cultural Revolution," without which we would have scored far greater achievements for our cause. Although we suffered from sabotage by the counterrevolutionary Lin Biao and Jiang Qing cliques during the "Cultural Revolution," we won out over them in the end. The Party, the people's political power, the people's army, and Chinese society on the whole remained unchanged in nature. Once again history has proved that our people are a great people and that our Party and socialist system have enormous vitality.

In addition to the above-mentioned immediate cause of Comrade Mao Zedong's mistake in leadership, there are complex social and historical causes underlying the "Cultural Revolution," which dragged on for as long as a decade.

★ RADICAL REFORM ★

Once Deng had outmaneuvered and disposed of Hua Guofeng and other neo-Maoists, by 1982 he and his principal protégés, Hu Yaobang and Zhao Ziyang, were given a relatively free hand to experiment with and adopt a wide variety of reformist policies. During the mid-1980s the most radical of these were adopted. All policy spheres were affected—the economy, education, science and technology, the military, culture, and so on. Even the Communist Party itself underwent radical revision of its membership and the way it operated.

Whenever societies and staid institutions are subjected to such sweeping reforms, resistance is to be expected. Throughout this period Deng and his associates encountered subtle but strong opposition from those who believed the reforms were going too far and too fast. When student demonstrations erupted in late 1985 (see Chapter 2), Deng's opponents made him pay a price by forcing CCP General Secretary Hu Yaobang to resign. Hu was replaced by Premier Zhao Ziyang. After an initial hesitancy, Zhao resumed and accelerated the radical reforms initiated by Hu.

ZHAO ZIYANG,
ADVANCE ALONG THE ROAD OF SOCIALISM
WITH CHINESE CHARACTERISTICS

At the Thirteenth Congress of the Chinese Communist Party in October 1987, Premier Zhao Ziyang unveiled his blueprint for even more sweeping and fundamental reform in China's economic, social, and political systems. Although Zhao was purged in 1989, much of his economic and social agenda was subsequently adopted—while his radical ideas for political reform were abandoned.

This selection was originally published as a special supplement to the Beijing Review *in November 1987.*

Comrades,

omrades,
As requested by the Twelfth Central Committee of the Communist Party of China, I shall now make a report to this congress on the work of the Committee.

Historic Achievements and the Tasks of the Current Congress

The Twelfth National Congress of the Party upheld and developed the line of the Third Plenary Session of the Eleventh Central Committee by setting forth a program designed to create a new situation in all fields of socialist modernization. Since that congress, the Central Committee of the Party has convened seven plenary sessions and a national conference. At these meetings timely, correct policy decisions were made which did much to promote reform, the opening to the outside world, and the effort to achieve both material progress and cultural and ideological progress.

It has been a period of nine years from the time of the Third Plenary Session of the Eleventh Central Committee through the Twelfth National Congress to the present congress. During these nine years, on the basis of the great achievements scored in socialist construction since the founding of the People's Republic of China, we have opened up a new period of development in the Party's history, and profound changes have taken place in the country.

By concentrating on economic development, we have brought about sustained, stable growth in the national economy. During these nine years the gross national product, state revenues, and the average income of both urban and rural residents have all approximately doubled. Therefore, we are fully assured that by the end of this century we will attain the objective of economic development set by the Twelfth National Congress.

With the growth of production we have started to solve, or found ways for solving, certain serious social and economic problems which had long plagued us:

• The overwhelming majority of our one billion people have secured a life with enough food and clothing. People in some areas are beginning to become well-off. There are still certain areas where the problem of food and clothing has not yet been solved, but even in those places there has been some improvement.

• We have created job opportunities on an extensive scale in both urban and rural areas. As a result, 70 million people in cities and towns have been newly employed, while in the countryside, where village and township enterprises have emerged as a new force, 80 million peasants have now shifted full time or part time from farming to industry.

• Market supplies have greatly increased. We have basically put an end to acute and long-lasting shortages of consumer goods.

• The serious imbalance between major sectors of the national economy has been markedly reduced, and the economy has gradually been set on a course of more or less coordinated development.

It should be said that in the last nine years the national economic strength has increased more rapidly and the people have obtained greater material benefits than in any other period since the founding of the People's Republic. This is in sharp contrast to the situation in the period of twenty years from the late 1950s to December 1978, when the Third Plenary Session of the Eleventh Central Committee was held. During those years, under the influence of the Left guiding ideology, "class struggle" was taken as the "key link," economic development met frequent setbacks, and the people's standard of living improved only slightly.

All these achievements in economic development over the past nine years are inseparable from the resolute efforts we made, after we had restored things to order, to advance the all-round reform and the open policy.

The Primary Stage of Socialism and the Basic Line of the Party

A correct understanding of the present historical stage of Chinese society is of prime importance for building socialism with Chinese characteristics, and it is the essential basis on which to formulate and implement a correct line and correct policies.

Our Party has already made a clear and definite statement on this question: China is now in the primary stage of socialism. There are two aspects to this thesis. First, the Chinese society is already a socialist society. We must persevere in socialism and never deviate from it. Second, China's socialist society is still in its primary stage. We must proceed from this reality and not jump over this stage. Under the specific historical conditions of contemporary China, to believe that the Chinese people cannot take the socialist road without going through the stage of fully developed capitalism is to take a mechanistic position on the question of the development of revolution, and that is the major cognitive root of Right mistakes. On the other hand, to believe that it is possible to jump over the primary stage of socialism, in which the productive forces are to be highly developed, is to take a utopian position on this question, and that is the major cognitive root of Left mistakes.

China used to be a semicolonial, semifeudal country. During the more than one hundred years since the middle of the last century, repeated trials of strength between various political forces, repeated failures of the democratic revolution of the old type, and the final victory of the new-democratic revolution have proved that the capitalist road is a blind alley for China and that the only way out is the socialist road, which China is now taking under the leadership of the Communist Party, having overthrown the reactionary rule of imperialism, feudalism, and bureaucrat capitalism. But precisely because our socialism has emerged from the womb of a semicolonial, semifeudal society, with the productive forces lagging far behind those of the developed capitalist countries, we are destined to go through a very long primary stage. During this stage we shall accomplish industrialization and the commercialization, socialization, and modernization of production, which many other countries have achieved under capitalist conditions.

How do things stand in China, now that socialism has been developing here for more than three decades? On the one hand, a socialist economic system based on public ownership of the means of production has been instituted, a socialist political system of people's democratic dictatorship has been established, and the guiding role of Marxism in the realm of ideology has been affirmed. The system of exploitation and the exploiting classes have been abolished. China's economic strength has grown enormously and educational, scientific, and cultural undertakings have considerably expanded. On the other hand, the country has a huge population and a poor foundation to start with, and its per capita gross national product still ranks among the lowest in the world. The picture is very clear: Out of a population of more than one billion, 800 million people live in rural areas and, for the most part, still use hand tools to make a living. A certain number of modern industries coexist with many industries that are several decades or even a century behind present-day standards. Some areas that are fairly developed economically coexist with vast areas that are underdeveloped and impoverished. A small amount of science and technology is up to the highest world standards, while the scientific and technological level as a whole is low, and nearly one-quarter of the population is still illiterate or semi-literate. The backwardness of the productive forces determines the following aspects of the relations of production: socialization of production, which is essential for expanded socialist public ownership, is still at a very low level; the commodity economy and domestic market are only beginning to develop; the natural economy and seminatural economy constitute a considerable proportion of the whole; and the socialist economic system is not yet mature and well developed. In the realm of the superstructure, a number of economic and cultural conditions that are necessary if we are to promote a high degree of socialist democracy are far from ripe, and decadent feudal and capitalist ideologies and the small producers' force of habit still have widespread influence in society and often corrode Party cadres and public servants. All this shows that we still have a long way to go before we can advance beyond the primary stage of socialism.

Building socialism in a big, backward Eastern country like China is something new in the history of the development of Marxism. We are not in the situation envisaged by the founders of Marxism, in which socialism is built on the basis of highly developed capitalism, nor are we in exactly the same situation as other socialist countries. So we cannot blindly follow what the books say, nor can we mechanically imitate the examples of other countries. Rather, proceeding from China's actual conditions and integrating the basic principles of Marxism with those conditions, we must find a way to build socialism with Chinese characteristics through practice. Our Party has explored ways of doing this and has achieved major successes. But the road it has traversed has taken many twists and turns, and this has cost us dear. Beginning in the late 1950s, under the influence of the mistaken Left thinking, we were too impatient for quick results and sought absolute perfection, believing that we could dramatically expand the productive forces by relying simply on our subjective will and on mass movements, and that the broader the scale and the higher the level of socialist ownership, the better. Also, for a long time we relegated the task of expanding the productive forces to a position of secondary importance and continued to "take class struggle as the key link" after the socialist transformation was basically completed. Many things which fettered the growth of the productive forces and which were not inherently socialist, or were applicable only under certain particular historical conditions, were regarded as "socialist principles" to be adhered to. Conversely, many things which, under socialist conditions, were favorable to the growth of the productive forces and to the commercialization, socialization, and modernization of production were dubbed "restoration of capitalism" to be opposed. As a consequence, a structure of ownership evolved in which undue emphasis was placed on a single form of ownership, and a rigid economic structure took shape, along with a corresponding political structure based on over-concentralization of power. All this seriously hampered the development of the productive forces and of the socialist commodity economy. This state of affairs has taught us that it is of prime importance to have a clear understanding of China's basic conditions and of the present stage of socialism in China.

What, then, is this historic stage, the primary stage of socialism in China? It is not the initial phase in a general sense, a phase that every country goes through in the process of building socialism. Rather it is, in a particular sense, the specific stage China must necessarily go through while building socialism under conditions of backward productive forces and an underdeveloped commodity economy. It will be at least one hundred years from the 1950s, when the socialist transformation of private ownership of the means of production was basically completed, to the time when socialist modernization will have been in the main accomplished, and all these years belong to the primary stage of socialism. This stage is different from both the transitional period, in which the socialist economic basis was not yet laid, and the stage in which socialist modernization will have been achieved. The principal contradiction we face during the present stage is the contradiction between the growing material and cultural needs of the people and backward production. Class struggle will continue to exist within certain limits for a long time to come, but it is no longer the principal contradiction. To resolve the principal contradiction of the present stage we must vigorously expand the commodity economy, raise labor productivity, gradually achieve the modernization of industry, agriculture, national defense, and science and technology, and, to this end, reform such aspects of the relations of production and of the superstructure as are incompatible with the growth of the productive forces.

In short, the primary stage of China's socialism is one in which we shall gradually put an end to poverty and backwardness. It is a stage in which an agricultural country, where farming is based on manual labor and where people engaged in agriculture constitute the majority of the population, will gradually turn into a modern industrial country where nonagricultural workers constitute the majority. It is a stage in which a society with the natural and seminatural economy making up a very large proportion of the whole will turn into one with a highly developed commodity economy. It is a stage in which, by introducing reforms and exploring new ways, we shall establish and develop socialist economic, political, and cultural structures that are full of vitality. Lastly, it is a stage in which the people of the whole country will rise to meet the challenge and bring about a great rejuvenation of the Chinese nation.

Comrades! The basic line of our Party in building socialism with Chinese characteristics during the primary stage of socialism is as follows: to lead the people of all our nationalities in a united, self-reliant, intensive, and pioneering effort to turn China into a prosperous, strong, democratic, culturally advanced, and modern socialist country by making economic development our central task while adhering to the four cardinal principles and persevering in reform and the open policy. Adherence to the four cardinal principles—that is, keeping to the socialist road and upholding the people's democratic dictatorship, leadership by the Communist Party, and Marxism-Leninism and Mao Zedong Thought—is the foundation underlying all our efforts to build the country. Adherence to the general principle of reform and the open policy has been a new development of our Party's line since the Third Plenary Session of the Eleventh Central Committee and has added to the four cardinal principles new content appropriate to our time. The two basic points—adherence to the four cardinal principles and adherence to reform and the open policy—are interrelated and mutually dependent, and they are integrated in the practice of building socialism with Chinese characteristics. We must not interpret the four cardinal principles as something rigid, lest we come to doubt or even reject the general principle of reform and opening to the outside world. Neither can we interpret reform and the open policy as something bourgeois liberal, lest we deviate from the path of socialism. In the primary stage when the country is still underdeveloped, the tendency toward bourgeois liberalization, which rejects the socialist system in favor of capitalism, will persist for a long time. Unless we overcome hidebound thinking and pursue reform and the open policy, we will not be able to demonstrate convincingly the superiority of socialism and to enhance its appeal, and this failure will encourage the spread of bourgeois liberalization. The struggle to eliminate the interference and influence of the two erroneous tendencies—hidebound thinking and liberalization—will last throughout the primary stage of socialism. Since the old Left habits of thought are deep-rooted and since they are the main source of the obstacles to reform and the open policy, the major task for quite a long time will be to overcome hidebound thinking. In short, the need to be guided by the two basic points and to make economic development our central task is the principal thing we have learnt through experience and the main content of our Party's basic line in the primary stage of socialism.

Reforming the Political Structure

The deepening of the ongoing reform of the economic structure makes reform of the political structure increasingly urgent. The process of developing a socialist commodity economy should also involve the building of a socialist democracy. Without reform of the political structure, reform of the economic structure cannot succeed in the end. The Central Committee of the Party believes that it is high time to put reform of the political structure on the agenda for the whole Party. Comrade Deng Xiaoping's speech "On the Reform of the System of Party and State Leadership," delivered to an enlarged meeting of the Political Bureau of the Central Committee in August 1980, is a guide to reform of the political structure.

The purpose of reforming both the political and economic structures is, under the leadership of the Party and the socialist system, to better develop the productive forces and to take full advantage of the superiority of socialism. In other words, we shall catch up with the developed capitalist countries economically and, politically, we shall create a democracy that is of a higher level and more effective than the democracy of those countries. We shall also try to produce more and better-trained professionals than they do. The merits of the reform should be judged on the basis of whether these objectives are attained.

China is a socialist country under the people's democratic dictatorship, and its basic political system is good. However, there are major defects in our system of leadership, in the organizational structure, and in our style of work. Chief among these defects are overconcentration of power, a serious degree of bureaucratism, and feudal influences that are far from eliminated. The purpose of reforming the political structure is to promote what is beneficial and eliminate what is harmful and to build a socialist democracy with Chinese characteristics. The long-range goal of reform is to build a socialist political system with a high degree of democracy and a complete set of laws, a system that is effective and full of vitality. And that is something which cannot be achieved without sustained effort.

Like the development of a socialist commodity economy, the building of a socialist democracy is a gradual, cumulative process. Confronted as we are with the complicated social contradictions that arise in the drive for modernization, we need a peaceful social and political environment. We shall never again allow the kind of "great democracy" that undermines state law and social stability. The system of the people's congresses, the system of multiparty cooperation and political consultation under the leadership of the Communist Party, and the principle of democratic centralism are the characteristics and advantages of our system. We shall never abandon them and introduce a Western system of separation of the three powers and of different parties ruling the country in turn. In the reform of the political structure, we must handle properly the relationship between democracy and stability and between democracy and efficiency. We must overcome bureaucratism and feudal influence so as to promote the reform of the economic structure and the policy of opening up both internally and externally. The immediate objective of reform is to institute a system of leadership that will help to raise the efficiency, increase the vitality, and stimulate the initiative of all sectors of society. Every measure taken in the reform should serve this objective and help to solve those problems for whose solution conditions are ripe.

SEPARATING PARTY AND GOVERNMENT

The Communist Party is the leading force in building socialism in China. In the new situation the Party's leadership can be strengthened only by improving the system, methods, and style of leadership. In the last few years we have worked hard to improve the Party's leadership and have achieved some progress. But one long-standing problem has not yet been completely solved: the lack of distinction between the functions of the Party and those of the government and the substitution of the Party for the government. Until this problem is solved, Party leadership cannot be really strengthened and other reform measures cannot be smoothly carried out. Therefore, the key to reforming the political structure is the separation of Party and government.

This means the separation of the functions of the Party and the government. It was under the Party's leadership that a Constitution was drawn up for the country and laws were enacted, and the Party must conduct its activities within the limits prescribed by that Constitution and those laws. It was under the leadership of the Party that organs of state power, mass organizations, and all kinds of economic and cultural associations were established, and the Party must ensure that those organs exercise their functions to the full. It should respect mass organizations, enterprises, and institutions and not monopolize the conduct of their affairs. The Party exercises political leadership, which means that it formulates political principles, points the political direction, makes major policy decisions, and recommends cadres for the key posts in organs of state power. The principal method by which it exercises political leadership in state affairs is as follows: through legal procedures what the Party advocates becomes the will of the state, and the people are mobilized by the Party organizations and the good example of Party members to implement the Party's line, principles, and policies. The Party and the organs of state power differ in their nature, functions, organizational forms, and methods of work. It is necessary to reform the system of Party leadership, to distinguish between the functions of Party organizations and those of state organs, and to rationalize relations between the Party organizations and the people's congresses, the governments, the judicial organs, mass organizations, enterprises, institutions, and various other public organizations, so that each performs its own functions. These relations should gradually become institutionalized.

As conditions are different in the central departments, the localities, and the grassroots units, the concrete methods they use to separate the Party organizations and the government departments should be different. The Central Committee should make policy decisions on such important questions as China's internal affairs, foreign affairs, the economy, and defense, recommend persons for leading posts in the supreme state organs, and exercise political leadership in all fields. The local Party committees at the provincial, municipal, and county levels should exercise political leadership in local work, carrying out the line formulated by the Central Committee and ensuring that the decrees of the central government are implemented. Their principal responsibilities should be to carry out directives from higher Party organizations and from the Central Committee; to ensure the implementation in their local areas of directives from governments of higher levels and from the State Council; to propose policy decisions on important local issues; to recommend cadres for key posts in local state organs; and to coordinate activities of the various local organizations. The relations between local Party committees and state organs at the same level should be worked out through practice and gradually become standardized and institutionalized. The separation of Party and government should not be carried out at village and township level until it has been done at county level. In enterprises, Party organizations should supervise the work and ensure that it is accomplished. Instead of attempting to provide centralized leadership, they should support the directors and managers in their assumption of overall leadership. In institutions, Party organizations should play the same role once a system is introduced under which administrative heads assume full responsibility.

The Party's organizational form and executive organs should be adjusted to conform to its new form of activity and new methods of leadership. Henceforth the Party committee at a given level will not designate a full-time secretary or member of its standing committee, who holds no government post, to take charge of government work. The executive organ of the Party committee should be smaller but more efficient, Party departments that overlap their counterpart government departments should be abolished, and the administrative affairs they are now managing should be transferred to competent government departments. The present practice in government departments of making leading Party members' groups responsible to the Party committees of the next higher level which have approved their establishment is not conducive to unity and efficiency in government work; such groups should therefore be gradually abolished. The Party's commissions for discipline inspection at all levels should not deal with breaches of the law or infractions of administrative regulations but should concentrate on fostering a strong sense of discipline, thus helping Party committees to cultivate fine conduct on the part of their members. The practice of making Party organizations in enterprises and institutions directly responsible to the Party organizations of higher administrative departments should be gradually changed so that in future they will be led by local Party committees.

Separating the functions of Party and government is a major reform in the system of Party leadership. It must be pointed out that when there is no distinction between Party and government, the Party's position is in fact lowered and its leadership weakened; only when the two are separated is it possible for the Party to ensure its leadership and improve its methods. When there is no distinction between Party and government, the Party has no time or energy to attend to Party building; only when the two are separated is it possible to see that "the Party handles Party affairs." When there is no distinction between Party and government, the Party has to bear the burden of administrative work and may easily become one opposite of a contradiction or even the focal point of many contradictions; only when the two are separated is it possible for the

Party to handle contradictions with ease, assume overall control of a situation, and coordinate the work in all fields. When there is no distinction between Party and government, the Party becomes the executive body; only when the two are separated is it possible for Party organizations to exercise better supervision and effectively prevent or overcome bureaucratism. All members of the Party should eagerly plunge into the reform in order to bring about this historic change.

DELEGATING POWERS TO LOWER LEVELS

Overconcentration of power is manifested not only in the concentration of all power of administrative, economic, and cultural departments and mass organizations in the hands of leading organs of Party committees but also in the concentration of all power of grassroots units in the hands of leading organs at higher levels. On the one hand, our leading organs have taken charge of many matters which they should not and cannot handle, or cannot handle efficiently, getting bogged down in routine work. On the other hand, the grassroots units lack the power to make decisions, and it is hard to fully arouse the initiative of the people. The way to solve this problem is to delegate power to lower levels. This devolution of power has proved effective in rural reform and should be carried out in all other fields.

Decisions and functions that can be properly handled at lower levels should be handled there. This is a general principle. In the relations between the central authorities and the local authorities, it is essential to gradually distinguish between the duties of each, while ensuring that decrees of the central government are implemented across the country. Thus local matters will be handled by local authorities, while the central authorities determine major policies and exercise supervision. In the relations between the government and enterprises and institutions, it is essential to delegate powers of operation and management to the latter so as to let them manage their own affairs with full authority. The function of the government is to provide service for enterprises and to supervise them, in accordance with laws, regulations, and policies. In the relations between the Party and the government on the one hand and mass organizations on the other, it is essential to give full play to mass organizations and to self-managed mass organizations at the grassroots level [i.e., residents' and villagers' committees—*Tr.*] so that the people will handle their own affairs always in accordance with the law. Localities, departments, and units should all take the overall interests into account and conduct their affairs strictly in accordance with laws, regulations, and policies. In delegating powers to lower levels, we must focus on expanding the power of major cities, enterprises, and institutions, in order to revitalize enterprises and to give cities a greater role in developing a socialist commodity economy. Once it has been decided that certain powers are to be delegated to cities, enterprises, and institutions, they must not be withheld by intermediate administrative levels. This devolution of power is an important means of breaking down barriers between different departments and regions.

Delegating powers involves the reform of many rules and regulations. To transform their functions and reform their working organs, departments at different levels should make investigations, listen attentively to the opinions of grassroots units, and work out detailed provisions.

REFORMING GOVERNMENT ORGANS

Bureaucratism remains a serious problem in the political life of our Party and the state. For economic, cultural, social, and historical reasons, our struggle against it will last a long time. Separating the functions of the Party from those of the government, delegating more powers to lower levels, and developing socialist democracy will all help overcome bureaucratism. It should be noted that overstaffing, overlapping, and unwieldiness of government organs, confusion of their responsibilities, and buck passing are also major causes of bureaucratism. We must therefore resolve to reform these organs from top to bottom.

To consolidate the achievements of structural reform and to institutionalize administrative management, we must improve administrative legislation, drawing up basic norms and procedures for administrative work. We should improve current regulations governing administrative organs and formulate rules specifying their size, in order to control the establishment of such organs and their manning quotas through legal and budgetary means. We should devise an administrative responsibility system at various levels to improve work quality and efficiency. We should formulate an administrative procedural law, strengthen supervision over administrative work and personnel, and investigate cases of neglect or dereliction of duty and other breaches of law or discipline by administrative personnel.

REFORMING THE PERSONNEL SYSTEM RELATING TO CADRES

We cannot stimulate the cadres' energy, efficiency, and initiative without reforming the personnel system. Over the past few years we have taken some important measures and accumulated some useful experience in this regard, but serious defects still exist in the personnel system relating to cadres. These are mainly as follows: The concept of the "state cadre" is too general and lacks a scientific classification; the power of cadre management is overconcentrated and the people who handle personnel affairs lack professional knowledge; the methods are outdated and simplistic, which hinders the intellectual growth of talented people; the management system is flawed; and there are no laws governing the way personnel are used. As a result, we have for a long time been faced with two major problems: First, it is difficult for promising young people to fully display their talents; and second, it is difficult to avoid malpractices in the use of people. To reform the personnel system relating to cadres we must alter the single category of "state cadre" and convert the current unified central management into a scientific system of management by establishing a number of categories. We must abandon the current practice of managing all personnel according to the same single pattern applied to Party and government cadres and institute different management systems for different categories of cadres. And we must change the present personnel system, which is not governed by legislation or democratic means, into a system governed by law and supervised by the general public.

The emphasis of the current reform of the personnel system relating to cadres is on establishing a system of civil service. This means formulating laws and regulations for the scientific management of government personnel who exercise the administrative power of the state and perform official duties. These civil servants are to be classified in two categories: those handling political affairs and those doing professional work. Civil servants in the political affairs category, whose tenure in office will be for a specified period of time, must be managed strictly in accordance with the relevant provisions of the Constitution and the Organic Law and be subjected to supervision by the public. The Central Committee of the Party and local Party committees at various levels will recommend candidates in the political affairs category at the corresponding levels to the national or local people's congresses, through legal procedures, and will supervise and manage those civil servants in this category who are Party members. Civil servants in the professional work category, whose tenure in office is to be permanent, will also be managed in accordance with the law governing civil servants. For posts in this category, people will have to pass a statutory examination in open competition. The job responsibilities of such civil servants will be clearly defined and their performance will be evaluated in accordance with statutory standards and procedures. Their promotion, demotion, reward, and punishment will be based mainly on their work results. Their rights to training, wages, welfare, and retirement will be guaranteed by law. The implementation of this new system governing civil servants will make it easier for the Party to reinforce and improve leadership over personnel work, facilitate the growth of outstanding cadres in both categories who possess political integrity and professional competence, and help to improve the efficiency of government work and the stability of state administration. It will be a considerably long process to establish and develop such a system. We should lose no time in drafting rules and regulations concerning public servants, working out supporting measures, setting up institutions to manage such personnel, and making preparations to found a state administrative college.

ESTABLISHING A SYSTEM OF CONSULTATION AND DIALOGUE

To correctly handle contradictions and reconcile various social interests is an important task in a socialist society. Only when the leading bodies at all levels listen attentively to the views of the masses can they gear their work to actual conditions and avoid mistakes. And only when they let the people know what they are doing and what difficulties they face can they secure the people's understanding. There should be channels through which the voices and demands of the people can be easily and frequently transmitted to the leading bodies, and there should be places where the people can offer suggestions or pour out any grievances they may have. Different groups of people may have different interests and views, and they too need opportunities and channels for the exchange of ideas. It is therefore imperative to develop a system of consultation and dialogue, so that what is going on at higher levels can be promptly and accurately made known to lower levels and vice versa without impediment, thus enabling people at all levels to understand each other.

The basic principle for establishing a system of consultation and dialogue is to carry on the fine tradition of "from the masses, to the masses" and to make public the activities of the leading bodies, letting the people know about important events and discuss important issues. The first thing to do now is to formulate regulations regarding consultation and dialogue. These should clearly define which problems are to be solved by which units or organizations, through consultation and discussion. The consultation and discussion on issues that are important at the national, local, or grassroots level should be conducted at that level.

Leading bodies at all levels should make this a top priority in their work. While opening new channels for consultation and dialogue, we should make better use of existing ones. We should provide wider coverage of the activities of the government and the Party through all forms of modern mass media, to give scope to the supervisory role of public opinion, to support the masses in their criticism of shortcomings and mistakes in work, to oppose bureaucratism, and in general to combat all unhealthy tendencies.

IMPROVING A NUMBER OF SYSTEMS RELATING TO SOCIALIST DEMOCRACY

The essence of socialist democracy is that the people are masters of the country, genuinely enjoying all citizens' rights and the power of administering the state, enterprises, and institutions. In building socialist democracy at the present stage, we should place emphasis on practical results and on arousing the initiative of the grassroots units and the people. We should start with things we are able to do, concentrating on improving a number of basic systems.

The system of people's congresses is the fundamental system of government in China. In recent years the people's congresses at various levels have made much progress in their work. In the years ahead, they and their standing committees should continue to improve the way they function and to strengthen their work of legislation and supervision through law. They should maintain closer contact with the people in order to be better able to represent them and be supervised by them. Meanwhile, the National People's Congress, and particularly its Standing Committee, should be strengthened organizationally, and the committee members should gradually become younger in average age and serve full time. In addition, the Standing Committee and the special committees of the Congress should improve their rules for discussion and their working procedures, so that they will have adequate rules and regulations to abide by.

The Chinese People's Political Consultative Conference is a patriotic united front organization that comprises all of China's democratic parties, the people's organizations, and outstanding individuals from all walks of life. It should strengthen itself organizationally so as to make political consultation and democratic supervision a regular practice where important policies of the state and major issues of the people's life are concerned. While upholding the principles of "long-term coexistence and mutual supervision" and of "treating each other with all sincerity and sharing weal or woe," we should improve the system of multiparty cooperation and consultation under the leadership of the Communist Party, with a view to promoting the role played in China's political life by democratic parties and patriots without party affiliation. The trade unions, the Communist Youth League, the Women's Federation, and other mass organizations that have always been a bridge linking the Party and government with the working class and other sections of the people have an important role to play in the implementation of socialist democracy. It is essential for Party and government departments to maintain harmonious relations with these mass organizations so that the latter can carry out their work independently in light of their own characteristics. This will enable them to better express and defend the specific interests of the masses they represent, while safeguarding the overall interests of the people throughout the country. The mass organizations, too, should undertake organizational reform, changing their pattern of functioning by actively participating in consultation and dialogue, democratic management, and democratic supervision and focusing their attention on the grassroots units. And if they want to win the trust of the people, especially those at the grassroots level, they should also rid themselves of their official airs and overcome the tendency to become mere administrative institutions.

In the past few years China's elections have become more and more democratic. However, the electoral system has not been fully and effectively implemented and needs to be improved. We should respect the will of the voters and ensure that they have more options in elections. We should continue the practice of holding elections with more candidates than posts, as prescribed by law, and improve procedures for nominating candidates and methods of publicizing them. For instance, the present practice of setting rigid quotas for different geographical areas when nominating candidates for the election of deputies to congresses at various levels tends to prevent the election from fully reflecting the will of the voters. In order to have candidates who represent broader sections of the people, therefore, we shall introduce the practice of electing deputies not only from geographical areas, as is done at present, but also from different walks of life.

Institutionalizing democracy in grassroots units provides the foundation for ensuring that the working class and other sections of the people are masters of the country, as well as for mobilizing the initiative of people in all quarters and maintaining stability and unity in society. Since from time to time the rights of the masses are encroached upon, we should enact laws governing the press, publication, association, assembly, and procession, and establish a people's appeals system, so as to guarantee the citizens' rights and freedom as stipulated by the Constitution. At the same time, we should put an end to abuses of those rights and freedoms. It must be pointed out that leadership characterized by feudal, patriarchal practices is still found in some departments and grassroots units. To eliminate the conditions that allow such practices to persist, we should formulate rules and regulations promoting a rational flow of personnel, build a labor arbitration system, and promote the socialization of public welfare services.

As China is a multinationality country, safeguarding the unity of the motherland, upholding equality and solidarity among the nationalities, and promoting their common prosperity are of vital importance to the country's future. It is therefore imperative to enhance the regional autonomy of minority nationalities and devote great effort to training cadres from among them. We should continue to consolidate the great unity of all our nationalities, develop socialist relations of equality, solidarity, and mutual assistance among them, educate all Party members in implementing the Party's policy concerning nationalities, and encourage them to do their best in this regard.

STRENGTHENING THE SOCIALIST LEGAL SYSTEM

Socialist democracy is inseparable from a socialist legal system. Without stability and unity throughout the society, we can succeed neither in economic development nor in the reform of economic and political structures. In exercising democracy and dictatorship in all spheres of activity—political, economic, and social—we should see to it that there are laws to abide by, that laws already enacted are observed and enforced to the letter, and that violators are brought to justice.

We must attend to legislation and to economic development and reform at the same time. During the whole process of reform we must go on building our legal system. On the one hand, we should improve legislation and the procedures for law enforcement, enable the judicial organs to exercise independent authority, as prescribed by law, and enhance citizens' awareness of law; on the other hand, we should see to it that legislation guarantees good order in economic development and reform and consolidates achievements scored in reform. We should try to define, in terms of laws or rules, what should be encouraged and what should be rejected. Only in this way can we bring about a new standard for political, economic, and social activities. And only in this way can we institutionalize various aspects of the society: the relations between Party and government departments on the one hand and public organizations on the other; the activities within government departments; the relations among the central authorities, local authorities, and grassroots units; the training, selection, employment, and replacement of personnel; democracy at the grassroots level; and consultation between leadership and the rank and file. In short, through reform we should gradually establish a legal framework for our socialist democracy and institutionalize it. This is a fundamental guarantee against a recurrence of the "Cultural Revolution" and for lasting political stability in the country.

Our current political structure, which took shape during the revolutionary war years, was basically established in the period of socialist transformation. It developed in large-scale mass movements and in the process of constantly intensified mandatory planning. It is no longer suited to our drive for modernization in economic, political, cultural, and other fields under conditions of peace, or to the development of a socialist commodity economy. We should make a historical analysis of this state of affairs. The political structure was the product of the historical conditions of the time, but today things have changed. The cause of the Party has progressed, and it is therefore necessary to reform this structure. This is a difficult and complex task, so we must adopt resolute yet cautious policies, trying to implement them in a guided and orderly way and to advance the reform as steadily as possible. In this period of transition from the old structure to the new, we should make special efforts to ensure that work is coordinated and conflicts are avoided. In pursuing reform, we must stress experimentation, encourage exploration, seek practical interim methods and measures, and advance one step at a time. Because conditions are different in different areas, we cannot simply ask all areas to do the same thing at the same time. In the autonomous minority nationality areas and outlying districts in particular, we should adopt prudent measures which suit the local conditions, while in the special economic zones we can afford to be more flexible. In the army the reform has already achieved important results. Since things are different there, plans for further reform will be studied and decided upon separately by the Military Commission of the Central Committee.

The immediate objective for the reform of the political structure is limited. However, when that objective is achieved, it will lay a sound foundation for socialist democracy and for the realization of our long-range objective. This is a magnificent undertaking, and all Party members should take the initiative in the reform. Party organizations at all levels are expected to provide more effective leadership over the reform and to take the lead by reforming themselves.

Strengthening Party Building While Carrying Out Reform and the Open Policy

The Chinese Communist Party is a party armed with Marxism-Leninism and Mao Zedong Thought, a strong party that has been tempered in long years of struggle. To accomplish the arduous and complicated tasks defined at this congress and to better shoulder the great historic responsibility of leading the people in building socialism with Chinese characteristics, we must study the theory and practice of Party building under new conditions and further change those ideas and practices that do not meet the needs of the new situation, so as to effectively strengthen our work in this area.

Since Party building has always been closely connected with the Party's basic political line, all Party work in the new period must ensure the implementation of that line. This means that Party building must undergo changes in order to suit the new circumstances brought about by reform and the open policy. This guiding ideology should be embodied in the Party's ideological education, its organizational building, and its work style.

In ideological education, the Party must propagate its entire basic line, emphasizing the central task of economic development and the two basic points, namely, adherence to the four cardinal principles and implementation of reform and the open policy. Party schools and Party organizations at all levels should conduct regular, intensive education among members, in the light of the realities prevailing in the primary stage of socialism, helping them to learn more about the Party and its basic line. Our goal is that all Party members, and particularly leading cadres, should be united in their thinking and action and become vanguard fighters who work conscientiously to accomplish the Party's tasks, as well as better-educated, self-disciplined model workers with high ideals and moral integrity. To reform the Party's work in propaganda and in ideological education, we must get rid of formalism and emphasize practical results. We can never go back to the closed society of the past, when people were forbidden contact with ideological trends of different sorts. Still less can we evade problems of understanding that may arise among the people in the course of construction and reform. We must abandon empty Party jargon and conduct propaganda and education utilizing the personal experiences of the people in a way that they can appreciate and understand, so that the four cardinal principles and reform and the open policy will truly take root in their hearts.

Reform and the open policy and the growth of the socialist commodity economy require that we stress and improve the Party's ideological and political work. The process of reform and opening to the outside world liberates people's thinking to an extraordinary degree, and that is a good thing and a natural historical phenomenon. But it also means that we must carry on the fine tradition of the Party's ideological and political work and make a success of such work in all fields of construction and reform, employing effective means adapted to the new situation. Thus we shall stimulate people's socialist initiative, creativity, and dedication and rally the whole nation to the magnificent cause of building socialism with Chinese characteristics.

The quality of our cadres is decisive for the implementation of the Party's line. In conformity with the political line formed since the Third Plenary Session of the Eleventh Central Committee, we set forth the principle of making the ranks of cadres more revolutionary, younger, better educated, and more professionally competent. That principle has proved correct in practice. The most important criterion for judging whether a cadre is revolutionary is whether he is firm in implementing the Party's basic line. We should place in important positions those cadres who have both ability and political integrity and who are fair and honest, that is, cadres who are loyal to the Party's line and can implement it creatively, rather than those who indulge in empty talk and do nothing practical for socialist modernization because they have little enthusiasm or sense of responsibility for it. A cadre's merits are to be judged by his performance in adhering to the four cardinal principles and to reform and the open policy. We must not hesitate to promote those who have made actual contributions to reform and the open policy and to socialist modernization and who have won the recognition and trust of the people. We should have the courage to place heavy responsibilities on outstanding younger cadres. We should cherish and support cadres who dare to explore new ways in reform, allow them to make mistakes, and help them sum up their experience constantly so that they will enhance their ability and learn and mature through practice. That is the only way to revitalize leading bodies at all levels. In our efforts to promote younger cadres to leading posts, we should now focus on members of the central leading bodies. We propose that this congress take a major step in this direction. While the leading members of the

Party's local and grassroots organizations should be younger, we should not rigidly demand that the average age of leading groups be lowered progressively at provincial, prefectural, county, and grassroots levels. Attention should be paid to the age structure within each leading group. While persevering in the effort to make the cadre ranks better educated and more professional, we must also take into consideration the different requirements of different jobs. Progress has been made in recent years in the cooperation between old and new cadres and the succession of the new to the old, and the leading groups at all levels are now basically up to the requirements of our Party's policy. We should continue to strengthen and improve the leading groups, making appropriate adjustments while maintaining stability.

To consolidate and develop the Party's correct line, to make its decision-making process more democratic and scientific, and to give full play to the enthusiasm and creativity of Party members and organizations at all levels, it is of vital importance to strengthen the systems of the Party. Furthermore, promoting democracy among the people through the example of inner-Party democracy is a feasible and effective way to develop socialist democracy. Strengthening the Party's collective leadership and democratic centralism should start with the Central Committee. This should chiefly include the following:

• Establishing a system of regular work reports to the Political Bureau of the Central Committee by its Standing Committee and to the plenary sessions of the Central Committee by the Political Bureau

• Appropriately increasing the number of plenary sessions held by the Central Committee each year so that it can play a greater role in collective decision making

• Formulating work rules and a system for holding democratic meetings of the Political Bureau, its Standing Committee, and the Secretariat of the Central Committee, so as to institutionalize collective leadership and place Party leaders under more strict supervision and control. Local Party organizations at all levels should formulate and improve corresponding rules of procedure, including a voting system and a system for democratic meetings. The inner-Party electoral system should be reformed and improved, and explicit provisions should be worked out for nominating procedures, with more candidates for election than there are posts to be filled. In the near future this practice of presenting more candidates than posts should also be applied in the election of deputies to Party congresses at all levels, members and secretaries of grassroots Party committees, members of local Party committees and their standing committees, and members of the Central Committee. The democratic rights of Party members as prescribed by the Party Constitution should be protected by specific rules. Infringement of the rights of Party members is a violation of Party discipline, and in such cases disciplinary measures should be taken. Channels for inner-Party democracy must be widened and democratic activities improved so as to enable members to keep better informed about inner-Party affairs and have more opportunities to involve themselves directly in them.

When a party is in power, its members tend to become divorced from the masses, and that is much more harmful to the people than it would have been before the party came to power. Under the new circumstances of reform and opening to the rest of the world, it has become even more important to improve the Party's work style. Since the Third Plenary Session of the Eleventh Central Committee in December 1978, the Party has restored its fine tradition of integrating theory with practice, maintaining close ties with the masses, and conducting criticism and self-criticism. Its line and policies have embodied the supreme interests of the people and promoted the growth of the productive forces. Reform and the open policy have helped to substantially reduce negative practices that were common in the past, such as subjectivism, coercion, and commandism, practices that resulted in setting excessively high targets, giving arbitrary directions, and resorting to struggle and punishment without good reason. Party organizations at all levels as well as individual Party members, including the vast majority of cadres, have been faithfully and enthusiastically serving the people, doing solid work, and demonstrating their creativity. It should be recognized that the ties between our Party and the people have been greatly cemented. Reform of the economic and political structures and separation of Party and government will help prevent the emergence of bureaucratism inside the Party and indeed make our Party a staunch force in the struggle against it. The people complain a great deal now that a small number of Party members, particularly leading cadres, have abused their power for private gain at the expense of the people's interests, hindering the smooth progress of the reform and implementation of the open policy and damaging the Party's prestige. This is a grave problem which we must take seriously and tackle in earnest.

Damage wrought by the "Cultural Revolution" made it necessary for us to concentrate for a certain period of time on consolidating the Party.

In general, over the past few years Party consolidation has been success-ful. At the same time, however, it must be recognized that remedying defects in the Party's ideology, organization, and work style is a regular, long-term task. It is impossible to solve all the problems merely through a certain period of Party consolidation, because new problems will con-tinue to crop up after the old ones are solved. Now that our Party is in power, it must stand the test of power. Now that it is providing leadership for reform and for opening to the outside world, it must also stand the test of that endeavor. This is a crucial test which we must undergo in Party building during the new period. In our judgment, the Party as a whole can stand severe tests, and it is strong enough to combat all kinds of negative and decadent phenomena. But we must recognize that a small number of Party members may fail these tests. In the past few years there have been frequent cases of tax evasion, smuggling, trafficking in smuggled goods, bribery, extortion, embezzlement and theft, moral degradation, violation of the law by persons in charge of executing it, divulgence of state secrets and economic information, breach of disci-pline in dealings with foreigners, favoritism in making appointments, and vindictive attacks on others. We certainly must not change our gen-eral principles and policies of reform and opening to the outside world just because of these few cases of corruption, or bring our work of eco-nomic development and reform to a halt in order to concentrate on sweeping the bad practices away. Nevertheless, we must combat them as we go on with that work. The inner-Party struggle against corruption is unavoidable when we are carrying out reform and the open policy. If we tolerate decadent elements in the Party, the whole Party will decline. We should, of course, educate Party members who have failed to stand the tests by talking with them in a kindly way. But experience has shown that we cannot completely solve the problem through education alone; we must also be strict with Party members and enforce rigorous Party dis-cipline. Corrupt members who have done harm to the cause of the Party and the people must be resolutely expelled. Once discovered, such peo-ple must be removed immediately, no matter how many they are. We can in no way tolerate or connive at their wrongdoing.

The strength of a proletarian party and the role it can play are decided not by the number of its members but by their quality, by their firmness in implementing the party's line, and by their loyalty to the cause of communism. For a long period in the past there was a tendency to neglect the quality of new members admitted to the Party. As a result, there are some members who are not qualified or not fully qualified for membership. Therefore, in order to maintain high standards and improve the quality of Party members, we must not only expel the few degenerate members but also concentrate on educating the great majority. The Party is the vanguard of the working class, a vanguard with a strong sense of organization and discipline. To be a Party member, one must meet the qualifications for membership, subject oneself to strict Party discipline, and play the exemplary role required. Even stricter rules should be applied to Party members who work in leading Party and government organs, especially those in principal positions. In the years of revolutionary war, Party members had to go through the test of risking their lives. Today they must stand the test of holding office and working for reform and the open policy. Unlike non-Party people, they must at all times be ready to sacrifice their personal interests for the benefit of the state and the people. It is in this sense that the title of Party member is glorious. The requirements set in the Party Constitution obviously are not meant for non-Party people, but they must be met by Party members. Those who fail to meet them, who fail to fulfill the duties stipulated in the Party Constitution and refuse to mend their ways in spite of education, should be persuaded to withdraw from the Party or have their names struck from the Party rolls. This is necessary to maintain the Party's status as vanguard of the working class. Party organizations at all levels should sincerely unite with those who have left the Party and should in no way attack or discriminate against them. They can remain good citizens and as such give their best to society. Some may even continue to hold appropriate leading posts. We should constantly recruit into the Party advanced people who have emerged in the course of the reform and opening to the outside world and who are qualified for membership. Only by upholding the good can we suppress the bad. We should promptly commend those comrades who are staunch Party members with a spirit of voluntary devotion, who serve the people wholeheartedly, putting the interests of the people above everything else, and who implement the Party's policies and accomplish the Party's tasks in an exemplary way. As their principal day-to-day work, grassroots Party organizations should provide constant education, maintain strict supervision, carry out criticism and self-criticism, strengthen Party discipline, expel degenerates, and properly handle those who are not entirely qualified for membership, admit excellent people, encourage healthy practices, and resist unhealthy ones. Through the exemplary vanguard role of Party members, the grassroots organizations will be able to unite the people around themselves and become a powerful fighting force.

Leading organizations of the Party are responsible for guiding the grass-roots organizations in this work. If the day-to-day jobs are done well, it will mean that under the new historical circumstances we have discovered a new approach for Party building through reform and through the establishment of new systems, instead of through political movements.

Reforms, particularly reform of the political structure, will bring our Party fresh vitality. We must adapt ourselves to the tremendous change and do a good job of building this great Marxist Party of ours. Only thus can our Party, sound and strong, remain in the forefront of reform and the modernization drive, a vigorous Party that has the courage to undertake reform, a Party that is strictly disciplined, honest, and fair-minded in performing its functions, a Party that serves the people with outstanding success by selecting and appointing talented, capable people.

Striving to Win New Victories for Marxism in China

Socialism with Chinese characteristics is the product of the integration of the fundamental tenets of Marxism with the modernization drive in China and is scientific socialism rooted in the realities of present-day China. It provides the ideological basis that serves to unite all the Party comrades and all the people in their thinking and their action. It is the great banner guiding our cause forward.

Marxism is a science that keeps developing in practice. In the contemporary era it is generally recognized that Marxism needs further extensive development. The world is undergoing tremendous change, civilization is advancing very rapidly, and new vistas are opening before the working class and the laboring people. All this requires Marxists to widen their vision, develop new concepts, and enter a new realm.

The historic contribution of Marx and Engels is that they transformed utopian socialism into scientific socialism. In theory and in practice—the practice of building socialism in one country, the practice of building it in many countries, and the practice of introducing reforms in socialist countries in the contemporary world—scientific socialism broadens and deepens the understanding of socialism by integrating the scientific theory of socialism with the practice in various countries and with the developments of the times. In this process, it is only natural that people will discard some theses which are utopian because they were formulated by our predecessors within the limits of their historical conditions. It is also natural that people will reject dogmatic interpretations of Marxism and erroneous viewpoints imposed on it, and will further develop the theory of scientific socialism on the basis of new practice.

The integration of Marxism with practice in China has been going on for more than sixty years. During this time there have been two major historic leaps. The first took place during the new-democratic revolution, when the Chinese Communists, after repeated experimentation and learning by trial and error, found a way to make revolution based on China's particular conditions and led the revolution to victory. The second took place after the Third Plenary Session of the Eleventh Central Committee, when, having analyzed both the positive and negative experience of more than thirty years since the founding of the People's Republic and studied the experience of other countries and the world situation, the Chinese Communists found a way to build socialism with Chinese characteristics, thus ushering in a new period of socialist development in the country.

The crucial point here is that we must discard historical idealism, which deals with socialism in abstract terms without any consideration of the productive forces, and make a fundamental distinction between scientific socialism and all forms of utopianism.

Marxist historical materialists have held all along that the productive forces are ultimately the decisive factor in social development. Only when the relations of production and the superstructure conform to the mode of the productive forces can they promote such growth. Unless the productive forces are developed, there can be no socialist society, and socialism cannot advance from one stage to another until the realization of communism. As early as the revolutionary war years, our Party already made it clear that in the last analysis the impact, good or bad, great or small, of the policy and practice of any Chinese political party upon the people depends on whether and how much it helps to develop their productive forces, on whether it fetters or liberates those forces. At that time we had to take class struggle as our central task, because if we wanted to liberate the productive forces we had first of all to overthrow the rule of the reactionary classes so as to free the laboring people from political oppression and economic exploitation. Now that the exploiting classes have been abolished, however, things are different: the laboring people have become masters of the country, and we have entered the stage of socialist development. Developing the productive forces has therefore become our central task. Our ability to make China prosperous and strong, to make the people rich, to make education, science, and culture flourish, to consolidate and expand public ownership and the state power of people's democracy—in a word, our ability to take full advantage of the superiority of socialism and to steadily enhance its appeal—hinges, in the final analysis, on the growth of the productive forces. Whatever is conducive to this growth is in keeping with the fundamental interests of the people and is therefore needed by socialism and allowed to exist. Conversely, whatever is detrimental to this growth goes against scientific socialism and is therefore not allowed to exist. In these historical circumstances, the growth of the productive forces is the immediate and decisive criterion.

Great practice requires great theory. The one billion Chinese people are devoting themselves to the grand cause of modernization and reform. This rich, lively practice provides us with an inexhaustible source of creative theoretical generalizations. At present, however, the study of Marxist theories in the Party lags far behind the progress of our great undertaking. Reform and the open policy have been pursued for several years, but little has been done to study them theoretically or to explain them to the general public. One of the major tasks confronting all Party members, especially senior and middle-level cadres, is to master the stand, viewpoint, and method of Marxism through earnest study, and to better integrate Marxism with China's development and reform and with the realities prevailing in every field of endeavor and in every region. Our Party is at a critical historical juncture, with large numbers of new comrades joining, and new cadres replacing older ones in leadership positions at all levels. At this moment it is of immediate and far-reaching importance to understand the general contemporary need to greatly develop Marxism, to call on the entire Party membership to study and enrich Marxism-Leninism and Mao Zedong Thought in the course of practice, and to build a contingent of Marxist theoretical workers, including a large group of newly rising creative thinkers.

China's revolution and development represent an important component of the progressive cause of mankind. The founding of the People's Republic of China, which shook the world, has strengthened the progressive forces of the world and expanded the influence of Marxism. With the success of its socialist modernization, China will unquestionably make a new contribution to world peace and to the progress of mankind and further increase the appeal of scientific socialism. Having triumphantly taken the first step toward the grand objective of socialist modernization, we shall work hard to take the second and third steps and win greater victories. We are convinced that the road of socialism with Chinese characteristics will become wider and wider.

★ T H E   T I A N A N M E N   C R I S I S ★

The radical reforms of Zhao Ziyang produced an unprecedented opening of society and the economy. But they also produced intensified inflation and corruption. In mid-1988 many conservative leaders began to
call for economic austerity measures to cool down the overheated economy and stem inflation. Some called for an even more sweeping rollback of Zhao's open policies; others even demanded Zhao's resignation.
The leadership agreed to implement price controls and other fiscal
measures, but these policies were never fully adopted. High prices and
uncertainty about the future concerned many Chinese citizens
throughout the winter of 1988–89. Then, in mid-April 1989, in the midst
of a Politburo meeting convened to discuss the situation, Hu Yaobang
collapsed and died of a heart attack. Within hours of learning the news,
students began to eulogize Hu—whom they revered as a liberal who
had sought to improve the lot of intellectuals and change the authoritarian nature of the Communist Party. As the days went by, increasing
numbers of students marched to Tiananmen Square to praise Hu while
denouncing the inflation and corruption that plagued China. These
demonstrations quickly mushroomed (see Chapter 2) and broadened
their appeals to include increased freedom of the press, transparency
and accountability of government, and democracy.

Over the next six weeks the demonstrations swelled to unprecedented proportions. As they did the leadership was paralyzed by factional divisions over how to deal with this assault on Communist Party
supremacy. After much deliberation the twin decisions were taken to
purge Zhao Ziyang and declare martial law and call in military forces to
clear Tiananmen Square and Beijing of demonstrators. The consequence has become history—another dark mark in the annals of imperial and modern China. Hundreds, perhaps thousands, of unarmed
civilians were shot down by elite units of the People's Liberation Army
(mobilized from all seven military regions).

While some of the selections in Chapter 2 highlight the atmosphere
and politics leading up to the "Beijing massacre," those in this section examine the inner politics and propaganda of the period immediately following the crackdown. As they reveal a great deal about how
the Communist Party leadership dealt with the situation—some en-
tries providing unprecedented looks into Politburo discussions—they
also provide a great deal of detail about how events unfolded before

June 4 (or, rather, how the authorities viewed the genesis of these events).

CHEN XITONG,
REPORT ON CHECKING THE TURMOIL AND QUELLING
THE COUNTERREVOLUTIONARY REBELLION

Following the People's Liberation Army's assault on Beijing and clearing of Tiananmen Square on June 4, 1989, and subsequent days, the Communist Party and government launched a propaganda offensive aimed at justifying the use of force in suppressing the Beijing Spring demonstrators and citizens of the capital. The man charged with spearheading the Orwellian offensive to reinterpret history was Beijing Mayor Chen Xitong (himself convicted in 1998 on charges of corruption, massive embezzlement, fraud, and official malfeasance). In a lengthy address to the Standing Committee of the National People's Congress on June 30, Mayor Chen set forth the official interpretation concerning the "turmoil and counterrevolutionary armed rebellion" and the events that contributed to it. Chen's speech will go down in history as one of the greatest examples of propaganda doublespeak (what Chinese refer to as "calling a deer a horse").

This selection was excerpted from the full text released by Xinhua News Agency on July 6, 1989.

During late spring and early summer, namely, from mid April to early June, of 1989, a tiny handful of people exploited student unrest to launch a planned, organized, and premeditated political turmoil, which later developed into a counterrevolutionary rebellion in Beijing, the capital. Their purpose in plotting turmoil and rebellion was to overthrow the leadership of the Chinese Communist Party and subvert the socialist People's Republic of China. The outbreak and development of the turmoil and the counterrevolutionary rebellion had a profound international background and social basis at home. As Comrade Deng Xiaoping put it, "This storm was bound to happen sooner or later. As determined by the international and domestic climate, it was bound to happen and was independent of man's will." In this struggle involving the life and death of the Party and the state, Comrade Zhao Ziyang committed the serious mistake of supporting the turmoil and splitting the Party, and had the unshrinkable responsibility for the shaping and development of the turmoil. In the face of this very severe situation, the Party Central Committee made correct decisions and took a series of resolute measures, winning the firm support of the whole Party and people of all nationalities in the country. Represented by Comrade Deng Xiaoping, proletarian revolutionaries of the older generation played a very important role in winning the struggle. The Chinese People's Liberation Army, the People's Armed Police, and the police made great contributions in checking the turmoil and quelling the counterrevolutionary rebellion. The vast numbers of workers, peasants, and intellectuals firmly opposed the turmoil and the rebellion, rallied closely around the Party Central Committee, and displayed a very high political consciousness and the sense of responsibility as masters of the country. Now, entrusted to do so by the State Council, I am making a report to the National People's Congress Standing Committee on the turmoil and the counterrevolutionary rebellion, mainly the happenings in Beijing and the work of checking the turmoil and quelling the counterrevolutionary rebellion.

The Turmoil Was Brewed and Premeditated for a Long Time

Some political forces in the West always attempt to make socialist countries, including China, give up the socialist road, eventually bring these countries under the rule of international monopoly capital, and put them on the course of capitalism. This is their long-term, fundamental strategy. In recent years they have stepped up the implementation of this strategy by making use of some policy mistakes and temporary economic difficulties in socialist countries. In our country, there was a tiny handful of people both inside and outside the Party who stubbornly clung to their position of bourgeois liberalization and went in for political conspiracy. Echoing the strategy of Western countries, they colluded with foreign forces, ganged up among themselves at home, and made ideological, public opinion, and organizational preparations for years to stir up turmoil in China, overthrow leadership by the Communist Party, and subvert the socialist people's republic. That is why the entire course of brewing, premeditating, and launching the turmoil, including the use of varied means such as stirring up public opinion, distorting facts, and spreading rumors, bore the salient feature of support by coordinated action at home and abroad.

This report will mainly deal with the situation since the third plenary session of the Thirteenth CCP Central Committee. Last September the Party Central Committee formulated the policy of improving the economic environment, straightening out the economic order, and deepening the reform in an all-round way. This policy and the related measures won the support of the broad masses and students. The social order and political situation were basically stable. Firm evidence of this was the approval of Comrade Li Peng's government work report by an overwhelming majority (with a mere two votes against and four abstentions) at the National People's Congress in the spring of this year. Of course, the people and students raised many criticisms of some mistakes committed by the Party and the government in their work, corruption among some government employees, unfair distribution, and other social problems. At the same time, they made quite a few demands and proposals for promoting democracy, strengthening the legal system, deepening the reform, and overcoming bureaucracy. These were normal phenomena. And the Party and government were also taking measures to resolve them. At that time, however, there was indeed a tiny bunch of people in the Party and society who ganged up together and engaged in many very improper activities overtly and covertly.

Collaboration between forces at home and abroad intensified toward the end of last year and early this year. Political assemblies, joint petitions, big- and small-character posters, and other activities emerged, expressing fully erroneous or even reactionary points.

Student Unrest Was Exploited by the Organizers of Turmoil from the Very Beginning

This turmoil found expression first in the wanton attack and slanders against the Party and the government and the open call to overthrow the leadership of the Communist Party and subvert the present government as contained in the large quantity of big- and small-character posters, slogans, leaflets, and elegiac couplets. Some of the posters on the campuses of Beijing University, Qinghua University, and other schools abused the Communist Party as "a Party of conspirators" and "an organization on the verge of collapse"; some attacked the older generation of revolutionaries as "decaying men administering affairs of the state" and "autocrats with a concentration of power"; some called [out] the names of leading comrades of the CCP Central Committee one by one, uttering such nonsense as "the man who should not die has passed away while those who should die remain alive"; some called for "dissolving the incompetent government and overthrowing autocratic monarchy"; some cried for "the abolition of the CCP and the adoption of the multiparty system" and "the dissolution of Party branches and removal of political workers from the mass organizations, armed forces, schools, and other units"; some issued a "declaration on private ownership," calling for "sounding the death knell of public ownership at an early date and greeting a new future for the republic"; some went so far as to "invite the Kuomintang back to the mainland and establish two-party politics," et cetera. Many big- and small-character posters used disgusting language to slander Comrade Deng Xiaoping, clamoring, "Down with Deng Xiaoping."

This turmoil, from the very beginning, was manifested by a sharp conflict between bourgeois liberalization and the four cardinal principles. Of the programmatic slogans raised by the organizers of the turmoil at the time, either the "nine demands" first raised through Wang Dan, leader of an illegal student organization, in Tiananmen Square or the "seven demands" and "ten demands" raised later, there were two principal demands: one was to reappraise Comrade Hu Yaobang's merits and demerits: the other was to negate completely the fight against bourgeois liberalization and rehabilitate the so-called wronged citizens in the fight against bourgeois liberalization. The essence of the two demands was to gain absolute freedom in China to oppose the four cardinal principles and realize capitalism.

Echoing those demands, some so-called elitists in academic circles, that is, the very small number of people stubbornly clinging to their position of bourgeois liberalization, organized a variety of forums during the period and indulged in unbridled propaganda through the press. Most outstanding among the activities was a forum sponsored by the *World Economic Herald* and the *New Observer* in Beijing on April 19. The forum was chaired by Ge Yang and its participants included Yan Jiaqi, Su Shaozhi, Chen Ziming (director of the Beijing Institute of Socioeconomic Science), and Liu Ruishao of the Hong Kong *Wen Wei Po* Beijing office). Their main topics were also two: one was to "rehabilitate" Hu Yaobang; the other was to "reverse" the verdict on the fight against liberalization. They expressed unequivocal support for the student demonstrations, saying that they saw therein "China's future and hope." Later, when the Shanghai municipal Party committee made the correct decision on straightening things out in the *World Economic Herald*, Comrade Zhao Ziyang, who consistently winked at bourgeois liberalization, refrained from backing the decision. Instead, he criticized the Shanghai municipal Party committee for "making a mess of it" and "landing itself in a passive position."

This turmoil also found expression in the fact that, instigated and engineered by the small handful of people, many acts were very rude, violating the Constitution, laws, and regulations of the PRC and gravely running counter to democracy and the legal system. They put up big-character posters en masse on the campuses in disregard of the fact that the provision in the Constitution on "four big freedoms" (speaking out freely, airing views fully, holding great debates, and writing big-character posters) had been abrogated and turning a deaf ear to all persuasion; they staged large-scale demonstrations day after day in disregard of the ten-article regulations on demonstrations issued by the standing committee of the Beijing municipal people's congress; late on the night of April 18 and 19, they assaulted Xinhuamen, headquarters of the Party Central Committee and the State Council, and shouted "Down with the Communist Party," something which never occurred even during the "Cultural Revolution"; they violated the regulations for the management of Tiananmen Square and occupied the square by force several times, one consequence of which was that the memorial meeting for Comrade Hu Yaobang was almost interrupted on April 22; ignoring the relevant regulations of the Beijing municipality and without registration, they formed an illegal organization, "solidarity student union" (later changed into "federation of autonomous student unions in universities and colleges") and "seized power" from the lawful student unions and postgraduate unions formed through democratic election; disregarding law and school discipline, they took by force school offices and broadcasting stations and did things as they wished, creating anarchy on the campuses.

Another important means that the small number of turmoil organizers and plotters used was to fabricate a spate of rumors to confuse people's minds and agitate the masses. At the beginning of the student unrest, they spread the rumor that "Li Peng scolded Hu Yaobang at a Political Bureau meeting and Hu died of anger." The rumor was meant to spearhead the attack on Comrade Li Peng. In fact, the meeting focused on the question of education. When Comrade Li Tieying, member of the Political Bureau, state councillor, and minister in charge of the State Education Commission, was making an explanation of a relevant document, Comrade Hu Yaobang suffered a sudden heart attack. Hu was given emergency treatment right in the meeting room and was rushed to a hospital when his condition allowed. There was definitely no such thing as Hu flying into a rage.

On the night of April 19, a female foreign language student of Beijing Teachers' University was run down by a trolleybus on her way back to school after attending a party. She died despite treatment. Some people spread the rumor that "a car of the communist police knocked a student to her death," which stirred up the emotions of some students who did not know the truth.

In the small hours of April 20, policemen whisked away those students who had blocked and assaulted Xinhuamen and sent them back to Beijing University by bus. Some people concocted the rumor of "April 20 Bloody Incident," alleging that "the police beat people at Xinhuamen, not only students, but also workers, women, and children," and that "more than 1,000 scientists and technicians fell in blood." This further agitated some people.

On April 22, when Li Peng and other leading comrades left the Great Hall of the People at the end of the memorial meeting for Comrade Hu Yaobang, some people perpetrated a fraud with the objective of working out an excuse for attacking Comrade Li Peng. First they started the rumor that "Premier Li Peng promised to come out at 12:45 [local time] and receive students in the square." Then they let three students kneel on the steps outside the East Gate of the Great Hall of the People for the purpose of handing in a "petition." After a while they said, "Li Peng went back on his word and refused to receive us. He has deceived the students." This assertion fanned strong indignation among the tens of thousands of students in Tiananmen Square and came very close to leading to a serious incident of assault on the Great Hall of the People.

Confused and incited by the rumors, the antagonism of young students against the government was greatly intensified. Using this antagonism, a very small number of people put up the slogan "The government pays no heed to our peaceful petition. Let's make the matters known across the country and call for nationwide class boycott." This led to the serious situation in which 60,000 university students boycotted class in Beijing and many students in other parts of China followed suit. The student unrest escalated and the turmoil expanded.

This turmoil was marked by another characteristic, that is, it was no longer confined to institutions of higher learning in the Beijing area; it spread to the whole of society and to all parts of China. After the memo-

rial meeting for Comrade Hu Yaobang, a number of people went to contact middle schools, factories, shops, and villages, made speeches in the
streets, handed out leaflets, put on slogans, and raised money, doing
everything possible to make the situation worse. The slogan "Oppose
the CCP" and the big-character poster "Long live class boycott and
exam boycott" appeared in some middle schools. Leaflets saying "Unite
with the workers and peasants, down with the despotic rule" were put up
in some factories. Organizers and plotters of the turmoil advanced the
slogan "Go to the south, the north, the east, and the west" in a bid to
establish ties throughout the country. Students from Beijing were seen
in universities and colleges in Nanjing, Wuhan, Xian, Changsha,
Shanghai, and Harbin, while students from Tianjin, Hebei, Anhui, and
Zhejiang took part in demonstrations in Beijing. Criminal activities of
beating, smashing, looting, and burning took place in Changsha and
Xian.

Reactionary political forces in Hong Kong, Taiwan, the USA, and
other Western countries were also involved in the turmoil through various channels and by different means. Western news agencies showed
unusual zeal. The Voice of America, in particular, aired news in three
programs every day for a total of more than ten hours beamed to the
Chinese mainland, spreading rumors, stirring up trouble, and adding
fuel to the turmoil.

The facts listed above show that we were confronted not with student
unrest in its normal sense, but with a planned, organized, and premeditated political turmoil designed to negate the Communist Party leadership and the socialist system. It had clear-cut political ends and deviated
from the orbit of democracy and legality, employing base political
means to incite large numbers of students and other people who did not
know the truth. If we failed to analyze and see the problem in essence,
we would have committed grave mistakes and landed ourselves in an
extremely passive position in the struggle.

The Government Had No Alternative but to Declare
Martial Law in Parts of Beijing, a Correct Measure

To safeguard the social stability in the city of Beijing, to protect the
safety of the life and property of the citizens, and to ensure the normal
functioning of the Party and government departments at the central
level and of the Beijing municipal government, the State Council had
no alternative but to declare martial law in parts of Beijing as empow-

ered by Clause 16 of Article 89 of the PRC Constitution and at a time when police forces in Beijing were far too inadequate to maintain normal production, work, and living order. This was a resolute and correct decision.

The decision on taking resolute measures to stop the turmoil was announced at a meeting called by the central authorities and attended by cadres from the Party, government, and military institutions in Beijing on May 19. Comrade Zhao Ziyang, persisting in his erroneous stand against the correct decision of the central authorities, neither agreed to speak at the meeting together with Comrade Li Peng nor agreed to preside over the meeting. He did not agree even to attend the meeting. By so doing, he openly revealed his attitude of separating himself from the Party before the whole Party, the whole country, and the whole world.

Prior to this, members of the Standing Committee of the Political Bureau of the Party Central Committee met to discuss the issue of declaring martial law in parts of Beijing on May 17. On the same day, a few people who had access to top Party and state secrets gave away the information out of their counterrevolutionary political considerations. A person who worked at the side of Comrade Zhao Ziyang said to the leaders of the illegal student organization: "The troops are about to suppress you. All the others have agreed. Zhao Ziyang was the only one who was against it. You must get prepared."

As a result of the close collaboration between a small number of people who had access to top Party and state secrets and the organizers and schemers of the turmoil, the organizers made timely adjustments to their tactics. That night, forty-five minutes before the meeting called by the central authorities and attended by cadres from the Party, government, and military institutions in Beijing, they changed the hunger strike to a sit-in in a bid to mislead the people and give them the false impression that since the students had already ended their hunger strike it was not necessary for the government to declare martial law. By so doing they also gained time to organize people and coerce those who were in the dark to set up roadblocks at major crossroads to stop the advance of the troops and to continue to mislead public opinion and confuse people's minds. While cursing viciously Comrade Deng Xiaoping and other proletarian revolutionaries of the old generation, saying that "we don't need Deng Xiaoping's wisdom and experience," they lavished praise on Comrade Zhao Ziyang by saying that "the country is hopeless without Ziyang as the Party leader" and "Give us back Ziyang."

They also plotted to rally forces for greater turmoil, claiming that they were going to mobilize 200,000 people to occupy Tiananmen Square and to organize a citywide general strike on May 20. Harmonizing with Comrade Zhao Ziyang's three-day sick leave, which started on May 19, they spread the word that a "new government" would be established in three days' time.

Under the extremely urgent circumstances, the Party Central Committee and the State Council decided resolutely to declare martial law in parts of Beijing, starting at 10:00 A.M., May 20, to prevent the situation from worsening and to grasp the initiative to stop the turmoil so as to give support to the broad masses who were opposed to the turmoil and longed for stability. However, as the organizers and schemers of the turmoil had learned of our decision before it was implemented, there were tremendous difficulties and obstacles for the troops in entering the city.

On the eve of the declaration of martial law and on the first two days after it was declared, all major crossroads were blocked. More than 220 buses were taken away and used as roadblocks. Traffic came to a standstill. Troops who were to enforce the martial law were not able to arrive at their designated places. The headquarters of the Party Central Committee and the State Council continued to be surrounded. Speeches inciting people could be heard everywhere on the streets. Leaflets spreading rumors could be seen everywhere in the city. Demonstrations, each involving several tens of thousands of people, took place one after another, and Beijing, our capital city, fell into total disorder and terror. During the following few days, the martial law troops managed to enter the city by different ways. Meanwhile, the armed police and police continued to perform their duties by overcoming tremendous difficulties. Urban and suburban districts organized workers, residents, and government office workers, as many as 120,000 people altogether, to maintain social order. The outer suburban counties also sent out militiamen. The concerted efforts of the troops, police, and civilians helped improve transport, production, and living order in the capital, and people felt more at ease. But the very small number of people never stopped for a single day their activities to create turmoil and never changed their goal of overthrowing the leadership of the Communist Party. Things were developing day by day toward a counterrevolutionary rebellion.

One of the major tactics of the organizers and schemers of the turmoil after martial law was declared was to continue to stay on Tiananmen Square. They wanted to turn the square into a "center of the student movement and the whole nation." Once the government made a decision, they planned to stage a "strong reaction at the square" and form an "antigovernment united front." These people had been planning to incite incidents of bloodshed on the square, believing that "the government would resort to suppression if the occupation of the square continues" and "blood can awaken people and split the government."

To ensure that the situation on the square could be maintained, they used funds provided by reactionary forces both at home and abroad to improve their facilities and install advanced telecommunications devices, spending 100,000 yuan a day on average. They even started illegal purchase of weapons. By using the tents provided by their Hong Kong supporters, they set up "villages of freedom" and launched a "democracy university" on the square, claiming that they would turn the university into "the Huangpu military school of the new era." They erected a so-called goddess statue in front of the Monument to the People's Heroes. The statue was named initially the "Goddess of Liberty," but its name was later changed to "Goddess of Democracy," showing that they took American-style democracy and freedom as their spiritual pillar.

Fearing that the students who took part in the sit-in could not hold on, Liu Xiaobo and other behind-the-scenes schemers went up onto the front stage and performed a four-man farce of a forty-eight- to seventy-two-hour hunger strike so as to pep up the students. They said, "As long as the flags on the square are still up, we can continue our fight and spread it to the whole country until the government collapses."

Taking advantage of the restraint that the government and the troops still exercised after martial law was declared, the organizers and plotters of the turmoil continued to organize all kinds of illegal activities. Following the establishment of the "autonomous students' federation of Beijing Colleges," the "Beijing autonomous workers' union," the "fasting contingent," the "Tiananmen Square headquarters," and the "union of the capital's intelligentsia," they set up more illegal organizations such as the "patriotic joint conference of people from all walks of life in the capital for upholding the constitution" and the "autonomous union of Beijing residents." In the name of the Research Institute for Restructuring Economic System, the Development Institute of the China Rural Development Research Center under the State Council, and the Beijing Association of Young Economists, they openly sent telegrams to some of the troops in an attempt to incite defection. They were engaged in such underground activities aimed at toppling the government as organizing a special team in charge of molding public opinion and making preparations to launch an underground newspaper.

They organized their sworn followers in taking a secret oath, claiming, "Under no circumstances should we betray our conscience, yield to autocracy, and bow to the emperor of China of the 1980s."

Organizers and instigators of the turmoil also unbridledly agitated for and organized violent action. They enlisted local hooligans, ruffians, and criminals from other parts of the country, ex-convicts who had not turned over a new leaf, and people with a deep hatred of the Communist Party and the socialist system to knock together so-called dare-to-die corps, flying tiger teams, the volunteer army, and other terrorist organizations, threatening to detain and kidnap Party and state leaders and seize state powers by means of "attacking the Bastille." They distributed leaflets to incite counterrevolutionary armed rebellion, advocating that "a single spark can start a prairie fire" and calling for establishing "armed forces that might be called the people's army," for "uniting with various forces, including the Kuomintang in Taiwan," and for "a clear-cut stand to oppose the Communist Party and its government by sacrificing lives."

All this shows that the turmoil planned, organized, and premeditated by a few people could not be put down merely by the government making some concessions or just issuing an order to impose martial law, contrary to the imagination of some kindhearted people.

They had made up their minds to unite with all hostile forces overseas and in foreign countries to launch a battle against us to the last. All one-sided goodwill would lead only to their unscrupulous attack against us, and the longer the time the greater the cost.

How Did a Small Minority of People Manage to Incite the Counterrevolutionary Rebellion?

The Chinese PLA undertakes not only the sacred duty of "strengthening national defense, resisting aggression, and defending the motherland" but also the noble responsibility of "safeguarding the people's peaceful labor, participating in national reconstruction, and working hard to serve the people," which are provided for in Article 29 of the Constitution of China. It was precisely to carry out the tasks entrusted to them by the Constitution of China that the troops entered the city proper and safeguarded social order.

After the announcement of martial law in some areas of the capital on May 20, the troops, despite repeated obstructions, were mobilized to march toward the city proper in accordance with a deployment plan and by different ways to take up appointed positions.

Just after midnight on June 3, while the martial law troops were heading for their positions according to schedule, agitators urged crowds to halt military and other motor vehicles, set up roadblocks, beat soldiers, and loot trucks of materials at Jianguomen, Nanheyan, Xidan, Muxidi, and other crossroads. Some twelve military vehicles were halted by crowds near Caogezhuang. Soldiers marching past the Yanjing Hotel were stopped and searched by rioters, and military vehicles parked in front of the Beijing Telegraph Office had their tires slashed and were surrounded with road dividers.

Around dawn, military vehicles on the Yongdingmen bridge were overturned, others at Muxidi had their tires slashed, and a group of 400 soldiers in Chaoyangmen was stoned. In the Liubukou and Hengertiao areas, military vehicles and soldiers were surrounded by unruly crowds.

Around 7:00 A.M. some rioters swarmed over military vehicles which had been halted at Liubukou and snatched machine guns and ammunition. From Jianguomen to Dongdan and in the Tianpiao area, martial law troops were cut off, surrounded, and beaten. On the Jianguomen flyover some soldiers were stripped and others severely beaten.

Later in the morning, troops in the Hufangqiao area were beaten by rioters and some were blinded. The mob prevented injured soldiers from reaching hospitals by deflating ambulance tires, and the victims were dragged from the vehicles. From Hufang Road to Taoranting Park, twenty-one military vehicles were surrounded and halted. Policemen escorting the soldiers were beaten and wounded by the rioters.

From noon onwards, many of the soldiers trapped by mobs and barricades at the Fuyoujie, Zhengyilu, Xuanwumen, Hufangqiao, Muxidi, and Dongsi crossroads were injured, and their equipment, including helmets, military caps, raincoats, water containers, and bags, was stolen. At Liubukou policemen tried several times to recover a military truck loaded with arms and ammunition from an enraged mob but failed. The consequences, had they been stolen or exploded, would have been dreadful. They were then forced to use tear gas to disperse the rioters and recapture the dangerous cargo.

About the same time, mobs began to surround and assault buildings, state housing organizations, and establishments of vital importance, including the Great Hall of the People, the Propaganda Department of the CCP Central Committee, and the Ministry of Radio, Film, and Television, as well as the West and South Gates of Zhongnanhai. Dozens of policemen and guards there were injured.

As the situation rapidly deteriorated, the instigators of the upheaval became more vicious. At about 5:00 P.M., the ringleaders of the illegal organizations known as the "Beijing Federation of Autonomous Students' Unions of Universities and Colleges" and the "Federation of Autonomous Workers' Unions" distributed knives, iron bars, chains, and sharpened bamboo sticks, inciting the mobs to kill soldiers and members of the security forces. In a broadcast over loudspeakers in Tiananmen Square, the "Federation of Autonomous Workers' Unions" urged the people "to take up arms and overthrow the government." It also broadcast how to make and use Molotov cocktails and how to wreck and burn military vehicles.

A group of mobs organized about 1,000 people to push down the wall of a construction site near Xidan and stole tools, reinforcing bars, and bricks, ready for street fighting. They planned to incite more people to take to the streets the next day, a Sunday, to stage a violent rebellion in an attempt to overthrow the government and seize power at one stroke.

At this critical juncture, the Party Central Committee, the State Council, and the Central Military Commission decided to order troops poised on the outskirts of the capital to enforce martial law to forcibly march in and quell the counterrevolutionary rebellion.

How Did the Counterrevolutionary Rebels Injure and Kill People's Liberation Army Men?

. . . The especially unbearable thing was that the mobs not only frenziedly attacked military vehicles and took part in beating, smashing, looting, and burning in an unbridled way, but they also murdered soldiers in various bestial ways. At about dawn on June 4, some mobs beat up soldiers with bottles and bricks at the Dongdan crossroads. At Fuxingmen, a military vehicle was surrounded and twelve soldiers were dragged off the vehicle. They were searched and severely beaten. Many of them were badly injured. In Liubukou, four soldiers were surrounded and beaten up, and some were beaten to death. In the Guangqumen area, three soldiers were severely beaten. One was rescued by some bystanders, and the other two have not yet been found. In Xixingsheng Lane in Xicheng district, more than twenty armed policemen were beaten up by mobs; some were badly injured, and the others' whereabouts are unknown. In Huguosi, a military vehicle was halted, and soldiers on it were beaten up and detained as hostages. Submachine guns were snatched. A truck full of bricks was driven from Dongjiao Minxiang to Tiananmen Square, and people on the truck shouted, "If you are really Chinese, come up to smash the soldiers."

After dawn, the rioters' atrocities toward the PLA soldiers became extremely detestable. A police ambulance was carrying eight injured soldiers to a hospital when it was halted by mobs. They beat a soldier to death and shouted that they would do the same to the other seven. In front of a bicycle shop in Qianmen Street, three soldiers were severely beaten by hooligans, who threatened anyone who tried to rescue them. On Chang'an Avenue a military vehicle broke down suddenly and was attacked right away by about 200 rioters. The driver was killed inside the cab. About thirty meters to the east of the Xidan crossroads, another soldier was beaten to death. Then the mob poured petrol over his body and set fire to it. In Fuchengmen, another soldier's body was hung over the flyover after he had been savagely killed. In Chongwenmen, a soldier was thrown from the flyover and burned alive. The rioters wildly clamored that it was "lighting a heavenly lantern." Near the Capital cinema on West Chang'an Avenue, an officer was beaten to death, disemboweled, and his eyes plucked out. His body was then strung up on a burning bus.

In the several days of the rebellion, more than 1,280 military vehicles, police cars, and public buses were wrecked, burned, or otherwise damaged. Of the vehicles, over 1,000 were military vehicles, more than 60 were armored personnel carriers, and about 30 were police cars. More than 120 public buses were destroyed as well as more than 70 other kinds of motor vehicles. During the same period, arms and ammunition were stolen. More than 6,000 martial law soldiers, armed police, and public security officers were injured, and the death toll reached several dozens. They sacrificed their blood and even their precious lives to defend the motherland, the Constitution, and the people. The people will remember their contributions forever.

Such heavy losses are eloquent testimony to the restraint and tolerance shown by the martial law troops. The PLA is an army led by the CCP and serves the people wholeheartedly. They always are ruthless to the enemy but kind to the people. They were able to defeat the 8 million Kuomintang troops armed by U.S. imperialism during the war years and able to defeat U.S. imperialism which was armed to the teeth to effectively safeguard the sacred territory and territorial waters and airspace of our country. So why did they suffer such great casualties in quelling the counterrevolutionary rebellion? Why were they beaten and even killed, even when they had weapons in their hands? It is just as Comrade Deng Xiaoping pointed out: "It was because bad people mingled with the good, which made it difficult for us to take the firm measures that were necessary." It also showed that the PLA love the people and are unwill-

ing to injure civilians by accident. The fact that they met death and sacrificed themselves with generosity and without fear fully embodies the
nature of the PLA. Otherwise how could there be such a great number
of casualties and losses? Doesn't this reflect that the army defends the
people at the cost of its own life?

In order to quell the counterrevolutionary rebellion and to avoid
more losses, the martial law troops, having suffered heavy casualties and
been driven beyond forbearance, were forced to fire in the air to open
the way forward after repeated warnings.

During the counterattack, some rioters who wreaked havoc were
killed. Because there were numerous bystanders, some were knocked
down by vehicles, some were trampled on or were hit by stray bullets.
Some were wounded or killed by ruffians who had seized rifles.

According to the information we have so far gathered, more than
3,000 civilians were wounded, and over 200, including 36 college students, died during the riot. Among the nonmilitary casualties were rioters who deserved the punishment, people accidentally injured, doctors,
and other people who were carrying out various duties on the spot. The
government will seriously deal with the problem arising from the deaths
of the latter two kinds of people.

Due to a rumor spread by the "Voice of America" and some people
who deliberately wished to spread rumors, people talked about a
"Tiananmen bloodbath" and that "thousands or even tens of thousands
of people fell in a pool of blood." The facts are that, after the martial
law troops reached Tiananmen Square at 1:30 A.M., the Beijing municipal government and the martial law headquarters issued an emergency notice, which stated: "A serious counterrevolutionary rebellion
occurred in the capital this evening" and "all citizens and students in
Tiananmen Square should leave immediately to ensure that martial law
troops will be able to accomplish their tasks." The notice was broadcast
repeatedly for three hours through loudspeakers. The sit-in students
gathered around the Monument to the People's Heroes in the southern
part of the square. At around 3:00 A.M., they sent representatives to the
troops to express their desire to withdraw from the square voluntarily,
and this was welcomed by the troops.

At 4:30 A.M. the martial law headquarters broadcast the following
notice: "It is time to clear the square, and the martial law headquarters
accepts the request of the students to be allowed to withdraw." At the
same time, another notice on quickly restoring normal order to the
square was issued by the municipal government and the headquarters

and broadcast. After hearing this, the several thousand students organized hand-in-hand pickets and started to leave the square, in an orderly
manner, carrying their own banners and streamers at about 5:00 A.M.

The troops vacated a wide corridor in the southeastern corner of the
square to ensure the smooth and safe departure of the students. At the
same time, a few students who refused to leave were forced to leave by
martial law troops in accordance with the demand of the "notice." By
5:30 A.M. the square-clearing operation had been completed.

During the whole operation no one, including the students who
refused but were forced to leave, died. Tales of "rivers of blood" in
Tiananmen Square and the rumor mongers themselves "escaping from
underneath piles of corpses" are sheer nonsense.

The counterrevolutionary rebellion was put down with Tiananmen
Square returning to the hands of the people and all martial law enforcement troops taking up their assigned positions.

During the quelling of the counterrevolutionary rebellion, the PLA
and the police regardless of sacrifice fought valiantly and performed
immortal feats. Many people gave first aid to the wounded and rescued
besieged soldiers, rendering their cooperation and support to the martial
law enforcement troops. Many good people said touching deeds
emerged during the event.

Due to the counterrevolutionary rebellion, Beijing has suffered
heavy losses in its economy, and losses in other fields cannot be counted
in terms of money. Workers, peasants, and intellectuals are now working
hard to retrieve the losses. Now, order in the capital has fundamentally
returned to normal, and the situation throughout China is also tending
to become smooth, which shows that the correct decision made by the
Party Central Committee has received support from the Chinese people
of all nationalities. Yet, the unrest and the rebellion are not completely
over, as a handful of counterrevolutionary rioters refuse to recognize
defeat and still indulge in sabotage, and even dream of staging a comeback.

In order to achieve thorough victory, we should mobilize the people
completely, strengthen the people's democratic dictatorship, and spare
no effort to ferret out the counterrevolutionary rioters. We should
uncover instigators and rebellious conspirators, and punish the organizers and schemers of the unrest and the counterrevolutionary rebellion,
that is, those who obstinately stuck to the path of bourgeois liberalization and carried out political conspiracies, those who colluded with
overseas and other foreign hostile forces, those who provided illegal

organizations with top secrets of the Party and state, and those criminals who committed the atrocities of beating, smashing, grabbing, and burning during the disturbances. We should make a clear distinction between two different types of contradictions and deal with them accordingly, through resolute, hard, and painstaking work. We must educate and unite people as much as possible and focus the crackdown on a handful of principal culprits and diehards who refuse to repent. On this basis, we will retrieve all the losses suffered in the unrest and the counterrevolutionary rebellion as soon as possible. For this, we must rely on the people, try to increase production, practice strict economy, and struggle arduously.

Chairman, vice chairmen, and Standing Committee members, our country's just struggle to quell the unrest and the counterrevolutionary rebellion has won the understanding and support of the governments and people of many countries. We extend our wholehearted gratitude for this. However, there are also some countries, mainly the USA and some Western European countries, which have distorted the facts, spread slanderous rumors, and even uttered so-called condemnations and applied sanctions to our country to set off an anti-China wave and wantonly interfere in our country's internal affairs. We deeply regret this. As for all the outside pressure, our government and people have never submitted to such things, not this time nor any time. The rumors will be cleared away and the truth and facts will come out.

Our country will unswervingly take economic construction as the central task and persist in the four cardinal principles and in reform and opening up to the outside world. Our country will, as always, adhere to our independent foreign policy of peace, continue to develop friendly relations with all countries in the world on the basis of the five principles of peaceful coexistence, and make our contributions to the safeguarding of world peace and the promotion of world development.

DENG XIAOPING, SPEECH TO OFFICERS AT THE CORPS LEVEL AND ABOVE FROM THE MARTIAL LAW ENFORCEMENT TROOPS IN BEIJING

There was no one more responsible for the Beijing massacre of 1989 than Deng Xiaoping. Deng and other retired elder leaders of his generation saw their life's efforts to build Communist Party power in China threatened by the popular protests of the preceding six weeks. They also undoubtedly recalled similar instances of mass unrest in Tiananmen and across China during the chaotic Cultural Revolution decade (1966–1976). Deng was the one who defined the protests as "counterrevolutionary" and decided to use force to suppress them. Throughout his career Deng never failed to suppress dissent, and he believed that such challenges to the Party's power posed by the demonstrators warranted a firm response. "Kill the chicken to scare the monkey" is an ancient Chinese aphorism, and Deng no doubt believed that if the demonstrations in Beijing were not dealt with severely, they would continue to spread (unrest had already occurred in thirty-three cities). This selection is the clearest example of Deng's own interpretation of the events of 1989 and his rationale for using force. It was delivered two days after the massacre, on June 6, 1989, to some of the military commanders who enforced martial law (not all commanders did, and those who did not were subsequently court-martialed for insubordination).

This selection was excerpted from Propaganda Trends (Xuanchuan Dongtai), *June 14, 1989, and first appeared in translation in* Chinese Law and Government, *Spring 1992.*

You comrades have been working hard! (Warm applause)

To begin, I would like to express my profound condolences to the officers and soldiers of the People's Liberation Army (PLA), the officers and soldiers of the People's Armed Police, and public security officers and police who died heroic deaths in this struggle! Allow me to convey my sincere solicitude for the thousands of officers and soldiers of the People's Liberation Army, the officers and soldiers of the People's Armed Police, and public security officers and police who were injured in this struggle! I also extend my cordial greetings to all the officers and soldiers of the People's Liberation Army, the officers and soldiers of the People's Armed Police, and public security officers and police who took part in this struggle!

I propose that all rise and stand in silent tribute for those martyrs. (All rose and stood in silent tribute.)

Now let me take the opportunity to say a few words.

This disturbance would have come anyway. Dictated by both the international climate and the domestic climate in China, it was destined to come, and the outbreak of this disturbance is independent of man's will. It was just a question of happening sooner or later, and of how serious the aftermath would be. It is to our advantage that this disturbance has broken out now. The most favorable factor for us is the existence of a large group of veteran revolutionaries who have experienced many disturbances and understand how to weigh the advantages and disadvantages of affairs. They support our adopting resolute actions against the rebellion. Although some comrades do not understand it for the time being [the necessity of adopting resolute actions to suppress the rebellion], they will eventually understand and support the decision of the party central leadership.

The nature of this disturbance was already determined to be turmoil in the April 26 editorial of *People's Daily*. The two characters *dongluan* (turmoil) are apt [for the nature of this disturbance]. Some people opposed the two characters and demanded they be revised. Practice has proven that the determination [of the nature of this disturbance] is correct. It is inevitable for the state of affairs to have developed to counterrevolutionary rebellion. We have a group of veteran comrades who are still alive, including those in the army, and we also have groups of backbone cadres who had joined the revolution in various periods. Therefore, it was relatively easy for us to control the state of affairs when the disturbance broke out recently. What is difficult for us to handle in this case is that we have never before faced such a situation. A small number of evildoers were among the vast numbers of young students and the masses of onlookers. For a while the alignment was unclear. All those made it difficult for us to put into effect many measures we should have taken. Without the support of so many veteran comrades in our party, it would have been difficult even to define the nature of this incident. Some comrades cannot see the nature of the issue and believe it is simply a problem of dealing with the masses. In fact, the opponents are not only the masses who cannot distinguish right from wrong but also a group of reactionaries and a large segment of the dregs of society. They are attempting to subvert our state and overthrow the Communist party, which is the essence of the issue. If we do not understand this fundamental problem, it means we are not clear about the nature of the issue. After making conscientious efforts in our work, I believe we will be able to win the support from the overwhelming majority in the party for determining the nature and handling of the issue.

It all became clear once the incident broke out. They have two key slogans: one is to overthrow the Communist Party, the other is to topple the socialist system. Their aim is to establish a bourgeois republic totally dependent on the West. We certainly accept the people's demand of opposing corruption. We will even have to accept as fine words the so-called anticorruption slogan by some people with ulterior motives. Of course, this slogan serves merely as a foil, and its crux is to overthrow the Communist Party and topple the socialist system.

In putting down the rebellion, many of our comrades were injured or even killed, and their weapons were stolen. Why did all this happen? It was also because the evildoers were mixed among the good ones, which made it hard for us to put into effect the measures we should have taken resolutely. It was a severe political test for our army to handle this incident. Practice shows that our People's Liberation Army has passed the test. Using the tanks to run over (the demonstrators) would have brought about confusion in the entire country regarding right and wrong. Therefore, I must thank the PLA officers and men for their attitude in handling the incident of rebellion. Although the loss was painful and distressing, it helped win the people over and change the opinions of those who could not distinguish between right and wrong. It showed everyone what type of people the PLA soldiers really are, whether there was a bloodbath in the square, and who really shed blood. If questions are made clear, we will gain the initiative. Although it was painful and distressing that many comrades laid down their lives, analyzing the whole process of the incident, the people will have to admit that the PLA is an army made up of the sons of the people. It will also help the people understand the measures we took in this struggle so that if the PLA should face difficulties in the future, their measures will be supported by the people. By the way, we will not allow our weapons to be stolen next time. All in all, this has been a test, and one that our army has success-fully passed. Even though there are not any veteran comrades in the army and most of the soldiers are youngsters of eighteen, nineteen, and twenty years of age, it is still an army genuinely made up of the sons of the people. While their lives were in danger, our army officers and men did not forget the people, the Party's teaching, and the interests of the state. Facing death, they showed no ambiguity. They are worthy of the statement that they went to their deaths like heroes and died coura-geously for a just cause. By saying that they passed the test, I mean that the army is still an army made up of the sons of the people and is a qual-ified one. This army carries on the tradition of the old Red Army. It has passed the true test of politics and of life and death, which is not easy indeed! This shows that our people's army is truly a bastion of iron for the Party and state. It shows that no matter how great a loss we may suf-fer, and no matter how many generations may be replaced, our army is always the army under the leadership of the Party, the defender of the state, the socialist system, the people's interests, and the most beloved men! At the same time, we should never forget how cruel our enemies are, and we should not forgive them even in the slightest way.

This incident has impelled us to consider the future, as well as the past, with a sober mind. This incident, bad as it was, may enable us to carry forward our reform and our opening to the outside world more steadily, and to correct our mistakes and better carry forward our strong points. I cannot elaborate on this issue today but only raise a few questions for study.

The first question is whether the lines, guiding principles, and policies, including the "trilogy" of our development strategy, formulated at the Third Plenary Session of the Eleventh Central Committee of the Chinese Communist Party are correct. Are questions raised about the correctness of our lines, guiding principles, and policies because of this turmoil? Is our objective a "leftist" one? Will we continue to regard it as our objective of struggle in the future? We must respond to these major questions with clear-cut and positive answers. We have already accomplished our first objective of doubling the national product; it will take twelve years to accomplish our further objective of doubling the national product for a second time; in the following fifty years, it will only require a growth rate of little more than 2 percent per annum for us to attain the level of an average developed nation. These are our strategic goals. I do not believe we have made a "leftist" judgment or set a too hasty goal on this. With regard to answering the first question, therefore, we ought to say that, at least up to now, the strategic objective we set is not unsuccessful. It is an extraordinary thing for a country with a population of 1.5 billion to achieve in sixty-one years the level of an average developed nation. We are able to realize this objective. One cannot conclude that our strategic goal is wrong because of this incident that is taking place. The second question is whether "one center, two basic points," set by the Thirteenth National Party Congress, is correct. Or whether the two basic points, namely, adhering to the Four Cardinal Principles and the policies of reforms and opening up, are wrong. Lately, we have been constantly thinking over this issue. We are not wrong. Adherence to the Four Cardinal Principles itself is not wrong. If anything is wrong, it is that we have not been consistent enough in adhering to the Four Cardinal Principles, and have failed to make it a fundamental thinking to educate the people, the students, cadres as a whole, and Communist Party members. The nature of the recent incident is bourgeois liberalization and opposing the four principles. It is not that we did not emphasize enough adherence to the four principles, ideological and political work, and opposing bourgeois liberalization and spiritual pollution, it is the lack of consistency and action regarding the problem, and we even talk little about it. The mistake does not lie in adherence to the four principles itself but in the fact that we did not adhere to them all along, and in the poor performance of our educational, ideological, and political work. On New Year's Day of 1980, I made a speech to the Political Consultative Conference in which I talked about the "four guarantees," including "the pioneering spirit of hard work." Hard work is our tradition. We will attach importance to the education of hard work and plain living for another sixty to seventy years. The more developed our country is, the more emphasis will be placed on building the nation through arduous efforts. To advocate the spirit of building the nation through arduous efforts will also help overcome corruption. We have been emphasizing hard work since the founding of the republic. When life improved after a time, high-level consumption was promoted, and the phenomenon of waste of all aspects was spreading. In addition, the weakness in ideological and political work, the imperfection of the legal system, and the phenomena of lawbreaking, violation of the principles, and corruption all surfaced. I mentioned to foreigners that the biggest mistake over the ten years was made in education; by that I meant the education of the people. We did little to educate the people in terms of building the nation through hard work and about the kind of state China is and will be. That is our big miscalculation.

Is the basic point of reform and opening up wrong? No, it is not. How could we be where we are today if there had been no reform and opening up? The people's living standards have been raised considerably over the past ten years, and we can say that we are now a step further. Despite inflation and other problems, the achievements of our ten years of reform and opening up should be amply evaluated. Of course, along with the reforms and opening up many bad influences of the West inevitably seeped into our country, and this we have never underestimated. In the beginning of the 1980s, when the Special Economic Zones were first established, I talked with the comrades from Guangdong Province on stressing two things simultaneously. On the one hand, I told them to attach importance to reforms and opening up; on the other hand, I told them to emphasize sternly cracking down on economic crimes and also to emphasize ideological and political work.

That is the theory of two basic points. Looking back, however, we find there have been obvious shortcomings. We have been strong on the one hand and weak on the other. The strength of one and weakness of the other do not fit together or cooperate well. Discussion on this point may benefit our future principles and policy making. Moreover, we will continue to keep unchanged the policy of adhering to combining a planned economy with market regulation. In practice, we strengthen or put more efforts on the planning feature in times of adjustment, and put more efforts on market regulation at other times. We should be more flexible in our work. In the future we will still combine planned economy with market regulation. What is important is that we never build China into a closed nation. It is extremely unfavorable to us to practice a closed-door policy as we would not even have access to information. Now people are talking about the importance of information, and it is important indeed. Without access to information, it is as if those in charge of administration have a stuffed nose, deaf ears, and blind eyes. We will never go back to the old times when the economy was extremely handicapped and tightly controlled. I propose that the Standing Committee of the Party Central Committee conduct research on this suggestion. It is a considerably pressing issue that needs attention. This has been a summary of our work over the past ten years. Some of our fundamental concepts, from our developmental strategies to the guiding principles, including reforms and opening to the outside world, are correct. If anything has been carried out insufficiently, it is in the area of reforms and opening up. The difficulties we have encountered in our reforms are far more than those in opening up. One thing we are sure of is that, in the aspect of reforming the political system, we must adhere to the practice of the system of a congress of people's representatives instead of the system of the American-style tripartite balance of power. In fact, not all the Western nations practice the system of tripartite balance of power. The Americans accused us of suppressing the students, while they themselves sent out police and troops to arrest people and allowed them to shed blood just the same in handling the student upheavals and unrest in their own country. They were really suppressing the students and the people, while we were only cracking down on counterrevolutionary rebellion. What right do they have to criticize us! Yet, in the future, in handling this type of issue, we must take care to prevent a trend from spreading when it first appears.

What should we do in the future? I believe we should maintain unchanged the basic lines, guiding principles, and policies we formulated before. We should carry our work firmly forward. Although a few changes need to be made in terminology, our basic lines and basic principles and policies will remain the same. This issue has already been raised, which requires your conscientious consideration. As far as some of our methods of work are concerned, such as the direction of investment and the direction of the funds to be used, I agree to strengthening our basic industries and agriculture. We need to increase investment in the basic industries for another ten to twenty years, including the industries of raw and processed materials, transportation, and energy. We will do so even at the cost of going into debt. This is also a policy of opening up. We need to be more audacious in these areas, and nothing can go badly wrong with that. If we generate more electricity, and build more railroads, highways, and ships for transportation, we can do a great many things. Now we have (a yearly production of) nearly 60 million tons of steel and are halfway to our future need of 120 million tons estimated by the foreigners. If we remodel our current plants and increase production by 20 million tons, we will be able to cut down the import of steel. Borrowing foreign money to be used in those areas is also reform and opening up. The question now does not lie in whether reforms and opening up are right and whether we should carry them forward, it lies in how, where, and in which aspects to carry them forward.

We must resolutely implement the series of lines, guiding principles, and policies formulated since the Third Plenum of the Eleventh Central Committee and conscientiously sum up our experience and carry on what is right, correct what is wrong, and make efforts to improve what is unsatisfactory. In a word, we must sum up the present and look forward to the future.

★   POLITICS IN THE NINETIES   ★

The Beijing massacre left the Chinese leadership with their most severe crisis since the Cultural Revolution. Sanctioned by Western nations and isolated abroad, the Communist Party and its leadership also lacked legitimacy and authority at home. Having used brute force to maintain themselves in power, and having turned the "people's army" against the people, the Party had, in the minds of many Chinese citizens, lost its mandate to rule. Yet China's leaders only intended to consolidate their rule while restoring "stability and unity" across the land.

MICHAEL D. SWAINE,
CHINA FACES THE 1990S: A SYSTEM IN CRISIS

In addition to their crisis of legitimacy, China's leaders in 1990 faced other pressing problems: rampant corruption, high inflation, decline of government revenue, bureaucratic inertia, a stagnant state industrial sector, declining central control, a factionalized military, rising crime, increasing social inequality, and further complex demographic, social, and environmental problems. In this selection the RAND Corporation China specialist Michael Swaine outlines these and other issues confronting the Chinese leadership in the aftermath of the Beijing massacre.

This selection was originally published in Problems of Communism, *May–June 1990.*

One year after the tragedy of Tiananmen, the leadership of the People's Republic of China remains committed to reestablishing the authority of the centralized socialist state. For a few observers, this effort marks the revival of full-blown totalitarianism in China, including most of the harsh measures of the Mao Zedong era. The implication of this view is that China is experiencing yet another historical swing of the pendulum, back toward monolithic central Party control, thoroughgoing repression, and central economic planning. This view can be labeled the "totalitarian revival" paradigm.

For a much larger number of China analysts, however, what we are witnessing in the People's Republic today is nothing less than the last gasp of a moribund system and its aged, reactionary leaders. These analysts view the current regime as merely marking time until the passing of Deng Xiaoping and his senior colleagues precipitates its collapse, most likely along with the entire communist system. Implicit in this view is the notion that, as in Eastern Europe, the forces of economic and political reform are irresistible and guarantee a relatively quick renewal of the upward climb in China's developmental curve. This view can be termed the "irresistible reform" paradigm.

Although these two views are contrasting perspectives on China's future, they nevertheless share one rather troubling assumption: that the central leadership is the key variable determining change, with developments along a reform-reaction continuum occurring largely as a function of a high-level internal power struggle between reformers and conservatives at the top. Such a perspective grossly oversimplifies the overall situation, underestimating the challenges China faces while overestimating the ability of *any* type of Chinese leadership to formulate and carry out policy effectively.

The Chinese system is at a critical juncture in its development. Economically, neither China's reform effort nor the corrective actions of the austerity program in effect since September 1988 have addressed the most fundamental deficiencies of the Chinese system. These deficiencies center on basic structural flaws related to the critical shortage of key resources (including intermediate goods such as energy and transport, and factor inputs such as capital and technology, management, and marketing skills) and, more important, increasing inefficiencies in the use of those resources. Politically, a decade of limited, piecemeal reforms has created as many problems in the system as these reforms have resolved, undermining the ostensible goals of stability, predictability, and strengthened regime legitimacy. Tiananmen was merely the most momentous of a series of social disruptions caused by such partial political reform. Because of it, the political crisis now greatly exacerbates the economic one, and the two have become inseparable.

To break this impasse and achieve further progress requires the formulation and implementation of much more innovative economic and political policies than those that have been proposed so far, almost certainly involving increased social unrest and political instability. Yet, on the other hand, the ability of the system to meet the challenges facing it through the development of innovative policies has never been weaker.

What we see in China are enormous problems in all areas comprising the key indices of regime capability: leadership at the very top is divided and without vision; the basic-level Party apparatus in both urban and rural areas is compromised and irresolute, often unable or unwilling to comply with central demands; the mid- and upper-level state and Party apparatuses are structurally fragmented and in conflict, while the interests and beliefs of their leaders have been altered in ways detrimental to central control; and the military, the ultimate guarantor of order, is embroiled in a major internal crisis, the dimensions of which are only dimly reflected in the public media.

The overall picture suggests that for an indefinite period of time, and regardless of the immediate consequences of the leadership succession, the center may be unable either to develop a program of fundamental political and economic reform or to reestablish central control. Instead, we may witness a third alternative, namely, a prolonged, relentless slide into state impotence, confusion, and disarray, in which the center is able only to suppress certain political, economic, and social activities, not guide and inspire them.

An Irresolute and Co-opted Party

Even the most casual observer of the Chinese scene recognizes that the overall organizational integrity and doctrinal authority of the Chinese Communist Party has eroded immensely since 1949. Much of this erosion is related to the oft-mentioned process of routinization occurring under the pressures of economic modernization, the persistent leadership strife since the early 1960s, and the passing of most of the original generation of revolutionary leaders. Only under the past decade of reforms, however, has this decline in the vitality of the Party taken a decidedly qualitative turn for the worse.

The decline has occurred largely because of the combined impact upon the Party of three interrelated phenomena basic to the reforms: (1) the general easing of controls on thought and discussion and the related opening to the outside world; (2) the economic changes occurring in the countryside, which have had a profound impact on the functions and outlook of basic-level rural cadres; and (3) a transformation in the nature of midlevel party elites.

In the cities, Party members at all levels have been strongly influenced by the process of political liberalization. As a consequence, many Party members share with broad urban elements a strong alienation from the regime, as indicated by the fact that many of the former participated in the spring 1989 pro-democracy demonstrations. Moreover, many individuals in the urban Party apparatus strongly doubt the official line that the Tiananmen demonstrations constituted a "counterrevolutionary rebellion" and that former Party General Secretary Zhao Ziyang sought to split the Party by encouraging the turmoil of the spring.

Having equally serious implications for central control over the Party apparatus is the fundamental transformation in the functions and interests of Party cadres that has occurred as a result of a decade of rural reforms. Before the 1980s, cadres on the grassroots level generally carried out the center's policies, gaining recognition, prestige, and, in some cases, advancement up the Party hierarchy for their efforts.

However, after some initial resistance to privatization and marketization, huge numbers of rural cadres became heavily involved in various schemes for making money. They did this both legitimately, as entrepreneurs and middlemen bringing peasant goods to market, and illegitimately, as corrupt parasites using their control over information and administrative procedures to engage in blackmail, extortion, and influence peddling. Eventually, these individuals became entrenched as essential bulwarks of the new reform economy, often working closely with those peasants who had profited most from the changed economic environment.

Instead of feeling angered or frustrated by the loss of their traditional sources of influence in the villages, most rural cadres have worked to establish very significant alternative sources of power and prestige outside the Party administrative hierarchy. The implications of this situation for central Party control are obvious. Even before Tiananmen, but particularly since then, Party sources have called attention to the thoroughly disorganized state of the entire Party apparatus in general and of rural Party organs in particular.

Compounding this crisis in the basic Party apparatus is the change that has occurred in the makeup of those midlevel Party elites ruling the large municipal regions (areas containing over half the population). In the past, such midlevel leaders were older, less educated cadres from rural areas, with experience in agriculture, Party organization, ideology, and military affairs, who gained promotion through participation in political mobilization and revolutionary campaigns. . . . Almost entirely as a result of the reforms, these positions are now overwhelmingly filled by younger and better-educated urban cadres (most with technical degrees), who have been recruited largely from the localities they govern.

This dramatic change in central control has, perhaps, been felt most keenly in the government sector, where it has led to strengthening of ongoing trends toward economic localism and general bureaucratic immobilism, both of which we shall discuss below. On the Party side, however, the promotion of individuals with backgrounds in administrative, industrial, and technical fields into elite positions reinforces the overall tendencies toward ideological decay and the related elimination of distinctions between Party and state functions and interests, and thus furthers the decline in the vitality of the central Party structures for mobilization and control.

State Bureaucratic Fragmentation

In the state sector, bureaucratic organizations have become cellular and fragmented, and thus both undermine the ability of the leadership to assess problems accurately and weaken the capacity of the state apparatus to implement policy. This fragmentation and diffusion of bureaucratic authority, although evident during the Mao era, intensified because of the reforms, which enhanced and sharpened the interests and capabilities of formal bureaucratic organizations and increased their overall role in the policy process.

On many important policy matters, an unprecedented degree of cooperation and coordination is now required among different functional bureaucratic systems, different hierarchical levels and regions, and different individual leaders for the government to function. Hence, decisions are usually not the outcome of a process limited to a single bureaucratic agency but the result of an ongoing series of smaller, reinforcing actions involving extensive bargaining among relevant organizations, each of which controls separate resources and seeks to promote distinctive interests.

For example, the policy process involved in the formulation and implementation of major economic policy lines often displays extensive conflict and competition among different vertical bureaucratic "systems" (*xitong*); horizontal, territorial governing bodies; separate bureaucratic units of differing rank; and various central and local officials. Among these entities, bargaining and lobbying within a wide range of policy areas often take place, especially before, during, and after major national planning and finance conferences. In this complex process, the interests of individuals and organizations associated with the development of heavy industry are often pitted against those representing light industry, agriculture, and fiscal conservatism.

As a result of the protracted negotiating necessary to placate the demands of all interested bureaucratic agencies, bold initiatives are often transformed into modest programs or negated altogether. Extensive organizational fragmentation and the resulting bargaining and consensus-building efforts of economic ministries and concerned government and Party leaders have resulted in the absence of a cohesive, consistent policy for national energy development.

Specific major projects in the energy sector such as the Three Gorges Dam hydroelectric project and the exploration and development of China's offshore oil resources displayed the effects of intensified bureaucratic competition. In these cases, several energy-related ministries contended with each other and with a wide array of additional relevant central ministries, central planning bodies, and various local officials over issues of project size, funding, location, equipment procurement, technical design, supply and distribution channels, and the level and type of foreign involvement to create a protracted policy debate that frustrated the intentions of the center while leaving most participants generally dissatisfied. The same general pattern of intensified bureaucratic contention over project development can be seen in politics surrounding the importation and construction of China's massive Baoshan steel complex near Shanghai from the late 1970s through most of the 1980s.

Diffuse Bureaucratic Interests

Closely related to the problem of structural fragmentation is the transformation of the interests and priorities of key state administrators that has further added to the decline of the center's ability to enforce compliance with its policies. Of particular importance are those changes affecting the outlook of top officials within ministries and commissions of the State Council's economic bureaucracy.

Because of their past dominant role within the centralized planning apparatus, economic ministries and commissions are often viewed as formidable allies of the current leadership in its attempt to strengthen central control over the economy. However, support for such recentralization among high-level officials of these organs may not be as strong as many assume.

The lack of support for recentralization is suggested by the recent organizational reforms that establish industry corporations and investment companies of ministries and commissions. Industry corporations were set up to utilize various forms of economic contracts in order to secure the production of goods governed by their parent ministries. In addition, these corporations are instructed by the government to make money by engaging in profitable activities but not necessarily in the same sector as the one administered by their parent ministry. Industry investment companies, by contrast, are to provide funding to the industry corporations for major state-approved projects, particularly in the areas of energy and transportation. As with the industry corporations, the responsibility to support major state goals is combined with the requirement to show a profit. These new entities are often staffed by high-level ministerial officials (in the case of industry corporations) or members of the State Planning Commission (in the case of investment companies), many of whom retain close ties to their former units.

Because of their need both to strike contractual (and other) deals and to make a profit, these new organizations in the period immediately before the Tiananmen massacre had expanded their links within the economic bureaucracy beyond the vertical, branch-line administrative command system of the past, toward the development of new types of horizontal, quasi-market relationships with various entities. The result was the formation of complex, often informal ties across industrial sectors and among various geographic areas.

The opportunities these ties created for central economic officials to profit financially from new business activities, plus the status and prestige that go with being a top officer in a new corporation or company, provide the basis for new interests supporting the continuation of more freewheeling, personally lucrative economic contacts basic to the hybrid economy. Moreover, under the new system, complex deal making and a greater concern for economic development within regions and localities have become more important. Consequently, it is increasingly problematic to assume that the interests of central economic organs such as the industry corporations and the investment companies lie in the strengthening of the rigid, centralized planning system as such. It is also problematic to assume, in turn, that the industrial corporations and the investment companies are hostile to the interests of specific regions.

Loss of Government Resources

Of even greater importance than the changes that have occurred in bureaucratic structures and interests is the tremendous erosion in the central government's control over basic financial and administrative levers essential to the effective implementation of *any* economic policy line, whether it is to reinvigorate centralized planning or to introduce more market-oriented reforms. The government's weakness is due to two interrelated developments: (1) a major decline in Beijing's control over essential economic resources combined with a concomitant rise in central financial burdens; and (2) the emergence of a range of informal relations and transactions existing outside both administrative and market-based channels and directives.

In 1979 government revenue as a whole accounted for 31.9 percent of national income; by 1984 that rate had dropped to 26.0 percent, and by 1988, to 19.2 percent. Moreover, the percentage of such revenue controlled by the center also fell from a high of 70.0 percent in the 1950s to 60.0 percent in the early 1980s and to 42.8 percent in 1989. Also by 1988 the proportion of foreign exchange under the control of the central authorities accounted for only 40 percent of the total; and the amount of foreign exchange held by governmental entities below the center had dropped as well. These trends suggest an overall increase in control over foreign exchange by nongovernmental sources.

The level of extrabudgetary funds controlled by local enterprises has been growing at the rate of more than 20 percent per year since the mid-1980s. In fact, by late 1989 the Ministry of Finance announced that almost as much money was circulating outside the state budget as within it. This loss of financial revenues by the center has also been exacerbated by the emergence of widespread currency hoarding in China. Hoarded currency may total as much as 200 billion renminbi, equal to about 40 percent of all currency in circulation. The result is a growing pool of funds existing totally outside the banking system.

In an attempt to rein in an inflation rate that had climbed to 30 to 40 percent in many urban areas by mid-1988, the center tried in late 1988 to reestablish its control over the money supply, credit, and the banking system. However, the existence of such an enormous pool of hoarded currency and other funds outside state control hampered the government's efforts by encouraging the creation of huge local markets in lending, which offered informal credit and loan arrangements. Since these local lending markets filled many of the funding shortfalls produced by the government's retrenchment policy, localities were able to resist Beijing's initial attempts to reduce drastically investment levels in late 1988 and early 1989.

Added to the decline in state capabilities created by the loss of financial resources is the increase that has occurred under the reforms in state outlays, especially subsidies. Such increases hinder the ability of the state to devote resources to other, more urgent needs. In 1989 Beijing reportedly paid out approximately 100 billion RMB in price subsidies and supports to state enterprises, nearly one-third of the state's budgetary expenses.

The explosive growth in the level of foreign economic relations that has taken place under the reforms has also reduced central economic control by increasing dependence on external sources of finance, trade, and investment. From 1979 to 1988, foreign capital inflow increased from nearly nothing to U.S.$47 billion, or about 10 percent of state fixed investment during that period. Foreign trade has also sharply increased by an average of 17 percent a year since 1978, with the share of exports rising from 5 to 14 percent of gross national product by 1987. By 1989 the total value of foreign trade exceeded $110 billion, a figure equal to at least 20 percent of China's gross national product.

Beijing's overall control of the economy has also been undermined by the emergence of township and village enterprises, which formed the core of industrial growth under the reforms. Developed largely outside of state control and responsive to the quasi-market forces of China's hybrid economy, these mainly small-scale enterprises have experienced phenomenal growth, particularly in the past five to six years. Approximately 18 million town and village enterprises, which employ more than 90 million people, or nearly 25 percent of the total rural labor force, have emerged since the reforms were initiated. According to recent official Chinese sources, such enterprises provide fully half of peasant income. Equally important, these entities reportedly turned over 114 billion renminbi in taxes to the state during the past decade. From the perspective of both financial revenues and employment, these production entities have come to play a very significant role in the Chinese economy.

Informal Transactions and Local Power

One might think that the erosion of Beijing's influence over its economic resources could be reversed simply by reassigning certain administrative and financial prerogatives that had been delegated to the localities under the reforms back to central economic organs. As the leadership in Beijing is discovering, however, recentralization is a far more complex and difficult task than it might first appear.

For one thing, the loss of central financial resources and the increased dependence on economic activities outside the state sector are the results of the limited successes of the reform period. But expanding the state sector and reestablishing direct control over key economic activities (by abolishing or attempting to absorb town and village enterprises, for example) or reducing the extent of involvement in the world economy would lead to reduced output and increased unemployment, thus prompting an even greater economic crisis.

More important, however, are the basic systemic and political obstacles to the reassertion of central control over resources. The former relate to the transformation of basic economic and administrative interactions under the half-plan, half-market structure of partial reform. As Jan S. Prybyla has observed, the economy of the PRC is a "dismantled planned economy with uncoordinated, unlinked, and imperfect markets existing here and there for individual goods." What holds the economy together is a wide range of informal transactions. Under the complex financial responsibility system of the reforms, informal, personal deals are struck between enterprises and factories, local bank managers and heads of local economic bureaus, and local governments and central ministries over levels of profit retention, taxation allotments, and investment financing. The same pattern of behavior is seen in the enterprise responsibility system, in which many types of production units, suppliers, and distributors bargain over planned targets, inputs, and outputs, often exchanging favors and engaging in payoffs to ensure fulfillment of contracts. In such a system, economic success depends on political bargaining skills and connections (*guanxi*), not knowledge of the market and attention to efficiency. The result is what Prybyla calls "socialist feudalism," where complex, interlocking, and interdependent networks of informal contacts exist in almost every product sector of the economy.

Networks of informal bargaining and exchange undermine central control over the economy. They resist pressures produced either by price fluctuations (the market) or by administrative orders (the plan). They also greatly enhance the incentives and opportunities for individual and group corruption. But to dismantle this system in the process of reestablishing central controls would lead to even greater chaos for the regime.

The political obstacles to the reassertion of central control over economic resources emerge largely out of the combined effect both of the new network of informal transactions and of the overall decentralization of economic decision-making authority under the reforms. These two developments combine with the transformation of midlevel elites during the 1980s, due to the decision to choose them primarily from the native population of a given area, to create a formidable array of local and regional interests with strong stakes in maintaining and even expanding their control over resources. Local governments usually stand at the center of the basic-level network of informal transactions and bargaining. Enterprises, factories, and other commercial and industrial entities depend upon them for information on and access to essential production inputs, funding, and markets. In addition, local governments make decisions regarding taxation levels, amounts of foreign exchange retained, venture approvals, et cetera. Local governments also mediate between the central government and production units in decisions regarding tax collection and other financial matters, often bargaining with Beijing over the amount the center is to receive through the system of "tax farming" established under the financial responsibility system. Finally, they have strong links with local financial institutions and an ability to manipulate prices under the irrational, two-tier pricing system.

As a result, in many places local political elites have established political machines that control local economic monopolies and engage in sometimes fierce competition with one another over scarce raw materials, goods, and funds. Local governments in the coastal regions are especially powerful as a result of the successful activities of the town and village enterprises in their jurisdictions and the expansion of foreign economic relations, which favored their regions.

The competition among these local "speculator-bureaucrats" for control of key resources adds to the general inefficiencies of the Chinese system and intensifies the "balkanized" structure of China's economic system. Moreover, as indicated above, China's emerging regionalism has played a role in the changing interests of central economic officials, whose involvement in wheeling and dealing through industry corporations and investment companies has a definite regional component.

A Divided Military

The disarray and immobilism that characterize the Chinese party, government, and economy today can also be seen in the military. In the case of the People's Liberation Army (PLA), however, such phenomena have emerged more recently, largely as a result of a major internal dispute brought on by the Tiananmen massacre and its aftermath. This dispute has drawn the military more directly into the political process.

The declaration of martial law and the subsequent violent crackdown of June 3–4, 1989, were highly divisive events for the Chinese military. Although attempts were made to create an impression of a responsive army, this was not the reality. Considerable hesitation and resistance existed, which were largely overcome only through the active involvement of Deng Xiaoping and other elder leaders. Over a period of weeks, officers and soldiers alike participated in the pro-democracy demonstrations of spring 1989, and, after May 20, many refused to obey orders to implement martial law. As a result, thousands of military men are reportedly under investigation, and arguments over Tiananmen continue within the ranks of the military.

As the longevity and severity of the dispute suggest, the problems in the PLA go far beyond differences over Tiananmen. The central rift is an intensified version of the controversy between the adherents of politicization that has plagued the military since the late 1950s. During the past decade, forces favoring greater professionalization clearly had gained the upper hand, as reformers deemphasized the past importance of ideology, politics, and Party control within the PLA in favor of the formation of a more Western-style national defense army under the control of the government.

This move toward greater professionalism reflected the very deep-rooted changes occurring in the Chinese military. At the center of this change are the younger officers at the middle and upper-middle levels of the PLA. These individuals, promoted to important positions under the reforms and actively involved in the movement to professionalize the military, have strong career and policy-related reasons to maintain a stress on modernization. Although it is impossible to estimate the exact number of these officers, some analysts have suggested that they comprise a significant body that could become dominant within the military once the senior leadership is gone. This view is at least partly confirmed by the high number of negative references to such officers found in the media after Tiananmen, suggesting that these people are of great concern to the current leadership.

A more precise indication of this generation of officers' positions and outlook is provided by interviews undertaken prior to the Tiananmen events with twenty generals, all of whom rose to power over the past ten years. Most were under fifty years of age, and many had visited foreign countries. These respondents expressed strong concern over the decline of the PLA's combat effectiveness. They sharply criticized the obstacles to modernization posed by elements within the PLA hierarchy, especially unnamed senior PLA leaders who resisted the application of science and technology to the military because of their own ignorance and support for tradition. They were also strongly opposed to the continued interference in military affairs of many supposedly retired PLA officers.

It is also very likely that the navy and the air force, which have benefited the most from military-related contacts, exchanges, and trade between China and the West over the past decade, have become strong supporters of professionalization. This support reflects a general shift that has occurred in the overall force posture of the PLA, away from an interior land-based defense strategy to a coastal-based one keyed to the importance of naval and air capabilities.

Interests favoring professionalization have now come into direct conflict with more orthodox conservatives within the party and army who seek to consolidate their political and ideological control over the PLA by reversing recent trends.

Conclusion

The complex process of systemic change that has taken place in China, largely under the reforms, has had a major adverse impact on the capacity of the center to develop the kind of innovative policies needed to overcome its enormous problems, thus casting doubt on the applicability of either the "totalitarian revival" or the "irresistible reform" paradigm. One might assert that the examples of policy failure cited above simply reflect broad-based resistance to a return to the past by forces favoring continued political and economic reforms, rather than any fundamental incapacity of the regime. Yet, as this article has attempted to show, the elements within the state and Party apparatuses that obstruct the center (both intentionally and unintentionally) in most cases derive their strength and durability not from a dedication to further change but from a defense of the status quo rooted in the distortions, inefficiencies, localist structures and attitudes, and informal transactions of China's partially reformed economic system. Drastic changes in this system toward either more open or more closed structures would threaten these interests.

So where does this leave China? After the passing of Deng Xiaoping and the conservative elders, we may see the emergence of a far more decentralized system than anything previously experienced under Chinese communism. This system could be marked by a weak central government locked in prolonged political struggle, yet held together by the strong fear of chaos, most clearly expressed by the military; a balkanized economy with pockets of continued progress existing alongside areas of growing deprivation, each controlled largely by local political machines concerned more with protecting and enlarging their respective economic resources than with challenging the ultimate political authority of Beijing; and continued social frustration and discontent, moderated by periods of limited economic progress and weakened doctrinal control from Beijing.

Of course, the emergence of such a scenario is by no means inevitable. Much depends on the specific degree to which many of the systemic changes discussed above hold true over time, especially the emergence of regional and local power (both formal and informal); the fragmentation of bureaucratic structures; and the altered interests of basic-level cadres, central officials, and urban elites. The key element in this scenario, or any future scenario, will be the actions of the Chinese military. As indicated above, the military is the only major part of the system that has a significant number of relatively powerful, progressive leaders, suggesting that it could become a force for genuine change. Yet support for modernization and professionalization cannot be assumed to be support for democracy and a market economy (indeed, some segments of the PLA are deeply involved in corruption and deal making). Moreover, in addition to the primary politicization/professionalization debate, other serious, albeit secondary personal and institutional divisions within the PLA undermine its ability to act as a force for positive change. The only interest that can possibly bridge these differences is the commitment of the military, as an institution, to the maintenance of order in China, but under current conditions order spells stagnation.

ANONYMOUS,
THE TEN-THOUSAND-CHARACTER MANIFESTO

Even before Deng Xiaoping died in February 1997, domestic critics of his reforms were raising objections in the press, sponsoring journals, convening conferences, and circulating documents inside the Party. In 1996 several lengthy tracts were so circulated. Since they were roughly 10,000 Chinese characters in length, they became known as the Ten-Thousand-Character Manifestos (wan yuan shu). One of the more prominently circulated manifestos is reproduced here. It was allegedly written under the auspices of the leftist critic Deng Liqun, but the identity of the authors is unknown. This document details many of the negative features that had appeared as consequences of economic reform.

This translated selection first appeared in the British Broadcasting Corporation's Summary of World Broadcasts/Far East *and was republished in* The China Quarterly, *December 1996.*

The Chinese Communist Party Central Committee with Comrade Jiang Zemin as the core has worked out a series of correct plans for the major issues concerning state security since 1989. Since the beginning of this year, the CCP Central Committee has again made a number of important proposals and adopted some correct measures.

For various reasons, however, there are still some factors in China at present which are disadvantageous to state security. In order to draw a lesson from the "1989 disturbance" and prevent a repetition of the toppling of the political power of the proletariat of Eastern Europe and the Soviet Union, we must conduct a careful analysis of all factors affecting China's state security.

Instead of analyzing all the factors affecting China's state security, this article will only focus on the factors of domestic economy, politics, and culture. Of the economic, political, and cultural factors, this article will analyze the factors at a deeper level which might affect China's state security within the next decade rather than the factors which may affect China's current state security but be eliminated by the efforts made in the next two to three years.

The factors include ownership structure, class relationships, social awareness, and the situation of the ruling party.

Changes in Ownership Structure

In light of the status quo of China's productive forces, the CCP Central Committee has decided to restore the economic sector of private ownership so that it can play a useful supplementary role to socialist public ownership. Since the implementation of this policy decision, major changes have been effected in China's ownership structure.

Of the total industrial output value from 1980 to the end of June 1994, the proportion of the state sector dropped from 76.0 percent to 48.3 percent, while that of the collective sector (which possibly included some of the private sector that used the name of the collective sector) increased from 23.5 percent to 38.2 percent and that of the private and individual sector and foreign-funded enterprises increased from 0.5 percent to 13.5 percent. Of the total volume of retail sales, the state sector dropped from 51.4 percent to 41.3 percent, the collective sector dropped from 44.6 percent to 27.9 percent, and the private and individual sector and foreign-funded enterprises rose from 0.7 percent to 30.8 percent. The proportion of the public sector is continuously dropping through the means of leasing, sale, mergers, and the shareholding system. It is estimated that in gross industrial output value, by the year 2000, the state sector will drop and account for only one-quarter of the total, while the collective sector will rise and account for 50 percent, and the private and individual sector and foreign-funded enterprises will rise and account for one-quarter. Of the volume of retail sales, the state sector will drop and account for only one-third, while the collective sector will drop and account for one-sixth and the private and individual sector (including retail sales by peasants to nonfarming residents) will rise and account for 50 percent. The growth in the private sector at the present stage will be conducive to the development of social production, make things convenient for the people, and increase employment. However, if the proportion of the private sector exceeds a certain extent, it will exert an adverse influence on the nature of China's social economic basis.

Thanks to the introduction of the shareholding system and corporate property rights, the remaining state enterprises are also faced with the problem that they will not be totally owned by the state. For example, Zhejiang's Hangjiahu and Wenzhou have allowed individuals to join the public sector through the shareholding system. Through reform, Sichuan will no longer have state enterprises in its county economy. The state enterprises, whose proportion has been drastically cut through such reform, will not be directly managed by the government and they will not be owned exclusively by state units.

Over the past three years, the leading cadres of many localities have regarded the development of the private sector as the main channel for boosting economic growth. Disregarding the public sector, they have put their energy, cadres, funds, materials, and markets into private enterprises, vied with one another in offering preferential treatment to private and foreign-funded enterprises, and proposed several "restriction-free" measures for the development of the private economy. The Heilongjiang Party committee put forward the slogan of "opening up a second battlefield" and went all out to accelerate the development of the private sector. Although these comrades have not stressed the theory of privatization, they have taken practical action to boost privatization.

In the course of such change effected in the ownership structure, there has been a drain of over 500 billion yuan of state assets since 1982, an average of over 50 billion yuan a year and over 100 million yuan a day. Some people have even estimated that the drain on China's state assets exceeds 100 billion yuan a year. These state assets which have been turned from public to private are the main source of the primitive accumulation of the new bourgeoisie. We can say that the new bourgeoisie are fed with the toil and sweat of the people of the whole country over the past forty years.

The private sector has played a positive role at the present stage, and it should be allowed to exist and develop. Our problem is not whether the private sector should be developed but whether it is necessary to bring the quantity and scope of the private sector under control, whether its role should be restricted to one supplementary to the public sector, and whether its negative role should be acknowledged and restricted.

The predominance of the public sector over other economic sectors and the leading position of the public sector in the national economy are the decisive factors determining that China's economy is socialist in nature. For this reason, the shrinking of the public sector and the privatization trend of the social economic structure will inevitably affect and undermine the security of the socialist economic foundation.

The public sector is the economic mainstay of the political power of the proletariat. The public sector not only houses China's industrial workers but also is the main source of China's revenue. The drop in the proportion of the public sector and the shrinking of public ownership will inevitably weaken the Party's leading position, the authority of the central government, and the ability of the state in handling contradictions and resolving problems. Moreover, it will menace the consolidation of the proletarian dictatorship.

The newly emerged private sector will also serve as the economic backing of the political demands of the newly emerged bourgeoisie. Historically, based on the principle of "no taxation without representation," the European bourgeoisie won the political power of the state from the feudal rulers. Now the agents of the new bourgeoisie have also proposed "paying taxes to 'purchase' from the government the 'public goods' such as the legal system, public order, national defense, and democracy which they cannot obtain from the market."

Moreover, the output value of the 80,000 foreign-funded enterprises which had gone into operation accounted for 30.0 percent of China's gross national product by the end of 1993, and the volume of their imports and exports accounted for 34.4 percent of the country's total. The proportion of foreign-invested enterprises in China's economy is growing rapidly. The growth in foreign capital is conducive to China's economic development, but it will also make China's economy more dependent on other countries. Compared with the past, we will easily be manipulated by others. When there is confrontation between China and the countries concerned, it will affect China's state security.

Changes in Class Relationships

With the restoration and development of the private sector in recent years, private entrepreneurs and individual operators have again emerged in China.

According to statistics, by the end of June 1994, China had 328,000 registered private entrepreneurs hiring an average of more than eight workers. A total of 5,008,000 were involved in private enterprises, with a registered capital of over 104.1 billion yuan.

Each enterprise had an average of 14.2 workers, with a registered capital of 317,000 yuan. Of these, private enterprises with capital of over 1 million yuan exceeded 5,000 by the end of 1992. Some people say that the figure exceeds 1 million. There are also a small number of millionaires and billionaires. In some of the coastal provinces, there are private enterprises hiring over 1,000 workers. According to a typical survey conducted by the Research Office of the State Council, the actual number of private entrepreneurs is 100 percent more than the registered figure. If this figure is taken into consideration, the actual number of private entrepreneurs will be far more than the number registered.

During the initial period of the People's Republic of China's founding, the standard set by China for private entrepreneurs was possessing 2,000 yuan of capital and three workers hired by factories or two staff members hired by commercial organizations. According to statistics based on the standards of the "Report Requesting Separation of Laborers from Industrial and Commercial Owners" ratified by the central authorities in 1979, China had only 160,000 registered private entrepreneurs before the 1950s.

It is generally acknowledged that there was a national bourgeoisie in China before 1955. A comparison of the current situation with the one before 1955 shows that the number of private entrepreneurs in China at present far exceeds that of the period before 1955 in terms of both absolute number and economic strength. What is more, the criterion for determining private entrepreneurs in terms of the number of workers hired is far higher than that in the initial period of the PRC's founding. Hence, we can say that a nongovernmental bourgeois class has taken shape economically. It is at least a class-in-itself. This is an indisputable fact. (Those with Marxist knowledge know that the bourgeois class is not limited to the private entrepreneurs; it includes the family members and the intellectuals who depend on them. This is the case with the bourgeois in the 1950s as well as in the 1990s. Herein lies the purpose and the comparison of the main portion of the bourgeois class, that is, the figures of the private entrepreneurs is sufficient to prove the point [sentence as published].)

According to statistics, by the end of September 1994, the number of individual industrial and commercial owners hiring an average of less than seven workers totaled 20.15 million. A total of 34.38 million people were involved, with a registered capital of 114.67 billion yuan. Therefore, a small bourgeois class, namely, a class of individual operators, has taken shape, of which some are the reserve force for the nongovernmental bourgeois class.

Since we have decided to restore the private sector, the emergence of a bourgeois class and a petty bourgeoisie is inevitable and normal. The question does not lie in whether the bourgeois class and petty bourgeoisie are allowed but in whether we can correctly understand the fact, correctly handle the relationship with the bourgeois class, unite and at the same time wage struggles, and regard the handling of such a relationship as an important component part of the Party's political line in the new period.

With the development of the private sector, foreign capital, and the individual economy, the number and economic strength of the nongovernmental bourgeoisie and petty bourgeois class will further expand. The embryo of a bureaucrat bourgeoisie and a comprador bourgeoisie has emerged.

As some state enterprises are facing difficulties, the living standards of the staff members have declined. The workers employed by the private enterprises (including foreign-funded enterprises) are again oppressed and exploited by the private owners. As a result, many workers have cast doubt on the leading position of the working class and the direction of the state's socialism. Moreover, they are pushing themselves away from the Party.

At present, the private entrepreneurs in China are "bending down to pick up the golden apple" on the one hand and have gradually raised independent political demands to protect their economic interests on the other hand. There are now 5,401 private entrepreneurs who are people's deputies above county level, 8,558 who are members of the Chinese People's Political Consultative Conference [CPPCC] above county level, 1,357 who are members of the Youth League above county level, and 1,430 who are members of the Women's Federation above county level. Some private entrepreneurs are still not satisfied with these figures. A general manager of a Shenzhen company said that the entrepreneur class has not fully expressed itself on the future trend of China's society. A private entrepreneur from Fujian's Jinjiang said: "The innovation of China's political system will start along with the development of the private sector and expansion of the ranks of the private entrepreneurs. In the future, large numbers of private entrepreneurs will enter the leading bodies of the government at all levels. We should no longer regard private entrepreneurs as political vases like the people's deputies and CPPCC members." Some private entrepreneurs said: "If there are mayors from among private entrepreneurs in the government, we will not have to worry about our legitimate rights." In 1988 more than twenty private entrepreneurs from Fujian's Shishi said: "We must recommend figures from political circles who can represent us to take part in the elections." They also jointly nominated candidates for the election of mayor. In order to become a standing committee member of the people's congress of a city, a private entrepreneur in Zhejiang entertained people everywhere. He openly declared that he would offer 1,000 yuan to those who cast their vote for him. As a result, he was elected. Some 21.3 percent of the private entrepreneurs of a prefecture in Hebei entered the grassroots level organs of political power and assumed leading posts. In Hunan's Shimen, 198 private entrepreneurs assumed leading posts, of which 86 were village directors and 67 were secretaries of village Party branches. "Chambers of private enterprises," "guilds of nongovernmental enterprises," "youth chambers," "nongovernmental enterprise clubs," "foreign-invested associations," and other private enterprise organizations have emerged in a number of localities. At the same time, some private entrepreneurs have proposed running newspapers and having their own "mouthpieces." There are now newspapers, including *Minying Qiyejia Bao* [*Nongovernmental Entrepreneurs*], *Qiyejia Bao* [*Entrepreneurs*], and *Changzhang Jingli Ribao* [*Factory Directors and Managers Daily*], which directly reflect their interests and demands.

In the ideological field, some agents of the bourgeois class said: "In the future, we will have to rely more on money to determine human value and talent." "The quantity and quality of tycoons is the hallmark by which to judge whether a country's economy is developed. Hence, there are few and not too many tycoons in China." "Businessmen from the West want a bridge to enter China, that is, large numbers of compradors." "If we have new compradors, China's opening up will smoothly escalate to a new stage." Some people questioned the saying that the only role of the nonpublic sectors is to supplement the public sector. Some proposed including "the protection of private property in the Constitution." Some asserted that reform in the future should "reduce the proportion of state enterprises" through the means of "leasing," "change," and "auction sales." "Reduce the scope of state enterprises so that they will exist in the field of production of public goods merely as an ineffective market tool and the field that natural monopolized trade and other private enterprises are incapable or are not willing to enter." In other words, they should play a supplementary role to the private sector. "The fission of property rights of state enterprises is the sensible and general trend." Some people urged "the government to change its position and stand at the side of the nonpublic enterprises." Some proposed setting up an "inhabitants' community" based on the predominance of the capitalists. They also asked for permission to run private newspapers and freedom of assembly. It is estimated that once the situation permits, these people will not need much time to openly form a bourgeois political party.

Some private entrepreneurs or those in charge of collective enterprises who insist on taking the capitalist road are subsidizing the bourgeois liberals in running newspapers and magazines, and establishing their so-called nongovernmental research, consultative, and intermediary organizations. The private entrepreneurs and the bourgeois liberals have started to form an alliance in the ideological field. Without doubt, such an alliance will accelerate the change of the bourgeois class from a class-in-itself to a class-for-itself.

Wan Runnan [a pro-democracy businessman who fled abroad in the wake of the June 4, 1989, incident], a representative of the bourgeoisie, who is in exile abroad, hit the nail on the head: "Standing in opposition to the existing system of the CCP, the newly born middle class wants to protect its own interest." "On the one hand, the middle class hates this system; on the other hand, they have to cooperate with this government in order to make money. Herein lie their interests. They use money and materials to corrupt the government and promote change in the society from the negative side." "In order to seek development, they will have to adopt various means and mainly use money to push, operate, and lubricate the rigid bureaucratic CCP system. As a result, the CCP regime becomes irremediably corrupt. It is the money of the middle class that has made the CCP corrupt. The more corrupt the regime is, the greater the possibility of a change in society. When the newly born middle class can maintain a certain economic status, they will expect the right to know and discuss political affairs and will further participate in political affairs. This is the process of political democratization." These remarks penetratingly illustrate the political consequences arising from the bourgeoisie.

Although major struggles took place on several occasions within the CCP in the thirty years before the mid-1980s, they were carried out in an environment without the bourgeoisie outside the party. Hence, no matter how the struggles proceeded within the CCP, its leadership over the state was not directly menaced. The reemergence of the bourgeoisie at present has fundamentally changed this environment. The interests of the bourgeoisie are fundamentally against the dictatorship of the proletariat, and this antagonism is independent of the cooperation or confrontation between the bourgeoisie and the proletariat. If the bourgeois class wants to change its economic position from a supplementary to a dominant one and change its political position from a subordinate to a leading one, it will share and even monopolize state power. Therefore, the formation of the bourgeois class constitutes a latent threat to China's proletarian dictatorship. When the conditions are not yet ripe, the bourgeois class will vigorously involve themselves in inner-Party struggles, attack the reformers within the Party who take the socialist road, and support the reformers within the Party who take the capitalist road. Once the conditions are mature, they will "completely destroy" the Communist Party with the cooperation and backing of the international bourgeoisie and openly and directly use bourgeois dictatorship to replace the proletarian dictatorship. Therefore, the bourgeois class is the main object we should take note of in our domestic political and security work in the next decade.

Changes in Social Awareness

Bourgeois liberalization and the Four Cardinal Principles have been engaged in a seesaw battle for more than a decade since 1977. Bourgeois liberalization gradually got the upper hand after 1992. Apart from a small number of Marxist periodicals, articles criticizing bourgeois liberalization have disappeared from the media. Bourgeois liberalization has not only revived but also intensified. Its depth and breadth have exceeded those in the period before the 1989 disturbance.

In the theoretical field, bourgeois liberalization has been mainly manifested in the following: Applying the theory of modern market economy to resist the theory of socialist market economy, which actually advocates developing a market economy similar to the capitalist market economy; denying that public and private ownership constitute the fundamental difference between socialism and capitalism so as to prove that private ownership is compatible with socialism and is a component part of socialism; attacking public ownership of the means of production and saying that it is "wild and ultraleftist socialism"; calling for the implementation of private ownership on the grounds that public ownership is incompatible with the market economy; saying that public ownership is not the goal and that the predominant position should not be self-claimed in order to oppose the predominance of public ownership and call for further cuts in the proportion of public ownership until the public sector is forsaken; proposing that state property be turned to private property through the shareholding system and the transfer of property rights to individuals; urging China to "fundamentally" reform its political structure; calling for the establishment of an inhabitants' community based on capitalists so as to get rid of the proletarian dictatorship, which protects socialism and restricts capitalism and create[s] conditions for replacing the proletarian dictatorship with a bourgeois one; totally negating the achievements of socialist construction over the past thirty years since PRC's founding and the explorations made in the building of the socialist road by the CCP under Mao Zedong's leadership; regarding the sixty-year history of the CCP as one in which "leftism" ran wild and which brought disasters to China; negating Marxist theories of class struggle and proletarian dictatorship; negating the theory of scientific socialism and regarding it as a traditional and outdated theory, and declaring that Marx's vision of the communist society was utopian and an illusion; advocating Westernization and Confucianism and applying these to replace Marxism; suggesting that the "postmodernist school" and "mass culture," namely, vulgar culture, be applied to "eliminate the mainstream ideology," that is, Marxist ideology; and attacking the training of a "new type of selfless person," saying that it is "utopian" and a "false humane spirit" which "ignores the true active person." These bourgeois liberalization proposals have spread unchecked under the cover of the anti-"leftism" banner. The theoretical encirclement and suppression of the Four Cardinal Principles will directly shake the theoretical grounds for proletarian dictatorship and undermine the foundation of our cause.

In literary and artistic works, the main expression of bourgeois liberalization is manifested in intentionally depicting China's poverty and backwardness over the past thirty years since the PRC's founding and sparing no efforts to exaggerate the shortcomings and mistakes made in the sixty years since the CCP's founding, describing the Party cadres and members who have taken the socialist road and the revolutionary masses who have followed the Party as negative figures and certain targets of socialist revolution and new democratic revolution as positive figures. In the works reflecting reality, workers, peasants, soldiers, and Party organizations have disappeared. The Party's cadres have become typical examples of rigidity and conservatism who hinder reform, while the private entrepreneurs and upstarts have become vanguards of reform and heroes of the times who incorporate all sorts of virtues. At the same time, audio-video products from Hong Kong, Taiwan, and Western capitalist countries which are immersed in a bourgeois outlook on life, values, and political concepts have flowed into the cultural market in China's urban and rural areas. The spread of these literary and artistic works has shaken people's faith in the Four Cardinal Principles. Many young people who have not experienced past history will mistakenly believe that the socialist revolution and new democratic revolution led by the CCP, as described by the authors of some works, were mistakes in history.

By reviewing the lessons drawn from the "1989 pro-democracy movement," the bourgeois liberal forces within and outside the Party are sounding out the atmosphere at home and abroad, and have developed relatively systematic and definite views over the past two years. They believe that the only wise and realistic option for China and the only feasible way for the CCP to save the Party and the nation is starting from "nonideology in the propaganda and ideological field," namely, diluting Marxism, gradually giving up the Four Cardinal Principles, effecting a change in the economy to a free market economy of private ownership and a change politically to a multiparty parliamentary democracy, and steadily effecting a "peaceful evolution" to capitalism through "reform" in a step-by-step manner. In cooperation with the Western capitalist countries and the hostile forces abroad by tacit agreement, they are adopting outflanking tactics to spread the influence of such political viewpoints within and outside the Party.

Influenced by the trend of bourgeois liberalization over the past three years, a change in direction has been effected in China's social awareness: The things which were regarded as correct in the past (of which some were proved to be correct) are now regarded as wrong; the things which were regarded as wrong in the past (of which some were proved to be wrong) are now regarded as correct; and the things newly built through socialist revolution are regarded as traditional old stuff, while pawn and auction sale agencies which existed long ago in the old society are regarded as things newly emerging in the course of reform. At the same time, marked changes have taken place in China's social mood. Some people who have suddenly became rich through means other than labor vie with one another in eating, drinking, visiting prostitutes, and gambling, which strongly stimulates the masses and sets examples. Luxurious hotels and shops, nightclubs, golf courses, saunas, massage parlors, and brothels, specially designed for tycoons, have been set up in the prosperous economic regions. Money not only is the condition for material comfort but also has became the criterion for the media to judge a man's social value and career. Ultraegoism, hedonism, and money worship have become the main theme of life and the creed pursued by an increasing number of people. Imitation of decadent Western lifestyles has become a fashion. Tycoons have become the target of public respect. Shops, hotels, and amusement centers vie with one another to use "VIP," "magnate," "mogul," "boss," and "emperor" as their names (the names of shops are the measure by which to judge their social status). Rational incomes obtained through hard labor are no longer regarded as the norm in life, and making money through speculation has become the ideal of an increasing number of people.

Many people mock the moral character of selflessness. A worker from Shanghai said: "Alas, I have woken up. Diligence cannot lead to affluence. I must change my concepts, wipe out my past thinking, and try to engage in business." In the past, people regarded "going to factories, rural areas, and the places where the motherland needed them most" as an honor, but now they want to "go to companies, foreign countries, and places where they can make money." "Party members are very serious" is replaced by "where ignorance is bliss, 'tis folly to be wise" and "having no regrets for wasting one's life" by "why not play through life?" Speculation in stocks and real estate, trading of false invoices, pornography, production and selling of counterfeit goods, and

even smuggling have become active mass movements in some localities. For a time, China held the "world title" for abduction of women
and children, highway robbery, and plane hijacking. With the inflow of
culture from Hong Kong, Taiwan, and Western countries, the mentality
of imitating Hong Kong and Taiwan culture, worshiping everything foreign, and yearning for the capitalist world has been passed from ignorant young people to some intellectuals and Party and government
cadres. Learning to speak the Cantonese dialect, vying with one another
for "lucky numbers," and regarding the wearing of shirts and caps with
U.S. stars-and-stripes designs as fashionable are the external expressions
of this mentality. It is conceivable that when there are confrontations
between China and the United States or other countries, we can hardly
expect people with such a mentality to support the government and
serve the motherland. On the contrary, they are likely to betray the interests of the motherland and directly undermine China's security.

The aforementioned changes in social awareness not only are a
reflection of some of the current social reality but also will have a negative effect on China's social being.

Changes in the Situation of the Ruling Party

Weakening of Party organizations. In the past, Party organizations were
like clenched iron fists and fighting bastions. Not only could they
promptly and comprehensively keep abreast of conditions concerning
Party members and the people around them but also they could carry
out correct ideological work among the Party members and the masses.
Consequently, they served as the leading core in a unit or locality and
effectively implemented the Party's principles, policies, and strategic
and tactical intentions. Now, not only have many Party organizations
failed to arrange for or encourage Party members to report about themselves and the people around them but the Party members themselves
have failed to report their own ideas to Party organizations. Even if the
Party members know something about the people around them, they do
not report it to the Party organizations either. Some grassroots Party organizations have in fact become "deaf" and "blind," unable to know anything or play any role. The fact that during the "1989 disturbance" some
problems which previously could have been controlled and resolved by
Party organizations had to be directly controlled and resolved by state
security and public security departments was precisely an outcome of
the weakening of Party organizations. The weakening of Party organiza-

tions is like osteoporosis. It greatly reduces the Party's combat effectiveness, making it impossible for the Party to exercise strong leadership over the masses of the people. Following the disintegration of the collective economy and the flow of peasants in some rural areas, many Party branches have sunk into a weak, lax, and paralyzed situation. A small handful of rural Party branches are controlled by religious or other evil forces. Such a situation has endangered stability in rural society and shaken the foundation of the Party's work in rural areas.

Changes in the ideas of some Party members. In the wake of the abandonment of the planned economy, the partial restoration of private ownership, and the collapse of the socialist system in Eastern Europe and the Soviet Union, major changes of orientation have taken place in the ideas of some Party members under the impact of the erroneous proposition of "upgrading belief" (a call issued by Li Wei of the Economics Institute of Beijing University on Beijing Television's BTV Evening Talk program). In their view, socialism has failed, the socialist path is a blind alley, communism is a fantasy, and Marxism-Leninism–Mao Zedong Thought is outdated. Some college teachers and students in Shanghai said: "Now Communist Party members talk less about ideals and the principle of Party spirit and more about money." Some Party cadres even praise peaceful evolution and call for privatization. Some Party members have started looking for "room for maneuver" outside the Communist Party. Taking advantage of the conveniences that are still available in the Party, some Party members have rushed to turn their children and even themselves into newly born bourgeois elements and new money-bags. If such ideological changes spread within the Party, it would be hard to expect the vast numbers of Party members to step forward bravely and fight for the Party should a situation occur similar to that of the "August incident" in the Soviet Union. By that time, our 50 million Party members will count for nothing. Moreover, those Party members who have thoroughly changed their minds are likely to break away from the Party, turn against their own side, and serve as a daring anticommunist vanguard, as happened in the Communist Party of the Soviet Union.

Changes in the Party's relations with the worker and peasant masses. At present, with the restoration of the private economy, the gap between rich and poor in China is widening and polarization is developing. By February 1994, the bank deposits of rich people, who accounted for 2 percent of the total number of depositors, comprised 80 percent of the total deposits of 1,300 billion yuan. According to a survey conducted by the All-China Federation of Trade Unions in 1993, of the 140 million workers and staff members across the country, the average monthly family income of 5 percent of them, involving a total population of 20 million, was only 62.19 yuan and, with the monthly expenditure standing at 67.50 yuan, they could not make ends meet. According to a survey conducted by the Propaganda Department of the Jiangxi Provincial CCP Committee, more than 60 percent of workers and staff members think that the status of the working class as masters of their own affairs has not been realized and 32.6 percent of workers and staff members think that the status of the working class has declined. A Xinhua reporter said: "The industrial worker groups who have always been looked upon as 'masters' have a sense of being abandoned. A female worker in charge of looms who checked the quality and quantity of the products said: 'We work hard for a year but our pay is less than a self-employed businessman who works for only two days. This is extremely unfair.' "

In the first half of 1994, there were 225 strikes across the country involving 37,900 people. They included 71 strikes at state-owned enterprises and 82 strikes at foreign-funded enterprises. There were also 4,000 cases of people collectively applying for an audience with the higher authorities to appeal for help. During their demonstration in February 1993, the workers at Hunan's Jinzhushan mine raised the slogan "We want to eat and we want to live." Now, labor-management conflicts have emerged in some private and foreign-funded enterprises. It is hard to completely avoid poverty for some workers and labor-management conflicts under the present conditions. The problem now is the Party's attitude toward the conflicts. As a British reporter put it, faced with conflicts between Chinese workers and foreign bosses, "the trade unions are almost prohibited from carrying out their activities because this may scare potential investors." The Taiwan general manager of Yuenzu Company in Shanghai attacked and hurled invective at the Communist Party. In spite of this, the department concerned in Shanghai's Hongkou District gave in to him again and again, prohibiting the company's workers, staff members, and Party members from reporting to the higher authorities, and forcibly ordering the workers and staff members who had applied for a ruling to the Labor Disputes Arbitration Commission to withdraw their application.

In the rural areas, in 1991 the per capita annual income of 9.4 percent of the peasant households across the country was less than 300.0 yuan, and the average annual income of some 20 million people was only

150.8 yuan. A peasant in Renshou County, Sichuan Province, said: "The Communist Party now loves rich rather than poor people." As the French *Le Figaro* put it, the Chinese "peasant dissatisfaction is likely to be explosive and may break out at any moment."

The working class and impoverished peasants may be disappointed with the Communist Party because of the decline in their economic, social, and political status. At least a considerable number of workers and impoverished peasants feel that the Party represents the interests of those who have knowledge, capability, and wealth rather than their interests, and they have a centrifugal tendency. If the Communist Party does not take action to improve its relations with the working class and impoverished peasants, it will be very hard for the Party to gain their support. The estrangement between the Communist Party on the one hand and the working class and impoverished peasants on the other is likely to leave the Party in an isolated and helpless position at a critical moment as the Communist Party of the Soviet Union was during the "August 1991 incident."

The corruption of some Party and government cadres. Over the past dozen years or so, corruption in China has reached two new levels. Before the 1970s, corruption remained at the low level of offering cigarettes and wine and "getting in by the back door" on such questions as joining the army, recruiting workers and students, and transferring someone to another post. In the 1980s, in an effort to obtain extra budgetary funds, raw and semifinished materials, energy, railway wagons, or markets, township and town enterprises, as well as private enterprises, set off the practice of giving "money wrapped in red paper envelopes" and "rebates," driving up corruption to the first new level. Since the beginning of the 1990s, guided by the ideas of "not bothering about whether it is socialist or capitalist in nature" and "looking at everything in terms of money," embezzlement, bribe taking and bribe offering, smuggling, selling of contraband, manufacture of fake products, pornography, and prostitution have been as rampant as water from a burst dike, driving up corruption to another new level. Almost all ugly phenomena of the old society prior to the establishment of the republic have been revived, and no Party cadre can be totally proof against every ugly phenomenon. Between September and December 1993, procuratorial organs throughout the country investigated and handled 6,790 major cases involving more than 10,000 yuan in corruption and bribery, a 2.1-fold increase over the same period in 1992; handled 1,748 major criminal cases involving more than 50,000 yuan in embezzlement of public money, a 2.7-fold increase over the same period in 1992; and penalized 715 cadres at the county (section) level or above for economic crimes, a 6.8-fold increase over the same period in 1992, including 61 cadres at the provincial department (bureau) level, an 11-fold increase over the same period in 1992.

Between September and December 1993, the courts tried economic criminal cases involving 13,110 people, an increase of 25.67 percent over 1992. When economic crimes and corruption cases are exposed, officials then protect one another. Under the banner of protecting reform and opening up, some law enforcement organs often pass lenient sentences on serious cases. For example, recently Jiangxi Province invariably gave light sentences to several dozen cadres guilty of economic crimes. They were given either a suspended sentence or a fine for their crimes. Even if they were sentenced to imprisonment, they were issued false hospital certificates to enable them to be released on bail for medical treatment. Although the Party Central Committee and the State Council have repeatedly issued injunctions against corruption and formulated some codes of discipline and rules, a good way to fundamentally resolve this issue has not been found.

Originally, the corruption of some Communists was caused or made possible by the bourgeoisie (as was pointed out by Wan Runnan). However, because the purpose of the Communist Party is fundamentally at variance with the interests of the bourgeoisie, the bourgeoisie still does not trust the Communist Party even if some Communists have degenerated as the bourgeoisie has desired, and it still wants to thoroughly overthrow the Communist Party. During the "1989 disturbance," the bourgeoisie incited the masses to pound at the Communist Party in the name of "fighting corruption." Therefore, not only has corruption made the Communist Party divorce itself from and set itself against the working-class and the broad masses of the laboring people but also it has given the bourgeoisie a pretext with which to attack the Communist Party and subject it to attack from front and rear.

Changes in the political quality of Party and government leading bodies. The developments cited above indicate that the next decade cannot possibly be an uneventful one politically and is likely to be one in which the bourgeoisie at home and abroad launches a decisive onslaught against our Party and the dictatorship of the proletariat. Economic development cannot by itself imperceptibly eliminate or prevent political turmoil. The situation in the future will set higher demands than at present on the political quality and leadership capability of the comprehensive Party and government leading bodies at all levels.

In the periods immediately after the founding of our Party and of our country, we had a small number of intellectuals-turned-career-revolutionaries who had a very high level of accomplishment in Marxist theory, the art of political struggle, and political leadership capability. We also had a large number of cadres promoted from workers, peasants, and soldiers who also had a firm proletarian stand and strong, practical political skills. Formed of these people, the leading bodies of the Party, government, and army at all levels dealt remarkably with the situation at that time and ensured the founding of the PRC, the accomplishment of socialist transformation, and the consolidation of the socialist system.

Since the start of reform a dozen years or so ago, after repeated adjustments of leading bodies at all levels, the cultural and specialized knowledge levels of the comprehensive Party and government leading bodies at all levels have been raised extensively and their capability in managing economic activities has also been heightened. This is in keeping with the central task of our Party and state at the moment. However, the overall political leadership capability has dropped slightly. Over the past few years, Party and government leading bodies at all levels have engrossed themselves in specific work, such as contending for and distributing investments, starting projects, approving land allocations, carrying out urban construction, running development zones, and holding talks with foreign businesses, as well as attending dinner parties, going abroad, and cutting ribbons, but they have little time to think and do not know much about various issues, such as the conditions of social classes, popular ideas, and social contradictions. In the course of their work, the leading bodies of some localities have actually turned the two "basic points" of our Party into one "basic point."

In selecting leading cadres from among intellectuals, there is a one-sided understanding about specialization. Consequently, many of those joining the local comprehensive leading bodies have studied science, engineering, medical science, or agriculture, few have studied the liberal arts, and fewer still are specialized in basic Marxist theory. It is said that 80 percent of the students at the Central Party School with a college degree or above majored in science, engineering, medical science, or agriculture. Such a pattern approximately reflects the professional knowledge pattern of the Party and government leading bodies at the provincial and city levels. We do have intellectuals-turned-cadres majoring in basic Marxist theory, but most of them work in Party schools, institutions of higher learning, or social sciences research departments, and very few of them have been inducted into the local comprehensive leading bodies at various levels. As "an understanding of economy and management" has been stressed in the selection of leading cadres in the past three years, they are not included. In the eyes of some leaders and organization departments, it is as though only science, engineering, medical science, agriculture, foreign trade, banking, and law can be regarded as specialties, while Marxist philosophy, Marxist economics, scientific socialism, the history of the international communist movement, and the history of the CCP cannot be regarded as such; it is as though comprehensive Party and government leading bodies at all levels only need those specialized in science, engineering, medical science, and agriculture rather than those specialized in basic Marxist theory, and only need those specialized in economic and administrative management rather than those specialized in political leadership.

Many leading cadres (including those at the provincial and ministerial level or above) have studied at Party schools, but they are clear and logical only when talking about specific business and become frivolous and even speechless when touching on Marxist theory. Some of them even erroneously take the concepts of Western Marxist and even bourgeois liberalization as Marxist concepts and pay lip service to them. If such a situation should continue and spread, it will be hard to preserve the Marxist characteristics of our Party.

The local comprehensive Party and government leading bodies at all levels are different from those of specialized departments. Apart from dealing with economic construction issues, they should also deal with a series of political issues. Given the circumstances cited above, the local comprehensive Party and government leading bodies may still be able to cope with the situation at a time of political stability, but they can hardly do so at a time of political turmoil. As it is, the professional knowledge pattern of the local Party and government leading bodies at all levels does not conform to the political situation in the next decade.

The CCP is a political party rather than a mass organization of another nature. According to Marxism, politics chiefly refers to the handling of relationships between classes, groups, and people. If our Party cannot correctly understand and handle classes, class contradictions, and class struggle, we may not be able to hold on to state power. If we lose power, we shall be unqualified to manage the economic activities of the society and unable to go on taking economic construction as the

Party's central task. For this reason, it is imperative to change the situation in which the political leadership capability of comprehensive Party and government leading bodies at all levels is declining. To this end, apart from paying more attention to and stepping up the study of political issues, we should also increase the proportion of people specialized in basic Marxist theory and politics in the leading bodies.

It is understood that, due to incorrect guiding ideas on the part of some leaders, some phenomena have emerged in some localities and units, such as pushing out and attacking comrades who are firmly opposed to turmoil or riots and take an active part in uncovering and screening-out work; and promoting and putting in important positions those who sympathized with the "1989 pro-democracy movement" and support bourgeois liberalization. These phenomena have inspired many people who participated in the "1989 pro-democracy movement," refuse to change their stand and hold on to bourgeois liberalization. These people cherish the illusion of relying on so-called forces from within the structure to reverse the verdict on the "1989 pro-democracy movement." On the other hand, those comrades who persisted in struggle on the front line when the republic was in dire peril at that time feel depressed. If there is a similar struggle in the future, some of them will probably hesitate to move forward and will not be as resolute and advance as bravely as before. Such a situation is extremely unfavorable to our Party and state security. It is estimated that in the next year or two hostile forces at home and abroad are very likely to take reversal of the verdict on the "1989 pro-democracy movement" as a point of breakthrough in attacking the leadership of the Communist Party and the dictatorship of the proletariat. Only by withstanding this attack and passing this test can the third-generation central leading collective of our Party be regarded as gaining a firm foothold and be in a position to talk about the future. Therefore, if the aforesaid situations are not rectified from now on, the number of people daring to stand on the side of the Party and government will probably drop, while the number of those opposing the Communist Party and the government as well as those observing neutrality to protect themselves will grow. When a political storm does come and we find ourselves in an unfavorable situation, it may be too late to change the situation.

★ CHINA AFTER DENG ★

On February 18, 1997, after a lengthy illness, Deng Xiaoping "went to meet Marx" (as he once phrased it to a visiting dignitary). The following selection looks backward and forward—recalling Deng's legacy as well as identifying the multiple challenges that his successors confronted in the immediate aftermath of the patriarch's passing.

ELLIS JOFFE, RULING CHINA AFTER DENG

Deng Xiaoping's successors, led by Jiang Zemin, inherited a far more complex country than Mao bequeathed to Deng. The challenges that the leadership faced at the outset of the 1990s (as described in Michael Swaine, "China Faces the 1990s") were magnified by the late 1990s. In this selection the eminent Israeli Sinologist Ellis Joffe catalogs the interconnected issues that challenged China's post-Deng rulers.

This selection was originally published in The Journal of East Asian Affairs, *Winter–Spring 1997.*

Of all the factors that will shape developments in China in the post-Deng period, none is more important than the capacity of its new leaders to rule effectively. In most countries, such a capacity is taken for granted. In China, it is far from self-evident.

Ruling China is a monumental task at any time, given its size, population, diversity, and the traditional strength of regionalism. The greatest achievement of the Communist regime under Mao and Deng, and the essential prerequisite for all its undertakings, has been its remarkable success, however reduced over time, in coping with this task. But, as China passes through a potentially disruptive political and economic transition to the post-Deng period, similar success is not assured for their heirs, who lack the personal authority and institutional power which had formed the basis for the effective rule of the revolutionary godfathers. Given this uncertainty, any assessment of China's internal developments and foreign policy in the coming years has to begin with a cardinal question: Will the new leaders have the capacity to rule China effectively?

This capacity consists of five interconnected core components: (1) at the top: leadership politics; (2) below the top: the political system; (3) in the cities and villages: the political system and the people; (4) in the provinces: the specter of regionalism; (5) in the wings: civil-military relations.

At the Top: Leadership Politics

The capacity of China's new leaders to rule effectively depends first of all on the unity of the leadership itself. The leadership at this level is composed of two groups. The smallest and most important consists of a core leader and the twenty-five to thirty-five most powerful political personalities in China—the members of the Politburo—who perform a dual function: they formulate China's major national and international policies and they oversee clusters of bureaucracies which implement these policies. The second group consists of several hundred powerholders who occupy the uppermost executive positions in the bureaucracies which make up China's power structure. These two groups of leaders — the Center—constitute the inner wheel which turns all the other wheels of China's ruling mechanism. If the functioning of the Center is seriously disrupted, the other ruling organs will lack the central direction that is essential for effective government. And nothing can disrupt its functioning more than the breakdown of leadership unity.

Clearly such unity is only one of several conditions for effective government, but its importance is elemental. Without it, none of the other conditions can be fulfilled. Unity at the apex leads to purposeful activity at all levels, whereas polarization leads to paralysis or infighting.

This is borne out by the record of the regime. Its first decade—from its establishment until the Great Leap Forward began to falter in 1959— was marked by leadership unity, which provided determined direction from above and facilitated dynamic implementation below. As a result, the regime achieved remarkable success in political control, economic development, and social revolution (albeit at a high cost in human suffering). Underlying this unity, more than anything else, were two interconnected reasons: the imposing figure of Mao and policy consensus among the leaders.

Maoist China was a totalitarian one-Party regime, and in such a regime the standing of the paramount Party leader was of supreme significance.

Even a leader of Mao's standing could not ensure the unity of the leadership under all circumstances. This was because policy consensus among the top leaders, which had held up until the Great Leap Forward began to falter, could not survive its failure. It had held up because until then all the leaders believed that China's road to development could combine revolutionary aspirations with their desire for modernization. And it broke down because after the failure of the Great Leap they concluded—unlike Mao and his supporters—that modernization had to take precedence over revolutionary purity. As long as the consensus held up, disagreements could be worked out within its framework without hindering policy implementation and sparking power struggles. But when it broke down, the gap between policy formulation and implementation opened up, leading to deadly infighting.

This did not happen under Deng Xiaoping. After he assumed supreme power in 1979, leadership unity was restored. One reason was Deng's leadership style. Although Mao's position was unmatched, Deng's was also underpinned by towering personal authority. Like Mao he could draw on achievements as a revolutionary leader, and on a successful Party career after the revolution. He also could draw on networks of ties that had been built up during these times. However, unlike Mao, he was more a practical politician than a dictator, and his ruthlessness was tempered by collegiality. Also unlike Mao, his political style tended toward consultation rather than coercion, toward coalition building rather than imperious rule. Mao stood above the leadership, but Deng was the great balancer between leadership groups. He worked out compromises with his critics and created a framework of consensus which ensured leadership unity.

Underlying this consensus was a basic belief which guided Deng's reforms: the objectives of rapid modernization should take precedence over the preservation of Mao's revolutionary vision. This belief was shared by all the top leaders, although they differed over how fast and how far the reforms should proceed. These differences were sharp during the 1980s, when the elders—front-rank revolutionary leaders of Deng's generation—were active in influencing policy. However, while these differences slowed down some of the reforms, they never broke through the boundaries of consensus. They, therefore, did not seriously hinder the implementation of the reforms and did not culminate in cut-throat struggles. This accounts for the sustained momentum of the reforms under Deng and for their many achievements.

Nonetheless, this decade ended in the Tiananmen disaster. One central reason was the division between Li Peng, the premier, and Zhao Ziyang, the Party general secretary, over the course of the reforms. This division spilled over into the political arena and prevented a forceful response by the leadership to the burgeoning demonstrations in Tiananmen Square. The absence of such a response fueled resistance to the government and became a prime factor in the process of escalation that terminated in the massacre. It also terminated in the purge of Zhao and the elevation of Jiang Zemin to the post of Party general secretary.

As Deng fades into history, what is the state of elite politics under Jiang Zemin? Jiang's stature is ambiguous. On the one hand, his personal leadership qualities are hardly notable. Most observers in China believe that within the Chinese hierarchy Jiang's presence does not inspire much awe or respect. His political career has been relatively short. Before becoming mayor of Shanghai in 1985, Jiang was a technical administrator. As mayor of Shanghai, he was reportedly known as a "flowerpot"—decorative but ineffective. As paramount leader, he has not articulated a grand vision of China's future. More importantly, Jiang cannot draw on two essential sources of personal authority that Mao and Deng had: a revolutionary record of achievements and long-standing ties and loyalties. When this void is added to Jiang's unproved leadership abilities, the result is that his personal authority is questionable.

On the other hand, Jiang has great assets in his institutional posts— by 1992 he had become Party general secretary, chairman of the Military Affairs Commission, and president of China. The first two mean that he stands at the apex of the most powerful hierarchies in China, while the third adds luster and international exposure. Despite the primary importance of personal authority in Chinese political culture, it also sets great store by institutional standing, because it emphasizes hierarchical compliance, and those at the top of the hierarchy command symbolic prestige, which in itself is a major source of power. Institutional standing also gives Jiang the invaluable privilege of installing supporters in key posts.

Whatever his personal weaknesses, Jiang is hardly a political wimp. A leader does not survive in the rough alleys of Chinese elite politics, even if backed by (an increasingly feeble) Deng, without substantial political skills. Although he had no power base when he was catapulted to the top position in 1989, Jiang has effectively expanded his base by appointing supporters to key posts and getting rid of rivals, such as the Beijing party chief.

Also working in Jiang's favor is the element of time. The succession process will not reach a climax until Deng dies, and the longer the transition period stretches out, the stronger Jiang becomes. This is because time takes its toll on the Party elders, whose personal standing towered over that of Jiang and his colleagues, and enabled them to intervene in decision making even though they no longer held official posts. The new leaders moving into top positions belong to Jiang's generation and are his equals in terms of seniority.

Moreover, Deng's final days are much more favorable to a successor than were Mao's. Mao's successor—the hapless Hua Guofeng—was hastily anointed and hardly had a claim on legitimacy. Even worse for him, the real strongman, Deng Xiaoping, was waiting in the wings to displace him. In contrast, Jiang has had time to consolidate his position. More importantly, he has no visible rival for the paramount position.

Jiang's uncertain personal qualities are thus offset by other strengths, and this obviously accounts for his apparent success as of 1996 in working out a consensus among the top leaders under his direction. This consensus is based on a commitment to continue the transition to a market economy started by Deng. Since the 1992 Party Congress under Jiang's leadership endorsed this line, the Center has adopted guidelines to implement it—such as, for example, the decisions to reform the state enterprises, as well as the banking, financial, taxation, and foreign trade systems. In short, as China moves into the post-Deng period, its leadership appears to be working in a unified and cooperative fashion under Jiang.

Will this pattern persist? As in the past, this will depend primarily on policy consensus and the standing of Jiang Zemin—and there are forces pulling in opposite directions. One force in favor of elite consensus is the militant nationalism that has dominated the outlook of Chinese leaders in recent years. Springing from a feeling, whether genuine or contrived, that China is obstructed by the United States from pursuing its rightful place as a major power, this outlook, as one example, accounts for the unified stand of the Chinese leadership during the Taiwan crisis of 1995–96. However, its importance is limited, since no leader will question policies that are suffused with strong nationalistic emotions.

This is not the case with respect to two other factors—the economy and social stability—which, more than anything, will shape relations between the leaders. This is because they know full well that their economic policies have to deliver the goods—sustained development and a promise of a better life for most Chinese—if they are to gain the active support of the lower levels and the acquiescence, if not the support, of the population. On the other hand, if the economy falters badly, unity will probably disintegrate. If that happens, and especially if economic setbacks cause social unrest, the leadership will probably split over alternate policy proposals. Such a split might lead to infighting and instability, or even spark an attempt to replace the Jiang group. The severity of the split will be contingent on the dimensions of the economic difficulties and their consequences, but also on the position of Jiang.

Since Jiang is a postrevolutionary figure, his administration will be much less personal and more bureaucratic than that of Mao or Deng. His personality, therefore, will not be as critical as that of his predecessors, and his position will depend to a large extent on his bureaucratic assets. These, as noted, are formidable, most notably the power of appointments. At the apex of the power structure he has already surrounded himself with supporters from Shanghai—the "Shanghai clique"—who are bonded by common coastal origins and shared technocratic values. He has also filled numerous positions with his followers in the Party, the mass media, and, to a lesser extent, the army.

Nonetheless, in an authoritarian regime, even a bureaucratically inclined one, the authority of the leaders is still central. Since Jiang's is not firmly established, he has to share power with other individuals and constituencies. As a result, his colleagues undoubtedly have a much greater say in policy making than under Deng. This may not be problematic as long they agree with Jiang on policy matters, but serious disagreements will pose a threat to Jiang's position, since his opponents are apt to be unusually assertive in their opposition.

This also holds true with respect to the military or groups of regional leaders. Because of Jiang's vulnerability, top military commanders are positioned to play a greater role in domestic and foreign affairs. Their backing greatly enhances the security of Jiang's position, and he has made strenuous efforts to ensure it. However, if disagreements drive the military to switch their support to a rival leader—and this, as will be seen, is not a move that will come easily under ordinary circumstances—Jiang's chances for political survival will plummet. Regional leaders have also acquired new power as a result of the decentralization mandatory in a growing market economy. If several of them—from the coastal provinces, for example—form a coalition which defies the central leadership on critical issues—and this, as will also be seen, is likewise not a move that will come easily under ordinary circumstances—Jiang's position will be severely undermined.

Even if the economy continues to grow in the near future, coping with the deleterious effects of this growth—inflation, corruption, unemployment, and mass migration, to name a few—will require tremendous leadership resources. And lurking behind the immediate problems are the perennial ones of population pressure on food supply and ecological devastation.

The political future of the leadership thus remains an open question. But this much is closed: The state of politics at the top in the coming years will be decisively determined by the fate of the economy at the bottom.

Below the Top: The Political System

Even if the leadership is united and resolute, its decisions will have little effect if they are not implemented properly. This is the responsibility of the political system—that huge conglomerate of governmental organizations controlled by the Party. The relationship between the top leadership and the system below is symbiotic. One cannot function adequately without the other. The unified action of the leadership is the first step in moving the ruling mechanism. The responsive and proficient operation of the political system is the second. This means that power holders at all levels must have the will to implement central policies and the organizational skill to do so.

As the experience of the regime has shown, only when these conditions were met satisfactorily did its policies produce the desired results on the ground. Its ability to produce such results has fluctuated in direct proportion to the ups and downs of the political system. Although the system has changed extensively over the years, its importance as a core component of effective rule has not.

One of the outstanding features of the Party during the regime's first decade was that most cadres managed to maintain relatively high moral and organizational standards, due to the strength of ideology and the periodic cleansing campaigns launched by the leadership. These standards began to decline as the post–Great Leap Forward demoralization set in and were completely shattered during the Cultural Revolution. On top of that, the deadly struggles of the Cultural Revolution left the Party with a legacy of bitter and irreparable divisions, which were exacerbated by the continued split at the top between its radical and moderate wings. As the Maoist period entered a twilight zone, Party standards sank to an unprecedented low point.

Although the Party apparatus was rebuilt under Deng, it was not easy to reconstitute its standards. Looser control from the Center, which was essential for the success of the reforms, and the spirit of rampant materialism, which the reforms generated, provided the environment for the growth of abuses by Party cadres. Corruption, nepotism, indiscipline, and greed—these were the more conspicuous ills that have plagued the Party in the era of reforms. The problem was particularly serious because these ills reached into its upper recesses and involved veteran high-level cadres and their families.

To combat the abuses, Deng set up a Central Discipline Inspection Commission, which launched several rectification campaigns, but despite impressive reports, its work was apparently less than successful, because a new task force was set up for the same purpose in 1987. A striking indication that all these efforts also did not achieve substantial results was that corruption and arrogance of Party cadres were among the main grievances of the Tiananmen demonstrators in 1989. Jiang Zemin has continued these efforts, but despite harsh punishments that are periodically meted out to transgressors, especially high-ranking ones, corruption in its many forms persists as a major defect in the Party.

It is not the only one. Another has been the already-mentioned tendency of the Party to usurp governmental functions. The negative effects were twofold: professional decisions were made not by specialists but by unqualified Party cadres on the basis of political considerations; and promotions of Party cadres in governmental organizations were made on the basis of political rather than professional criteria. The Deng leadership responded to this problem by transferring responsibility from Party to governmental organizations, especially in economic decision making. The Party continued to supervise the work of government but withdrew from day-to-day administration. This division of functions gave the government substantial autonomy and was a major reason for the success of the economic reforms.

However, even if the Party no longer maintains direct control of government, it still wields enormous power in Chinese politics and society. Formally, it makes policy and oversees its implementation, but there is nothing to stop it from intruding into governmental affairs except exhortation and self-restraint. Proposals in the mid-1980s by radical reformers to put institutional limits on the Party's power were rejected. Thus, despite the changes, the Party remains the central pillar of rule in China. And it is this pillar that is being corroded by the abuses of power.

Will it survive? More specifically, will the leaders be able to stamp out the severe ills that afflict the Party, or at least reduce them to levels that will not undermine its leadership role? And will Party cadres be able to adjust adequately to the new circumstances dictated by the transition to a market economy? A case can be made for both positive and negative possibilities.

The Party's strongest chances for survival and rejuvenation lie in the vested interest of its millions of members—some 54 million in 1996—to hold on to power and the privileges that go with it. These members are entrenched in an enormous nationwide network, which has deep organizational roots and a tradition of rule that goes back to the early days of the Communist movement. This organization will not collapse easily, especially since its leaders and many of its members are obviously aware that change is mandatory for survival and have made efforts in that direction.

But change will not come easily. One reason is the loss of ideological identity. A prime reason for the Party's robustness during its halcyon days was Marxist ideology, which imbued its members with a historical calling and bonded them with a shared belief. Those days are gone. In the era of reform, Marxist ideology has become a dead letter as China moves to a market economy and its leaders uphold the virtues of capitalism as the ideal path to economic development. Yet this same leadership professes a commitment to this discredited ideology as the basis for its political rule. As a result, ideology is widely disregarded by cadres and people alike, and the prevalent attitude toward it is cynicism.

Another reason is the loss of power by Party cadres. This also has been an inevitable result of the economic reforms. In the millions of private firms that have been established in China's cities, Party cadres have no say. Their leadership role has been taken over by the new entrepreneurs who are propelling China's economic surge. In the thriving township and village enterprises that blanket the country, cadres either are ineffectual or have joined the new elite. In the countryside, after the institution of the "family responsibility" system, rural cadres no longer have the authority to tell farmers how to work or what to do with their income. In short, while the Party apparatus has remained intact, especially in the countryside, its power has waned.

Nowhere was this displayed more dramatically than in the initial stage of the Tiananmen demonstrations. These demonstrations could never have grown as quickly as they did had the Party reacted forcefully before they got out of control. One reason was wavering among the top leaders. But another was the ineffectiveness of the Party, which could not stem the rising tide.

The third obstacle to change is the difficulty faced by the leaders in recruiting qualified personnel into the Party. The Party keeps growing, but it does not usually attract the best and the brightest of China's youth. Unlike in earlier years, when the Party was the main, if not the only, ladder to success, in the late Deng period the new members are not in most cases the talented ones in society. These can readily find lucrative careers in the enormous private sector. In the prevailing climate, most of those who join apparently do so because of the benefits that Party membership offers, and not out of idealism.

Finally, there is the already-mentioned corruption, which is a major threat to the future of the Party, and by extension, to the political system. No party can survive indefinitely as a viable and effective institution if corruption in its many forms gnaws at its sinews the way it appears to be doing in China of the mid-1990s. However, as the new leaders take over, there is no convincing indication that they have been successful in substantially stemming it. On the contrary, the very factors that fuel the economic drive—looser control, a freewheeling milieu, a growing market economy, and cadre involvement in it—these same factors foster the growth of corruption. And, according to numerous reports from China, it has grown high and wide.

To a decisive degree, therefore, the future of the Party—and the entire political system—depends on the leadership's ability to reverse these trends. Given the fact that they draw strength from the economic reforms, there is no way to predict how this will work out. But the outcome will be crucial in determining whether or not the Party, and with it the entire system, will get a new lease on life after Deng.

In Cities and Villages: The Political System and the People

The capacity of the leadership to rule ultimately hinges on the attitude of the people. It requires that the people accept the regime—with active support at best, with passive consent at least. If they do not, the regime will not be able to function properly. Rejection, depending on its form and extent, can cause anything from passive resistance to the implementation policies, to large-scale demonstrations, and even the collapse of the regime.

Where does popular acceptance derive from? From two main sources—the legitimacy of the political system, as symbolized by the paramount leader, and its performance in satisfying the people's basic desires. The interaction between these two sources has been clearly demonstrated by the history of the Communist regime in China. It has been most effective when both were strong, but to some extent one can compensate for the inadequacy of the other. Mao's legitimacy—though not his power within the system, and not that of the system itself—was solid enough to survive the terrible post–Great Leap Forward famine and upheaval of the Cultural Revolution. Deng did not have the attributes on which Mao's legitimacy rested, but his legitimacy was greatly strengthened by the success of his economic reforms. Jiang's is not yet firmly established, so his future, and that of the political system under him, depends primarily on performance.

The tragedy of Tiananmen did not affect Jiang Zemin's personal standing, because he was brought into the central elite only after it occurred. As mayor of Shanghai, he handled demonstrations in his city with restraint and prudence, which prevented the outbreak of violence. The other top members of the new elite were likewise not affected, either because they joined it later or because they did not share in the responsibility of the elders. The only leader who was severely blemished by the event is the prime minister, Li Peng, who is blamed for a tough attitude toward the students, and for cooperating with the elders.

The legitimacy of Jiang's personal position is thus not connected to the Tiananmen events. It suffers from other previously discussed weaknesses: his problematic personality, and the absence of revolutionary achievements and long-standing connections. These weaknesses are offset to some extent by Jiang's institutional posts, his new connections, and the imperatives of Chinese political culture.

Nonetheless, unlike Mao, and, to a lesser extent, Deng, Jiang will have to rely much more on performance—on the results achieved by the top leadership's policies and by the political system below. In this context, two questions are of crucial importance, the same questions that stand out as most pertinent to other components of effective rule as well. Will the economy advance sufficiently to satisfy people's desires and ensure stability? Will the transition to a market economy and a looser society give rise to groups which will challenge the political monopoly of the political system?

The economy will not be discussed here, but a few pertinent points need to be made. On the importance of the economy for political rule and social stability there is no disagreement among observers. However, on the prospects for the economy there are wide disagreements, which can be divided into two groups, with many nuances in between.

On the optimistic end of the spectrum is the view that China's economic growth will continue for years at a steady pace (7 to 9 percent or so a year) until China becomes the world's largest economy by about the year 2020. In the course of this growth, China will become an enormous market for foreign goods and an increasingly attractive place for foreign investors. The obstacles already encountered by the economic growth, and the difficulties caused by it, are seen as surmountable. They are explained as natural in an economy that has recently been decentralized, in which market forces are rapidly growing stronger, and which is becoming more complex all the time.

At the other far end of this spectrum is the view that China's economic boom is bound to collapse. It is based not on solid foundations but on easy money, huge speculations, financial and monetary indiscipline, and quick profits. The central government lacks the fiscal levers and legal system to guide and control a market economy.

No one can predict at what point between these two ends the Chinese economy will end up, not even China's leaders. What can be predicted with confidence is that the reforms started by Deng—the essence of which is the transition to a market economy—will continue. There may be obstacles that will slow them down, but the direction is not likely to be turned back toward a centrally planned economy. On balance, the reforms have been a major success, and they have spawned far too many important and entrenched interests to be reversed.

The realistic question, then, is not whether or not reforms will continue but how the leadership will cope with the obstacles in their path. Will the market economy produce forces which will compel the government to adopt political reforms? Limited reforms from above that do not lead to pluralism and the establishment of real democratic institutions should not be ruled out after the new leaders consolidate power. In fact, Deng viewed such reforms—more open, responsive, and restricted government—as necessary for economic development, and for the Party to retain its monopoly on political power.

This has given the average citizen much more freedom than before to lead a life with little government interference. However, a more liberal society will not necessarily produce a civil one—composed of groups whose new wealth will generate demands for power sharing. There are no signs that this is happening in China. Private economic bodies seek government sanction and support—as in traditional China—not autonomy and concessions. Only a handful of brave democratic activists make such demands, but they are powerless and the government has cracked down on them.

Given the force of tradition, the limited aspirations of most reformers, the imperatives of governing China, and the slow growth of potentially autonomous organizations, a threat to China's new political elite is not likely to come soon from a civil society. However, such a threat is widely believed to come from elsewhere.

In the Provinces: The Specter of Regionalism

No threat to the ruling capacity of the central leaders is seen by many observers as more dangerous than the threat of regionalism, which derives from the changes that have occurred in central-regional relations as a result of the economic reforms. According to these observers, the decentralization of economic functions, which has been essential for carrying out the reforms, has also led to a devolution of political power to such an extent that the capacity of the central government to rule over the regions has been brought into doubt.

This capacity has always been qualified, because of China's size, local diversity, and the staggering growth of its population in the last century. As a result, centrifugal tendencies have been the rule rather than the exception in China's political system in the modern period. At their worst, these tendencies gave rise to the terrible dozen years of "warlordism," between 1916 and 1928, but even after that, China was only nominally unified under Chiang Kai-shek. Real political unification was not achieved until the Communists came to power. Without it, the new rulers could not have undertaken the transformation of China, so it still stands out as their most impressive achievement.

However, even at the height of their power, central rule was necessarily limited by decentralization, local autonomy, and some circumvention of central directives. This did not reflect trends toward regionalism in the sense of open and prolonged defiance of the central government by local leaders, who had the capacity to act autonomously on major issues. Regionalism in this sense obviously undermines the central government, but limited departures from its directives do not. On the contrary, such departures have been essential for the operation of China's sprawling political system. They did not bring into question the capacity of the Center to rule—until Deng's reforms got well under way.

The only exception was the Cultural Revolution, when the military was compelled to intervene in the nationwide struggles and was given contradictory directives to maintain order and to support revolution. Military commanders displayed remarkable discipline and followed central orders to back off from openly crushing troublemaking mass organizations (only one commander refused) but did so indirectly and refrained from openly defying the capital. They thereby preserved the framework of national unity, no matter how fragile, and stemmed the potential tendencies toward regionalism which the turmoil let loose.

Have such tendencies been revived by Deng's reforms, and do they threaten the rule of his successors? Observers point to substantial signs of growing regional autonomy. Provincial leaders have acquired a greater say in personnel appointments in their areas. They have gained economic resources, in the form of a larger share of national tax revenues and profits from state enterprises, as well as greater control of investments and foreign trade. This has given them more independence from the central government and an enhanced influence in national politics, which they have used to pursue provincial interests. This has been reflected in their opposition to national policies which they see as inimical to local needs, and in bargaining with the central government over financial remittances from the provinces to the national treasury.

Moreover, provincial leaders have gone further than that. They have avoided implementing central policies not to their liking and have acted against central policies on matters such as obtaining loans and credits, establishing interprovincial trade barriers, setting up stock markets, and creating special development zones in excess of government guidelines.

Will such trends lead to regionalism that will eventually undermine the central government, and even contribute to its collapse? This prospect may be reinforced by other factors. One derives from the possibility that if leadership disunity leads to paralysis and a preoccupation with elite struggles, the power of local leaders will be greatly enhanced. This will also happen if leadership fails to reform the political system, which is its primary organizational means of controlling local leaders. In short, the weaker the central leadership, the more it will have to share power with local strongmen.

Another possibility is that several provincial leaders with common local interests—from the coastal provinces, as the most conspicuous example—will form an alliance and confront the central leadership with a united front. And if the economy breaks down, the central leadership will be discredited, and one result may well be the devolution of power to the provinces.

However, working against regionalism are several powerful ties that bind Center and regions. One is modern Chinese nationalism, which has emerged in recent years with new force after the virtual end of Communism as a viable ideology. The overriding aim of the nationalist factor in the outlook of the Chinese Communists, throughout their revolutionary struggle and after, was the unification of China. This was the precondition to making it strong enough to ensure its rightful place among the great powers. Therefore, no leader, even of the younger generation, will consciously take action which will destroy the great achievement of the Chinese Communists, and which is of supreme significance to all Chinese nationalists in the post-Communist era.

Beyond this, the central leadership has other measures at its disposal. One is the power of appointments and dismissals, which carries great symbolic value, and is not lightly defied. Another is its control over economic resources, which are needed by provincial leaders. A third is its ability to co-opt regional personalities into the central elite and to reduce their attachment to local interests, a measure the Jiang leadership has already used, as evidenced by the large infusion of provincial leaders into the Politburo and the Central Committee in the 1990s. In addition, the Center can invoke the support of poorer provinces, which need it for the allocation of resources, against richer ones, which may try to gain more independence.

If all else fails, the Center can use the armed forces against unyielding local leaders. Resorting to such extreme action assumes that in a crisis of the most severe dimensions in central-regional relations, the military will side with the Center, and will carry out orders to remove local leaders. There are several reasons to support such an assumption—including the power of nationalism in the Chinese officer corps, its professionalism and discipline, and the effectiveness of political control and coercive measures.

In sum, the strength of these countervailing forces to the regional trends will be a critical element in determining two outcomes: first, whether or not the Jiang regime will survive in its present form; and, second, whether or not China will survive as a unitary entity.

In the Wings: Civil-Military Relations

Unlike the other components, the military do not have a direct bearing on the leadership's ruling capacity. But their support is indispensable; without it, the political leadership cannot survive. This is because they command the forces which may be used to determine the outcome of an elite power struggle, displace rebellious local figures, put down a mass uprising, or even carry out a coup. The military show their support for the political leadership in several ways: they praise the leaders and their policies at the highest level; they demonstrate their backing symbolically to the nation; they educate the troops accordingly; they refrain from any action that might undermine the leadership; and they take action to support it if the need arises. Under Mao and Deng such support was taken for granted, but as the Jiang leadership takes over, it is no longer self-evident. A look back into the previous periods will help explain why this is so.

The most important reason for the pivotal political role of the Chinese army, and for its unconditional support of the Mao and Deng leaderships, was the close integration of political and military leaders at the uppermost level of decision making. The roots of this integration lay in the long revolutionary period, when the Party and the army were intertwined and Communist leaders performed both political and military functions.

After the establishment of the regime in 1949, rival hierarchies developed within the vast Chinese power structure, but at its apex the distinction between the roles of top leaders remained blurred. This was because their authority continued to be highly personalized and derived essentially not from institutional affiliation but from their individual stature, which had been built up during the revolution and was supported by vast networks of personal ties. Thus, despite a functional differentiation, Party and army leaders continued to regard themselves—and were regarded—as national figures standing above solely parochial concerns. These leaders, particularly those who headed the Party, saw it as natural and legitimate to cross the boundaries between the two institutions.

The most important result of this integration was that the nation's paramount leaders, Mao and Deng, were also supreme and active commanders of the armed forces. Their special standing enabled them to use the army as a power base in elite politics. They knew—and all key participants in the political system knew as well—that when it came to the crunch, they could count on the total support of the military. Their use of the military was mostly implicit, but at times it was also direct. The most direct and dramatic uses of the army for political purposes were its prolonged embroilment in the Cultural Revolution and its lightning suppression of the Tiananmen demonstrations.

This does not mean that the army has been prone to political intervention. While China's top leaders did involve it in politics, military commanders never tried to use it for advancing the army's sectoral interests. More importantly, these commanders never intervened in politics on their own initiative, only when the initiative came from outside. Although they responded to orders—readily in the Cultural Revolution, reluctantly in the Tiananmen crisis—both interventions were opposed by senior commanders, who foresaw the dangers. The Chinese army, in short, has not been an army eager for political action.

This was because of the way it developed after the end of the revolution. While the distinction between Party and military leaders at the top level remained blurred, at lower levels they developed as distinct entities. The army went through a far-reaching period of Soviet-inspired modernization, which laid the groundwork for the growth of military professionalism and which became a cause for an enduring Party-army conflict. This conflict—over the relative importance of political and military considerations in determining the army's development and daily activities—waxed and waned over the years, depending on the political situation and on the intensity of the Party's efforts to intervene in military affairs. But it never endangered the ultimate control of the Party over the army—control that was rooted in the army's traditions and reinforced by its professional discipline and the vast political apparatus in the armed forces.

So what has changed after Deng? First and foremost, the stature of the paramount leader. In the Chinese system, his status is of unique importance, because its strengths or weaknesses determine his relations with other groups and institutions, foremost among which are the armed forces. Jiang Zemin, as already observed, does not—indeed cannot—have the attributes which endowed Mao and Deng with their extraordinary personal authority in the military. For this reason, as China moves into the Jiang era, its military is positioned to exercise unprecedented influence in domestic and foreign affairs. This is the defining feature of post-Deng civil-military relations.

However, this feature has to be qualified. The new capacity of military commanders to influence policy does not mean—as was frequently claimed in the press during the Taiwan crisis of 1995–96—that they have become the dominant political force in China's internal or foreign affairs. Far from it, because their influence is counterbalanced by several factors.

One is a generational change that is taking place in the armed forces. Jiang has undoubtedly been in a difficult position in relation to military leaders of Deng's generation, who are nominally his subordinates, because he did not have a revolutionary record, any military experience, or connections in the armed forces. But this is changing as the new military leaders moving into top positions belong to Jiang's generation, and do not derive their standing from revolutionary exploits. They cannot pull the rank of seniority on him and cannot criticize him on the basis of lifelong achievements. In fact, many of the new military leaders are Jiang's supporters and owe their appointment to him.

Another factor is the inner working of the military organization. This is a hierarchical organization that operates according to standard procedures. For this reason, Jiang is not subjected to pressures from many quarters in the military on critical issues, as he was frequently portrayed in the press during the above-mentioned Taiwan crisis. Chinese officers are disciplined professionals who are not inclined to commit themselves openly to positions that are at variance with those of the current leadership. They do not go outside channels and do not act like cowboys. If they express views, this is likely to be within the confines of the military hierarchy. Jiang, therefore, does not have to deal with an influential but unruly army, only with its top leadership.

This leadership will command a military establishment that is becoming more complex, specialized, and professional—which constitutes another limit on its political influence. This is because as its modernization advances, it will become more inward looking and separated from the Party in interests, function, and outlook. Separation will strengthen its inclination to avoid political entanglement, which can only be inimical to its corporate well-being. This inclination will also be reinforced by the new differentiation at the highest leadership level, which will make it more difficult for Party chiefs to embroil the armed forces in internal political struggles.

In sum, civil-military relations will be determined, first and foremost, by the interaction between political and military leaders at the apex of the Chinese power structure. This relationship is complex. On the one hand, to restate, the military is stronger politically than ever before and its capacity to influence policy is unprecedented. On the other hand, while Jiang has certainly courted the military, he does not have to haggle constantly with them for support and to pay for it with concessions. He can count on such support as a matter of course—due to tradition, military professionalism, the institutional power of the paramount leader, and the instruments of coercion at his disposal.

But what if matters swerve off course? The crucial question, then, is: What might cause this to happen? One possible reason could be the rejection of military demands for more funds, but until now the military has not made any move against the Party leaders for sectoral objectives.

Another reason could be military dissatisfaction with the position of the civilians on core foreign policy issues that involve intense nationalistic emotions, such as Taiwan, but until now there have been no rifts on such issues.

Barring these possibilities, what may impel the military to move against the new Party leadership is a severe crisis on the national scene. An economic collapse that sparks social unrest, as already mentioned, could destroy Jiang's legitimacy and motivate a rival group to replace him. In that event, the military will probably be drawn into the struggle, most likely because the rival group will appeal for their support. Their stand will presumably be determined by their weighing the instability caused by the crisis against the disruption caused by their political intervention. In any case, given the military's long-standing subordination to the political leadership, this is not a move that they will take lightly. And given Jiang's support in the armed forces, it is also not one that will be pulled off easily.

The above possibilities for and against military support for Jiang are predicated on two essential preconditions, which have existed so far: that the military remains united in its dealings with the Party leadership, and that the lower ranks remain obedient to the high command. If the military splits at the top or if there is insubordination at the bottom, then all bets are off.

Concluding Remarks

This article has attempted to identify and analyze the components that will shape the ruling capacity of the post-Deng leadership in China. As stated at the outset, it has not attempted to predict how this capacity will fare in the future, only to assess the factors that will shape it—those that might strengthen it and those that might operate in the opposite direction. It is not possible to forecast how the balance between them will be worked out, only to use past patterns and current trends in order to follow this process as China passes through the difficult transition to a new political period.

II. OUTER-PARTY POLITICS

━━━

When the Chinese Communist Party came to power in 1949 and imposed its Leninist system of "democratic centralism" (which called on all officials and citizens to adhere to the "correct line" once Party leaders had spoken), for all the outside world could tell China became a land of political and ideological unity. Behind the scenes, however, intra-party political struggles regularly raged over China's political direction. On several occasions these debates spilled out of the back rooms of the top leadership, and for short periods of time ordinary people were able to deliver their own public verdicts on and critiques of how their country was being governed.

For those who felt that China's future depended on radical reforms away from the model of "big leader" authoritarianism, these occasions were hopeful signs that the Chinese people were, at last, becoming emboldened enough to speak out and that China was evolving away from the kind of one-party dictatorship that had marked the Mao years. But for hard-line Marxist-Leninists who had spent their whole lives "making revolution," these spontaneous upwellings of popular political expression were a dangerous prelude not only to the Party's demise but to potential political and social chaos as well.

Invariably these periods of "outer-Party" political expression arose out of special circumstances, usually a period of liberalization that allowed reform-minded officials and intellectuals to feel less fearful about the consequences of dissent. But they were inevitably followed by crackdowns as Party leaders, ever fearful of the consequences of allowing spontaneous mass agitation to go unchecked, moved to silence dissenting voices.

The selections in this chapter are from the three major episodes of popular dissent during the years of Deng Xiaoping's reforms: the Democracy Wall movement in 1978–79; the student protests of 1987; and the Tiananmen Square demonstrations of 1989.

⋆ D E M O C R A C Y   W A L L   ⋆

In December 1978, as Deng Xiaoping regained power after having been purged during the Cultural Revolution, thousands of Chinese began congregating at an unprepossessing wall around a bus yard in Beijing. Here at "Democracy Wall" they traded political views, delivered speeches on China's future, and put up "wall posters" criticizing the Party and its leadership in a free exchange of ideas that was unprecedented in socialist China.

ORVILLE SCHELL, THE DEMOCRACY WALL MOVEMENT

Once Deng Xiaoping had heralded his new era of reform at the 1978 Third Plenary Session of the Eleventh Central Committee, the suddenness with which ordinary citizens began voicing long-repressed grievances caught many off guard. The major venue for such expressions was Democracy Wall, and it quickly became the center of a new movement calling on China to democratize itself politically as well as to develop itself economically.

This selection was excerpted from coeditor Orville Schell's book Discos and Democracy: China in the Throes of Reform, *published in 1988.*

Ⅰn 1977, just after Mao's death, the fall of the Gang of Four, and the return of Deng Xiaoping to power, China's newspapers began to proclaim publicly the need for democracy. The *People's Daily*, reborn with a completely new voice, declared that if China's socialist bureaucracy remained unchecked by elections and other democratic institutions, it might again run amok and degenerate into "feudal fascism." That June, in an important speech at an army political conference, Deng told incredulous delegates that it would no longer do for China just to "copy straight from Marx, Lenin, and Chairman Mao"; henceforth criteria for truth should be sought in facts rather than in politics.

By February 1978, a new constitution had been adopted whose Article 45 guaranteed "freedom of speech, correspondence, the press, demonstrations, and the freedom to strike," as well as what the Chinese came to refer to as the four big freedoms, namely the right of people to "speak out freely, air their views fully, hold great debates, and write big-character posters."

Hu Yaobang, Deng's protégé and the new chief of the Party's Organization Department (he became Party general secretary in 1980), launched a far-reaching program to rehabilitate the tens of millions of Chinese who had been slandered, persecuted, and imprisoned for being landlords, rich peasants, rightists, counterrevolutionaries, bad elements, antisocial elements, and capitalist roaders. Tens of thousands of people were released from jail as, that fall, commentators in the press began exhorting Chinese to "break through all spiritual shackles" and "emancipate their minds" in order to carry out Deng Xiaoping's new slogan, "Practice is the sole criterion of truth."

At a Central Work Conference held that November, Deng stated, "Some people say that we must do what Chairman Mao said. But actually there are many things that the Chairman did not say. Engels never rode in a plane. Stalin never wore Dacron. Practice is developing. We must study the new situation and solve new problems."

Not surprisingly, 1978 was a time of enormous ferment and excitement as Deng went about the task of repudiating the Cultural Revolution. After ten years of political suppression and terror, the new sense of freedom and excitement in the air was palpable. Chinese intellectuals who had lived in a state of almost perpetual fear once again became emboldened to speak out. "Literature of the wounded," a new genre of writing that recounted the horrors of the Cultural Revolution, began to be published. Before long, this new sense of freedom began to translate itself into political sentiment, producing a crop of wall posters expressing a variety of long-pent-up ideas and complaints.

The epicenter of this cultural and political tremor was an unprepossessing stretch of brick wall in front of a streetcar yard, located near the intersection of the Avenue of Eternal Peace and Xidan, one of the capital's main shopping streets. There, for several months during the winter of 1978–79, behind a scruffy hedge and under a row of leafless sycamore trees, Democracy Wall flourished. Here, people spent hours at a time reading, talking, and listening with an openness never before seen in the People's Republic. What brought them were *dazibao*, "big-character posters," a form of public expression to which Chinese have long turned when denied access to government-controlled media. During the fall of 1978, *dazibao* suddenly began to appear on Democracy Wall, their content becoming bolder and bolder as the weeks passed, so that by the middle of November young activists had covered and re-covered the wall with savage attacks on the Cultural Revolution, the Gang of Four, and sometimes even Mao himself. Before long, they even began bringing up the taboo subject of democracy, proclaiming:

> It is incredible that in a People's Republic there should still be among the officials to whom the people have entrusted national sovereignty, executioners and murderers, whose hands are stained with the blood of the people. . . . In China . . . a country of proletarian dictatorship armed with the Great Thought of the Era, we certainly do not measure up to the people of ancient times or to foreign countries. . . .

> Citizens of China do not want just a paper constitution. We don't want hunger. We don't want to suffer anymore. We want human rights and democracy.

> However great and wise a leader might be, he certainly cannot be immune from making mistakes. Several thousand years of feudal history and over a hundred years of the people's dauntless struggles have taught us one truth: We must place our hope in a healthy, effective, scientific, and democratic system, so that both the common people and the public servants they elect are bound by this system and strive for the well-being of the people . . .

> To make people think that democracy and human rights are only slogans of the Western bourgeoisie and that the Eastern proletariat needs only dictatorship . . . is something that cannot be tolerated anymore.

> The Chinese people want to learn more than just technology from the West. They also want to learn more about Western democracy and culture. We demand the opening of the gates that have been locked against us for so long, and to let true liberty blow across the land.

As the movement progressed, some Democracy Wall activists even began shouting their messages through hand-held bullhorns:

We must uphold the Party! But we must also supervise the Party and make it the public servant of the people!

We demand democracy! We demand freedom!

By the end of December 1978, when the Third Plenum of the Eleventh Party Central Committee published its pathbreaking communiqué on reform and "opening up" to the outside world, Democracy Wall had been in existence for five weeks. Thousands of people flocked to it each day to see what had been written the night before and to join throngs of activists in heated discussion groups or to listen to spontaneous speech making. This unruly liberated zone of free expression was not closed down by the authorities because the activists initially supported Deng Xiaoping. Still consolidating his position against his opposition, Deng found his interests well served by having a cadre of such activists in the streets ready to protest against his opponents at a moment's notice.

"Putting heaven and earth in harmony, opening doors, establishing order, discipline, and great democracy, Vice Premier Deng is openminded, humble, and honored by the entire world," wrote one Democracy Wall scribe, extolling Deng as a classically benevolent Chinese ruler. "His greatness, beauty, and success in seizing the seat of government are hailed in the north and the south. . . . [Under him] the nation will be rich and strong, and the economy will be pushed ahead."

To encourage the protesters, on November 26, 1978, Deng told the visiting chairman of Japan's Democratic Socialist Party that wall posters were "a normal phenomenon, a manifestation of a stable situation in our country . . . [which] is permitted by our constitution. . . . The masses should be allowed to vent their grievances. . . . We should not check the demands of the masses to speak."

A short time later he bluntly told the American reporter Robert Novak, "Democracy Wall is good." Echoing these sentiments, the *People's Daily* proclaimed, "Let the people say what they wish, the heavens will not fall. A range of opinions from people is good for a revolutionary party leading the government. If people become unwilling to say anything, that would be bad. When people are free to speak, it means the Party and the government have strength and confidence. . . . If a person is to be punished for saying wrong things, no one will say what he thinks. . . . The suffocation of democracy produces bad results."

Predictably, these Democracy Wall activists grew more and more outspoken and soon began to criticize the whole Chinese political system rather than just the Gang of Four and the Cultural Revolution. But at the point where they began to blatantly level their fire at Mao himself, they had outlived their usefulness for Deng. Perhaps fearing that he would be their next target, Deng was reported to have said, "The masses have their doubts on some questions, [but] some utterances are not in the interest of stability and unity."

"Vice Premier Deng, you are wrong, completely wrong!" wrote one displeased protester. "There is no doubt that a long time ago the Chinese people took note of Chairman Mao's mistakes. Those who hate the Gang of Four cannot fail to have grievances against Chairman Mao."

As the focus of the posters began to switch from criticisms of the Cultural Revolution to broadsides against Mao and increasingly strident calls for democracy, the marriage of convenience between Deng and the Wall activists chilled rapidly. Soon plainclothesmen began disrupting activities at the Wall, and rumors circulated that Party leaders had branded the democracy movement as "underground." Then, on January 18, the first arrest was made. The honeymoon had been short-lived. Paranoia and disillusionment quickly replaced the earlier optimism and ebullience of the protesters. Rumors were soon rampant that a struggle between reformers and hard-liners over both Democracy Wall and the new Party line was raging within the leadership.

As *Explorations*, one of the democracy movement's most outspoken underground journals, put it, "Some bigwigs in the Beijing Municipal Party Committee are afraid that the people might be able to enjoy true democracy." The editor of *Explorations*, Wei Jingsheng, a young ex-soldier who worked as an electrician at the Beijing Zoo and whose family had suffered grievously during the Cultural Revolution, was one of the most radical and eloquent advocates of democracy during these hectic months. His now famous wall poster, "Democracy: The Fifth Modernization," had first appeared on the Wall and was later published in *Explorations* (see next selection). It not only called for basic reforms in China's system of government but expressed a bitingly cynical attitude toward Deng's four modernizations (of agriculture, industry, science, and defense). Like other reformers before him, Wei set out to ascertain why Chinese society was so backward and weak. He concluded that the cause of that weakness lay in the country's lack of democracy.

Although a passionate and devoted advocate of democracy, Wei tended to justify democracy as "the condition on which survival of productive forces depends." This traditionally utilitarian Chinese cast to

Wei's argument for democracy did nothing, however, to mitigate the reaction of China's Party leaders to his criticisms. The leadership had already been increasingly unsettled by what was being written on the big-character posters by upstart democrats like Wei, not to mention what had begun to appear in the more than fifty underground journals now being published in Beijing.

In February 1979, Deng Xiaoping made his historic trip to the United States to celebrate the establishment of diplomatic relations with Washington. Once back home, with his own leadership position secure, Deng made his move. On March 16 he claimed that protesters had used the issue of democracy to fan old resentments from the Cultural Revolution, that they had formed secret cabals with agents from Taiwan, and that they had had unauthorized relationships with foreigners. In short, Deng cast his lot with those hard-liners who had long agitated for an end to the Wall and at the same time delineated his Four Cardinal Principles (to uphold socialism, the dictatorship of the proletariat, the leadership of the Communist Party of China, and Marxism-Leninism–Mao Zedong Thought), which henceforth became the new ideological standard of the Party.

On March 25, hearing through the grapevine that a crackdown was imminent, Wei and his colleagues rushed out a special edition of *Explorations* entitled "Do We Want Democracy or a New Dictatorship?" in which they savagely attacked Deng's statement of March 16 and accused him of having "metamorphosed into a dictator." On March 29 new regulations were issued by the government forbidding "slogans, posters, books, magazines, photographs, and other materials that oppose socialism, the dictatorship of the proletariat, the leadership of the Communist Party, Marxism-Leninism–Mao Zedong Thought" from being publicly displayed. Almost instantaneously, Party propaganda organs began churning out diatribes against "extreme democracy" (*daminzhu*) and in favor of socialist democracy and the Four Cardinal Principles.

On the same day, Wei was arrested on charges of publishing counter-revolutionary materials. According to the soon-to-be-minted Chinese criminal code, counterrevolution was defined as any act undertaken "for the purpose of overthrowing the political power of the dictatorship of the proletariat and the socialist system and jeopardizing the People's Republic of China."

"For the past four months Wei has been active in the spontaneous democracy movement," wrote the other editors of *Explorations* by way of an epitaph.

He has fiercely criticized all backward factions that he thought prevented China's modernization, including the obstructive role that he thought was played by Marxism and the Thought of Mao Zedong. Because of that, the Chinese government arrested him for the crime of counterrevolution.

Where is the freedom of speech in China?. . . . All criticism is fiercely suppressed as being contrary to socialism and to the dictatorship of the proletariat. So much for democratic freedom under the Chinese government! What brutal hypocrisy!

"Some people have the audacity to say that there is no democracy in the whole of Beijing, or even the entire country," rejoined the *Beijing Daily*. "These words not only show ignorance, they are out-and-out slanders and distortions. . . . If we allow [people like Wei] to promote their so-called democracy, we will do harm to the democratic rights of the masses of people."

Why had Wei persisted against such futile odds? "Because I know that democracy is the future of China, and if I speak out now there is a possibility that I can hasten the day when the Chinese people will enjoy democracy," he had optimistically told the British diplomat and author Roger Garside before his arrest. "Two years ago it would have been pointless for us to speak or write as we do now, for we would have been arrested as soon as the words were out of our mouths. Now, through our posters and journals we can make our voices heard."

By April 1979 some thirty other Democracy Wall activists were rounded up. That October, Wei Jingsheng was brought to trial and accused of "supplying military intelligence [on China's war with Vietnam] to a foreigner and of openly agitating for the overthrow of the government of the dictatorship of the proletariat and the socialist system in China."

At his trial, Wei declined to be represented by a government lawyer and instead spoke in his own defense. Answering the government's indictment that he had "put forth the banner of so-called freedom of speech and the demand for democracy and human rights to agitate for the overthrow of the dictatorship of the proletariat," Wei eloquently replied, "I must point out that freedom of speech is not a wild demand, but something that is guaranteed in black and white in the Constitution. The tone in which the prosecutor talks about this right shows not only that he is prejudiced in his thinking but that he has forgotten his responsibility to protect the democratic rights of citizens." Instead of trying to defend himself against his indictment by claiming that his acts were not counterrevolutionary, Wei attacked the very notion of a "counterrevolutionary crime":

> Some people have the following view: that it is revolutionary if we act in accordance with the will of the leaders in power and that it is counterrevolutionary to oppose it. I cannot agree with this debasement of the concept of revolution. . . . Revolution is the struggle between the new and the old. . . . To label the will of the people in power as forever revolutionary, to wipe out all divergent views and theories, and to think of power as truth — this was precisely one of the most effective tools of the Gang of Four in the past twenty years. . . .
>
> The current historical tide is a democratic tide, one that opposes feudal fascist dictatorship. The central theme in my articles, such as "Democracy: The Fifth Modernization," is that without democracy there can be no four modernizations. . . . How can such a central theme be counterrevolutionary?

Wei concluded his impassioned defense with an unrepentant restatement of his belief that the Constitution guaranteed him the right to criticize the government. "Criticism cannot possibly be nice and appealing to the ear, or even always correct. Requiring criticism to be entirely correct, and inflicting punishment if it is not, is the same as prohibiting criticism and reform. It is tantamount to elevating leaders to the position of being deities."

For his outspoken views, Wei was given fifteen years in jail.

In December 1979, by belatedly banning further displays of posters on Democracy Wall, the Party authorities formally ended Beijing Spring, just twelve months after it had begun. When later asked for his views on the whole movement, Deng replied, in his characteristically terse way, "As to the so-called Democracy Wall, the demonstrations and the sit-ins cannot represent the genuine feelings of our people."

On September 10, 1980, at the direction of Deng Xiaoping, the Third Session of the Fifth National People's Congress rescinded the four big freedoms, which had been written into Article 45 of the 1978 Constitution. The vote was unanimous except for one defaced ballot, which, Andrew Nathan has noted, "was unusual enough to merit front-page comment in the *People's Daily*, which welcomed the anonymous delegate's courage as a sign of the new vigor of democracy in China." As Deng Xiaoping observed after the sentencing of Wei, China could never develop if "so-called democrats and dissidents such as Wei Jingsheng and his ilk," who are openly opposed to the socialist system and to Party leadership, obstruct the "unity and stability" of the country.

WEI JINGSHENG, DEMOCRACY: THE FIFTH MODERNIZATION

One of the most eloquent Chinese voices to come out of the Democracy Wall movement was that of a former soldier and young electrician from the Beijing Zoo named Wei Jingsheng. Because of his biting critiques of Mao Zedong, the Communist Party, and its leaders—including Deng Xiaoping (whom he described as a dictator)—Wei was arrested and sentenced to fifteen years in prison. Released briefly in September 1993, he was rearrested in April 1994, and not given his freedom until November 1997, shortly after President Clinton invited Chinese Party Chief and President Jiang Zemin to the White House for a state dinner. The condition of Wei's release was that he go into immediate exile.

Wei's Democracy Wall movement manifesto, "Democracy: The Fifth Modernization," posted on December 5, 1978, is one of the most cogent and uncompromising documents to come out of the movement. It calls on the Party to add democratization to the list of "four modernizations" (industry, agriculture, science and technology, and national defense) that the leadership was then advocating.

This selection was translated by Simon Leys and published in The Burning Forest: Essays on Chinese Culture and Politics *(1983).*

If newspapers and the radio have now stopped bashing our ears with their deafening propaganda catchwords on the theme of "class struggle," it is partly because this was the magic abracadabra of the "Gang of Four." But mostly because the masses were fed up with it; you cannot make people march anymore to that tune.

There is a law of history according to which as long as the old does not disappear, the new cannot come into existence. Now that the old is gone for good, everyone is scanning the horizon in the hope of seeing the emergence of the new. As the saying goes: "God would never disappoint the faithful." Hence, a fantastic new formula was invented and is being served to us now. They call it "The Four Modernizations." Chairman Hua (our "wise leader") and Vice Chairman Deng (who, in the eyes of some people, is even wiser and greater) managed to defeat the "Gang of Four," thus making it possible again to dream of democracy and prosperity—a dream for which heroic people shed their blood in Tiananmen Square on April 5, 1976.

After the arrest of the "Gang of Four," the people ardently hoped for the return of Deng; and in their delusion that he would "restore capitalism," they turned him into the living symbol of their movement. Eventually, Deng was reinstalled in the central leadership of the State and of the Party: and this event was greeted by the entire nation with indescribable enthusiasm and emotion.

After that, alas! our odious political system was not amended in the slightest. As for the freedom and democracy that the people expected, even the very words cannot be mentioned. The living conditions of the population have not changed; "salary increases" were largely canceled by the astronomical rising of prices. As for "capitalist restoration," it seems that the system of production bonuses is going to be reintroduced—precisely what the Fathers of Marxism-Leninism used to stigmatize as "the invisible whip under which workers suffer maximum exploitation." It is now announced that the methodical policy of "cretinization of the masses" has been abandoned. Though the people are not to be kept anymore under the authority of a "Great Helmsman," they are now under the direction of a "Wise Leader," who will see to it that they "catch up with and overtake the most advanced countries of the world," such as England, the United States, Japan, and ... Yugoslavia! To "make revolution" is not fashionable nowadays. Now, if you wish to achieve a brilliant career, the best way is again to work for a university degree. The people need no longer suffer the wearisome drivel of "class struggle." Now it is the "four modernizations" that have become the new panacea. Needless to say, we still must obey the orders of the central authorities. Follow the guide dutifully, and all your beautiful dreams will materialize.

There is an old Chinese saying that tells of "feeding the people by painting cakes," and there is another one of "quenching thirst by contemplating plums." The satirical spirit of this old wisdom truly reflects long political experience. If history is actually a constant progression, how could one still hope today to swindle the public with those same crude stratagems that had already been exposed long ago by our ancestors? And yet there are still people who believe they can cheat the world with such tricks, and who actually proceed in this fashion.

Thus, during these last few decades, the Chinese people docilely followed a "Great Helmsman" who fed them with cakes that he painted by using a brush called "communism," and who quenched their thirst by dangling in front of their noses plums that were called "Great Leap Forward" or "Three Red Flags." And the people kept on bravely marching forward, tightening their belts. . . . After having suffered this regime with considerable fortitude for thirty years, the people eventually understood: like the monkey who attempts to grasp the moon, they were condemned to remain forever empty-handed. That is why, as soon as Vice Chairman Deng launched his new program, "Back to Reality," the masses supported him with enthusiasm, showing their approval with a voice as formidable as the roaring of the ocean. Everyone expected that Deng, applying his famous principle "to reach truth from facts," would submit the recent past to critical investigation, and that he would lead the people toward a worthy future.

And yet, what is actually happening now? Some gentlemen come to warn us earnestly: "Marxism-Leninism and Mao Zedong Thought remain the foundation of all there is on earth; no valid utterance can be formulated without referring to it." Or again: "Chairman Mao is the savior of the people," and "Without the Communist Party, there would be no New China"—which amounts to saying, "Without Chairman Mao, there would be no New China." Now, if anyone questions these affirmations, there are good medicines to cure him of his skepticism! Some others lecture us: "The Chinese people need to be led by a strong man. If the modern despot is even tougher than his feudal predecessors, this merely shows his greatness. The Chinese people have no need for democracy, except when it comes properly 'centralized'; in any other form, it is not worth a penny. You have little faith? As you wish. For your kind of people, there is always room in our jails. . . ."

Nevertheless, they still leave you one open path. *Forward march!* Within the framework of the "four modernizations," close all ranks, and cut out the nonsense, all you dutiful packhorses of the Revolution! At the end of the road you will reach Paradise—the utopia of Communism—with the "four modernizations." Furthermore, well-meaning persons still come forward to lavish their wisdom on us: "If these perspectives still fail to stir your enthusiasm, apply yourselves seriously to the study of Marxism-Leninism and Mao Zedong Thought! Your lack of enthusiasm results from your deficient theoretical understanding, and the very fact that you do not understand the theory precisely proves its sublime depth. Come on, be good fellows now—anyway, the authorities that be, ordained by history, will not allow you any alternative. . . ."

I beg you all—do not let these political swindlers cheat you yet again! Rather than swallow what we know to be a dupery, why not, for once, simply rely on our own resources? The cruel experiences of the Cultural Revolution have opened our eyes. Let us try to discover by ourselves what is to be done.

Why Is Democracy Necessary?

This question has been discussed at length now for many centuries. More recently, the various people who put forward their views on the Democracy Wall explained thoroughly why democracy is infinitely better than despotism.

"The people are the masters of history"—is this true, or is it an empty phase? It is both true *and* an empty phrase. We say that it is true because without the people's strength, without the people's participation, no history is conceivable (with or without "the Great Helmsman" and other "Wise Leaders"). From this point of view, it is obvious that without a new Chinese people there could be no "New China"; and it is no thanks to Chairman Mao that this "New China" came into existence. Vice Chairman Deng thanked Chairman Mao for having saved his life—we can understand and forgive his reaction—however, should he not rather thank the *people*, who, with their outcry, succeeded in returning him to office? How does he dare to say now to the people: "You should not criticize Chairman Mao—after all, he saved my life!" From such an episode, it appears clear that a saying such as "the people are the masters of history" is mere hollow chatter. Its emptiness is plain, because we see that, in fact, the people are deprived of any possibility of determining their fate according to the wishes of the majority. All the achievements of the people are always credited to someone else, all the rights of the people are confiscated to weave a garland for someone else. In these conditions, can we still say that the people are the masters? They look rather like docile slaves. Even though the people remain theoretically creators and masters of history, in actual fact their role is merely to provide legions of respectful and silent servants, and to serve as clay in the hands of the real masters.

The people need democracy. When they demand democracy, they

simply demand that which originally belonged to them. Whoever dares to deny them democracy is nothing but a shameless bandit, even more despicable than the capitalist who robs the workers' sweat and blood.

Do the people now enjoy democracy? No. Is it that the people do not want to be their own masters? Of course they do! It is precisely for this reason that the Communist Party defeated the Kuomintang. After its victory, what came out of all the earlier promises? First they changed the slogan of "People's Democratic Dictatorship" into "Dictatorship of the Proletariat." And then the last democratic leftovers, which a tiny handful of people were still enjoying at the top, disappeared too, to be replaced by the personal despotism of "the Great Leader." Thus, on "the Great Leader's" orders, Peng Dehuai was dismissed and dragged in the mud, for having dared to vent some grumbles at an internal gathering of Party leaders. So it was that a new formula appeared: "Since the Leader is so great, a blind faith in his person could only bring increasing happiness to the people." At the time, the people accepted this formula, partly because they were forced to do so and partly because they were willing. But what is the situation now? Are the people really happier, more prosperous?

The inescapable truth is that today the people are more miserable, unhappy, and backward than before. How could such a situation develop? This is the first question we should examine. What should we do? This is the second question we must study.

Today it is perfectly irrelevant to try to determine the balance account of Mao Zedong's achievements and mistakes. Originally it was he himself who suggested such an assessment; for him, this was a defensive maneuver. The question that the people should now be asking is this: Without Mao Zedong's personal despotism, could China ever have fallen as low as we see her today? Or are we to believe that Chinese people are stupid or lazy or devoid of any desire to improve their lot? We know very well that this is not the case. Then what happened? The answer is obvious: the Chinese have taken a path they should never have entered; if they followed it, it is because a despot, who knew how to peddle his trash shrewdly, simply took them for a ride. On the other hand, he did not leave them very much choice: "You disagree? Then you will be given a personal dose of dictatorship!" Moreover, the people were kept in complete ignorance of all alternatives, and were persuaded that this was the sole feasible way. What a swindle! Is there still any point in calculating exactly how many kudos should be awarded to its perpetrator?

What is this way called? I am told it is called "the socialist way." According to the Marxist theoreticians, under socialism the masses — also known as the "proletariat" — hold all political power. Go and ask Chinese workers: "Apart from the wretched salary that you are given every month, just to prevent you from starving, what rights do you have? What power do you have? Whose masters are you? Alas, you can control nothing — not even your own marriage!"

Socialism is supposed to guarantee to every producer the right to enjoy the fruits of his own labor after he has discharged his duties toward society. And yet, for you, is there any limit to the burden of your duties? What is allocated to you is precisely this wretched salary, "barely enough to sustain the energy necessary to meet production requirements"! Socialism is supposed to ensure that every citizen has the right to be educated, to develop his individual talents, and many other rights — but we see no trace of all this in our lives. The only thing we can see is "the dictatorship of the proletariat" and this new variation of the "Russian-style despotism," which is now "Chinese-style despotism." Who can really believe that this socialist way contains any recipe for the happiness of the people?

Is this the kind of socialism that Marx envisioned and that the people are hoping for? Obviously not. What is it, then? We would laugh if it were not so sad — it resembles precisely the kind of "social feudalism" described in the *Manifesto*, a kind of feudal monarchy in socialist garb.

Do we need to continue suffering such slavery and misery? If we wish to break away from it, there is only one way — democracy. In other words, if we want to modernize our economy and science and defense and the like, we must first modernize our people. We must first modernize our social system.

The Fifth Modernization — Which Democracy?

What is genuine democracy? It is a system that allows the people to choose, at their own will, representatives who administer in the name of the people, in conformity with the people's will and interests. The people must retain the right to dismiss and replace their representatives at any time, to prevent them from abusing their powers and turning into oppressors. Is such a system actually feasible? In Europe and the United States, the people enjoy precisely this type of democracy. At will, they were able to dismiss their Nixon or de Gaulle or Tanaka, and if they so wish they can as well call them back, without any force interfering with the free exercise of their democratic prerogative. But, in our country, if in a private conversation you merely express the slightest doubt concerning the historical sublimity of our "Great Helmsman," Mao Zedong (even though he has already passed away), you immediately see in front of you the gaping gates of a jail where various special treatments, all quite beyond imagination, are awaiting you. If one compares the "democratic centralism" of the socialist countries with the democracy of the "exploiting classes" in capitalist regimes, one sees a difference as great as between night and day!

Is it true to say that if democratic rights were granted to the people, there would be a danger of falling into disorder and anarchy? On the contrary. Newspapers in our country recently exposed all the scandalous abuses that our despots, large and small, could perpetrate precisely because we have no democracy—*that* is the real disorder, the *real* anarchy! The problem of how to maintain democratic order is a problem of internal politics with which the people alone are competent to deal, and there is no need to call upon some feudal gentlemen, equipped with special powers, to take care of this problem for the people (for the purpose of these gentlemen is not to protect democracy but to find a pretext to divest the people of their rights). Of course, these problems of internal politics are not simple, and to solve them will require a lengthy process during which mistakes will inevitably be committed, needing constant rectification.

But this is *our* business, and such a system is still a thousand times better than the arrogant tyranny of our present feudal aristocracy, providing no recourse against constant injustice. As for the people who worry at the idea that the establishment of democracy might produce chaos, they remind me of those who, just after the 1911 Republican Revolution, believed that a China without emperors would sink into chaos. Their conclusion is, "Let us patiently suffer oppression. . . ." Are they afraid that without a tyrant riding on their back, they might stumble and fall?

To those who entertain such worries, let me merely say this, very respectfully: We want to become the masters of our own destiny. We need no gods and no emperors; we believe in no savior; we want to direct our own lives. We do not want to be mere tools in the hands of despots with expansionist ambitions, who wish to use us to carry out a modernization geared to their own advantage. What we want is a modernization of the people's living conditions. The only reason we want to achieve modernization is to ensure democracy, freedom, and happiness for the people. Without this "fifth modernization," all other "modernizations" are nothing but lies.

Comrades, I launch this appeal to you: Let us all unite under the flag of democracy! Do not let us be cheated again by those slogans of "unity in stability" of which our despots are so fond. Totalitarian fascism can bring us only disaster. Entertain no more illusions concerning these people. Democracy is our only hope. If we give up our democratic rights, it is as if we fasten onto ourselves our own chains. Trust your own forces! We alone create human history! As for those who award themselves the titles of "Great Leaders" and "Great Teachers," and who have swindled the people of their most precious rights for several decades now, may they all go to hell!

I firmly believe that if production is put under control of the people, it will certainly increase, because the producers will work in their own interest. Life will become beautiful and good, because everything will be geared toward the improvement of the workers' living conditions. Society will be more just, because all rights and powers will be democratically wielded by all the workers.

I have no illusions — this ideal will not be reached without strenuous efforts; and in order to achieve it, the people must not count on the intervention of some providential hero. Yet I know that the Chinese people will not be discouraged by the many difficulties they will encounter on the way. The main thing is that the people must acquire a clear vision of the goal and an accurate assessment of the obstacles, and must, without hesitation, be able to crush the pathetic insects that try to hinder their progression.

Forward Toward Modernization: Establishing Democracy

If the Chinese people wish to modernize, they must first establish democracy, they must first modernize China's social system. Democracy is not what Lenin says, a mere consequence of a certain stage of development of society. It is not merely the necessary product of a certain degree of development of the productive forces and the production relations. It is also the condition on which depends the very survival of the productive forces (and the production relations in this phase of development, or in a situation of superior development). Without democracy, society would sink into a stage of stagnation, and economic growth would encounter insuperable obstacles. Thus, as is shown by historical precedents, a democratic social system was always the prerequisite for any real development. Without this preliminary condition, not only would it be impossible to achieve any progress but it would even be difficult merely to preserve the achievements obtained at a given level of development. The best evidence is provided by the situation to which our great country has been reduced after these last thirty years.

Any struggle waged by the people to ensure happiness, peace, and prosperity must necessarily begin with a struggle to obtain democratic rights. Similarly, for a people to resist oppression and exploitation, the most essential objective must be the establishing of democracy. Let us bring all our strength into this battle for the establishment of democracy! The people's will is democratic; depotism, dictatorship, and totalitarianism are its most direct and most dangerous enemies.

Will these enemies let us establish democracy? Of course not. They will try by all means to hinder the progression of democracy. One of their most efficient methods is to cheat and deceive the people—all fascist despots keep repeating, "You enjoy the very best conditions in the whole world!"

Will democracy emerge by itself at the end of a natural and necessary evolution? Certainly not. On the way toward democracy, the smallest victory will exact a terrible price; let us have no illusions; democracy will be reached only after bloody sacrifices. The enemies of democracy try always to deceive the people telling them: "The emergence and the disappearance of democracy are phenomena that result from an inner necessity; there is thus no need to spend any effort to bring it into existence. . . ."

Look rather at the teachings of history, true history, not the history written by Party hacks: genuine democracy, the only valid democracy, is nourished with the blood of martyrs and with the blood of tyrants. Every step forward toward democracy must overcome the frantic counterattacks launched by reactionary forces. The fact that democracy succeeds in defeating all these obstacles shows how dear it is to the people; it is the embodiment of all their hopes, which endows it with the irresistible impetus of a tidal wave. The Chinese people fear nothing; once they have clearly recognized which orientation they must follow, they will be able to overthrow their tyrants.

Can the struggle for democracy mobilize the Chinese people? During the Cultural Revolution, for the first time they became aware of their own strength when they saw all the reactionary powers shaking with fear. But at that time the people still did not have a clear idea of the way they should proceed, and thus the democratic trend could not predominate. Hence it was all too easy for the tyrant to dominate, manipulate, and divert most of these struggles; he neutralized the movement by using in turn provocations, seductions, lies, and violent repression. Since the people, at that time, still had a religious respect for despots, they became the powerless toys and victims of the ruling tyrant as well as of all the other tyrants to come.

Twelve years later, however, the people have now identified their goal, they see clearly the way they should follow, they finally acknowledge their true banner—the flag of democracy.

The Democracy Wall in Xidan became their first fortress in the struggle against all reactionary forces. In this struggle, we shall overcome. As the propaganda phrase used to say: "The people will certainly liberate themselves"; but this time that worn-out slogan is being given a new meaning. Blood will be shed, there will be new martyrs, persecution will become even more sinister; but the reactionary forces will never again succeed in obliterating our democratic flag in their poisonous mist. Let us all unite under this flag, which is great and true; let us march forward to secure peace and happiness for the people, to win our rights and our freedom, and to make our society truly modern!

★ THE STUDENT ★
DEMONSTRATIONS OF 1986-87

A second wave of popular protest arose in 1985 and 1986, during one of the most liberal and intellectually open periods of the Chinese Communist revolution. Aroused by the host of new political ideas they had been absorbing from abroad over the past few years, in 1986 students took to the streets of Beijing and twenty other cities demanding more rapid political reform and a greater quotient of democracy. Although the demonstrations ended without significant violence, Party Chief Hu Yaobang was unceremoniously purged from office by Marxist hardliners and reformers were put on notice that there were still limits to dissent.

FANG LIZHI,
DEMOCRACY, REFORM, AND MODERNIZATION

Fang Lizhi was a well-known astrophysicist in the tradition of the Soviet Union's Andrei Sakharov, whose interest in freedom of expression grew out of having had his scientific work censored by Party propagandists. As a scientist and vice president of the prestigious University of Science and Technology, Fang became dedicated to the principle of open inquiry and academic freedom. Predictably, the speeches he began giving and the articles he began writing in the mid-1980s put him at loggerheads with Party regulars. After students began demonstrating in December 1986, Fang was fired from his job and expelled from the Party.

Fang's speech "Democracy, Reform, and Modernization," given at Shanghai's Tongji University on November 18, 1986, had a profound impact after it was circulated throughout China because it reminded students and more senior intellectuals that "rights" are the common heritage of all people and not something that can be given by a government or party.

This selection was excerpted from a collection of Fang's writings, Bringing Down the Great Wall: Writings on Science, Culture, and Democracy in China, *edited by Jim Williams (1991).*

Our goal at present is the thorough modernization of China. We all have a compelling sense of the need for modernization. There is a widespread demand for change among people in all walks of life; and very few find any reason for complacency. None feel this more strongly than those of us in science and academia. Modernization has been our national theme since the Gang of Four were overthrown ten years ago, but we are just beginning to understand what it really means. In the beginning we were mainly aware of the grave shortcomings in our production of goods, our economy, our science and technology, and that modernization was required in these areas. But now we understand our situation much better. We realize that grave shortcomings exist not only in our "material civilization" but also in our "spiritual civilization"—our culture, our ethical standards, our political institutions—and that these also require modernization.

The question we must now ask is, What kind of modernization is required? I think it's obvious to all of us that we need complete modernization, not just modernization in a few chosen aspects. People are now busy comparing Chinese and Western culture—including politics, economics, science, technology, education, the whole gamut—and there is much debate over the subject. The question is, do we want "complete Westernization" or "partial Westernization"? Should we continue to uphold the century-old banner of "using Western methods but maintaining the Chinese essence," or any other "cardinal principle"? Of course this is not a new discussion. A century ago, insightful people realized that China had no choice but to modernize. Some wanted partial modernization, others wanted complete modernization, and thus they initiated a debate that continues down to the present day.

I personally agree with the "complete Westernizers." What their so-called complete Westernization means to me is complete openness, the removal of restrictions in every sphere. We need to acknowledge that when looked at in its entirety, our culture lags far behind that of the world's most advanced societies, not in any one specific aspect but across the board. Responding to this situation calls not for the establishment of a priori barriers but for complete openness to the outside world. Attempting to set our inviolable "essence" off limits before it is even challenged makes no sense to me. Again, I am scarcely inventing these ideas. A century ago people said essentially the same thing: Open China up and face the challenge of more advanced societies head on, in every aspect from technology to politics. What is good will stand up, and what is not good will be swept away. This prognosis remains unchanged.

Why is China so backward? To answer this question, we need to take a clear look at history. China has been undergoing revolutions for a century, but we are still very backward. This is all the more true since Liberation, these decades of the socialist revolution that we all know firsthand as students and workers. Speaking quite dispassionately, I have to judge this era a failure. This is not my opinion only, by any means; many of our leaders are also admitting as much, saying that socialism is in trouble everywhere. Since the end of World War II, socialist countries have by and large not been successful. There is no getting around this. As far as I'm concerned, the last thirty-odd years in China have been a failure in virtually every aspect of economic and political life.

We need to take a careful look at why socialism has failed. Socialist ideals are admirable. But we have to ask two questions about the way they have been put into practice: Are the things done in the name of socialism actually socialist? And, do they make any sense? We have to take a fresh look at these questions, and the first step in that process is to free our minds from the narrow confines of orthodox Marxism.

I have been in academia for a long time, so I've been subjected to a lot of propaganda. I've always had the feeling, even though we claim that Marxism embraces all contributions to civilization down through the ages, that when you really get down to it, we're saying that only since Marx has anyone known the real truth. Sometimes even Marx himself is tossed aside, and all that counts is what's happened since Liberation. Everything else is treated very negatively. Anything from the past, or from other cultures, is denigrated. We are very familiar with this attitude. When a historical figure is discussed, there is always a disclaimer at the end: "Despite this person's contributions, he suffered from historical limitations." In other words, he wasn't quite of the stature of us Marxists.

This is typical. When scholars of other races or nationalities make great discoveries, we'll say that they've done some good things, but due to the limitations of their class background, thus-and-so. In one area after another, it is made to appear that only since Liberation have truly great things been accomplished. This is parochial and narrow-minded in the extreme. What became of embracing the contributions of other cultures? We see ourselves towering over the historical landscape, but the fact is, nothing can justify such a claim. Only religions view their place in history in this fashion.

Our narrow-mindedness is a consequence of feudalism and its associated attitudes: No one but yourself is legitimate or worthy of respect. We must forsake this narrow framework and open our eyes to the world. We should look with humility at what others have to offer, and what is good we should try to incorporate. Complete openness, allowing the outside world to challenge our way of doing things, is the only way to change our society. We need to take an objective look at what's really out there, and then decide what to believe and what we want or don't want. But not before then. When I saw East and West Berlin with my own two eyes, I couldn't help but be affected by it. If we could quit bolting our doors and proclaiming that everything here is wonderful, and instead open our eyes to the richly varied outside world, we would not remain so narrow-minded.

We've talked about the need for modernization and reform, so now let's consider democracy. Our understanding of the concept of democracy is so inadequate that we can barely even discuss it. With our thinking so hobbled by old dogmas, it is no wonder we don't achieve democracy in practice. Not long ago it was constantly being said that calling for democracy was equivalent to requesting that things be "loosened up." In fact the word "democracy" is quite clear, and it is poles apart in meaning from "loosening up." If you want to understand democracy, look at how people understand it in the developed countries, and compare that to how people understand it here, and then decide for yourself what's right and what's wrong.

I think that the key to understanding democracy lies first of all in recognizing the rights of each individual. Democracy is built from the bottom up. Every individual possesses certain rights, or to use what is a very sensitive expression indeed in China, everyone has "human rights." We seldom dare to utter the words "human rights," but actually human rights are very basic.

What are these human rights? That everyone from birth has the right to live, the right of existence. From birth I have a right to think. Of course, I have a brain; a severely mentally handicapped person may not be capable of possessing this right. I want to learn, and I have the right to an education. I have the right to find a mate, to get married. And so forth. This is what human rights are. In China we talk about human rights as if they were something fearful, a terrible scourge. In reality they are commonplace and basic, and everyone ought to acknowledge them.

But perhaps we are starting to view the spiritual aspects of civilization a little differently. We are beginning to see "liberty, equality, and fraternity" as a positive spiritual heritage. Over the last thirty years it seemed that every one of these good words—liberty, equality, fraternity, democracy, human rights—was labeled bourgeois by our propaganda. What on earth did that leave for us? Did we really oppose all of these things? If anything we should outdo bourgeois society and surpass its performance in human rights, not try to deny that human rights exist.

Democracy is based on recognizing the rights of every single individual. Naturally, not everyone wants the same thing, and therefore the desires of different individuals have to be mediated through a democratic process, to form a society, a nation, a collectivity. But it is only on the foundation of recognizing the humanity and the rights of each person that we can build democracy. However, when we talk about "extending democracy" here, it refers to your superiors "extending democracy" for you. This is a mistaken concept. This is not democracy.

"Loosening up" is even worse. If you think about it, what it implies is that everyone is tied up very tightly right now, but if you stay put, we'll loosen the rope a little bit and let you run around. The rope used to be one foot long, now we'll make it five feet. This is a top-down approach. Democracy is first and foremost the rights of individuals, and it is individuals that must struggle for them. Expression like "extending democracy" and "loosening up" would have you think that democracy can be bestowed upon us by those in charge. Nothing could be further from the truth.

The newspaper often refers to National People's Congress (NPC) representatives coming for an "inspection" tour. At times we speak sloppily ourselves, talking about "inspections." But think about it: Why should a visit from a People's Congress representative be called an inspection? We have become accustomed to talking this way, but it couldn't be more mistaken. These people are our elected representatives, who supposedly listen to us and speak on our behalf at the People's Congress, so why should their visit be called an "inspection"? Simply to use the word "inspection" reveals contempt for democracy. But of course, our NPC representatives do not actually represent our opinions, and in fact I don't even know who my representative is.

Why bother with this comparison? At one time I thought that it was perfectly natural for big officials from the NPC to come "inspect" us. But during the first half of this year, I was at the Institute for Advanced Study, in Princeton, New Jersey, doing research in cosmology. While I was there I received a mailing from our local member of Congress, explaining what Congress had been up to lately and what he had been doing during the session. He wrote quite a bit about his voting record, explaining what he'd voted for and against. He spoke about his achievements in office, how he had gone on the record for this or that, and why he had done so. In short, he was "reporting" to us. Although I was only a temporary resident, he had sent me this material, showing respect for anyone living in his district. He wanted us to know how he stood on the issues, and whether we agreed with him; if not, we could raise our concerns and he could turn around and express these in Congress. Despite representing a "false democracy," this man was clearly accounting to me for his actions.

Now what about our "true democracy"? I have never received any document telling me what issues my representative talked about, or how he or she voted at the NPC. I have never known what my representative supported or opposed, or what his or her accomplishments in office were. And the next time I have to go cast my vote for this person, I will still be totally in the dark. Our "true democracy" had better get on the ball until it can do better than their "false democracy"! I lived in China a long time without being aware of these problems. But when I went abroad and was finally able to see for myself, the contrast was glaringly obvious.

In democratic countries, democracy begins with the individual. *I* am the master, and the government is responsible to *me*. Citizens of democracies believe that the people maintain the government, paying taxes in return for services—running schools and hospitals, administering the city, providing for the public welfare. . . . A government depends on the taxpayers for support and therefore *has to be* responsible to its citizens. This is what people think in a democratic society. But here in China, we think the opposite way. If the government does something commendable, people say, "Oh, isn't the government great for providing us with public transportation." But this is really something it *ought* to be doing in exchange for our tax money.

In democratic societies, democracy and science—and most of us here are scientists—run parallel. Democracy is concerned with ideas about humanity, and science is concerned with nature. One of the distinguishing features of universities is the role of knowledge; we do research, we create new knowledge, we apply this knowledge to developing new products, and so forth. In this domain, within the sphere of science and the intellect, we make our own judgments based on our own independent criteria.

This is the distinguishing characteristic of a university. In Western society, universities are independent from the government, in the sense that even if the money to run the school is provided by the government, the basic decisions—regarding the content of courses, the standards for academic performance, the selection of research topics, the evaluation of results, and so on—are made by the schools themselves on the basis of values endemic to the academic community, and not by the government. At the same time, good universities in the West are also independent of big business. This is how universities must be. The intellectual realm must be independent and have its own values.

This is an essential guarantee of democracy. It is only when you know something independently that you are free from relying on authorities outside the intellectual domain, such as the government. Unfortunately, things are not this way in China. I have discussed this problem with educators. In the past, even during "the seventeen years" [1949 to 1966, the era prior to the Cultural Revolution], our universities were mainly engaged in producing tools, not in educating human beings. Education was concerned not with helping students to become critical thinkers but with producing docile instruments to be used by others. Chinese intellectuals need to insist on thinking for themselves and using their own judgment, but I'm afraid that even now we have not grasped this lesson.

In physics, for example, you'd assume that the evaluation of physicists is what matters in determining the merits of one's research. But in China, the work of physicists has long been subject to the evaluation of officials who know nothing about physics, and moreover we're ecstatic if they deign to say a few good words about us. This leads to a "docile tool" mentality that is still a major problem. Things are even worse in the social sciences. Naturally, we physicists check out the latest "philosophical" writings in order to keep ourselves out of hot water, but much of the writing of philosophers and social scientists in this country is little more than recapitulation of the latest official pronouncements. If our leaders were experts in philosophy—or experts in anything, for that matter—their words might carry some weight as academic authorities. But if they aren't philosophers, what is the value of quoting them? This is a worthless enterprise, and it doesn't prove a thing, but we quote the leaders nonetheless because we need the sanction of political authority before we dare to open our mouths.

The opposite relationship obtains in the West. At Princeton I met with some Chinese economists. They delved into their subject in whatever manner they saw fit, and they came up with whatever theories they found appropriate, without any interference. But contrary to our situation in China, when the American government was making policy, it requested the opinions of these academics; the government wanted to know if they had obtained any relevant results on which to base policy. What a far cry from our situation—officials needing the sanction of college professors to lend them credibility! This is what I mean by intellectual independence. Knowledge must be independent from power, the power of the state included. If knowledge is subservient to power, it is worthless.

When it comes to our fields of knowledge, we must think for ourselves and exercise our own judgment about what's right and wrong, and about truth, goodness, and beauty as well. We must refuse to cater to power. Only when we do this will Chinese intellectuals be transformed into genuine intellectuals, and our country have a chance to modernize and attain real democracy. This is my message to you today.

DENG XIAOPING, TAKING A CLEAR-CUT STAND AGAINST BOURGEOIS LIBERALIZATION

These remarks were made by Deng Xiaoping after student demonstrations had swept the country. They represent the increasingly hard line Deng adopted toward political protest, or "bourgeois liberalization," code words for any kind of political reform that challenged the Party's grip on power.

This selection was excerpted from Deng's speech to "leading members" of the Chinese Communist Party's Central Committee on December 30, 1986. It was originally published in Fundamental Issues in Present-Day China, 1987.

The recent student unrest is not going to lead to any major disturbances. But because of its nature it must be taken very seriously. Firm measures must be taken against any student who creates trouble at Tiananmen Square. The rules and regulations on marches and demonstrations promulgated by the Standing Committee of the Municipal People's Congress of Beijing have the force of law and should be resolutely enforced. No concessions should be made in this matter. In the beginning, we mainly used persuasion, which is as it should be in dealing with student demonstrators,. But if any of them disturb public order or violate the law, they must be dealt with unhesitatingly. Persuasion includes application of the law. When a disturbance breaks out in a place, it's because the leaders there didn't take a firm, clear-cut stand. This is not a problem that has arisen in just one or two places or in just the last couple of years; it is the result of failure over the past several years to take a firm, clear-cut stand against bourgeois liberalization. It is essential to adhere firmly to the Four Cardinal Principles; otherwise bourgeois liberalization will spread unchecked—and that has been the root cause of the problem. But this student unrest is also a good thing, insofar as it is a reminder to us.

I have read Fang Lizhi's speeches. He doesn't sound like a Communist Party member at all. Why do we keep people like him in the Party? He should be expelled, not just persuaded to quit. There are some people who still hold to their opinions but who say they will not get involved in student disturbances. That's fine. You can reserve your opinions, so long as you don't take part in activities against the Party or socialism. We have to admit that on the ideological and theoretical front both central and local authorities have been weak and have lost ground. They have taken a laissez-faire attitude toward bourgeois liberalization, so that good people find no support while bad people go wild. Good people don't dare to speak out, as if they were in the wrong. But they are not in the wrong at all. We must stand up for the Four Cardinal Principles and especially the People's Democratic Dictatorship. There is no way to ensure continued political stability and unity without the people's democratic dictatorship. People who confuse right and wrong, who turn black into white, who start rumors and spread slanders can't be allowed to go around with impunity stirring the masses up to make trouble. A few years ago we punished according to law some exponents of liberalization [including Wei Jingsheng] who broke the law. Did that bring discredit on us? No, China's image was not damaged. On the contrary, the prestige of our country is steadily growing.

In developing our democracy, we cannot simply copy bourgeois democracy, or introduce the system of a balance of three powers. I have often criticized people in power in the United States, saying that actually they have three governments. Of course, the American bourgeoisie uses this system in dealing with other countries, but when it comes to internal affairs, the three branches often pull in different directions, and that makes trouble. We cannot adopt such a system.

In carrying out the open policy, learning foreign technologies, and utilizing foreign capital, we mean to promote socialist construction, not to deviate from the socialist road. We intend to develop the productive forces, expand ownership by the entire people, and raise the people's income. The purpose of allowing some regions and some people to become prosperous before others is to enable all of them to prosper eventually. We have to make sure that there is no polarization of society—that's what socialism means. We work for common prosperity, but we permit certain disparities of income.

Without leadership by the Communist Party and without socialism, there is no future for China. This truth has been demonstrated in the past, and it will be demonstrated again in future. When we succeed in raising China's per capita GNP to $4,000 and everyone is prosperous, that will better demonstrate the superiority of socialism over capitalism, it will point the way for three-quarters of the world's population, and it will provide further proof of the correctness of Marxism. Therefore, we must confidently keep to the socialist road and uphold the Four Cardinal Principles.

We cannot do without dictatorship. We must not only affirm the need for it but exercise it when necessary. Of course, we must be cautious about resorting to dictatorial means and make as few arrests as possible. But if some people attempt to provoke bloodshed, what are we going to do about it? We should first expose their plot and then do our best to avoid shedding blood, even if that means some of our own people get hurt. However, ringleaders who have violated the law must be sentenced according to law. Unless we are prepared to do that, it will be impossible to put an end to disturbances. If we take no action and back down, we shall only have more trouble down the road.

The struggle against bourgeois liberalization will last for at least twenty years. Democracy can develop only gradually, and we cannot copy Western systems. If we did, that would only make a mess of everything. Our socialist construction can only be carried out under leadership, in an orderly way and in an environment of stability and unity. That's why I lay such emphasis on the need for high ideals and strict discipline. Bourgeois liberalization would plunge the country into turmoil once more. Bourgeois liberalization means rejection of the Party's leadership; there would be nothing to unite our 1 billion people, and the Party itself would lose all power to fight. A party like that would be no better than a mass organization; how could it be expected to lead the people in construction?

China must take its own road and build socialism with Chinese characteristics—that is the only way China can have a future. We must show foreigners that China's political situation is stable. If our country were plunged into disorder and our nation reduced to a heap of loose sand, how could we ever prosper? The reason the imperialists were able to bully us in the past was precisely that we were a heap of loose sand.

Disturbance can be checked if the leaders take a strong stand.

★ THE TIANANMEN SQUARE ★
DEMONSTRATIONS AND THE BEIJING MASSACRE

The third wave of popular protest during the Deng era arose in 1989, as thousands of students and ordinary people gathered in Tiananmen Square during mid-April to commemorate the death of Hu Yaobang, the liberal former general secretary of the Chinese Communist Party. It was not long, however, before the commemoration broadened into a full-blown protest movement, venting public anger over official corruption, the lack of freedom of expression, and the Party's dictatorial form of governance.

ORVILLE SCHELL,
CHINA'S SPRING

The Tiananmen Square demonstrations began just after the death of the former Party Chief Hu Yaobang on April 15 and ended with the Beijing Massacre on June 4. In the tradition of the May 4 demonstrations of 1919, when Chinese intellectuals had first taken to the streets in a protest movement that helped several generations of Chinese intellectuals define themselves politically, the 1989 demonstrations ended up being the largest and most prolonged mass outpouring of public disaffection in Chinese history. At their height over a million people from all walks of life flooded the square and paralyzed Beijing (as well as many other cities).

This selection was excerpted from an article in The New York Review of Books, *June 29, 1989, by coeditor Orville Schell, who was in Beijing until after the declaration of martial law.*

To stand, in early May, atop the Gate of Heavenly Peace, which guards the entrance of the Forbidden City, and look across the vast crowd of people jammed into Tiananmen Square was to have a historically new sense of what Mao called "the broad masses." It was to this ancient gate that Mao himself came on October 1, 1949, almost forty years before, to greet the adoring "broad masses" upon the defeat of the Nationalists of

Chiang Kai-shek and the founding of "New China." Just the day before, in a declaration for the First Plenary Session of the Chinese People's Political Consultative Conference, he had proclaimed that "we are holding this session at a time when the Chinese people have triumphed over their enemies, changed the face of their country, and founded the People's Republic of China. We the 475 million Chinese people have now stood up, and the future of our nation is infinitely bright."

It was to be a new beginning, which for many Chinese promised the hope of delivering their country from the warfare, corruption, economic ruin, and seemingly endless and humiliating failures that had plagued every aspect of its history for so long. Through the selfless devotion of its people to socialism and country, Mao promised that China would be uplifted from its status as the "poor man of Asia." He went on in his declaration to proclaim defiantly that his new government would "organize the overwhelming majority of the Chinese people in political, military, economic, cultural, and other organizations and put an end to the disorganized state characterizing the old China, so that the great collective strength of the masses may be tapped both to support the People's Government and the People's Liberation Army and to build a new China, independent, democratic, peaceful, unified, prosperous, and strong."

This past May, Mao's dreams for China seemed far away indeed. Not only had most of the main principles of his revolution been annulled by reformers, but now Tiananmen Square was filled with hundreds of thousands of dissident free thinkers deriding the very Party Mao had helped found and challenging the very notion of the "dictatorship of the proletariat." Morever, instead of marching in lockstep from a single direction with resolute socialist smiles as they had done in the past, people now were spilling spontaneously down the Avenue of Eternal Peace from both east and west, where, with flying banners extolling bourgeois democracy, they converged chaotically like two turbulent rivers, and in the confluence of the square became a roaring crowd that swirled and eddied in changing configurations. Even in back alleys and surrounding neighborhoods of the city one could hear their clamor reverberating like the roar from a faraway cataract. The only place I had ever heard a sound like the one that rose from the vast square below me was in a crowded football stadium in America.

This historic upheaval started in mid-April with the death of former Party Chief Hu Yaobang, who had been accused of being too liberal in his treatment of intellectuals and students, and was unceremoniously dismissed by Deng Xiaoping in January 1987 shortly after demonstrations for democracy—relatively mild ones involving perhaps 50,000 people—had last shaken China. This time a group of students from several schools of higher education in Beijing, particularly Beijing University and Beijing Normal University, seized on Hu's death as a symbolic moment to vent their long-pent-up dissatisfaction with the slowness of political reform and the lack of freedom of expression in China, and the endemic corruption that has riddled the Party and government. When they marched on Tiananmen Square to mark Hu's passing, they were joined by about 20,000 other young people. If nothing further had happened, this one demonstration alone against the Deng regime would have been a historic event.

But the students did not stop here. After several more protest demonstrations in the square, the new student movement faced its first direct challenge from the government. On April 27 it was attacked in the official Party paper, the *People's Daily*, in an editorial that called the protests an "organized conspiracy to sow chaos" led by "people with ulterior motives," whose purpose was "to poison minds, create national turmoil, and sabotage the nation's political stability." In response some 150,000 angry students defied government prohibitions and marched again. After several tense moments, they succeeded in peacefully breaking through police lines and triumphantly reached Tiananmen Square once more. But what was so striking about this march was that all along their route from the Haidian section of Beijing, for the first time the students were greeted by onlookers who not only cheered them but gave them free food and drink. Never had the capital seen such bold support for political opposition. A Chinese journalist told an American reporter, "It was the first time in history that ordinary Chinese people won such a great victory. The date will live in history."

On May 4 there was another march, again of more than 100,000 students, and from then on, Tiananmen Square, the symbolic heartland of the capital and the country, became a nonstop theater of dissent. The next important act began on May 13, when, in anticipation of Mikhail Gorbachev's visit two days later, 1,000 students entered the square to go on a hunger strike. The large crowds that immediately began gathering to support them would have been beyond the imaginings of Mao, who built the one-hundred-acre square for rituals of loyalty, not discord. They wore three-piece suits and neckties, headbands, and acid-washed jeans, T-shirts inscribed with the words "Science and Democracy," short skirts and funny hats, and they created an almost festive atmosphere in the square in spite of the seriousness of the fasting students' cause. The crowds seemed to become more intense as they carried on discussions and made speeches, and each day the number of people grew larger, and it included more and more diverse groups until, by the third week in May, they became one of the largest and most representative bodies of urban Chinese society ever assembled in one place.

The students' immediate demands were at this point quite simple. They wanted direct talks with high-ranking leaders, the right to establish an independent student union, and the retraction of the editorial in the *People's Daily* of April 27 denouncing them for "conspiracy" and "sabotage."

Indeed, talking to those student protesters at the time, one had little sense of them as revolutionaries bent on deposing the government or Party, or even of their having unappeasable resentments toward the leadership. What was most noticeable about them was not their iconoclasm but their yearning to be listened to and taken seriously by the government and leaders they were criticizing. Their demand that the Party retract its hard-line editorial reflected the prevailing sentiment among many students: far from wishing to be seen as unpatriotic troublemakers, they just wanted the government to acknowledge that they, too, were constructive citizens, albeit critical ones, with something to contribute. The Western reporters visiting the square, more familiar with hostile student protesters elsewhere who view their governments and police as unalterable enemies, were often startled and even sometimes touched by the sense of self-sacrifice, and by the sweet and almost naive moderation they found among these Chinese students, many of whom had even earnestly made out their wills in case the government reacted violently.

Had Deng Xiaoping, Premier Li Peng, and the other top leaders been able to compromise even by acknowledging the editorial in the *People's Daily* as a mistake, there would have been an immediate outpouring of goodwill from the students, and it is not unlikely that the gesture would have headed off the precipitous events that followed. But the editorial had, according to reliable reports, been written by Deng Xiaoping himself, who, in spite of his lack of official titles, remained China's behind-the-scenes supreme leader; therefore, according to the still prevailing convention of Communist leadership, it could not be reversed.

Deng and Premier Li and their allies were not only preoccupied with Gorbachev's visit, they were unaccustomed to redressing grievances articulated with such forcefulness from people at the bottom. Zhao Ziyang, the more liberal General Secretary of the Chinese Communist

Party, and some of his supporters, took a more conciliatory line than Deng and Li Peng, and even urged that talks with student leaders take place. Even though Zhao had in recent months been attempting to reassure the Politburo of his loyalty to the Party by taking an increasingly intolerant view of political dissent himself, he was still viewed by hardliners with great suspicion for advocating that Chinese economic and political reform move at a quicker pace.

Deadlocked at the top, the leadership was simply unable to respond to the events taking place outside the Great Hall of the People and to student demands. And so, with each passing day, the crowd in Tiananmen Square grew, until by Wednesday, May 17, five days after the fasting students had arrived, more than a million people gathered there. At this point Li Peng finally agreed to speak with representatives of the hunger strikers in the Great Hall of the People. But when he actually met with the de facto student leaders—who included two brazen and unrepentant twenty-year-olds, Wuer Kaixi, from Beijing Normal University, and Wang Dan, from Beijing University—during a bizarre nationally televised "dialogue" on May 18, he very quickly became intransigent. Refusing even to make reference to the demands of the protesters, Li lectured the fasting students, several of whom had come directly from the hospital clad in pajamas and were breathing through oxygen tubes, saying, "We have to defend socialism. . . . I don't care whether you are happy to listen to this or not."

Li and Deng and most of the other Party leaders seemed incapable of understanding that the students, by articulating their own grievances, had touched a nerve of disaffection with the current government that ran through almost all of Chinese society. Being the first to protest publicly, the students had inadvertently become representatives of the as yet unarticulated sentiments of other groups as well. Intellectuals were frustrated by the slow pace of political reform, by restrictions on what they could publish, and by their dismally low salaries. Workers on fixed incomes were angry at the way their buying power had been reduced by inflation, which had been running at well over 30 percent. Students in China were fed up with squalid living conditions, dull curriculums, and the government's refusal to make adequate investments in education. And students returning from abroad were dispirited to find that the older cadres often had all too little use for them or their skills and were more interested in protecting their positions and saving face than in modernizing and developing China.

Young people were angry at being assigned to dead-end jobs or being without jobs at all. Engineers, doctors, economists, teachers, and other professionals who still worked for the state were distressed that their counterparts in private enterprises earned ten, sometimes twenty times more than they did. And virtually everybody one talked to was fed up with the rampant corruption and nepotism that had invaded all branches of government and the lack of possibilities for advancement for people who lacked "connections."

Walking in the square on Sunday, May 14, just after the hunger strikers arrived, I remember wondering if the disaffection of other groups in the city would not soon cause them to join in the protest. That the students would link up in protest with other parts of society was the Party's undoubted nightmare. Activist intellectuals and journalists had in the past months already begun circulating and signing petitions calling on the government to release political prisoners and to grant more freedom of expression. What if they began to take up the cause of workers?

By Monday, May 15, as more and more students began flooding into the square, a kindling point seemed to be reached. That night, after Gorbachev's arrival, a large and spontaneous crowd of local private street vendors, unemployed young people, workers, and people who were obviously poor suddenly came together in front of the Museum of Chinese History and Revolution, on the east side of the square. Beneath a crude banner proclaiming themselves simply as *shimin*, or "citizens," they began enthusiastically to march in a procession around the square as onlookers roared in approval.

By Tuesday more and more groups of intellectuals, journalists, and teachers were joining in. By Wednesday hotel employees, hospital nurses, middle- and grade-school students, and even sizable groups from China's national airline, the Foreign Ministry, the police, and the Party's school for cadres had begun to appear. And by Thursday bus and taxi drivers, employees from the state railroad, workers from factories, even night soil collectors and peasants from the outskirts began to pour into the city and to drive with almost reckless abandon through the streets in commandeered trucks and buses. For all that anyone could see, the government had lost control of the capital. Moreover news reports claimed that the protest had spread to almost every major city in China.

As the size of the crowd kept growing, student organizers suddenly found themselves forced to become amateur urban planners, traffic policemen, communications specialists, accountants, and logistics experts. With a rapidity and skill that amazed everyone, they soon succeeded in organizing the tens of thousands of protesters camped at the center of the square into a city within a city. They used plastic packing string and rows of seated students to cordon off the hunger strikers who lay under tent flies, and they laid out broad "life-line" roads running through the center of the crowd so that ambulances could get collapsed students to city hospitals; they also set up a medical dispensary, established a communications headquarters with battery-powered loudspeakers, organized print shops with silk-screen machines on which leaflets could be duplicated, a finance office to handle contributions, encouraged groups of students to distribute all the water and drinks and food that were being contributed in great quantities by local vendors and stores. They even devised a system of passes to prevent unauthorized people from entering roped-off areas where the students who had emerged as the leaders of the moment met to discuss strategy.

Everywhere there were flags inscribed with the names of the protesters' universities and academic departments, and banners emblazoned with pro-democracy and antigovernment slogans fluttering in the spring breeze. The place looked more like a fairground than the site of an insurrection, and there was a palpable feeling of relief at the idea of being, at least for now, so defiantly beyond the reach of the Party. Until Thursday, May 18, when the first torrential downpour fell, so balmy was the spring weather, so elated were those in the square, that no task seemed impossible.

By then, thousands of volunteer nurses and doctors had arrived to take care of the hunger strikers. Concerned professors had come to shore up the spirits of their fasting students. Parents who came in hopes of dissuading their sons and daughters from continuing their fast left in tears, talking about their newfound pride in their children. Outside the space that had been roped off for the hunger strikers, small groups gathered everywhere in tight clumps to listen to political debates. Older Chinese who had in the past suffered torments at the hands of the Party watched and listened with cautious curiosity, marveling at the temerity of this new generation of Chinese, who suddenly seemed so bold and confident in their challenge to authority. Everyone knew that the world was now watching China. Even Dan Rather, in his khaki-colored Banana Republic jacket, had become a regular visitor to the square. The sense of accomplishment and pride seemed to serve as a powerful cure for the feelings of hopelessness that had been such a dominant feature of China's landscape for the last few years. Never in fifteen years of visiting Beijing had I seen so many people smiling and looking happy as in Tiananmen Square this May.

If one needed proof that things were at least for the moment different, all one had to do was leave a bicycle unlocked in the square and find that no one had stolen it. Even *liumang*, or hooligans, were reported to have gotten together and agreed to stop their petty thievery in favor of working with students. I saw some of them helping to direct traffic and collecting food. That there were virtually no incidents of crime in the square only contributed to the heady feeling of openness and triumph pervading the crowd.

But this feeling of ebullience also created a strangely unreal atmosphere in which some of the protesters seemed tempted to believe that nothing could now hurt them. One young man only half-jokingly told me, "We are like the Boxers of 1900. We believe that not even bullets can pierce us!"

It was, indeed, hard to imagine any force powerful enough to disperse so many well-organized and confident people. How could there be danger when lovers were walking arm in arm, and entire families were riding through the middle of the square on their three-wheel bicycle carts with their wide-eyed children sucking Popsicles? In this self-contained universe where with impunity one could read political leaflets denouncing the Party, or listen to political speeches in which the leadership was reviled as hopelessly corrupt and incompetent, it was hard even to imagine the outside world, much less a military crackdown.

Although the young protesters were demonstrating in the name of democracy and freedom of expression rather than Maoist socialism, there was a suggestion in the air of the same insular confidence that former Red Guards describe as having possessed them during the Cultural Revolution, when China was as much a world unto itself as Tiananmen Square was now. Insulated for a historical instant from the immense difficulties of actually changing China, young protesters—and even Western journalists—were all too easily swept up in the immediacy of what was happening around them. In the intoxication of the moment it was not difficult to believe that a state of revolutionary immortality had been attained and that some important but indefinable success was just around the corner. The atmosphere, however illusory it might ultimately prove to be, recalled Woodstock in its nonviolence and sense of giddy liberation, and the Paris Commune in the conviction among the demonstrators that the "people" had finally risen up to secure the country's heartland from forces of reaction.

It was this infectious new sense of elation and invincibility that later seemed to give ordinary people the courage and conviction to sit down in front of armored vehicles. But the protest also had its own restrained tone, partly because the self-sacrifice of fasting became central to its symbolism. So far, at least, the students had avoided the kind of violence and brutality that was inflicted on many of their own families during the Cultural Revolution. In this sense their peaceful hunger strike was a hopeful break with China's long history of politics through brute force.

As the days progressed, students continued to keep the situation in the square organized and to persevere in their nonviolent approach. But as the students became increasingly frustrated and angered by the government's refusal even to consider their demands, the slogans on the banners became bolder and people became more irreverent. Whereas in the first few days they modestly declared "Democracy Is Our Common Dream" and "Long Live Democracy—Long Live Freedom," by the time martial law was declared at the end of the week, on May 20, people began carrying effigies of Li Peng in a Nazi uniform and slogans proclaiming, "Deng Xiaoping, Your Brain Is Addled! Retire and Go Back to Playing Bridge!"

The Beijing students may have had more support from adults than in any other student rebellion to take place in modern times. "Of course, I am for the students," a scholarly looking elderly man told me almost indignantly after he saw me observing him giving a fairly large amount of money to one of the many student bands that roved the city asking for donations. "They say and do what I have only dared think. They're the ones who represent my feelings, not the government." Merchants sent in food, drinks, clothing, sun hats, rain gear, paper, medicine, whatever they could offer. Pedicab drivers hauled students to bus stops free of charge. Cab drivers, normally among the surliest and greediest people in Chinese cities, were suddenly giving free rides and decorating their cabs with graffiti. One read, "Why Has Heaven Given the Soviet Union a Gorbachev, While It Has Only Given Us a Deng Xiaoping?" and "Strangle the Dictator Li Peng."

Even Beijing's citizens, long notorious for being among the most ungracious in the world, began to act more politely. There was less pushing and shoving in lines, people began to say "Excuse me" if they bumped into you on the street, or to say "Thank you" for some small gesture of deference. Drivers no longer cut you off rudely in traffic. People contributed effusively to students with collection boxes. Everyone, it seemed, wanted to do something for the students. How long would it last? When I asked this question of a young man with a headband inscribed with the words "Democracy or Death," he said, "We will never be silent again! They will never again succeed in intimidating us to submission."

In retrospect his statement sounds overblown, but at that moment, it had a convincing ring. In such an environment, where people had been saying and doing the unthinkable for so many days, where they had been openly defying the government, the police, and then, finally, the military itself, it seemed almost unimaginable that the old stifling order that had made Chinese feel eternally afraid of speaking out could ever again reassert itself. Even the façade of elephantine socialist buildings that ringed the square and had once looked so imposing now seemed clunky and out of date. The massive Great Hall of the People, which had been built during the 1950s by thousands of volunteers working around the clock for a year, now, with an enormous crowd moving about in front of it, looked unimposing and old. The Museum of Chinese History and Revolution opposite it was draped with so many banners of different sizes proclaiming democracy and freedom that it looked as if someone were using it to put laundry out to dry. And even Mao's Memorial Mausoleum—closed until further notice—now looked forlorn.

Although the students tried to make their demands specific by calling, for instance, for dialogue with government leaders or for the retraction of the April 27 editorial, when pressed to be more precise about their vision of reform or their notions of how democracy might work in China, they tended to become vague and even flustered. What they did know was that they wanted basic human rights guaranteed by the Chinese constitution and still denied them—freedom of the press, speech, assembly, and travel—and that they did not feel represented by the current government. As one student only half-facetiously said, "I don't know exactly what we want, but we want more of it."

What was unprecedented was not the ability of students to suggest a new political system for China but the fact that they had succeeded in standing up in such numbers to oppose the discredited vision that China's old guard revolutionaries still proclaimed as workable. Even if the Tiananmen movement ended up winning nothing at all by way of its specific demands, it was still changing the existing chemistry of relations between the Chinese people and their government in ways that would deeply affect the future of politics in China. Through the highly contagious symbolic act of taking to the streets, Chinese had declared that their days of waiting compliantly for the Party to reform itself democratically from the top were over. In doing so Chinese intellectuals and students, and perhaps other key segments of urban society as well, gained a new sense of independence, confidence, and strength, qualities that were quickly discernible to anyone who entered the square.

At last, I heard people say, China had done something right. It had spawned one of the largest and best organized nonviolent political protest movements the world had ever seen. It was no small wonder, then, that for a moment at least, Chinese, without even quite knowing what they had accomplished, felt a new and exhilarating sense of self-respect that would be central to their defiance when Li Peng finally declared martial law on May 20 and troops began arriving on the outskirts of Beijing to put down the protest that he patronizingly described as "anarchy."

Once again the Chinese astounded the world, and probably themselves as well. Instead of a pitched battle in the streets between soldiers and people, the global village of television viewers watched as students, along with China's *laobaixing*, or ordinary people, brought the entire military caravan to a grinding halt by sitting down in front of the advancing vehicles. Then, instead of excoriating the soldiers as the enemy, bands of civilians formed on the spot, only a few of them students, and offered drinks and bowls of soup to the weary and doubtless frightened men. They read to them from newspapers, hoping that the same kind of moral didacticism that had stood Chinese from Confucius to Mao in such good stead might now also prove effective. And when no troops reached the heart of the city, it was more tempting than ever to believe that the Chinese citizen-protesters might continue to defy all the laws of Realpolitik and somehow bring about a new kind of peaceful revolution against armed dictatorship. The Party leaders who had for so many years been able to count on the Chinese people to obey them and follow them out of respect now could not be certain that people would follow orders, even out of fear of retaliation.

On May 18, just two days before martial law was declared, I went down to the square one last time before leaving Beijing. Standing on a bicycle cart just in front of the portrait of Mao in Tiananmen Square, I watched while hundreds of thousands of newly arrived demonstrators surged down the Avenue of Eternal Peace, many of them students who had just come from the train station after traveling from remote parts of China. What seemed incontrovertible was that even if the Party were somehow able to get rid of the million-odd demonstrators everywhere around me, even if Deng Xiaoping and whatever allies he chose were able to hold on to power, and even if all the visible signs of the huge protest were removed from Tiananmen Square, still China would not be the same as before.

1989 WALL POSTERS

Because the major organs of the Chinese media have always been under official Party control, whenever spontaneous protest movements have arisen, those wishing to communicate their ideas to the public have been forced to do so by means of dazibao, *or "big-character wall posters," put up around Beijing and other cities. As so often in the past, during the spring of 1989 university campuses and other major meeting places quickly became festooned with such posters.*

The first of these selections was excerpted from a wall poster that appeared on May 2 at Beijing Normal University, and the second from a poster that appeared on May 17 at Beijing University. They were published in Cries for Democracy: Writings and Speeches from the 1989 Democracy Movement, *edited by Han Minzhu (1990).*

Pluralism in the hands of one-party leadership is like a free man dancing in chains. If we do want democracy, it is necessary that we destroy the one-party autocracy or establish genuine democratic institutions capable of truly representing the interests of all social strata (such as nongovernment-controlled labor unions). And if we want democracy and freedom, the only thing to do is to give legislative power to the people. Only by following the principle of legislation by the people can there be true freedom of press and true freedom of speech.

I believe that the only way to change the current political situation in China is to fight for democracy—to emphasize that all people are equal before the law, and that no one is above the law. Political change requires that the right of legislation truly belongs to the people. It means that laws will not be made by a small handful of government officials, and that they shall reflect the common will of the people.

The primary objective of legislation is freedom and equality. Only when people equally abide by laws that reflect their common wishes can there be freedom. Only when genuine rule by law replaces rule by autocracy, which is monarchy in disguise, can there be genuine democracy, and can it be possible for our society to overcome the defects of feudalism. The government is only an administrator of the people's sovereign will, an institution to which the people grant administrative power and entrust law enforcement power. If the National People's Congress is truly to reflect the people's will, the electoral procedures for its representatives must be changed.

In the absence of a genuine people's supervisory organ, a government [with unchecked power to] implement the law will become corrupt.

Let us greet the coming of a genuinely democratic, free spring with our actions!

—By a Nonrevolutionary of
Beijing Normal University, May 2, 1989

Reflections on the Chinese Communist Party

The Chinese Communist Party has been an excellent carrier of the genes for dictatorship and bureaucracy; the latter is not only a true-to-the-original copy of the former but also its logical extension. Today, after so many years, the Party still maintains the organizational form that existed when our nation had not yet been founded, a structure shaped by security considerations and based on military models. [This structure] stipulates that "the individual obeys the organization, subordinates obey their superiors, the entire Party obeys the Central Committee, and the Central Committee obeys one person or a few persons." In short, "to obey orders is a duty." How could this type of closed organization be anything but a breeding ground for dictatorships, patriarchies, and personality cults? . . . In a country such as ours, it is not at all surprising that, under the lengthy centralized leadership of a single party which founded itself on such principles and methods, dictatorship and bureaucracy should arise again and again. Nowadays, many people are placing their hopes in the possibility that one or two wise and capable individuals might arise from within the Party. The idea is absolutely terrifying; have we not had enough of handing over the lives of a billion people to one or two leaders? So many times has the Party said the simple phrase "in the end, our great Party always brings order to chaos," but this is nothing but [a justification for] at the cost of several decades of their lives for hundreds of millions of people (half their lives); the cost of the lives of hundreds and thousands of others, and the cost of pushing history back several decades, or several hundreds of years (as did the Cultural Revolution in China, and Stalinist revisionism in the Soviet Union). Now, if a party has been committing unpardonable errors for most of its time, and yet we continue to place the fate of a billion people into its hands instead of their own, how does it differ from gambling? . . .

The Party, instead of establishing its political program through national elections, and instead of having its will expressed through the mechanism of the National People's Congress, has placed itself high above what the Constitution has designated as the supreme organ of state power—the National People's Congress—and the supreme administrative body—the State Council. If the National People's Congress and the State Council are its machines, what's the point of adding the word "supreme" to them? And if the "representative assembly" that the people has elected is only the Party's machine, isn't the phrase "all power resides with the people" superfluous? Better just to get it over with and acknowledge that all power lies in the Party and the "Party's Gestapo." Indeed, when a few statements of a certain individual from the Party, who is neither an organ of state power nor an administrative body, can for a few years determine the directions or policy decisions of a country, does this not alarm us and make us bristle with anger? . . .

We should recognize that the people and the national government come first and that the Party comes last. It is absolutely not the other way round, where we recognize not the people and the government but a Party which represents nothing at all!

—Big-character poster
at Beijing University, May 17, 1989

A HUNGER STRIKE MANIFESTO

As it became evident that moderate students would be unable to negotiate an agreement with liberal leaders in the government and as mass interest in the Tiananmen Square demonstrations began to ebb at the beginning of May, more radical students hit upon a hunger strike as a means of refocusing attention on their demands. On May 13, several thousand students marched into Tiananmen Square and began a fast. The effect was galvanic.

By the beginning of June, however, the student movement was once again falling into disarray with many students in favor of leaving the square. As interest flagged four young intellectuals—the pop singer Hou

Dejian, the literary critic Liu Xiaobo, and two friends—began a hunger strike of their own. Their joint manifesto, largely penned by Liu, was one of the most searching statements to come out of the student movement.

This selection was excerpted from the manifesto as published in Cries for Democracy: Writing and Speeches from the 1989 Democracy Movement, *edited by Han Minzhu (1990).*

We are on a hunger strike! We protest! We appeal! We repent!

Death is not what we seek; we are searching for true life.

In the face of the irrational, high-handed military violence of the Li Peng government, Chinese intellectuals must dispose of their age-old disease, passed down over centuries, of being spineless, of merely speaking and not acting. By means of action, we protest against military control; by means of action, we call for the birth of a new political culture; and by means of action, we express our repentance for the wrongs that have been the doing of our own age-old weakness. The Chinese nation has fallen behind; for this, each one of us bears his share of responsibility.

Our hunger strike is no longer a petition, but a protest against martial law and military control! We advocate the use of peaceful means to further democratization in China and to oppose any form of violence. Yet we do not fear brute force; through peaceful means, we will demonstrate the resilience of the democratic strength of the people, and smash the undemocratic order held together by bayonets and lies.

The thousands of years of Chinese history have been a story of violence met with violence, of learning to hate and to be hated. Entering the modern era, this "enemy consciousness" [where one separates the enemy from the people] has become the legacy of the Chinese. The post-1949 slogan "Take class struggle as the key link [to all human struggles and as the motive force of history]" has pushed to the extreme this traditional mentality of hatred, this enemy consciousness, and the practice of meeting violence with violence. This time, the imposition of military control is but another manifestation of the political culture of "class struggle." It is because of this that we are on a hunger strike; we appeal to the Chinese people that from now on they gradually discard and eradicate [our] enemy consciousness and mentality of hatred, and completely forsake [our] "class struggle" form of political culture, for hatred generates only violence and autocracy. We must use a democratic spirit of tolerance and cooperation to begin the construction of democracy in China. For democratic politics is a politics without enemies and without a mentality of hatred, a politics of consultation, discussion, and decision by vote, based on mutual respect, mutual tolerance, and mutual accommodation. Since as premier, Li Peng has made grave mistakes, he should be made to resign according to democratic processes.

However, Li Peng is not our enemy; even if he steps down, he would still enjoy the rights that citizens should have, even the right to adhere to his mistaken beliefs. We appeal to all Chinese, from those in the government down to every ordinary citizen, to give up the old political culture and begin a new one. We ask that the government end martial law at once. We ask that both the students and the government once again turn to peaceful negotiation and consultative dialogue to resolve their differences.

The present student movement has received an unprecedented amount of sympathy, understanding, and support from all sectors of society. The implementation of martial law has turned a student movement into a national democracy movement. Undeniable, however, is the fact that many of those who have supported the students have acted out of humanitarian sympathy and discontent with the government; they have lacked a citizen's sense of political responsibility. Because of this, we appeal to all [members] of [Chinese] society gradually to drop the attitude of [merely] being onlookers and simply expressing sympathy. We appeal to you to acquire a sense of citizen consciousness. First of all, this citizen consciousness is the awareness that [all citizens] possess political rights. Every citizen must have the self-confidence that one's own political rights are equal to the rights of the premier. Next, citizen consciousness is a consciousness of rationalized political involvement—of political responsibility—not just a sense of justice and sympathy. It means that every man or woman cannot only express sympathy and support but also must become directly involved in the construction of democracy. Finally, citizen consciousness means self-awareness of one's responsibilities and obligations. In the construction of social politics bound by rationality and law, every one of us must contribute his part; likewise, where social politics are irrational and lawless, each bears his share of responsibility. Voluntary participation in the political life of society and voluntary acceptance of one's responsibilities are the inescapable duties of every citizen. The Chinese people must see that, in democratized politics, everyone is first and foremost a citizen, and then a student, a professor, a worker, a cadre, or a soldier.

For thousands of years, Chinese society has followed a vicious cycle of overthrowing an old emperor just to put up a new one. History has shown that the fall of a leader who has lost the people's support or the rise of a leader who has the backing of the people cannot solve China's essential political problem. What we need is not a perfect savior but a sound democratic system. We thus call for the following: (1) all [sectors of] society should establish lawful, autonomous citizens' organizations, and gradually develop these organizations into citizens' political forces that will act to check government policy making, for the quintessence of democracy is the curbing and balancing of power. We would rather have ten monsters that are mutually restrained than one angel of absolute power; (2) by impeaching leaders who have committed serious errors, [we should] gradually establish a sound system for the impeachment of officials. Whoever rises and whoever falls is not important; what is important is how one ascends to, or falls from, power. An undemocratic procedure of appointment and dismissal can only result in dictatorship.

In the course of the present movement, both the government and the students have made mistakes. The main mistake of the government was that, conditioned by the outmoded political ideology of "class struggle," it has chosen to take a stand in opposition to [the position of] the great majority of students and residents, thus causing continuous intensification of the conflict. The main mistake of the students is that, because the organizing of their own organizations left much to be desired, many undemocratic elements have appeared in the very process of striving for democracy. We therefore call on both the government and students to conduct levelheaded self-examination. It is our belief that, on the whole, the greater fault for the present situation lies with the government. Actions such as demonstrations and hunger strikes are democratic ways through which people express their wishes; they are completely legal and reasonable. They are anything but "turmoil." Yet the government ignored the basic rights of the people granted by the Constitution; on the basis of its autocratic political ideology, it labeled the student movement as "turmoil." This stand led to a series of wrong decisions, which then led to the growth of the movement and rising antagonism. The real catalyst for the turmoil is therefore the government's wrong decisions, errors of a gravity no less than [those committed in] the "Cultural Revolution." It was only due to the great restraint shown by the students and people of Beijing and to impassioned appeals from all sectors of society—including the Party, the government, and the military—that wide-scale bloodshed has been avoided. In view of this, the government must admit to and examine these mistakes it has made. We believe that it is not yet too late to correct the mistakes. The government should draw some painful lessons from this major movement. It should learn to become accustomed to listening to the voice of the people, to allowing people to express their desires through the exercise of the constitutionally granted rights, and to governing the country in a democratic way. This nationwide movement for democracy is a lesson for the government in how to govern society by means of democracy and the rule of law.

The students' mistakes are mainly manifested in the internal chaos of their organizations and the lack of efficient and democratic procedures. Although their goal is democracy, their means and procedures for achieving democracy are not democratic. Their theories call for democracy, but their handling of specific problems is not democratic. Their lack of cooperative spirit and the sectarianism that has caused their forces to neutralize each other have resulted in all their policies coming to naught. More faults can be named: financial chaos; material waste; an excess of emotion and a lack of reason; too much of the attitude that they are privileged, and not enough of the belief in equality; and so on. In the last hundred years, the great majority of the Chinese people's struggles for democracy have remained at the level of ideological battles and slogan shouting. Enlightenment is much talked about, but little is said about the actual running of a democracy. Goals are discussed, but not the means, the procedures, or process through which they will be achieved. We believe that the actual realization of a democratic political system lies in the democratization of the process, of the means, and the procedures of operating such a system. For this, we appeal to the Chinese people to forsake this tradition of "empty democracy," a democracy of only ideology, slogans, and [abstract] goals, and begin the construction of the process, means, and procedures for the operation of a democracy. We ask you to transform a democratic movement focused on ideological enlightenment into a movement of democracy in action; this must be done by starting with each specific matter. We call for the students to begin a self-examination that should focus on the overhaul and reorganization of the student groups in Tiananmen Square.

The government's grave mistakes in its approach were also reflected in its use of the term "a handful of persons" [to refer to participants in pro-democracy protests]. Through our hunger strike, we would like to tell the media, at home and abroad, who this so-called handful of persons [really] is: they are not [a bunch of] students but citizens with a sense of political responsibility who have voluntarily participated in the present nationwide democratic movement led by the students. All we have done and all we are doing is lawful and reasonable. In this combat of opposing political cultures, of character cultivation and of moral strength, the hunger strikers intend to use their wisdom and actions to make the government feel shamed, to make it admit and correct its wrongdoings. We also intend to encourage the autonomous student organizations to improve themselves daily in accordance with democratic and legal procedures.

It must be acknowledged that democratic governance of the country is unfamiliar to every Chinese citizen. And every Chinese citizen, including the highest officials in the Party and the government, must learn it from the bottom up. In this learning process, mistakes by both the government and the people are inevitable. The key is to admit mistakes when they become evident and to correct them after they appear; to learn from our mistakes and turn them into positive lessons; and, during the continuous process of rectifying our mistakes, to learn gradually how to govern the country democratically.

> *We don't have enemies!*
> *Don't let hatred and violence poison wisdom and the process of*
>   *democratization in China!*
> *We all must carry out a self-examination!*
> *Everyone bears responsibility for the backwardness of China!*
> *We are above all citizens!*
> *We are not seeking death!*
> *We are searching for true life!*

YANG JIANLI, THE BEIJING MASSACRE

On the night of May 19, 1989, Premier Li Peng declared martial law. But when People's Liberation Army troops tried to enter the city to clear Tiananmen Square, they were halted by tens of thousands of unarmed citizens blocking the streets.

On the night of June 3–4, a much stronger and more determined force was assembled and commanded to retake the square at all costs. When this assault force again met with determined popular resistance, troops opened fire, initiating what has come to be known as the Beijing Massacre.

This selection was excerpted from an eyewitness account of one of the bloodiest confrontations, as troops moved from the west down the Avenue of Eternal Peace (Chang'an Avenue) toward Tiananmen Square. Its author, Yang Jianli, was a University of California, Berkeley, doctoral student in mathematics at the time. It was originally published in Children of the Dragon: The Story of Tiananmen Square, *by Human Rights in China (1990).*

When we got to the square, we saw no sign of panic. By now, after all the excitement, I decided that I had lost my fear. I said to H., "This afternoon, I was still afraid of being hit by a billy club. But now I think we ought to fight with them. Let's get ourselves a pair of clubs. Tear gas and water cannons won't kill anyone. It's summer, you know." While I was going on in this vein, I heard a sharp noise from the west side of Chang'an Avenue. "A gunshot!" I said. Suddenly my heart was in my throat. I couldn't speak. A middle-aged woman shouted at us, "Don't go any farther! They've already started firing!"

"Let's turn back," I said to myself, but H. was saying "Hurry up!" and pedaling toward the gunfire. I forced myself to follow him.

Gradually, we saw that there were fires at the Xidan intersection. The buses that people set up yesterday as barricades were now on fire. Tanks and truckloads of soldiers armed with machine guns were rolling in one after another toward the square. At the intersection, we heard perhaps a thousand people shouting, "Down with fascism!" We threw our bicycles aside and joined the crowd. We made our way to the very front and began shouting together with the rest, "Down with fascism!" Flashes spouted from the muzzles of the soldiers' rifles. We ran back a bit and threw ourselves onto the pavement. "Did they really fire?" I said to H. "I still can't believe it." Some people continued to stand up, saying nonchalantly, "Don't be frightened, they're only using rubber bullets." Before they had finished speaking I heard someone scream, "Look out! There's a cart coming through!" Two men with gunshot wounds were being carried away. Someone swore and gasped, "They aren't rubber bullets at all!" One man had been shot in the leg; the other was hit in the stomach and died on the cart. We stood beside the cart, staring at him, and burst into tears. All this time the army trucks kept on passing in front of us in a line. As the crowd shouted, "Fuck you, Deng Xiaoping, fuck you!" it pressed on toward the middle of the road. Suddenly there was more gunfire, and we dropped to the ground again; my heart jumped from sheer fright.

A voice screamed, "Get another cart!" I felt a great rage well up in me. I began gathering bricks and throwing them at the trucks. "Let's get them!" I shouted. Then the soldiers fired again, and another three or four men were carried away. H. wept and shouted, "They're dead, but we're still alive. . . . I'll fight with them to the death!" He started running forward. But I pulled him back tightly. "Don't die for nothing!" I said.

"Let's get out of here," I heard someone say from below. I looked up the street and saw twenty to thirty soldiers coming at us with fixed bayonets. Two tear-gas shells exploded, and a thick, yellowish smoke quickly spread through the crowd. I began to cough; our noses and eyes ran. My hands hurt, and I lost my voice.

Gradually the smoke cleared. An endless line of army trucks had now jammed Chang'an Avenue. For a moment there was complete silence. Then, little by little, the people collected again and inched their way toward the trucks until they could touch them. They begged, they cursed, they swore. "You are the People's Army, you can't open fire on the people!" some protested. Others were sarcastic, saying, "You're very good at killing unarmed civilians! You've turned yourselves into killing machines for those old bastards! But when they finally die, you'll all be executed!" Then a hoarse voice began to lead the crowd in singing the "Internationale." We all wept. The soldiers were stone-faced; you could see from their eyes the stupidity, the apathy, the cruelty. The crowd grew angry again and shouted, "Down with the fascists!" and "Bury Yang Shangkun's army!" Some people from the back passed us bricks and stones. An officer took out a pistol and shot a young man just a few feet away, and I stood there and watched him die in front of me.

Another young man was walking alongside the army vehicles, talking to the soldiers. "Four of my best friends died in my arms today," he said, "why don't you kill me, too?" He patted his chest. "Come on, open fire!" he insisted. "Open fire." Later we learned that he was a student from Xinjiang. He had walked the two miles from Muxidi with the troops. His blue T-shirt was soaked with blood. Finally, somebody grabbed him and dragged him off the street.

"Get that officer!" someone shouted. Dozens of people had encircled a jeep. H. wanted to go up close, but I held him back. People were now pounding the jeep with their fists. There was a round of gunfire from a truck in front of us. I saw five people fall. H. dropped facedown, sobbing. "I don't want to live anymore! I don't want to live!"

A man came over to us, shook us, and said, "Where did you get hit?" He thought we had been wounded. His concern made us cry even harder.

Then an ambulance arrived. The doctor inside waved a Red Cross flag as the vehicle approached the soldiers, but they aimed their weapons at the ambulance and signaled it to retreat. The doctor waved the Red Cross flag even harder. More soldiers pointed their weapons at the ambulance until, finally, it began to retreat. I heard someone shout through clenched teeth, "They're not even letting people be saved now! From now on, when we see a soldier, let's kill him!"

At that moment, the crowd suddenly began to shift wildly about. A mob chased two soldiers, and one of them was caught.

I yelled, "Beat him to death!" and struck him. H. kicked him. The soldier cried, "It wasn't me!" When we heard this, we stopped beating him.

My heart softened, and I could tell that H. felt the same way. We turned around and walked back hand in hand, but the two soldiers were quickly beaten to death by the civilians anyway.

DING ZILIN,
WHO THEY WERE

Ding Zilin was the mother of one of the students who died on the night of June 4. Her seventeen-year-old son, Jiang Jielian, was a sophomore at People's University, where Ding herself taught philosophy. Instead of keeping silent after her son's death, Ding publicly bore witness to the dead by compiling and publicizing a list of civilians who were wounded or killed, something that the government had steadfastly refused to do.

This selection was excerpted from an open letter Ding wrote to the World Conference on Human Rights in Vienna, held in 1993; it was published in China Rights Forum, *Summer 1994.*

Since June 4, the Chinese government has talked constantly about respecting its citizens' "right to exist." Yet five years ago guns and tanks deprived countless outstanding young Chinese men and women of their "right to exist" in a single night. This is nothing but hypocrisy.

As the mother of a victim, there is no way for me to forget these boys and girls and men and women, including my own son, who died in pools of blood. I want the people of the world to know that they once lived in this world, that this world once belonged to them, and why and how they disappeared from it.

Late in the night of June 3, 1989, the West Road martial law troops came in from the western suburbs of Beijing along Wukesong and Cuiwei Roads, shooting and killing as they made their way east to the head of the bridge at Muxidi. There they were blocked by over 10,000 people. Just past 11:00 P.M., the sound of machine gun fire began again and my seventeen-year-old son, Jiang Jielian, a second-year student at People's University High School, was in the first group of people to fall. Downed around the same time was Hao Zhijing, thirty, a science and technology policy and management researcher at the Chinese Academy of Sciences. He had returned from a visit to the United States in 1988 and had been married less than a year. He too was his parents' cherished only child. He was shot in the chest and taken by local citizens to Fuxing Hospital, where he died. His family did not find his body until July 4. Also among the mass of bodies that fell one after another in the continuous spray of machine gun fire at Muxidi was Xiao Bo, a young instructor in the Chemistry Department at Beijing University who had turned twenty-seven that day. He had gone to Muxidi expressly to urge his students to return to school. Xiao Bo died leaving behind a pair of twins not yet seventy days old.

Also brought down at the same time was twenty-seven-year-old Yuan Li, an engineer in the Electrical Machinery Department of the Beijing Machinery Industry Research Institute who had just received a visa to visit the United States. He was shot in the chest not long after leaving his home in Ganjiakou at 11:00 P.M. Soon afterward, his corpse was labeled "Unknown Body 2" by the Naval General Hospital and placed in storage until his family found where it was on June 24. Stored together with Yuan Li's corpse was "Unknown Body 3," later identified by his family as Wang Chao, thirty, an employee of the Stone Corporation who had been married only a month. "Unknown Body 1" turned out to be nineteen-year-old Ye Weihang, a third-year student at Beijing Middle School Number 57 and student association chairman. He was shot in the right shoulder and chest at 2:00 A.M. on June 4 but did not die until, after falling, he was shot again in the back of the head. Twenty-seven-year-old Lu Chunlin, who entered the master's program of the Philosophy Department at People's University in 1986 and was the son of a southern Jiangsu farm family, was also shot at Muxidi. Just before he died, he used the last of his energy to give everything he was carrying with him to a passerby to take back to the university and report his death.

As the troops charged toward Tiananmen, the number of sons and daughters of China stripped of their "right to exist" increased. Duan Changlong, a graduating senior majoring in applied chemistry in the Chemistry Department of Qinghua University, had just found a job. His forty-six-year-old father had only this one beloved son. That evening, Duan had left an experiment unfinished in the school laboratory and ridden his bike from Houhaijia to the vicinity of the Palace of Nationalities at Xidan. There he came across the martial law troops blocked by the crowd. He pushed forward and was hit in the chest with a bullet. People took him to the nearby Postal College, where he stopped breathing before receiving any medical care. Also dying alongside Duan Changlong at the same time in the Postal College Hospital was a nineteen-year-old girl, Zhang Jin. She was a student majoring in foreign trade at a vocational high school and was training to work at the International Trade Center. Seeing the gunfire and killing, Zhang Jin and her boyfriend had hidden in a small alleyway near the Palace of Nationalities, but they were unable to avoid the slaughter. Just past midnight, Zhang Jin was shot twice in the head and fell at her boyfriend's feet. She died shortly after being taken to the Postal College Hospital around 1:00 A.M., June 4. Among the other bodies at the Postal College Hospital was that of a senior in the Industrial Management Department at the People's University, Wu Guofeng. He was the only university student from his remote district in Sichuan Province. He had left the school carrying a camera on the evening of June 3 and never returned.

The Killing Continues

The argument has been made that the slaughter of June 3 and 4 was necessary to clear Tiananmen Square. Then why did the indiscriminate killing of innocent people continue for several days after the martial law troops had already occupied the square? On or about June 5, Zhang

Xianghong, a second-year student in the International Politics Department at People's University, went to the end of the alleyway near her home with her sister-in-law, as they were anxious about Zhang's brother who was going out. They were chasing behind him, calling for him to return home when Zhang was hit by a round of ammunition fired by the martial law troops. Zhang died instantly in the arms of her sister-in-law. An Ji, thirty-one, of the Chinese Architectural Technique Research Center of the Construction Department and editor of the Rural Planning and Design Division's journal, *Township Construction*, was killed under similar circumstances. At a bit past 11:00 P.M. on the evening of June 7, An Ji and a group of friends were seeing off another friend to Yangfangdian. As they passed the Beijing Children's Hospital near Yuetan Park, martial law troops shouted at them to halt. An Ji and several other young men ran to hide and in a burst of gunfire, he and another man in his thirties surnamed Wang were hit and killed. Both of them left behind old mothers, wives, and young children.

These young men and women are only a small number of the victims of June 4 that I know of. Relatives of some victims, fearful of official pressure, are unwilling to reveal publicly the names and circumstances of the deaths of their loved ones, and thus they bear an even greater pain.

The June 4 Massacre is already five years in the past and the dead are long gone, but what has it meant for the living—aging parents, widows, and orphans? An epitaph on a tombstone in the Wan'an Public Cemetery west of Beijing reads:

> *Crying in sorrow for my son*
> *who not yet reaching thirty*
> *abruptly left this world.*
> *Our family's star of hope*
> *suddenly fell from the sky.*
> *How is the God in Heaven so unfair*
> *to call away a righteous youth*
> *and leave behind his parents in their seventies?*
> *Our son was born on the seventh of July*
> *and ascended to heaven on the third of June.*
> *A brief short life*
> *unfortunate from beginning to end.*
> *The entire family is heartbroken*
> *forever bereft of happiness and laughter*
> *we erect this memorial in our grief.*

These words articulate the anguished cries of the families of those killed. For the relatives of these victims, there is no longer any laughter. The only thing left is pain and tears. One elderly couple who lost their cherished son wear expressions of indifference and seldom speak, but deep in their hearts they are uneasy. They have only one wish, and so they pray that they can live a bit longer to see with their own eyes the day when the clouds will open and the fog will clear.

The government has adopted a policy of forbidding discussion and making people forget June 4. With the passage of time, the warmth and solicitude of people around the families of victims grows increasingly sparse while longing for lost loved ones can be suffocating. There is one mother who has gradually grown quiet over these past five years. It is a fearful silence, and she is unable to talk about the nineteen-year-old son she lost. She acts as though none of it ever happened, but in her heart she is suffering terribly and her whole personality seems to have been transformed. Another mother is so pained that she does not want to go on living; she is close to having a nervous breakdown. When she can no longer control herself, in the middle of the night she goes to a deserted area and cries and screams madly. There is another mother who normally restrains her sorrow, but at the Qingming grave-sweeping festival and on the anniversary of her son's death, she falls before his grave and cries ceaselessly. On these anniversaries, yet another mother is unable to stay in the house where her son once lived and walks aimlessly through the streets and alleyways, unwilling to return to her home for long periods. One widow found it impossible to hold back her bitterness and hoped to meet others with whom she could share her pain. So once when she was attending to the grave of her husband, she quietly left her address on the funeral urns of others she did not know who had died in the same way. In this way she broke through her loneliness and helplessness.

I suffered the same fate as these mothers and wives and endured many grim, sad days and nights after June 4. My spirits and health were seriously damaged, and I suffered repeated bouts of heart trouble. When I could bear it no longer, I broke my silence on the eve of the second anniversary of June 4 by agreeing to an interview with ABC Television in which I pointed out the errors of fact in Premier Li Peng's interpretation of the June 4 incident. I paid a heavy price for this, bringing on more than a year of persecution. On the eve of the third anniversary of June 4, I was expelled from the Chinese Communist Party and deprived of my job as a graduate student adviser.

The Government's Response

How did the Chinese government behave toward the families? A month after the massacre, the Chinese government–controlled Hong Kong newspaper *Wen Wei Po* published a story saying that appropriate funeral arrangements had been made for those mistakenly killed in Beijing. Deputy Secretary of the Beijing Municipal Government Yu Xiaosong was quoted as saying that "the government is undertaking conscientious and careful arrangements" for their relatives and that they would be given compensation of between 10,000 and 20,000 yuan. Yu indicated that the children of victims would be supported by the government until they reached eighteen.

However, despite repeated requests, no government official has ever announced the official verdict on whether my son was mistakenly wounded or was a "rioter." One mother I know of angrily requested that the authorities list her deceased daughter as a "rioter," saying that that was better than just leaving the cause of death completely unclear. Of all the relatives of victims I know of, not one has obtained an official conclusion on their loved one's cause of death or received any compensation.

During the political study and investigation which followed the June 4 Massacre, the CCP political department in each work unit pressured the families of victims to take part in "study" sessions to raise their understanding, to maintain unanimity with the central government, and to acknowledge that "pacifying the uprising" was reasonable. The families of some victims were forbidden to make their status as relatives of victims public and prohibited from accepting press interviews under threat of being expelled from their deceased relative's work unit housing.

We have suffered from unimaginable material, spiritual, and physical pain. We have lost the right to enjoy a normal life and lost the right to express our opinions and viewpoints. Human rights, which should be universally enjoyed by all human beings, remain a luxury in present-day China, especially for those of us who are relatives of the victims of June 4.

EDUCATION, MEDIA, AND CULTURE

___

III. EDUCATION AND RESEARCH

The People's Republic of China was founded on the concept of an educational system and an artistic establishment that were beholden to the state. Thus the job of educators and "cultural workers" has been not to train free thinkers and independent artists but to train new generations of young people who would be dedicated to socialism and loyal to the imperatives of the revolution.

Nonetheless, as Deng began initiating his reforms, many recognized that without changes in both conception and organization, China's educational and arts institutions would not be up to the challenges of modernizing the country and making it a competitive world player. This ambiguity of roles left students, educators, scholars, and artists in a contradiction. During periods when more liberal leaders came to power and emphasized *fang*, or "loosening up," and Party policies encouraged a greater degree of academic and artistic freedom, intellectuals were able to be more adventuresome. However, during times when hard-line leaders were ascendant and emphasized *shou*, or "tightening down," intellectuals were forced to be more mindful of Party dogma.

DENG XIAOPING, SPEECH AT THE NATIONAL CONFERENCE ON EDUCATION

As he returned to power in 1978, one of the first things Deng Xiaoping did was address educational reform. While this speech, delivered on April 22,

calls for a new realism and a less ideological curriculum, it is also a mas-
terpiece of political ambiguity. Deng urges teachers to help students "seek
truth from facts," but reminds them that they are also bound to "foster rev-
olutionary ideals and communist morality."

This selection was excerpted from Deng's April 22, 1978, speech, pub-
lished in volume 2 of The Selected Works of Deng Xiaoping (1975–1982),
1984.

Comrades,

There have been many new developments on the educational front
since the smashing of the Gang of Four and particularly since the college enrollment system was reformed and the "two appraisals" were criticized. These achievements should be fully recognized. Still, both in
educational circles and in society at large, people are hoping for even
faster progress in this sphere. There are many problems to be solved and
many things to be done in this connection. Today, I would like to offer
some opinions on the subject.

First, we must improve the quality of education and raise the level of
teaching in the sciences, social sciences, and humanities so as to serve
socialist construction better.

Our schools are places for the training of competent personnel for
socialist construction. Are there qualitative standards for such training?
Yes, there are. They were stated by Comrade Mao Zedong: We should
enable everyone who receives an education to develop morally, intellectually, and physically and become a worker possessed by both socialist
consciousness and a general education.

The Gang of Four were opposed to placing strict demands on students in their study of the sciences, social sciences, and humanities, and
to making such studies the main concern of the students. They made
the ridiculous claim that that would be "putting intellectual education
first" and thus "being divorced from proletarian politics." They declared
that they would rather have laborers without education and that the
more a person knew, the more reactionary he would become. What is
more, they slandered all working people or children of working people
who had received some education, calling them "bourgeois intellectuals." Even today, much effort is still needed to eliminate the pernicious
influence of these absurdities spread by the Gang.

Lenin emphasized time and again that the workers should not for a minute forget their need for knowledge. Without knowledge, he said, they would have no way of defending themselves, while with it they would be strong. The importance of this truth stands out even more clearly today. We must train workers with a high level of scientific and general knowledge and build a vast army of working-class intellectuals who are both "red and expert." Only then will we be able to master and advance modern science and culture and the new technologies and skills in every trade and profession. Only then will we be able to attain a productivity of labor higher than that under capitalism, transform China into a modern and powerful socialist country, and ultimately defeat bourgeois influences in the superstructure. Proletarian politics demands that all these be done.

Beyond all doubt, schools always attach first importance to a firm and correct political orientation. But this doesn't mean they should devote a great many classroom hours to ideological and political teaching. Students must indeed give top priority to a firm and correct political orientation, but that by no means implies that they should abandon the study of the sciences, social sciences, and humanities. On the contrary, the higher the students' political consciousness, the more consciously and diligently they will apply themselves to the study of these subjects for the sake of the revolution. Hence the Gang of Four not only were being utterly ridiculous but were actually negating and betraying proletarian politics when they opposed efforts to improve the quality of education and to raise the students' scientific and cultural level on the basis of a firm, correct political orientation and declared that that was "putting intellectual education first."

It is not good to put too heavy a load on students, and we should continue to take effective measures to prevent this bad practice or remedy it. But it is equally obvious that we will not be able to raise the level of our scientific and cultural knowledge substantially unless we maintain the work style of the "three honests and four stricts," and unless demands are exacting and training rigorous. If we are to catch up with and surpass the advanced countries in science and technology, we must improve not only the quality of our higher education but, first of all, that of our primary and secondary education. In other words, the primary and secondary school courses should be enriched with advanced scientific knowledge, presented in ways the pupils at these levels can understand.

Examinations are a necessary way of checking on the performance of students and teachers, just as the testing of factory products is a necessary means of quality control. Of course, we must not put blind faith in examinations or consider them the only method for checking up on study. Conscientious research and experimentation are required to improve the form and content of examinations and make them serve their purpose better. Students who don't do well on their examinations should be encouraged and helped to continue their efforts instead of being subjected to unnecessary psychological pressure.

Second, our schools must make an effort to strengthen revolutionary order and discipline, bring up a new generation with socialist consciousness, and help to revolutionize the moral tone of our society.

Not only did the sabotage of education by the Gang of Four cause an alarming decline in the quality of scientific and cultural education; it also did grave damage to ideological and political education in the schools, undermined school discipline, and sapped the revolutionary spirit of socialist society. The Gang shouted to high heaven about the importance of politics, but in fact their politics were counterrevolutionary and antisocialist. They used the most decadent and reactionary exploiting-class ideas in their attempt to poison the minds of our young people and turn them into illiterate hooligans. The eradication of the Gang's pernicious influence is a political task which is of the utmost importance and which has a direct bearing on the consolidation of the dictatorship of the proletariat in China.

We should foster revolutionary ideals and communist morality in young people from childhood. This has always been a fine tradition in our Party's educational work. During the years of revolutionary wars, members of the Children's Corps and the Communist Youth League performed stirring deeds of heroism. After Liberation, young people were encouraged to carry on this fine tradition by the schools, the Young Pioneers, and the Youth League. For a long time, our children and young people studied well and made progress every day. They were filled with love for their motherland, for the people, and for labor, science, and public property, and they struggled heroically and resourcefully against bad elements and enemies, setting the tone for a new era. The revolutionary spirit in our schools helped foster a revolutionary spirit in our whole society. This spirit was unprecedented in Chinese history and won the admiration of people the world over. We hope that not only the comrades working in education and related fields but also every family in our society will pay close attention to the ideological and political progress of our children and young people, so as to revive and enrich the fine revolutionary traditions which the Gang of Four undermined. Comrade Mao Zedong once said: "All departments and organizations should shoulder their responsibilities in ideological and political work. This applies to the Communist Party, the Youth League, government departments in charge of this work, and especially to heads of educational institutions and teachers." The responsibility for training young successors for the revolutionary cause rests particularly heavily on the primary and secondary school teachers and on kindergarten personnel. We should strive to inculcate in our young people the revolutionary style of diligent study, observance of discipline, love of labor, pleasure in helping others, defiance of hardships, and courage in the face of the enemy. In this way they can become fine and competent people loyal to the socialist motherland, to the proletarian revolutionary cause, and to Marxism-Leninism and Mao Zedong Thought. Thus, when they finish their schooling and take up their jobs, they will be workers imbued with a strong sense of political responsibility and collectivism and a firm revolutionary ideology; their style of work will be to seek truth from facts and follow the mass line, and they will observe strict discipline and work wholeheartedly for the people.

We hope that everyone will do his best to make progress because, when all is said and done, progress depends on individual effort. Collective effort is the sum of individual efforts. And individual effort will continue to differ even in communist society. Comrade Mao Zedong once said that 10,000 years hence there will still be a gap between the advanced and the backward. Therefore, while we encourage and help everyone to do his best, we have to recognize that differences in the abilities and character of different people will manifest themselves in the course of their development. We must take these differences into account and do everything possible to enable each individual, in accordance with his particular circumstances, to keep pace with the general movement of society toward socialism and communism. At the same time, conscientious efforts must be made and strict measures taken to correct and reform those who seriously undermine revolutionary order and discipline and refuse to mend their ways after repeated efforts to educate them; in no case should we let a handful of such persons harm our schools and society as a whole.

From now on, it is not only the secondary schools and institutions of higher education that should examine applicants in an overall way — taking into account their moral and intellectual qualities and the state of their health — and admit only those who are best qualified. All units should gradually follow suit and recruit only those job applicants who are best qualified. This will require that students be enabled to develop morally, intellectually, and physically and to become workers with both socialist consciousness and a general education. Thus the policy put forward by Comrade Mao Zedong to the same effect will be thoroughly implemented in all aspects of social life. This system of selection will be most useful in raising the political, scientific, and cultural levels of our working personnel, in meeting the special needs of different trades and professions, and in creating, among the young people and throughout our society, a revolutionary atmosphere in which everyone is eager to make progress and work hard and is unwilling to lag behind.

Third, education must meet the requirements of our country's economic development.

To train qualified personnel for socialist construction, we must try to find improved ways of combining education with productive labor, ways that are suited to our new conditions. Marx, Engels, Lenin, and Comrade Mao Zedong all laid great stress on combining education with productive labor. They considered this to be one of the most powerful means for reforming society under capitalism. They also believed that after the seizure of political power by the proletariat, it should be the fundamental way to train a new generation that would integrate theory with practice, unite study with practical application, and develop in an all-round way, and they looked upon it as an essential measure for gradually abolishing the distinction between mental and manual labor. As early as eighty years ago, Lenin said: "Neither training and education without productive labor, nor productive labor without parallel training and education [can] be raised to the degree required by the present level of technology and the state of scientific knowledge." In our own day, rapid economic and technological progress demands rapid improvement in the quality and efficiency of education. This includes steady improvement in the methods of combining study with productive labor and of selecting the type of labor appropriate for this purpose.

To this end, educational institutions of all types and levels must make appropriate decisions as to what kind of labor the students should engage in, which factories and rural areas they should go to and for how long, and how to relate their labor closely to their studies. More important still, education as a whole must be in keeping with the requirements of our growing economy. If, on the contrary, what the students learn isn't suited to the needs of their future jobs, if they study what they aren't going to apply or if they can't apply what they study, won't this flatly violate the principle of combining education with productive labor? And, if that is so, how can we arouse the students' enthusiasm for study and work and how can education meet the enormous demands placed on it by the new historical period?

As our economy develops in a planned and balanced way, we must also carefully plan the training of future workers and professionals to meet its needs. We must bear in mind not only immediate needs but future ones as well. We must make plans that take into full account not only the needs of growing production and construction but also the trends in modern science and technology.

The State Planning Commission, the Ministry of Education, and other organizations should collaborate in making education an integral component of the national economic plan. We should coordinate the development of various types and levels of educational institutions, and, in particular, we should plan to increase the number of agricultural secondary schools and vocational and technical secondary schools. We should also consider what types of institutions of higher learning to build up, how to readjust the specialties offered, how to institute the courses on basic theory, and how to improve teaching materials. We must take steps to accelerate the development of modern media of education, including the radio and television. Broadcasting offers an important means of developing education with greater, faster, better, and more economical results, and we should take full advantage of it. We should study and find ways of coordinating productive labor and scientific experiment and research more effectively in our schools so as to better meet the needs of our economic and educational plans. In order to speed up the training of qualified personnel and to raise the overall level of education, we must consider concentrating our forces and strengthening key colleges and universities and key primary and secondary schools, thus raising their level as quickly as possible.

From now on, the state will be trying to open up new productive enterprises and new lines of work so as to serve the four modernizations more effectively. In working out our educational plan, we should coordinate it with the state plan for the utilization of labor and consider how to meet the needs for increased employment.

Lastly, I would like to say a few words about ensuring respect for the labor of our teachers and about improving their qualifications.

Teachers are the key to a school's success in training personnel suited to the needs of our socialist construction, that is, its success in training workers who have both socialist consciousness and a good general education and who are highly developed morally, intellectually, and physically.

In the past two decades and more, we have built up a contingent of 9 million teachers devoted to serving the people. The overwhelming majority of teachers and other school personnel love the Party and socialism. They work industriously to provide a socialist education and so have made great contributions to the nation and the proletariat. Educational workers who serve the people are high-minded workers for the revolution. We salute this multitude of educational workers for their painstaking efforts and express our appreciation to all of them and especially to the primary school teachers, who have worked tirelessly under particularly difficult conditions to bring up successors for the revolutionary cause.

We must raise the political and social status of teachers. They should command the respect not only of their students but also of the whole community. We urge students to respect their teachers and teachers to love their students. Respect and love, with teacher and student learning from each other—that is the appropriate comradely, revolutionary relationship between teachers and students. Outstanding educational workers should be commended, rewarded, and widely acclaimed.

The present pay scale for teachers, especially those in primary and secondary schools, should be reviewed. Proper steps should be taken to encourage people to dedicate their whole lives to education. Particularly outstanding teachers may be designated "special-grade teachers." Owing to our country's economic limitations, we cannot bring about a marked improvement in the material life of teachers and other school personnel for the time being, but we must make every effort to create the conditions needed for this. The Party committees at all levels and the administrative authorities in charge of education should, first of all, do everything possible to provide better collective welfare services.

All Party committees and Party organizations in the schools should take a warm interest in the teachers' ideological and political progress. They should help the teachers to study Marxism-Leninism and Mao Zedong Thought so that more of them will have a firm proletarian, communist world outlook. We must make a point of recruiting outstanding teachers into the Party. The tasks of education are becoming heavier and heavier. All educational units must strive to raise the capabilities of teachers and improve the quality of instruction. The Ministry of Education and local educational departments should adopt effective measures to train teachers, making full use of radio and television, setting up training classes and advanced courses of various kinds, compiling reference material for teachers, and so forth. We hope that all teachers will work hard to steadily raise their political and professional levels and become increasingly socialist minded and professionally competent.

Comrades! I hope that some of the major issues in educational work will be fully discussed at this conference. We urge you to proceed in the revolutionary spirit of daring to think and speak. It doesn't matter if opinions differ. We can compare the different proposals. We must follow the mass line in everything we do. Good ideas can be produced only if democracy is practiced fully within the ranks of the people. Of course, a good idea will not turn into reality by itself. Bright prospects remain merely idle talk unless we devise practical measures and work hard to implement them. If we are to achieve the Four Modernizations within a reasonable length of time, we must insist on a practical, revolutionary style of work that will gradually help us turn lofty ideals into reality.

I believe that if—under the leadership of the Central Committee of the Party—we rely on the efforts of the teachers, students, administrators, and other school workers, carry through to the end the struggle to expose and criticize the Gang of Four, and approach our work in a practical way, we will see more and more people of a new type emerge. Good news will pour in from the educational front as our work in this domain thrives the way it is doing in all others.

GEREMIE BARMÉ, A SMALL MATTER OF TRUTH

For historical researchers in China, the late 1980s were a halcyon period when intellectuals confronted less official control than at any other time over the previous forty years. Nonetheless, as the military historian Zhang Zhenglong learned, the principle that the Party is the ultimate arbiter of the meaning of history was never fully abandoned. Indeed, it was reasserted as the guiding principle of historical research in the aftermath of the Beijing Massacre.

This selection was excerpted from an article by the Australian National University research scholar Geremie Barmé published in Australian Literary Review, *February 1991.*

Zhang Zhenglong had been in an ideal position to investigate the story. As a trusted member of the armed forces in the northeast, he found many local old military men and civilians willing to speak to him. Years of writing reportage, a form of investigative journalism popular in China since the mid-1980s, gave Zhang a confident and fluent style. And the boom in publishing of the late 1980s that led publishing houses to search out new and sensational books encouraged him to believe— like so many others—that he enjoyed a new freedom of expression. An official imprimatur was given to the project when the PLA publishing house included his book in a series on the revolutionary wars.

White Snow, Red Blood presents a historical account of the Party's army that conforms entirely with what the population learned about the People's Liberation Army in June 1989. For many army people the most controversial aspect of the book is the detailed account of the martial feats of the "renegade" Lin Biao, the military commander of the campaign (who was later designated Mao Zedong's chosen successor, only to die mysteriously in 1971) and an objective description of Chiang Kai-shek's Nationalist army. However, for the average reader the most devastating section of the book must certainly be Part 14, "City of Death," which describes in chilling detail how, in 1948, the PLA laid siege to Changchun, the provincial capital of Jilin, and starved it into submission. An estimated 150,000 civilians are said to have died in this standoff between the Communist and Nationalist forces that was previously described as a "bloodless victory."

Despite the explosive nature of the material and the author's provocative antiwar commentary throughout the narrative, the book continued to be sold for some months, surviving for a time the general purge of the publishing industry initiated by the Party in August 1989. Even the leading pro-government apologist "intellectual" He Xin praised the book in conversation with this writer and cited its continued sale as proof that the cultural purge was aimed at specific "turmoil-related" elements only. Then in August 1990 came the rumors of Zhang's work being subject to internal review, and the detention of the head of the PLA publishing house for questioning. By November the Hong Kong and Taiwan press reported the rumors and published excerpts from the book.

Zhang was fully aware of the danger of pursuing independent historical research in China. Some of his informants were all too mindful of the explosive nature of their knowledge. Zhang, however, was anxious to get them to speak before it was too late. "Time is no longer our friend," he reflects in his introduction, written in February 1989. He compares some of the reticent old soldiers (some reveal that they have the information he wants, but they can't possibly tell him) to the black box or flight recorder in an airplane disaster. "Imagine that after incredible difficulties you actually manage to locate the black box only to discover you can't open it!" While many other writers were attracted to historical topics as a kind of escapism, Zhang says, he had found in history numerous "forbidden zones" and "dangers lurking at every turn." "Sometimes I just wanted to run away." He even speculates about the need for "political insurance" for China's reportage writers, if indeed any insurance company would sell such a policy.

By revealing so many unsavory details of the supposedly most glorious chapter in the PLA's history, Zhang has so tarnished the image of the Party's "Great Wall of Iron" that no amount of insurance could have kept him safe.

Historical writing and research in China enjoyed a period of unrivaled development in the 1980s. Many saw a key to understanding and dealing with the dilemmas of contemporary China in the past, especially in the history of the last century. Although the Party presented its own definitive view of post-1949 history in a document released in 1981, a body of works that constitutes the basis of a "parallel" history gradually appeared throughout the 1980s.

With the increasing publication of documentary materials and personal recollections, autonomous views of the past began to emerge, confounding the Party's interpretation of events and even challenging its legitimacy as the sole source of historical truth. Investigative journalists, previously interested predominantly in contemporary issues, also began to delve into the past, and from the mid-1980s produced some of the most widely read works. Of these writers, the woman journalist and fiction writer Dai Qing is perhaps the most outstanding.

Dai produced long investigations of two "historical mysteries" which involved the silencing and eventual death of outspoken intellectual critics of the Party. One was Wang Shiwei, the main object of attack in the ideological struggles in the Party's wartime guerrilla base of Yan'an in the early 1940s. Dai uses this case—the first cultural purge carried out by the Party—to dissect the nature and style of such campaigns, revealing in the process that Wang was beheaded in 1947. The other was Chu Anping, a journalist and famous liberal who spoke out against the Party's monopoly of power in 1957. He disappeared in the early days of the Cultural Revolution in 1966. Both remain unrehabilitated. Dai's writings, part of a longer series of historical investigations, had one main thrust. As she put it:

> I'm writing for the sake of the present. If it weren't for this I wouldn't bother writing about these cases. In my opinion the situation is exactly the same today, that's why I wanted to tell the truth about these incidents; so people can read about them and think: how come nothing's really changed, why hasn't there really been any progress?

History-related works that have been outlawed since the massacre range from the serious, such as Dai's writings, to the sensational, such as Su Xiaokang's account of the Lushan Conference of 1958, which many see as the prelude to the Cultural Revolution, and Yan Jiaqi and Gao Gao's history of the Cultural Revolution, and even the sacrilegious, such as *Their Struggle—From Marx to Hitler*.

Independent historical writing both contributed to and profited from the ideological collapse of China in the 1980s. On May 13, 1989, a petition signed in Shanghai by a group of poets and literary critics declared publicly that writers had a "right to history." Different from any of the other appeals supporting the student demonstrators in Beijing, it read in part:

> Writers must have the freedom to analyze, explain, and publish their views on all aspects of Chinese reality both historical and present, in particular political incidents. For a party official to use his position or administrative powers to restrict or interfere with writers or deprive them of their freedom of expression or publication is not only an abuse of power but illegal.

The rewriting of history has been an important feature of the Party's efforts at self-justification since June 1989. The official description of the carnage of the Beijing Massacre as a riot by hooligans is the most obvious case in point. The media have also been used extensively to prove the "historical necessity" of Party rule and socialism in China. The most notable example of this has been *On the Road*, a four-part documentary series first screened in August 1990. Glossing over the "errors" of Party rule, it affirms that China's salvation lies in socialism. There have been other such programs, like *Love for the Republic*, which deals with the commitment of scientists to the motherland, and *The Spirit of China*.

The response to the sprouts of independent history writing that appeared in the late 1980s among orthodox Party historians is perhaps best reflected in comments the leading ideologue Hu Qiaomu made on March 8, 1990, at a national meeting on Party history. Hu, the man directly in charge of overseeing the production of an official Party history for the seventieth anniversary of the founding of the Party this year, said that "the study of Party history . . . is not oriented to the past; it is to confront the present and face the future. . . . Like other areas of the Party's ideological work, our endeavors are concerned with supporting the leadership of the Party, it is part of the struggle for the socialist enterprise in China." In other words, the task of history or historiography is didactic; history is to be used to illustrate, not to establish, the truth.

In that speech Hu Qiaomu attacked the activities of feral historians like Dai Qing and Su Xiaokang in a classic passage of doublethink:

> Our struggle is that of science against antiscience, the struggle of truth against lies. Originally the true face of history was like this, but inimical forces are dead set on obliterating, distorting, and slandering the truth about the past revolutionary struggles of the Party and the people. It is for this reason that we must use a scientific attitude, scientific methodology, and scientific proofs to elucidate the various basic questions of our Party's history.

In the summer of 1988 Zhang Zhenglong, who was writing *White Snow, Red Blood*, was inspired by the news from the Soviet Union that high school history examinations were being canceled and texts revised. He reflected on the relationship between the makers and inheritors of history in China:

> That final war [of 1948] laid waste to the black earth of the northeast. But since then what has continued to defile it? As it's the grown-ups who've thrown the family chronicle into chaos, how can we ever hope that our children will continue it? . . . If you expect sincerity from your children, you must be honest yourself.

The dissident historian can thus be as threatening as the political activist or pamphleteer.

IV. MEDIA

In the traditional Marxist-Leninist scheme of things, the media are supposed to act as mouthpieces for the Communist Party, not as independent, inquiring voices. Thus, even as economic reforms proceeded at an ever quickening pace and China was bombarded with ideas from abroad extolling the virtues of a free press, Party leaders remained reluctant to alter their conception of the media. Nonetheless, throughout the 1980s journalists waged a constant struggle with the Party over the media's role in Chinese society. Those who supported reform and liberalization believed that China could never become a fully modernized country without codified laws that guaranteed a more independent status for journalists. Those who resisted reform and liberalization were fearful that an open press would be the undoing not only of the Communist Party but also of Mao's whole "revolutionary" edifice.

As increasingly permissive media policies were tested, it did not take long for hard-line Party leaders to realize that whenever they gave up a significant measure of control, long-pent-up grievances escalated from minor criticisms into sweeping indictments of the political status quo. Many "veteran revolutionaries" quickly came to view freedom of the press not only as a direct challenge to their right to rule unilaterally but also as a recipe for political instability, possibly even chaos.

Serious public debate over creating new press laws ended in 1989, as conservative hard-liners reconsolidated their grip on the media and vowed not to allow them to escape control again. Yet as market forces and outside influences continued to change the face of Chinese society, the media themselves continued to change in ways that left the question of press freedom in a constant state of tension.

ALLISON JERNOW,
THE PRESS IN THE 1980S: TESTING NEW GROUND

In the decade before the Tiananmen Square demonstrations, many hoped that China was on the verge of growing beyond the idea that the press was the official voice of the Party and government. The former People's Daily editor in chief Hu Jiwei, who had pioneered a resurgence of investigative journalism in the early 1980s, became one of the leading advocates for a reconception of the press's role in society. He called not only for press reform but respect for intellectual dissent. "Freedom of the press for citizens," he reminded Chinese, "is their right to be kept informed as masters of the house."

This selection was excerpted from "Testing New Ground in the 1980s" by Allison Jernow with the Committee to Protect Journalists, published in 1993.

In 1977, when Deng Xiaoping picked Hu Jiwei to be the editor in chief of *People's Daily*, China was about to embark on an unprecedented path of modernization and opening to the outside world after a decade of Maoist insularity. Hu Jiwei, a veteran journalist and Communist Party cadre, seemed a good choice to help fulfill the vision of a bold new China. Six years later, he had been ousted from his position. The story of his fall from grace is common enough among Chinese journalists but no less tragic for its familiarity.

People's Daily is the one newspaper in China whose bureaucratic rank is equivalent to a ministry. Its editor enjoys the prestige and privileges, and the unique responsibility to the Party, of a minister—known in Chinese as *dangxing*. *People's Daily* is the oracle of Zhongnanhai, the compound in Beijing where China's highest leaders live and work. Many of the newspaper's front page commentaries are written in Zhongnanhai and then are reprinted by other papers and broadcast by radio and television stations, so the voice of *People's Daily* literally reverberates throughout the country.

Hu Jiwei was not only a member of the Communist Party and editor in chief of the Party's most influential newspaper, he was a *zhishifenzi*, a word that translates as "intellectual" but carries much more weight. In Chinese tradition, *zhishifenzi* assume responsibility for the fate of the country. Lacking the checks and balances of parliamentary systems, China depends on its intellectuals to keep the rulers aware of the people's needs. Intellectual dissent is presumed to be loyal and not rebellious.

By the time Hu Jiwei became editor of *People's Daily*, he was all too aware that the Party made mistakes. His patriotism and his Party loyalty were no longer synonymous, and he was forced to choose. *People's Daily*, Hu Jiwei decided, had to live up to its name. It had to reflect not only the policies of the Party but also the will of the people. Luckily for him, the moment was ripe.

The early 1980s were a time of sweeping economic and political change. Under Hu Jiwei's leadership, *People's Daily* published some of the best investigative journalism China had ever seen. An exposé on the sinking of the Bohai oil rig led to the resignation of the minister of petroleum. Other articles revealed that the model people's commune of Dazhai was in fact not such a exemplar and that the minister of commerce dined out at public expense. In 1982, at the apogee of his career, Hu Jiwei delivered a speech in which he called on newspaper editors to publish the opinions and criticisms of their readers.

Hu Jiwei's belief that newspapers should speak for the people was later called his "conspiracy," both by Party bureaucrats who felt threatened by the loss of control and by fellow journalists who admired his aims. But his intent was not to replace the Party's voice with his own. He believed the press should offer diverse, even conflicting, thoughts and opinions. He used accepted Communist terminology to present the idea, novel in China, of independent journalism.

Overstepping the boundaries that govern the rules of intellectual dissent carries a high price. In 1983, during the Anti-Spiritual Pollution Campaign, Hu Jiwei was forced to resign. *People's Daily* staff members refused to endorse the new campaign, and many editorials were written instead by the conservative Deng Liqun, the head of the Propaganda Department.

Hu Jiwei, sidelined from the paper but still a member of the Standing Committee of the National People's Congress, became an even more outspoken advocate for press freedom. He led the debate about the need to reform journalism and in the mid-1980s was charged with drafting a press law. He frankly told foreign correspondents that he wanted a law to "protect the freedom of the press."

In one of the last articles he wrote for a mainland newspaper, Hu Jiwei said, "Freedom of the press for citizens is their right to be kept informed as masters of the house, their right of political consultation, their right of involvement in the government, and their right of supervision." After the June crackdown, Hu Jiwei was ostracized and publicly denounced. In August 1989 one newspaper accused him of taking press freedom to mean "the freedom to oppose the four basic principles," which include upholding the socialist system and the leadership of the Communist Party. He was stripped of his position as a member of the Standing Committee and only narrowly escaped being expelled from the Party. For now, his voice has been silenced, but his ideas are very much in the minds of China's journalists.

Journalists in China must live daily with the contradiction between speaking for the Party and speaking, in a plurality of voices, for the people. It is an acute and deeply felt tension. "What we must write we cannot write; what we want to say we cannot say" is a common saying that captures the feelings of many. Journalists carry the weight of the government's demands, the people's expectations, and their own professional consciences. Such an occupation is fraught with hazards and offers few rewards.

Journalists Work for the Government

Efforts by Hu Jiwei and others to loosen government and Communist Party control of the press have proceeded unevenly. The Chinese state exerts its authority in a variety of ways, and journalists have developed almost as many means of resistance. Nevertheless, state supervision remains pervasive and effective.

Despite the recent expansion of the private sector, news organizations remain state organs, and, like other work units, they are part of the government apparatus. None are independent. One reporter at a major daily newspaper describes how it works: "It's true there is no formal censorship system, but the Party . . . does control newspapers. They control through personnel changes. If you're fired, you lose your housing, your privileges, everything."

Television and radio stations fall under the jurisdiction of the Ministry of Radio, Film, and Television, which answers to the Central Propaganda Department of the Communist Party. Party organizations at various levels and of various types own and manage newspapers. Every provincial and municipal Communist Party committee has a newspaper, and sometimes more than one. For example, the Shanghai Municipal Party Committee publishes *Liberation Daily*, and the Guangzhou Province Party Committee puts out *Southern Daily*. These committees provide funding, appoint staff, and establish editorial policy.

Newspapers are also published by government agencies, trade groups, and political organizations. The Ministry of Culture, the All-China Federation of Industry and Commerce, the Communist Youth League, the State Council Science and Technology Commission, and the People's Liberation Army all publish papers that are part of the mainstream press. Party propaganda departments at the municipal, provincial, and central levels oversee their work. A third kind of newspaper is internal reference. Marked by varying degrees of confidentiality, the highest is circulated only among top Party officials, and the lowest is available to almost any member of a work unit. These internal papers present fairly straightforward digests of foreign news and reports on topics considered too sensitive for general consumption. Most of the articles are written by journalists who work in the public media.

Except in times of extreme repression, control is rarely overt. Proofs of articles are not regularly sent to a government censor for prepublication approval as they are in some countries. Instead, censorship is embedded in the entire process of producing a news story, from the assignment and writing of it to the editing and layout. An article on a sensitive subject might be shown to the local Party chief for review, but critical articles are not likely to be written at all. Self-censorship, not censorship, is the norm.

The system works, explained a deputy director of one paper's editorial department, "because the Party and state own the means of production and Party cadres control the daily business of news organizations. The party has 'branch' committees in practically all news organizations . . . [to] closely monitor personnel and to recruit new staffers. . . . The political and administrative staff is often much larger than the editorial staff."

Propaganda departments hold regular meetings for newspaper editors and issue bulletins that do not so much proscribe topics as suggest what should be emphasized. Consistency is also enforced by reducing the number of officially sanctioned sources. Rather than write their own stories and risk errors of judgment on delicate subjects, newspapers often recycle stories from *People's Daily* and Xinhua, the government news agency. Reprinting of important policy editorials is mandatory. In times of crisis, the Propaganda Department of the Central Committee will instruct all newspapers to use the Xinhua version. Newspapers thus display a united propaganda front.

Flexible control mechanisms make the press responsive to political realignments. Instead of defining limits in advance, Party committees prefer to discipline those who cross invisible lines. Such arbitrary and sometimes retroactive punishment requires journalists to develop acute political antennae and a sense of caution. Not surprisingly, informal censorship makes for a very nervous newsroom.

Cycles of Repression

In 1978 a newly rehabilitated Deng Xiaoping directed China away from the class struggle of the Cultural Revolution and toward modernization. The press began to change, too. Reflecting the permissive attitude at the top, *People's Daily*, the flagship publication of the Chinese Communist Party, became a trailblazer. Investigative reporter Liu Binyan recalls the excitement of the period and says that "readers enjoyed *People's Daily* more than ever" as circulation rose to a height of 7 million.

In the fall of 1983, the political winds shifted. A leftist-backed movement to "eradicate spiritual pollution" was launched in October with a commentary in *People's Daily* targeting those who "mistrust socialism." The campaign, although brief, caused heads to roll, and press reformers lost crucial ground.

One reason the Anti-Spiritual Pollution Campaign died quickly was that memories of the Cultural Revolution were still fresh in the minds of Party leaders. They did not want to reignite ideological witch-hunts, purges, and violence. When the political sloganeering and public denouncements began to threaten Deng's economic reforms, the hardliners retreated. By February 1984, Liu Binyan was able to publish his famous article "People or Monsters?" about a Party cadre's gross abuse of power in Heilongjiang Province.

A twice-purged journalist and Party member who had spent years in internal exile, Liu Binyan gained fame writing about the long-neglected grievances of common people. Petitioning Liu Binyan and other reporters was a means by which victims of various wrongs could achieve some form of redress. Lacking direct access to those in power, people sought to use the press to reach their rulers. Indeed, one of the duties of newspapers was to forward complaints to appropriate officials, and journalists took the liberty of publishing readers' letters on injustices that they could not directly address themselves.

In October 1985, Liu Binyan wrote "A Second Kind of Loyalty" about one of his petitioners, an unrepentant dissident named Ni Yuxian. In the article, he supported the right to "espouse political opinions that differed from the Party or Mao." The article was considered too inflammatory for *People's Daily*, and he published it instead in a new magazine called *Kaituo*. A few months later, when the political atmosphere changed once again, both author and magazine were severely criticized. *Kaituo* folded, and in January 1987 Liu Binyan was expelled from the Party.

This second wave of repression was in response to student demonstrations that broke out in Shanghai, Beijing, and other cities in December 1986. (See "The Student Demonstrations of 1986–87.") Party leaders feared a return to the ideology-driven tumult of the Cultural Revolution, but they also regarded with dread any hint of popular discontent. The movement against "bourgeois liberalization" was launched. Hu Yaobang, general secretary of the Chinese Communist Party and one of Liu Binyan's political sponsors, was forced to retire. Also ousted from their positions were the writer Wang Ruowang and the scientist Fang Lizhi, both outspoken reformers, and Propaganda Minister Zhu Houze, who was regarded as a liberal.

On January 25, 1987, *People's Daily* reported that "as a result of Liu Binyan's serious errors, the Disciplinary Inspection Committee of the *People's Daily* Branch of the Chinese Communist Party came to a decision to strip Liu Binyan . . . of his Party membership. . . . He has often . . . opposed the four basic principles and encouraged bourgeois liberalization." A commentary the same day said Liu Binyan had done "his utmost to vilify and oppose the leadership of the Party."

Most journalists fought the new political campaign with passive resistance. Instead of writing what they did not believe, they refused to write at all. Wu Guoguang, an editor at *People's Daily*, recalls the fine art of stalling. When writers in his Commentary Department received propaganda directives they disliked, they delayed action on them for as long as possible. During the Anti-Bourgeois Liberalization Campaign of 1986–87, rather than write their own editorials, the editors reprinted ones from other newspapers.

Thinking as Independent Agents

Press freedom suffered setbacks during the Anti-Bourgeois Liberalization Drive, but a process of internal transformation had begun among journalists. Having had a chance to speak and write with more autonomy, they began to see themselves as independent agents, something more than Party puppets. Throughout the 1980s, journalists discussed the need for press reform—a topic that never would have been broached before—in seminars and study groups. The debate even took place in the pages of *News Front*, a journal devoted to analyzing the profession.

A new generation of journalists was at work. These were people who had been schooled in programs like that of the Chinese Academy of Social Sciences' Institute of Journalism, which emphasized professionalism, not propaganda. Their teachers included Liu Binyan, Hu Jiwei, and Wang Ruoshui—senior journalists who believed in an independent press and were trying to figure out how best to achieve it. Young journalists also had increasing exposure to the West, as the number of exchange students multiplied and as foreign news, films, and literature became more accessible. They often knew journalists from the West and from Hong Kong, and they learned by example. No longer creatures of the Party, they strained against the controls the Party imposed.

In October 1987 journalists detected yet another warming trend. Zhao Ziyang, who had replaced Hu Yaobang as general secretary of the Chinese Communist Party, told the Thirteenth Party Congress that public opinion was needed to supervise public officials, and he specifically encouraged critical reporting. Zhao said the public should know about important events and debate important topics. Chinese journalists responded enthusiastically.

The late 1980s saw a rise in investigative, analytical, and independent reporting. Articles and journalists were criticized from time to time, and more libel cases were being filed, but openness prevailed. This was due in part to the protection of reformers like Zhao Ziyang high in the Party structure. Debate on the need for a press law, and the form that law would take, became more public and more heated. Newspapers like the *World Economic Herald* and the *Asia-Pacific Economic Times* grew increasingly bold. In 1988 Chen Ziming and Wang Juntao, two independent social scientists, took over *Economics Weekly*. As these papers reported on China's uneven steps toward a market economy, they inevitably covered political and social affairs as well. They became widely read forums for opinions about reform, and they served as inspirations and models for other publications.

When the protest movement began in the spring of 1989, China's journalists had come too far down the road toward independence to beat a hasty retreat. They had too much at stake: their own autonomy and editorial integrity, and their desire to report history in the making.

The student demonstrations challenged them to become the kind of journalists they had always wanted to be.

SETH FAISON,
THE PRESS DURING THE 1989 DEMONSTRATIONS

As the protest movement in Tiananmen Square gathered momentum, the Chinese press began to speak out in ways that were unprecedented in the People's Republic. During a short period of time newspapers, radio, and television were able to publish and broadcast reports about the tectonic events taking place in Beijing and elsewhere around the country without interference. For the first time in most people's memories, China enjoyed a press that was free from the strictures of Party dictates.

This selection was excerpted from "The Changing Role of the Chinese Media," published in The Chinese People's Movement: Perspectives on Spring 1989, *edited by Tony Saich (1990). Seth Faison, later the New York Times Shanghai bureau chief, was then a South China Morning Post Beijing correspondent.*

It was already late evening when two young editors at the *Renmin Ribao (People's Daily)* approached the office of Tan Wenrui, the paper's editor in chief. It was unusual for the men to visit their boss at a late hour, but it had been an unusual day. More than 1,000 determined students from Beijing University had marched overnight on April 17, 1989, to Tiananmen Square, where they laid wreaths for the former party leader Hu Yaobang, who had died of a heart attack two days earlier. It was the largest student march since late 1986, and the newsroom was abuzz with speculation that even larger protests would follow. The young journalists were now wondering: Would the *People's Daily*, official mouthpiece of the Chinese Communist Party, report on the day's remarkable events?

Tan, a slim, soft-spoken man in his late sixties, was talking on the telephone. He motioned the two editors to come into his office, a spacious room whose walls were covered with citations and photographs accumulated during Tan's thirty-nine-year career as a loyal soldier for the Party paper. When Tan hung up the phone, one of the journalists

handed him a handwritten draft of a news article about the demonstration put together by a couple of *People's Daily* reporters who witnessed
the daring march. Tan read it in silence. He knew that the editors were
seeking his approval to publish it, something they had never done
before. Like other official newspapers, the *People's Daily* had to follow
Party instructions when assigning, reporting, and especially publishing
stories. Any deviation from the norm could endanger the careers of
reporters and editors involved. Tan remained silent. The editors got up
and left, their plea silently made.

Tan sat quietly for several more minutes, then continued his nightly
round of telephone calls to editors at other newspapers to see how they
were playing the officially sanctioned stories of the day: a report on
industry in Jiangsu Province, another on rising workers' incomes, a third
on an education conference. Tan may have discussed the student
demonstration with other senior editors or government officials, but he
did not have to ask anyone whether publishing would be seen as a direct
challenge to the Party's leaders. The next day, neither the *People's Daily*
nor any of the other major papers carried anything about the march.

It appeared that censorship, exercised by veteran editors like Tan, had
once again prevailed. But when newspapers arrived in mailboxes
around Beijing the next morning, there was surprise. The *Keji Ribao*
(*Science and Technology Daily*), a state-controlled newspaper that usually limited its coverage to nonpolitical news, had published a factual
account of the scene in the square alongside a large photograph showing students, some with clenched fists, packed around a huge banner
that proclaimed, "The Soul of China." No one else had dared touch the
story, let alone publish a picture portraying the students sympathetically.
Copies were quickly pasted up on bulletin boards at Beijing University,
drawing huge crowds all day. Journalists at other papers reacted with
pride and a touch of envy. "It seemed like such a natural step; I remember thinking, 'We will all be doing this soon,'" a reporter from the
Zhongguo Qingnian Bao (*China Youth News*) said later.

Sure enough, the *Science and Technology Daily*'s coverage, like a
tiny leak in the dike of official control, led to further journalistic risk taking, which eventually turned into a flood of reports on the peaceful
protest movement. In the following days, balanced articles on the
spreading demonstrations appeared in the *Gongren Ribao* (*Workers'
Daily*), the *Nongmin Ribao* (*Farmers' Daily*), and *Beijing Qingnian Bao*
(*Beijing Youth News*). Within a few weeks, journalists joined students to
march for greater press freedom, arguing that it was a cornerstone of

long overdue political reform. Inside newspaper offices, reporters—including those at the *People's Daily* whose initial attempt to cover the movement had been frustrated by their cautious editor—petitioned their superiors to begin reporting accurately. Finally, after a massive demonstration on May 4, with support from the liberal faction of the Party, even the *People's Daily* started to report on the protests in a fair, if limited, way. Everyone followed suit, and by mid-May the dike of censorship itself seemed to have been washed away. . . .

Chinese Press Freedom and the Case of Qin Benli

By 1988, minor signs of change [had already] begun to appear. A handful of nonofficial newspapers—set up independently but still liable to censorship by propaganda departments—were pushing the limits of what was acceptable. A growing number of reports on sensitive economic issues were published; if somewhat one-sided, they at least brought touchy subjects out into the open, a clear step forward.

Other issues, including political ones, eventually came under journalistic scrutiny as well. One blockbuster appeared in December 1988, when the progressive, nonofficial, Shanghai-based journal the *World Economic Herald* published an article by the theoretician Su Shaozhi that sharply criticized government policy toward intellectuals.

The *Herald*'s editor, a feisty, chain-smoking journalist named Qin Benli, quickly came under fire. The Shanghai authorities, who had clashed with Qin off and on ever since the paper was launched in 1980, called him in to discuss his "resignation." Qin, with thirty years of experience in debating propaganda officials, argued that Su was an old personal friend. When he offered the *Herald* an essay he had written, how could Qin refuse? The essay was based on a speech Su had delivered at a national conference in Beijing. If it was allowed there, Qin argued, shouldn't it be published for readers in Shanghai as well?

The matter was appealed to the Shanghai Party secretary Jiang Zemin, whose loyalty to Beijing would six months later yield a big promotion, to replace Zhao Ziyang as general secretary of the CCP. Jiang had warned Qin in 1987, when the *Herald* was criticized for printing an interview with the dissident astrophysicist Fang Lizhi, that the newspaper could continue publication on the condition that it stick to economic issues and avoid politics. Now he lectured Qin again, saying that "many comrades" thought it might be time for Qin, age seventy-two, to retire. But his departure might be delayed, Jiang said, if Qin wrote a statement explaining why the *Herald* had run Su's article so that superiors in Beijing could consider the issue. Qin wrote the memo and was allowed to travel to the United States in February 1989, pending a decision from the capital.

In Washington, Qin accepted an interview with the Voice of America, where he said that he was still the *Herald*'s editor but that retirement might beckon "sooner or later," a signal to Beijing that he was adequately humble but hoped to retain his position. Qin also was able to meet President George Bush, with whom he shared a four-sentence conversation on the receiving line of an official breakfast. President Bush had just announced plans to travel to China later that month, and Qin authorized a front-page story in the *Herald* on the "interview with President Bush." Qin knew it would not look good if, when Bush arrived in Beijing, the authorities had just sacked a progressive editor Bush himself had met so recently in Washington. Talk of Qin's retirement was put aside.

When Hu Yaobang died suddenly in April, Qin saw an opportunity to broach sensitive political issues the same way students had. He authorized the *Herald*'s Beijing bureau to invite several prominent and outspoken intellectuals to a special forum to mourn Hu Yaobang and consider his legacy. For professors and writers disgruntled with the bumpy course of reform, the debate over Hu Yaobang's sudden dismissal after the last round of student demonstrations was precisely the kind of talk the government did not want to hear.

The *Herald* prepared a special edition with the most potent extracts from the forum. Wu Mingyu, a former government official, discussed how Hu once said he had two regrets in life: his failure to protect a colleague during the antirightist campaign of the 1950s and his agreement to make a self-criticism when he was dismissed in January 1987. Others called for a clearing of Hu's name and an honest explanation about why he lost his job—in effect, calling on the government to account for its authoritarian ways.

"The main problem China has had, up to today, is a lack of democracy. A handful of people can just talk among themselves, put aside the interests of the people, and reach an unpopular decision," said Yan Jiaqi, a political scientist who was later to escape from China to lead the Paris-based democracy movement in exile. Such statements became commonplace in the weeks that followed, but to have printed them openly in a newspaper in late April was still a risk.

When Shanghai authorities got word that the *Herald* was preparing a special edition on Hu Yaobang, they telephoned Qin to make sure their censors would get a preview, as usual. Qin said yes, and on April 21 newspaper proofs were sent over accordingly. A municipal Party official called Qin the following day and ordered him to delete the most sensitive parts of the edition. Summing up the government's view of the press, the official said, "It is not allowed to publish openly any opinions that differ from the official decisions of the central authorities, especially in the current circumstances when students have taken to the streets."

To the official's surprise, Qin refused. "I want Deng Xiaoping to examine these himself," Qin said of the proofs, according to the government's account of the meeting later published by Xinhua. "The earlier he looks at them, the earlier he will enjoy popular support. If he'll examine them, we will follow his decision."

Alarmed by Qin's open defiance, the official contacted Jiang Zemin, the Shanghai party chief. According to one account, Jiang exploded when Qin walked into his office in downtown Shanghai, hurling a stream of abuse at the editor that only subsided as Jiang got around to discussing the possible ways the *Herald* staff might suffer if Qin did not agree to amend the controversial edition. Eventually Qin appeared to agree and headed back to the newspaper to review the edition. Jiang later found out, however, that printing of the original edition had already begun before his meeting with Qin. In all, the government later claimed, 160,000 copies of the banned edition were printed, several hundred of which found their way to Beijing, where they were leaked to Chinese and foreign journalists. The unsuccessful attempt to stifle the *Herald* was reported around the world.

Jiang was livid. He ordered Qin dismissed immediately and sent a "work team" to the offices of the *Herald* to supervise subsequent issues. Jiang may have taken encouragement from Beijing, where Deng Xiaoping had spelled out a hard line against demonstrations that was carried in a *People's Daily* editorial on April 26. According to one account, Deng personally reviewed a draft of the editorial, crossing out each use of the phrase "student movement" and replacing it with the politically charged "turmoil," effectively branding the student demonstrators as political enemies.

Only one day later, the political outlook in Beijing was muddied again, at least as far as Jiang was concerned. Student leaders, angered at being called enemies in the editorial, pulled off an extraordinary well-organized march of 100,000 fellow students, piercing police blockades with a seemingly miraculous absence of injuries. Traffic in the capital was paralyzed, and onlookers could be seen cheering the students all over the city. The government announced that some sort of dialogue with the students would be held. Deng's orders to use violence to suppress the marchers had been stymied by unwilling officials and police. The students were triumphant.

In the uncertain political climate, Jiang probably did not want to risk closing the *Herald* down entirely. He was under heavy enough criticism from the reformers as it was. But the paper's staff was not cooperating in putting out subsequent editions. For the next week's paper, the staff prepared several hard-hitting articles on a variety of topics, believing that the censors would not be able to ban everything. Arguments broke out over the final proofs. An edition was eventually prepared with a page one headline, "In Memory of May Fourth," but when it came back from the printer, a new headline had been substituted: "We Need an Atmosphere Where We Can Speak Freely." When the "work team" tried to pin down who had replaced the headline, printing staff all said they could not remember. After two more editions produced nonstop bickering, the newspaper was shut down.

Meanwhile, the Qin Benli incident became a cause célèbre in Beijing. When students again marched in huge numbers on May 4, they were joined by several hundred journalists who openly paraded under banners with the names of their newspapers and carried signs proclaiming, "Newspapers Should Speak the Truth," "Press Freedom," and "Reinstate Qin Benli." It seemed at the time that the string of uninterrupted antigovernment protests would certainly succeed in extracting some liberal concessions from the government, the first of which, many felt, would be a freer press.

The Chinese Press Opens Up

On the morning of May 5, it was clear which side the main newspapers were on. The *People's Daily* carried large photographs of the massive demonstration held the day before, the first time the paper had done so. In contrast to the minimal stories on the march of April 27, which had been described as illegal and improper, those published on May 5 reported accurately on the student chants for democracy and science. A photograph appearing on the front pages of many papers showed a banner that urged, "Support the *World Economic Herald*." For ordinary readers outside Beijing, it was the clearest news yet on the demonstrations. For sophisticated readers all over China, it demonstrated the depth of the political crisis that was unfolding.

On May 5, Zhao Ziyang told Hu Qili and his fellow Secretariat member Rui Xingwen that there was "no big risk in opening up a bit by reporting the demonstrations and increasing the openness of news." This statement was later used by the government as evidence that Zhao supported the protest movement; indeed, an exhibition in the Military Museum on the "quelling of the counterrevolutionary rebellion" highlighted Zhao's words, though few viewers would likely consider a call for more press freedom to be a crime. In fact, Zhao's comment simply gave official recognition to what had been a reality in the press since the previous day. An editor such as Tan Wenrui did not need to have spelled out what he had read between the lines in Zhao's May 4 speech. And Tan may have had quiet instructions from a higher authority.

Whatever the politics behind the scenes, journalists all over Beijing seemed convinced that an irrevocable step toward press freedom had been taken.

It is still unclear what role Hu Qili played in the dramatic explosion of press coverage that took place on May 17, 18, and 19. For those three days, the *People's Daily* looked as though its censors had melted away. Reporters believe Hu was so caught up in the late-night meetings with other leaders that he simply did not worry about media coverage. Long, detailed, and sympathetic articles on the demonstrations and hunger strikers showed no signs of the paper's earlier caution. For readers of the *People's Daily*, that was as good as official permission to go out and join the demonstrations.

At least one million people jammed Tiananmen Square and the surrounding streets on May 17, derailing parts of Mikhail Gorbachev's visit. Reporters and editors from every major newspaper joined the marches, openly parading under the banners that called for a more open press. "One Million from All Walks of Life Demonstrate in Support of Hunger-Striking Students" screamed the main headline on the May 18 *People's Daily*. "Save the Students, Save the Children," read a headline over a separate story. The newspaper ran six page-one articles on the boisterous demonstration. A small corner at the bottom of page one noted the historic Gorbachev visit, which under normal circumstances would have dominated the news.

"Over 1,000 reporters and workers from our own paper took part in the demonstrations, with several renowned and respected writers and editors at the head of the line," said a page-one story from one leading newspaper. Another national paper, the *Guangming Daily*, ran seven different stories on its front page about the demonstrations in Beijing and other cities. "The condition of the students and the future of the country touched the heart of every Chinese who has a conscience," said one.

As astonishing and unprecedented as such reporting was, it was not completely free. What was happening on the streets was being reported accurately and fully, but the power struggle within Zhongnanhai was left untouched. When Qian Liren, the director of the *People's Daily*, attended a meeting chaired by Li Peng on May 18, the premier is said to have exclaimed, "We have lost control of your newspaper!" Qian apparently responded that his paper included "not one small bit" of bourgeois liberalism and was still upholding the basic principles of the CCP.

Li Peng had more pressing matters at hand. He met the student leaders Wu'er Kaixi, Wang Dan, and others that day and apparently did not pursue the argument with Qian. When martial law was declared on May 20, Qian checked into a hospital, the face-saving way of avoiding responsibility when the ax is about to come down. Tan Wenrui also entered a hospital, as had Zhao Ziyang the night before.

Li Peng's meeting with the unruly students was, for many Chinese viewers, one of the high points of recent television coverage, which, like newspaper reporting, had been selective and tame until May 17. Beijing residents had heard about Wu'er Kaixi and Wang Dan, and the exceptional organization of student marches on April 22 and 27 and May 4 had made them something of folk heroes. But although the two mavericks welcomed interviewers from the foreign press, they had remained invisible to the vast majority of Chinese. Their requests to see Li Peng were finally granted at noon May 18 and broadcast after the nightly 7:00 P.M. news.

Looking nervous and exhausted, Li's appearance contrasted sharply with the smooth, if dull show he gave during a televised meeting with Gorbachev two days prior. After hurriedly shaking hands with the seven student representatives, commenting with forced sympathy on the hunger striker Wu'er Kaixi's need to wear hospital pajamas, Li launched into a rambling, disorganized speech. He appeared confused about how to talk without a prepared agenda, especially to students whom he had until that day referred to as unworthy renegades. "My youngest child is older than all of you. . . . I have three children . . . not one does official profiteering, but they're all older than you . . . you are all like our own children, like our own flesh and blood."

Wu'er Kaixi promptly interrupted him. "Premier Li, we don't have time to talk like this. . . . It was not you who invited us here, but rather it was the huge number of us in the square who asked you to come and talk about several issues. It should be for us to decide about what."

Chinese viewers had never before seen one of their top leaders talked to in such a manner, much less by a twenty-one-year-old student. If television has an equalizing effect, putting debaters on a seemingly equal footing, Wu'er Kaixi's brash, charismatic manner made him look far more authoritative than Li. Other students spoke rationally, consistently, and to the point. Li was mumbling incoherently even as he left. It seemed shocking that Chinese television would allow such embarrassing footage to be broadcast to hundreds of millions of viewers across the nation, but one of Li's aides personally went to China Central Television's studios that afternoon to approve an unedited version.

The reason such footage was shown, damaging or not, became clear in Li's final statement. He warned that serious consequences would follow if the students did not leave the square immediately. But without any major concessions from the government, no amount of pleading would get the students to leave the square. Some viewers, offended by Wu'er Kaixi's rudeness, felt he may have forfeited the students' one shot at real negotiation. But in fact a decision had already been made by the time the meeting was held. Unknown to the students, Li had the previous day agreed with other leaders—without Zhao—to declare martial law in Beijing. By meeting the students, Li apparently tried to give the impression that the government was willing to offer them one last chance. But it was already too late.

The Chinese Press Back on the Leash

After martial law was declared on May 20, it took two full weeks before the freewheeling situation in Tiananmen Square was brought under control. At the *People's Daily*, it took one day. Qian Liren and Tan Wenrui were gone, and a "work team" made up of order-obeying editors and plainclothes soldiers entered the newspaper compound, many of them dressed as doctors in ambulances to avoid being blocked at the gate. Two reporters and five print-shop workers were arrested for their complicity in putting out an unofficial edition of the newspaper that urged on the protesters. Several senior editors told friends they would resign rather than continue working at a newspaper that would now once again toe an embattled, anachronistic party line.

But few actually did. Instead, the vast majority of reporters and editors stayed on and found ways to signal their resistance to the central authorities by sneaking irreverent news items through the censor's net. The first example occurred on May 21, only one day after martial law was declared. Coverage of the demonstrators was reined in, but at the bottom of the front page, where the one or two international news items rarely attracted the censor's attention, editors ran a story on the resignation of a prime minister in Italy. No careful Chinese reader could fail to understand that it was a swipe at China's own prime minister, Li Peng. The following day, the censors had apparently not yet caught on, for in the same space was an item on a Hungarian leader's statement that Stalinist tactics of violence should not be used to suppress the people.

The new ideologues now supervising the *People's Daily* gradually tightened their grip. A box that appeared on page one to remind readers each morning how many days the as yet unenforced martial law declaration had been in effect was eventually scrapped. Photographs of demonstrators stopped appearing in any form. By June 3 officials had effectively stifled any overt signs of sympathy for the popular expression on the streets. After June 4 there were no more overt signs to report.

On that fateful night, when soldiers were finally ordered to shoot their way into Beijing, hundreds of journalists risked their lives to see and record the tragedy for posterity. They knew by then that their own newspapers would print nothing of the truth of what they saw. Photojournalists who witnessed the killings in Muxidi, Fuxingmen, and Xidan later hid their photographs or had them confiscated by the authorities.

One woman photographer bravely held her ground beside a line of students at Xidan, watching them fall as approaching soldiers mowed them down. After a moment of shock, she began to run down a side street, only to be fired at from behind. A bullet ripped through her back, piercing her right lung before it exited above her breast. Somehow she kept running, until she fell into the arms of bystanders who carried her to a hospital. Her shirt was soaked in blood. As a medical worker cut through her clothing to inspect the wounds he found her black journalist card and told a doctor. She was immediately taken to a hidden room in the hospital basement, where she was given immediate attention ahead of a long line of other casualties. "We have to serve you first," she remembers the doctor telling her as he dressed her injury. "We have to protect the witnesses."

Chinese journalists were indeed witnesses to the Beijing uprising of 1989, witnesses who would have to remain silent, during the repression that followed, about what they had seen. But they are unlikely to forget.

ORVILLE SCHELL,
THE SECOND CHANNEL

Although harsh controls were reimposed on the media as part of the crack-down after June 4, when Deng Xiaoping made his nanxun, or "tour of the South," in 1992 and once again encouraged market forces to take the lead, media entrepreneurs went back into high gear. It was not long before a world of commerce-driven media began springing up beneath the veneer of Party-controlled outlets as a quasi underground.

This selection was excerpted from "Letter from China" by coeditor Orville Schell, which appeared in The New Yorker *in July 1994.*

When I met Jia Lusheng at a Beijing restaurant in the spring of 1989, as the demonstrations in Tiananmen Square were building, there was little about him to suggest that he was a well-known writer, much less in the forefront of a whole new style of Chinese journalism. Unlike the typical pale-faced urban intellectual, Jia had dark skin and unkempt hair, which, along with a less than stylish manner of dress, conveyed the impression of someone who did not spend his life behind a desk. And, in fact, he told me that he felt far more comfortable in the provinces among ordinary people than in the meeting halls of Beijing's intelligentsia. Jia was one of a group of emerging writers who had used the relative openness of the 1980s to pioneer a bold new kind of investigative journalism known as *baogao wenxue*—literary reportage. This genre, something akin to New Journalism in the United States, proved popular and helped encourage writers to *ganyu shenghuo*, or "delve into life" and expose its "dark sides," rather than just *fenshi shenghuo*, or "cosmeticize life," as writers of socialist realism had been forced to do for four decades. By going underground for months at a time among beggars, petty criminals, street urchins, mentally unbalanced drifters, entrepreneurial hustlers, prostitutes, political outcasts, and prisoners, Jia began revealing aspects of Chinese society that had largely been ignored by more conventional writers. The result was a corpus of long, agenda-setting investigative pieces such as "Travels with Beggars," about living with China's drifters, and "The Language of Thieves," about street lingo, that, when they were published in the late 1980s, in the journal

Baogao Wenxue, pulled back the shroud from an enormous underclass, which neo-Maoist Party hard-liners were far from pleased to see highlighted.

Jia and other contributors to *Baogao Wenxue* prided themselves on fearlessly covering topics that ranged from underground political movements and the conditions in prisons to malfeasance in office and the abject poverty of China's dispossessed.

Even though the late 1980s were a period of relative liberalization, because of his exposés Jia was accused of engaging in "yellow journalism" and in 1988 was expelled from his official "work unit," the Shandong branch of the Chinese Writers' Association. "Since I no longer have an 'iron rice bowl' and very few people want to have much to do with a writer who has no unit, the only way I can survive now is to give my stuff to the 'second channel'," he said, smiling self-deprecatingly. "It's not so much that I want to be underground as that I have no choice." In fact, just before his expulsion, *Baogao Wenxue* published an article in which he described a group of book and magazine publishers and distributors who were starting to form this shadowy underground. It was a subject worthy of Jia's attention, because the second channel had begun to do something long thought impossible in China: it had begun to challenge the state's control over the printed word.

Before Deng Xiaoping began allowing whole sectors of China's economy to privatize and to become regulated by market forces, the publication and distribution of books and periodicals had been a state-run monopoly. While there were hundreds of different publishing houses, all were controlled by the State General Publishing Administration (SGPA), an organization that was under the thumb of the Party Central Committee's Propaganda Department and had a branch in each of China's provinces. The government also regulated the allocation of paper and saw to it that all publications were distributed through the state-owned Xinhua Book Distribution Company, which had the exclusive right to supply the thousands of retail outlets that composed the country's network of Xinhua Bookstores. Writers, too, were a part of this vertical state monopoly. Each writer was carefully screened before being admitted to the official Chinese Writers' Association, whose branches existed in every province and major city, and paid a member's salary and provided his or her housing, health care, and pension. Since it was rare for a writer who wasn't in the association to be published regularly, and since publishing abroad was unthinkable, it was virtually impossible for anyone to make a living as a writer outside the system. Just to maintain one's status as a "literary worker" and to be successful at the kind of self-censorship that was required demanded an almost intuitive sense of where shifting ideological boundaries were at any given moment.

Only after manuscripts passed muster at an official publishing house did the SGPA assign them *shuhao*—book-registration numbers, which in 1987 became China's International Standard Book Numbers. Without such a number, no volume could be legally printed, published, or distributed in China. In 1987, after student demonstrations rocked the country, the oversight body was renamed the State General Press and Publications Administration (SGPPA) and, in an effort to tighten and centralize controls, was given the responsibility for regulating newspapers, magazines, and other periodicals as well as books.

Even so, although the Party still controlled all major publishing houses and newspapers during the late 1980s, a host of trashy tabloids and works of pulp fiction aimed solely at making money began appearing and eroding the old system of control. The growing laxity also allowed serious muckrakers like Jia to explore previously taboo subjects. At the same time, foreign works began to appear in abundance; the writings of Nietzsche, Freud, Jung, Adam Smith, Locke, Jefferson, and even Orwell were soon competing for space at outdoor bookstalls with the autobiographies of Ronald and Nancy Reagan and Lee Iacocca.

When I asked Jia in 1989 how publishing had changed in China, he laughed and said that the situation was "really screwed up" but that he liked to describe it as consisting of three different routes, each of which had its own characteristic color. The "red route" was the old government monopoly. The "white route" consisted of private entrepreneurs and a network of nongovernmental distributors, who, although they technically had government permission to distribute a restricted variety of publications within a prescribed region (the restrictions differed wildly from place to place), often secretly branched out, linking up with each other to form extensive, quasi-clandestine distribution systems that Jia described as being like an "irrigation system spread out across our vast country among millions of people." The "black route" was made up of unlicensed, illegal, fly-by-night deal makers, underground printers, and private distributors operating without any government sanction, who tended toward the production of racy tabloids, pornography (a very lucrative business in Deng's China), and quickie reproductions of *neibu*, or "for internal circulation only," books published by the Party for high-level cadres on a need-to-know basis. *Neibu* publications included such things as classified government documents, translations of critical foreign views of China, inner-Party critiques of past policies, and even occasional unflattering accounts of purged leaders. Needless to say, the word *neibu* gave a book great cachet and almost guaranteed a tremendous boost in sales, making black-route operators only too glad to take the risk of printing such knockoff editions.

By "the second channel," Jia meant a combination of the quasi-legal white route and the illegal black route, which often overlapped. Both centered on what he called *shuwang*, or "book kings," many of whom were ordinary young Chinese who had made their initial scores as entrepreneurs in the profitable business of distributing publications. By 1989 some book kings had started commissioning new manuscripts on hot topics that they deemed to have market potential. Since the advances and royalties they offered were usually far higher than those paid by state publishing houses, and since second-channel books could be produced much more quickly than officially approved books—editing was a notoriously hasty and cursory process—book kings were able to capitalize on market trends far more readily than the bureaucratic state-run houses. It was not surprising that writers were willing to be published via the second channel. Nor was it surprising that some writers, after churning out a hasty potboiler, adopted pen names to avoid damage to their reputations, or even prosecution.

Once a book king had received a completed manuscript, he had to make an important choice. If the topic was too controversial or too sexual, he might steal a *shuhao*, or else arrange for the book to be printed illegally without a number and then distributed as a black-route publication. Otherwise, he would usually negotiate with a state-run publishing house for the use of its name and one of its *shuhao*. Although the payments for these services were essentially bribes, they did help a book maintain at least a semblance of legality.

According to Jia, some private township industries, which had proliferated as Deng's economic reform movement accelerated in the 1980s, were soon entirely devoted to the production of illegal publications. Upon visiting one of these operations, in Shandong Province, he was stunned to find printing presses hidden literally underground, in cellars, and the whole town—children as well as adults—consecrated to the task of laying out, printing, and binding illicit books and magazines.

Such industries were able to flourish because it became increasingly difficult for the government to continue controlling publishing when free market economic reforms in other areas were allowing, and even encouraging, other Chinese to become more entrepreneurial. And as market forces came to dominate more and more sectors of the economy and government subsidies were progressively cut back, even state-owned publishers were forced to pay close attention to profits and losses. Eliminating the second channel altogether would have deprived publishers of an important, though illicit, source of income.

After a brief, though tense, post–Tiananmen Square hiatus, book kings began picking up where they had left off, and by sticking with works that were largely nonpolitical in content, they were soon cautiously expanding their operations again. Then, in the climate of rampant capitalist expansion that began sweeping China after January of 1992, when Deng Xiaoping signified his approval of a new great leap in the development of China's market economy, . . . publishing and every other form of independent business raced to embrace the market with new, unalloyed vigor.

By early 1993, China was on fire with commercial zeal, and entrepreneurs were harder than ever to control. Since consumers were spending more money on leisure activities, it was possible for publishers to make fortunes playing to people's fascination with the latest fashions, occult practices, military lore, pop music styles, and new household conveniences. How-to books on improving one's sex life and redecorating one's bathroom abounded. Tracts with titles like "183 Tricks to Playing the Stock Market" sold like hotcakes. A magazine I picked up in Kunming called *Legal Stories* had a cover emblazoned not with legal briefs but with a girl in a bikini surrounded by a phalanx of helmeted, gun-toting police, and contained such pieces as "Bar Girls!" and "Beautiful Women Flashy As Female Wolves." It was a runaway seller. The magazine *Deer Call* offered such articles as "Female Teacher Buried Alive by Sexually Perverted Hoodlums" and "Porno Fantasies Cause a Life to Be Lost.". . . Almost every publication seemed to pander to prurience, greed, violence, or power. One enterprising Shandong book king even bought a *shuhao* to publish a Chinese translation of *Mein Kampf*—although he changed the title to *The Footprints of the Fighters*.

Even organs of the Chinese government decided to "jump into the sea of commerce." In a move to contain the second channel and profit from it at the same time, officials began renting out space to private entrepreneurs in Xinhua Bookstores and setting up new kinds of book outlets of their own. For example, in Beijing the Chaoyang District People's Government and the Beijing Press and Publications Bureau got together with the Beijing Chaoyang District City Construction Comprehensive Development Company to open the Beijing Magazine and Book Wholesale Trade Mart, on a dead-end street in the eastern part of the capital near the *People's Daily* office. In spite of the fact that each stallholder must pay a monthly rent of approximately $230 and that vendors were easy prey for tax collectors and Industry and Commercial Bureau inspectors collecting licensing fees, the mart has quickly become a beehive of activity. A hundred booths and more than 200 different private and state-owned publishers and distribution companies are represented, selling everything from books and magazines to cards and calendars.

Wherever there is money to be made, some mogul now has a way of popping up. Book kings, who have begun referring to themselves by the slightly more dignified name "book traders," now find themselves in competition with a new generation of upstart operators, including some who have been dubbed *feixing daxia,* or "flying knights." Many of these *feixing daxia* are uneducated youths who got their start by operating private bookstalls on the streets, where they gained a keen sense of the way rapidly changing trends influence what sells, as well as the entrepreneurial skills needed to make deals. This new breed of publishers includes illiterates, hoodlums, and even ex-cons; they rarely have offices or permanent phone numbers, so they are almost impossible to track down and hold accountable. Some, operating out of hotel rooms, simply appear at the homes of popular writers and offer them suitcases full of cash to crank something out posthaste. With manuscript in hand, a *feixing daxia* will jump on a train or plane to rendezvous with an underground provincial printer with whom he has personal connections and who is willing to start rolling his presses without payment. Then, to raise the capital to pay the printer, the *feixing daxia* begins soliciting prepaid orders through second-channel distributors. By the time his book is printed and bound, the scheme, if it's successful, has produced enough not only to pay the printer but to create a fat premium for the flying knight as well. In a matter of weeks, the book is in the distribution system, and its progenitor has dropped out of sight.

By the end of 1993, the general manager of Xinhua Bookstores, Deng Yun, was lamenting in the SGPPA's official organ, *China Press & Publishing Journal,* that about a third of the 90,000 titles that had appeared the year before in China were published through illicit private channels. An editorial in the *Journal* had likened what was happening in publishing to a form of "slow suicide" and warned that if China didn't bring its maverick book kings to heel, "the Communist Party and the state will lose control over the leadership and management of publishing." The official *Guangming Daily* quoted Deng Xiaoping himself expressing concern, by chastising "some persons in the fields of the arts, publishing, and antiquities who have simply become businessmen motivated only by profit."

Jia Lusheng was probably one of the people Deng was referring to, for Jia indeed survived the 1989 crackdown quite nicely. Embracing Deng's unlikely slogan "To get rich is glorious" with new ardor, by 1991 he was working out of Zhengzhou, the capital of Henan Province, and had transformed himself into a mover and shaker in a world where successful entrepreneurs enjoyed expensive banquets, drove Mercedeses, and clinched distribution deals over car phones. His first post-1989 book, an investigation of China's then-faltering economy, was banned but nonetheless reportedly sold almost a million copies. His next book, *The Sun That Never Sets*, was about the Mao phenomenon that swept the country just before the hundredth anniversary, in December of 1993, of the Chairman's birth. I picked up a copy at a private bookstall in Shanghai and read on its title page that it had been put out by the Central China Peasants Publishing House, printed by the Loyang Yuxi Printing Company, and distributed by the Henan branch of the Xinhua Book Distribution Company. However, as in the case of most products of the second channel, its title page did not necessarily tell its real pedigree. Still, whether it had come up along the red, white, or black route was not what mattered to Jia. What mattered was that before the sun set on this book it is said to have sold hundreds of thousands of copies.

Radio and television have traditionally been the media most tightly controlled in China, and the stations have always been state owned. By the beginning of 1994, however, even radio and television had begun to develop a set of shadow institutions that in certain ways seemed to take their cue from publishing's second channel.

Until recently, each Chinese city had only one locally controlled radio and television station. In 1992, however, under the sponsorship of the entrepreneurial-minded Gong Xueping, formerly the director of the Shanghai Bureau of Radio and Television and later the city's vice mayor in charge of culture, Shanghai was allowed to set up a second station, East Radio, and then, in 1993, a new TV channel, Oriental Television. Although both operated under the aegis of the Shanghai Bureau of Radio and Television, they were to support themselves with commercials. But what was really unique about them was that they instituted a new style of programming, which included live shows and call-in talk programs—a mixture that the *China Daily* recently described as "revolutionizing China's conservative broadcasting format."

Refreshing as this new format is, hosts have had to be very careful to stay away from political controversy. "General political problems are out, but cultural, family, and city problems are in," I was recently told in Shanghai by an editor in Oriental Television's "reporting department," a nattily dressed twenty-seven-year-old named Wu Chaoyang, who has a master's degree in physics from Nanjing University. "In" subjects include civic problems like traffic and housing; consumer rights lawsuits; advice to the lovelorn; sports news; tips on personal finances; and information on consumer products. In addition, programs offer discussions of sexual problems and, of course, a rich diet of titillating crime stories. *Dongfang 110*, for instance, a program featuring actual criminal cases, is noteworthy in that not only is it produced with the Shanghai police, but it features a uniformed cop as an anchorwoman. As Wu put it, Oriental Television programming ranges "from economics to murder."

When I asked Wu about politics and government control, he immediately became more hesitant. Indeed, this is a subject that most people in the media still do not like to discuss on the record, especially with Western journalists. "Government interference is growing less and less," he said, somewhat unconvincingly. "We have our own regulations, but, in essence, we regulate ourselves. But it's hard to say anything about the future. Since I don't maintain terribly high hopes, there is little frustration. All I can say is that we are basically happy with our present living situation, so we don't think much about politics."

According to Wu, as soon as East Radio began broadcasting, the station "just made it overnight. No one imagined it would be so successful. Its founding is really a revolution in Chinese history." One of its most popular daytime shows is *Emergency Room Hotline*, which broadcasts a mixture of Western pop tunes and phoned-in consumer queries. A late-night program, listened to by taxi drivers and insomniacs, is a music and talk show called *Accompany You Till Dawn*. With a potential audience in the hinterland around Shanghai of roughly 100 million, Chinese talk radio has stirred such enthusiasm that sometimes thousands of callers have dialed in to East Radio at once. Occasionally, even local government leaders call in.

Politically bland as these radio and television shows still are, they have nonetheless revolutionized Chinese broadcasting. What is perhaps most important, they have given Chinese their first opportunity to voice their thoughts or problems in a direct and public way. This type of programming can now be heard on radio stations in almost every major city, so the call-in and live-interview format has been getting listeners all across the country accustomed to the notion of open discussion, and even some remonstration (although at this stage their remonstrations usually sound more like complaining than dissent). However, Wu's disclaimers notwithstanding, it is not difficult to imagine the role that such shows might play should some future wave of national protest sweep the country.

Despite the vast audience for radio, television has, not surprisingly, become the most influential medium of public communication. Although there are not yet any truly independent television channels in China, the issue of independence has been rendered somewhat moot because VCRs are ubiquitous. This means that large numbers of Chinese are now able to play any cassette they can get their hands on—whether hard-core pornography, MTV rock music videos, BBC documentaries, or Hong Kong kung fu movies—in the privacy of their own homes.

In addition, tens of thousands of parabolic satellite dishes have appeared on rooftops during the last few years, enabling citizens of the People's Republic to tune in to CNN and StarTV; the latter, partly owned by Rupert Murdoch, broadcasts to millions of Chinese households everything from *The Simpsons* and *The Oprah Winfrey Show* to the BCC World Service news and international sporting events. The list of those benefiting from the unregulated sale of satellite dishes is a telling one. Just as many state-run publishers have become dependent on income from the second channel, so some state-owned enterprises and government agencies have profited from the manufacturing of potentially subversive electronic products like satellite dishes; in fact, even such government organs as the PLA General Staff Department and the Ministry of Electronics have been engaged in marketing dishes to the public. And dishes have been sold not only on the street by venders who operate in much the same way as the private-bookstall owners, but also in state-owned department stores and electronics shops. Needless to say, all the manufacturers and retailers have acquired a vested interest in keeping the Chinese satellite dish industry uncontrolled.

What is more, over the past year or so a rapidly growing number of local work units and Party-sponsored block committees have also gained an economic interest in the industry's survival, by setting up thousands of minicable networks, which rely for programming on satellite feeds from StarTV as well as on videotapes of such things as foreign movies smuggled in from abroad. By buying a dish and then selling closed-circuit subscription hookups to other people in a given building, compound, or neighborhood, enterprising individuals have found a simple way to make a handsome return on a relatively small investment. In 1991, it was estimated that more than 10,000 of these community cable services had sprung up, and the government itself admitted that things were "out of control."

Shanghai Cable, a $115 million venture approved by the Shanghai Bureau of Radio and Television in 1992, is a good example of the Party's new policy of allowing the market to sate viewers with TV programming, provided that the programming is not politically provocative. It is set up to offer individual subscribers twelve new channels of entertainment for a hookup fee of about twenty-five dollars and a monthly charge thereafter of less than a dollar. Already some 700,000 homes in Shanghai have subscribed and been linked via fiber-optic cables. "When it's finished, it will be the biggest cable network in the world," Ye Zhikang, the vice director of the Shanghai Radio and Television Bureau, boasted to a Hong Kong monthly, *Asia, Inc.* "Then no one will need a satellite dish." Wu Chaoyang worried that "all these new cable channels will present even more competition for us at Oriental Television. Now the problem is that there is no shortage of programming, just a shortage of good programming."

China's expanding TV market has filled many overseas media merchants with visions of profit as rosy as those which gripped the nineteenth-century British industrialists who calculated they could keep the mills of Lancashire spinning for a generation if only every Chinese would add one inch to his shirttail. It has also been tempting for outsiders to believe that such a dynamic market would inevitably triumph over politics. But in early October of 1993 Premier Li Peng, who had been sidelined for months by heart trouble, signed State Council Proclamation 129, which made it illegal for individuals living in China to sell, buy, install, or use satellite dishes without obtaining government permission. According to the *People's Daily*, the object of the ban was to protect "socialist spiritual civilization"—or what was left of it.

Unsurprisingly, Li Peng's ban proved ineffective. By the time of the decree, there were so many satellite dishes in use that regulating them would have required the launching of a vast census operation to check every city dwelling, rooftop by rooftop.

The reality of China today is that issuing edicts against the sale of satellite dishes, banning books, fining second-channel publishers, and even imprisoning the occasional book king have done little to slow down the commercial forces that are driving China's quasi-underground media forward. Instead, the media seem to have co-opted aspects of Mao's theories on "people's war" and used them to become a kind of postmodern guerrilla operation, infiltrating official state structures with entrepreneurial energy. There is one enormous difference, however: the impetus behind this media revolution has almost nothing to do with ideology. "What has changed in China is the market," Zhang Weiguo, the former Beijing correspondent for the *World Economic Herald*, told me emphatically. "It is now money, rather than politics, that is in command, and there are such enormous fortunes being made in publishing underground newspapers, magazines, and books, and now in radio and television as well, that I don't think it's any longer realistic for the government to think in terms of completely stopping these second channels."

A clerk at a shop run by several university presses at the Beijing Magazine and Book Wholesale Trade Mart told me while I was browsing there one day this spring, "Oh, sure, officials come in here and confiscate stuff from time to time, but there's no longer any way they can actually control what's really going on. The most they can hope to accomplish is to scare people who mess with sensitive subjects."

THE BATTLE FOR CYBERSPACE

As China has become ever more integrated into the world market system, it has become increasingly reliant on the free flow of economic and technical information via such international communications systems as the telephone, fax, and Internet. At the same time ideological watchdogs have been made extremely wary about the political contagion that can enter China through these networks.

In December 1997, China adopted regulations designed to control access to the Internet as well as the kinds of politically "incorrect" information that they could bring into China. Whether such measures could effectively clamp down on this infamously nonauthoritarian form of communication was another question.

This selection was excerpted from "Regulations on the Security and

Management of Computer Information Networks and the Internet," *approved by the State Council on December 11, 1997.*

Chapter 1: Comprehensive Regulations

• In order to strengthen the security and the protection of computer information networks and of the Internet, and to preserve the social order and social stability, these regulations have been established on the basis of the "People's Republic of China Computer Information Network Protection Regulations," the "PRC Temporary Regulations on Computer Information Networks and the Internet," and other laws and administrative regulations.

• The security, protection, and management of all computer information networks within the borders of the PRC fall under these regulations.

• No unit or individual may use the Internet to harm national security, disclose state secrets, harm the interests of the state, of society, or of a group, the legal rights of citizens, or to take part in criminal activities.

• No unit or individual may use the Internet to create, replicate, retrieve, or transmit the following kinds of information:

1. Inciting to resist or breaking the Constitution or laws or the implementation of administrative regulations
2. Inciting to overthrow the government or the socialist system
3. Inciting division of the country, harming national unification
4. Inciting hatred or discrimination among nationalities or harming the unity of the nationalities
5. Making falsehoods or distorting the truth, spreading rumors, destroying the order of society
6. Promoting feudal superstitions, sexually suggestive material, gambling, violence, or murder
7. Terrorism or inciting others to criminal activity; openly insulting other people or distorting the truth to slander people
8. Injuring the reputation of state organs
9. Other activities against the Constitution, laws, or administrative regulations.

• No unit or individual may engage in the following activities which harm the security of computer information networks:

1. No one may use computer networks or network resources without getting proper prior approval.

2. No one may without prior permission change network functions or add or delete information.

3. No one may without prior permission add to, delete, or alter materials stored, processed, or being transmitted thorough the network.

4. No one may deliberately create or transmit viruses.

5. Other activities which harm the network are also prohibited.

• The freedom and privacy of network users is protected by law. No unit or individual may, in violation of these regulations, use the Internet to violate the freedom and privacy of network users.

Chapter 2: Responsibility for Security and Protection

• Units and individuals engaged in Internet business must accept the security supervision, inspection, and guidance of the public security organization. This includes providing to the public security organization information, materials, and digital documents, and assisting the public security organization to discover and properly handle incidents involving law violations and criminal activities involving computer information networks.

• The units mentioned above have the responsibility to report for the record to the local public security organization information on the units and individuals which have connections to the network. The units must also report in a timely manner to the public security organization any changes in the information about units or individuals using the network.

• The public security computer management and supervision organization is responsible for pursuing and dealing with illegal computer information network activities and criminal cases involving computer information networks. Criminal activities in violation of section 4 or section 7 should, according to the relevant state regulations, be handed over to the relevant department or to the legal system for appropriate disposition.

Chapter 4: Legal Responsibility

• For violations of law, administrative regulations, or section 5 or section 6 of these regulations, the public security organization gives a warning and, if there is income from illegal activities, confiscates the illegal earnings.

• For more serious offenses, computer and network access can be closed down for six months, and if necessary Public Security can suggest [the revocation of] the business operating license of the concerned unit or the cancellation of its network registration. Management activities that constitute a threat to public order can be punished according to provisions of the public security management penalties articles. Where crimes have occurred, prosecutions for criminal responsibility should be made.

Chapter 5: Additional Regulations

• These regulations should be consulted with regards to the implementation of the security, protection, and management of computer information networks connecting to networks in the Hong Kong Special Administrative Region as well as with networks in the Taiwan and Macao districts.

• These regulations go into effect on the day of promulgation.

V. CULTURE

As Mao wrote in his "Talks at the Yan'an Forum on Art and Literature" in 1942, "In the world today all culture, all literature and art belong to definite classes and are geared to definite political lines. There is in fact no such thing as art for art's sake. . . . Proletarian literature and art are part of the whole proletarian revolutionary cause; they are, as Lenin said, cogs and wheels in the whole revolutionary machine."

One of the most distinctive changes that occurred during Deng's reform era was that both "high" and "low" culture acquired more independence. Novelists became freer to write about "the dark side" of life; filmmakers were able to engage in a cautious new realism; artists began to paint ironic, and often even macabre, depictions of life and revolutionary iconography; and musicians could compose and perform music that was not purely didactic. As long as cultural works were not overtly political, artists were often able to escape official censorship.

However, the fact that the Party still controlled most of the major cultural outlets meant that artists whose sensibilities collided with the official view of things were forced to the margins or into pop culture. Indeed, while the world of "high culture" was quite moribund during the 1980s and '90s, "low culture" gained a rough vibrancy. In fact, pop culture became one of the main surrogate venues through which Chinese could air opposition sentiment, if not outright dissension.

★ H I G H   C U L T U R E   ★

Unlike Maoist views, Western notions of culture have traditionally centered on the idea that at the heart of any great work of art is the sensibility of an individual. If culture was to escape the Party and its "political line," it was first essential to reestablish an environment in which an individual artistic sensibility could be expressed without being persecuted. Indeed, one of the most significant but indirect aspects of Deng's reforms was the way the Party's retreat from everyday aspects of private life allowed space for such sensibilities to take tenuous root.

ORVILLE SCHELL, THE REEMERGENCE OF THE REALM OF THE PRIVATE

In assessing the depth of changes in China's cultural environment during Deng's tenure, it is essential to understand how deeply rooted systems of thought control had become in the psyches of a people who had endured long periods of forced ideological conformity. It would not be too extreme to say that Chinese intellectuals were kept obediently silent by their own acquiescence and eagerness to support "the revolution" as much as by the Party's organs of coercion. What distinguished the 1980s was a striking change in this state of passivity.

This selection was excerpted from an essay by coeditor Orville Schell, published in The Broken Mirror: China After Tiananmen, *edited by George Hicks (1990).*

For a decade in the 1980s we were regaled in our morning papers with news of one monumental change after another that embraced almost every aspect of Chinese life from culture and politics to the economy and environment. But there was one other change that, while not quite so palpable or directly measurable as the number of private vendors in the street, the variety of avant-garde publications for sale at newsstands, or the recrudescence of fashion in clothing, nonetheless had an impact on Chinese society of the most profound nature. This was a psychological change of heart that involved a transformation of the way Chinese began to feel about themselves. It was a transformation that changed the very chemistry of human and social relations.

When I visited Beijing in October 1989, four months after the June 4 massacre, martial law remained in effect and Tiananmen Square was still occupied by goose-stepping troops from the People's Liberation Army. Although I felt anxious to know firsthand how old friends and colleagues were faring under the crackdown, out of fear of causing them trouble, I decided not to look any of them up. Democracy movement suspects were still being detained, jailed, and even executed, while ordinary people continued to be herded into study sessions, forced to write out detailed diaries of where they had been and what they had done during the crucial days of April, May, and June, and in many cases to write confessions.

Over the preceding years, as China opened up and relaxed, I had slowly become accustomed to moving about with more and more impunity; to visiting whomever I wished with little concern for either their safety or my welcome as a visitor. But, this time, with such free and open interchange suddenly denied me, on arrival I found myself feeling alien and isolated, very much as if I was back in the China I remembered from the latter days of the Cultural Revolution, when Mao lived and the "Gang of Four" still held sway. Even now I remember with perfect vividness how perplexed I was upon arriving in Beijing in 1975 and finding that even though I spoke Mandarin and had spent years mixing with Chinese elsewhere in the world, I was now as unabsorbable as oil on water. No one, literally no one, was willing to speak with me as a foreigner, even to exchange pleasantries about the weather. . . . The Party and the state did not shine kindly on unauthorized personal relationships. It goes without saying that in this environment of suspicion and mistrust, where "unofficial" contact with foreign "imperialists" and "capitalists" might land a Chinese in prison, a visitor did feel positively leprous.

As I later came to appreciate, however, it was not just foreigners who were kept at arm's reach. Chinese were also afraid of each other. For unprogrammed liaisons or spontaneous encounters between them also raised the specter of conspiracy and could portend disastrous consequences. In fact, it is not too much to say that during these bitter years a whole generation of Chinese lost touch not only with the outside world of foreigners, but with each other as well. So defoliated of trust had the landscape become that almost any kind of personal friend with whom confidences could be safely shared became suspect.

Curiously, the distance between people was not maintained exclusively by secret police peering over shoulders and hectoring and bullying their charges into doing the bidding of the Party. Quite the contrary, as a measure of self-defense, most people learned how to police themselves. But, alas, by doing so they slowly lost the habit of seeing themselves as separate and distinct human beings entitled to a private life free of state scrutiny.

This dissolution of the realm of the private and of the self was aided and abetted by another compelling historical circumstance. The emphasis on the virtues of collectivized life and on "serving the people" rather than oneself had been so prevalent in the early years of the Communist Revolution that Chinese were provided with compelling rationalization for surrendering themselves to "selflessness" and their country. Of course, these ideals not only were Maoist but also enjoyed a good deal of resonance with older Confucian values of service and sacrifice to country and culture. Fragile enough in ordinary times even in the West, where individualism is lionized, the boundary that ordinarily exists between the realms of the public and the private became even further eroded by this new exaggerated Chinese ethic of sacrifice and selflessness. It is no small wonder, then, that in the People's Republic, where service to the Party and "people" was touted as the highest and most "correct" aspiration, and where attention to oneself was deemed "bourgeois" and antisocial, few people were able to maintain even a rudimentary sense of entitlement to the notion of a private life.

But perhaps the most powerful weapon the Party wielded in this collectivization of the Chinese psyche was guilt. By making its subjects feel responsible for their alleged "ideological crimes," the Party was able to manipulate them into blaming themselves even for those accusations that it chose to bring against them. This willingess—or perhaps it would be better to describe it as vulnerability—of intellectuals to blame themselves for charges leveled against them by the Party apparatus was perhaps the most destructive force of all to the preserve of a private world in which a "self" might safely reside. In this Alice-in-Wonderland universe, the accused unwittingly and horribly became complicitors in their own downfall. By taking part in what the intellectual historian Sun Longji describes in his book *The Deep Structure of Chinese Culture* as the "disorganization of the self," they ended up becoming their own accusers. Rather than reject the charges of being "rightists," "capitalist roaders," or "bourgeois individualists," those who had been attacked and "struggled against" tended to internalize the charges.

"The infallible Party cannot be wrong, therefore I must be wrong," was the common presumption. Such self-judgment led the victims to draw the charges toward themselves as if they were magnets, and then painstakingly to try to locate the seat of their alleged wrongdoing within themselves. The orgy of self-criticisms and confessions that China produced as a result of this perverted system is ample testament to a society that, having destroyed all vestiges of individualism, was left with an intellectually and morally defenseless populace passively accepting the Party's charges of ideological unhealth. The results were destructive and disastrous.

In his recent autobiography, Liu Binyan, one of China's most respected journalists, recalls his own long ordeal during the antirightist campaign of the late 1950s. Under repeated accusation, he writes:

> I began to lose confidence. Was I without fault? Of course not. And all my faults, in the final analysis, boiled down to "bourgeois individualism." Could I honestly say that I had joined the Party solely for the liberation of the Chinese people with no ulterior motives? Of course not. There was at least some element of self-fulfillment. And then there was my writing. Could I honestly say that I never had any eye on publicity and profit? Of course not.

After repeated assertions that one is a "rightist" with a "wrong attitude" and a "reactionary point of view," even the most stalwart person begins to have grave doubts about his own innocence. "All these [accusations] were very effective in adding to our load of guilt," Liu writes of the reaction between the accused in his own group of exiled rightists.

> In criticizing one another, we judged each other by the criteria of Communist Party members. . . . Thus, the criteria we set out were grandiose, but in the end, it always boiled down to "insufficient awareness of one's own guilt," "insufficient resolution to undergo thorough and complete reform of the self," as was in keeping with our "rightist" status.

The psychological effects of such incessant attack are obvious. As Sun Longji reminds us, "This intrusion into and control of private lives has no other function than to eradicate individual personality."

Looking back on all the political campaigns that he was forced to endure, Liu remembers being "preoccupied with a sense of humiliation that silently reminded me that I was the lowest of the low. That I had injured my wife and children. That I had no hope of exoneration in this life."

There were some notable exceptions of defiance in China. The writer Nien Cheng, author of *Life and Death in Shanghai,* comes to mind. But, it must be added that she had spent many years abroad, was a Christian, and had a very highly evolved sense of self, not to say of justice and indignation. But she was the exception rather than the rule. The way in which most Chinese ended up surviving was by internalizing the guilt, by blaming themselves for those charges and accusations that the Party and revolution leveled against them. The fact that to most of these victims the charges now seem nothing short of bizarre and preposterous suggests simply the nightmarish world of Franz Kafka's fiction, where characters labor eternally under vague but damning charges leveled against them by some apparat on high. Unable to understand the logic of their indictments, and thus unable to rebut them, they are left with no recourse other than guilty torment and the unsatisfying purgative powers of self-blame. That is, of course, the equivalent of mental self-immolation. In such a world, maintenance of a private reserve within which one's own psyche has any expectation of survival is unthinkable.

In *The Castle,* Kafka's antihero Land Surveyor K. and in *The Trial,* Joseph K. both find themselves in situations that most Chinese intellectuals would immediately recognize. Under a vague but menacing indictment, they are plunged into unfathomable circumstances that they are powerless either to understand or to ameliorate. Rather than rebel against the injustice of their plights—which would be useless and probably suicidal as well—both become paralyzed by confusion and uncertainty compounded by a sense of their own culpability. The Czech writer Milan Kundera, who became a refugee himself from a Communist country after the failure of Prague Spring in 1968, has written a grimly insightful essay about this dilemma. In "Somewhere Behind," from his collection *The Art of the Novel,* Kundera underscores the relevance of Kafka's fiction to modern Communist totalitarianism. Describing Kafka's inverted heroes as being caught in an "autoculpabilization machine," he analyzes how they seek to punish themselves as a last resort in order to expunge their overpowering if unfathomed sense of guilt for their alleged crimes.

"Raskolnikov cannot bear the weight of his guilt, and to find peace he consents to his punishment of his own free will," writes Kundera.

It is the well-known situation where *the offense seeks the punishment*. In Kafka the logic is reversed. The punished person does not know the reason for the punishment. The absurdity of the punishment is so unbearable that to find peace the accused needs to find justification for his penalty: *the punishment seeks the offense*. [In fact,] in this pseudotheological world, *the punished beg for recognition of their guilt*.

Once one is in such a mind-set, the burden of being jury, judge, and executioner is paradoxically shifted away from the accuser to the accused. Just to remind us that we are not dealing with any purely Kafkaesque literary abstractions here, Kundera states that "totalitarian states, as extreme concentrations of these tendencies, have brought out the close relationship between Kafka's novels and real life." In short, it would not be too extreme to say that intellectuals in countries such as China have all too often found themselves as interchangeable with the likes of Joseph K. Having learned to internalize accusations against themselves, they live in a state of eternal guilt and self-loathing, a bizarre state in which they are compelled to reject themselves much as the body sometimes finds itself seized by a violent allergic reaction.

Kundera describes these victims of the state who, robbed of all dignity and independence, have turned into their own enemies:

All their lives they had entirely identified themselves with the Party. When it suddenly became their prosecutor they agreed like Joseph K. to "examine their whole lives, their entire pasts, down to the smallest details" to find the hidden offense and, in the end, to confess to imaginary crimes.

What Kafka's characters highlight is the understandable human yearning to have one's "case" resolved, even if that means surrendering to the accuser by confessing to "imaginary crimes." What is important about this "Kafka syndrome" from the perspective of Chinese society is the way in which over the past few decades the Party's relentless scrutiny of individuals led to a virtual dissolution of the realm of the private. This "rape of privacy," as Kundera calls it, led to a helpless and supine attitude among the citizenry. It was a phenomenon that ironically saved the Party many burdens of oversight. For when people have learned to control themselves by means of an internal psychological mechanism that turns them into their own suppressors, the state may justifiably feel a sense of triumph.

In this world, where there were and are no provisions against arbitrary mental search and seizure, where holding even any small part of the human self inviolate from official ideology is a crime, and where the prying arms of state are ubiquitous, it is impossible for an individual to maintain any meaningful sense of the self. Unless a person has a defiance made of steel, without the cushion and protection of a modicum of privacy, this aspect of a human being can only perish.

As Kundera bluntly puts it:

> Totalitarian society, especially in its more extreme versions, tends to abolish the boundary between public and private; power, as it grows ever more opaque, requires the lives of citizens to be entirely transparent. The ideal of life without secrets corresponds to the ideal of the exemplary family: A citizen does not have the right to hide anything at all from the Party and state, just as a child has no right to keep any secret from his father or his mother.

What makes Kundera's notions about "autoculpabilization" and the "rape of privacy" so important to an understanding of China in the 1990s is that they help us comprehend the suppressive psychological mechanism against which the Chinese intellectuals have been struggling to refoliate their lives with an interior dimension. During the past decade of reform, there has been a slow but steady process of incubation in which this dimension of life has at last been able to develop in a rudimentary way. And what was so important about the protests and demonstrations that rocked China during the spring of 1989 was not just their exterior political message, which was amazing enough, but their subliminal message. What they were announcing—without actually saying it—was that many Chinese were now ready to resist, sometimes only cautiously, further incursions by the Party and state into the legitimately private side of their lives.

RELIGION MUST SERVE THE STATE

Religion has been part of almost every great world civilization. But as Communists, China's leaders have been deeply distrustful of religion as a form of glorified superstition. When they have allowed it at all, they have sought to keep it under careful Party and state control. Even by the mid-1990s, when the freedom to worship had become more expansive than ever before in China, the Party's distrust of independent religious institutions remained.

This selection was excerpted from a report by Human Rights Watch, Asia, published in 1997.

There is nothing trivial about religion. The management of religious problems is deeply concerned with politics, government policy, and the masses. . . . We must definitely adopt Lenin's attitude on such questions: "Be especially cautious," "Be most rigorous," and "Think things over carefully."

—Ye Xiaowen, head of the Religious Affairs Bureau, March 14, 1996

Since early 1996 Chinese leaders, in government and Party documents, speeches, and articles in official publications, have consistently reiterated the three guiding principles for management of religion: adaptation to socialist society, supervision according to the law, and correct and comprehensive implementation of the Party's religious policy. At the same time, they have made repeated reference to China's official atheism, its policy of separation of church and state, and the need for religion to serve economic development.

Adaptation to Socialist Society

The Chinese government insists that religion must serve the state and adapt—or be adapted—to socialist society. According to one analysis, this means highlighting moral teachings and curbing religious "extremism." It also means a religion must adjust its "theology, conception, and organization" and interpret its canon and doctrine "in the interests of socialism." According to Li Ruihuan, the Politburo member in charge of culture, this means that religious groups should help promote economic reform, or as a senior government official in Xinjiang put it, "Ancient traditions and religions cannot become obstacles to development."

The principle of adaptation undermines freedom of religious belief by insisting that any principles and doctrines of the five recognized religions that do not conform to socialism should be changed. Expressions of faith that the government does not recognize as "normal" are subject to punishment. Article 36(3) of the Constitution of the People's Republic of China reads: "The state protects normal religious activities. No one may make use of religion to engage in activities that disrupt public order, impair the health of citizens, or interfere with the educational system of the state." No definition of "normal" appears in any of the published regulations pertaining to religion, but in materials provided to Tibetan monks undergoing reeducation, saying prayers or celebrating religious festivals is considered "normal" while "any action that is prompted by ignorance and superstition or that undermines the interest of the state and people's lives and property" is considered "irreligious."

Supervision According to the Law

Increasingly the government is citing violations of Chinese law as its pretext for dismantling churches, monasteries, mosques, temples, or congregations that refuse to adapt, especially targeting those individuals and organizations that attempt to operate outside official bureaucratic control.

The emphasis on law—including the Chinese Constitution, the criminal code, and various administrative regulations and policies—to control religion is a relatively new development that emerged in the 1990s. Broadly worded laws, such as those on "counterrevolution," were, of course, in place long before and used against religious activists. But it was only in 1994 that a series of regulations on registration procedures for religious organizations and management of their activities was promulgated by the State Council.

The emergence of these regulations may have been a response to what was seen by the government as a growing danger. It may have reflected an awareness on the part of the Chinese leadership that violence and force would neither succeed in preventing the growth of religion in China nor destroy religion's influence in society. It may also have been designed to appeal to the international community, which had generally applauded China's tentative steps toward legal reform. But the government appears to have concluded as well that the regulations work, and that their enforcement is a feasible alternative to harsher methods of repression. The stress during the last two or three years thus has been less on punishment of individual offenders than on "lawful supervision" and strict regulation of religious organizations. There has been an emphasis as well on strengthening officially approved religious organizations and workers, with particular focus on the need to build up a younger generation of patriots.

This is not to suggest that the central government has succeeded in eradicating the use of extralegal means to limit religious activity or that the laws in place are in accord with international human rights standards. But with surveys indicating that the faith of Chinese in the Party and trust in a socialist future have declined, and with more and more people turning to religion, the government appears to be changing its methods of control and allowing its citizens to express their faith within the confines of the "law." The laws themselves, however, are the problem.

Dangers of Destabilization

The Chinese leadership argues that religion must "conduct its activities so as to safeguard the unity of nationalities and national unification" and resist "exploitation of religion by hostile domestic and foreign forces." In 1991, well aware of the declining force of Marxism and the social dislocations brought about by economic reform, it launched a five-year "socialist spiritual civilization" campaign, with an emphasis on ideological education, patriotism, self-abnegation, dedication to the Party, and rejection of bourgeois-liberal values. In November 1994, Zhao Puchu, president of the official Chinese Buddhist Association, noted at a seminar that by "guid[ing] everyone to set up correct ideals, convictions, and beliefs, a worldview, and a set of values," the Party hoped to check discontent brought on by discrepancies in economic development and by the center's demands on the provinces. Zhao noted that "patriotic education" was the means for "inspiring the national spirit" so as to overcome obstacles and to "strengthen national cohesion."

On August 11, 1996, Wang Zhaoguo, the director of the Party Central Committee's United Front Work Department, not only warned against splitism but inveighed against the use of religious issues by hostile international forces as "a breakthrough point" to "Westernize" China. While stressing that the religious situation in China was stable, he tied "recent" problems to changes in domestic and international relations. The same viewpoint was expressed in the same language in an article analyzing China's religious problem which appeared in 1996 in a restricted circulation *(neibu)* magazine, one of the publications of *Qiushi*, the Chinese

Communist Party's official theoretical journal. Wang's remarks followed a ten-day conference in northeastern China at which religious leaders discussed measures to strengthen patriotism among believers and to replace the aging clergy and religious staff with well-trained young and middle-aged leaders. In May 1997 an article in *Tianfeng,* the magazine of the official Chinese Christian Church, called on all Chinese believers to see patriotism as their Christian duty.

The danger that religion poses comes not just from the West in the view of Chinese leaders. On June 14, 1997, in a listing of seven factors that could destabilize the country, top Party officials included "foreign radical religious forces [which] have greatly enhanced their influence in some areas occupied by minority nationalities." One such area is Xinjiang Autonomous Region in the northwest, with a majority Muslim population and a good percentage of Party members openly professing adherence to Islam. The region, once known as East Turkestan, has an armed separatist movement led by members of the Uighur ethnic group. While the movement is primarily nationalist and not religious, the Chinese government believes the rebels are receiving support from radical Muslim groups abroad. The Xinjiang government chairman clearly believes religion and disunity are linked. "The biggest danger threatening stability," he said, "comes from separatism and illegal religious activities."

Similar charges have been made with respect to Tibet, where the Chinese leadership has put a high priority on preventing collusion between the "Dalai clique" and "international reactionary forces." Again and again Tibetan and Chinese officials accuse the Dalai Lama, Tibet's exiled leader, of using religion to engage in "political infiltration" and to sell his separatist ideas. The Chinese government likewise views the Catholic Church as a potential destabilizing force, given its role in the overthrow of Communism in Eastern Europe. It is deeply suspicious of Protestantism, officially called Christianity in China, because of the overseas connections of its missionary organizations, not only to the West but to Taiwan and South Korea as well.

HONG YING, SUMMER OF BETRAYAL

Because politically sensitive things that cannot be said in nonfiction can be said obliquely through fiction, literature in China during the 1980s and '90s was often more politically revealing than explicitly didactic writ-ing. The Sichuan-born novelist Hong Ying suggests that one of the most important forms of rebellion against China's authoritarian society during this period was manifest in the quest of many Chinese for hedonism and sexual excess.

This selection is the opening chapter, "June 4, 1989: Sunday," from Hong's book Summer of Betrayal, *published in the United States in 1997.*

Lin Ying fled through a city alight with flames. Heavy, gray gun smoke wrapped about her like mist, stinging her skin. Her face twitched, her hands shook uncontrollably. From time to time, her stomach turn-ing, she staggered like a pendulum gone crazy. She ached to stop, lie down, vomit herself clean, but her legs disobeyed, dragging her forward. She kept on, one dash and then another and then another.

Surely this was a scene in some movie, a fabrication. Bloody battles like this happened only in nightmares. She had only to wake up, to call out with relief, "It's not true!" Right now the important thing was to hurry home to bed, to awaken in his arms and find that all of this hadn't happened.

Like a human tide, people dodging bullets had flowed into the alleys and lanes on the north side of the Avenue of Eternal Peace. After run-ning first in one direction, then in another, she found she was separated from anyone she knew. She dashed down a twisting lane that headed east, where the sound of gunfire seemed to be lighter.

When she thought she was out of danger, she suddenly found herself at a major boulevard. It was thick with soldiers, all wearing identical hel-mets, submachine guns at the ready, young faces covered with ashes and sweat, none showing a flicker of emotion. Tank after tank thundered by at measured speed. Anything in the way of the tanks was flattened or overturned: bicycles, carts, iron railings, buses. Vehicles were bursting into flames, shaking the earth and the sky and making the buildings on either side look as if made of paper, as if at any moment they might ignite and float heavenward. The smell of scorched asphalt assaulted the nose, mixed with the stench of burned bodies and blood.

Frightened shadows sped by.

She gripped the wall, not allowing herself to fall. Another string of footsteps pounded along from behind, and a voice cried out, "Run!" A sharp instrument seemed to be twisting in her brain. She pulled herself together, then continued, hugging the wall to avoid bullets and never looking back. Only when the tanks and other people had passed and nobody was around did she allow herself to slow down. Dragging her exhausted body, she limped through smoke-filled streets like a dog being chased, sniffing the ground, trying to find a corner to hide in.

Must flag down a car. For the past few weeks, Lin Ying had gotten used to sticking out her hand and quickly getting an enthusiastic driver ready to give her a free lift. Now the streets were strewn with obstructions—buses, taxis, lorries overturned, smashed, twisted. Except for the tanks and the army trucks that followed right behind them, no vehicles were on the road.

Abandoned bicycles leaned against walls under the yellow streetlights, against trees, by the entrances to alleyways. Here before her eyes was a ready-made means of transportation, but Lin Ying, raised in a mountain city, had never learned how to ride a bicycle. She had regretted this in the year or so she had been in Beijing. "It can't be that hard," she muttered to herself now.

After the desperate flight through half the city, her body was rebelling. Her flesh and blood seemed congealed, as though she might shatter at any moment, crumble and fall around her own feet like pieces of plaster. "Really, what could be so hard about it?" At this second thin, hoarse utterance, she recognized her own voice.

Should she return to Balipu, to the dormitory where students in the university's writing program lived? Or to her own home, at Chen Yu's? No need even to ask. Chen Yu would be waiting for her, worried, standing by the telephone in case she called.

There was a telephone booth across the road. Reaching into her skirt pocket, she discovered that her purse had fallen out at some point, probably when she'd stumbled and fallen. Her wristwatch was also gone. She couldn't find any change to make a call. A coin would have been useless anyway, since most of the phone booths in the city were broken. She went on. A storefront displayed the symbol for public phones, but the door was locked. Her light blue skirt was spattered with patches of someone's blood. The spots were coated over with mud that had dried and begun to crumble.

Early-morning light began to penetrate the smoke and haze in the streets. She was approaching a large traffic intersection in the east. She had put the sound of gunfire and burning behind her, to the west.

Faces began to reveal themselves behind windows and doors. People flitted through the little byways between buildings, between the clumps of shrubs and bushes along the road. Unconsciously she straightened her clothes, brushed back her shoulder-length hair, rubbed off the dirt and soot and sweat that streaked her face. Ready, she headed in the direction of human beings.

Those people who had hidden during the night now, at dawn, were venturing out to learn what had happened. Several army trucks, lined up neatly in a row, stood patiently in the middle of the road emitting heavy smoke. The soldiers had long since abandoned them. A number of people were throwing soda bottles into the flames, others were picking up empty gunshells. About a dozen people were standing silently near a mailbox and a parked three-wheeler. After a moment's hesitation, Lin Ying walked over to them. Unprepared, she abruptly caught sight of a body lying in a strange position on the sloping ground. One eye was bulging out like a small round ball; the other eye was squashed to a slit. Dark red blood looked as though it had been deliberately splattered on the man's white undershirt, his blue underpants, his graying hair and beard. White brain matter mixed with blood seemed to be oozing onto the ground.

Lin Ying had run madly though the night, herself pursued by death. This was the first time she had seen the savagery of death in the light of day. Her stomach churned and this time doubled her up in pain. She pushed away from the crowd. Leaning against an electric pole at the sidewalk, she began to vomit. Her temples were throbbing, people and things whirled before her. She held tightly to the pole, panting and vomiting in turn. Whatever was still in her stomach after the night came out as thick, stinking bile. When she had emptied herself, an uncontrollable dry heaving continued.

A middle-aged woman stopped with her bicycle. "Young lady, what's the matter?" she asked, concerned.

Lin Ying struggled to lift her head and point to the people surrounding the corpse. The woman parked her bike and gently patted Lin Ying on the back. She looked like a worker. "That was an old widower," she said, "who shouldn't have come out on his balcony last night to see what was happening. He was hit by a stray bullet."

The touch of a human hand comforted Lin Ying. Supporting herself against the pole, she asked the woman for a ride to the Yellow Temple. Lin Ying felt she could walk no farther.

"Get on, little one, get on!" The woman got onto her bicycle. "I can't go to work anyway. I'll take you. Oh my, what a sin! What a sin!" She kept repeating this as they rode along. "What they've done! What a mess they've made!"

Lin Ying sat on the back, holding on to the woman's waist. She shut her eyes, calmer now, the terror subsiding. The bicycle bounced as it went over bumps. Lin Ying opened her eyes to see the high, gray walls of a building near the Yellow Temple, just visible on the street corner. She had the feeling that the striped curtains she knew so well were fluttering for her from every window. After a night of madness she would soon sleep.

Security was tight at the entrance to the *People's Daily* compound. A sentry post had been installed. The soldier on guard stopped and questioned Lin Ying. She said she lived there.

"Which block, which doorway?"

She specified the number. Fortunately the guard did not scrutinize her clothes—his gaze remained on her face. Finally, reluctantly, he let her in.

Trees lined both sides of the main entryway and marched down the endless avenue. Neatly mown lawns separated the trees and the buildings. Lin Ying staggered at each step. Just get to Chen Yu. He would hold her, take her in his arms, and put her to bed. Lie down. Be comfortable. He would bring her the milk with honey she loved so, then caress her and keep her company while she slipped into peaceful slumber. The day he had met her at the train station, he had said, "Little Ying, my poor little thing, you need a good rest. When you've woken up, everything will be the way you want it to be." Gazing at Chen Yu back then, she had slowly closed her eyes and thought, From now on, I will no longer be tossed on the waves.

The boulevard was unnaturally silent, empty of people. A bird flew past, soundless, its wings stirring the still air. She passed a dry water fountain, her legs unbearably heavy. Whatever you do, don't stop, she told herself. Hold on. You'll be home in a minute. The word "home" was like a pool of light pushing back terrors, holding her securely in its warm depths.

Lin Ying finally went into one of the gray buildings. Each stairway landing was crowded with padlocked bikes and garbage cans. She climbed the stairs with difficulty, holding the banister with her left hand while her right loosened a key chain tied around her neck. By the last flight of stairs, at the top of the building, she could hardly catch her breath, but her feet kept moving along the corridor to the first door. She inserted the key in the lock and turned it to the left three times. The door opened, she went in and shut it behind her.

She crossed the tiny entryway in five steps, past a small table, and pushed open the bedroom door.

The curtains were drawn. Chen Yu was lying on the bed in the darkened room. He must have waited for her all night and only now fallen asleep. Lin Ying could no longer stand, her body swayed, and she knew she was going to fall. If so, she should fall into his arms. She took a step toward the bed and collapsed beside it on the carpet. Her body went limp as her eyes closed and her head came to rest on his chest.

The clock on the wall ticktocked, back and forth. "Yu," she called, almost silently. He had not woken. The only sounds seemed to come from her own pulse, her breathing, and the ticking of the clock.

Surely nothing had happened! With great effort, she forced her eyes open.

The room already seemed less dark. She now saw that Chen Yu was staring at her, that distress and horror filled his face.

Do I look so terrifying? Confused, she pushed against the bed as she brought her right leg underneath her and slowly raised herself up.

Chen Yu's head turned ever so slightly toward his back. Lin Ying's gaze automatically moved in that direction, and now she saw that something else was on the bed: a woman, her head buried in the bedding but some of her disheveled hair showing, as well as part of her naked back. Chen Yu slowly pulled his hand out from under the woman's body.

Lin Ying sprang to her feet, speechless. She could not believe the fact before her eyes: Chen Yu in bed with another woman. Her entire being felt as if turned to ice; even the scream inside her was frozen.

Two hands of despair began pulling her inexorably backward, forcing her toward the door. Her eyes stayed fixed on Chen Yu, and only when she bumped against the door did she know she'd been moving. She turned abruptly and ran from the bedroom. The stool by the table clattered as she knocked it going through the hall. She pulled open the front door and took the stairs at a run. Outside the building, she stopped, panting, by the trees, their two straight green lines like soldiers at attention, holding rifles. Coming off parade, they now advanced toward her, step by step.

She shrank back, but behind her was a sheet of flames and smoke. The glowering sky darkened; gunfire, shouting, and the growl of tank engines merged in a cacophonous crescendo.

She had nowhere to run to.

Lin Ying heard Chen Yu saying her name, sometimes clearly, sometimes muffled, as she moved in and out of consciousness. Her clenched fist opened and she felt the rough fabric on the couch; only then did she realize where she was. Chen Yu was wiping her face with a damp towel. She pushed him away and tried to stand, but he held her down.

She fought back and struggled to sit up. Her feet found her sandals, covered with ashes inside and out. The green striped curtains of the window had been pulled open, but the room was still quite dark. The bed was made up with an ivory-colored bedspread. A woman in tight black pants sat on a chair opposite. She had short hair, the left side slightly longer than the right. Her eyes glittered in the darkness and she didn't say a word.

Clearly, this was the woman who had been lying in the bed. Lin Ying herself must have been carried back upstairs by Chen Yu. The whole recent scene had effectively stemmed the tears that should have come after her night of exhaustion and terror escaping from the shooting. What might have poured out was now returned to the deepest recesses of her mind. The only signs of what she had been through were her nostrils cracked with dryness and her painfully aching throat. One nightmare had been followed by another; the stage was different, the actors were different, but the nightmares went on.

Lin Ying reached out both hands to a cup of tea on the table near the sofa. She drank one mouthful slowly, then all the rest. Her throat felt better. The other woman drew circles with her finger around the top of a glass ashtray. Chen Yu smoked, one cigarette after another. The smoke from his mouth, joining smoke drifting up from incompletely extinguished cigarette butts, screened the woman, blurring the contours of her body so that all Lin Ying really saw were her eyes.

Lin Ying straightened up, away from the back of the sofa. She brushed back a lock of hair and smoothed her short-sleeved jacket and skirt. She looked at the ashtray on the table and paused a moment, then reached out to take a cigarette from the pack. The tobacco was too strong — she took one drag, then let the cigarette smolder between her fingers. The three of them sat in silence, as though the air in the room were solid, as though the room were completely silted up.

Chen Yu's mouth twitched once, but he said nothing. His eyes were deep-sunken and bloodshot, and he looked as though he hadn't shaved in the several days Lin Ying had been away. He was haggard and thin, and his shirt was wrinkled.

In the end it was the other woman who broke the silence. "I've always wanted to meet you." She said this slowly and deliberately, in a light, low voice. Her daring to speak relaxed her; the two others in the room sat frozen. "I even dreamed of you a few times." She put her hands in her pockets, casually.

Lin Ying placed the filter of the burned-out cigarette in the ashtray. She realized this was Mei Ling, the wife whom Chen Yu said he had been living apart from for two years and whom he was in the process of divorcing. In the year that Lin Ying had been living with Chen Yu in Beijing, she had never known them to have any contact, not even a phone call, let alone an actual meeting. When Chen Yu had talked of his unsatisfactory marriage, it was as though he were discussing educational materials in a course on the Communist Party. The only thing that remained between them, he said, was the final signatures on the divorce papers.

Lin Ying's face was ashen—not with jealousy, not with anger at any deceit, for she hadn't had time to think of these things. Instead, she felt total emptiness.

Chen Yu silently examined the glowing end of his cigarette. He hardly resembled the Chen Yu who had had her try on a wedding ring. He seemed far removed. Lin Ying became aware that what she wanted at this moment was not a man who loved her; what she wanted was an unshakable, immovable form of trust, the kind that could give stability in this upside-down world, an unchanging, steady diamond pivot.

She stood up and said softly, "I'm going."

Nobody objected.

Mei Ling also stood up, grinding out her cigarette. "Wait just a moment, I'll be going too."

Only Chen Yu continued to sit and smoke, without even looking up. The women seemed to have found the strength to act; he was left not knowing what to do.

Lin Ying took the key chain from around her neck and put it on the sofa. Woven of blue and green silk threads, it was something parents might hang around a child's neck, and when Chen Yu had first given it to her, she'd been overjoyed. Now it seemed vulgar—so clearly a trap, falsely pretending to be a symbol of home. Like other symbols, it said, Look, here I am! You should be satisfied! Lin Ying shook her head. Even now, her childhood hopes for life did not seem so outrageous: a lamp glowing at the window, a spot of yellow warmth in a lacquer-black expanse of wilderness.

Mei Ling looked at the keys, perplexed.

Lin Ying moved around the table with a determination that surprised even her. Without a word, without glancing at Chen Yu, she turned and left the room.

No shops were open on the streets, no vendors were hawking wares on the sidewalk. The occasional pedestrian hurried along. Bicyclists and peddlers with their three-wheeled carts kept their noses pointed straight ahead, their mouths open and breathing hard.

Lin Ying went through the central gate of the editorial department of the *People's Daily*. She walked in a daze along the road from the Yellow Temple in the direction of Balipu. After a while, she could no longer lift her feet. She leaned against a willow tree, then sat on the small ridge of earth beside the sidewalk.

A young person wearing sunglasses rushed past without stopping but called out to her, "Soldiers coming from that side. Quick, get out of here!"

Lin Ying didn't move. She couldn't move. If they are coming, let them come.

She might be able to endure Chen Yu's sleeping with other women. But that it was Mei Ling, the person Chen Yu said he most despised, was something else. He had said he couldn't tolerate her. That she was vain, superficial, ignorant, a chatterbox. Hearing all this, Lin Ying couldn't help being amused at first, but as the repetition of faults continued, she hadn't been sure what to believe.

If there had been no disaster last night, she might still be keeping vigil at the square, full of feelings like everyone else — happy, excited, indignant, hopeful — feelings that, good or bad, had to do with more than just her own self. Or if she'd fallen in the rain of bullets, none of the nightmare would have happened. Then she wouldn't have learned what sort of a person Chen Yu was. What age am I? she wondered. She had long since passed the age of girlish sentimentality and had encountered a fair dose of deceit. As a woman with knowledge of the bittersweet world, did she actually still believe that people had self-restraint? Did she still give any weight to love's promises? She should long ago have understood that lying and doing evil are the basic ways the world goes round.

The absurdity! That she could have hoped it would be into Chen Yu's arms that she finally collapsed!

★ L O W   C U L T U R E ★

The aftermath of the 1989 demonstrations left China both under martial law and in a depressed state of mind. While people were still relatively free to speak privately, any dissenting political views uttered in public quickly became grounds for greater Public Security Bureau scrutiny and/or arrest and imprisonment for crimes such as "counterrevolutionary propaganda and incitement." However, just as it was possible to express dissonant views through fiction with greater freedom than through public political discourse, greater latitude was afforded those who used pop culture as a vector for their expressions of disenchantment and rebelliousness. Popular music, video art, modern dance, fiction, TV soap operas, underground films, contemporary art, fashion, and even nightlife all became areas of everyday culture in which the state of China's mind was indirectly able to manifest itself without triggering the wrath of either censors or the constabulary.

Sometimes it almost seemed as if the Party had decided that it was better to allow some mechanism through which disaffection, especially among young people, might find release so that it would not build up and spill out through direct political action. And so, even while the early 1990s were a time of relatively severe political repression, one found a surprisingly fecund, and often darkly provocative, world of pop culture coexisting alongside very straitlaced official political culture.

ORVILLE SCHELL,
SHAKE, RATTLE, AND ROLL

Perhaps because officials did not understand its obliquity, pop music was one of the areas of Chinese culture where errant forms of self-expression were best tolerated.

This selection was excerpted from a piece by coeditor Orville Schell on Cui Jian, one of China's most subtle and popular rock stars during the 1980s and '90s; it was published in the Los Angeles Times Magazine *in November 1992.*

In the crowded streets of downtown Nanjing, it looked as if the entire city were flooding toward the concert at the 30,000-seat Wutaishan Sports Arena. Along the way, clumps of police stood watching the seemingly endless procession of young Chinese flow by. Outside the stadium gates, crowds of teenagers negotiated anxiously with scalpers for tickets that cost as much as U.S.$25, five times their original price and more than half the monthly income of the average Chinese worker. The event was the last of three May concerts given in Nanjing by China's best-known rock and roll star, Cui Jian. The series represented the first time in two years that Cui had been allowed to perform with official sanction in such a large venue. It was not that the Communist Party particularly approved of Cui's dark, enigmatic, hard-driving music but simply that Cui had agreed to donate the proceeds from the shows to Project Hope, which would help send rural children to school; such tithe paying had forged a curious alliance between this new cultural Chinese rebel and the old Chinese political establishment.

Inside the arena, the fans ecstatically waved hand-lettered banners and cheered wildly. One claque from a city almost 1,000 miles away held up a sign that read, "Cui Jian: Your buddies from Lanzhou are here!" Another group had organized itself so that when each of its members raised a placard inscribed with a single character, they created a collective message: "From your fans in Nanjing!"

When a slender, pale, and almost expressionless young man wearing blue jeans and a white tank top strode onto the stage amid a blaze of flashing colored lights and billowing clouds of theatrical smoke, the audience rose to its feet, screaming. With his band behind him, Cui Jian looked around the stadium and proudly proclaimed, "Nanjing is another of my liberated areas!" When Cui hit the first earsplitting chord of "Rock and Roll on the New Long March" on his white electric guitar, the crowd exploded as if the home team had just scored a last-minute tiebreaking point.

On the stage, electric guitars, synthesizers, woodwinds, and brass shared space with traditional Chinese instruments such as the oboelike *suona*, the zitherlike *guzheng*, and the reed pipe *sheng*, blending Western rock riffs with Oriental flourishes. In the audience, a young man swayed back and forth, waving his arms over his head. "I love it here because I don't have to behave!" he cried out. "This is the only place I can go where I don't have to act like a gentleman."

As he smiled beatifically, all around him thousands of other young Chinese whooped, clapped, gyrated, and cheered en masse. Set against the repression and enforced political silence of post-Tiananmen China, the concert was a stunning moment of exultant mass catharsis.

"I feel something like I imagine the old guard of revolutionaries must have felt on the Long March," Cui Jian would tell a journalist from the Hong Kong–based *China Times* weekly after the concert. The old guard, he explained, in a way that made it hard to tell if he was being facetious, realized their dreams despite being "chased and embattled." "I want to study their spirit," he said, "so that perhaps I, too, can succeed in creating something rare in this world."

Cui didn't bother to define precisely what he meant by "something rare in this world," but it was clear that the Long Marchers would hardly have approved of what he was stirring up this night at the Wutaishan sports area. In fact, as the crowd danced and shouted, one block of the audience—Nanjing dignitaries attending the benefit in their official capacities—sat almost motionless in a special section near the stage. Isolated amid the sea of fans, they looked as if they had been anesthetized by some mysterious, highly selective chemical agent.

Their only counterparts in the hall were hundreds of silent, still police, watching the crowd nervously and clinging to their walkie-talkies like drowning men to lifelines. The more excited the crowd became, the more jittery the police grew. Once or twice, they tried to restrain youths who had jumped to their feet to dance in the aisles. But against the music and the crowd's frenzy, such gestures of authority seemed almost hopeless.

"Now my heart is like a knife that wants to pierce your mouth, to kiss your lungs," Cui sang, coming to the end of "Like a Knife," one of his most popular songs. The government officials remained as opaque as ever. But when he broke into "The Last Shot," I thought I saw a flicker of recognition sweep across their faces. Undoubtedly they were, like everyone else, thinking of the Beijing Massacre.

Cui Jian has insisted that "The Last Shot" is about the 1979 Sino-Vietnamese war. The lyrics consist of only two lines: "A wild shot hit my chest/and at that moment everything from my life surged through my heart," followed by the title sung again and again like an incantation. During the concert, periodic bursts of machine gun–like fire rolled from the drummer's snare, and the song closed with a plaintive, taps-like trumpet solo. Like so many of Cui's songs, the words were packed with images of weapons, blood, anger, wounds, and loss, and as he sang, his fans began to light candles in the classic gesture of rock and roll solidarity.

When the concert ended, the Nanjing dignitaries appeared even more lifeless and frozen than before. I supposed that their glumness was not simply caused by Cui's violation of that most fundamental of Maoist precepts—namely, that all art and literature should serve party politics—but also by the inescapable evidence that China's youth had become hopelessly indifferent to the older generation's socialist pretensions. Stranded in the center of a liberated zone of counterculture where tens of thousands of young people stood mesmerized by a thirty-one-year-old singer, those stony-faced cadres must have recognized just how irrelevant the Communist Party had become for this generation of Chinese.

In the suffocating environment of China since 1989, many young Chinese—Cui Jian among them—sought refuge in what some observers now call *huise wenhua,* or "gray culture." *Huise wenhua* is a distinctive universe, defiantly separate from official Party culture. Its signal components are rock and roll, pulp fiction, pop art, and punkish fashion. Rooted in China's pre-Tiananmen thaw, this counterculture not only survived the postmassacre crackdown but also blossomed, providing one of the few arenas in which the Chinese could still express their frustrations and alienation.

In his article "The Graying of Chinese Culture," published in the *China Review,* Australian Sinologist Geremie Barmé described *huise wenhua* as a phenomenon mixing "hopelessness, uncertainty, and ennui with irony, sarcasm, and a large dose of fatalism." It is less a movement than a state of mind, and it is the province of a rebellious generation that, for the moment at least, has abandoned any thought of directly confronting China's political establishment.

Instead, says Andrew Jones, whose monograph *Like a Knife* chronicles the Chinese pop music scene, "Rock parties, wild lyrics, and slam dancing have replaced megaphones, sit-ins, and rock throwing as the preferred means of protest." In China, being politically subversive can still land you in jail, but those who merely subvert the culture are, to some degree, tolerated—at least for now. Ducking and weaving to avoid the Party's counterblows, gray culturalists are co-opting the system rather than trying to change it.

Cui Jian is one of the most prominent figures in this shadow culture.

"I don't want to talk about politics," he told the Agence France-Presse. "I engage in culture. Politics is not my work." As much as he insists on the apolitical nature of his music, to many Chinese youths his songs are almost as important as Mao's Little Red Book was to their parents. "If one likens rock and roll in the West to a flood," he said at a 1989 concert in Beijing, "then Chinese rock and roll must be likened to a knife. Let us stick this knife into our own land."

As in the American '60s, rock music provides a focal point for a burgeoning counterculture. One of the other main constituents of *huise wenhua* is China's so-called *liumang*, a word that is difficult to translate into English. *Liumang* are the mustachioed young men who float around the cities of China late at night, wearing looks of vapid boredom, shooting endless games of snooker, drinking, chain-smoking, and chasing girls in karaoke bars. Lately, they have gotten into drugs—opium from Yunnan Province's poppy crop and hashish from Xinjiang can be bought in almost every major city in China. *Liumang* keep their various habits satisfied with one illicit hustle or another. Many are *getihu*, or private street entrepreneurs, the progeny of Deng Xiaoping's economic reforms launched in the early '80s.

Not long ago, the word *liumang* was a pejorative term similar to "punk" or "hoodlum." Today, however, it has expanded to embrace almost any kind of alienated urban rebel who aspires to distance himself or herself from official culture. Particularly among young people, the word has lost much of its negative connotations of indolence, dishonesty, and criminality and now describes an attitude that includes desirable attributes such as individualism, defiance, and independence. It has even taken on some of the romance associated with the *jianghu haojie*, the Robin Hood–like knights-errant in Chinese literature who have embodied China's "outlaw ideal" for hundreds of years. Being called a *liumang* in China is now almost the equivalent of being called "hip" or "cool" in Western culture.

The extent to which gray culture has successfully defied and even infiltrated official culture was graphically illustrated in May. The Central Ballet, China's most prestigious classical dance troupe, scheduled a program that included selections from "Swan Lake," "Sleeping Beauty," "The Red Detachment of Women," and a work called "Four Romantic Pieces." On the night of the performance, the audience was astonished to find that the last was set to the music of Cui Jian.

It was a major coup for Chinese gray culturalists. Not only did the Central Ballet bring indigenous rock music into China's temple of classical ballet for the first time, but the choreography also contained just the sort of veiled political subtext that defines *huise wenhua*. In one piece, dancers came onstage like walking apparitions, holding candles to their chests while Cui's well-known "Nothing to My Name" boomed out. Later, they broke into a frenzy of stylized fist shaking that evoked an angry protest demonstration. The piece ended when the dancers, seeming to wipe away tears, moved across the stage in a dirgelike procession of unmistakable sadness.

Cui Jian first burst on the Chinese scene in 1986, when he was invited to appear on a nationally televised pop music competition. Then twenty-five, Cui was already one of the country's rock pioneers. His father, a member of the army band, had taught him to play the trumpet. After graduating from the Beijing Industrial Institute High School, Cui, an accomplished musician on several instruments, won a position as trumpeter with the prestigious Beijing Philharmonic Orchestra in 1981. But after hearing the music of John Denver, Simon and Garfunkel, and Andy Williams—whose records were among the first nonclassical Western music to enter China, in the early 1980s—Cui started drifting into pop music. Playing hooky from his duties at the Philharmonic, he formed his own band with six other classical musicians and made a few recordings. "I worked hard, said farewell to my old life, and started a new life from zero," he said.

By 1986 he was listening to the Beatles, the Rolling Stones, the Talking Heads and Sting. When he showed up at Workers' Stadium in Beijing for the televised music competition, he was wearing a pair of tattered army fatigues, and his style had moved from smooth pop to gravel-voiced, hip-gyrating rock. At first, he dumbfounded the studio audience. But by the time his set had ended, the crowd was cheering wildly and dancing in the aisles. It was not long before bootlegged tapes of his performance began appearing all over China, and other concert offers flooded in.

Even though some of the Party's cultural pooh-bahs were grudgingly willing to exploit certain seductive aspects of Western culture to survive, they far preferred to pacify young people with *tongsu yinyue*, or "popular music," rather than *yaogun yinyue*, literally "shaking and rolling music." The former tended toward traditional ballads, insipid love songs, and uninspired imitations of Western disco, avoiding any hint of the kinds of complex social and political issues that rock and roll tended to focus on.

Once the Party opened its arms to pop music, however, officials discovered they had made a Faustian bargain. The line between *tongsu yinyue* and *yaogun yinyue* proved impossible to hold.

Not that they didn't try. When the government censured Cui Jian and expelled him from the Philharmonic, it also denied him his "iron rice bowl"—the salary, housing, and medical care guaranteed to all employees of the state. Party leaders must have hoped such punishment would silence Cui, but instead it afforded him an unprecedented degree of freedom to develop both his music and a new outlaw lifestyle. As he told *Billboard* magazine in 1992, "Of course, when you are the first, there are a lot of problems. But I also think one is lucky because no one will control you. You can do anything you want."

Still, the problems were real. In 1987 Cui was living a hand-to-mouth existence in his cramped Beijing apartment decorated with posters of Elvis and John Lennon. At about that time, he began playing regularly with a new band, ADO: a bass player from Hungary, a guitarist employed at the Madagascar embassy, and several Chinese dropouts.

With ADO, and sometimes without, Cui managed to support himself by playing at private parties for foreigners, in restaurants, bars, small hotels, and the after-hours club at Pierre Cardin's Maxim's restaurant, which had ushered night life into Beijing.

Cui's ability to survive without a Party-sanctioned job was another result of Deng's economic reforms. As China's economy privatized and diversified, the margins of society steadily expanded, creating areas where nonconformists, entrepreneurs, and even rock and rollers could find refuge and work beyond the reach of government interference. For a society that had allowed no such sanctuaries for more than four decades, these fringe zones represented a real milestone in the history of the People's Republic.

And as the reform movement weaned more and more state-run businesses away from government subsidies, life for a rock musician could only get easier. Recording companies, like other businesses, had to start making a product that turned a profit. Cui was suddenly in demand.

The new market-driven reality even meant that when political considerations collided with commerce, commerce often won. Though Cui had been censured by the government, his first rock album, *Rock and Roll on the New Long March*, was released in 1987 by the state-run China Tourism Publishers of Audio-Visual Materials. Official radio and television might not play his music, but his album was a steady seller.

Cui's growing underground popularity stemmed from his ability to skillfully articulate deep levels of political frustration, sexual confusion, and social alienation. While he avoided overt political references in his songs, he often toyed with Party symbols or alluded to Party themes. Like Bob Dylan in the '60s, Cui captured the chaos of his times without becoming mired in didacticism or romantic escapism. In his song "It's Not That I Don't Understand," he sang:

> *Looking back I can't tell good from bad*
> *I can't even remember the decades gone by*
> *What once seemed so simple is now unclear*
> *And I suddenly feel the world has no place for me.*

Some critics have been frustrated by Cui's habit of sidestepping what they see as the obviously political dimension in his work. "If you want to understand me, you only have to listen to my songs," he has insisted. "Everything I want to say is in these songs." It is precisely this evasiveness that makes Cui a gray culturalist par excellence. He has said that the music represents nothing except "the truth, the modern truth . . . about our life in China." The songs are simply an expression of "the serious things in my heart, people's lives, including love, of course." Cui has been content for each person to define that "truth" for himself.

Whatever Cui's denials, he has walked a fine line between art and politics. When "Nothing to My Name"—which obliquely suggests that after forty years of socialism the Chinese still have "nothing"—was released in Hong Kong and Taiwan in early 1989, the notes made a strong claim for Cui's outlaw role. "He is a reflection of what is going on in Chinese culture, and because he criticizes Chinese culture to this degree, he has become a spokesman for a generation," the notes point out. "One could also say that he brought the situation of the last few decades, in which there has been such a scarcity of individuality and individual thought in art, to an end."

Early in 1989, Cui was finally allowed to give major concerts in Beijing. In April, just prior to the outbreak of demonstrations in Tiananmen Square, Cui's musical reputation had grown to the point that he signed with EMI Music in Hong Kong and was invited to England to participate in the First Asian Popular Music Awards at London's Royal Albert Hall. By the time he returned to Beijing, the student movement was in full swing, and "Nothing to My Name" had become one of the demonstrators' anthems: "I've given you my dreams, given you my freedom/But you always just laugh at my having nothing."

As the dramatic events unfolded, Cui finally could not resist going to Tiananmen Square. And when a wire service photo showed him performing before a huge crowd of students, wearing a blood red blindfold, Cui became irrevocably identified with the protest movement in the minds of Party officials. After the Beijing Massacre, Cui, like so many other young Chinese, dropped out of sight.

Although the crackdown bludgeoned the political dissidents, officials found it more difficult to get the gray culture genie back into the bottle.

After lying low following the massacre, an absence from the scene that spawned rumors that he had been detained by police, Cui Jian finally reemerged unscathed. But with the Party initiating yet another campaign against bourgeois liberalization, Cui found it impossible to give formal concerts. On the fringes again, he survived by selling his tapes and playing with outlaw bands at private gatherings.

By then, China's leaders were desperate to reenter respectable global society, and they looked to the 1990 Asian Games, scheduled for Beijing, as a showcase opportunity. When Cui agreed to do a series of benefit concerts to help the games make up their huge budget deficit, the authorities were hard put to turn down his offer.

But all over China, Cui performances were met by ecstatic fans who raised clenched fists in defiant solidarity and flashed the "V" for victory sign, the symbol of the Tiananmen Square Protest. Government censors were particularly offended when Cui donned the red blindfold and his guitarist put on a gag while performing the song "A Piece of Red Cloth."

Halfway through the ambitious ten-city benefit tour, the honeymoon ended. In April 1990, the Party abruptly canceled the remaining shows.

Cui continued performing with outlaw bands, appearing often in all-night jam sessions in an abandoned Beijing movie theater known as the Titanium Club. His companions in the underground included Yellow People, the hard pop Black Panthers, all-female Cobra (whose lead singer, Wei Hua, had been an anchor on CCTV's English-language news until she lost her job in 1989 for giving interviews to foreign television reporters), and He Yong, an angry new-wave punk rocker whose song "Garbage Dump" contained the memorable line "First we eat our consciences, then we shit ideology."

China's gray culture, it seemed, was gathering momentum.

Just after dark, the rented bus crammed with musicians and hangers-on rattled to a stop in front of a large, walled enclosure somewhere on the outskirts of Beijing. It was last May, three years after the Tiananmen protests, and Cui Jian was making a movie. A sort of Chinese version of Penelope Spheeris's punk documentary, *The Decline of Western Civilization, Beijing Bastards* was being produced with Hong Kong money and directed by Zhang Yuan, an avant-garde filmmaker, who had made Cui's video. The idea of the film was to capture in cinema verité style the freewheeling gray cultural elite, using Cui and other habitués of the rock underworld as stars.

What Zhang had in mind for this night's shoot was a rock bacchanal—complete with nude dancing, according to a rumor—staged at a horse track about an hour outside of Beijing. In the flickering light of bonfires that had been lit in the middle of the riding ring, two iron caldrons waited for freshly killed goats that had been hung from a hitching post nearby. Knots of young men in high black boots, tight trousers, and black T-shirts mingled with attractive young women in modish outfits.

The production crew was laying tracks for a camera dolly as the party began. The scene was like a diorama of the new underground, with alienation, ambiguity, black leather, cigarettes, beer, and rock music replacing discussions about democracy and idealistic demonstrations. Those on the "set" were about as far removed from the official Communist Party version of Chinese youth as they could be.

Cui Jian was unobtrusively seated on the ground next to one of the bonfires, vamping on an acoustic guitar in the midst of a throng of buddies. Finally, after the goat carcasses had been hacked into pieces and thrown into the caldrons by two shirtless young men, someone rushed out with a clap stick to start the shooting. But the presence of a rolling camera seemed almost irrelevant to the partygoers.

How had Zhang Yuan dealt with securing official approval for *Beijing Bastards*? He smiled conspiratorially. "Well, we sort of got it," he said slyly.

"The whole point of the film is to portray the kind of hand-to-mouth lives these guys live," piped up a young woman whose connection to the film was unclear. She gestured to the crowd that by now was roasting huge chunks of boiled goat meat over the open fires. "The government says that it wants to encourage private entrepreneurs as part of Deng's economic reform movement. So these musicians are just taking the government at its word by extending the notion of private enterprise to include rock and roll." She gave a little chirrup of laughter.

It seemed safe to assume that the Ministry of Radio, Film, and Television, whose job it is to keep strict account of all movies made in China, would have been more than a little reluctant to approve the script, if indeed there ever was a formal script, for *Beijing Bastards*. In all my years of visiting China, I had never encountered anything quite so bizarre as this film shoot, and it made me wonder if Chinese authorities had any idea what was going on here.

It was well past midnight when Cui's band finally began warming up. As bats flew overhead and huge moths did kamikaze dives into the lights, the music reverberated over the dark fields around the horse track, loud enough to wake up everyone in the surrounding villages, including the police. But neither the crew members nor anyone dancing in the firelight seemed agitated. Then, out of the corner of my eye, I caught some movement in the shadows near the entrance gate. Two men wearing Public Security Bureau uniforms were watching the proceedings. I braced for a confrontation. But once again, no one in the crowd of merrymakers evinced even the slightest alarm.

Finally, two young men who looked as if they were part of the production team sauntered over to the two policemen. Five minutes later the officers quietly turned to leave. I asked a long-haired young man standing beside me if he knew what had happened.

"Aw, they're just locals," he replied without concern. "Unless there is some order from above, they won't bother us," he said, pointing upward with his index finger. "Anyway, I guess they've been taken care of, so it's no big deal." He took a swig from a can of Qingdao beer and for a moment stared off at the dancers. Then he looked up and smiled. "Hey!" he said. "We're just a bunch of *liumang!* We do what we want!"

Although the party and filming of *Beijing Bastards* went on well past sunrise, I left about 2:00 A.M. I later learned that the nude dancing never did materialize, but I was stunned enough by what I had seen of China's new underground culture. What was so unique about it was that despite its iconoclasm, it chose to manifest itself in an indirect and nonconfrontational way that, compared to the protesters of 1989, seemed almost Taoist. A new kind of youth revolt seemed to be taking root on the free market edge of society, free and clear of Party politics and political manipulation, neither the Party's creature nor its hostile adversary.

On the eve of the Tiananmen demonstrations, Cui Jian had told an interviewer, "We do not rebel. We fight for personal liberation." But in a society where the political reins are so tightly held by the state and where the human cost of direct political dissent is still so high, the kind of liberation sought by Cui and his comrades puts them perhaps unwittingly in the vanguard of a strong new revolution. As Mao Zedong presciently warned: "There may be some Communists who are not conquered by enemies with guns . . . but will be defeated by sugar-coated bullets."

Whether Cui cares to admit it or not, he is a veritable machine gun of sugar-coated bullets.

Sang Ye, Computer Insects

Because cyberculture is essentially antiauthoritarian, as it spread in China during the 1990s it often tended to merge with the cynicism of youth culture. Dealing as they do in the global free flow of information and lending themselves to the kind of unbridled entrepreneurialism that was already sweeping China, hackers, computers, and the Internet looked as if they might be shaping up as one of the most subversive forces of China's established political order.

Although the government required all Internet users to register (see "The Battle for Cyberspace"), and although it sought to limit what entered China from the outside world through government-controlled "gateways," it was difficult to imagine that the Party would ultimately be able to control access to the World Wide Web or the activities of so-called computer insects, who had grown up in cyberspace and were merging entrepreneurialism with politically heterodox ideas.

This selection was made from an interview in the Chinese-Australian writer Sang Ye's latest volume of oral histories, Chinese Time: The People on the People's Republic *(forthcoming, 1999), conducted with a computer program pirater in Beijing. It was translated by Geremie R. Barmé and published in* Wired *magazine in July 1996.*

I studied at Qinghua University, specializing in computer databases. It was boring as hell, and I barely managed to avoid turning into a machine myself. DBP, DBA—it's all about data-based machines. That wasn't for me, so I dumped it and hooked up with a small company to get some money together. If you specialize, you just end up in some government research job or working for a big company. It might sound all right, but at best you can make only a few hundred yuan (U.S.$36) a month. It's chicken feed, and you end up sitting in front of a machine all day long. You've got to be kidding!

At my present company, or rather, at *our* company, I'm the development manager. That means I manage my own development. There are only ten people in this company; one boss, eight managers, and that secretary sitting there. She's called the office manager. We've all got fancy titles. It's good for business, and our main business is selling hardware. Small companies like ours can only push software by selling hardware. Although I've got a reputation as a pirate, that's really my after-hours career.

I've been with this company for more than a year. The pay is OK, a steady two grand (U.S.$240) a month. But there's not always stuff around to pirate—not stuff that'll make a profit. A program like CCHD 6.0 contains more than 1,000 ready-made 3-D images of interiors. A licensed copy sells for 2,700 renminbi (U.S.$323). But I can strip it down in over an hour and make as many copies as I want. Actually, I was working on that a few days ago. I was doing it for a friend, so I charged only 6,000 renminbi (U.S.$718), less than my normal fee.

It was cheap at that price. My friend can sell my pirated version for ages and make back what he spent on me many times over. To employ me for an hour costs about 100 renminbi (U.S.$12); the rest went to buy my skill. If it was someone else, they might not have been able to break the program code even in 10,000 hours. Anyway, I didn't learn what I know for free. I have to make back the money I invested in going to university.

The way I see it, pirating software is no big deal. Hong Kong, Taiwan, Korea, and Singapore created all their wealth and prosperity by pirating. Tell me what those little shits in Hong Kong have ever invented? Zilch. They're just a bunch of pseudo-foreign devils who started out as tailors and cobblers. Everything they know about computers comes from having learned how to pirate stuff.

PCs are made up of parts from everywhere. Open up any machine and you'll find components manufactured in a pile of different countries. Plus there are always a few things without any labels made by guerrilla outfits. It's the same for software. I rip you off, then you rip me off. Popular software products—regardless of who developed them—all contain some fishy things. So much intermarriage has gone on over the years that nowadays everyone's related.

It's ridiculous for these stinking foreigners to pick on China like they do. We're just following the general trend by pirating some of their stuff.

And they're up in arms, carrying on about intellectual property infringement and making a fucking stink all over the world about us.

Foreign devils are just plain unreasonable. To be honest, they've been ripping off the Chinese for ages. What's all this stuff about intellectual property? Whose ancestors got everything going in the first place? I don't think there are any cut-and-dried answers, but just ask yourself: What's the basic element of computing? Binary notation! That's the theory of yin and yang. Everything in the universe is made up of yin and yang, and the Chinese discovered that. Let's forget the hardware aspect of all this.

And what about electricity and magnetic fields? Who discovered magnetism? Pardon me, it was the Chinese! Then what are you supposed to do with your data? How do you record it? You need hard copy after all. Well, it's obvious, you need paper to print a hard copy and without Cai Lun (the legendary Chinese inventor of paper), those foreigners would still be writing on parchment. Can you cut parchment into A4 size and print on it? No way! These fucking foreigners don't have a clue. They can't face up to the fact that they owe us for copyright infringement. When we were advanced, they ripped us off left, right, and center. Now that they've managed to get ahead, they won't let us have a go. As soon as they struck it rich, they began lording over everyone else. Well, I'm going to go right on copying whatever comes my way.

They can hit China with as many sanctions as they want. Besides, they're only punishing the central government, it can't touch any of us. At least the foreign devils got that right—the Chinese government is the one to go after. Boy, do they make a heap from pirating! You can make a bundle if you pirate really clever software. But only the government can get away with it. I couldn't copy programs for heavy-duty machines, even if I wanted to. I don't have any originals to work with, nor do I have the know-how, equipment, or access to a market. I've got no alternative but to let the government make the real killing.

The government raided us a few days ago just to give the Yanks some face during the latest round of Sino-U.S. intellectual property talks. Go for it! All they got was a few disks. We still have software coming out our ears. Our pigs were just putting on a show for the Yankee devils. If they really wanted to enforce a ban, they'd hit the National Defense Science, Technology, and Industry Commission or the Academy of Sciences. All we get are their leftovers. The government has been breaking the same laws we have. If they don't give a damn, why should we be scared? Besides, if they nabbed me I'd play dumb, I'd just say that I was ripping off the foreign devils to help the Communist Party save some money on advanced technology from abroad!

Everyone along Thieves Alley (where software pirates hang out in Beijing) does the same thing. If we're selling to a government organization or state-owned company, we charge through the nose. What the heck? State-run companies aren't worried about money. As long as their middlemen get a commission, you can do what you want. Small private companies are more uptight about the bottom line, but it doesn't matter. They're computer illiterate, so you can tell them they need a pile of software and they'll believe you.

My first job wasn't on Thieves Alley, it was with an advertising company in Beijing's Eastern District. That was back in 1992, while I was working my way through my third year at university. At the time, my dad was only making 200 to 300 renminbi (U.S.$24 to $36) a month, and he saw me make a few grand for one night's work. It blew him away. He said to me, "You never know when you're going to make that much again, so you'd better not let your girlfriend spend it all." But he could tell I could make that kind of money easily, and he hated my guts for it. The old prick hasn't gone anywhere in life, and here was his little sperm, up and running.

I'm running all right. I'm making a killing, and I've got a real street cred: they call me one of the Four Heavenly Kings of Hacking here in Beijing. My old man can't believe it.

Before I went to college, I didn't take much notice of people in my dad's generation. You can forgive them for not knowing anything about computers, but I never spoke a common language with them. At the time of the June 4 incident back in 1989, I was in my last year of middle school. I went out to muck around in Tiananmen Square, but I didn't burn any military vehicles, let alone kill any of our blood brothers in the People's Liberation Army. Besides, only a fuckwit would ever admit to taking part in the riots.

My parents were freaking out because they were afraid I'd get into trouble in the square. "Politics is really complex," they said, "you don't understand." Fuck that for a joke. They didn't even stop to consider whether I'd been bitten by the politics bug in the first place. Those kids who got mixed up with politics were idiots or plain fools. Like I'd waste my time getting involved with any of them?

When I started university, the Maoists were in favor. They made all college students do military training. We lived in army barracks for months. But the more training we got, the worse we became. Geez, the government is full of idiots. They're always talking about trying to reform the way people think. Well, that's pretty dumb, if you ask me. The way you think is already programmed in your head, like a big mess of documents. You might be working with a fucked up application, but it's got its own internal logic. It's impractical to try and change it according to some master plan, document by document. It's more labor intensive than starting all over again.

If I started acting like our shit-for-brains government and spent all my time trying to change things, then everything would always go wrong. I'd always be crashing. Then I'd change some more and crash again.

My approach is just to copy, without changing anything. I'll leave your mistakes where they are. I won't even touch the trademark. It's not worth changing things. I'll sell whatever the market wants. I just have to make sure I can outsell everyone else.

Generally speaking, I've been in the right place at the right time. After my third year at university in 1992, I was pretty much free to do what I wanted. I had a chance to exploit my talents to the fullest. Didn't have to worry about a scholarship or finding a job. You have to rely on yourself, and that's just what I've been doing. That's why I'm different from my parents: I don't owe the Communist Party anything, and the Party doesn't owe me. The Party makes money their way; I make it mine. It's all money after all. We've just got a different approach.

I'm only responsible for myself. It's not my duty to save the nation or the People. I couldn't do it even if I wanted to. I'm clean and serene. All that propaganda about "the People sent you to university," or you should "serve the People"—it's a load of old crap. Couldn't even be bothered to ignore it. I got into university because I passed the entrance exams. For me it was an investment, pure and simple. Once I graduated, I didn't have to pay anyone back.

We're not living in a moral society or a moral age. As the old saying goes, "Only when you have enough to eat and wear do you think of frugality and shame." We're at the stage of accumulating capital. We're going through a baptism of blood and fire. It's far too early to get onto a moral high horse. Anyway, I'm sick of being poor. This society's never given me anything, so I don't care what they say now. Sorry, it's too late.

I'm better read than your average computer insect. I like reading and going to karaoke bars when I have the time. I've even read some Freud! But those brain-dead characters who waste their time in research institutes or big companies are satisfied to interface with machines all day long. If the authorities really want to wage a campaign against pornography, then they should go after those computer dweebs. All they know how to do is write programs. They have difficulty relating to people. Their lives suck. So they spend their leisure time reading about people screwing each other. Even in their free time, they pirate other people's lives.

I'd prefer not to go into much detail about my income. My salary's about 20,000 to 30,000 renminbi (U.S.$2,395 to $3,592) a year. Then there's my gray income on top of that. I don't do too badly. I belong to the income group that can afford to buy a car but can't yet buy an apartment. Luckily, my girlfriend has a place of her own. Her dad works in the government housing administration, and he got it for her. We all have to live off what we've been given, and her family can get housing. Her dad can rip off housing, cars, and villas from the state. It's easy to do, and completely legal. That's what they mean by the saying, "The dog that barks doesn't bite, while the dog that doesn't bark does."

Here, I'll give you a disk, you can use it as evidence against me. You're into IBMs; I'll give you an IBM disk, though of course I have Apple by the cartload, too.

You really think I'm stupid enough to let you use my real name? If my name ever appears in print, I'll sue you for defamation.

Take a good look, these CDs are all pretty crude—there's lots of rubbish printed on the case. But don't worry: you won't find my name or the name of the real producer anywhere. In fact, you won't even find the words "Made in China."

THE ECONOMY

VI. BUILDING AN ECONOMIC SUPERPOWER

Visits to Japan in 1978 and the United States in 1974 and 1979 convinced Deng Xiaoping of something he appears to have anticipated: China had fallen far behind the ranks of the global industrial powers during its quarter-century experiments with Maoist autarky and social engineering. Not only the gap between China and the West but that between China and its regional neighbors had significantly grown since the Second World War. China had completely missed out on the "East Asian Miracle." Its economy was ossified, largely devoid of new scientific and technological inputs, and still primarily preindustrial. Socialist central planning and high rates of reinvestment had stifled new growth, while the absence of market mechanisms had rigidified a multitude of distortions in the pricing and supply systems and throughout the economy. The Chinese economy was in dire need of overhaul.

The selections in this chapter illuminate many of the key elements in China's two decades of successful reform. The first three are taken from the 1995 report of the Joint Economic Committee of the U.S. Congress on the status and future of the Chinese economy. The final selection discusses the problem of what Chairman Mao defined as the "key link": grain.

BARRY NAUGHTON,
THE PATTERN AND LOGIC OF CHINA'S ECONOMIC REFORM

*In this selection the economist Barry Naughton provides an overview of
China's economic reforms and assesses the distinctiveness of the Chinese
approach to industrialization, agricultural development, market enhancement, and price reform. He shows that China's reformers did not operate
from a blueprint or master guide but proceeded incrementally by experimenting with different methods—which Chinese leaders describe as* mo
shitou guohe *(crossing the river feeling from stone to stone). Naughton
also argues that China's economic reforms are far from complete, and the
country faces many remaining obstacles.*

*This selection was first published in the U.S. Congress Joint Economic
Committee report* China's Economic Future: Challenges to U.S. Policy
in 1995.

China's economic reform process has succeeded in fundamentally
transforming the Chinese economy. Before reform, all important economic decisions were made by bureaucratic actors who were insulated
from most of the direct economic consequences of their actions,
and who did not in any case have meaningful prices to guide them in
decision making. China differed from more traditional Soviet-style
economies in that decision making was more decentralized, and central
planners did not dispose of the same level of detailed control over the
economy as in those countries. But the fundamental fact that decisions
were bureaucratically made and without real accountability was common to all of the formerly socialist economies. Today, economic decisions in China are made by a broad and diverse group of economic
agents, who respond to market prices and are overwhelmingly accountable for the economic consequences of their actions. It is in most fundamental respects a market economy. Moreover, China made the
transition from a bureaucratic to a market economy without experiencing a large transition-related economic contraction. Instead, economic
growth accelerated during the transition process. Saving and investment
have remained robust, and human resources have adapted rapidly to
the needs of a market-driven economy. Today, the fundamentals are in

place for a sustained period of high-growth development, extending well into the next century.

Despite the impressive achievements, China's economy continues to display some peculiar features and faces some important challenges. The most unusual aspect of the Chinese economy is the continuing involvement of government at all levels in decisions that would be made by private individuals in most market economies. Governments from the village to the national level own and operate factories. The central government remains committed to a national "industrial policy" that it hopes will guide development patterns in a number of industrial sectors. Governments interfere with bank credit decisions to ensure support for favored firms and projects. The pervasive involvement of government in the economy is matched by the relatively weak record in institutionalizing some of the key roles that government needs to play in a market economy. Despite an important tax reform in 1994, tax revenues continue to erode as a share of gross domestic product and many activities manage to avoid taxation with the collusion of local government sponsors. Despite passage of an impressive body of commercial law, enforcement of property rights remains weak and recourse to the legal system is not in practice available to all. Weak institutionalization and pervasive government involvement in business open the door to corrupt practices.

The key element that has kept the reform process on course has been the steadily increasing impact of market forces. Reform has proceeded through the gradual but persistent injection of market competition into progressively more crucial sectors of the economy. In a competitive context, the costs of government support for poorly performing firms or grandiose projects have become increasingly obvious; and the limitations on government resources in this still relatively poor country have eroded support for projects that cannot pay their own way. Regions, sectors, and local governments compete in a context in which success is determined primarily by market performance. In this context, national and local governments cannot fully shelter poorly performing client enterprises from the imperatives of the marketplace. Most economic organizations have been forced to recognize that they must pay their own way, whether they are private or governmentally sponsored. The following sections briefly outline the process of reform and then outline the main elements of the reform strategy and the lessons to be drawn from it.

Successive Waves of Market Competition

The traditional socialist economy was not simply a bureaucratic economy; it was also a protected economy, in which key sectors were reserved for government actors. Most critically, industry and foreign trade were protected sectors where the government used its monopoly power to ensure high prices and high profits. During the Chinese reform process, the government cautiously, but progressively and systematically, opened these sectors to market competition. As it did so, it maintained a planned sector in place over the medium run in order to ensure economic stability and allow the government to achieve a few of its priority objectives. Gradually, as the market sector developed, the planned sector was frozen, and then cut back. In successive waves of reform, marketization spread to nearly every sector of the economy.

During the first wave of reform, beginning at the end of 1978, important initiatives were launched simultaneously in urban and rural industry, agriculture, and foreign trade and investment. It is not quite true that Chinese reforms "began in agriculture," since the earliest reforms were quite broad based. But it was in agriculture that reforms reaped early and undeniable success. Incremental reforms of the agricultural collectives led steadily—and in retrospect inexorably—to a system by which land was contracted to individual households. The rural reform was radical in the willingness to devolve managerial policy all the way down to the household level but conservative in maintaining ultimate ownership of the land with local collectives, and in maintaining state control of the marketing channels for agricultural inputs and output. Farmers responded to their new freedoms with a surge of output, doubling farm incomes over six years and moving China out of centuries of food shortage.

The early reform with almost as much long-run impact as the agricultural reforms was that which allowed rural industries to expand into virtually any product line. Rural industries already existed, but they had been constrained to a narrow "serve agriculture" orientation that prevented their emergence as a core element of local development. In late 1979 rural industries were freed from these constraints. Following a multitude of development strategies—including subcontracting with urban factories, producing building materials and consumer goods for newly affluent rural households, and locating "niche markets" of unmet urban demand—rural industries grew into an important part of the industrial base. Rural industries gradually grew to provide significant competition with urban, state-owned industry. Those urban industries had, in the meantime, been given expanded autonomy and improved incentives. Factories were allowed to retain some profits and sell additional output above plan targets. Although initially modest, these early reforms began to prepare factory managers for more radical departures. Moreover, a whole new corps of factory managers was brought in, as Cultural Revolution–era political appointees were replaced by a new group of younger and more competent managers.

Among the earliest of the first-wave reforms were those which opened up parts of southern China to foreign, and especially Hong Kong, businesses. The Special Economic Zones attracted the most attention, but equally important were measures that allowed the duty-free import of inputs for export processing contracts. These measures created a sphere of the Chinese economy that was externally oriented and freed of the constraints of the state-run economy. Initially modest in size and carefully circumscribed from the main domestic economy, the export-oriented sector was poised for explosive growth.

The second wave of reform, roughly 1984–1988, was given impetus and legitimacy by the success of rural reforms, and built on the accomplishments of the first wave. In industry tentative early policies were knit together into a coherent program to improve the operation of state industry. Most important were the steps taken to replace a plan with market operations. The absolute size of plan targets was "frozen" at the end of 1984 for most goods. State-owned factories were instructed to procure all their above-plan inputs and sell all their above-plan output independently on the market. Market prices came to regulate a significant portion of state factory output, as well as the bulk of rural industrial output. Crucial to this strategy was the commitment to freeze the absolute size of the plan: this implied that all growth would take place in the market sector, permitting the industrial economy to "grow out of the plan." Factory managers were given much more powerful incentives, and experiments with leasing and auctioning of managerial rights were carried out on a large scale.

In foreign trade reform, the initial export-oriented economy was given a vastly expanded scope with the adoption of the Coastal Development Strategy in 1987–88. This policy allowed foreign investment and duty-free import for export producers through a large swath of the southern coastal region. In addition, the official exchange rate was devalued, and a secondary market for foreign exchange was established. These measures allowed exporters anywhere in the economy partial access to foreign currencies, and improved incentives to export.

Only in agriculture were the second-wave reforms less impressive. An attempt to rapidly marketize agricultural procurement and input supply in 1985 failed in the face of a surge of inflation. While that initial inflationary episode was tamed, a subsequent outburst in 1988 led to a crisis of confidence in reform and a political backlash that extended to the Tiananmen episode in 1989. During 1988–89, it appeared to many in China that reform had led to inflation and instability, without clearly improving economic performance. Conservatives sought to roll back reforms in the wake of the Tiananmen tragedy.

However, this rollback lasted for less than two years. Attempts to reinstate planning failed miserably, while the performance of the new market-oriented sectors was, in the face of adversity, clearly superior to that of traditional state-run sectors. The stage was soon set for a third wave of reforms. Beginning in 1992 China passed a series of economic reform milestones. In rapid succession China abolished most of the remnants of central planning and relaxed the bulk of price controls. Foreign investors were given significant access to the Chinese domestic market. At a Communist Party Congress in November 1993, a program for a broad move to a market economy was officially adopted. Immediately following this important meeting, several crucial reform measures were adopted that were designed to regularize China's economic procedures and build substantially more effective institutions. The two most significant of these were the adoption of a new tax and fiscal system, and the devaluation and unification of exchange rates. Both of these important measures were put into place on January 1, 1994.

One of the significant achievements of the third reform wave was the development of labor markets. During most of the first two waves, state workers had remained within their existing enterprises and rural workers had remained within their own communities. During the 1990s there has been a surge of labor mobility. Attracted by opportunities in the emerging private and foreign-invested sectors, well-educated young urban dwellers began changing jobs. New social security and unemployment funds have been created that make job changing less traumatic than in the old system of enterprise-specific social benefits. At the same time large-scale interregional migration began, as peasants began leaving farms for work in the booming coastal regions. By 1995 some 60 to 80 million workers were estimated to be working outside their home villages. The growth of the economy gradually began to provide occupational choice and opportunity for a substantial segment of China's population.

Reforms have perhaps been least thorough in the financial sector. State-owned banks still dominate that sector, and bank credit is still the predominant form of financial intermediation. Allocation of credit is influenced by government officials, notwithstanding attempts to segregate policy lending into three "policy banks," thereby freeing up the remaining banks to operate according to commercial principles. The banks carry many bad loans on their books and are in urgent need of restructuring. Undoubtedly, China will need to carry out further banking and fiscal reforms, or else face financial crises that may disrupt future growth, at least temporarily.

Overall, however, it is remarkable how much China has achieved. One marker of the changes in the economy is that state-owned industry accounted for only 31 percent of industrial output value in 1995. Another 3 to 4 percent of industrial output was produced by joint stock companies in which government organizations have controlling interests, so perhaps 34 to 35 percent of output is from the state sector overall. Moreover, the bulk of state ownership is now concentrated in sectors such as utilities and resource extraction, or in capital- and scale-intensive industries such as chemicals, steel, and transport machinery. The pattern of state ownership is now fairly similar to that in developed, "mixed" market economies. This has been achieved without massive privatization of government-owned factories, simply by preferentially encouraging the growth of private, foreign-invested, and rural collective enterprises.

The Chinese Approach as a Strategy of Economic Reform

China's reform is typically categorized as a gradualist approach. This is true, in the sense that reform has been protracted and cautious. The Chinese leadership has acted as if it were constrained to maintain both inflation and open urban unemployment within fairly narrow limits. The Chinese have acted as if minimizing short-run adjustment costs (at the expense of prolonging the overall adjustment process) were an important argument in their overall transition strategy. Yet it is important to distinguish Chinese gradualism from the tentative reforms which were tried in the European socialist economies in the 1960s. Those reforms, which I prefer to call "rationalizing reforms," were never designed to be a strategy for transition to the market. Instead they involved a strategy to improve or "perfect" the planning system. Rationalizing reforms maintained the fundamental framework of the existing system, most crucially the state monopoly over the critical core sectors of the economy. Reformers hoped the computation of optimal prices could be combined with improved reward functions to create a planned economy with the efficiency of a market economy. They were after a "computopia" that would combine the best aspects of plan and market, and in which perfect computation would substitute for real competition.

By contrast, it should be clear from the preceding narrative that Chinese reforms involved the injection of market forces and market prices into the economy from the earliest stages. Competition with the "core" state-run industrial sector was permitted once rural enterprises were allowed to produce according to market dictates. From the beginning the Chinese reform process involved introducing market elements where they could be introduced without disrupting the economy as a whole. In the overwhelming emphasis on marketization as such, the Chinese reform pattern shares a basic kinship with "Big Bang" transitions in Eastern Europe (most notably Poland). Both involve quick acceptance of market-determined prices and large-scale entry of nonstate producers. Because of this dynamic, both involve a sharp decline in the government's direct control over resources, as measured by budgetary revenues as a share of gross national product, and a concomitant increase in control over resources by households and enterprises. The Chinese transition differs from those in Eastern Europe in the specific sequence with which policies were adopted, and in particular transitional institutions, rather than in the ultimate objective. Both strategies ultimately led to the creation of a market economy, even if this was not known (or could not be openly proclaimed) in China at the outset.

Key Features of the Chinese Approach

Since the Chinese approach differs from other transitional strategies primarily in the way that specific elements of transition are sequenced and organized, it is worthwhile to briefly outline the distinctive features of the Chinese approach, as follows.

THE DUAL-TRACK SYSTEM

The first distinctive element of the Chinese reform process is the "dual-track system." This refers to the coexistence of a traditional plan and a market channel for the allocation of a given good. Rather than dismantling the plan, reformers acquiesced in a continuing role for the plan in order to ensure stability and guarantee the attainment of some key government priorities (in the Chinese case, primarily investment in energy and infrastructure). Having a dual track implies the existence of a two-tier pricing system for goods under that system: a single commodity will have both a (typically low) state-set planned price and a (typically higher) market price.

It is important to stress that the dual track refers to the coexistence of two coordination mechanisms (plan and market) and not to the coexistence of two ownership systems. By the mid-1980s most state-owned firms were still being assigned a compulsory plan for some output but had additional capacity available for production of above-plan, market goods. Thus, the dual-track strategy was one that operated within the state sector—indeed, within each state-run factory—as well as in the industrial economy at large. This was essential, because it meant that virtually all factories, including state-run factories, were introduced to the market and began the process of adaptation to market processes. The dual-track system allowed state firms to transact and cooperate with nonstate, marketized firms, allowing valuable flexibility.

GROWING OUT OF THE PLAN

The mere existence of a dual-track system is not itself sufficient to define a transition strategy. All planned economies have something of a dual-track system, in the sense that none of them ever completely eradicates various kinds of black market trading that, inescapably, takes place under market-influenced prices. Thus, it is a crucial feature of the Chinese transition that economic growth is concentrated on the market track. I coined the phrase "growing out of the plan" in 1984 after Chinese planners in Beijing had described in interviews their intention to keep the size of the overall central government materials allocation plan fixed in absolute terms. Given the obvious fact that the economy was growing rapidly, this implied that the plan would become proportionately less and less important until the economy gradually grew out of the plan. Planners concurred in this description: Chinese policy makers were making a generally credible commitment to freeze the size of the traditional plan. The commitment to growing out of the plan was of great importance for the individual enterprise as well. With their plans essentially fixed, enterprises faced "market prices on the margin." Even those firms with compulsory plans covering the bulk of capacity were in the position that future growth and development of profitable opportunities would take place at market prices. The plan served as a kind of lump-sum tax on (or subsidy to) the enterprise, and decisions would be based on market prices.

ENTRY

The central government's monopoly over industry was relaxed. In China the protected industrial sector was effectively opened to new entrants beginning in 1979. Large numbers of start-up firms, especially rural industries, rushed to take advantage of large potential profits in the industrial sector, and their entry sharply increased competition and changed overall market conditions in the industrial sector. Most of these firms were collectively owned, and some were private or foreign owned. But local governments also sponsored many new start-up firms during the 1980s, and these firms were often "state owned." The crucial factor is that the central government surrendered in practice its ability to maintain high barriers to entry around the lucrative manufacturing sectors. This lowering of entry barriers was greatly facilitated in China by the nation's huge size and diversity, and the relatively large role that local governments play in economic management even before reform. Large size and diversity meant there was scope for competition among firms in the "public sector," even if each of these firms remained tied to government at some level.

PRICES THAT EQUATE SUPPLY AND DEMAND

Flexible prices that equated supply and demand quickly came to play an important role in the Chinese economy. Beginning in the early 1980s, a significant proportion of transactions began to occur at market prices, and in 1985, market prices were given legal sanction for exchange of producer goods outside the plan. This meant that state firms were legally operating at market prices, since virtually all state firms had some portion of above-plan production. Gradual decontrol of consumer goods prices—initially cautious—steadily brought most consumer goods under market price regimes. An important benefit of the legitimacy given to market prices was that transactions between the state and nonstate sector were permitted, and they developed into a remarkable variety of forms. Simple trade was accompanied by various kinds of joint ventures and cooperative arrangements, as profit-seeking, state-run enterprises looked for ways to reduce costs by subcontracting with rural nonstate firms with lower labor and land costs.

INCREMENTAL MANAGERIAL REFORMS IN THE STATE SECTOR

This market framework for the state firm facilitated the maintenance and incremental reform of the management system of state enterprises. As state firms faced increasing competitive pressures, government officials experimented with ways to improve incentives and management capabilities within the state sector. This experimental process focused on a steady shift in emphasis away from plan fulfillment and toward profitability as the most important indicator of enterprise performance. It is characteristic of China's reform that the improved, and in some ways intensified, monitoring of state enterprise performance was an alternative to large-scale privatization. Logically, there is no reason why privatization cannot be combined with a dual-track transitional strategy, but practically there are obvious reasons why they would tend to be alternatives. Urgent privatization tends to follow from a belief that state sector performance cannot be improved, and often leads to a short-run "abandonment of the enterprise" as the attention of reformers shifts away from short-run performance and to the difficult task of privatization. Conversely, the sense that privatization is not imminent lends urgency to the attempt to improve monitoring, control, and incentives in the state sector.

DISARTICULATION

Along with measures to reform the core of the planned economy, Chinese reforms also advanced by identifying economic activities that were the least tightly integrated into the planning mechanism and pushing reform in these limited areas. Chinese reform might thus also be labeled a strategy of "disarticulation," in which successive sections of the economy are separated from the planned core, which persists. This was clearly not an intentional strategy, but rather one that emerged from the nature of the policy process and from the concern of Chinese policy makers not to disrupt the core economy. The early establishment of Special Economic Zones is the most obvious example of such policies—export-oriented enclaves were created that had, initially, almost no links to the remainder of the economy. This approach is also one of the reasons that reforms succeeded first in the countryside. Policy makers realized that it was not necessary that all the countryside be integrated into the planned economy. Beginning with the poorest areas, some regions were allowed to detach from the planned economy. So long as the state could purchase sufficient grain to keep its storehouses full, it could afford to let the organizational form in the countryside devolve back to household farming.

INITIAL MACROECONOMIC STABILIZATION ACHIEVED THROUGH THE PLAN

Macroeconomic stabilization and reorientation of development strategy were initially carried out under the traditional planned economy. Rather than combining stabilization and reform into a single rapid but traumatic episode, the Chinese used the instruments of the planned economy to shift resources toward the household sector and relieve macroeconomic stresses at the very beginning of reform. This dramatic shift in development strategy created favorable conditions for the gradual unfolding of reform. Particularly striking is the fact that reforms began with a strengthening of the government's guarantee of full employment to all permanent urban residents. Indeed, the initial shift toward a more labor intensive development strategy was motivated in part by the need to provide jobs for a large group of unemployed young people.

MACROECONOMIC CYCLES THROUGHOUT THE REFORM PROCESS
After the beginning of reforms, a pattern developed in which bold reform measures tended to be implemented after stabilization had achieved some success. Reform measures then contributed to renewed macroeconomic imbalances, eventually leading to a new period of macroeconomic austerity. As a result, macroeconomic policies have been of fundamental importance in determining the success or failure of reforms during individual periods.

At the same time the alternation between expansionary and contractionary phases of the macroeconomic cycle has contributed to marketization of the economy over the long run. Periods of macroeconomic austerity led to relative abundance of goods and the temporary elimination of shortages. Under those conditions, the demand for planning was reduced, and the position of markets strengthened. More generally, the planning apparatus has been buffeted by the rapid change in economic conditions, and its importance receded as a result of its inability to respond rapidly to quick changes in the economic environment. The almost intractable task of planning an economy can only be carried out in conditions of artificially imposed stability; without that stability, the inadequacy of attempts to plan the economy became increasingly evident.

CONTINUED HIGH SAVING AND INVESTMENT BY HOUSEHOLDS
Steady erosion in government revenues—ultimately traceable to the dissolution of the government industrial monopoly—led to a sustained reduction in government saving. At the same time, though, steady increases in household income and the increasing opportunities in the economic environment led to a rapid increase in household saving. These offsetting changes meant that total national saving remained

high, sustaining high levels of investment and growth. One consequence has been a vastly enhanced role for the banking system, serving as an intermediary channeling household saving to the enterprise sector. While this process has been relatively smooth, it has been difficult for the government both to acquiesce in and to manage the decline in its resources, and macroeconomic policy making has become more complex and more difficult.

Together, these factors gave the Chinese transition process an ex post coherence. That coherence did not derive from an early blueprint for reform; nor did it derive from a simple realistic and empirical approach on the part of Chinese policy makers. Rather it derived from a consistent approach to economic problems. This approach sought to minimize economic disruption while gradually and systematically substituting market competition for planned regulation. On balance, and despite a stormy political evolution, this approach has served China well, and succeeded in bringing the Chinese economy to the market.

HANG-SHENG CHENG, A MIDCOURSE ASSESSMENT OF CHINA'S ECONOMIC REFORM

This selection takes stock of the first fifteen years of China's economic reforms. Hang-Sheng Cheng details the considerable progress made but also identifies the limits of reforms in many key sectors: partial decentralization, incomplete marketization, limited financial liberalization, and inadequate market infrastructure. In addition, he notes the problems posed by insolvent state-owned enterprises, an inadequate social welfare system, a weak taxation system, foreign exchange irregularities, a debt-ridden financial system, and inadequate legal structure. He suggests that without prompt and sustained attention to these and other pressing problems and parallel development of market-supportive institutions, China's heretofore rapid economic growth will not be sustainable. Needless to say, these concerns became even more pronounced in 1998 as an economic meltdown threatened all of Asia.

This selection was first published in the U.S. Congress Joint Economic Committee report China's Economic Future: Challenges to U.S. Policy *in 1995.*

China's economic success has dazzled the world. Since reform began in 1979, China has maintained the highest output growth rate in the world, attaining an annual average of 12.5 percent from 1992 to 1995. Among the developing countries, it has been the largest recipient of foreign direct investment, amounting to $38 billion in 1995. Some observers are speculating that China could replace Japan as the second largest economy in the world by the year 2010.

Yet, paradoxically, many respected scholars and policy advisers in China are quite concerned about the country's economic future. In private conversations, they marvel at the outside world's enthusiasm and note, with a smile, how its views have swung from dire pessimism at the beginning of this decade to unbounded optimism a mere six years later, when basically not that much has changed in China.

What is the reason for this contrast in assessment? Are the outside observers naive, as the insiders seem to believe? Or are the insiders seeing only the trees, not the forest, as the outsiders seem to think? What is the true picture of China's economy today and its prospects in the foreseeable future?

China has reached a midpoint in its economic reform. Past reforms have produced rapid output growth and improved the living standard for the majority of its people. Yet, the task is only half completed. Many of the constraints to growth remain, and the underlying foundation for sustainable growth is yet to be laid.

Past Reforms and Problems

China's impressive economic progress in the last seventeen years is a familiar story that needs no repeating. Instead, three principal features of the reforms that began in 1979 will be sketched to help review the past and assess the present. They are decentralization, marketization, and financial liberalization.

Decentralization means a devolution of economic decision making from the central authorities to lower levels of the government. During the thirty years prior to 1979, twice decentralization had been tried, first in 1958–1960 and then in 1967–1976, both times ending in disaster. The third attempt in 1979 differed in that decentralization this time was extended down to the level of individual production units, rather than stopping at the provincial government level, in a gradually liberalizing market environment.

Marketization means the replacement of central planning by the free play of market forces. Internationally, an open-door policy ended thirty years of self-imposed insulation from the rest of the world and opened the economy gradually to competition, new technology, and new markets through foreign trade and foreign investment. Domestically, by 1994 more than 85 percent of agricultural prices and more than 95 percent of industrial consumer prices were free of government control, and the scope of mandatory production planning fell to only 5 percent from 95 percent of total industrial output prior to reform. In addition, the rise of township and village industries and of private enterprises, including wholly or partially foreign-owned businesses, has greatly increased opportunities for entrepreneurship and competition in the economy.

Lastly, financial liberalization means the switch from government-budgeted investment financing to lending through banks. Because in China banking control is much weaker than government fiscal control, the change has significantly loosened the budget constraint on the financing of investment and production. Together, these three factors released a torrent of powerful productive forces that had been dammed up by central economic planning. Over the past seventeen years, this newly unleashed vitality has gathered momentum to create spectacular output growth, especially in the last four years.

The question facing China now is, how long can this momentum be sustained?

To answer this question, we must draw a distinction between economic growth and economic development. Economic growth refers to output growth, while economic development refers to the development of public and private institutions and conventions that are essential for sustaining economic growth. A nation can achieve rapid output growth by increasing capital investment and acquiring new technology—as the former Soviet Union did in the 1930s and China in the 1950s—as well as by more efficient use of its resources through domestic and international marketization—as China has done since 1979. But, without developing the essential market-supportive institutions and conventions, output growth will inevitably lead to chaos, wastefulness, and eventual exhaustion of the sources of growth.

This, I believe, is where China stands today. On the surface, everything looks fine: businesses are booming, high-rises are going up everywhere, and foreign capital keeps pouring in. But, internally, both its society and its economy have deep-seated problems.

These problems may be summarized under the same three headings used above to characterize past reforms: decentralization, marketization, and financial liberalization—plus market infrastructure. Past reforms, in each of these areas, carried the signature of a piecemeal, experimental approach. This approach has brought about clear signs of malfunction of a half-market, half-government-controlled economy—with plenty of vitality but not much rule and order. Pundits have aptly labeled it an economy of the "Wild East."

PARTIAL DECENTRALIZATION

Devolution of business decision making has not been carried through to all enterprises. For ideological as well as practical reasons, this has been especially true with respect to the state-owned enterprises (SOEs), which to a large extent continue to be directly managed or tightly controlled by various government agencies. However, despite preferential treatment in the supply of energy, transportation, and raw materials, about one-half of the 100,000 SOEs sustained losses in the business-boom year of 1994. Although accounting for only about 40 percent of the nation's total industrial output, they absorbed two-thirds of total domestic credit and received subsidies amounting to two-thirds of the large government budget deficit that year.

The SOE problem is only the tip of the iceberg of a much larger and more general problem of the nation's industrial organization. Virtually all domestic businesses of any significant size are either owned and operated by some government agencies or indirectly connected with some government units. Though government related, these business enterprises exist not to carry out government policies as before reform but to make money, to get rich, for their own workers and the respective government agencies and their staffs.

Moreover, the majority of businesses are in some way tied to the local government. Local interests often prevail over business interests. Local protectionism in terms of the sourcing of productive inputs, allocation of credit, distribution of tax concessions, and enforcement of court decisions has built up a tight and cozy relationship between businesses and the local bureaucracy.

In this environment, connections reign over productive efficiency as the key to economic success. Corruption is rampant, and influence peddling is a way of life. The cost of doing business in this environment, to individual businesses and the society, is enormous, compared to that in a market economy.

Another consequence of decentralization has been the steady deterioration of government finance. The share of government revenue in gross domestic product (GDP) fell steadily from 34 percent in 1978 to only 14 percent in 1993, compared to an average of 32 percent in developing countries and 48 percent in industrial countries. Inadequate government revenue and the associated perennial budget deficits have meant underfunding of major priority areas such as education, public health, poverty alleviation, environmental protection, transportation, pension reform, and unemployment assistance—with adverse impacts on social stability in the short run and on economic growth in the long run.

INCOMPLETE MARKETIZATION

Marketization has also been far less than complete. Internationally, although the open-door policy has succeeded in attracting large inflows of foreign direct investment and in developing a dynamic, rapidly expanding export sector, by 1993 the economy was still shackled by a deep-rooted mercantilist mentality of export promotion coupled with protectionism against imports. Almost one-half of imports were subject to licensing, and a high tariff system was structured to favor imports of raw materials and intermediate products against finished goods, resulting in retarded development of domestic high-quality intermediate-product industries and low domestic content of exports. In addition, an exchange control regime coupled with a dual exchange rate added another layer of mercantilist policy to the trade restrictions.

Domestically, marketization has been almost entirely on the output side of the market and little on the factor-input side. Although by the end of 1993 the prices of most goods and services were market determined, for the factor inputs—land, capital, labor, and technology—there were hardly any markets to speak of. The nation's constitution stipulates that all land is state owned. Since 1979 farmers have leased land from the state, but the leases are not transferable. Experiments with urban land leases, also nontransferable, are just beginning. Until recently capital was allocated by state-owned banks in accordance with the credit plan. And the annual volume of capital raised in the emerging capital markets is negligible. Labor mobility is hampered by the household registry system, which has kept surplus farm labor in the countryside, though with decreasing effectiveness. A more effective barrier to labor movement has been the employer provision system, which still provides to permanent employees cradle-to-grave welfare—including housing, medical care, child education, vacation travel, old-age pension, funeral and burial services. Technology is also not marketable. A patent law was passed in 1985 and a copyright law in 1990, to encourage inventions and innovations. But enforcement remains a remote hope.

LIMITED FINANCIAL LIBERALIZATION

The shift from government-budgeted financing of investment to bank financing is a far cry from the deregulation of the financial system in market economies. In fact, after seventeen years of economic reform, although central planning of physical production has largely disappeared, until recently the credit plan remained the central guiding principle of credit allocation in China. Under the plan, the central bank directly controlled the total volume and the direction of bank loans to enterprises as well as the magnitudes of individual securities issues in the capital market. Interest rates today are still regulated by the central bank under the direction of the State Council.

The result of this government direct control of all financial activities has been a banking system that operates purely as a government bureaucracy, and a stunted growth of money and capital markets. Despite the phenomenal expansion — in variety and in volume — of financial institutions and financial assets in the last seventeen years, functionally finance remains the most unreformed area in the Chinese economy today. Thus, in this partially reformed economy, while most of the prices and production decisions are now market determined, the all-important allocation of credit and supply of money was until recently still controlled by economic planning.

The incongruity of marketized production and plan-controlled finance has become more evident, as decentralization expanded both the sources and the magnitude of political pressure on the central bank for easy monetary policy. The increased pressure has made the central bank's management of the annual credit plan increasingly difficult. Moreover, as was to be expected, the market has developed many ways to get around the credit plan, in the form of a variety of nonbank financial institutions and informal money markets. The result has been less effective monetary control.

Moreover, under political pressure, the central bank has not followed a stable monetary policy. When it succumbed to pressures and allowed rapid growth of credit and money supply, inflation followed; when it tightened credit and reduced monetary growth, the economy slowed down and pressures for reversal of the policy remounted. The resultant stop-go monetary policy has been the principal cause of China's macroeconomic instability and accelerated inflation during the past seventeen years.

INADEQUATE MARKET INFRASTRUCTURE

Foremost among the market-supportive institutions essential for sustainable economic growth are law and the court system. Civil law has never had much of a tradition in China. Whatever tradition there had been the Communist revolution in 1949 destroyed almost entirely. The 1979 reform reawakened an appreciation of the importance of law in a market economy. A series of basic laws have been enacted, governing foreign joint ventures (1979), business contracts (1981), trademarks (1982), patents (1984), environment protection (1989), copyrights (1991), corporations (1993), foreign trade (1994), and arbitration (1995).

Efforts have been concentrated on legislation, however, rather than on enforcement. The latter depends on the lower courts and the local police, both of which are either directly under the local government or closely tied to it. Court judgments against local businesses under local government protection have little chance of being enforced.

Current Reform: Programs and Implementation

Recognizing the problems arising from the piecemeal, experimental approach to past reforms, the authorities in 1994 launched a bold, comprehensive, and integrated reform program designed to complete the reform process and construct a "socialist market economy with Chinese characteristics" by the year 2010. It covers a wide spectrum of areas. Instead of examining it in detail, I shall focus on a few areas to illustrate the general characteristics of the program and the difficulties of implementation.

STATE-OWNED ENTERPRISES

The authorities recognized the need to complete the decentralization process by insulating the SOEs from government interference and giving them complete autonomy in management. Out of the 100,000 SOEs, 10,000 were selected to adopt new accounting standards, 1,000 large SOEs to adopt new state asset management regulations, and 100 large and medium-sized to be incorporated as shareholding companies operating under their own boards of directors. In addition, eighteen cities were chosen to experiment with comprehensive reform programs, including corporate restructuring and municipal provision of social insurance services to workers. Recently, in March 1996, the government announced its intention to concentrate reform on 1,000 large SOEs and dispose of the roughly 90,000 small SOEs through mergers, leasing, or sale.

Given the magnitude and complexity of the task, it is not surprising that progress has been limited. Of the 100 selected for incorporation, 61 have done so, but altering the form of corporate structure is the easiest part of the program. Among the eighteen cities selected for reform experiments, several have successfully completed bankruptcy proceedings on loss-making enterprises and laid off hundreds of thousands of workers without incident. However, out of the 100,000 SOEs and the estimated 15 million redundant workers, this is a very small beginning.

HOUSING AND SOCIAL WELFARE

The largest obstacle to enterprise reform has been the employee welfare system that guarantees the workers cradle-to-grave benefits. These benefits are provided directly by the SOEs and constitute a heavy burden on them, especially in the face of increasing market competition from other types of firms—such as collectives, township-and-village enterprises, and foreign-owned businesses—which are not similarly burdened. To create a level playing ground, the SOEs must be relieved of these burdens.

Reforms in housing, medical care, children's education, and old-age pension were started before 1994; some of these have been accelerated since. Besides vigorous housing construction in all major cities, rents have been raised and experiments with sales have begun. Although little progress has been made on medical care and education because of lack of funds, reportedly 70 percent of the urban workers have joined some sort of pension system, and 53 percent are now covered by unemployment insurance. In addition, 50 million rural workers have joined a national rural old-age pension plan. Out of a total rural population of 900 million, this is a mere fraction. Nevertheless, it is a significant beginning.

TAXATION

Another major component of the reform program is a complete overhaul of the nation's taxation system, launched in 1994. The goal was a modern taxation and revenue-sharing system based on the principles of equality of tax burden, simplicity of tax administration, and buoyancy of tax revenue with the expansion and contraction of the national income. The new tax system introduced a unified single income tax for all enterprises, a broad-based value-added tax (VAT) covering almost all goods and services, excise taxes on a few selected commodities, and a business tax on services not covered by the VAT. Revenue sharing between the central and local governments is now clearly defined, and a national tax administration has been established to collect central taxes as well as tax revenues to be shared with the local governments.

The implementation of tax reform is an enormously difficult task. Old habits of tax evasion are hard to change, and fraud is rampant. For instance, in 1995 the total amount of export tax refund under VAT exceeded the total VAT collected from their production. The difficulties of implementation are also reflected in the continued fall in the government revenue as a ratio to GDP, slipping from 13.8 percent in 1993 to 12.4 percent in 1994, and 11.3 percent in 1995.

FOREIGN TRADE AND FOREIGN EXCHANGE

In its bid to enter the World Trade Organization (WTO), China has reduced its import tariff rates to an average of 23 percent from 40 percent in 1992 and eliminated two-thirds of the import quotas and other quantitative restrictions. In addition, a unified exchange rate was established in 1994 to replace the previous dual exchange-rate system. The exchange rate is now determined by the market through the banks, with central bank participation in the market to help stabilize the rate. Moreover, the onerous foreign-exchange certificate imposed since 1980 on tourist and foreign business spending in China has been abolished. And exchange controls on trade and all trade-related transactions have been removed. Recently, the authorities declared that the national currency would become convertible on all current-account transactions by the end of 1996, thereby making China one of the International Monetary Fund's "Article VIII" member countries.

THE FINANCIAL SYSTEM

On the domestic side, one of the most important marketization programs is the reform of the financial system. The authorities intend to overhaul the entire financial system in order to free it from vestiges of the old command economy and transform the system into one operated according to market principles. First, the central bank has been given more independence, but still functions under the State Council's direction, in carrying out its responsibilities. Monetary policy is now explicitly aimed at price stabilization. Second, banks and nonbank financial institutions are required to operate on a commercial basis. Policy loans are to be shifted to three policy banks specifically created for that purpose. Third, the central bank is charged with fostering the development of competitive money and capital markets under its supervision and regulation, for the provision of liquidity and efficient allocation of capital.

Thus far, the basic legal framework for financial reform is largely in place. Accounting and auditing procedures for banking operations have been formulated, and staff training programs have been started. The credit plan has been abolished, and an interbank fund market has been restarted under close central bank supervision. The three policy banks—an export-import bank, an industrial development bank, and an agricultural financing and development bank—are in operation. However, the problem of policy loans remains unresolved, and banks must continue to provide policy loans. Interest rates are still regulated by the central bank. And, despite claims of the economy's successful "soft landing" in 1995, the end of stop-go monetary policy is not yet in sight.

LAW

With the 1994 reform, the pace of legal reform accelerated. The People's Congress set a goal to complete the basic legislation for a "socialist market economy" by the end of the century. In 1995 alone it passed thirteen laws of fundamental importance to the economy, including laws on the central bank, commercial banks, insurance, securities, taxation, corporation, and environmental protection. Also notable were new laws on local election, the court system, the police, education, food standard, science, and technology. The rapid increase in the number of lawyers in China is another sign of the growing importance of law in the society. There were 82,000 in 1995 compared to less than 50,000 in 1992 and less than 1,000 in 1980. Progress toward effective law enforcement, however, remains very limited.

Conclusion

The question on China's economic prospects by 2010 can now be answered. The answer is implicit in the analysis above. Nonetheless, it is useful to make it explicit, together with a consideration of China's role in the world economy.

First, economic growth is not the same as economic development. In the past seventeen years, China has achieved rapid economic growth, but made little progress in economic development. Without the essential parallel development of supporting market institutions and conventions, eventually the economic costs of growing chaos and wastefulness will override whatever remains of the economy's growth potential.

Second, the comprehensive reform program launched in 1994 reflects the authorities' recognition of the numerous basic deficiencies in the economy, requiring correction. In the last two years, considerable progress has been made in foreign trade and foreign exchange liberalization, the development of a modern tax code, and revenue-sharing arrangements, as well as in social and economic legislation. However, despite these impressive achievements, enormous difficulties continue to confront enterprise reform, housing and social welfare, tax administration, financial reform, and law enforcement.

Hence, the answer to the question posed in this article must be a conditional one: China's output growth is sustainable into the next century, say, to 2010, if and only if it succeeds in implementing its current comprehensive reform program. Predictions of China's becoming a great economic power by the year 2010 are greatly exaggerated. At best, it could become another newly industrialized country. Nevertheless, because of its sheer size China remains an attractive market for businesses that are experienced in trading with or investing in developing economies.

Anthony Y. C. Koo and K. C. Yeh, The Impact of Township, Village, and Private Enterprises' Growth on State Enterprises Reform: Three Regional Case Studies

This selection examines one of the key components of China's economic success: private and collective township, village, and private enterprises (TVPs). After 1978 many rural workers moved into this sector and powered an export boom in light industrial manufactured goods. To a significant extent the TVPs have been the engine that drove China's rapid economic growth during the initial phases of the reform era—thus offering counterevidence to the central state–centric "East Asian development model." The fiscal relationship of TVPs to local governments has had a key reciprocal dimension, as local governments have pumped bank funds into TVPs while extracting tax revenues from them. The TVPs have demonstrated extraordinary entrepreneurship and production flexibility in meeting both domestic and foreign demand. At the same time there is no single TVP model. Anthony Koo and K. C. Yeh usefully distinguish among three distinctive versions of the TVP experience: the Wenzhou, Sunan, and Pearl River Delta models.

This selection was first published in the U.S. Congress Joint Economic Committee report China's Economic Future: Challenges to U.S. Policy *in 1995.*

This study examines the causes and patterns of growth of rural enterprises in three regions and explores their implications for enterprises reform. The analysis suggests that, unless the Party leadership decides to suppress its growth, the very factors that contributed to the rise of rural enterprises are likely to remain effective in sustaining their future growth. These factors include the vigorous entrepreneurship of the local businessmen, the active support of the local cadres, and rapidly expanding domestic and external markets. While the rural enterprises compete with the state-owned enterprises for markets and resources, they also pressure the latter to perform more efficiently. At the same time, some rural enterprises complement the state-owned enterprises through backward and forward linkages. Furthermore, the rural enterprises contribute substantially to state budget revenues, thus enhancing the capability of the government to finance the restructuring of the state-owned enterprises. More significantly, the rural enterprises keep chipping at the old system and introduce institutional innovations that help to establish ground rules for a market economy in which the state-owned enterprises must eventually learn to survive and grow.

One striking feature in China's economic transition is the sharp contrast in the development of the state-owned enterprises (SOEs) and the township, village, and private enterprises (TVPs). While the output of the SOEs continued to grow steadily, their performance paled in comparison to the soaring success of the rural enterprises. To redress the imbalance, the government has concentrated its effort in revitalizing the SOEs and at times has curbed the growth of the TVPs, particularly the private enterprises. Thus far, the approach has not been successful. An interesting question arises. Is it possible that the optimal path to reform exhibits a turnpike property, in that, to restructure the SOEs, it might be more effective to go by an indirect route of nurturing the TVPs' growth instead of concentrating all the resources and effort on transforming the SOEs? Much depends, of course, on the extent to which the TVPs generate pressure on, as well as support for, the SOEs and thereby accelerate the latter's growth and reform. This article explores this issue on the basis of the experience of TVP growth in three regions in China: Wenzhou, Sunan, and the Pearl River Delta.

Township, village, and private enterprises exist all over China. Besides the three cases under study, there are other "models" such as Baoji in Shaanxi, Zhangte in Hunan, Minquan in Henan, Kengce in northern Jiangsu, and Kaoyang in Hebei. However, the three selected regions were the first to develop and the most important in terms of their shares in total output of rural enterprises in China. By and large, they are representative of rural enterprises in the coastal regions, where both the TVPs and SOEs are far more developed than their counterparts in the interior. The inferences based on these case studies should be useful in better understanding the growth of an important sector and its implications.

This article addresses the following three questions respectively: How did the rural enterprises grow so rapidly? Is their growth sustainable? And what effects have the rise of the rural enterprises had on the SOEs in particular and on China's economic transition in general? The final section presents some concluding remarks on the implications of TVP growth for the reform of the SOEs.

Sources and Patterns of TVP Growth

The phenomenal growth of the rural enterprises has been one of China's major economic achievements since the Party leaders embarked on a program of reform and opening to the outside world. The upsurge is all the more striking if we recall that the rapid development occurred under some very unfavorable conditions. In the late 1970s rural per capita income was rather low, the peasants had little education, savings, or capital stock, and state investments in the rural areas were minuscule. How did the peasants overcome these difficulties and develop rural enterprises into a leading sector almost overnight?

Several hypotheses have been advanced. The common theme is that rural poverty and chronic unemployment drove the peasants to develop rural enterprises, and this was made possible by the central government's momentous decision to liberalize controls of the economy, and by the active support of the local governments. While these factors undoubtedly have a part to play, there are others that have been overlooked, or their emphasis has been misplaced. We propose the following alternative working hypothesis. During the initial stage of China's transition from a centrally planned system to an open, market economy, many supply-demand gaps in the economy began to surface. There were supply gaps originating partly from the pent-up demand for certain consumer goods that had been in short supply for decades, partly from the increase in the peasants' income after agricultural reform, and partly from the inefficient distribution system, a legacy of the past. Then there were also demand gaps. The peasants who prospered from agricultural reform had accumulated some savings, but outlets for their investment were limited. The most important demand gap was in the demand for the farm labor. In localities like the ones under study, entrepreneurs emerged to fill these gaps by exploiting the comparative advantages of each locality. They were the key figures who initiated the development of the rural enterprises. With the support of local cadres, these entrepreneurs pressed forward the opening of markets (as in Wenzhou), and markets in turn opened new horizons for the entrepreneurs (as in Sunan). In short, the peasants were highly motivated to increase their incomes, the surplus workers were eager to seek employment, the economic transition provided the opportunity, the entrepreneurs led the drive, and the local officials lent their political support for the rural enterprises to develop, at a time when the central authorities allowed, albeit hesitantly, the transition to proceed in the rural areas.

Who were the entrepreneurs in the three cases and from where did they come? In Wenzhou, they were the thousands of salesmen and purchasing agents who wove a nationwide network of marketing outlets and sources of material supply. Wenzhou has a long history of a large number of its people traveling all over China as traders and craftsmen. In the period prior to 1978, their business activities were suppressed for ideological reasons. But once the state-imposed restrictions on trade and other private business were lifted, the dynamism of Wenzhou's enterprising traders burst out. Not only did they provide services as middlemen linking the consumers with the producers across China, they organized the family enterprise system, mobilizing local capital and labor to produce for the market on which they had accumulated extensive information. In Sunan, the entrepreneurs were largely the managers of former commune and brigade industries. Many of these industries were built in the 1960s and 1970s so that these managers had some management experience. Moreover, Sunan lies in the vicinity of large cities, and many managers had close political connections with those of the SOEs in the big cities, drawing from the latter the management and technical skills they needed. In the Pearl River Delta, the entrepreneurs came largely from nearby Hong Kong. Many businessmen in Hong Kong have family ties with residents in this region. It was natural for them to organize joint ventures with the local people, combining their capital, technology, and management expertise with local labor, land, and other domestic resources.

Although the origins of these entrepreneurs were different, the basic functions that they performed in all cases were the same. Essentially they initiated the growth process by identifying and developing markets for products that they could produce at relatively low cost because of the comparative advantages each locality had. And they built new institutions to fit the political environment and economic needs. As their comparative advantages and local needs differed, their development paths also varied.

CREEPING CAPITALISM: THE WENZHOU MODEL

In Wenzhou, the development has been based on farm family units in a rural environment of small towns and villages where local entrepreneurs played a crucial role. Its major comparative advantage, the Wenzhou people's craftsmanship and marketing skills, stems from a long tradition of its handicraftsmen and merchants emigrating to other parts of the country. The emigration originated in the peasants' attempt to supplement their meager income by exporting labor. The economic consequences, however, were profound. These wandering craftsmen and peddlers brought back new concepts, ideas, business experience, and accumulated savings. Many have become enterprising traders, roaming all over China and forming a nationwide network supplying market information, goods, and technology. In the late 1970s, Wenzhou had over 100,000 such traders. By the time the Party leaders opened the door to reform, they were well positioned to move forward. At first, they simply played the role of middlemen linking the producers with the consumers. As such, they were actually developing a new distribution system. But, being entrepreneurs, they quickly moved beyond simple trading. With their knowledge of the markets, they obtained orders from buyers outside and farmed them out to local family factories to manufacture the products. In the process, they negotiated contracts, scheduled production, searched for raw materials, equipment, and parts, and financed the deals.

In Wenzhou, the basic business unit is the privately owned family factory. In the late 1980s, Wenzhou had 133,000 such factories. They produced mostly petty commodities indispensable to people's daily lives, which the large SOEs overlooked either because their costs were higher or because the state planning departments did not bother to include them in their production plans. The production of these products generally required a relatively small amount of capital and simple technology, so that it was easy for the family factories to get started and, once established, to quickly respond to changing market demands. Examples are such products as buttons, medals, badges, plastic flowers, plaited baskets, sign boards, footwear, zippers, and apparel. Production costs were relatively low not only because of the cheap family labor, but also because they often utilized discarded or surplus materials of the SOEs. Furthermore, as markets expanded, specialization and division of labor became possible, for example, in the form of product specialization by different localities and functional specialization in the production and marketing process.

Expansion in trade and manufacturing inevitably created demand for supporting services, such as telecommunications, transportation, packaging, information, technology acquisition, hotels, and restaurants. Consequently, the tertiary sector vigorously grew along with the rural industries.

Crucial to the development process was the emergence of Wenzhou's markets. The markets were spontaneously established by the traders to facilitate exchange of goods and services between producers and consumers, a basic function which the distribution system under state planning had failed to perform. At the beginning, the traders set up roadside stalls to sell various petty commodities like watchbands and gloves. Subsequently they opened shops and stores, established a nationwide network of salesmen, and organized specialty markets. By the late 1980s, Wenzhou had 415 specialty markets, of which 10 were nationwide wholesale markets where buyers and sellers from all over China came to trade. Each specialty market had a relatively complete assortment of products. Prices were competitive and the volume of transactions relatively large.

As the commodity markets developed, factor markets also emerged, albeit still in a formative stage. For example, various forms of a labor market have been developed. In the city, the government has set up labor exchanges. Then there were private placement services. And workers sometimes directly applied for jobs and enterprises advertised their openings in the local newspapers. The markets were as yet imperfect, but they facilitated a higher degree of labor mobility than ever before. The surplus labor in the less developed parts of the county flocked to the towns. Skilled workers and trained experts from the cities sought employment in the rural areas. Among them were those from SOEs, as the pay scale in the private sector was higher than for comparable jobs in state enterprises. Many other SOE workers had second jobs with the rural enterprises.

Of particular significance was the development of financial markets. Prior to the 1980s, in Wenzhou as in other areas, the rural financial system consisted of the state-owned Agricultural Bank of China and the rural credit cooperatives. The interest rates for deposits and loans were fixed at relatively low rates so that there was excess demand for credit at these subsidized rates. The household enterprises, being privately owned, had low priority in the credit plans of the state banks and thus had a hard time getting credit. Meanwhile, the demand for financial services by the rural enterprises increased sharply as their output surged forward. Again a gap appeared, and not surprisingly, the private sector rose to fill the gap. Private banks, money shops, credit associations, and pawn shops were opened, offering credit at interest rates that reflected supply and demand at the local money market. These floating rates were considerably higher than the fixed rate set by the state banks and credit cooperatives. Subsequently, the financial market in Wenzhou expanded beyond the county boundary. Credit unions in different villages within the county extended credit first to each other and later to those in other provinces. Toward the late 1980s a long-term credit market was in the making. In 1986 the local government issued regulations for stocks and bonds as some enterprises and credit unions were ready to reorganize into stockholding companies. The banks provided negotiable savings certificates and other financial instruments. In sum, Wenzhou was moving far ahead of many other areas in developing financial markets.

By the mid-1980s, economic growth and institutional reform had dramatically changed the economic landscape in Wenzhou. What used to be primarily a rural community had now become highly urbanized. Many small towns sprang up. The reason for the proliferation of small urban centers is not hard to find. At the initial stage of development, the peasants could "leave the soil without leaving the villages." But as the economy expanded in scale and complexity and the workers' living standard rose, transaction costs under conditions of industrialization without urbanization became unduly high. The growth of small towns in the rural areas is a natural outgrowth of the rise of rural industries, as the entrepreneurs continuously searched for ways to maintain their competitive edge by lowering costs. It is interesting to note that in Wenzhou the local residents, rather than the government, funded the construction of new towns and expansion of old ones.

Apart from initiating rural industrialization and fostering urbanization, the entrepreneurs in Wenzhou had yet another major role to play: as institutional innovators they constantly introduced organizational changes that enabled them to thrive in the midst of political uncertainties during the transition. In the past, Wenzhou's economic fortunes have varied with political winds. Even though economic reform has been accepted as the long-term goal for China, there have been vacillations in the Party leaders' attitude and policy toward economic liberalization. Wenzhou's market economy suffered setbacks when the conservatives gained power and vice versa. One major problem has been the ideological bias against private ownership that dominated the Wenzhou economy. As fear of revival of private business among the Party leaders remained strong, many individual operators registered with the local authorities as collectively owned units under the local administration to avoid political harassment. Others attached themselves to established public enterprises, paying a fee for the use of the latters' name, stationery, and bank account numbers. Similarly, new institutional changes were adopted on the basis of economic needs.

However innovative and enterprising the Wenzhou businessmen might be, they probably could not have succeeded so dramatically without the support of the local cadres. The local officials on various occasions covertly rejected central directives that were detrimental to private business and tried to institutionalize rules of the game for the newborn market economy. There appeared to be good reasons for their support. To a considerable extent the economic interests of the local government coincided with those of the private enterprises. A growing economy would mean increases in the revenues of the local government. Reduction in unemployment would mitigate the pressure on the local government to deal with the problem. Economic prosperity would bring social stability and political clout to the local officials. In any case, the private businessmen and the local cadres became partners working together toward the common goal of fostering economic growth and reform.

THE SUNAN MODEL

When we turn to Sunan, we find a somewhat different pattern of development. Unlike Wenzhou, Sunan is by no means isolated but located in an area with good connections to some large cities nearby and to the rest of China through a network of railroads, highways, and waterways. Its agricultural resources are better than most other regions in China. Yet in the late 1970s it faced the same problems as Wenzhou: low per capita income under the commune system and a large surplus farm labor. The same pressure from poverty and unemployment drove the peasants in Sunan to develop rural enterprises. And, in no time, Sunan became one of the highest income areas in China.

Just as Wenzhou had its comparative advantage in the thousands of traders who turned into entrepreneurs, Sunan had a fairly strong initial industrial base with its commune and brigade industries. Although these industries had roots that dated back to the 1950s, they never really blossomed, partly because of their technological backwardness and partly because their products were oriented toward the local market that was quite limited at that time. In the 1970s a unique opportunity occurred. There were an opening in the urban markets nearby and an inflow of technicians and urban youths from the cities in the aftermath of the Cultural Revolution. The history of Sunan's rural enterprises during the initial period is simply one of commune and brigade industries expanding rapidly by employing rural labor and imported technicians to produce for urban markets in Shanghai, Wuxi, Chengjiang, and Xuzhou. More specifically, the rural enterprises in Sunan developed close relationships with the SOEs in the cities. The two cooperated in several ways. For example, the rural enterprises produced parts for the SOEs and became subcontractors as shortages of land, labor, and capital in the cities forced the SOEs to move some of their manufacturing activities to the rural areas, just as Hong Kong's businessmen moved their manufacturing facilities into China. Furthermore, the rural enterprises depended heavily on the SOEs for technology. In other cases, the rural enterprises supplied raw materials to the SOEs.

As in Wenzhou, the local cadres contributed immensely to Sunan's growth through credit subsidies, supply of raw materials, and assistance in land acquisition and borrowing from outside sources. But unlike Wenzhou, the local officials were more closely connected to the TVPs because of the predominance of community ownership, and the relationship created several problems. First, they were more committed to an egalitarian policy in income distribution. It was in part because of this deliberate policy that the income gaps between farmers and workers diminished, a distinctive feature of the Sunan model. However, this policy may have some adverse effect on incentives. Second, the local government being politically sensitive to the development of private enterprises, had an ambiguous policy toward those enterprises. They were hesitant to open channels for free entry and exit. They encouraged the existing private enterprises to merge with other rural enterprises, thus reducing competition. Third, the local governments often acceded to requests of unsuccessful TVPs for financial rescue, softening their budget constraint. Finally, to protect the TVPs in the region, the local governments often suboptimized by restricting the free flow of capital, labor, and goods into or out of the region.

Despite these shortcomings, Sunan was able to sustain rapid growth after the initial takeoff because of two major developments. One was the expansion of domestic and export markets for their products, due to rising urban and rural incomes, a vastly improved distribution system, and the policy of opening to the outside world. Sunan's close connection with Shanghai, a major seaport with a long history of international trade, added to its advantage. The other factor was the development of a new crop of entrepreneurs. The original group of managers were mostly local cadres who were accustomed to administrative practices under a planned system. They were forced to learn management techniques and marketing skills essential to operate independently in a competitive environment, through training programs and learning by doing. Younger and better educated management personnel also gradually replaced the older ones.

THE PEARL RIVER DELTA

Six major factors contributing to the economic success in the Pearl River Delta have been identified: growth in agricultural output, expansion of foreign trade, the inflow of foreign capital, flexible and innovative development policy, proximity to Hong Kong and Macao, and overseas Chinese as a human resource. One highly simplified way of tying these factors together is to view the development process in this area as essentially a case of offshore manufacturing brought about primarily by the substantial difference in wages and rent in this area and those in Hong Kong, Taiwan, and Japan. Many investors, particularly those in Hong Kong, facing high rental and labor costs at home, transferred their manufacturing facilities to the Delta, where land and labor were relatively cheap and tax rates lower than in other countries. The foreign investors moved their factories to the Pearl River Delta for yet another purpose: to position themselves to enter China's domestic market. Most of the investors, especially those in nearby Hong Kong, have family ties with people in the Delta. They provided the financial and human capital to help build and run the rural enterprises, the output of which were destined for the world market. But again, all this could not have happened without a flexible and innovative development policy and the liberalization of export and exchange controls by the government.

To the local residents and governments in this region, the benefits have been many. A large volume of the surplus farm labor has been absorbed into the foreign-funded enterprises, since the industries moving in were mainly labor-intensive industries sensitive to wage differentials among regions. In addition, the development of service industries supporting manufacturing increased employment further. For the government, the rise of the largely export-oriented industries raised tax revenues and foreign exchange earnings. And, over the longer term, the inflow of capital, technology, and management skills undoubtedly has positive spillover effects.

The natural outcome of the cooperative effort between the foreign investors and the people in the region was rapid development of rural enterprises. One type of partnership was export processing (processing raw materials supplied by the foreign investor, manufacturing products according to the foreign investors' samples, or assembling parts provided by the foreign investor) and compensation trade. This type of arrangement was quite prevalent between the rural enterprises in Dongguan and the businessmen in Hong Kong, partly because of Hong Kong's proximity and partly because many businessmen in Hong Kong were natives from this area. Another type of cooperation was foreign direct investment in the form of joint ventures, cooperative enterprises, and wholly owned foreign enterprises. The foreign-funded enterprises in the western part of the Delta (Nanhai, Shunde, and Zhongshan) were mostly of this type, possibly because the traditional rural industries were more developed here than in the eastern part, and thus the industrial base made it easier to transplant foreign technology to these enterprises.

When placed in a broader perspective, the development process in this region is not really that different from Wenzhou or Sunan. Fei Xiaotong characterizes the present form as "a store at the front and a factory in the back," the front being Hong Kong and the back being the Pearl River Delta region. The observation captures the essence of the development process common to all three cases. Hong Kong, the store at the front, is crucial to the development because the businessmen in Hong Kong provide the marketing channels for the products of the rural enterprises, just as the traders from Wenzhou provide the sales network for the local family factories, and the big cities like Shanghai provide the market for Sunan's products. Also, the rural enterprises in the Pearl River Delta benefit much from its proximity to Hong Kong in terms of technology transfer, information flows, and learning about urbanization, just as those in Sunan have from their connections with Shanghai.

Summary

To sum up, a comparison of the three cases suggests some common characteristics in their development. One striking feature is that they all went through a process of development and reform from below. Measures for economic growth and reform were basically initiated and carried out locally rather than by orders from the central authorities. For example, the initial capital for developing the rural enterprises came from sources outside the government. In Wenzhou, investments were financed by the savings of the local peasants, the wandering craftsmen, and merchants. In Sunan, it was mainly the accumulated funds of the former commune and brigade enterprises that financed their own expansion. In the Pearl River Delta, foreign investors, particularly the overseas Chinese, provided the bulk of the initial capital. Similarly, institutional changes have been introduced on the initiatives of the local businessmen, often without prior government sanction. The opening of specialty markets and the introduction of flexible interest rates in Wenzhou are examples. The implication is that in the current transition, there may well be a workable alternative to development and reform from above which the government has doggedly emphasized thus far.

To portray what happened in these three clusters as development and reform from below raises the question: who at the micro level initiated the process? This brings us to the second similarity in the three cases. The initiatives came primarily from the entrepreneurs and secondarily from the peasants and the local cadres. The entrepreneurs were motivated to innovate because they could claim most, if not all the residual income or profit from their operations. The peasants, being underemployed on the farms, were eager to support a movement that provided them opportunities to increase their incomes. Moreover, unlike the SOEs, the rural enterprises generally paid their workers according to their contributions, without any bureaucratic restrictions. The local cadres patronized the entrepreneurs because the growth of rural enterprises directly or indirectly benefited the local government. In short, under the new incentive system, the three groups all had reasons to embark on a new course of development.

As noted earlier, the development paths of the three cases were markedly different. Nonetheless, one distinctive feature common to all stands out. Rural enterprises that sprang up profusely in all three clusters were predominantly industrial enterprises. In other words, the key to their economic success was rural industrialization. Only after the rural industries took root did other sectors such as transportation, finance, and construction follow suit. Rural industrialization was by no means new in China. During the Great Leap and the 1970s, tremendous efforts had been made to industrialize the rural areas. What is new in the present case is that rural industrialization was primarily market driven rather than centrally planned. In Wenzhou, the very existence of the family factories depended heavily on the opening of nationwide markets by the traders. In Sunan, rural industries had their roots in the commune and brigade enterprises of the 1970s, but their growth did not accelerate until shortfalls in the urban markets nearby opened up opportunities for them to expand. In the Pearl River Delta, the rise of rural industries has been largely the result of offshore manufacturing organized by foreign investors. Like Wenzhou, the processing industries produced on orders from traders outside. Others produced mainly for the world market.

While the markets led to the rise of the rural industries, the expansion of rural industries in turn pushed the development of markets to new levels. As markets are interdependent, the expansion of commodity markets fostered the growth of markets for services, labor, and capital. Such developments can be vividly seen in Wenzhou, but similar experiences are also found in the Pearl River Delta and Sunan.

Perhaps the most significant feature common to these cases is the outgrowth of a similar set of rules of the game for the emerging market economy, such as freely fluctuating commodity and factor prices, relatively free entry and exit from markets, and tacitly defined property rights. Of these, the property rights issue is of paramount importance. When we consider the ownership of the rural enterprises in the three cases, we find a heterogeneous pattern. In Wenzhou, private enterprises are predominant. In Sunan, the rural enterprises are mostly collectively owned. In the Pearl River Delta region, there are more foreign-funded enterprises than in most other areas. It would appear that ownership as such is immaterial in their growth. However, these differences should not obscure a major point: the growth of rural enterprises in all three cases depended heavily on, and at the same time demanded, the demarcation and protection of private property rights in the rural economy, regardless of their ownership. For example, a common characteristic of the rural enterprises in the three clusters is that their management is largely autonomous and relatively independent of government interference in decision making. This is feasible only if the right of the enterprise managers to utilize the property is recognized. The right to use property and to dispose of returns therefrom is evident in the leasing of land to the foreign investors in the Pearl River Delta. And the movement of farm labor into the rural enterprises raises the issue of the right to transfer land-use rights to the peasants who stay behind. At this stage, these property rights are generally implicit and fuzzily defined, and their effective protection is still not assured. A case in point is the private financing of urbanization in Wenzhou. It raises the issue: does the private financing give the investors legitimate ownership claims to the land and/or the right to use it? But however imprecise the definitions may be, these preliminary steps toward institutionalizing the rules of the game have been indispensable to the growth of the rural enterprises by lowering transaction costs and thus enhancing the competitive edge of these enterprises.

In this connection, the contribution of the local cadres must be recognized. In an important sense, the local cadres are political entrepreneurs. By creating adaptable policies and institutions to take advantage of local conditions and special treatment by Beijing, they have opened the door to new areas where the business entrepreneurs can operate and prosper. One cannot deny that the central government too contributed to the growth of the TVPs by passively allowing them to grow, by sanctioning institutional changes after the fact, and in some cases, by actively providing fiscal stimulus packages, e.g., tax concessions to attract foreign investment in the Pearl River Delta. But it seems fair to say that the development of rural enterprises was never on the leadership's initial reform agenda. In fact, the TVPs' upsurge was a total surprise to the leaders. It was not until after 1984 that the central government first recognized the rise of the TVPs as a major force in the reform movement. Even then, the TVPs remained second to the SOEs as far as policy focus or resource allocation was concerned. To the extent the government has played a direct, positive role, it was the local, rather than the central government.

FREDERICK CROOK,
GRAIN GALORE

During the early 1960s Chairman Mao used to exhort his countrymen to "grasp grain as the key link!" This was because China had just experienced the Mao-made famine of the Great Leap Forward, which killed 10 to 20 million people. Today China is awash in grain and other agricultural products. As the China agriculture specialist Frederick Crook observes, the People's Republic is the world's largest producer and consumer of agricultural products such as cotton, pork, potatoes, rice, tea, vegetables, and wheat. In this selection Crook details China's agricultural scene and predicts that the abundant conditions will continue.

This selection was originally published in The China Business Review in September–October 1997.

China's agricultural economy is a giant. The People's Republic is the world's largest producer and consumer of such agricultural products as cotton, pork, potatoes, rice, tea, vegetables, and wheat. China also is a leading exporter of fruits, vegetables, and processed foods, and is a major importer of grains, cotton, and edible oils. Despite the historical importance of agriculture in China, the fundamental trend of the country's development in the twentieth century has been a shift away from an agrarian to an industrially based economy. The contribution of agriculture to China's national output has declined steadily from well above 50 percent in 1956 to 20 percent in 1996.

As China industrializes, many are watching to see how changes in PRC agricultural demand and supply conditions affect world commodity markets. Of most interest will be output changes in grain, China's main agricultural commodity, since fluctuations in China's demand and supply of grain have sometimes dramatically affected world commodity markets. For example, the 1992 reduction in the PRC government subsidy paid to farmers to hold grain stocks contributed to PRC wheat import declines in 1992 and 1993 of 57.6 percent and 35.8 percent, respectively.

Grain Stocks and Food Security

Since ancient times, China's leaders have defined food security—processing sufficient stockpiles of food to feed the populace—in terms of having enough grain. The Book of Rites, written in the fifth century B.C., cautioned that less than nine years of grain stocks were insufficient; less than six years of reserves created a tense situation; and less than three years of stocks pointed to a government in decline. In the 1990s, maintaining a healthy level of grain stocks (wheat, rice, corn, sorghum, millet, barley, oats, soybeans, potatoes, and pulses) remains a top priority of the Chinese government.

From the mid-1950s to the early 1990s, government-owned institutions managed the distribution of agricultural products from farm gate to consumer. The Grain Bureau of the former Ministry of Commerce (which merged with the Ministry of Materials to become the Ministry of Internal Trade in 1993) purchased, transported, stored, milled, and retailed grain. The ministry purchased grain from farmers at low prices to provide cheap grain to urban consumers through its ration system.

In 1992, Beijing introduced market reforms, in part to ease the financial burden of the grain subsidy policy, but also to boost the economic efficiency of China's grain market. By year-end 1993, twenty-eight out of thirty-one provinces had begun phasing out the grain ration system, leaving urban consumers to purchase grain at market prices. Meanwhile, China's leaders also started to consider relaxing national grain self-sufficiency standards by allowing imports to account for up to 10 to 12 percent of the country's total grain consumption requirements, compared with the 1 to 5 percent previously permitted. With its large labor force and wide-ranging agricultural climates, China's comparative advantage lies in producing more labor-intensive goods for export, rather than land-extensive crops such as grain. Thus, to many observers it appeared in the early 1990s that China was ready to pursue a grain policy based more on free market principles and comparative advantage.

Reversing the Trend

Between 1993 and 1994, several developments prompted China's leaders to reassert government control over grain markets and veer away from the principle of comparative advantage. Attributing the stagnant grain production growth rate of the early 1990s to the decrease in land area sown with grain, PRC officials implemented policies to stabilize the amount of farmland devoted to grain production. A sharp rise in rice prices and other inflationary pressures in 1994 prompted Beijing to reinstate grain price controls, even though the inflationary price increases had little to do with agricultural conditions. Rather, the price escalation resulted largely from the Ministry of Finance's increase of the money supply to aid inefficient state-owned enterprises and boost wages and bonuses of urban workers. But price stability has always been important to China's central leaders, many of whom witnessed the country's devastating hyperinflation at the end of World War II. When faced with the conflicting objectives of maintaining price stability and raising farm incomes, China's leaders have tended to choose price stability.

Also factoring into Beijing's decision to limit agricultural market reforms and encourage grain production were reports published in 1994 by both PRC and foreign analysts that questioned the country's capacity to produce enough grain to meet growing consumption requirements. The steady decline in the PRC's total arable land—from 99.5 million hectares in 1979 to 94.3 million hectares in 1996—has coincided with a reduction in the percentage of area sown with grain and an increase in the area either farmed with more profitable crops, such as fruits and vegetables, or used for nonagricultural endeavors. By 1995 officials were again espousing "limited self-sufficiency" in grain and capped imports at 5 percent of total consumption. Though no subsequent policy statements have emerged to change the 5 percent import cap, actual PRC grain imports have continued to decline, accounting for a mere 1.1 percent of grain consumption in 1996 (see Table 2).

Transferring Responsibilities

In an attempt to increase government control over the grain economy, bolster grain production, and limit grain imports, Beijing initiated the "governors' grain bag responsibility system" (*mi daizi shengzhang fuzezhi*) in late 1994. The grain bag policy has shifted most responsibilities for the supply, use, and financial management of grain from the State Administration for Grain Reserves, the State Council, and the State Planning Commission to the provinces. Though the policy applies to all grain crops, the purchase quotas for corn, rice, and wheat are more strictly enforced, and trade in these grains is centrally controlled. The policy assigns provincial governors with responsibility for stabilizing the area sown with grains in their respective provinces; guaranteeing investment in inputs, such as chemical fertilizers, used to stimulate grain pro-

Table 2. PRC Grain Imports,* 1986–1996

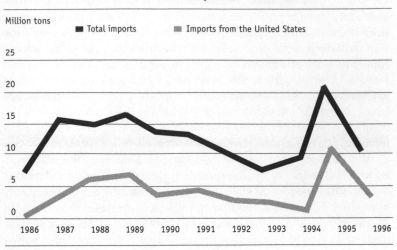

Million tons

■ Total imports   ■ Imports from the United States

Sources: PRC General Administration of Customs, U.S. Census Bureau
*Grain includes wheat, milled rice, corn, and soybeans.

duction; meeting central government targets for stock levels; ensuring the completion of grain transfers into and out of their respective provinces; stabilizing grain supplies to urban areas; minimizing inter-provincial grain and edible oil price differentials to curb excessive grain flows across provincial borders; controlling 70 to 80 percent of commercial grain sales; controlling wholesale grain market activity; raising commercial sales as a share of total grain sales; managing grain imports and exports; and elevating the level of grain self-sufficiency.

Though the policy outlines these goals for provincial governors, how the goals are reached is largely determined on a province-by-province basis. Provincial grain bureaus perform both policy and commercial operations to achieve grain bag policy objectives. Until provincial grain quotas are filled, farmers must sell grain at fixed prices to provincial grain bureaus.

The central government's role is now limited to subsidizing any losses incurred by the policy divisions of the grain bureaus and managing national grain stocks. County grain bureaus submit balance sheets of output and demand to the provincial grain bureau, which then makes arrangements for intraprovincial grain transfers and estimates whether the province will have a grain surplus or deficit. Governors report their provinces' grain status to the Ministry of Internal Trade. Using this data, the State Council orders the buildup or release of grain stocks and directs state trading firms such as China Cereals, Oils, and Foodstuffs Import and Export Corp. (COFCO) to import grains that are in short supply. The State Council also uses the data from the grain balance sheets to formulate quotas and prices for the following year's crops. In 1995 the central government purchased 50 million tons of grain from provinces at fixed quota prices and an additional 50 million tons at market prices.

Under the grain bag policy, provinces with frequent grain deficits, such as Guangdong, must agree to try to expand grain production in the next growing season by stabilizing or increasing the area sown with grain, increasing the supply of inputs to raise yields, or providing subsidies to grain producers. Grain-deficit provinces seeking to bolster supplies with imported grain must obtain an import license from the State Council and submit a list detailing the amounts and types of grain to be imported. Meanwhile, governors of provinces with surpluses are required to maintain sufficiency and facilitate sales of excess grain to grain-deficient provinces.

The Cup Runneth Over

Both self-sufficient and grain-deficient provinces have responded to the grain bag policy by increasing the area sown with grain, while surplus grain provinces have diversified their crop production. As a result, grain-sown land has expanded by 2.8 million hectares, bringing the nationwide total to 112.4 million hectares in 1996, a figure which includes multiple crop plantings on single plots. The increase in grain-cultivated area has resulted in record output levels, while cultivation and output levels of cotton, edible-oil crops, and hemp have dropped. Indeed, China's multiple-cropping ratio for grain—the area sown with crops as a portion of the amount of arable land, and an indication of intensity of land use—rose between 1994 and 1996 from 1.56 to a record 1.61.

Bumper grain harvests in 1995 and 1996 have caused market grain prices to fall. To provide farmers with a financial incentive to continue planting grain, provincial grain bureaus have been forced to purchase grain at above-market prices. The grain bag policy has become especially burdensome for provinces in 1997. Despite overflowing grain bins from 1996 harvests, provinces pushed farmers to increase grain-sown area in 1997, causing market prices to fall as much as 15 percent below the state-fixed quota prices in some provinces. Perhaps a reflection of the difficulty local governments are having in paying higher prices for grain, in July Beijing reiterated that local governments must continue to buy grain at fixed prices and not issue IOUs to farmers for grain purchases.

Demonstrating Commitments

The grain bag policy also pushed both central and provincial government departments to increase overall investment in agriculture. Total investment in 1996 in the agricultural sector — agriculture, forestry, animal husbandry, fisheries, and water conservation — registered 33.5 billion yuan (U.S.$4 billion), up 27.5 percent from 1995 levels. Agriculture's share of total national investment rose from 1.8 to 1.9 percent. Also benefiting the country's agricultural sector was Beijing's added investment in transportation and communications infrastructure, to 301.2 billion yuan (U.S.$36.3 billion) in 1996 — an increase of 22.1 percent over 1995.

Twenty provincial governments increased investment in agriculture by about 15 percent in 1995–96. Many provinces bolstered investment in agricultural extension, allocating funds for rural technicians to demonstrate new farming methods and teach courses on improving crop yields and farming efficiency. Such investments have resulted in the use of new seed varieties and more efficient irrigation and chemical fertilizer use.

Meanwhile, provincial governments have increased purchase prices for grains. According to a 1996 Ministry of Agriculture survey, nineteen of the twenty-five provinces surveyed added subsidies to the state-fixed quota grain purchase price, presumably as an inducement to farmers to plant grain. The subsidies ranged from 40 to 420 yuan (U.S.$5 to $50) per ton. Local governments also provided chemical fertilizer subsidies ranging from 100 to 640 kilograms of chemical fertilizer per ton of grain sold under the fixed quota system. As a result, chemical fertilizer application rose on a nutrient-weight basis from 33.1 million tons in 1994 to 35.9 million tons in 1995 and 38.2 million tons in 1996 — increases of 8.1 percent and 6.5 percent, respectively. Domestic chemical pesticide production rose from 268,000 tons in 1994 to 427,000 tons in 1996.

In 1995–96, provincial governments also funded water control projects to improve flood and drought mitigation measures. Provinces continued to mobilize rural laborers in corvée projects, requiring them to work on government water-works construction projects twenty to thirty days each year. In 1996 China effectively irrigated 50 million hectares, an increase of 1.5 percent over 1995.

Taking Stock

Though Beijing has been relatively successful in accomplishing most of the grain bag policy objectives (see Table 2), implementation of the policy has generated some problems. Inadequate grain storage and bumper crops have resulted in larger than normal grain losses and have pushed down the market grain price. High grain stocks have tied up capital that could be used to develop other parts of China's economy. Moreover, the grain bag policy has slowed the emergence of more market oriented, comparative advantage–based rural economic trends. Because the current and potential costs of the grain bag policy are high, China's leaders likely will be forced to make appropriate adjustments. Such changes might include importing more grain, improving the management of grain stocks and grain distribution, and promoting agricultural specialization according to China's comparative advantages.

On the Horizon

The U.S. Department of Agriculture (USDA)'s grain projections for China through 2005 predict a scenario in which the demand for food and feed grain outpaces supply, despite grain production increases. According to USDA estimates, China will import roughly 27.4 million tons of grain (8.9 million tons of corn, 2.3 million tons of barley, 14.7 million tons of wheat, and 1.5 million tons of milled rice) and export only about 700,000 tons (300,000 tons of corn and 400,000 tons of milled rice) in 2005. Though China probably will continue to be a net grain importer in the coming decade, its dependence on world grain markets will probably be marginal and PRC trade should not disrupt the world grain trade. China basically will feed itself.

China's net import levels for cotton and soybeans also are likely to rise in the near term. PRC net cotton imports during the next ten years are estimated to grow from 1.6 million 480-pound bales in 1996–97 to 2.3 million bales in 2005–6. China's net imports of soybeans are expected to increase from 1.0 million tons in 1996–97 to 3.5 million tons in 2005–6. And as domestic demand for protein meal for livestock feed rises, net soybean meal imports are predicted to reach 2.9 million in 2005–6, up from 1.6 million tons in 1996–97.

Already one of the world's largest exporters of horticultural products, China likely will expand its exports of such goods. The variety of China's horticultural output has expanded rapidly in the last decade, supplying foreign as well as domestic consumers with a growing array of vegetables, fruits, spices, tea, and other specialty products. In 1994 net horticultural exports totaled $2.7 billion, compared with net grain exports of $255 million. At the end of 1995, net horticultural exports had grown to $3.3 billion, while China's grain trade balance registered a $3.5 billion deficit. In 1996 PRC horticultural exports to the United States alone totaled $295 million.

Though China's agricultural trade should yield short-term benefits, the PRC could encounter difficulties over the next thirty years in trying to feed its citizens, unless proper policies are implemented. Northern China likely will experience water shortages unless the government introduces more water conservation programs, raises water prices, or increases investment in water transfer projects. Investment in infrastructure projects such as cold storage networks, grain handling facilities, and food processing and packaging facilities also could fall short of needs, resulting in continued food loss between farm gate and consumer. The decline in investment during 1980–95 in new seed development stands to constrain crop yield improvements for the coming decade, since new seed varieties take a certain amount of time to move from the laboratory to the fields. To increase yields, Beijing will have to increase funds for domestic seed technology development, import improved seeds, or create an investment climate conducive to foreign seed companies.

Decisions over the size of grain stocks appropriate for China's conditions also could prove problematic for PRC policy makers. Choosing to hold large stocks entails a heavy financial burden that denies scarce capital for other uses. Low stock levels, however, may risk contributing to civil unrest if Chinese citizens lose faith in Beijing's ability to manage China's food system. Policy makers also must decide on the degree to which grain markets will function independently of the government, thus forcing Beijing to choose between the merits of developing a globally competitive agricultural sector and maintaining national grain self-sufficiency. While China has the capacity to feed itself, the government's policy decisions will affect China's actual levels of grain production, consumption, imports, and exports.

Ripe Opportunities

Growth in China's rural economy over the next ten years should provide a wide range of opportunities for U.S. companies, in areas such as the following:

High-yield seeds. Because China is a relatively land-poor country on a per capita basis, improving grain yields—by importing or developing high-yield seeds—is crucial.

Fertilizer. Though grain imports have fallen under the grain bag policy and may remain low in the short term, chemical fertilizer imports have gone up, suggesting that chemical fertilizer may be an indirect import substitute for grain. Strong demand for fertilizers likely will continue, and China no doubt will continue to purchase such products in the international market. China's chemical fertilizer industry also may seek greater foreign investment.

Water-saving and waste-treatment technology. Though improved irrigation has contributed significantly to China's relatively high crop yields, industrialization and urbanization threaten to deplete agricultural water supplies. Currently, about half of China's cultivated land is irrigated. As water needs rise, the demand for foreign water-saving and waste-treatment technology and equipment also should increase.

Machinery. Though China has the world's largest agricultural labor force, farm labor shortages still occur during wheat harvests and preparation for summer corn planting. The need for plowing, seeding, and harvesting machines and inexpensive vehicles at such crucial times should present opportunities for foreign machine and vehicle manufacturers.

Storage equipment and technology. Though China is one of the world's largest exporters of horticultural products, millions of tons of fruits, grain, and vegetables perish each year because of inadequate food packaging, processing, and storage facilities in China. In the coming decades, China will be in the market for grain storage and handling equipment, as well as packaging, cold storage, and food-processing equipment and technology.

Alternative power-generating systems. Because rural residents tend to rely on wood and crop residues rather than electricity or natural gas for household energy needs, foreign manufacturers of energy-efficient stoves, combustion technology, and alternative power-generating systems also should find a market in China.

Agriculture and the WTO

If China joins the World Trade Organization (WTO), the volume of the PRC's agricultural trade will expand over time, though initially the change will not be great. In time Beijing may have to change some of its policies, including the grain bag system, which runs counter to WTO principles. Producers and consumers inside and outside of China stand to benefit once China commits to pursuing its comparative advantages in agriculture. Adjustments in the agricultural sector of China and other countries will be required, though what form these adjustments will take is difficult to foresee. On the whole, the United States will continue to have a comparative advantage in exporting land-extensive crops such as wheat, corn, soybeans, and certain processed food items. China's vast work force, meanwhile, puts the PRC's advantage squarely in exporting labor-intensive agricultural products such as fruits, vegetables, and processed foods.

SOCIETY

VII. THE SOCIAL CONSEQUENCES OF REFORM

In many important ways the social effects of China's economic reform were as tectonic as Mao's earlier revolution that had nationalized industry and collectivized agriculture. By reprivatizing large sectors of China's economy, reform created new avenues of social mobility. Whereas previously the only means of gaining status, power, and prestige were through the Party hierarchy, now Chinese were able to make an end run around the Party by acquiring individual wealth in the marketplace. And whereas once decision making was centralized in the highest organs of the Party and state, under Deng Xiaoping's reforms much of the state's authority began to devolve to the regional and local levels.

At the same time that the economy was being privatized and decision making decentralized, more and more individual initiative in the marketplace was being allowed. As the number of jobs in the private sector grew, people began to ignore the old *hukou*, or "household registration" system, that had kept Chinese firmly rooted to the place where their state-owned "work unit," or *danwei*, was located. As they started to move about at will in search of employment in coastal China's booming new industries, Party control and social cohesion weakened. At the same time crime and corruption increased.

Moreover, as the economy grew environmental problems multiplied, and as wealth accumulated the gap between the rich and poor yawned ever wider. In short, although the benefits that Deng's economic reforms brought were impressive, they also generated a darker side, confronting the government with a host of new and unfamiliar challenges.

⋆ R I C H A N D P O O R ⋆

During the early phase of his regimen of economic reform, Deng proclaimed, "It is all right for some people to get rich first." In essence, he was countermanding Mao's long-heralded notion that the Chinese Communist Revolution could only succeed if all the people—whether they be workers in the cities or peasants in the countryside, intellectuals in the universities or manual laborers on construction sites—developed and advanced equally.

Indeed, it was not long before some enterprising Chinese, especially in coastal cities that had been declared "special economic zones" or "open ports," did become "Ten-Thousand-Yuan Households." Soon there were millionaires, even billionaires with growing business empires, fleets of foreign cars, networks of new homes, and schedules crowded with international travel.

However, as some "got rich first," others, especially in impoverished inland regions, remained poor. As the People's Communes were dismantled and state-owned enterprises began to fail, depriving people of their so-called iron rice bowls, some even became poorer. Whereas once Chinese society had been strikingly equalized, even if it was the equality of poverty, with the recrudescence during the 1980s of a new middle class, China saw the rise of precisely the kind of class system against which Mao had consecrated his revolution. While China was undeniably wealthier as a result of Deng's reforms, Chinese society also became more clearly denominated into rich and poor, with all of the points of tension that grow out of economic disparities.

ANTOINE KERNEN,
OUT OF WORK IN THE STATE SECTOR

As private factories and township and village enterprises boomed, many state-owned enterprises floundered and were forced to xiagang, *or "sideline," millions of workers. Their disaffection created the potential for serious social and political unrest that alarmed leaders as much as protesting students had during the 1980s. What they feared was not new protests like the ones that had filled Tiananmen Square in 1989, but protests by lumpen workers and peasants who had lost their jobs and the socialist wel-*

fare net that had once guaranteed them a lifetime of security. Indeed, by the end of 1990 an increasing number of inchoate peasant and worker demonstrations had arisen from Sichuan to Liaoning.

This selection, by a Ph.D. candidate at the Institute of Political Science in Paris, was excerpted from "Surviving Reform: Former 'Socialist Pioneer' City Copes with New Poverty," published in China Perspectives, *June–July 1997.*

For more than ten years, China has experienced one of the highest rates of economic growth in the world. However, this growth has been unevenly distributed across the whole country. Comparing China's southern regions with the North, the differences are enormous. In northeast China, the country's original industrial base is lagging behind in the reform process. The region's three provinces, Heilongjiang, Liaoning, and Jilin, are plodding toward a market economy with some difficulty. In this process it is the workers in the state-owned enterprises—once the privileged of the Communist regime—who are paying the highest price in the transition. Many workers and their families are living in hardship, sometimes in such disastrous situations that certain Chinese researchers do not hesitate to use the term "new urban poverty" to describe the phenomenon.

Among the big cities of the Northeast, Shenyang is experiencing the most problems. The capital of Liaoning Province, this city located 600 kilometers northeast of Beijing was once one of the richest cities in China. Known as a pioneer in heavy industry, Shenyang had a glorious past. After the Chinese Communist Party took power in 1949, the provinces of the Northeast became the country's principal industrial base with its uniquely developed infrastructure. This was built as a result of the colonization of the region by the Russians and then the Japanese, and particularly during the latter, between 1931 and 1945. As the center of one of the nation's most advanced industrialized regions, Shenyang helped finance the development of other cities. While the central government used the profits of this early industrialization to support development in other parts of China, it did not put sufficient funds into modernizing the old plants in the area.

Today, the Northeast needs help from the general government if it is to restructure the unwieldy edifice of its state-run economy. But such assistance has not been forthcoming. In the absence of substantial help from the central government, the region has generally been left to pull itself out of the morass by its own bootstraps. On government orders, banks have offered a certain amount of credit to state-run firms for restructuring, but this is far from sufficient. Now, after long hesitation, the Chinese government appears to have decided to solve the problem of loss-making state-run enterprises. To this end, the central government has decentralized the management of state-owned enterprises to the provinces and municipalities. Consequently, the state-owned enterprises have been forced to restructure and, as part of this process, have had to lay off some of their employees. Following these changes state-owned enterprises across China are facing difficulties. But in a region where 50 percent of the urban workforce is still employed in the state sector, and with these enterprises in particularly bad shape, the reforms have reached a crisis point.

Since the beginning of the reform period the Chinese government has experimented with various reform strategies that all share the same goal: to improve the management and the quality of the products of the state-owned enterprises. The state enterprises have thus been undergoing gradual change. But the authorities have always been reluctant to alter the social role of the state enterprises. To date, they have continued to make an important contribution to social stability in the cities by providing most of the urban jobs. So even though a bankruptcy law was passed in 1986, the authorities have been extremely reluctant to use it. But the ever-increasing losses piled up by state enterprises continue to exact a heavy price for this stability. The government has now decided to tackle this problem head-on, but quite how it will go about this is, as yet, unclear.

Fake and Real Jobless

On arrival in Shenyang, the abundance of street markets and stalls at first seems surprising considering the desperate economic condition of the city. But these are not an expression of the economic dynamism seen in southern China. Nor are they the result of an influx of rural migrants attracted by cities. The street hawkers and peddlers are workers from state-owned enterprises trying to survive. Most of them are still officially employed in the city's state-owned sector. They did not choose to "swim in the sea" of the market *(xiahai)* as is so much the rage elsewhere in China, but they have been unintentionally thrown into it. These casualties of the state-run economy do not have any other choice than to sell what they have to improve their situation.

Everything imaginable is for sale in the street markets of Shenyang. The accumulated possessions of a lifetime are on display: books, clothes, crockery, household appliances, and so on. Other sellers have collected what they can find in their enterprises: tools, screws, nuts, pipes, radiators, lamps. . . . Factories with no cash to pay their employees try to make enough for the salaries from their sales in the street markets. When night falls there is a change of faces as another group of laid-off workers from state-owned enterprises markets their families' goods or objects purchased from the city's wholesale markets on the same streets and pavements.

Many of the workers peddling their wares in the street market in Shenyang are on "extended holiday" *(fangchangjia)* or have been granted "early retirement" *(tiqian tuixiu)* by their employers. These are actually disguised forms of underemployment or unemployment.

Accurate figures for the number of workers who have fallen victim to the restructuring of state-owned enterprises are virtually impossible to find. Many types of people who might be considered as falling into this category (including those on extended holiday and early retirement) are not included in official statistics for layoffs or unemployment. As one Chinese researcher wrote in Shenyang's *Social Sciences Quarterly* last year: "Our statistics are not compiled in the same way as in other countries. In terms of the unemployment rate, we don't include the surplus laborers in the countryside and the cities. If we added all these people, the unemployment rate in our country would go far above that of most countries in the world." Thus the figure for the urban unemployed is officially composed only of workers who have lost their jobs following a bankruptcy and are receiving an allowance directly from the state. So in the Northeast official urban unemployment is just a bit higher than the national 3 percent rate.

According to official statistics, at least 10 million workers in the country have been laid off, but most of them are still officially part of a state-owned enterprise *(xiagang)*. In 1996, 1.4 million workers in Liaoning Province were laid off from state-owned enterprises, but officially most of them have found a new way to earn a living. The impact was felt the most in the manufacturing industry, as well as in mines, textiles, and construction. In the mining towns of Chaoyang and Fuxin, the official rate of unemployment has risen to more then 7 percent. Reports in the press early this year said that in Shenyang more than 206 enterprises had gone bankrupt, including 12 large concerns. Furthermore, in Liaoning Province as a whole, there were some 367,000 surplus workers in about 5,000 enterprises which were either losing money or actually bankrupt. In the province as a whole, 1.7 million state enterprise workers are receiving only part of their monthly salaries or are not being paid at all, representing a total of 2.8 billion yuan in unpaid wages in 1996. In Shenyang, total unpaid wages in the city's state-owned enterprises amount to as much as 600 million yuan. And only 5 percent of enterprises pay workers' salaries on a regular basis. According to a recent investigation, 60 percent of the city's factories have closed down part of their operations. In Suihua, a small town in the Northeast, production had completely ground to a halt at 30 percent of the city's enterprises, while unpaid wages in the town totaled some 20 million yuan, according to a recent report in the *Heilongjiang Daily*.

The reason it is so hard to obtain statistics that reveal the true extent of the economic crisis in the Northeast is that the authorities deliberately conceal the impact by such tactics as failing to categorize large groups of people who are effectively unemployed as being so and by issuing even more inaccurate data than in other areas of the economic scene. But certain effects can be inferred from the fact, revealed in the annual *Blue Book* on the economy produced by the Chinese Academy of Social Sciences, that the profits of state-owned enterprises fell by 85.4 percent in the first six months of 1996, while 46 percent of state-owned industrial enterprises are running at a loss.

The New Urban Poor

While many analysts have focused on the emergence of the "nouveau riche" in Chinese cities, few have noticed the creation at the same time of a large group of low-income people now present in all of China's urban areas. "According to recent statistics and international estimations, this new relative poverty affects at least 12 to 15 million citizens in China," a group of Chinese researchers on poverty wrote recently. Most of the new urban poor have fallen into this group as a consequence of the reform of state-owned enterprises. Together with the elderly and the disabled, they constitute a new class in urban society which is excluded from the benefits brought by the reforms. State factory workers, women, and those approaching retirement age are generally the first victims of the restructuring process.

Women have been disproportionately affected by the crisis in state-owned enterprises, and according to figures from 1996, they now make up 60 percent of the unemployed in Liaoning Province. Officially, 49,316 women workers in Shenyang have been laid off. An investigation conducted by a woman sociologist revealed that a large proportion of those laid off were women aged over thirty-five with little education. The management in a big Shenyang machinery factory were straightforward in admitting that women were particularly likely to be sent home on reduced pay for "extended holidays." "They are too much of a burden for us. If they take early retirement, a lot of them are happy because they can take better care of their children," asserted one of the firm's high-ranking cadres. Such attitudes and experiences are far from an isolated affair. From 1994 onwards the policy of "early retirement" has been widely adopted by enterprises in the city. In some big factories, the retirement age has been lowered to forty-two for women and fifty-two for men. Certain companies have encouraged their female employees to take extended maternity leave of up to seven years.

Thus the management policies of Shenyang enterprises generally have the effect of gradually depriving women of their access to the job market. The women who have been pushed to retire early generally do not share their former employers' view of their situation: most did not wish to quit their jobs and are far from happy about their fate. While they receive a small monthly payment of 80 to 120 yuan, they have lost a large part of their salary and social benefits of various kinds. To compensate for this loss and to survive, many of them run small market stalls or try to find other jobs.

When enterprises go bankrupt, 95 percent of women cease to look for work, according to the study by the woman sociologist just mentioned, even if the government encourages them to find a job transfer. Some of the women do not want to accept the new jobs they can find, because the pay is often lower than in their previous employment, and the work may be harder and farther away from their homes. In such circumstances, certain women prefer to earn a little money as street vendors and live on the meager unemployment allowance.

The city's Women's Federation is now making an increasingly important contribution in helping women to cope with the changes in their situation. Interestingly, in taking up this challenge the Women's Federation has had to move away from its previous role as a simple conveyor belt for the authorities' policies in order to become an advocate for the interests of divorced and jobless women facing serious financial hardship, reminding the municipality of their plight. However, while the

Federation's degree of autonomy has increased somewhat as a result of the crisis, it still sticks to the Party line in its work.

Strong Resentment Among Workers

In conversations workers are surprisingly frank about their attitudes toward the recent changes. "We miss the Mao period when the city was prosperous. . . . The only thing the reforms have brought to us is the bankruptcy of enterprises all over the city. In the past, we were rich, now we are just surviving." This former employee of a pharmaceutical factory is unequivocal about who are the culprits: "The bosses say that they do not have enough money to pay our salaries, but they always have enough to buy lots of cars for themselves. They have so many cars that the commuters cannot even find any place to park. Now they do not pay our wages anymore. But it does not mean a problem for them. They have already saved enough for themselves. They have plundered the enterprise, and today we have nothing at all!" A former ball-bearing plant worker added: "The son of our director opened a business in Shenzhen, no need to ask where the money came from! Workers today suffer under both socialism and capitalism!"

In a climate of rising social tension, workers have frequently staged demonstrations demanding payment of their salaries in front of city government buildings. According to a summer 1996 news report citing the central Public Security Bureau, some 12,000 public demonstrations, petitions, and sit-down protests were staged in 1995, and 80 percent of these cases were related to urban poverty. In some cases even the official labor union has taken part in the protests, as was the case last year in a dispute which occurred in an automobile plant which is part of the Golden Cup group in Shenyang. However, in Shenyang today workers appear indifferent to such actions because they know that marches and protests will not change their fate. For this reason relative peace and quiet has now returned to the streets of the city. But an increase in other social problems is still proof of the crisis in the city: suicide, crimes, divorce, and prostitution are on the rise.

Managing Poverty

Just as in the late 1970s, when the cities had to find ways to cope with the increased unemployment resulting from the return of the people Mao had sent to the countryside to their urban homes, the private sector is seen as the principal solution to the crisis. However, the economic situation now is entirely different: the 1970s shortage of labor in the service sector no longer exists, which means that the private sector cannot be the sole solution to urban unemployment. While 80,000 enterprises had been created in Shenyang by 1996, 42,000 had closed down. Competition in the market is growing ever fiercer. New entrants into the arena of small private business cause a decrease in the income of those who came before them, not to mention the impact of former state employees given licenses to trade on the city's pavements.

The state also clearly sees philanthropy and economic laissez-faire as the main solutions to the problem of poverty, but some efforts have also been put into creating an elementary social safety net. Municipalities in the Northeast have set a poverty line, and people whose incomes fall below it may apply for assistance from the government. The local authorities then issue the family with a "Certificate of Household in Extreme Poverty" (*tekun huzheng*), which allows poor families to buy necessities at discounted prices and to benefit from allocations of free grains and clothes. In Shenyang some 10,000 people were receiving such benefits in the beginning of 1996, according to press reports.

The government does not directly take charge of alleviating poverty but mostly delegates the task to the labor union and the Women's Federation. These Party organs, which originally were mostly engaged in political work, are now dispensing aid to needy families. The union and the Women's Federation are thus engaging their networks, which reach down to the grassroots level, for a new purpose. They have created more than one hundred professional training centers for the jobless in Shenyang. Such centers not only give courses but also help with finding work. Assistance to the poor is primarily oriented toward helping them to reenter the job markets as entrepreneurs through the creation of markets for other poor people and through the establishment of service centers in residential areas.

In order to assuage widespread resentment among the workers, the Shenyang city government has made much of its sympathy for the most deprived. As in other Chinese cities, Shenyang has developed a rich political folklore. Every Chinese New Year, the mayor visits poor families together with his colleagues. They bring with them coal, fruit, cakes, and money. Throughout the year campaigns to "bring warmth" (*song wennuan*) are given a great deal of publicity. Generally, these campaigns involve each cadre pairing with one poor family and acting as their "guardian" (*duijiezi*). The cadre is responsible for paying regular visits to the family and for helping them to resolve administrative difficulties, the educational problems of their children, or presenting gifts or money. In an effort to improve the image of its cadres, the local government has also organized campaigns against corruption and bad morals, forbidding officials from holding banquets or frequenting the massage salons which are so often fronts for prostitution. As a sign of the government's determination to combat corruption, in 1996 more than twenty luxury cars were sold at a public auction.

In addition, "good" cadres are featured prominently in the media, and the spirit of solidarity and mutual assistance is lauded. Newspapers and television often carry anecdotes stressing the importance of mutual aid within neighborhoods. The entire population is engaged in raising funds for the poor. In Harbin, the capital of Heilongjiang Province, schoolchildren are urged to help their peers who are in difficulties. They give daily necessities like clothes, books, and stationery. Whenever there is a natural disaster like a flood or a fire, the authorities have always appealed to the private sector for relief funds. Private entrepreneurs or individual merchants are expected to give generous donations on a regular basis. Sometimes they are pressured to employ former workers of state-owned firms who have been made redundant rather than the rural migrant laborers who are usually more hardworking and expect lower wages than city folks.

In order to ensure its stability, the city of Shenyang has sought for quick answers to the extent of urban poverty. The administration acts as a fireman dispensing some humanitarian assistance to the people facing the harshest situations, thus helping some citizens to survive the crisis, but does not really have a strategy for finding a way out of it.

The losses in the state-owned sector are due not merely to these enterprises' lack of efficiency but also to growing competition in the Chinese market. State enterprises now have to compete with collective businesses, in which wages, costs of social benefits, and taxes are lower, as well as with foreign-funded enterprises. In such an unfair race, without a more interventionist policy to help them rise to the challenge, the state enterprises will close one by one, causing massive social dislocation.

PATRICK TYLER,
RURAL POVERTY

While coastal China boomed, many areas in inland China remained mired in backwardness and poverty, creating a potentially explosive discontinuity between rich and poor areas.

This selection was excerpted from an article by the former New York Times *Beijing bureau chief Patrick Tyler, "Deng's Economic Drive Leaves Vast Regions of China Behind," published in* The New York Times *in December 1995.*

Chen Xianhe is not a revolutionary. He is just a down-on-his-luck peasant whose wife has run away to escape the poverty here and whose only cow fell off a cliff in May and died.

But Mr. Chen, thirty, and many of his neighbors in this remote and desperately poor region of southwestern China, speak a language of disaffection that is worrying China's Communist Party leaders.

No one is predicting a rebellion here, but it is hard for anyone, including the Party bosses in Beijing, to understand where the limits of tolerance are for 1.2 billion Chinese.

Last year at this time, tens of thousands of peasants roared out of their villages and rioted in the cities of Kaili and Tongren in Guizhou Province, and army units were sent to restore order.

The grievances there were similar to the ones in Dongwang: crushing tax burdens, brutish population control, and a sense of hopelessness about escaping poverty, about feeding and schooling families, about living in something more than a reed house swagged on a limestone hillside.

As China's economic miracle continues to leave millions behind, more and more Chinese are expressing anger over the economic disparities between the flourishing provinces of China's coastal plain and the impoverished inland, where 70 to 80 million people cannot feed or clothe themselves and hundreds of millions of others are only spectators to China's economic transformation.

On a recent morning, during a pause from stacking cornstalks, Mr. Chen easily unburdened the frustrations of his impoverishment to visitors, as many of his neighbors joined in.

"I am really angry," he said, squatting on a short wooden stool in front of his dirt-floor hut. "This year I wanted to get electricity for my hut, but I didn't have the money."

Submission is a strong tradition in China, but so is rebellion.

When the riots hit Tongren, Communist Party officials blamed a handful of agitators who went from village to village to whip up antigovernment sentiment.

Unofficial accounts said "many deaths" had occurred. Even Guizhou's Communist Party newspaper seemed breathless in reporting that "illegal elements openly smashed vehicles, illegally took hostages, and robbed public security cadres and police of their firearms, thus causing serious consequences" that "shocked the entire province."

But what are more shocking to many peasants are the tales of China's new millionaires exploiting the tax breaks, child labor, and financial privileges created for "special economic zones" in coastal provinces.

These stories have nurtured a deep resentment among an inland population that has been eagerly waiting its turn under the economic reform policies of Deng Xiaoping.

With Mr. Deng, ninety-one, infirm, the very success of his reforms has revived the latent passion of a long debate in China about egalitarianism. It pits the era of Mao with all of its Communist idealism of a level society—an idealism still very much alive across several generations of Chinese—against the reform era of Mr. Deng.

In the Deng era, the wonders of capitalism have re-created in China great inequalities, dislocations, and the scourge of corruption and vice that many Chinese, whether they still believe in Communism or not, deeply loathe.

For sixteen years, ever since Mr. Deng set China on the path of economic reform, hundreds of millions of peasants in the interior have suffered under his admonition that some areas would have to get rich first while others persevered in poverty.

Millions of peasants in Mr. Deng's native Sichuan Province and in Yunnan, Guangxi, and here in the Mashan region of Guizhou, about a hundred miles south of the provincial capital, Guiyang, are among those who have been waiting. Now, many of them are seething.

Mr. Chen is raising his two daughters by himself in an open-air hut where temperatures dip to freezing this time of year and make it even harder to haul water up the mountain on a shoulder pole or get any sleep under a thin quilt after an unnourishing dinner of cornmeal gruel.

The local government has just taken the equivalent of two years' income from Mr. Chen to bring electricity to his house, which for Mr. Chen means two sixty-watt lightbulbs to illuminate the squalor of his life.

"I don't have much faith in anything," Mr. Chen said. "My misfortunes seem to never come alone. We don't have money to buy fertilizer, I don't have a cow or ox to cultivate the land, and the soil is barren.

"My biggest wish," he added, "is that the government will change its policies and help us get rich, because living in this kind of poverty makes us too embarrassed to even go out of doors."

To a great extent, China's Communist Party leaders have tried to alleviate poverty, and they can claim a measure of success.

Since 1978, when Mr. Deng pushed through China's first agricultural reforms, freeing the peasants to expand their private plots and markets, more than 170 million Chinese have climbed above the "absolute poverty" line of $43 a year per capita.

But as the World Bank pointed out this year, "the quick reductions of poverty through agricultural growth" in China "were largely exhausted by the end of 1984.

"Most of the residual poor have remained trapped in more remote upland areas where agricultural productivity gains have proven far more problematic," the bank's agricultural division said in a report issued in May.

Reducing poverty further will require a much greater commitment from the central government, which has mobilized many small-scale antipoverty projects with the World Bank, the United Nations Development Program, and numerous charities, but the main task of poverty reduction remains largely unaddressed.

Using a Chinese expression, a Communist Party official in Guizhou said that when the government talks about investing new financial resources in central and western China, "the thunder is huge, but the raindrops are tiny.

"I don't expect a lot from the central government, because they don't have a lot of money," said the official, who has worked inside Guizhou's Party bureaucracy for thirty years.

Even within Guizhou Province, the disparities are significant. The provincial capital, Guiyang, glitters at night under the lights of new hotels, restaurants, and karaoke bars whose driveways are choked with the Cadillacs and BMW's of top government and police officials.

Corruption is widespread. The provincial chief of public security and the wife of the former governor were sentenced to death this year.

The governor's wife, Yan Jianhong, was executed on January 16 after she was convicted of embezzling hundreds of thousands of dollars in public funds to build a private restaurant, massage parlor, and spa for the thin upper crust of moneyed entrepreneurs and their Party patrons who run this province.

Three weeks after the riots in Tongren, she was paraded through the streets of Guiyang, standing shackled in the bed of a Liberation brand truck, which drove her to the provincial execution grounds. There, she was told to kneel to receive her executioner's bullet at a downward angle through the back of her head.

"I haven't knelt since Liberation," she said defiantly, before being forced to her knees and shot.

Within the Chinese Communist Party, some economic reformers fear that the strong emotional pull of egalitarianism is being exploited by Party ideologues and other opportunists to undermine Mr. Deng's reforms and his protégés in the government. But others disagree.

"If Deng Xiaoping knew the disparities were as big as they are, he would be more militant than I am in trying to eliminate them," said Hu Angang, a researcher at the Chinese Academy of Sciences in Beijing. "Every country has regional differences, but in China the regional differences are getting bigger, not smaller."

Mr. Hu, forty-two, has become, if not the most influential, at least the most vocal of Communist Party intellectuals sounding the warning that the inequities in China's reform program are breeding rebellion.

"In America," he warned, "the deep differences between the North and South more than one hundred years ago led to the Civil War."

He insisted that he and many like-minded Party apparatchiks were not seeking to undermine China's coastal engines of economic growth. "But since the coastal areas can now sustain their development and get rich, I don't think it is unreasonable to shift the focus to the undeveloped areas," he said, "if only from the point of view of justice and equality."

The debate over "justice and equality" has seized the Party's ruling Politburo all year. Last summer [1995], as China fired missiles off Taiwan's coast, threatening Asia with a military crisis, China's leaders closeted themselves for their annual informal gathering at the northeastern beach resort of Beidaihe. They debated whether to drop preferential tax policies that have been helping to make China's coastal provinces rich.

In their place many officials pushed for new policies to help lift the inland provinces out of poverty. The debate was intense, put China's new financial barons of coastal wealth on the defensive, and sent shudders through the foreign business sector, which has invested billions of dollars in factories that pay reduced taxes on their imported raw materials and production.

President Jiang Zemin and other top leaders are apparently heeding the warnings of some provincial leaders that rising crime, rebellion and warlordism will be the consequence of not addressing huge disparities. It now appears that many of the tax breaks will be eliminated beginning next year.

In his own speech to a special Communist Party Central Committee meeting in October, Mr. Jiang referred prominently to the dangers of the "widening gap between the eastern and the central-western regions.

"Achieving common prosperity is a cardinal principle and an essential characteristic of socialism," he said. "We should never waver about it."

But in Guizhou and many parts of inland China, the peasants continue to wait. Mr. Hu, who toured Guizhou this year, said, "It will be a long and hard struggle to bring those people out of their backward state, as long and as arduous a struggle as the Civil War in the United States."

★ THE "FLOATING ★
POPULATION"

By the mid-1990s more than 100 million unemployed "peasants" had migrated to China's large urban centers in search of jobs. They constituted the largest migration in human history and threatened to overwhelm the cities to which they had been drawn. However, they also helped fuel China's "economic miracle" with an inexhaustible supply of low-cost labor, making Chinese consumer products highly competitive on world markets.

CHENG LI,
200 MILLION MOUTHS TOO MANY: CHINA'S SURPLUS RURAL LABOR

At the same time that China's "floating population" helped spur rapid economic development, it augmented the populations of many large Chinese cities by one-third and substantially increased crime rates and the potential for social unrest and instability. Whereas previously peasants had been bound to their communes and villages by the "household registration system" (they could not even travel without official permission), this system of social control had by the mid-1990s almost completely broken down. And so, try as it did, the central government was not able to staunch this flow from the countryside into the cities.

This selection was excerpted from an essay published in Rediscovering China: Dynamics and Dilemmas of Reform, *1997.*

Anyone who has been observing socioeconomic changes in China should be aware of the problem of overpopulation. Indeed, few issues in the study of the nation's socioeconomic development over the past several years have generated as much public concern and sense of urgency as surplus rural laborers and consequent large-scale internal migration in the country. The so-called surplus rural laborers, as some Chinese scholars stated, are "actually the unemployed rural population."

The issue of surplus rural laborers in China is not new. Since at least the nineteenth century, Chinese rulers have been concerned about the lack of arable land and the flow of surplus rural laborers. China accounts for 22 percent of the world's population but has only 7 percent of the world's arable land. What is new, however, is that those surplus farmers are now free to move and are increasingly choosing to move to urban areas, owing to the rapid economic growth in Chinese cities during the past decade.

As with human migration elsewhere, China's ongoing internal migration is both a cause and a consequence of socioeconomic change. While no one seems to doubt the magnitude of the impact of migrants on the country, students of China differ profoundly in their interpretations of its politicoeconomic implications. The sociologist Jack Goldstone argues that China's surplus rural laborers and internal migration pose a major threat to the country's political stability and economic growth. As the agricultural economy becomes virtually incapable of providing more employment, and the industrial growth is not rapid enough to absorb the rural surplus, he expects China to have a "terminal crisis" within the next ten to fifteen years. Masses of unemployed peasants, according to Goldstone, are likely to be the catalysts if China descends into chaos.

In contrast, some other China experts believe that surplus rural laborers provide great human resources for the country to reconstruct the economy, accelerate urbanization, and further rapid economic growth. Gu Shengzu, a Chinese demographer, argues that this flow of surplus laborers is a key step in China's transition from a dual to a modern economy, from a backward agrarian country to an industrialized state. The implication of China's internal migration, as some believe, lies in the impulse not only to reduce the segregation between rural and urban areas that was institutionalized during the Mao era but also to narrow the widening gap between rich and poor regions during the Deng era. Instead of causing crisis and chaos, the ongoing internal migration will affect China's national integration constructively. Alan Liu, a political scientist, believes that these effects are the most intriguingly significant, especially insofar as they promote the economic interdependence between regions. Some Western scholars of Chinese politics also argue that the free movement of people will contribute to the formation of a civil society. Dorothy Solinger, for instance, argues that migrant laborers constitute a form of civil society because this social group "stands apart from and against the state."

The contrasting views about surplus rural laborers and internal migration reflect policy dilemmas for the Chinese government. It seems neither possible nor desirable for Chinese authorities to keep millions of surplus rural laborers on farmland, but rapid and large-scale internal migration is seen as politically dangerous to the regime. Not surprisingly, hard-liners in the Chinese government advocate controlling and restricting the flow of migrant workers. A best-selling book in China during the early 1990s, *China Through the Third Eye,* provides the rationale for these advocates of control. If the government loses control over the flow of migrant laborers, according to the author, it will lose its power to rule because migrants will lead the country to chaos. The author asserts that all Chinese dynasties, without exception, were destroyed by migrants (*liumin*) — those who lost or abandoned farmland.

In the past several years, the Chinese government has tightened its control of migrant laborers. During a recent "cleanup campaign" in a district of Shanghai, policemen caught over 500 migrants in a single day and immediately sent them back to their home areas. The Shanghai government recently issued an order that prohibits any firm in the city from hiring migrants who do not have three cards — identification, temporary residence, and work permit. In Beijing the government recently demolished more than twenty migrant enclaves and "vacuumed" the well-known Zhejiang Village — a migrant settlement that at one time housed over 100,000 migrants from Zhejiang Province. In late 1995 in Shenzhen, China's first special economic zone, the security force stepped into a dispute between 500 migrant workers from the central provinces and several hundred local residents. The security force opened fire to stop a bloody brawl during which several were killed and a dozen were seriously injured. These suppressive actions by the government, however, cannot really reduce the pressure of surplus laborers. On the contrary, they have increased the tension and conflict between the government and migrant laborers.

It is, therefore, crucially important to make a broad assessment of the nature, magnitude, dynamics, causal factors, and policy measures of China's surplus rural laborers and internal migration. A number of studies on China's internal migration have recently been published in the West, but most are either highly technical or largely normative. Any possible solution to the problem of surplus rural laborers should start with a better understanding of the reasons that drive people to migrate. One needs to know why, all of a sudden, rural China has so many surplus laborers. Some factors that induce China's internal migration are by now well-known, while some others are often overlooked. It is necessary to review briefly all the factors that have contributed to the increasing number of surplus rural laborers and internal migration.

Push Factors

The Lack of Arable Land as a Result of a Geographical Disadvantage. The phenomenon of surplus agricultural workers in China is a century-old problem. . . . Cultivated land now constitutes only 10.3 percent of China's vast territory. The arable land of China is only one-half of the arable land of the United States, but China has 120 times the number of rural laborers.

The Decrease of Farmland as a Result of Improper Land Use. Not only does China have a shortage of arable land in terms of the ratio of land to laborers but its cultivated land also has been disappearing at an alarming speed. From 1952 to 1988 the area under cultivation in China decreased from 1.5 billion *mu* to 1.4 billion *mu* (one *mu* is about 670 square meters). According to Chinese official statistics from 1949 to 1992 the cultivated land area declined by 2.51 percent. The per capita cultivable land dropped from 3.00 to 1.33 *mu*, which is much less than the world average of 6 *mu*.

Several factors have caused the loss of arable land. The preference for high-yielding cash crops over slower organic farming has led farmers to overuse fertilizers, which have caused soil deterioration. Desertification and deforestation have also been serious problems in China during recent decades. In the first three years of the 1990s, for example, China lost 9.37 million *mu* of land (about the size of Qinghai Province) mainly because of local officials' lack of environmental concern. These factors have reinforced each other and resulted in pollution and deteriorating fertility. In South China's hilly terrain, for example, the organic content of soil has fallen from 6 percent at initial cultivation to 2 percent now. Environmental pollution in rural areas caused by the spread of township and village enterprises has also aggravated the shortage of farmland. This fast loss of land is so threatening that both the Central Committee of the Chinese Communist Party and the People's Congress held special meetings to discuss the problem.

Another major cause for the decrease is the sale of farmland for industrial and commercial use. During the past three decades, China has converted a total of 15,000 hectares of arable land to industrial and other uses. This is equivalent to the amount of arable land of France and

Italy combined. The sale of farmland, which the Chinese call land lease or transfer of the land-use rights *(tudi pizu)*, has become an increasingly common practice in many coastal regions in the past few years as individuals or institutions are allowed to sell or lease property to foreign joint ventures or domestic companies. In Guangdong Province, for example, 100,000 *mu* of arable land were sold for 9.4 billion yuan in 1992. That represented 44.8 percent of Guangdong's revenue that year. China's arable land decreased by 0.5 percent during the late 1980s.

The National Increase of Agricultural Laborers. Agricultural laborers increased from 180 million in 1950 to over 400 million in 1988. Each year about 10 million agricultural laborers have joined the rural labor force. China now has 460 million agricultural laborers. It is estimated that their number will increase to 540 million by the year 2000.

The Effect of Agricultural Modernization. Because of both the increase in grain yield and the advance of agricultural mechanization, farm work requires far fewer laborers. China's grain yield increased from 163,920,000 tons in 1952 to 442,660,000 in 1992. The average annual growth rate from 1949 to 1992 was 3.5 percent. The increasing grain yield is likely to continue in the coming years. According to a recent study completed by Lin Yifu, an economist at Beijing University, the maximum potential of per unit yield in several decades will be about two to three times more than the present figure. While China has experienced rapid development in agricultural technology, especially the wider use of electricity, agricultural machines, and chemical fertilizers, the number of rural laborers has increased, and arable land has decreased.

The Effect of the Household Contract Responsibility System. The abolition of the People's Commune in the early 1980s "liberated" millions of Chinese peasants. Rural economic reforms, particularly the establishment of the household contract responsibility system, ended the "iron rice bowl" system in rural China and decentralized farming from the collective to the household level. As a result, efficiency increased and the number of laborers needed decreased.

Economists usually use the concept marginal product of labor to analyze whether a work unit, region, or country has surplus laborers. As more laborers are hired, the marginal product of labor will eventually fall. The work unit or country should stop employing laborers at the point at which any additional labor would cost more than it would produce.

How many laborers, then, does Chinese agriculture need at present? In other words, how many surplus rural laborers does China have? The exact number is difficult to estimate. This is partially because of rapid changes in the Chinese rural economy and partially because of the confusion caused by how the Chinese government defines rural population. In China the category *nongmin* (rural laborers or peasants) has been a residential identity rather than an occupational one. When the Chinese government compiles statistics, the "rural population" refers primarily to administrative location and not to occupation.

Mistakenly, people both in China and abroad often describe China as a rural country with 900 million peasants. This number actually refers to the total population of rural areas before the economic reform in the 1980s. According to the State Bureau of Statistics, since China's economic reform 110 million peasants have changed their status by moving to urban areas. The actual rural population at present is 797 million. This number includes 274 million children and aging people who are unable to work. Of the remaining 523 million laborers, 63 million are engaged in nonagricultural work, and 460 million are engaged in agricultural work.

China's agriculture today does not need 460 million peasants. According to the author of *China's Rural Reform: Retrospect and Prospect*, the portion of the gross national product devoted to agriculture decreased from 45.4 percent in 1950 to 19.7 percent in 1988, while rural laborers increased from 180 million in 1950 to over 400 million in 1988.

To make the situation even worse, over 10 million rural residents join the labor force every year as they become adults. But because of the structural change of the Chinese economy, the proportion of rural laborers in the total labor force is supposed to decrease from 57 percent at present to 45 percent in 2000. The burden of surplus rural laborers in China will become even worse.

One may argue that the notion of surplus is ambiguous, because one peasant's job can well be shared by three peasants. This has been the case in rural China for many decades, and this kind of practice may continue without causing any sociopolitical problems. But factors such as geographical disadvantages, improper use of farmland, environmental deterioration, the natural increase of agricultural laborers, and the effects of agricultural modernization are only *push* factors—there are also *pull* factors that cause China's rural to urban migration.

Pull Factors

The Widening Income Disparity Between Rural and Urban Areas.
The widening gap in income between areas and trades is one driving
force behind this migration. The population living below the poverty
line in China has declined significantly as a result of rural economic
reform in the past decade. However, Pieter Botteller, head of the World
Bank resident mission in China, believes that the opportunities for further reductions in poverty through agricultural growth and rural industries were largely exhausted by the mid-1980s. The rural-urban income
disparity grew from 1:1.71 in 1984 to 1:2.55 in 1994. In 1993 the income of
urban residents was 12 percent greater than that in 1992, while the
income of a peasant increased only 2 percent. Because of the widening
income gap, many peasants move to cities to seek a better life. This is
due in part to the soaring prices of fertilizers, insecticides, and machinery needed for agriculture, while farmers can still fetch only relatively
low prices for their goods. The government has failed to raise the prices
of farm products to keep up with those of manufactured goods. In 1993
the prices of fertilizer, fuel, and other farming necessities rose nearly
twice as fast as those of farm commodities.

Not only is the gap between rural and urban areas widening but also
the disparity is increasing between coastal and inland cities. According
to a Chinese Academy of Social Sciences survey of 20,000 urban households and a China's Worker Union survey of 50,000 urban households,
one-half of China's city and town dwellers live in poverty or *wenbao* (just
above the poverty line).

Under these circumstances, the waves of internal migration have
swelled rapidly. Statistics from Sichuan, Anhui, Hunan, Hubei, Henan,
and Jiangxi Provinces indicate that in 1982 fewer than 1 million peasants
"floated" into cities. A decade later the figure became a "tsunami" of at
least 24 million. As a Chinese journalist told me, in the first half of 1991
only 200,000 peasants left rural areas in Jiangxi Province, but in 1993
more than 3 million followed the tide

The Increased Demand of Urban Construction Projects. Construction
projects in urban areas need a great number of laborers. Shanghai, for
example, completed more municipal works in the past four years than it
did in the previous four decades. The city has witnessed over 1,000 new
skyscrapers due to the property boom of the past few years. Two bridges
and a new tunnel now link the east and west sides of the city. The Ori-

ental Pearl TV Tower and Yaohan building (two of Asia's highest buildings) pierce the sky on the east bank of the Huangpu River. In 1995 Shanghai opened its first subway line and its first overpass highway ring around the city. Migrants are the main source of the workforce for these urban projects. In Pudong, for example, about 4,000 new construction projects were started in 1994, and more than three-fourths of the construction workers were migrants from other provinces. Thousands of migrants have flooded into Pudong since it became a new economic zone a few years ago. Many migrants, however, cannot find jobs there.

The Increased Demand of the Nonstate Sector in Urban Areas. Not only urban construction projects but also urban private enterprises and foreign joint ventures have sought to hire cheap laborers. For the first three decades of the People's Republic of China, the government strictly restrained the existence of private enterprises. They began to reappear in the mid-1980s, but at that time each private firm was allowed to hire no more than eight workers. In the early 1990s private enterprises have been growing rapidly. By the end of 1992, approximately 7.7 million — 89 percent — of the retail sales outlets in China belonged to private firms or individually owned businesses. About 80 percent of the 140,000 shops and markets in Beijing, for example, are either owned or run by private entrepreneurs. The number of private enterprises in the country increased from 91,000 in 1989 to 420,000 in 1994.

The private sector has developed fastest along the southeast coast of China, where 70 percent of the country's private businesses are located. Another 19 percent are in central China, and only 1 percent are in the western part of the country. It is not clear how the number of workers employed in the private sector is divided between locals or migrants, but some case studies show that in the coastal area, migrants constitute an overwhelming majority of workers in the nonstate firms, including private, collective, and foreign-owned firms. As *China Daily* reported in 1994, in some economically advanced market towns in southern Jiangsu, the number of nonlocal laborers surpassed local residents.

Foreign companies or joint ventures, especially those from Hong Kong and Taiwan, have employed a large number of migrant workers. Dongguan, bordering the Shenzhen Economic Zone, is one of the leading counties in China in terms of foreign investment. The number of migrant workers in 1990 was 4.2 times the number in 1986. In Shenzhen out of the total population of 1.7 million in 1990, 980,700 were migrants.

The Changing Structure of Labor Markets in Urban Areas. The development of a market economy in urban areas has increased the demand for low-wage labor in service sectors. Permanent city residents, however, have become increasingly unwilling to do "dirty jobs" such as cleaning lavatories or collecting garbage. According to a recent newspaper investigation, migrant laborers have shouldered 80 percent of the "dirty, heavy, and dangerous jobs" in Shanghai. A large number of maids in Shanghai are from Wuwei County, Anhui Province. "Wuwei County," said a girl who works in my friend's house in Shanghai, "exports soldiers in wartime, maids in peacetime." Many of the garbage collectors in Shanghai are from Hunan, and most of them are just teenagers.

All these push and pull factors have contributed to the ongoing rural-to-urban migration. None will disappear in the foreseeable future. There is every reason to expect that the issues related to rural surplus laborers and internal migration will become even more acute, especially as China's urban unemployment rate increases. The crucial question for China is whether its cities are ready to absorb this huge number of laborers. Very few of the social scientists and government officials with whom I spoke seemed optimistic.

China has made rapid progress in urbanization during the past few years. Between 1988 and 1992 the number of population centers designated as cities increased from 223 to 517, with the urban population growing from 135 million to 320 million. Great pressure has already been exerted on the country's urban employment, infrastructure, transportation, health care, and social stability. China's urban areas seem totally unprepared for this large-scale migration.

"Just about the worse news that China can hear is that the urban unemployment rate is increasing at the same time that millions of rural workers are migrating to the cities. But that's the news we are getting from government reports," a scholar from the Shanghai Academy of Social Sciences said to me.

According to an influential Chinese newspaper, 80 percent of China's state-owned industrial enterprises currently have hidden deficits. The Chinese government has admitted that one-third of state-owned enterprises have overt deficits, and another one-third have hidden deficits.

These enterprises often lay off employees or persuade many middle-aged workers (in their midforties) to take early retirement. Many workers are ordered to stay at home while waiting for a job. The government uses the term "off-post" *(xiagang)*, to refer to those "job-waiting" workers. Off-post workers receive about 30 to 40 percent of their regular salaries.

The Chinese government does not give any indication of how many off-post workers China has now. According to the official Federation of China's Workers, some state-owned enterprises exist only in name. About 7 million workers live in poverty because of China's lack of a social welfare system. A Chinese official magazine estimated that China's state-owned enterprises have 25 million "urban surplus laborers."

I suspect that the real number of off-post workers must be an embarrassment to the authorities. Some of my middle-school classmates in Shanghai are off-post. In May 1994 I went to a wedding banquet for a relative of mine. Of the eleven people at my table, three were off-post.

Recently it has become common for state-owned enterprises to be unable to pay salaries to their employees on time. Zhu Rongji, the Politburo standing committee member who is in charge of China's economy and who became Premier in 1998, in 1994 traveled to Heilongjiang, Jilin, Liaoning, Henan, and Hubei Provinces, where a great many state-owned enterprises are located. Many enterprises there were behind in payments. Zhu said during the trip: "It is imperative to make a thorough survey of the enterprises, help them solve their problems, deepen their reform, and transform their operating procedures."

Zhu also dismissed several top provincial officials for their incompetence in dealing with the rise in the unemployment rate and other problems. The disciplinary committee of the Chinese Communist Party issued new regulations in 1994, stating that no county or municipal government could purchase cars if the local government is behind in paying employees' salaries. Those local governments that had purchased cars were required to sell them and use the money to pay salaries. It was reported that in Shandong and other provinces unemployed urban workers and migrants destroyed fancy cars parked on the streets.

Millions of migrant workers have deepened the problems of urban unemployment. The Chinese government seems not to have any effective measures to cope with these two integrated problems. Local governments in major cities have recently adopted some measures to constrain what they called the "reckless flow of job-seeking farmers [*mangliu*]." Earlier in 1994 the Shanghai municipal government issued a yearlong and renewable "blue card" *(wugongzheng)* system to permit migrant laborers to work in the city. Some officials in major cities have advocated that local governments should adopt a more restrictive policy to limit the flow of migrant laborers. But no measures seem to be effective in stopping the flow.

According to a recent report, China will face three "demographic peaks" at the turn of the century or during the early decades of the next century: (1) "population peak"—1.3 billion people by the year 2000; (2) "aging population peak" in 2024—300 million will be over sixty years old; and (3) "labor population peak"—rural laborers (age fifteen through fifty-nine) will be 660 million, actual rural laborers will number 590 million, and the total needed rural laborers will be 279 million, leaving a surplus of 311 million.

Furthermore, the massive internal migration has significantly affected birth control in the country. For over two decades every family in China has been allowed to have only one child. Local officials have been closely watching the effectiveness of "the one-child policy." But birth control is practically impossible to enforce among migrant workers. Some couples come to urban areas in order to avoid enforced birth control in their native villages. They have a female baby, but they still want a son. Many have two children or more. A newlywed couple migrated to Amoy nine years ago, and now they have nine children! It was reported that Shanghai had 430,000 young female migrant workers (*wailaimei*) in 1993. About 20 percent of them illegally "lived together" with men. Some became concubines. Altogether 12,000 bore children in 1993, accounting for 12.5 percent of the total births in the city.

According to another 1994 survey conducted in Shanghai, over 60 percent of migrant workers wanted to have two children. Unplanned childbirth among the floating population was thirty times higher than among Shanghai residents. Some urban officials are aware of this problem and want to adopt effective methods to control the birth rate of migrant workers. But when they do so, the migrant workers just "float" to other places.

"My wife and I will move repeatedly until we have a male baby," a migrant worker from Shandong told a reporter of a Shanghai newspaper.

There are no easy solutions to the pressure of overpopulation, particularly surplus rural laborers and the increase of urban unemployment. A top Chinese leader recently said to the media: "Agriculture and state enterprises are the keys to developing a healthy economy and maintaining a stable society." Unfortunately, both these key areas have been beset by serious difficulties.

"These two problems are like time bombs," said a sixty-six-year-old retired schoolteacher with whom I chatted in Wuhan. "These problems can be contained now, as China has continuously had a good grain harvest for the past few years, and the Chinese economy generally grows well. But who knows what will happen if rural China experiences a famine, or if urban China suffers another major unemployment hit, or if the Chinese government deliberates too long in establishing a responsive social welfare system, or if a large number of state-owned enterprises are unable to pay their employees, or if migrant women all want to have more children, as they were allowed to do during the Mao era, or if . . ."

PEOPLE'S DAILY COMMENTATOR,
STRENGTHENING MANAGEMENT OVER THE FLOATING POPULATION

What concerned the government most about the ballooning "floating population" was that if economic growth slowed, China's cities might find themselves awash with millions of unemployed, lumpen, and angry workers with no welfare safety net to rescue them and no place to go.

This selection was excerpted from a genre of writing often used in the People's Daily *to express official Party positions; it was published in July 1995.*

The problem of floating population is a common problem facing practically all developing countries. According to statistics, China currently has a floating population of approximately 80 million, of which 44 million are temporary residents registered with public security organs. Most of these temporary residents are people from rural areas engaging in industry and trade. The rational and orderly flow of the surplus rural laborers plays an important role in promoting economic development and social progress. It has boosted urban development and construction of some state projects; promoted the development of township and town enterprises in coastal and suburban areas, and the comprehensive development of agriculture; met the demand of enterprises, units, and households in urban areas for the workforce; and played a positive role in improving the quality of life for the peasants by helping poor areas shake off poverty.

However, due to outdated management measures and relatively

weak macroregulation and control, the floating population at the present stage is still in a blind and disorderly state to a certain extent, thus bringing some negative effects: It has caused a serious impact on the management order in inflowing localities and a serious imbalance in the workforce of some outflowing localities, making it difficult to carry out measures to boost agricultural production and grassroots infrastructural construction; it has given rise to the common phenomena in which the legitimate rights and interests of the people who have left their hometowns to engage in industry and trade have been infringed upon. If the blind and disorderly state in the population flow is allowed to go unchecked, it will lead to serious consequences.

The Party Central Committee and the State Council attach great importance to the strengthening of management work of the floating population, taking it as a very important task in the comprehensive management of public order this year. All sectors in society and the vast numbers of the people are also very much concerned about it. Doing a good job in the management of floating population not only contributes to the maintenance of social security and social stability but also helps promote economic development and ensure the smooth progress of reform, opening up, and the socialist modernization drive. In recent years all relevant local and central departments have conscientiously studied and actively explored the strengthening of the management over the floating population. They have done a great deal of fruitful work, thus laying a good foundation for the management of the floating population.

To do a good job in the management of floating population, first it is necessary to reach a common understanding. By proceeding from the overall situation of the work of the whole Party and the entire country and conforming to the inexorable trend of the flow of population, we should actively guide and strictly manage the shift of the surplus rural workforce, adroitly guide action according to circumstances, promote what is beneficial, and abolish what is harmful. The main way out for the resolution of the surplus rural workforce is to digest and absorb most of that workforce on the spot by strengthening the comprehensive development of agriculture, developing township and town enterprises, and developing small cities and towns. Under this premise, in accordance with the requirements of urban economic development, we can organize part of the surplus rural workforce to enter cities in an orderly way and gradually perfect the corresponding measures of management, education, and services. . . .

Through the strengthening of management over floating population, we should conscientiously keep abreast of the flowing situation of population, control the scale of the flow, and direct the orderly flow. It is necessary to safeguard the legitimate rights and interests of the floating population, prevent and crack down on criminal activities by a handful of people, maintain social security and the order of various kinds of management in accordance with the law so as to serve the reform, opening up, economic development, and social stability in a better way.

★ THE ENVIRONMENT ★

As China's economy boomed and the standard of living for hundreds of millions improved, the country's resource base began to be exploited and its environment degraded at an alarming pace. Whether China can expect to sustain the kind of unregulated growth that it relied on during the 1990s is a question whose answer will have global environmental consequences for the next century. Simply put, China's predicament is this: If it does not continue its high-speed development, it will be unable to employ those being laid off and sidelined as state enterprises are closed and as the "floating population" balloons, not to mention the 12 to 15 million new young people entering the job market each year.

To require new industries to incorporate the latest pollution control devices in their planning and construction, much less to retrofit or close the vast numbers of old industries that are serious polluters, would not only involve a vast expenditure but also impede China's industrial development. It is a trade-off that Chinese leaders have not yet felt able to make.

MARK HERTSGAARD,
OUR REAL CHINA PROBLEM

When the magazine journalist Mark Hertsgaard went to China to study its environmental situation, he found the dark side of its economic miracle. While there are many imponderables in China's transition from Maoist revolution to a more marketized and democratized society, one absolute limitation is the finiteness of the country's air, water, and other natural resources. Whether these can sustain such rapid continued exploitation and whether the health of the Chinese people can survive the environmental compromises required for such high rates of growth are questions that must be answered. But if environmental degradation continues over the next decade at the same rate that it has over the past decade, China's environmental problems could end up being more of an impediment to the well-being of its people and to the stability of the country than politics and other global issues.

This selection was excerpted from an article published in The Atlantic Monthly *in November 1997.*

China claims that its population is 1.22 billion people (as of the end of 1996). The true number is certainly higher than that. But even the official figure means that nearly one out of every four human beings on earth lives in China. The Chinese economy is ranked anywhere from the third to the seventh largest in the world, and is expected to be number 1 by 2010. Incomes have doubled since Deng Xiaoping initiated his marketplace reforms in 1979, and the environmental side effects have been devastating.

At least five of the cities with the worst air pollution in the world are in China. Sixty to 90 percent of the rainfall in Guangdong, the southern province that is the center of China's economic boom, is acid rain. Since nearly all the gasoline in China is leaded (Beijing switched to unleaded gas in June), and 80 percent of the coal isn't "washed" before being burned, people's lungs and nervous systems are bombarded by an extraordinary volume and variety of deadly poisons. One of every four deaths in China is caused by lung disease, brought about by the air pollution and the increasingly fashionable habit of cigarette smoking. Suburban sprawl and soil erosion gobbled up more than 86 million acres of farmland from 1950 to 1990—as much as all the farmland in Germany, France, and the United Kingdom. Farmland losses have continued in the 1990s, raising questions about China's ability to feed itself in years to come, especially as rising incomes lead to more meat-intensive diets.

Even the government's official policy pronouncements, which invariably overaccentuate the positive, admit that environmental degradation in China will get worse before it gets better. For China's new-found wealth has only whetted its citizens' appetite for more. China's huge population wants to join the global middle class, with everything that entails: cars, air conditioners, closets full of clothes, jet travel. Rising consumer demand has already resulted in chronic widespread electricity shortages. Thus China plans to build more than a hundred new power stations over the next decade, adding 18,000 megawatts of capacity every year—roughly the equivalent of Louisiana's entire power grid. By 2020 its coal consumption will have doubled, if not tripled. All this will not only worsen the country's acid rain and air pollution problems but endanger the entire planet by accelerating the global warming that scientists say is already under way.

China's huge population and grand economic ambitions make it the most important environmental actor in the world today, with the single exception of the United States. Like the United States, China could all but single-handedly make climate change, ozone depletion, and a host of other hazards a reality for people all over the world. What happens in China is therefore central to one of the great questions of our time: Will human civilization survive the many environmental pressures crowding in on it at the end of the twentieth century?

Like governments the world over, China's leaders have learned to say the right things about the environment. In 1992 China was an enthusiastic participant in the United Nations Earth Summit. In July of last year President Jiang Zemin and Premier Li Peng began to speak out against environmental destruction and to urge a shift toward "sustainable development." China has also adopted comprehensive environmental laws and regulations that on paper compare favorably with—indeed, were often modeled on—their Western equivalents.

But the future is shaped less by official rhetoric than by what actually happens on the ground, and environmental laws are often simply not implemented in China. This is no state secret; most of the dozens of government officials I interviewed acknowledged the pervasiveness of the problem, often without prompting. Sometimes the culprit is corruption: factory owners use *guanxi*—personal connections—or bribery to get local regulators to look the other way. Beijing either can't or won't stop them. As the ancient Chinese adage says, "The mountains are high, and the emperor is far away."

Even more common, and intractable, is the so-called soft-law syndrome. Under soft law the government excuses state-owned companies from full compliance with environmental laws and standards; the law is "softened" in order to spare the companies (and the state banks supporting them) from bankruptcy and to shield their workers from unemployment. In contrast to corruption, soft law is not something Chinese officials like to talk about.

Right after an explosion at [a local] paper factory I had lunch with Hu Jiquan, a top government economist in Chongqing. Keen to encourage foreign investment, Hu was pledging that the local environment would improve in years to come, thanks to tougher law enforcement. "We will close factories if we have to," Hu said. "We've already closed more than two hundred of them." Having just returned from seeing a "chlorine waterfall" [caused by a paper plant], I couldn't help challenging this rosy vision, and Hu was honest enough to concede that short-term economic considerations often do override environmental goals in China. "The trouble is, if we close that factory, many workers will lose their jobs, and our government would rather support the workers than protect the water," he said with a shrug.

Hu then extended his explanation, though he first told Zhenbing [my interpreter] not to translate this part for the foreigner. The government of Chongqing knew perfectly well that the paper plant should be closed immediately. In fact, it had tried to shut the plant months earlier, "but the local people and leaders complained a lot, so the government backed off. It was afraid of social unrest."

This is the crux of the Chinese environmental problem. The government knows the environment needs protecting, but it fears the social consequences. Bluntly put, it worries that doing the right thing environmentally could be political suicide.

A Long Nightmare of Deprivation

The government would like to protect the environment for a very simple reason: senior officials have come to realize that environmental degradation costs money — indeed, it threatens to derail China's entire economic modernization program. Li Yining, a grand old man of market economics who was one of the masterminds of China's transition to private enterprise, told me in an interview that "inadequate ecological protection" was one of the few things that could prevent China's economy from growing at 10 percent a year "for a very long time." Acid rain, for example, causes $2.8 billion worth of damage to forests, agriculture, and industry in China every year. Air pollution raises health-care costs and lowers workers' productivity. Deforestation worsens the floods that already kill thousands of Chinese every year. The list goes on. The official *China Daily* estimates that the annual cost of China's environmental degradation is 7 percent of the gross domestic product. Vaclav Smil, a geographer at the University of Manitoba and a leading expert on China's environment, calculates the cost at no less than 10 to 15 percent of gross domestic product. If Smil is correct, then the much-celebrated growth of China's economy is, in effect, being canceled out by associated environmental degradation. In short, the economy is running hard but poisoning its own future. The problem, of course, is that faithfully implementing environmental laws would require closing hundreds of thousands of factories and throwing tens of millions of people out of work.

The Chinese people have long and bitter experience with scarcity and are understandably eager to leave it behind. As recently as 1949 life expectancy was only thirty-nine years, a level not seen in Europe since the Industrial Revolution. All Chinese over forty have firsthand memories of the greatest manmade disaster of the twentieth century, the famine caused by Mao Zedong's Great Leap Forward campaign. As Jasper Becker, the Beijing bureau chief of the *South China Morning Post*, documents in *Hungry Ghosts* (1997), the famine killed some 30 million people from 1959 to 1961 and brought starvation, misery, and even cannibalism to rural China.

Today the average Chinese life span is about seventy years, yet scores of millions still live in desperate poverty. All this has left Party leaders determined to keep the economy growing no matter what. They believe that Tiananmen Square was not primarily about politics—about the issues of democracy and human rights that dominated Western news reports—but about economics. There is truth to this. Hundreds of thousands of average Chinese followed the students into the streets not only because they yearned to breathe free but also because they were angry about hyperinflation, corruption, and their own uncertain economic prospects. The Party saw its life flash before its eyes in 1989, and it got a second warning in 1991, when its erstwhile "big brother," the Communist Party in the Soviet Union, fell from power. The Chinese Communists are determined not to suffer the same fate. As Deng Xiaoping warned his fellow Party leaders after Tiananmen Square, if the Party cannot improve the welfare of the people, the people will go into the streets.

Environmental Revolts

But there is a Catch-22. The people, it seems, will also go into the streets if their local environment becomes intolerably polluted—if, for example, they are deprived of safe drinking water.

"There were social revolts along the Huai River, so the State Council [China's cabinet] *had* to react," one retired senior government official told me, recalling the most dramatic government crackdown on pollution to date. The Huai region, about 200 miles northwest of Shanghai, is the most densely populated of China's seven major river basins: 110 million inhabitants share 108,000 square miles of land. The river had been severely polluted for years, but it got drastically worse in July of 1994, when a sudden flood of toxins turned the river black and deadly for weeks. Hundreds of thousands of people were left without drinking water, several thousand were treated for dysentery, diarrhea, and vomiting, and 26 million pounds of fish were killed.

Popular outrage took many forms, including pelting local officials with eggs when they blocked foreign journalists from filming the river. The most extraordinary moment came when a top leader from Beijing, Song Jian, the elderly chairman of the State Council's environment committee, arrived to inspect the site. Somehow one brave and resourceful peasant managed to give Song a glass of river water to drink. Song took a sip of the putrid brew; then he turned to the local and provincial officials flanking him and shrewdly invited them to drain the glass. These officials had ignored earlier pleas to close the paper, leather, and dyeing factories whose waste fouled the Huai. Song told them they would be sacked if the offending factories were not shut promptly. Last summer the government closed 999 paper mills and untold numbers of other factories.

If Beijing fears social unrest so much, why did it shut all those factories? One reason, said the retired senior government official, was that "for years no boy from [certain villages in] the Huai River area has been healthy enough to pass the physical examination required to enter the army." Even more important, said other observers, these factories were township and village enterprises, or TVPs—small, privately owned plants that employed no more than a few dozen workers each. Such plants employed at most tens of thousands of moonlighting peasants who had never stopped working in their fields. Against that fact the government had to weigh the anger of the many hundreds of thousands of people who relied on the Huai for their drinking water—people who had already demonstrated a capacity for protest. There was no question which group should be placated.

Beijing went national with the campaign against TVPs in August of last year, when the State Council ordered some 60,000 heavily polluting factories to close. "That sounds like a big number, but in a country as large as China it amounts to only one percent of the total number of enterprises and workers," Ye Requi, a deputy administrator for the National Environmental Protection Agency, told me. Ye nevertheless argued that the closings "show the seriousness of the government in this area." Unfortunately, TVPs account for only a fraction of China's pollution—estimates range from 5 to 30 percent. To make a real dent in the problem, state-owned enterprises like the Chongqing Paper Factory would have to be closed. But fear of social unrest makes that problematic, as it does the recent pledge by Party leaders to end state ownership of 10,000 of China's 13,000 largest industrial enterprises.

Thus China's leaders find themselves in a box. They can, in the name of economic growth, leave the big factories and other environmental hazards essentially undisturbed and hope that the resulting pollution and ecological destruction do not trigger either unmanageable popular protest or long-run economic stagnation. Or they can clamp down, clean up, and face the double short-term risk of a stalled economy and a wrathful proletariat. Not an enviable choice, but for Chinese leaders not a difficult one either. As Chen Qi, the top environmental official in Liaoning, a region of bitter winter cold and 30 percent unemployment, explained to me, "Heavy pollution may kill you in a hundred days, but without enough heat and food you die in three."

The Collapse of the One-Child Policy

The most pervasive environment-related myth about China is that couples are allowed to have only one child. But in truth the one-child policy has long been "more slogan than reality," in the words of a top Chinese demographer. The Party was forced by popular resistance to back off from the policy—another example of social unrest driving government decisions. Enraged peasants were actually attacking and killing local Party leaders and their families.

Today the one-child family is all but unheard of in rural China, where nearly three out of four Chinese live. In my six weeks of travel, which took me from Liaoning and Hebei provinces in the north through Shanxi and Sichuan in the middle west to Hunan and Guangdong in the south, I talked with scores of peasant families. I was the first foreigner that some of these peasants, especially the children, had ever seen. Every family I met had at least two children; many had three or four, and some had five or more. In a village near the Pearl River I shot baskets with a boy of ten who shyly told me that he was the youngest of seven. It seems that the only Chinese who do adhere to the one-child target are urban dwellers—especially those who work directly for the government and thus can be easily monitored, and penalized through the withholding of salaries, promotions, and the like.

All of which casts strong doubt on official claims regarding China's population: that Chinese women average only two births each, that the population will not reach 1.5 billion until 2030, that it will peak at 1.6 billion in 2046. Although some newly affluent families are, in the familiar demographic pattern, having fewer children, the gross numbers are almost certainly greater. The truth is that no one knows exactly how big China's population is, or how fast it is growing.

Population growth is probably China's most important environmental issue, because it magnifies all others. For example, China ranks near the very bottom in global comparisons of per capita supplies of arable land, fresh water, and forests. This is in part because so much of China's land is arid, and in part because Mao, in his mad Great Leap Forward, ordered millions of trees to be cut down. But the country's gargantuan population makes a bad situation worse.

Beijing has so little water that Party leaders have questioned whether the city can remain the capital, according to Yu Yuefeng, the staff director of the Environmental Protection and Natural Resources Conservation Committee of the National People's Congress. With a nervous chuckle, Yu told me that the problem has eased in the past two years, thanks to higher than normal rainfall, but, he conceded, "This is a roll of the dice. We have to rely on the gods to keep the rains coming." In his privileged Party position, Yu can afford to laugh. The problem is not so amusing for some 50 million people in rural northern China who must walk for miles or wait for days to obtain any drinking water at all. As for farmland, population growth has reduced the supply per person to about the size of one-third of a tennis court.

Everywhere I visited, I noticed that China *felt* crowded. How could it not? China's population is five times that of the United States, even though the two countries occupy roughly the same amount of land area. But since deserts and mountains make the western half of China inhospitable to human settlement, 90 percent of its population lives in the east. Imagine, then, almost nine times as many people living east of the Mississippi as live there in real life. That is everyday reality in China.

In all the thousands of miles of scenery I observed during my travels, I cannot recall a single place without signs of intense human settlement. Open space was for farming, period, and was cultivated to within an inch of its life, with furrows reaching right to the edge of any road and curling into hollows as small as pitchers' mounds. In daylight hours the cities become churning masses of congestion. Although China has only one car for every 150 inhabitants (the United States has one for every 2), that still means a huge number of cars. Jockeying for space alongside them are sky blue cargo trucks, ancient city buses, an occasional horse-drawn wagon, and an endless fleet of bicycles—many of them three-wheeled cargo bikes, transporting everything from bulging sacks of fruit and vegetables to freshly skinned sides of pork to couches, toilets, and televisions.

The Meaning of Spitting

Walking down the sidewalk in China was a challenge not only because of all the people I had to dodge but also because of the puddles of spit they left in my path. Everyone, it seems, spits in China—on the sidewalk, in the classroom, on the train, in restaurants. The habit is universal. The Communists tried to eradicate spitting when they came to power in 1949; it was one of their first exhortations to the masses. They failed. Spitting lives on because it is a habit of peasant life, and the vast majority of Chinese are still peasants or only one generation removed. The habit apparently derives from the basic conditions of peasant life, which include rampant lung infections and other respiratory problems. These, in turn, result from a historical fact with enormous environmental implications: for centuries Chinese peasants lived with very little heat in wintertime. They burned wood if they were lucky, but more often they used dried leaves and crop stalks, as Zhenbing remembers his family doing exclusively before he turned ten, in 1976. Today peasants still rely on such "biomass" fuels for 70 percent of their energy consumption.

Coal therefore represents a great advance for the Chinese people: it keeps a body much warmer. But it does so at terrible cost: the Chinese are dying in frightful numbers from coal smoke. Twenty-six percent of all deaths in China are caused by respiratory disease. Coal smoke is not the sole cause of these deaths, but it is a major contribution. Outdoor air pollution, of which coal smoke is the main component, is second only to cigarette smoking as a cause of lung cancer in China's cities, where lung cancer has increased 18.5 percent since 1988. Coal is also a central element in the "indoor pollution" from home stoves that is the chief cause of rural lung cancer, especially among women.

There is little hope of relief. One of the few natural resources China has in abundance, coal accounts for three-quarters of total energy consumption. The country's power stations and manufacturing plants are fueled overwhelmingly by coal. Factor in coal's dominant role in keeping people warm, along with the primitive technologies often employed, and it's no surprise that Chinese cities, especially in the industrial, frigid north, have some of the filthiest air on the planet.

Levels of total suspended particulates, or TSP (soot and dust, in lay terms), are appallingly high in China—often four to nine times as high as the World Health Organization's guideline of 60 to 90 micrograms per cubic meter annually. Most American cities have readings in the 40-

to-60 range; New York measures 62. In some northern cities in China the level climbs as high as 400, 500, or even 800 in wintertime.

The Ghosts in Tiananmen Square

Visitors to Beijing can forget seeing blue skies in winter, except immediately after Siberian winds have roared through. By chance such winds struck the capital the night of my arrival. But two days later the winds calmed, and over the following week and a half I witnessed the sickening descent of the city into murk and gloom.

At noon on my third day, a Saturday, after barely twelve hours of still air, I took a bus across town to a luncheon interview, traveling the main east-west boulevard past Tiananmen Square. Directly above me the sky was still blue, but in the distance a fuzzy, pale gray layer of smog already frosted the skyline. When I came back outside a mere four hours later, the layer had nearly doubled in thickness, its blurry density giving the sky an otherworldly aspect as it melted into a sunset of vivid pinks and yellows. The pollution accumulated with each passing day, and by Thursday I was used to waking up to a dull gray-white haze that rested on the city skyline like a lid on a wok.

On Friday morning I took a taxi to the National People's Congress. Passing through the larger intersections of Beijing, I looked both ways down the cross streets, but my line of sight extended no farther than about 200 yards. When I reached Tiananmen Square, at 8:45, the sun hung white and barely visible above the southern gate to the Imperial Palace, like a dim lightbulb in a barroom full of cigarette smoke. Gazing north, past Mao's mausoleum, I could not see the far end of the square, much less the Forbidden City beyond it. The pedestrians crossing the square were like spectral figures, half ghost, half flesh, as they disappeared into the gritty mist.

During our travels beyond Beijing, Zhenbing and I fell into a running debate over which city in China had the nastiest air. Was it, in fact, Beijing? Zhenbing, a resident of the capital, wouldn't entertain the possibility. Was it Benxi, in Manchuria, whose pollution was so thick that in the 1980s the city had vanished from satellite photos? Possibly. Though Benxi was now visible again from outer space, local officials admitted that its TSP levels remained very high. What's more, my interviews with residents suggested that what progress had been made stemmed as much from widespread factory bankruptcies as from the government's vaunted cleanup campaign.

For a day I leaned toward Datong, an ugly, low-slung town known as China's coal-mining capital. Bad as the air was in Beijing, it was unusual there to see smokestacks belching copious amounts of pure black smoke; the pollution somehow seemed more dispersed. In Datong black emissions were routine and ubiquitous. . . .

Another formidable competitor was Xian, the ancient imperial capital known the world over for the enormous collection of terra-cotta warriors buried outside town. A splendid bell tower and massive city wall dating back to the Ming dynasty further enhance Xian's reputation as one of China's loveliest cities. But Xian's pollution screened these architectural treasures from view. Even on a sunny day the only sign of the orb itself was a patch of sky somewhat brighter than the rest. As a test I timed how long I could stare at the artificially veiled sun without hurting my eyes. After sixty seconds I stopped counting.

Astonishingly, the Chinese I met insisted that their health is not endangered by all this pollution. I developed a dry, rasping cough because I was a foreigner; they, on the other hand, were "used to it." I heard that phrase dozens of times, even from people who should have known better. One leading environmental scholar and advocate in Beijing, for example, assured me that his lungs could tolerate his daily jogs because he had been breathing Beijing's air for years. By that logic, of course, smoking cigarettes poses no health risk so long as one begins in early childhood. He granted the point but said that since he could not escape Beijing's air, he at least wanted to be as strong and fit as possible.

The biology of cancer seems to be unknown to many Chinese; even well-educated people appear to be unaware that the human body cannot build up tolerance against industrial carcinogens the way it can against the infections that cause influenza. But the lack of awareness goes deeper. "A tendency to deny unpleasant realities has become part of the Chinese personality in recent decades," according to Orville Schell, the author of many books on China. "A society that has for decades had to ignore so many unjust and irrational things in order to just get along—the injustices of the gulag, families ruined during the Cultural Revolution, other kinds of government barbarity, the lack of a believable news media—is one in which the capacity to avoid recognizing all sorts of problems, including environmental ones, has become essential to survive," Schell says. In addition, most Chinese accept the familiar idea that economic growth requires environmental damage, and they are quite ready to pay that price. "We have a saying in China," one journalist who has tried to raise public awareness of the subject told me. "'Is your stomach too full?' In other words, are you so well off you can afford to complain about nothing? This phrase is used for Americans who talk about saving birds and monkeys while there are still many Chinese people who don't have enough food to eat."

400 Green Chinese

The environmental movement in China, such as it is, thus faces a daunting challenge. The few individuals who dare to work on the issue say that by necessity education is the top priority. Liang Conjie, the founder and president of Friends of Nature, one of the very few independent environmental groups in China, told me that his organization got permission to operate because it registered as a cultural rather than a political group. He added that, with a mere 400 members, "Friends of Nature could never oppose the government directly, the way Greenpeace would—that will not work." Liang focuses instead on raising public consciousness, particularly by prodding Chinese journalists to cover environmental issues more attentively.

It would be hard to overstate the power that the government-run media exercise in China, so, not surprisingly, Liang was glad to see an increase during the past year in media criticism of environmental problems. Much of that increase has been orchestrated by the government itself, specifically the National Environmental Protection Agency. But there are definite limits to what the official media will say. "In my stories," one journalist told me, "I always have to begin with something positive—how NEPA has announced new policies to protect the air, for example—not with how the pollution got there in the first place and what its exact effects are. So people don't know how bad the situation actually is."

China is a greenhouse giant. It has already surpassed the former Soviet Union to become the world's second largest producer of greenhouse gases, trailing only the United States. With its immense coal reserves, huge population, and booming economic growth, China is very likely to triple its greenhouse emissions by 2020. Absent a radical shift in policies elsewhere in the world, that increase will accelerate global climate change, plunging the world into potentially catastrophic territory—melting polar ice caps, raising sea levels, causing more and nastier hurricanes, droughts, and blizzards. China will by no means be immune. Much of its coastline could face severe flooding; perhaps 67 million people could be affected.

Yet China has little patience with Western finger-pointing on the climate change issue, regarding it as a cynical means of constraining China's economic development. That is oversensitive, but it contains a kernel of truth. For all its nuclear weapons, grand ambitions, and mobile phone–wielding, expensively dressed business executives, China remains a poor country where hundreds of millions of people have no reliable supply of electricity. What's more, China emits a far smaller amount of greenhouse gases per capita than the rich nations whose earlier industrialization has already condemned the world to climate change. If outsiders want China to do something about global warming, they will have to pay for it. As one Western consultant with regular access to senior Chinese officials puts it, "They know very well they can hold the world for ransom . . . and whenever they can extract concessions, they will."

"The Americans say China is the straw that breaks the camel's back on greenhouse gas emissions," says Zhou Dadi, the deputy director general of the State Planning Commission's Energy Research Institute. "But we say, 'Why don't you take some of your heavy load off the camel first?' If the camel belongs to America, fine, we'll walk. But the camel does not belong to America. China will insist on the per capita principle [of distributing emissions rights]. What else are we supposed to do? Go back to no heat in winter? Impossible.

"China is not like Africa, you know—some remote place that's never been developed. We used to be the most developed country in the world. Now, after many decades of turbulence, civil war, revolution, political instability, and other difficulties, we finally have the chance to develop the country again. And we will not lose that chance."

A Terrible Dilemma

To get rich is glorious, in Deng Xiaoping's famous phrase. Although unrestrained growth can destroy the ecosystem on which all economies ultimately depend, the headlong pursuit of wealth is the cornerstone of modern Chinese life. The crowning irony is that even China's top environmental officials accept that economic growth must take precedence over environmental protection for years to come. Economic growth is essential not only to maintaining political stability—avoiding a return to the chaos and stagnation seen during the Cultural Revolution—but also to financing the environmental cleanup. "The money will come from the polluter-pays principle," explains Zhang Kunmin, another deputy administration of the National Environmental Protection Agency. "The enterprises and households must pay the costs of a cleaner environment, so they need more wealth."

"This is the terrible dilemma of China's environmental crisis," argues a Chinese environmental expert who must remain nameless. "Of course, rapid economic growth will cause additional environmental damage; some things in the environment are irreversible. That's why I think China will have to lose something—some species, some wetlands, something. We are working very hard to strengthen our environment. But, much as I regret it, you cannot save all the things you would like. You cannot stop a billion people."

THE WORLD BANK,
CHINA'S ENVIRONMENT IN THE NEW CENTURY

Although normally encouraged by a country's rapid development, the World Bank, too, has began to show a growing alarm about the environmental consequences it foresees of 1.3 billion Chinese joining the global consumer culture. It is questionable whether its proscriptions for a solution are realistic.

This selection was excerpted from a 1997 World Bank report titled Clear Water, Blue Skies.

Robust economic growth has brought immeasurable benefits to the Chinese people. Incomes have increased, poverty has fallen, and health indicators have improved. Yet the same unbridled growth that has lifted millions out of poverty has also caused serious environmental damage.

Over the past decade China has begun to curb this damage. New laws have established comprehensive regulations for the environment. The government has invested considerable resources in protecting air and water. And economic reforms have reduced the economy's energy intensity at an impressive pace. Although ambient concentrations of most pollutants are still unacceptably high, they have been kept in check.

Chinese leaders know that much remains to be done. Particulate and sulfur levels in major Chinese cities are among the highest in the world, exceeding World Health Organization and Chinese standards by two to five times. Pollution is one reason chronic obstructive pulmonary disease—emphysema and chronic bronchitis—has become the leading cause of death in China, with a mortality rate five times that in the United States. As Premier Li Peng noted last year, China has to not only "provide people with riches and material products but also gradually improve the quality of life, and environment is an important part of the quality of life."

This report's findings underscore the environmental concerns of Chinese leaders:

• An estimated 178,000 people in major cities suffer premature deaths each year because of pollution.

• Indoor air pollution, primarily from burning coal and biomass for cooking and heating, causes 111,000 premature deaths each year, mainly in rural areas.

• Each year some 7.4 million work-years are lost to health damages related to air pollution.

• Water pollution, a focus of recent Chinese policy, has contaminated 52 to 135 monitored urban river sections. These sections do not even meet the lowest standards necessary for irrigation water, rendering them mere waste sinks. Unless action is taken, future access to safe drinking water is threatened for tens of millions of people.

• Acid rain in the high-sulfur coal regions of southern and southwestern China threatens to damage 10 percent of the land area and may already have reduced crop and forestry productivity by 3 percent.

• Children in Shenyang, Shanghai, and other major cities have blood-lead levels averaging 80 percent higher than levels considered dangerous to mental development.

• Air and water pollution damages, especially the dangers fine airborne particulates pose to human health, have been estimated to be at least $54 billion a year—or nearly 8 percent of gross domestic product in 1995.

Despite the magnitude of the problem, China has an unprecedented opportunity to increase its environmental quality of life. Rapid economic growth makes clearer waters and bluer skies more attainable. High rates of investment can be used to develop cleaner, more energy-efficient industries. Policies that channel investment into cleaner production, encourage material and energy efficiency, and faster conservation of scarce resources could reduce emissions in 2020 below today's levels, improve air and water quality, and lower pollution-related health costs by 75 percent—even as China quadruples its output.

But these outcomes will not happen automatically. Indeed, they will require considerable effort. Although structural change and new technology will help reduce pollution per unit of output, without new policies the pressures from a growing economy will swamp these improvements, and may even undermine recent gains. The old pattern of growth, projected into the future, would generate rising health costs and dramatically raise the cost of cleanup to future generations.

A new growth strategy should aspire to

- Increase substitution of cleaner fuels—especially natural gas—for coal in household cooking and heating
- Improve energy efficiency and diversify energy supplies into non-coal sources
- Reduce emissions from industrial boilers and furnaces
- Curb indoor air pollution in rural households
- Increase wastewater collection and treatment from cities and towns and industrial enterprises, especially small enterprises
- Control increasing acid rain deposition in sensitive regions
- Prevent automobile-related air pollution.

Since current policies are fragmented across several government agencies with differing policy mandates, a serious assault on China's pollution problems will require not only more aggressive policies but also better integration of policies and implementation efforts.

China's increasing market orientation requires a strategy for future environmental protection that goes beyond the command and control measures of the past. The next generation of policy should be based on three principles:

- *China must harness the market to work for the environment, not against it.* This means accelerating economic reforms—reorienting state enterprises so that they respond to environmental penalties, adjusting the pricing system to ensure that it reflects environmental costs, liberalizing international trade to give Chinese industry access to the latest environmental technology, and developing capital markets to provide financing to firms and municipalities supplying environmental infrastructure. Harnessing the market also means recognizing that China, with its limited resource base, is underpricing energy and water. Prices of natural gas and water, for example, should be raised to reflect their scarcity. Finally, harnessing the market means that the government should expand the use of taxes on pollution to incorporate its enormous social costs. The real cost to society of coal—after its damages to human health are included—is 100 percent higher in Beijing than its current price. Environmental taxes on coal and gasoline and on pollutants would use the market to clean the environment.

• *China must harness growth for the environment by pursuing investments with the highest environmental benefits for future generations.* Better pricing makes investments in clean technology economic and imposes environmental discipline on firms. For example, Chinese industry today operates at 50 to 85 percent of the energy efficiency of countries in the Organization for Economic Cooperation and Development. Pricing energy correctly would create incentives for firms—state and nonstate—to invest in more efficient technology and abatement. If emission taxes and coal transport charges were correct, investment in coal wasting—a priority to curb particulate emissions—would be more economic.

Beyond this, public investments in natural gas to replace home use of coal would increase energy efficiency by two to five times and reduce urban air pollution. Public investments in research and development are critical for bringing new industrial technologies (such as efficient industrial boilers and renewable energy) to the market. Public investment in wastewater treatment is unavoidable and would be more financially viable if sewerage charges were universally introduced and gradually raised to full cost recovery levels. Investments in public transit systems would help avoid the emergence of automobile-based urban transportation systems, which lead to congestion and heavy pollution. Finally, public investments in wastewater systems, financed through increased cost recovery and better pricing, are crucial for conserving water resources and for cleaning China's rivers, lakes, and coastal waters.

• *China must harness its administrative capabilities for the environment.* At the national level better regulations and policy coordination could replace direct investment controls. Some regulations, such as phasing out lead from gasoline by 2000, are essential for environmental improvement. As markets grow regulations should spread to cover township and village industrial enterprises, which are an increasingly large source of pollution but are effectively exempt from regulation. If the government uses its powers to set national standards—for automobile and motorcycle emissions, the energy efficiency of buildings, and so on—it will achieve major improvements in environmental quality.

At the regional level effective management of water basins and airsheds requires setting up regional authorities to overcome the paralysis afflicting current policy making. Similarly, regulation of sulfur emissions, like that in the Air Pollution Prevention and Control Law of 1995, must target areas suffering from acid rain to have the maximum effect and to minimize control costs.

At the urban level environmental master plans could help remove dirty industries from downtown areas and allow for effective urban transportation, two measures that will reduce health damages and pollution loads in the years to come. By 2020 well-organized cities with good public transit could have half as many cars clogging their roads as poorly managed cities without public transit. Finally, environmental education, already under way, will increase citizen demands for a cleaner environment. These demands must find expression in wider community participation in environmental policy making.

Achieving these goals will require some sacrifices in the near term. Pollution control investments will have to double, to about 1 percent of GDP. Still, these costs are small relative to China's annual investments, which total 35 percent of GDP. They are also small relative to the future costs of cleanup if action is delayed. Most important, today's sacrifices are small relative to the enormous improvements in the quality of life that will accrue to future generations.

If China manages to grow by 6 to 7 percent a year for the next two decades or so, by 2020 its population will enjoy incomes roughly equivalent to those in Portugal today. New policies and careful investments made today mean China's children and grandchildren would also enjoy clear water and blue skies.

★ CRIME ★

As Chinese society has become less dependent on state-owned industries and collectivized agriculture, more mobile, less bound by either a
Confucian ethic or the "serve-the-people" ethic of Mao's revolution,
and ever more fixated on wealth as the measure of success, there are
fewer restraints on antisocial activity than at any time since the Party
came to power half a century ago. It is hardly surprising then that during
the two decades since Deng's reform program was initiated, crime rates
in China have spiraled upwards.

Because Chinese society is becoming less rather than more cohesive
as a result of its reform program, the effect of government efforts to bring
the surge of criminal activities under control has been minimal. Indeed,
by the late 1990s China had reached such a degree of decadence and
lawlessness that an increasing number of older people recalled the
1950s—when life under Mao's tutelage was spartan but orderly and
safe—with growing nostalgia.

China's leaders look on the explosion of crime in their country with
great trepidation. Organized crime is a kindred spirit of popular uprising, and everyone is familiar with the history of those dynasties brought
down by such rebellions.

ANGELINA MALHOTRA, SHANGHAI'S DARK SIDE

*When Mao's Communists came to power in 1949, they prided themselves
on having quickly suppressed Shanghai's notorious underworld. However,
as free markets began to create a new class of privately wealthy moguls,
China witnessed a rapid recrudescence of quasi-illegal night spots, gang-
sterism, drug dealing, secret societies, prostitution, and gambling, much of
it owned and run by the police and military.*

*This selection was excerpted from an article by the Indian writer
Angelina Malhotra published in* Asia Inc., *in February 1994.*

• At 2:00 A.M. at the Shanghai Moon Club, on Shanghai's Zhaojia-bang Road, Zhang Qing, a twenty-two-year-old prostitute, sips coconut milk, munches cashews, and talks about how caring her employers are: "I make 1,500 renminbi ($260) a month—about what it costs to live in Shanghai. My boss makes sure I get at least that much." And there's an added comfort: "It's extremely safe to work in this club, extremely safe." It certainly should be. The owner of this karaoke bar–brothel, according to well-informed diplomats, is the Public Security Bureau (PSB), China's national police force. Its closest commercial competitor, located opposite the nearby Jin Jiang Hotel, is a club owned by Shanghai's savior from sin of forty-four years ago, the People's Liberation Army (PLA).

• Customers wishing to enter the Huashan Bao Mi (literally, Protected Secret Club), a more exclusive brothel on Huashan Road, must first know the code: Rap twice and whisper a secret phrase. Finding the week's passwords isn't easy—it takes "about forty-eight hours of *guanxi* (connections) with a policeman friend from the PSB Reporting Station on Yan'an Road," says a dedicated Shanghainese nightclubber, an eye-catching *da ge da* (very large mobile phone) dangling in an imitation leather holster at his groin.

• In downtown Shanghai these nights, *da* (to dial) is more than simply a Chinese telecommunications term. *Da ge* can also mean "big brother" or "leader." Like their counterparts throughout Asia, Shanghai's fast-growing gangland community classifies members as big and small brothers. The question in Mandarin, *Da ge da zai na li?* translates literally to "Where is [your] mobile phone?" But to streetwise Shanghainese the sentence figuratively means, "Are you one with the big brothers?" (Is your triad *guanxi* good?)

Triads? Prostitution? Chinese officialdom involved in vice? In the People's Republic? Wasn't China's bloody revolution, especially in Shanghai, expressly intended to sweep away all such plagues? "Good-bye to all that," wrote Edgar Snow, Mao Zedong's Western journalist friend in 1960, a decade after revolutionaries had allegedly purged this "paradise for adventurers" of its notorious excesses. "Good-bye to all the night life; the gilded singing girl in her enameled hairdo, her stage makeup, her tight-fitting gown with its slit skirt breaking at the silk-clad hip . . . the hundred dance halls and the thousands of taxi dolls; the opium dens and gambling halls . . . the sailors in their smelly bars and friendly brothels on Sichuan Road; the myriad short-time whores and pimps busily darting in and out of the alleyways . . . gone the wickedest and most colorful city of the old Orient: good-bye to all that."

But Snow spoke too soon. Nowadays visitors to Siping Road, in Shanghai's northeast quarter, will come to a blue-glass, neon-crowned tower called Shanghai Taiwan City. Here the decadence, rapacity, the crowing vulgarity of old Shanghai has been reborn: high-slit cheongsam dresses, dimly lit karaoke rooms, male and female masseuses, higher-slit cheongsams, scarlet bathtubs built for two, taxi girls, drinks girls too young to know the characters for cheongsam but available for 580 renminbi ($100) or more a night.

"Preliberation behavior has returned," says a wealthy *tai zi* (or "princeling," a term for cadres' sons), sipping whiskey and smiling from the depths of a plush sofa at a disco elsewhere in the city owned by Hong Kong's Sun Yee On (New Righteousness and Peace) triad. Vice is back with a vengeance in Shanghai, perhaps without the style but with all the invincible swagger of the 1920s. Prostitution, bribery, gambling, extortion have all resurfaced. Old Shanghai's red-light district of Fuzhou Road has reappeared on Maoming Road, thirty blocks to the southwest. The thuggery of Blood Alley (the sailors' haunt mentioned by Snow) has moved fifteen blocks west to chrome-drenched Zhapu Road. Bathhouses are popping up on Shanghai's Dainty Delicacies Street (a most precise translation). It's difficult to find an opium den—though they're said to exist—but easy to buy opium and a silver pipe to smoke it in.

Reemerging, too, are the powerful old alliances among organized crime, the law, and the government. As in the days when Du Yuesheng, chief of Shanghai's Qing Bang (Green Gang), ran narcotics, gambling, and prostitution rackets from his desk at the Opium Suppression Bureau, police, PLA, and Party members are opening their own nightclubs and brothels and signing joint-venture agreements, often with criminal organizations from overseas.

For companies doing business in China, all this may seem a harmless enough repetition of the after-hours scene in any Asian city. But despite its current obsession with markets in all their forms, China's political system has puritan-messianic origins. The purge of old Shanghai was widely welcomed for reasons perhaps best known to Snow's "gilded singing girl." The return of capitalism's excesses strengthens those arguments and invites the return of people who are ferociously antibusiness—China's many remaining Communist diehards.

Nonetheless, the rot continues. "The money to be made through illegal rackets has proven irresistible to many [military and police officers]," observes a Western diplomat whose department tracks Shanghai's corruption. "For the Hong Kong and Taiwanese triads and Japanese yakuza, this is a chance to launder money and cozy up to the mainland government. If the PLA is a partner in your brothel, or the PSB shares the girls from your karaoke bar, who's going to crack down on you?"

No one, from the looks of the action on a recent Shanghai weekend. Some snapshots of the city after dark:

• At the Dedo Club in the Bailemen Hotel, Manager Bright Yan shouts through the reverberating bass: "You need a good partner to run a club in China, and the Public Security is a good partner." This pitch-dark, Berlin-inspired club was opened as a joint venture between the PSB and a consortium of Taiwanese businessmen. An anonymous Japanese group then officially bought out the Taiwanese. Yan formerly managed a nightclub at a PLA-owned hotel nearby; he was tapped to create the same atmosphere at the Dedo: lots of beeper-equipped, available women and free-spending businessmen.

"You have to have the women here," says Yan. "Look, I have a policy. The first time such a woman comes in, I treat her as a guest. The second time, if she behaves legally, I leave her alone. If she behaves illegally, I try to persuade her to leave. The third time, if she behaves illegally, I make her leave." What defines illegal behavior? "Well, doing PR work for herself is okay, but she should not overly harass my customers. Public Security wants this to look like a cultural place, not a red-light zone."

• At the Shanghai Moon Club, Zhang Qing and other PSB-employed girls are so certain of their invincibility that they have no qualms about being photographed or interviewed. The club is a textbook example of the bureau's niche in the world of Shanghai vice. A medium-sized brothel, the Moon caters to top-level PSB officers, mid-level cadres, *tai zi*, and wealthy Hong Kong and Taiwanese businessmen. The bureau allows its club employees to keep all the money they receive from clients; how much the ladies make depends on how fully they fill the old singsong girl's role as hostess, escort, geisha, artiste, whore. The PSB makes its money by charging outrageous prices for private rooms, beverages, and platters of mixed fruit. However, they will gladly provide receipts bearing the chop of the Shanghai Moon Bay Big Restaurant—presumably more acceptable on a cadre's expense report.

Asia, Inc., has learned that all PLA business in Shanghai, both over and under the table, is controlled by the Guard Army of Shanghai Garrison Headquarters (Shanghai Kanshou Jingbei Silingbu), headed by Senior Colonel Gu Siren. His men control the wholly owned PLA clubs as well as the joint-venture operations and collect rent from every vice operation in the city. The only other military group believed to share in the vice income is the well-connected Nanjing Military District Office, which reportedly collects commissions on under-the-table arms shipments and goods smuggled in and out of Shanghai ports.

Shanghai's corruption problem stems in part from Beijing's directive that government agencies should become more financially self-sufficient. An aide to Colonel Gu readily confirmed in a phone interview that the PLA owns Shanghai clubs, restaurants, and other commercial ventures. "Of course we earn a lot of money," he said. "With this money we can treat the army better."

The PLA's myriad commercial enterprises—from publishing to manufacturing to organizing exhibitions—added some $27 billion to its $57 billion 1993 budget, according to John Frankenstein, senior lecturer at Hong Kong University and author of a recent study on Chinese defense production. He believes the PLA splits its profits among commercial ventures, infrastructure upgrades, offshore investments, and the purchase of high-tech hardware. Says Frankenstein, "They've realized since the Gulf War that they need to upgrade their technology. And the budget allocated to them by the government isn't enough to cover the purchases they're looking at." The military's costly shopping list, and the desperation of the less entrepreneurial PSB, means any profitable business is good business. And karaoke brothels are great business—customers consistently drop from $5,000 to upwards of $25,000 a night for whiskey, women, and watermelon.

The PSB concentrates mainly on small and medium-sized brothels, opening them in obscure locations ranging from the Shanghai No. 9 Shop of 100 Things to the Public Security Reporting Station on Yan'an Road. They've opened just two exclusive brothels, the Moon Club and the Huashan Bao Mi. The PLA and the city government, on the other hand, operate at the high end of the price scale. They prefer joint-venture partnerships with Hong Kong's Sun Yee On triads and Taiwan's Four Seas and Bamboo Gang triads. While the PLA plays an active role in providing management and security, the PSB tends to favor so-called flip-over companies. For these, the city government donates the land, "flips over," or transfers, its privileges, and claims half the revenue.

"Joint ventures allow the PLA and the state to make money in clubs they couldn't possibly afford to build. At the same time, it makes them feel in control of vice operations," notes the diplomatic source. "What do the triads get out of it? Well, a relationship with the forces that control Shanghai. And a foothold within the People's Republic before China takes over Hong Kong in 1997, with a chance to recruit members from the police and Party cadre ranks."

The Sun Yee On has set up a number of nightclubs with the PLA on the stretch of Yan'an Road approaching Hongqiao Airport; on Beijing Road in the area of the Portman Shangri-La Hotel, and on Nanjing Road near People's Park. Taiwanese triads have so far confined themselves to the "Taiwan ghetto" area of Siping Road. Siping Road's rebirth as a dodgy area is credited to the Taiwan-based Bamboo Gang.

• A door pass to the Ming Ren (Famous People) brothel at 240 Beijing Road, ensuring nothing more than entry, costs 5,000 to 10,000 renminbi ($865–$1,725)—depending on your *guanxi*. As its name brazenly implies, the Ming Ren caters to high-ranking cadres. One of the few non-Party officials to have gained access to the club laughingly describes its nonegalitarian nature: "You enter the Ming Ren foyer, and in front of you is a very heavy door. In front of that is a beautiful hostess at a desk and on either side guards wearing pith helmets with feathers in them. The few people you see outside the private rooms look at you in this conspiratorial way. The exclusivity makes them feel special, and that feeling is addictive. They think they can control it [vice], but it's going to end up controlling them."

The *getihu* (small businessmen) running independent bars and restaurants claim that financial squeezing by the PSB, PLA, and triads has them coughing up 40 to 60 percent of their profits. Tom Yang, owner of Tom's Famous Grouse Bar behind the Hilton Hotel, complains that, aside from their monthly kickback, the PSB now arbitrarily issues fines. "They'll come and say, 'Oh, your light is too dim today, needs to be very bright, 50 renminbi fine,'" he grumbles. "The next day they say, 'Oh, your light is too bright today, 75 renminbi fine.' They can't be satisfied anymore."

Tommi Chan, manager of the Galaxy Entertainment Club, says he's getting it from all sides. Chan and seven other people, including the disc jockey Ali Wong, were brought over from Hong Kong last year to staff the $2 million club. Chan says the PSB is a partner in the club. But although the police still collect their share of the profits, they stopped giving the club protection after being paid off by wealthy Hong Kong gangsters, who took a liking to it. Without protection, the club is up for grabs.

Says Chan, "We have a big security problem. Local [Chinese] street gangs come and ask for a discount, free drinks, and threaten trouble. Then the Taiwanese gangs come and say, 'Hey, you have trouble, pay us to fix it.'" Now, Wong adds, pacing angrily about and stamping his silver-tipped boots, the PLA wants money to ignore the prostitutes who come in. "And recently I see the same triad gangs I saw in Hong Kong. They come in with choppers and guns and act the way they do in the clubs they control in Kowloon. They're the most scary."

The bartender at another PSB joint-venture nightclub concurs. "Chinese gangs are dangerous, but most trouble is coming from outside [Hong Kong and Taiwan] gangs," he explains. "The rule is, anyone who is not your partner is probably going to give you trouble because everyone is trying to expand their area of control. So you would be foolish to open a club without the PSB, PLA, city government, or a strong gang as a partner."

Foolish and, according to some Shanghai sources, needlessly moralistic. "Really, it's a knee-jerk Western reaction to gasp in horror at the whole thing," complains a longtime Western resident of Shanghai. "First, kickbacks are a part of life in China. Second, if you're going to have vice, who better to run and control it than the police? This allows the government to monitor triads moving into China."

But others hold that the triads control the mainlanders, blinding them with cash. One notable example occurred in 1991, when the Hong Kong film industry's triad-controlled sector raised millions of dollars for victims of China's floods. "Taking the money to Beijing gave triads a heaven-sent opportunity to make *guanxi*," says a Hong Kong–based intelligence source. In a startling admission at a Beijing conference last April, Public Security Minister Tao Siju revealed that a Hong Kong triad group "dispatched 800 of its members to guard our state leader against danger," a reference to an unidentified top cadre's overseas trip. The revelation that Siju met repeatedly with key Sun Yee On members in China last year—followed by his startling comments about Beijing's willingness to work with Hong Kong–based "patriotic triads"—struck fear in those who expect criminal societies to gain in power after 1997. "At this point I'm sure there are top people in each branch of [Hong Kong] government tied to triads," observes the intelligence source.

Such social deterioration in Shanghai, however, means that China once again risks alienating the city's poor and the intelligentsia. Our diplomatic source suggests that growing vice and corruption put the working classes in a 1989 state of mind: "It's the same sort of anger and frustration that fed Tiananmen. Continuing corruption could lead to an economic situation that would lead to a people's rebellion that could cause a central crackdown."

PATRICK TYLER,
CRIME (AND PUNISHMENT) RAGES ANEW IN CHINA

Throughout the 1980s and '90s, rising crime rates in China presaged a series of nationwide yanda, *"strike hard," anticrime drives in which millions of alleged offenders were imprisoned and tens of thousands executed. The vital organs of some executed prisoners were reportedly sold for transplant by avaricious Public Security Bureau officials.*

This selection was excerpted from an article by The New York Times's *former Beijing bureau chief Patrick Tyler, published in the* Times *in July 1996.*

The corpse of the taxi driver was still warm in the backseat when Liao Yongxiong, age twenty-nine, pulled up in front of the Lian Yuan Street branch of the Industrial and Commerce Bank here in the car he had just hijacked.

He concealed his pistol under his jacket and went inside. The three women tellers greeted him; he was a familiar face as one of the security guards who delivered cash each week from the main office. Perhaps he was smiling when he asked, "Could I use the restroom?" because the women were all too willing to unbolt the door to the security area where they were working.

He killed them swiftly, just as he had the taxi driver, with point-blank shots to the head and chest. Only one of the tellers, right before she died on the blood-spattered floor, was able to press the alarm button near her desk as Mr. Liao was escaping with a bag full of cash and securities.

Scenes like this one, which occurred on April 16 on a leafy side street here in this southern Chinese boomtown, Zhongshan, had been virtually unheard of in China during most of the last five decades. Now, suddenly, gangsters are staging a comeback in China, and major crime seems out of control. It has provoked the largest nationwide crackdown on crime in more than a decade and a wave of executions that has alarmed human rights organizations.

Serious crime and crimes involving firearms are rising at more than 20 percent a year, with more than a third of those cases involving gangs.

"We were used to seeing this kind of crime in the movies, but such things have never happened here," said Su Leting, who had just opened a new seafood restaurant and was concerned, as many members of the Zhongshan business community are, that fear of crime would drive foreign investors away. "Many foreigners have started to get nervous about social stability," said Hu Baishou, the editor of the *Zhongshan Daily*, whose front page carried the police composite drawing that led to Mr. Liao's arrest fifty-four hours after the robbery.

Before China opened to the outside world in the late 1970s, totalitarian social controls had all but eliminated major crime, drug trafficking, and prostitution. But with the decentralization of authority, the disappearance of Communist-organized neighborhood communities, and the reappearance of wealth, a criminal reawakening is under way.

Although the overall crime rate in China remains modest in comparison with those of United States and other Western countries, its rapid rise and a sudden surge in major crimes, including murder, armed robbery, and drug trafficking, have triggered a response from Communist Party authorities.

In December 1995 and February 1996, separate criminal gangs in Guangdong Province and in Beijing staged spectacular armored car robberies with precision planning and sophisticated arms. Together they netted more than $2 million in cash. The holdups prompted the Ministry of Public Security to rewrite its budget plan for the next five years to buy more armor, better alarms, and global-positioning devices that use satellite signals to pinpoint the location of cash-carrying vehicles, many of which are not even armored in China.

The day before the Zhongshan bank robbery, the police in Guangdong Province stopped five Jeeps and a truck trying to smuggle 1,200 pounds of heroin into Hong Kong for shipment to the United States and Europe. It was one of the largest single hauls of heroin in history.

In the country's rich coastal provinces, well-armed highway gangs have used prostitutes to lure drivers into robbery and murder traps. Kidnappers are preying on the families of China's new rich, and the heroin trade has spread to all of China's large cities.

But it may have been Mr. Liao's murderous bank heist in this city where Sun Yat-sen, the father of modern China, was born that shocked the Communist leadership in Beijing into ordering in late April a nationwide crackdown on major crimes and gangs.

The so-called Strike Hard crackdown has led in its first two months to tens of thousands of arrests and at least 1,000 executions, more than at any time since the 1983 crackdown on crime, when diplomats say about 10,000 were put to death within a few months.

One of those executed in the current campaign was Mr. Liao, who was shot in the back of the head on April 30 by a police executioner, fifteen days after the crime. Before he died, he was paraded before 5,000 Zhongshan residents at a sports stadium, where he was denounced as a "barbarian" by local Communist Party officials.

"This was a big case, so the masses' reaction was very serious," said Mr. Hu, the newspaper editor who doubles as the deputy chief of propaganda for the Communist Party committee in Zhongshan. "After Liao was arrested, the people were very happy, and they appealed to execute him right away."

Mr. Liao's last words to a state television interviewer were "I do not fear death," and his dramatic appeal to his older brother to care for his three-year-old son was captured by a local photographer.

Around the country so many city and provincial governments have been staging execution rallies that human rights organizations are having trouble keeping an accurate tally.

Even before the crackdown, the human rights group Amnesty International was estimating at least 2,000 executions a year in China, with the death penalty being applied in many cases "as a result of political interference" and "with hardly any safeguards against miscarriages of justice."

In Shanghai, China's largest city, Fu Changlu, an administrative judge of the city's First Intermediate People's Court, said in an interview that "within the realm of the law, we have to be as severe as we can" on the perpetrators of major crime. Anyone who may be executed will be executed, he said, adding, "We will not simply give capital punishment to all criminals, but those who deserve it will get it."

An internal Public Security document issued in April characterized the rising crime rate as a outgrowth of "the accumulation of social wealth and a growing gap between rich and ordinary people" that is "forcing us to take measures to more effectively track and crush crime."

Crime is also making news. Many local Communist Party newspapers have dropped some of the dull essays on Party theory from their front pages to make room for the latest criminal outrage.

One "vampire gang" in northeastern China, a newspaper reported, enslaved homeless children and sold their blood to hospitals. And, in Hebei Province, a night security guard was reportedly sentenced to life in prison for ringing up $6,000 in international charges to telephone sex lines in the United States.

Even the Communist Party flagship paper, the *People's Daily*, which likes to chronicle the sins of Western society, was forced to give prominent display last winter to the murder of Li Peiyao, the vice chairman of the National People's Congress, China's parliament. Mr. Li was murdered during the burglary of his home by one of his body guards from the People's Armed Police.

Chinese experts say the numbers of gangs and "secret societies" are growing faster than the police can count them. One nationwide police tally found that in 1991 there were about 500 known criminal gangs comprising a few dozen members to more than 100. By 1995 the tally had leaped to about 10,000 gangs with a total membership of 500,000 to 1 million members.

Cai Shaoqing, a professor at Nanjing University who studies China's criminal history, says most gangs are made up of unemployed youths and former prisoners.

Not since 1983, after the first stirrings of capitalism in China had revived criminal opportunities in a huge population accustomed to deprivation, have Communist Party leaders been so compelled to whip up a national campaign against crime. Their decision has prompted speculation about its larger political meaning.

Some experts say this crime wave provides the younger generation of Chinese leaders an opportunity to demonstrate their toughness on law and order issues, which are becoming more important as China's economy develops.

But the new campaign carries the unmistakable echoes of earlier power struggles in which popular revulsion to the seamy side of capitalism was exploited by Party conservatives to improve their standing. This revulsion was the impetus for the 1983 crackdown.

In the culture of the Communist Party, crime is associated with the chaos and corruption of the pre-Communist era. Even the family of Deng Xiaoping, the country's paramount leader, was a victim. As a young revolutionary, Deng got word in 1938 that his father had been set upon by bandits and killed in their native Sichuan.

But the crackdown has fostered alarm among legal scholars that China's efforts to establish the rule of law in its criminal justice system could be undermined by the overtones of a "mass movement"—a term associated with the political persecutions of the Maoist era—against crime.

"The leaders are not yet putting this crackdown forward as a movement," said Jiang Ping, one of China's most prominent legal scholars and former head of the Politics and Law University in Beijing, "but it has the smell of a movement because the whole party is behind it and the whole nation is involved."

Mr. Jiang, like many legal scholars, also questions whether China's heavy reliance on the death penalty has had any effect. "The first crackdown really began in 1984, and you could say that for these ten years or so the more we crack down the more serious the crime situation becomes," he said. "This time, the crackdown may be connected with the need to insure stability as the economic and social shortcomings emerge" in China's reform era and create "disaffection among the masses that can lead to the spark that sets off trouble."

For now, the crackdown appears to enjoy popular support. Even Mr. Liao's neighbors in the village of Wuguishan could not argue with the death penalty verdict against him. "It was fair," said a friend of the family, as he sat in Mr. Liao's courtyard home under portraits of his ancestors and the ashes of incense sticks recently burned before them. "If you kill a man, you should pay compensation with your life," he said.

VIII. THE RULE OF LAW, RIGHTS, AND PRISONS

■

Although Articles 35 and 36 of China's Constitution guarantee that Chinese citizens "enjoy freedom of speech, of the press, of assembly, of association, and of demonstration" as well as "freedom of religion," and although the government is a signatory of the UN-mandated Universal Declaration of Human Rights guaranteeing basic individual freedoms to all, state-sponsored violations of basic rights remain endemic in China. The Chinese government's and the Party's perceived right to interfere with the exercise of individual rights grows out of their original presumption that China is a "socialist state" governed by a "dictatorship of the proletariat" in which only members of the "revolutionary classes"—such as workers, peasants, and soldiers—technically enjoy legitimate rights. Even during the era of Deng's reforms, when the Party became so much less intrusive in the lives of ordinary people and some legal reforms were initiated, leaders continued to defend the theoretical right for the Party to rule in the name of the proletariat and to suppress so-called counterrevolutionaries, namely, anyone whose dissenting voice challenged Party hegemony.

During the Deng years it was over the question of human rights and the rule of law—especially after the Beijing Massacre, when Westerners were reminded of China's rights abuses in the most graphic way—that Sino-U.S. relations often turned and sometimes foundered.

Andrew Nathan,
Getting Human Rights Right

The questions of whether it is legitimate for one government to concern itself with the way another government treats its people and whether one country has the right to pass judgment on the human rights record of another have engendered repeated and contentious debates between China and the United States. These debates have arisen out of the almost evangelical belief of many Americans that, since "all men are . . . endowed . . . with certain unalienable rights," violations of people's rights in one country are the business of citizens in any country. This posture has collided directly with China's view of its right to sovereignty and to not be subject to "hostile foreign forces" "interfering in its internal affairs."

This selection was excerpted from an article by the Columbia University political scientist and rights scholar Andrew Nathan published in The Washington Quarterly, *Spring 1997.*

The State of Human Rights in China

The international law of human rights centers on the Universal Declaration of Human Rights, adopted by the United Nations General Assembly on December 10, 1948, and on the two covenants—one on civil and political rights, the other on economic, social, and cultural rights—adopted by the UN General Assembly in 1966. Like all nations, China is bound by the Declaration. Although it has not acceded to the two covenants, they represent appropriate standards against which to evaluate any country's behavior. China has acceded to and is bound by nine UN human rights conventions, including the one against torture, and a number of International Labor Organization (ILO) conventions related to workers' rights.

The international human rights regime requires individual liberty, but it does not require any particular kind of political or economic system. As the product of negotiations among all nations, the regime is not a weapon in the clash of civilizations. In light of Chinese fears of Western subversion, it is important to separate human rights from democratization and treat it as the international idea that it is, not as a code word for Westernization.

Under Mao Zedong, and even more rapidly since the beginning of Deng Xiaoping's reform, China made progress in supplying its citizens with economic and social rights. Living standards have increased, compulsory education has been extended to nine years, adult literacy stands at 79 percent according to official figures, and life expectancy at sixty-nine exceeds that of many middle-income countries. Nevertheless, the record may not be as good as it is generally thought to be. A recent World Bank study finds that more than 350 million Chinese live in conditions of grinding poverty. But pending more research the focus of foreign concerns is appropriately on the deprivation of civil and political rights.

In this realm pervasive and systematic violations occur, many of them carried out as matters of government policy. The violations that should be of central international concern are those that are conducted by government agents, transgress China's international obligations, and are indefensible under even the most culturally relativist standards. The fact that such violations are sometimes carried out under the auspices of Chinese law should not mislead policy makers. Many abuses transgress the clear language of the Chinese Constitution, the law of criminal procedure, and other enactments. Governments apply their own laws, but when they stretch the law beyond all sense they abuse, not interpret, it. A good example is [1989 dissident] Wang Dan's illegal pretrial detention and the four-hour show trial at which he was convicted.

Nor should the United States be dissuaded from recognizing rights violations by the fact that many Chinese citizens have gained new liberties of personal movement and private political expression under Deng's reforms, or by the fact that the victims of rights abuses are a minority. As in U.S. history, rights are not rights when they are limited to actions the government chooses to tolerate, or to speech by persons with whom the government agrees.

The major categories of rights abuses are as follows:

• Imprisonment, arbitrary detention, or forced exile of people who have not used or advocated violence but whose political beliefs counter those of the government. The victims include democracy movement activists arrested for such acts as writing articles and petitioning the National People's Congress, Tibetans detained for verbally supporting independence, Mongols detained for a cultural revival movement, people detained for protesting about personal grievances, and people accused of divulging state secrets for circulating publicly available information.

• Religious repression, including the arrests and beatings of adherents of the autonomous Catholic and Protestant movements; detention of Tibetans for religious practices: and the house arrest of a six-year-old child who was designated by the Dalai Lama as the incarnation of the Panchen Lama. Religious victims are often charged as counterrevolutionaries, yet in many instances they have carried out no political acts.

• Violations related to criminal procedure, including lack of procedural safeguards against police abuse, especially during the process of shelter and investigation *(shourong shencha)*; insufficient safeguards against unlimited detention without trial; failure to provide fair trials (no publicity, insufficient provision for notice to family and preparation of a defense, lack of a presumption of innocence); lack of independence of the judiciary; and the widespread use of "reeducation through labor" as a form of imprisonment at police initiative without benefit of trial (as in the recent case of Liu Xiaobo). The 1995 Judges Law and 1996 amendments to the 1979 Criminal Procedure Law addressed some of these issues, but they did not resolve them.

• Torture and abuse of inmates of prisons and labor camps, and imposition of forced labor on inmates. The Chinese government has signed the convention against torture, has intermittently campaigned against the use of torture by police and jailers, and reiterated the outlawing of torture in its 1994 Prison Law. But the practice remains prevalent. In the case of many political prisoners, it is evidently condoned by the central authorities. Prominent political prisoners recently or currently mistreated in prison included Wei Jingsheng, Liu Gang, and Xu Wenli; those denied adequate medical care included Chen Ziming and Bao Tong.

• Forced resettlement, suppression of dissent, and violation of labor rights in connection with work on the Three Gorges project.

• Forced abortion and sterilization as part of population-planning practices. These acts violate declared central government policy yet are carried out by local officials on what appears to be a widespread basis.

Other civil and political rights violations have been less noticed in the outside world but are also appropriate subjects of concern. These include denial of the right to strike, denial of the freedom of the Chinese and foreign press, mistreatment of homosexuals, eugenic practices, and state interference in the practice of Islam and Buddhism.

A number of issues that have drawn foreign attention are more debatable as rights violations. In dealing with them, Western policy should focus on the ways in which these actions clearly violate international law. Such issues include the following:

- *Capital punishment.* Its use is not against international or Chinese law. Yet China uses the penalty exceptionally widely and with grossly inadequate safeguards. Moreover, international law considers public execution, still widely practiced in China, to be a violation of human dignity.
- *Harvesting of organs from condemned prisoners for transplantation.* Organ transplant does not violate international law. But in China the need for organs reportedly leads to frequent violations of due process, and the authorities seldom obtain donor consent.
- *Kidnapping, trafficking, and abuse of women and girls.* The government has campaigned against these practices, yet they continue on a widespread basis, and some analysts plausibly argue this is only possible with the cooperation of local officials.
- *Export of prison labor products to the United States.* This violates U.S. law but not international law. But when prison labor is compulsory, as appears to be the case in Chinese prisons and labor camps, it is prohibited by ILO conventions.

Human Rights as Realpolitik

It is often noted that human rights represent Western values, and that no China policy that ignores them can achieve stable public support. It is less widely realized that promotion of human rights serves Western interests. Humanitarian sympathy and moral outrage can drive human rights policy, but consistency of purpose and clarity of focus must come from thinking through human rights as Realpolitik.

The United States has devoted increasing effort since the end of the Cold War to strengthening the international system of rules that benefit the West in such areas as arms proliferation, trade, and the environment. It should give equal attention to fortifying the international human rights regime, which was one of the earliest regimes the world started building after World War II. This regime provides the framework for countries to intercede peacefully against domestic abuses in other states that potentially have serious international consequences. It has growing utility in the post–Cold War world as part of an emerging new international order.

First, the theory of the "democratic peace" that goes back to Immanuel Kant remains a good guide to policy, even though it is not universally accepted by political scientists. The exercise of political rights by citizens is conducive both to reducing governmental misjudgments in foreign affairs and to creating a more peaceful, rational, and predictable foreign policy. Countries that respect the rights of their own citizens are less likely to start wars, export drugs, harbor terrorists, or generate refugees.

In China's case respect for human rights is a precondition for peaceful resolution of the Taiwan issue and successful management of Hong Kong's transition to sovereignty by the People's Republic on July 1, 1997. The human rights gap is a source of Beijing's difficulties in both situations.

Second, China's stability and prosperity have been declared interests of the West since the early 1970s, when Henry Kissinger was secretary of state and Richard Nixon was the first president to travel to Communist China. A stable and prosperous China will anchor a stable Asia and contribute to global prosperity through trade. A corrupt, unstable, economically stagnant China will contribute to regional disorder, pollution, and refugee flows, and in the extreme case could heavily tax outside resources for relief. China's rapid development has created such a mobilized and sophisticated population that the government can no longer legitimize itself without allowing a measure of political freedom and participation, and without legitimacy its political stability is at risk. The latest repressions testify to the fragility of the regime, which sees a handful of peaceful dissenters as an intolerable threat to its survival.

This is not to say that China should be pushed to adopt a particular model of political system. But long-term stability will elude it until it honors the political freedoms so wisely recognized in all four of its own constitutions since the founding of the People's Republic. This argument has been propounded within China by Party reformers since the mid-1980s. It is now being promoted by officials who are experimenting with village-level elections aimed at consolidating, not undermining, Chinese Communist Party power.

Third, it is sometimes argued that human rights violations are a necessary, temporary trade-off to achieve economic development. But few Chinese rights violations (for example, mistreatment of prisoners or violations of due process) have any plausible link to development. The few that have—such as deprivations of freedom of speech and political action, which may be considered necessary to keep political order—lead more often to developmental mistakes than to developmental achievements. Others, such as coercive population planning practices, are shortcuts to achieve targets that could be achieved equally well or better by legal methods, and probably with more secure results. Meanwhile, the violations in themselves worsen the quality of life and constitute a form of underdevelopment unmeasured in gross domestic product and other statistics.

The relationship between human rights and development is in fact the reverse. Systems that violate political rights tend to generate distorted communications and commit policy mistakes. Suppression of information contributed to a vast famine during the Great Leap Forward, devastation of forests, salinization of farmland, and a series of dam collapses in 1975. Repression need not be widespread to send a signal to all Chinese that they should remain silent. Rights violations throttle the channels of discussion that China desperately needs to manage its problems in the midst of rapid economic and social change. Enforced silence worsens corruption, removes checks to environmental damage, and clears the field for potential megadisasters like the Three Gorges Dam, which specialists think may do extensive ecological damage. Nor can China compete successfully in world markets in the age of information when it filters Internet access, tries to control financial reporting, censors the domestic and foreign press, and otherwise interferes with the flow of ideas.

Fourth, human rights diplomacy is often erroneously presented as standing in conflict with Western business interests. In fact, even at the height of the Most-Favored Nation (MFN) debates in the United States, U.S.-China trade boomed. In 1995, placing orders for European-made Airbus Industrie airplanes, Premier Li Peng indicated that the Chinese government was penalizing the competing U.S. supplier, Boeing, for U.S. human rights pressure. But most observers believe the Airbus decision was made for business reasons, with the human rights linkage tacked on later. I know of no other case in which the Chinese government discriminated against a U.S. company because of U.S. human rights activism. Continued U.S. division over human rights, however, may encourage the Chinese to start enforcing such linkages.

Rule of law is essential to protect U.S. and other foreign interests (business and otherwise) in China. Today those Chinese who make and enforce the laws (legislators, procurators, and judges) are chosen, promoted, and kept or fired at the pleasure of political authorities. They write, adopt, revise, and apply the laws under Party supervision, with little independent input.

Enforcement of the laws is arbitrary, and the courts have no autonomy. The lawlessness of the Chinese legal system is experienced as much by foreign businesspeople as by Chinese dissidents. What happened to Wei Jingsheng has happened in different forms to the Australian businessman James Peng, International Monetary Fund official Hong Yang, Royal Dutch Shell employee Xiu Yichun, and others.

If the law is a system of rules that are known in advance and enforceable by appeal to independent arbiters, then China's legal system will become a rule of law only when it incorporates respect for human rights. It is not, as some think, expanding the legal code that will solve the human rights problem but making advances toward a true rule of law and guarantees of human rights that will solve the problems with the legal code. A human rights–neutral improvement of the Chinese legal system is impossible.

The community of nations has a strategic interest in improving the human rights regime in all countries, not just in China. But China's demographic and geographic size, its strategic and economic importance, its status as a permanent member of the UN Security Council, and its position of leadership in the developing world make international interest in Chinese human rights practices greater than interest in many other nations' practices.

To be sure, the Chinese government fears it will be criticized and even overthrown when citizens are able to exercise freedom of speech. But repressing criticism is not a long-term strategy for stabilizing power, as many in the ruling party know. An old Chinese proverb says, "You can dam a river forever, but not the mouths of the people."

Shaping Policy

If the goal is to change China's behavior, the best means is to enforce and strengthen the international human rights regime. By disentangling human rights from democratization and "Western values," such a policy can avoid stimulating reactive nationalism and regain the polemical initiative lost to proponents of "Asian values" in China and Southeast Asia. By multilateralizing the human rights issue, the United States can work more successfully with allies and can more readily enlist the cooperation of sympathetic policy makers within the Chinese bureaucracy. Multilateralism would make it harder for the Chinese government to divide its critics abroad. But fundamentally, multilateralism is important because a major goal of human rights policy is to strengthen multilateral institutions.

Human rights are not invariably the highest priority of China policy, but their importance is greater than the present administration gives them. Unless human rights are pursued consistently, Washington will lose a prime opportunity for change. When trade-offs must be made to pursue other interests, the costs of failing to build a vital international human rights regime need to be weighed more accurately in the balance than they have been in the past.

Patience and persistence are crucial to a successful human rights policy, as they are to building any other international regime. The Chinese sometimes complain that Western human rights negotiators keep increasing their demands. In fact, the negotiation process regarding human rights should be no different from negotiating with China (or any other country) on issues related to other international regimes, such as arms control, intellectual property rights, or market access. Both sides should realize that the regime-building process is a long one; they should acknowledge long-term goals while pursuing urgent or achievable goals. The regime-building process has achieved much so far. Its further progress should not be sacrificed to a desire for smooth, conflict-free relations.

Conclusion

The Chinese government has succeeded in convincing many analysts that human rights pressure is counterproductive. Beijing has signaled that the subject cannot be part of normal diplomacy because of its need to "save face," succession politics and the rise of the military, national pride in recovered sovereignty after a century of neocolonialism and exploitation, and the nationalistic "feelings of the Chinese people." Beijing has persuaded many that it cannot negotiate over human rights.

It is always useful for a government to convince its interlocutors that it is too rigid to bend on an issue. But in fact, in its human rights diplomacy as in other areas of foreign policy, China has behaved as a realist power, making those concessions it perceived as necessary to influence states with which it was interacting and not making them when they were not deemed necessary. Since the late 1970s a Western human rights policy combining pressure and assistance has successfully supported an internal Chinese evolution toward improved human rights, achieving greater results when it was firm and lesser results when it was weak. The historical record suggests that the main obstacle to maintaining an effective human rights policy toward China is not Chinese intransigence but Western indecision.

China today understands the U.S. human rights policy as one of hostility, restriction, containment, and punishment. The policy should instead be articulated in a way that conveys that the United States accepts China's legitimate security and other needs but wants China to play by the international rules. It should also stress that the desire to build an international human rights regime is not a code word for subverting the Chinese system of government. At home the Clinton administration needs to articulate its strategic rationale and thus build a domestic consensus for including human rights in its China policy.

Of all the international regimes with which the outside world wants a rising China to comply—the missile technology control regime, intellectual property rights, the World Trade Organization, and others—the international human rights regime is the oldest and the best established in international and domestic Chinese law. Less real conflict of interest exists between Chinese interests and the international regime in human rights than is the case with other areas of dispute. Moreover, the human rights regime is easily grasped by the relevant domestic publics—U.S., Chinese, European, Japanese, and others—and it can serve as a symbolic anchor for the otherwise somewhat elusive idea that the West wishes both to acknowledge China as a great power and to insist on China's obeying world rules as a great power should. In dealing with a realist power like China, the West will do better in building the human rights regime if it acts as a realist itself and maintains a consistent stand on behalf of its own interests.

Yi Ding,
Opposing Interference in Other Countries' Internal Affairs Through Human Rights

Stung by foreigners' condemnation of their handling of the 1989 demonstrations, Chinese propaganda organs claimed that every nation has a right to put down "turmoil" and that overseas critiques of rights violations in China were misguided because there is no such thing as "universal and abstract rights" that take precedence over the legal codes of each sovereign country.

This selection was excerpted from a piece published in the Beijing Review *in November 1989.*

In the turn of spring and summer this year, turmoil and then a counterrevolutionary rebellion in Beijing attempted to overthrow the leadership of the Chinese Communist Party and subvert the government of the socialist People's Republic of China. At first the Chinese government imposed martial law in some sections of Beijing in accordance with the Constitution. Only later did it take drastic measures to crush the counterrevolutionary rebellion.

These actions were the proper, rational, and lawful actions of a sovereign nation and have been understood and supported by most countries in the world. However, some foreign forces made unwarranted charges and wantonly interfered with this country's internal affairs. This, of course, sparked great indignation and opposition from the Chinese people. Consequently, these foreign forces explained they were only showing their concern for human rights and that human rights have no boundaries. They maintained that concern for human rights in other countries does not constitute interference in those countries' internal affairs. This opinion is utterly unjustified.

No Abstract Human Rights Exist

First, there are no universal and abstract human rights. Countries with different ideologies and social systems and at different stages of development have different understandings of the basic concept of human rights.

The traditional Western view is that human rights are natural, inborn, and inalienable. But from the Marxist standpoint, all rights emerge historically and are based on economic relations in society. Accepted "human rights" are only those which have been recognized in law by the dominant class of a country.

As for the scope of human rights, the West's traditional view is to stress the individual's political and civil rights which are protected under law. But this view obviously does not consider different levels of economic development or political conditions in different countries. The third world countries, given their national conditions, stress collective rights. They regard collective human rights as the foundation of individual rights and the precondition for individuals to enjoy all rights and freedoms. They also consider that economic, social, and cultural rights cannot be separated from civil and political rights. These two aspects are equally important—full economic rights and guarantees are material conditions for realizing the civil and political rights.

Some Western scholars also recognize differences in the theory and concept of human rights. Hedley Bull, for example, contends, "We should remember how slender is the consensus that unites the governments of the world today in the matter of human rights" and that "the reluctance evident in the international community even to experiment with the conception of a right of humanitarian intervention reflects not only an unwillingness to jeopardize the rules of sovereignty and nonintervention by conceding such a right to individual states but also the lack of any agreed doctrine as to what human rights are."

Second, there are, fundamentally, no universal human rights that override the laws of various countries. The human rights we talk about today exist not only in theory but also in the concrete form of specific laws. In the international community, most countries outline the citizen's basic rights and freedoms through internal legislation, especially through their constitutions or related documents. These internal laws are the legal basis for the enjoyment and realization of human rights. Without these specific laws, the individual's rights and freedoms cannot be said to exist and individuals cannot ask for guarantees of their rights and freedoms.

Different concepts of human rights are evident in the way various countries draft their laws indeed. These laws are unique to each country and sometimes contradict the legislation of another nation.

According to the Western view, the right of property is an important component of human rights. For example, the idea that private property is sacred and inviolable appears in similar form in the constitutions of the United States, France, Japan, and the Netherlands. Property rights — as one aspect of human rights — are essential to maintain the capitalist system.

This principle is quite different from those of countries that pursue a socialist policy of public ownership. For example, in the constitutions of China, the Soviet Union, and Romania, the system of public and collective ownership is stressed. Public property is sacred and inviolable, while private property is protected according to the laws.

Given these differences in human rights legislation, where is the legal justification for saying there are no national boundaries for human rights?

Third, international documents relating to human rights do not supersede the laws of any country. Human rights documents adopted by the United Nations, such as the Universal Declaration of Human Rights,

International Covenant on Civil and Political Rights, and International Covenant on Economic, Social, and Cultural Rights have played a great role in promoting and encouraging respect for human rights and for fundamental freedoms. However, they have failed to create specific and common laws about human rights. The reasons are these:

1. Sovereign countries played a leading role in drawing up these international documents. Without their involvement and agreement, these documents would not exist.

2. International documents about human rights only state some general principles. The power of explaining and practicing these principles is in the hands of sovereign countries. In fact, each country practices these principles according to its unique situation. For example, British Chancellor Lord Denning said that the International Covenant on Civil and Political Rights "is so wide as to be incapable of practical application. So it is much better for us to stick to our own statutes and principles and only look to the convention in case of doubt."

3. International declarations on human rights must be implemented through the legislative, judicial, and administrative measures of each signatory. For example, the International Covenant on Civil and Political Rights stipulates that each signatory is permitted "to adopt such legislative or other measures as may be necessary to give effect to the rights recognized in the present Covenant."

The fact that many countries have reservations about international conventions on human rights also proves there is no such thing as rights that completely transcend national boundaries and legal limits. As a matter of fact, not a single international convention or agreement passed by the United Nations has been accepted without reservation by member states.

Pretext for Meddling in Other Countries' Internal Affairs

The theory that human rights know no national boundary is not only theoretically wrong and legally groundless but also very harmful politically and practically. The preachers of this theory say that they are merely concerned about human rights and do not intend to interfere in other countries' internal affairs. This runs counter to the facts. A certain country has used its embassy to provide shelter for a criminal [Fang Lizhi] wanted by the host country, intervening in the host's normal judicial activities; allowed wanted criminals to conduct activities aimed at subverting another government; discussed the internal affairs of another country in its own Congress and imposed economic sanctions on that country just because they share different values; and even set as a precondition for improving bilateral relations the lifting of martial law. Does this represent gross interference in another country's internal affairs?

On December 9, 1981, UN Resolution 36/103 adopted a Declaration on the Inadmissibility of Intervention and Interference in the Internal Affairs of States. The declaration stated, "No State or group of States has the right to intervene or interfere in any form or any reason whatsoever in the internal and external affairs of other States." It further added, "The duty of a State (is) to refrain from the exploitation and the distortion of human rights issues as a means of interference in the internal affairs of States, or exerting pressure on other States or creating distrust and disorder within and among States or groups of States."

Though favorable to peace and development, the world situation today is still complicated. Any attempt to impose one's values, political beliefs, and social systems on others will lead only to friction and tension in international relations. Only the Five Principles of Peaceful Coexistence, including the principle of noninterference in each other's internal affairs, provide a healthy guide for international relations.

The Chinese government has repeatedly stated that China will continue its independent foreign policy of peace and the policy of reform and openness. We believe that on the basis of the Five Principles of Peaceful Coexistence, the friendly and cooperative ties between China and other countries will be further strengthened and developed.

Xu Liangying, Chinese Officialdom's Miraculous and Unique Conception of Human Rights

Despite the risks inherent in publicly criticizing official Party policy in China, a few courageous voices have spoken out during the 1980s and '90s. Most have suffered consequences for their audacity. One such voice is that of the septuagenarian historian of science and translator of Albert Einstein, Xu Liangying. Since the 1980s Xu has repeatedly defended freedom of expression and mocked the Party's self-serving notion of sovereignty as retrograde and their abuses of human rights as a humiliation to all modern Chinese.

This selection was excerpted from an article published in China Rights Forum, *Summer 1994.*

When the British foreign secretary visited China recently, a high official said to him, "It is not fair to force the developed nations' view of human rights onto developing countries. China will certainly not accept America's concept of human rights." It is difficult to suppress laughter when officials make such enlightening remarks, since they are obviously in contradiction with the facts of the development of world civilization and of the history of China, and furthermore clearly violate the fundamental spirit and principles of the United Nations' Universal Declaration of Human Rights. As a citizen of what is, after all, called the "People's Republic," I cannot but feel ashamed and discouraged at hearing such braggadocio from those in power.

What can be meant by an "American concept of human rights" except what is stated in the 1776 United States Declaration of Independence: "We hold these truths to be self-evident, that all men are created equal, that they are endowed by the Creator with certain unalienable Rights, that among these are Life, Liberty and the pursuit of Happiness—That to secure these rights, Governments are instituted among Men, deriving their just powers from the consent of the governed"; and in the 1791 constitutional amendment which reads "Congress shall make no law respecting an establishment of religion, or prohibiting the free exercise thereof; or abridging the freedom of speech, or of the press; or the right of the people peaceably to assemble, and to petition the Government for a redress of grievances."

Are these human rights especially American? Certainly not! This conception of human rights was not exclusively grown on American soil but was also a product of the European Enlightenment of the seventeenth and eighteenth centuries and of the "Glorious Revolution" of 1688 in England, while the 1789 French Revolution's Declaration of the Rights of Man developed it even further. The Declaration of Independence and the Declaration of the Rights of Man are both milestones in the history of human progress, on which are carved humankind's ideals and principles of human rights and democracy. These principles are the foundation stones of modern civilization and apply everywhere, not merely within particular national borders.

Is this conception of human rights concepts applicable to "developing countries"? For the answer, let us look at some statistics. Two hundred years ago the United States and France were both agricultural nations, with no mechanized industry at all, only handicraft production. However backward China is today, it is at a level of economic development not even remotely comparable to that of England, the United States, and France 200 years ago. This shows that the human rights issue really has very little to do with the question of economic development; using an underdeveloped economy as an excuse for rejecting the universally accepted human rights concepts is a gross deception.

Will China "certainly not" accept these concepts of human rights? Only someone who knows virtually nothing about Chinese history could make such a strange statement. In 1905, years before this high official was even born, Sun Yat-sen included the idea of civil rights (actually human rights) as one of his three great guiding political principles, which together made up the Three People's Principles. The Provisional Constitution of the Republic of China (1912), which marked his establishment of the first republic in Asia, stated that the people enjoyed seven types of rights and freedoms, including "freedoms of expression, writing, publication, and of assembly and association." In the first issue of the magazine *New Youth* in 1915, Chen Duxiu (one of the founders of the Chinese Communist Party) issued a warning cry: "The reason for Europe's superiority in recent times," he wrote, was its achievements in science and human rights, which are "like the two wheels of a vehicle"; "if the people of this nation wish to escape these benighted times, . . . they must rise up immediately and pursue [a system] which accords respect to both science and human rights." Even Mao Zedong in 1945 openly declared that China "would put into practice Mr. Sun Yat-sen's Three People's Principles, Abraham Lincoln's principle of 'to the people, by the people, and for the people,' and Roosevelt's four great freedoms." After 1949, despite significant deficiencies in the articles of the Constitution concerning the rights of citizens, in essence they accepted the world's universal human rights principles. (As to whether they were ever put into practice, that is another story.) Bellowing that "China will certainly not accept" this kind of human rights conception ignores the facts of Chinese history and the Constitution currently in force. It is doubtful whether the "China" the official spoke of actually represents many people at all.

But the "miraculous conception" expressed by this member of the power elite does represent several articles of faith: that "having power, you have everything," and that once you have power in your hands, you can brazenly trample human rights underfoot, as Mao Zedong did. On the day when this official met with U.S. Secretary of State Warren Christopher, his power extended even to the entrance to my home, where, without any legal procedure at all, police were ordered to block the door and not to allow me to go out or to let my friends and relatives come in. I was under this type of house arrest for three days. Why? The reason was simply that *The New York Times*, in a report on March 11, published the "Call to Improve the Human Rights Situation in Our Country" that the seven of us had issued, and interviewed me. During our interview the reporter asked me whether I wanted to meet with Christopher. I replied, "Originally I did not plan to do so, but if he wants to see me, I would like to meet him." Because of our appeal and this one remark, the authorities deprived me of my personal freedom for three days, from March 12 to 14. On the afternoon of March 19, they again began to restrict my movements, and the police did not leave until March 21. The personal freedom of Ding Zilin (see Ding Zilin, "Who They Were") and Jiang Peikun, also signatories of the appeal, began to be restricted on March 10, and their telephone was cut off as well.

We made a reasoned appeal for improvements in the human rights situation, and as a result we immediately experienced flagrant violations of our own rights. This is a concrete and vivid manifestation of what is meant by the official "human rights conception" "with Chinese characteristics." This exclusive "human rights conception" of the power elite should really be called a "miraculous and unique human rights conception," since it has virtually nothing in common with the view of human rights generally accepted by the rest of humanity. This new aspect of China's human rights situation is worthy of note.

WANG YU, LIU GANG: STALWART RESISTANCE

Even in the more cosmopolitan China of the 1990s, the price of exercising freedom of political expression has all too often been arrest and imprison-

ment. If intimidation did not silence dissidents, they were dealt with in two major ways: (1) They were "administratively detained" and sent to "reeducation through labor" camps without formal charges, trials, or sentences being handed down. (2) They were charged with such nebulous crimes as having engaged in "counterrevolutionary propaganda and incitement" or having sought to "overthrow the Chinese government," tried in mock trials that were usually closed, and sent off to do long terms of "reform through labor."

After participating in the 1989 demonstrations, the Beijing University physics student Liu Gang was charged with "conspiracy to overthrow the government," sentenced to a six-year term, and imprisoned in the notorious Lingyuan No. 2 Labor Reform Detachment in Manchuria's Liaoning Province.

This selection was excerpted from an interview by Wang Yu with Liu Gang, published in China Rights Forum, *Fall 1996.*

WANG YU: How is your health now? What are your plans for the future?

LIU GANG: My health is good. I'm keeping myself very busy, studying English every day, returning home late. My life is quite regular.

In September I want to start a university course—I'm giving priority to my education right now so that I'll be able to provide for myself in the future. Of course I will continue the struggle for democracy and human rights.

WY: I've read that while you were in prison you suffered from a number of serious ailments. I know you endured great hardship in prison; did the torture and terrible living conditions cause these health problems?

LG: Before I went to prison, I had gastrointestinal problems after going on hunger strike, but I received treatment and everything was fine. But in prison they put me in solitary confinement and starved me, forced me to sit still on a narrow bench day after day, and stomped on my stomach. As a result my problems returned, but this time they were far more serious.

The heart problems were caused by beatings with the electric baton. In prison this type of torture is routine: every time we would go out to work, a few of us were beaten with the electric baton as a way of "killing the chicken to frighten the monkey"—punishing a few in order to warn the rest. When American journalists came to look at the prison, the prison authorities made sure that there were no electric batons to be seen, but in fact the use of electric batons is extremely common.

As for solitary confinement, we called it "prison within prison." You can imagine what kind of a place it was. There are strict regulations on solitary confinement—a prisoner is not supposed to be put there for more than half a month—but these regulations are ignored. After three months in solitary confinement, you are likely to develop hemorrhoids and anal fistulae. [Prisoners in solitary are generally forced to sit still for long periods.]

I had pain in my left ankle for many years because I was forced to wear leg irons for long periods.

WY: What sort of behavior would result in these types of brutal treatment?

LG: I think they had a problem with my attitude. Right after I arrived in prison, I took the lead in singing songs, staging hunger strikes, refusing to write self-criticisms or to cooperate when called in for interrogation. I was influencing the other prisoners, so they segregated me in the "strict regime" brigade and held me in a solitary confinement cell.

At the time my thoughts were, I can observe labor camp discipline, but I refuse to accept coercive inculcation and thought reform. I felt that I had not committed any crime, so why should I adopt the attitude of a criminal?

WY: In August 1992 the State Council Information Office issued the White Paper "The Situation of Criminal Reform in China," which discussed "the principal rights enjoyed by prisoners under current Chinese law," including the principle "under no circumstances shall human dignity be insulted or personal safety violated." Did you have a lawyer who could protest your treatment?

LG: I had a lawyer, but I was not permitted to see him until just two days before my trial. And he seemed to be more like the public prosecutor than even the prosecutor was. All he did was look for various ways to prove that I was guilty, to get me to confess. I demanded a new lawyer but to no avail. How could this sort of lawyer protest on my behalf?

When I was at Lingyuan being beaten, tortured with the electric baton, and shackled, my father went to talk to the prison authorities and was told, "There are no prisons where the inmates are not beaten."

When you are in prison, knowing that someone outside is paying attention makes all the difference in the world.

I remember once I found a way to get a letter to my brother to relay to the outside world. But after he got the letter, he kept it to himself. His intentions were good—he thought that if he relayed the letter, I would face repercussions in prison—but I was very angry when I found out. The police had cut me off from the outside—how could he hold back my letter?

WY: Did your refusal to cooperate while you were in prison create trouble for your family?

LG: A great deal. My mother was terminally ill, but because of what they called my poor attitude, they would not allow me to see her one last time before she died.

After I was transferred to Lingyuan, my brother tried to visit over a dozen times, but he was not permitted to see me even once. A year before I was to be released, they detained him. They gave him a choice: become a policeman or go to jail. Finally, the day after I was released, they released him, too. They told him, we've treated you this way just because you're Liu Gang's brother.

Also because of me, my brother had to leave his job as a teacher and find other work.

On November 11, 1993, my father came to Lingyuan to visit me but was turned away. The reason they gave him was "When family members visit there is a relatively strong reaction in Liu Gang's thinking which is not conducive to his reforming himself."

When my sister tried to visit, she was not permitted to see me and she was beaten up. The injuries she sustained were quite serious. She went to Beijing to complain about what had happened, but no one would take any notice.

WY: At first you were at Qincheng Prison, then you were transferred to two or three other locations, and finally you ended up at the Lingyuan. Can you contrast the conditions in the different places? Can you say a little about the conditions of your fellow sufferers?

LG: In Beijing they borrowed some cells in Qincheng to hold us. I was in custody in a detention center. The conditions were relatively good; as long as no one tried to escape, the guards did not beat the prisoners. Another reason was that the quality of the guards in Beijing was higher; and they really understood what had happened on June 4.

When I was transferred to Shenyang, my situation suddenly deteriorated. As soon as I arrived the guards started in with the beatings. I think that if Chen Xitong [former Beijing mayor, recently sentenced for corruption charges] were sent to that place, they would beat him too. This was a true prison as opposed to a detention center, and so the conditions were a lot worse. Prisons mean beatings, beatings to keep you afraid.

Lingyuan was just as bad—no one there had not endured beatings and torture with the electric baton. Guards would be looked down upon by the other guards if they did not use violence.

At Lingyuan I was put in a company which was part of a special study brigade for political prisoners who participated in the Democracy Movement. We tried to take a stand together to win reasonable treatment, staging hunger strikes and work stoppages. As a result some of us were sent to the "strict regime" brigade and some to solitary confinement. Others tried to compromise and ended up suffering the worst of all.

WY: You studied at the Chinese University of Science and Technology, where Fang Lizhi was a professor. Do you think your passion for activism has something to do with his influence?

LG: Yes, in particular his sense of dignity. The other teachers told me to listen to the Party; what the Party says goes. But Professor Fang was different. He had a doubting, critical spirit. And I think that this is exactly how a true scientist should be.

WY: What do you know about the regulations governing detention centers and prisons? Are these rules respected?

LG: Inside the prisons, there are rules for criminals undergoing reform, lots of them, and they were always making us recite them from memory.

The prisoners had a popular saying [which adapts an official statement of how guards are supposed to treat those under their charge]: "Guards are to prisoners as mothers to children—that is, stepmothers; Guards are to prisoners as doctors to patients—in a mental hospital; Guards are to prisoners as teachers to students—in a reform school."

WY: Were there libraries in the prisons and labor camps? Could prisoners find law books so that they could better understand the circumstances of their cases?

LG: Definitely not. They wouldn't even permit family members to bring books to prisoners. After I had been locked up for three months, they sometimes let me read the paper, but sometimes they wouldn't. You could always get some news from the broadcasts, although they were skewed. For example, the broadcasts on Soviet political reform told us to support the Soviet Communist Party, to oppose Yeltsin.

WY: After you were released, plainclothes police attacked you in broad daylight, beat you up, and stole your money, but the authorities paid no attention. Is it true that in Chinese society when an innocent person meets with this sort of injustice, the law provides no recourse?

LG: When the incident happened, some people on the street tried to come over and help, but the uniformed police who were watching held them back. In fact the uniformed police did more than just ignore my plight; they actually helped the ruffians—who were in fact plain-clothes police—beat me and rob me, all the while claiming that they were just "maintaining order." After the attack, when I demanded that the uniformed police bring the ruffians to justice, they said they were simply traffic police and could not help. I went to the local police station to file a complaint, but they just stalled. I also appealed repeatedly to the Liaoyuan City People's Congress Standing Committee, the city Politics and Law Committee, the Procuracy, the Traffic Police Brigade, the Public Security Bureau, and other relevant organs but got only doors slammed in my face or, at best, perfunctory treatment.

However, Yang Liu, head of the Office of Grievances of the People's Congress Standing Committee, took me seriously and filed a detailed report on my case. Later he also told me that there were a number of people in the People's Congress who were quite upset with the way my case had been handled. Yang wrote a memorandum to the chief of the municipal Public Security Bureau, Zhou Feng, ordering him to handle my case properly, and he also suggested that I go see Zhou myself to take the matter up personally. But when I tried to do this, Zhou refused to receive me. He had his people abuse me and then throw me out.

Although I am very angry that this case was never resolved, I have not lost heart. The reaction of some of the people in the People's Congress gives me hope that if individuals are persistent fighting for the rights which they are supposed to have through legal means, gradually society as a whole will be transformed and the rule of law will be realized.

WY: From your experience, what do you think people outside of prison can do for people inside?

LG: Give support; find any way to help. As I said before, when you're in prison, if you feel that no one from outside supports you, you feel utterly despondent. Let the outside world know what is happening to the people inside, and let the people inside know that they have support.

But ultimately you must rely on yourself to fight for your rights. If you are afraid to struggle for yourself, even if other people are willing to help you, it will be difficult to get anywhere.

WY: In prison you showed unflagging resistance; you endured inhuman persecution but never surrendered. People who hear of your courage are truly moved. What kind of inner power was it that enabled you to survive? Did you have moments of weakness? Did you ever wish for death? What is the deepest impression that your experiences in prison have left with you?

LG: I never wished for death.

Because prison guards and police officers in China don't believe in anything, their quality is very low. They are tools, lackeys. I have great contempt for them, and I do not fear them. I think, How can people of your quality defeat me? If you beat me up, the worst you can do is kill me. And if you don't kill me, I will keep coming back. This is the spirit by which I lived; I've taken the same spirit as the starting point in my fight for my human rights.

SECURITY
AND FOREIGN
RELATIONS

—

IX. THE MILITARY

Another antiquated institution that Deng Xiaoping inherited from Mao Zedong was the military. Although possessing nuclear weapons (since 1964) and ballistic missiles, the People's Liberation Army (as China's army, air, naval, and strategic rocket services are collectively known) remained largely of Korean War vintage. Twenty years later their capabilities have improved in some categories but overall still lag twenty to thirty years behind the state of the art.

In the early 1980s, Deng began to rebuild the PLA. He took personal charge of the mission — assuming the positions of chief of staff and chairman of the Central Military Commission. However, in doing so Deng dictated that military modernization must follow and benefit from China's overall economic, scientific, and technological modernization programs (military modernization was intentionally ranked last in the priorities of the four modernizations).

Modernizing China's military was not merely a matter of acquiring new equipment. It also required extensive changes in the command, control, and size of the PLA. When Deng took over, the PLA stood at nearly 5 million soldiers under arms — today it is half as large and still contracting. The PLA also suffered from extensive command problems — not the least of which was the fact that ranks had been abolished during the Cultural Revolution! The 1979 border war with Vietnam pointed up the extent to which Chinese military forces were slack and uncoordinated. They received a drubbing from a much smaller Vietnamese army.

China's military also needed to concentrate on soldiering—yet during the Cultural Revolution and before, PLA forces had become extensively engaged in the political arena. Indeed, the Cultural Revolution was brought to an end by the military—which essentially enforced martial law from after 1967 and ended the long national nightmare by arresting the "Gang of Four" in 1976. A large part of Deng's challenge to restore normalcy to the Chinese polity and society was to return the troops to their barracks. This was progressively accomplished by 1985, only for the military to be drawn into another sphere that distracted it from its core mission: involvement in the commercial economy. Deng's decision to call in the tanks and troops for domestic security purposes again in 1989 further postponed the PLA's separation from the political and commercial domains.

The 1991 Persian Gulf War reminded Deng and the PLA of how far China's military capabilities had fallen behind modern standards. Thereafter a more concerted effort was made to concentrate resources and training on military modernization while pulling the PLA out of politics and commerce. Even though in the fall of 1995 Party Chief Jiang Zemin ordered the military to liquidate its commercial ventures, this effort has not been fully successful, as the following selection makes clear, but it has afforded new progress in modernizing equipment, tactics, and command and control.

DAVID SHAMBAUGH, CHINA'S MILITARY: REAL OR PAPER TIGER?

As China's economy has developed, greater resources have been devoted to military modernization. This process has caused alarm in some quarters outside China, as the specter of a "China threat" has been raised. Is this assessment justified? What is the actual nature and magnitude of China's military modernization program? What is its defense doctrine? How should the United States and China's neighbors respond?

Coeditor David Shambaugh addresses these questions in this excerpted selection, originally published in The Washington Quarterly, Spring *1996.*

Few aspects of the People's Republic of China as a rising power trouble officials in Washington and world capitals as much as the modernization of the People's Liberation Army (PLA). While American officials wrestle with Beijing's burgeoning trade surpluses, ensuring market access and conditions for China's entry into the World Trade Organization, human rights concerns, the delicate Taiwan problem, how to pursue a policy of "comprehensive engagement" with the People's Republic, and other issues, it is the specter of an assertive, nationalistic, conventional and nuclear military superpower that has many worried.

For their part, China's leaders insist that the upgrading of its armed forces is overdue, minimal, underfinanced, and nothing for others to worry about. They and Chinese commentators vigorously rebut commentary about the so-called China threat. China's president, Jiang Zemin, told the Republic of Korea's National Assembly in November 1995 that "to allege that a stronger China will pose a threat to other countries is groundless. China will never take part in an arms race, never engage in expansion, and never seek hegemony."

While U.S. officials and intelligence agencies closely follow China's comprehensive force modernization program and monitor China's compliance with the Missile Technology Control Regime, Nuclear Nonproliferation Treaty, moratorium on nuclear testing, chemical and biological weapons stockpile treaties, and other arms-control agreements, the American news media have published numerous articles that fuel fears of a rising Chinese military threat. Academic analyses have been less alarmist as a rule, but they too detail developments that show China's military moving toward unprecedented levels of capability.

Are these concerns and fears justified or exaggerated? What is the actual nature of China's military modernization program, and how much progress is really being made? Does it constitute a military buildup, or is it simply a long-needed overhaul of a badly outdated force structure? What is the defense doctrine driving the program, and what are the impediments to realizing its ambitions? How might China's growing military prowess challenge American interests? How should the United States respond?

This article explores these questions and related issues. It attempts to do so in a balanced and dispassionate manner, because hardheaded realism is important in assessing China's growing military capabilities. Both wishful thinking about a benign China and exaggerated fears of a threatening China are distorting and destabilizing. Careful and rational assessments are called for. I conclude that to date there is more hype than reality in assessments of Chinese military modernization, and that discussion of a "China threat" is both inaccurate and irresponsible. The Chinese military does not now, and will not for the foreseeable future, have the capability to challenge U.S. national security directly. But at the same time the across-the-board progress being made in streamlining and modernizing the PLA must be recognized. Many aspects of this improving military capability do potentially threaten American national interests in Asia as well as those of China's neighboring states. These interests include maintaining Taiwan's security and integrity, freedom of navigation in the Pacific and Indian Oceans, and the security of long-standing U.S. allies and partners in East, Southeast, and South Asia.

The Nature of China's Military Modernization Program

Three interrelated elements of China's military modernization program merit attention: the PLA's expenditure, its doctrine, and its weaponry. Each is complex in its own right, and there is considerable debate among PLA watchers about the specifics in each category, but I shall present the principal trends where general consensus among specialists seems to exist.

CHINESE MILITARY EXPENDITURE

Probably the most contentious and least well understood aspect of China's military is its defense budget and expenditure. This is because there is no official transparency, as is commonplace in other countries. An increasing number of Asian nations publish annual defense white papers detailing expenditure and other categories of military development, but China does not. Its finance minister provides only an annual aggregate figure. For 1995–96 this amounts to 63.1 billion renminbi ($7.5 billion). This represents approximately 9.9 percent of total state expenditure and 1.5 percent of gross national product. Virtually no foreign analysts accept this as a plausible amount with which to maintain a force of 2.93 million in active service, with an additional 1.00 million strong paramilitary People's Armed Police and 1.20 million reserves, with enough left over to finance an across-the-board modernization of conventional and nuclear weaponry.

The lack of transparency makes foreign analyses inherently difficult and results in wide-ranging and often exaggerated estimates. Problems of calculation involve which categories of revenue and expenditure to include or exclude, uncovering and estimating allocations hidden in other state budgets, and whether to use dollar conversion or purchasing power parity methodology. The official budget not only ignores these extra revenue sources but explicitly excludes arms sales revenues; demobilization and pensions costs; maintenance of militia, reserves, and the People's Armed Police; commercial earnings; and defense industrial conversion expenditure. Many of the discrepancies in calculating Chinese military expenditure arise from differences in the categories of inclusion and exclusion. If one accepts the limited Chinese categories—which do not accord with North Atlantic Treaty Organization standards—the lower aggregate figure presented is more acceptable. What is clear is that the official Chinese figure has been climbing steadily in recent years. It grew 159 percent from 1986 through 1994, but when adjusted for inflation the budget increased by only 4 percent in real terms. Since 1988 the budget has increased annually at double-digit figures but when adjusted for inflation real growth has been about 40 percent.

The official defense budget primarily pays for operating and maintenance costs, plus most ordnance procurement and research and development. This does not mean that the defense budget pays for all operating and maintenance or research and development costs, because this is certainly not the case. China's military-industrial establishment earns three to four times as much from hidden budget allocations and commercial earnings as it does from the official defense budget.

Individual military units now meet a considerable portion of daily operating and maintenance costs through their commercial and sideline activities. This includes, importantly, food production. Salaries and a variety of daily maintenance costs are also topped up through proceeds from units' extracurricular activities. Similarly, procurement and research and development costs are also supplemented by a variety of secondary budget allocations—principally direct line allocations from the State Council to the five main defense ministries/corporations (Electronics, Ordnance, Nuclear, Aeronautics and Astronautics, and Shipbuilding). Research and development costs are topped up through allocations from the civilian State Science and Technology Commission and commercial earnings by research institutes themselves. The paramilitary People's Armed Police is primarily funded via the Ministry of Public Security budget, although some sources indicate that it is partially paid for out of Ministry of State Security funds. Allocations for garrisoning and maintaining regional force units (as distinct from main force units, which are maintained primarily by central funding) are paid partially through civilian provincial budgets, although a large percentage of the necessary funds (perhaps 50 percent) are now generated by individual units. Similarly, the militia and reserves are paid for by a combination of central, local government, and unit-generated revenue (the so-called three-thirds policy). Pensions and other costs associated with demobilization are met jointly by the Ministry of Civil Affairs and municipal governments. Since 1987 the PLA has demobilized over 1 million troops, of which approximately 10 percent have been officers who command large pensions, retirement bonuses, housing, travel funds, free health and hospital care, and often a car and driver. The final area of off-budget earnings for the PLA is central allocations for defense industry conversion and earnings by these industries. To be sure, many of China's estimated 50,000 military factories—which employ approximately 50 million—have not converted successfully. Hence they require substantial state subsidies. One report noted that 50 percent of defense industry production capacity remains idle and described such factories as "an unbearable burden on the national economy." Nonetheless, official Chinese sources claim that nearly 70 percent of military factories now produce civilian goods. During the Eighth Five-Year Plan (1991–95), the State Council earmarked 6 billion yuan ($1.14 billion) for facilitating further conversion.

The trend for increased defense outlays can be expected to continue in coming years. In 1994, before he fell ill, Paramount Leader Deng Xiaoping is reported to have promised double-digit growth rates to the PLA for the remainder of the 1990s. Although such increases are a reversal of the pattern seen during the 1980s, they must be kept in perspective. The PLA's operating revenue base is substantial, but it remains a fraction of the defense budgets of most developed countries and hardly enough to maintain a total force structure of 3 to 4 million. Given the rapidly growing Chinese economy, why should increased funds not be made available to modernize the backward PLA? Moreover, as the Chinese economy continues to grow at double-digit rates, inflation too has risen rapidly. Except in 1994 and 1995, the increases in official defense spending have not kept pace with inflation. It is also important to bear in mind that a substantial percentage of defense budget increases has gone to increasing salaries and improving living conditions for PLA personnel (especially officers).

What then is the operating budget of the Chinese military? The truth is that outside analysts do not know. And it is quite likely that the PLA itself does not know. Much more is known abroad about China's defense budget *process* and categories of hidden allocations than about actual expenditure. Estimates vary widely—ranging from two to twelve times the official figure (the higher-end estimates mostly employ purchasing power parity methodologies)—but a consensus is beginning to emerge among defense economists and leading Western experts that the PLA's total spending is in the $28 to $36 billion range (International Institute of Strategic Studies and Stockholm Institute Peace Research Institute estimates respectively), or four to five times the official budget.

While most nations are radically reducing their defense budgets and dismantling their military establishments in the post–Cold War era, China is doing the opposite. This is a source of anxiety for China's neighbors and is a cause for legitimate concern in the international community. But again this estimated expenditure must be kept in perspective—it is not a great amount to sustain a force of 4.0 million in active service (PLA and People's Armed Police) and 1.2 million reserves, as well as the comprehensive weapons modernization programs under way. Nor does it come close to the $53.8 billion spent by Japan in 1995 on a considerably smaller force structure.

Publication of a credible defense white paper would help to alleviate a number of the analytical problems noted here, help answer critics, and clarify uncertainties about Chinese defense spending, doctrine, and force deployments. Such increased transparency would be welcome. Persistent and probing efforts should continue to be undertaken by the Japanese government, the United States, the Regional Forum of the Association of Southeast Asian Nations, and other governmental and nongovernmental organizations to press China and the PLA to dramatically improve transparency concerning their military budget and overall revenue/spending. This should be a high priority.

CHINESE DEFENSE DOCTRINE AND WEAPONRY

Since the redefinition of China's strategic frontiers in the late 1980s—when a shift from continental to peripheral defense took place—the PLA has concomitantly revised its overall defense doctrine and force structure. Today and toward 2000 the PLA is attempting to implement a doctrine of flexible response for multiple missions based on high-technology weapons and a diversified—yet integrated—force structure. Officially the new doctrine is dubbed limited war under high-technology conditions (*jubu zhanzheng zai gao jishu tiaojian xia*) and active defense (*jiji fangyü*).

It is important, however, not to confuse ambition with capability—

the PLA's doctrinal desires at present stand in sharp contrast to its severely limited capabilities. Its current weapons inventory remains ten to twenty years or more behind the state of the art in almost all categories, although some gaps are being closed. It will lack the airlift and sealift capability vital for power projection and rapid deployment for probably two decades or more. Most knowledgeable analysts are extremely skeptical, even pessimistic, about overall conventional PLA capabilities. They describe it as an antiquated force of largely Korean War–vintage weaponry. The air force is seen as particularly backward, with China's naval forces being green-water capable at best. New systems are under development, and some advanced weapons are being purchased abroad (particularly from Russia), and these will enhance China's power extension capabilities, but on balance the PLA lags far behind the state of the art.

These relative gains in the PLA's capabilities are particularly important when viewed in the context of China's potential *regional* adversaries. Military power is not absolute but relative. It is not so much the United States or other modern militaries against which the PLA should be compared but rather regional militaries in Asia. When judged in this light, the PLA's order of battle appears stronger (and potentially more threatening). It will increasingly have the capability to exert force around China's periphery—against Taiwan, in the South China Sea, and in defense of its land borders.

The PLA's operative doctrine today is the product of a decade-long rethinking of the nature of contemporary war and conflict, the potential threats to China, and the concomitant adequacy of the PLA force structure. At first the new doctrinal orthodoxy was labeled people's war under modern conditions, but soon the realization set in that the Maoist strategy of people's war was wholly inadequate. Conflicts were not likely to take place on Chinese continental territory and could not be fought on the presumption of "luring the enemy in deep." Instead, Chinese defense planners began using new vocabulary and concepts to describe new contingencies and needs. "Limited war" (*jubu zhanzheng*) became the order of the day. Chinese defense analysts concluded that limited wars had a number of characteristics. They were often fought for ethnic, religious, or political reasons. They were generally short in duration, although some—such as the Iran-Iraq War—could drag on for several years. They were geographically localized and tended not to spread across neighboring borders. The combatants employed massive firepower, particularly airpower and short-range missiles. This did not mean that ground forces were not important—the Falklands and Iran-Iraq conflicts showed they were—but they were not seen as the mainstay or key to victory. All weapons in the disputants' inventory were seen as fair game for use—including chemical and tactical nuclear weapons—and successful armies practiced combined arms and had good command, control, communications, and intelligence systems (C³I).

Throughout the late 1980s the PLA began to adjust its doctrine, force structure, command and control systems, training, and weapons inventory to prepare for "limited warfare" contingencies. The Iran-Iraq conflict was China's model, and the PLA believed that it possessed certain comparative advantages in fighting such a war. The Lebanese and Afghan conflicts further convinced PLA commanders that small-scale, localized, and guerrilla warfare were not completely obsolete.

Then came the Persian Gulf War of 1991. This conflict had a jarring effect on the PLA. The military nature of Desert Storm and the swiftness of the allied victory stunned the Chinese high command. Before the war they had been predicting that U.S. forces would become bogged down in a ground war similar to the Soviets' experience in Afghanistan. Every element of the allied strategy and capabilities left the PLA aghast and hammered home as never before the backwardness of the PLA. The PLA was forced to confront the elements of modern warfare: precision-guided munitions; stealth technology; electronic countermeasures; precision bombing of military targets with minimized collateral damage; airborne command and control systems; in-flight refueling; the minimum loss of attack aircraft and life; the use of satellites in antiballistic missile defense, strategic targeting, and intelligence gathering; early warning and surveillance; the use of command centers half a world away; the use of antiballistic missile defense; massive airlift and rapid deployment capability; the ability of troops to exist in desert conditions; the use of special operation commando squads; and so on. This was the PLA's first exposure to a high-tech war, and they were stunned.

The Gulf War caused a thoroughgoing revision of doctrine and training in the PLA. But the most important impact has been on thinking about weaponry. Reversing Maoist maxims, weapons and technology are now thought to be decisive elements in modern warfare. Since the Gulf War military publishing houses in China have been turning out large quantities of books on high-technology warfare. This has meant increased attention to the development of combined arms, rapid deployment units (*kuaisu fanying budui*), force mobility, long-range force projection, and the development of airlift and sealift capability.

Both the PLA navy and air force have embarked on comprehensive modernization and professionalization programs around these objectives.

For the air force this has meant an emphasis on procuring long-range interceptors, aerial refueling, transports, and airborne early warning and guidance systems. Thus far China possesses minimal to nonexistent advanced systems in these categories. Its fighter inventory remains essentially of Korean War vintage. The purchase of forty-eight Sukhoi 27 fighter-bombers and ten Ilyushin transports from Russia has helped to plug deficiencies in certain areas, but they are far from sufficient to create a modern fleet capable of power projection or close air support. The PLA air force has no in-flight refueling or airborne warning and control (AWAC) capability. China is building a new-generation fighter designated the J-10. It is apparently modeled on a U.S. F-16 A/B, which Chinese aerospace technicians are trying to clone from a sample prototype reportedly provided to China by Pakistan. The avionics in this plane are not of the advanced F-16C version, and thus China has turned to Israel for assistance based on its aborted Lavi project. It must be said that China's record on reverse engineering aircraft has not been good, and it remains in doubt if this plane will ever join China's interceptor inventory (it is at least two years away from flight testing and seven to eight years away from deployment if all goes well). Although the air force has approximately 400 J-5s, 500 J-7s, and 100 J-8s in its inventory, the mainstay of the air force remains the J-6—a Chinese version of the MiG-23. This aircraft (approximately 3,000 are active) is at least twenty years out of date and no match for the principal interceptors in the inventories of the United States, Japan, South Korea, Russia, Taiwan, India, or several ASEAN states. This is also the case for the H-6, the PLA air force's principal bomber.

For the PLA navy the new doctrine has meant the development of a new generation of Luhu class destroyers (displacement 4,200 tons) and Jiangwei class guided missile frigates (displacement 2,250 tons). Thus far only one Luhu has been commissioned, with another near launching and two more reportedly under construction. But the Luhu's engines and onboard ship armaments are heavily dependent on foreign sources of supply (principally French)—which have been cut off as a result of the post-1989 sanctions. It will be difficult for the navy to build further Luhus without access to Western defense contractors. The Luhus would join refitted Luda III class destroyers, which are a vast improvement over their progenitor.

The navy is also building a new generation of guided missile frigates. The new Jiangwei frigate entered the fleet in 1991 (thus far four are in service with six more on order). They have many of the same characteristics as the refitted Jianghu III class frigates, except with more sophisticated radars (Thomson-CSF) and Crotale antiship missile launchers (capable of carrying up to twenty-six in a magazine). They also carry an indigenously made surface-to-air missile (the Hongqi-61M).

The PLA navy's submarine force is also improving with the first deliveries of Kilo class diesel submarines from Russia. It is unknown how many Kilos have been ordered, but it seems doubtful that the navy will have the hard currency to buy more than ten in the next few years. The purchased Kilos are reportedly the top-of-the-line variety used by the Russian navy, not the less capable export model. For a conventional diesel submarine, the Kilo is quiet and fast. It has a range of 6,000 nautical miles at seven to eight knots submerged and can stay at sea for up to sixty days. It is outfitted with eighteen Type-53 torpedoes (each with a 400-kilo warhead) and can reportedly carry enough replacements to reload twelve times. Russian experts are also working in China under the Five-Year Defense Cooperation Accord to improve the navy's long-plagued nuclear submarine force (Han class). Another important development was the launching in 1994 of the indigenously manufactured Song (a.k.a. Wuhan-C) diesel attack submarine. The Song is intended to supersede the aging Ming and Romeo classes and become the standard conventional submarine in the fleet. The PLA navy currently operates fifty-two submarines—including one nuclear-fueled ballistic missile submarine, five nuclear-fueled submarines, one non–ballistic missile submarine, one Kilo, and forty-four Romeo class coastal submarines.

Despite the existing and planned surface combatants and submarines, the navy remains very much a coastal patrol force. In recent years it has moved from a brown- to green-water capability, with minimal blue-water capacity. It has fifty-five surface combatants (although at present only three destroyers and four frigates approach modern standards), a few nuclear-fueled attack submarines, and a variety of minesweepers and light patrol craft. It will take considerable time and expenditure to build a blue-water navy of any significance.

Hence, with the exception of the submarine force, worries about the Chinese navy patrolling the Pacific and Indian Oceans appear exaggerated at present. What is really needed to achieve power projection, of course, is one or two aircraft carriers. There are numerous reports of indigenous aircraft or helicopter carriers being built, but confirmation has not materialized. Nor is China in a financial or political position to purchase a carrier abroad.

The PLA's new limited war doctrine had also meant the upgrading of short- and medium-range missile forces for use in conventional combat, as well as the further development of strategic and tactical nuclear forces. The East Wind (*Dongfeng*) ballistic missile series—especially the DF-15, 21, and 25—are all being adapted for use in limited conflicts. Although it is not useful in conventional conflicts, the Second Artillery is also upgrading China's entire strategic missile force. The new DF-31 (a solid-fueled, mobile, long-range intercontinental ballistic missile [ICBM] capable of striking anywhere in the United States) was successfully tested in 1995. By the turn of the century China's goals are to almost quadruple the ICBM force from the present eight to thirty; base them increasingly with fixed launchers in hardened silos; have them use solid fuel propellants; and hopefully outfit as many as possible with multiple independently targetable reentry warheads (China has not yet mastered this last technology). China's intermediate-range ballistic missile force is also being modernized, while improvement of submarine-launched ballistic missiles is also a very high priority. As part of its nuclear modernization program, China continues to defy the international moratorium on nuclear testing. The reason for this continued testing is that the Second Artillery seeks to develop a new generation of warheads that are smaller, "cleaner" (less collateral damage), and more accurate before China accedes to the renewed Nuclear Nonproliferation Treaty and the Comprehensive Test Ban Treaty in 1996. Once in force, China's nuclear arsenal will, in effect, be frozen.

Thus, the PLA is assimilating multiple lessons from the Gulf War. Doctrine, force structure, training, deployments, weaponry, and research are all undergoing substantial revision and streamlining. The PLA's goal is clearly to develop a multifaceted and technologically modern force structure capable of pursuing multiple missions. "Flexible response" is probably the most apt description of the PLA's evolving doctrine. The PLA seeks to develop the capability to meet a range of contingencies—including a conventional land invasion, strategic or tactical nuclear attack, the use of chemical weapons, air-to-air engagement over land and sea, coastal and deep-water naval battles, and forward deployment of forces. The PLA is developing and upgrading its entire force structure to contend with this range of contingencies. In terms of equipment and training, all PLA services and branches have a *long* way to go to reach modern levels of capability, but the trend line is apparent and the gap is being narrowed.

The United States and Asian nations should have no doubt about the *intentions* of China's military modernization program—to have a modern multifaceted force structure—but they must equally be sanguine about the PLA's *capabilities*. To be sure, there are substantial technological and innovative impediments to developing needed systems, but by the same token China's military-industrial complex has proven capable of producing a wide range of fairly sophisticated systems and has demonstrated particular adeptness in certain categories. Although at present backward and limited, China will continue to close the gap and develop a flexible and increasingly sophisticated force structure. The only questions are how quickly they can build it, to what ends it will be put, how China's neighbors will respond, and what the impact will be on American national interests.

The Impact on American Interests

The impact of China's military modernization program on U.S. national interests falls in four principal areas.

First, it is important to remember that the maintenance of China's own stability and security is critical to peace and stability in Asia. Modern Asian history has repeatedly proven that when China is unstable internally it invites pressure or aggression from outside, which in turn destabilizes the entire region. One of the greatest potential threats to Asian security would be civil conflict in China that would lead to economic retardation and a likely refugee exodus on a scale the world has never known. Many Asian countries know this well and accordingly work to ensure economic growth and internal stability in China. Human rights concerns (such as they exist) thus take a distinct backseat to deeper Asian concerns about promoting China's internal coherence, territorial integrity, social stability, and economic development. An economic recession in China could trigger the fissures they seek to avoid. For the United States, it is also important that China remain united and effectively and humanely governed. Similarly, as China's territorial and national security is vital to Asian security and stability, it is also central to U.S. national interests. A China that is secure from foreign threat or coercion, can adequately defend itself, and can protect its legitimate sovereignty is good for both Asian and American national interests.

The second aspect of how China's military modernization impacts

U.S. national interests is clearly the Taiwan issue. China's continued refusal to renounce the potential use of force vis-à-vis Taiwan is not conducive to the reunification of China, to peace and stability in Asia, or to U.S. national interests. The United States has long-standing ties with, and commitments to, the people of Taiwan. Military and other forms of coercive pressure by China against Taiwan only serve to escalate tensions and decrease the desire for reunification among the island's 21 million citizens. China's medium-range ballistic missile "tests" 90 kilometers off the coast of Taiwan during the summer of 1995 and the large-scale military exercises undertaken during the last two years are indicative of this counterproductive behavior. The United States has a commitment under the Taiwan Relations Act to ensure that Taiwan maintains an adequate defense, and this should be carefully monitored and maintained—even if it violates the 1992 U.S.-China Joint Communiqué on established ceilings of arms sales to Taiwan. Thus far, with two areas of exception, Taiwan has an adequate force to defend itself against a range of coercive scenarios. The two exceptional areas of vulnerability for Taiwan are in antiballistic missile defense and antisubmarine warfare. The Chinese missile "tests" during 1995 pointed up the first vulnerability, while the PLA navy's growing number of surface combatants and submarines point up the potential for a blockade against the island. In response, the United States has recently sold Taiwan some Patriot antiballistic missile systems and has leased it Knox class frigates with good antisubmarine warfare capability. The events of 1995 illustrate that the Taiwan problem continues to fester and has potential to erupt in armed conflict that could very well draw in the United States.

The third potential problem area is the impact that China's growing naval capability might have on freedom of navigation and shipping in East Asia. There is nothing to suggest that China has ambitions to disrupt the sea-lanes, quite to the contrary. But its contested claims in the South and East China Seas have the potential to cause such disruption, as would any Chinese blockade or other use of force against Taiwan. Most East Asian nations are heavily dependent on energy and merchandise imports and exports that pass through the shipping channels of East Asia.

Finally, China's military modernization affects America's allies in Asia insofar as those nations feel endangered by the growth in PLA capabilities. There is evidence that these concerns are rising regionwide, but to date they seem most acute in Japan and some Southeast Asian countries. The United States maintains security alliances with Japan, the

Republic of Korea, the Philippines, Thailand, and Australia. None can be said to be directly threatened by China, but all are concerned about the impact of growing Chinese military power on the regional balance of power.

Drawing the PLA Out and Bringing It into the International Order

For the United States to deal creatively and effectively with the rising challenges presented by Chinese military modernization, interrelated unilateral, bilateral, and multilateral responses are required.

Unilaterally America must maintain its current military presence on land and at sea in the Asia-Pacific region while shoring up the defense capabilities of its allies and partners in the region (including Taiwan) and keeping a careful eye on Chinese military developments. The maintenance of 100,000 U.S. troops in East Asia is conducive to peace and stability in the potentially volatile region and reassures U.S. allies. In recent years elements in the PLA and some Chinese security specialists have increasingly expressed the view that they no longer favor forward-deployed U.S. forces in East Asia. This is a source of concern and should be a central issue on the multinational dialogue agenda with Beijing.

Bilaterally, the United States must engage the PLA at all levels—seeking through dialogue to increase transparency in Chinese defense expenditure, doctrine, deployments, and security perspectives; exchanging personnel between national military units, service academies, and staff colleges; undertaking, in time, joint maneuvers and other confidence-building and transparency-enhancing measures; and maintaining an ongoing dialogue on international security trends and bilateral defense interests at the highest level of the two military establishments. Eventually the United States must again consider limited defensive weapon sales and technology transfers to China, because a situation in which such sales and transfers take place with nations around China's periphery but not China itself cannot be sustained indefinitely without fueling China's fears of containment.

Multilaterally, the United States must work with Asian and Western nations to integrate the Chinese government *and the PLA* into global and regional cooperative (as distinct from collective) security regimes. This should be done at both the intergovernmental level—by means such as the ASEAN Regional Forum, Missile Technology Control

Regime, Nuclear Nonproliferation Treaty, chemical and biological weapons conventions, United Nations Arms Register, et cetera—as well as the "Track 2" nongovernmental level. Again, the primary aim should be to incrementally but rapidly increase the transparency of the PLA and build trust and confidence between China and other nations through exchange of information and defense data.

Cooperation with China is the key, because a confrontational approach will surely create in Beijing a truculent rival at best and an enemy at worst. If the United States treats China as an adversary, it will become one. The United States cannot again afford to base its China policy on the flawed assumption of containment. That failed miserably during the Cold War, costing the United States over 100,000 lives in Korea and Vietnam as well as the opportunity for a generation of beneficial commercial and cultural contacts. Such a misguided policy would be stillborn today for lack of resources and the fact that none of America's allies and partners in Asia and Europe would go along with it. They have already made clear their choice on how to deal with China: cooperate bilaterally, discussing issues of mutual concern privately, while working multilaterally to enmesh China in a variety of regional and international regimes that will condition China's behavior domestically and externally.

China is at an important juncture in its international orientation. It has never before been more open to the world and exposed to international influences, yet in many ways it is not integrated into the international system. It is not yet a member of key international organizations such as the World Trade Organization and Missile Technology Control Regime, and in those in which Beijing is a member its participation is often passive. As long as China is not fully integrated into the international system, it has the potential and capacity to be a disruptive non–status quo power.

For more than a century China has pursued a policy of trying to gain from international exchanges while protecting its cultural distinctiveness and political sovereignty. Its approach to managing this duality has been ambivalent—often expressed as the *ti/yong* dichotomy—but many would say that China has tried to be a classic "free rider," deriving maximum benefits from the world while minimally abiding by international norms and conventions in return. Beijing is highly distrustful of international organizations with universalistic agendas, fearing that such organizations will penetrate into China while limiting China's sovereignty and freedom of maneuver externally. It fears being entrapped and manipulated from outside. For the same reason Beijing eschews alliances and close binding relationships with foreign countries. Such fears derive directly from modern China's experience before 1949 of territorial partition and impotence in the face of foreign imperialism— what it describes as the "century of shame and humiliation."

Thus China carries considerable historical baggage to its contemporary international relationships, which makes it highly suspicious of foreign entanglements. Chinese leaders are convinced that only wealth and power (*fu qiang*) will enable them to fend off manipulation by foreign countries or international organizations.

It is against this backdrop that many Chinese officials and specialists display deep distrust of the United States. The military brass are the most vociferous critics of what is termed "U.S. hegemonism," but there are also elements inside the Communist Party and state apparatus that see the United States as an enemy (using the translated term *diren*). They are still in a minority, but few describe the United States in friendly terms. For the majority of opinion in Beijing's official circles and think tanks the jury is still out, although it must be said that in 1995 the center of gravity demonstrably shifted toward viewing the United States as a growing adversary. Extensive interviews with, and publications by, China's international relations and security communities revealed what was believed to be a four-faceted strategy on the part of Washington to contain China strategically, frustrate its emergence economically, subvert it politically, and divide it territorially by trying to permanently separate it from Taiwan. As inaccurate as this conspiratorial image is, one can find evidence of these views in the U.S. Congress.

China does not seek a confrontation with the United States, but it is ready to reciprocate if that is what Washington pursues. Thus the United States and China must constructively engage each other on a variety of levels (including the PLA) and in a range of forums in order to address the panoply of difficult issues between the two sides. Otherwise, misperceptions will quickly harden and Washington and Beijing will awake one day soon to find themselves embroiled in an adversarial relationship neither seeks, needs, or can afford.

X. CHINA
AND THE WORLD

███

China's foreign relations have also been affected by the reform era. As the selections in this chapter illustrate, this can be observed and measured in a number of ways. China is now a global actor, if not a global power. It is now also largely a status quo power—in stark contrast to its destabilizing posture of the 1950s and '6os, when Beijing sought to foment revolutionary movements around the world.

As in other areas of reform, and perhaps more so in this sphere, Deng Xiaoping had much to do with formulating China's new strategy, style, and practice of foreign relations. The selections in this chapter illustrate several components of China's new external posture: its attributes as a great power, the sources of its seemingly erratic behavior, and Beijing's own view of its place in the world. The last two selections address China's most important, and most troublesome, relationship: with the United States.

SAMUEL S. KIM,
CHINA AS A GREAT POWER

That China aspires to be a "great power" is not doubted, but is it one? How will we know when it has achieved great power status? When it becomes a great power, will China behave as a "responsible" actor in world affairs? These are the questions explored in this selection by the Chinese foreign policy specialist and international relations theorist Samuel Kim.

This selection was originally published in Current History, *September* 1997.

The question of China's status as a "great power" in the international system seems elementary enough, yet the answer is far from obvious. During the Cold War, assessments of China's national power ranged from a "sleeping dragon" and aspiring "superpower candidate" to an actual major power—the much-coveted balancing third force—in global geopolitics. In the wake of the 1989 Tiananmen tragedy, many were prematurely pessimistic, predicting a declining if not collapsing China. Today a "rising China" has captured the American public's attention, and with it the question of China's great power status has resurfaced.

Although there is no "scientific" way of measuring state power and international rank in a rapidly changing world, an assessment of China as a great power must be informed by several factors. First, many states are subject to the relentless twin pressures of globalization from above and substate localization and ethnonational fragmentation from below. As a result, the capacity of states and their leaders to promote human security and well-being within an enclosed territorial space has been weakened. China is not exempt from the sovereignty-diminished dynamics of globalization from above and localization from below.

Second, assessing Chinese power at this critical juncture in world history is complicated by the profound domestic social, economic, and ecological transformations China is experiencing at a time when the global system of which it is a part is undergoing a structural transformation. In world politics the perception and credibility of national power matters as much as the reality of it. The perception of what constitutes power has changed significantly with the demise of the socialist superpower and the multipolarizing process in East Asia. And the Cold War illusion of a consensus on what constitutes a superpower has been shattered by the rise of Japan as a global power of a different kind (a one-dimensional global power), the sudden "third worldization" of the former Soviet Union (South Korea's gross national product now surpasses Russia's), and America's heroic but increasingly ineffective claim of global leadership without bearing the costs and the responsibilities.

Third, especially in an era of globalization, power needs to be seen in synthetic terms. The traditional military and strategic concept of power pays too much attention to a state's aggregate power (power potential as inferred from its as yet unconverted resources and possessions) and too little to the more dynamic and interdependent notions of power in an issue-specific domain—that is, power defined in terms of control over outcomes.

How then is a great power defined today? It is a state that easily ranks among the top five in the primary global structures—economic, military, knowledge, and normative—and that enjoys relatively low sensitivity, vulnerability, and security interdependence because of massive resource and skill differentials and relative economic self-sufficiency. A great power is a strong state with the ability to mobilize the country's human and material resources in the service of its worldview and policy objectives. There is also the normative-behavioral requirement of great power status: a great power is and becomes what a great power does.

China's Economic Power and Murphy's Law

China's economic power, measured in terms of the aggregate economic numbers, is impressive enough. Post-Mao China established an all-time global record in doubling per capita output between 1977 and 1987. According to the World Bank's purchasing power parity estimates, China, with a 1994 gross domestic product of just under $3 trillion, has become the second-largest economy in the world, after the United States. If we accept the projections of a 1995 RAND study, China's gross domestic product will reach $11.3 trillion by the year 2010 (in 1994 purchasing power parity dollars) compared with $10.7 trillion for the United States, $4.5 trillion for Japan, $3.7 trillion for India, and $2.0 trillion for a unified Korea.

The unpleasant downside is that this remarkable economic growth has been made possible by China's growing involvement in and dependence on the capitalist world economic system. China's expanded involvement in the global political economy more easily translates into greater vulnerability and sensitivity than into greater power. China's external debt stands at about $120 billion and is still growing. While China has had the fastest-growing economy in the world—its total output quadrupled between 1978 and 1995—its external trade dependence, defined as the sum of imports and exports as a percentage of gross national product, rose dramatically during the same period, from less than 10 percent to more than 56 percent (Beijing's foreign trade increased more than thirteen times during the same period, from $21 billion to $280 billion). That China registered a $39.5 billion surplus in its bilateral trade with the United States in 1996 speaks volumes about Beijing's sensitivity to Murphy's law.

Forecasting China's future economic growth is difficult because of the twin pressures of globalization from above and localization from below. Post-Mao China, with its opening to the forces of globalization from above and suppression of those associated with ethnonational fragmentation from below, has achieved remarkable economic growth, but its continuing success remains far from assured.

Indeed, because of localizing pressures from below, China will not so easily become the economic superpower that many have predicted. Recent World Bank data and estimates show that a larger part of China's burgeoning population is being left behind than was previously assumed, even as the overall economy continues to register impressive growth. More than one-quarter of all Chinese—about 350 million people—subsist on less than $1 a day; most are concentrated in the peripheral but strategically important areas of Tibet, Xinjiang, and Inner Mongolia. Moreover, for the first time a significant number of urban dwellers—15 million or more—are falling below the poverty line without a state welfare net to catch them. Some 100 million rural Chinese are part of a floating population that drifts from city to city, and hundreds of thousands of Chinese are escaping their homeland in search of better economic opportunities in foreign countries. A growing mismatch between population and resources, and a possible eruption of ethnonational conflict accompanied by domestic, social, political, demographic, and environmental problems, could make Beijing's march to the promised land daunting if not impossible.

Military Power and China Lebensraum

Its growing economic vulnerability and dependence notwithstanding, authoritarian China with a world-class-sized economy seems poised to mobilize significant quantities of resources for the exercise of power outside its borders. China is a member of the exclusive nuclear club, possessing the world's third-largest nuclear arsenal. It also maintains the world's largest standing army, with 3 million soldiers.

In the early 1990s Beijing began proclaiming that it enjoyed the best external security environment and the deepest peace since the founding of the People's Republic. At the same time it continued to increase its

defense budget at double-digit rates and beef up its military power projection capabilities. Using the official exchange rate of 8.29 renminbi to
the dollar, China's announced defense budget for the 1996–97 fiscal
year stands at $9.72 billion. The actual amount devoted to military
spending is generally estimated to be at least four to five times greater
than an official defense budget; this means that China's total military
spending for the 1996–97 fiscal year is between $38.60 and $48.25 billion
(it is not possible to give an accurate and universally accepted figure
because of the lack of transparency and the differences and discrepancies in the categories of inclusion and exclusion).

Translating military expenditures into military power projection
capabilities is even more difficult and controversial than estimating
actual military spending. Most analysts warn against overestimating
China's military power in terms of high-tech sophistication and power
projection capabilities. They note that as much as 30 percent of China's
military expenditures is used to stabilize inefficient military industrial
enterprises; that China's ambitions run ahead of its limited capabilities;
that the People's Liberation Army (PLA) is not in a position to project its
air and naval power in sustained combat for more than ninety days in
the South China Sea; that the PLA's weapons systems are roughly ten to
twenty years behind the state of the art in almost all categories needed
for the kind of war the PLA wants to fight and win within a few days—
high-tech, high-firepower, rapid-reaction local peripheral war; and that
an unfolding military revolution based on the application for information technology to weapons could put the already dominant United
States far ahead of its allies and adversaries alike.

Whatever the actual numbers, size, and sophistication, it is clear that
China's military power in quantitative and qualitative terms is growing.
For a more accurate and comprehensive account of China's overall military power, however, other factors need to be considered. One of these
is the belief that military power is the most important component of
"comprehensive national strength" (zonghe guoli), which is viewed as
indispensable in China's attempt to regain its status as a leading world
power and to defend against any threats, actual or imagined, to its territorial sovereignty and political integrity. Without sufficient military
power, it is argued, China will not be able to successfully project its
national identity as a great power or to play a more decisive role in world
affairs. The idea that sufficient military power buys both deterrence and
status reflects and effects internal debates about why China needs more
and better high-tech weapons systems.

One of the most remarkable and potentially dangerous developments in the post–Cold War era is the rise of the concept of *haiyang guotu guan* (sea as national territory). The Chinese people have been prodded to cultivate and cherish *haiyang guotu guan* in order to direct their attention to the unpleasant fact that it is China's maritime interests that have been encroached on in recent years. Chinese strategists now also discuss the need for *shengcun kongjian* (living space) and for strategic frontiers that extend into the Indian Ocean, the South China Sea and East China Sea, and even into outer space. A recent internal Chinese document states that the disputed island groups in the South China Sea, some of them situated nearly 620 miles (1,000 kilometers) south of China's Hainan Island province and most of them subject to conflicting jurisdictional claims, could provide lebensraum for the Chinese people. Consonant with these concepts, China's naval military doctrine has shifted from the coastal defense of the mainland to active defense of maritime economic and strategic interests. In line with the new doctrine, Beijing's naval exercises, gunboat diplomacy, and creeping maritime expansionism have extended outside coastal waters in the 1990s.

The irony is that the West has begun to sing the rise of China chorus at a time when Chinese leaders, bereft of their vaunted geopolitical swing value, are shifting from the pretense of being a global power to becoming the dominant regional military power in Asia. From Beijing's post–Cold War perspective, Asia is the center of Chinese power and influence, the nucleus of ever-expanding circles radiating in all directions. Today China relies on Asia, we are constantly told, for its status and role as "a special power in the world."

Brains, Not Brawn

Changes in science and technology have transformed the global structures of economic and military competitiveness, productivity, and hierarchy. Knowledge power—also called skill power—is believed to be increasingly more significant than "hard power" in the conventional sense. The changes in the nature and distribution of knowledge power between and among various social actors at all systemic levels, and how best to initiate or adapt to such changes, will have a direct bearing on China's march to great powerdom.

China is relatively weak and vulnerable in knowledge power. In the realm of ideas and information, China takes rather than creates, importing far more than it exports; China is not even among the top fifteen patent powers in the world. Virtually all of China's futuristic writings and policy pronouncements in the post-Mao era incorporate a hard technocratic globalism based on a nationalistic viewpoint that emphasizes the determining role of science and technological power in the rise and fall of great powers. According to this view, China has to be knowledge competitive with the stronger military and industrial powers if it is to beat them at their own game. A country's success in global competition is also said to depend on the development of its high-tech industries. If China is to become a world power, it must attend to these industries, as it once did to the development of nuclear weapons and satellite programs.

Not only is technology accepted by Beijing as a marketable commodity but it is often treated as a kind of global collective good—the more free rides China takes, the better. Nearly all the UN system's multilateral economic, science, and technology regimes have been reconceptualized as cost-effective "deliverymen" for global information and innovations. They have been allowed to enter, some by design and others inadvertently, the castle of Chinese sovereignty as conceptual Trojan horses. There they influence the process by which Chinese national interests are redefined and Chinese national priorities are restructured to better fit the logic of the global situation.

Making and Shunning the Rules

The concept of a great power has always implied a synergy of two kinds of power: material and normative. To say that China is a great power is to say not only that it has special rights and privileges and commands formidable muscle power but also that it has corresponding special duties and responsibilities and behaves like a responsible great power.

The apparent paradox of a China seeking great power status and attaching great power politics at the same time is explained by the Chinese differentiation between great power and hegemonic power. Hegemony is defined by China in motivational and behavioral terms rather than terms of the general criteria and attributes of a great power. This explains why China attacks hegemonic behavior rather than the great power state per se. Unlike imperialism, hegemonism is said to carry no special implications for the social system or class character; that is, hegemonism has nothing to do with the attributes of a national power but has everything to do with the nature of state behavior. The irony is that the world's principal aspirant to great power status has been none other than the world's principal critic of superpower hegemony, and that the world's principal antihegemonic champion has become the principal security and economic beneficiary of America's hegemonic structural power. Thus China's identity as a great power may be divided into two symbolic and substantive components: great power identity as defined by what China *is*, and great power identity as defined by what China *does*.

The UN Security Council, as a formalized institutional expression of great power cooperation in settling international disputes and enforcing international peace, allows us to assess China's normative power in world politics. China, along with the other four powers granted permanent seats on the Security Council at the end of World War II, was endowed with special rights and privileges (for example, permanent membership and veto power). The five permanent members enjoyed these rights and privileges—even though they ran counter to the principle of state sovereignty and equality—because they were believed to be in a position to make special contributions to the maintenance of international peace and security. In the post-Mao era, China has cultivated a self-image as a great power with China-specific rights and entitlements—but not the duties and responsibilities—commensurate with its status, based on Deng Xiaoping's simple sinocentric logic that "the stronger China grows, the better the chances are for preserving world peace." Indeed, it is increasingly difficult to find evidence of any symmetry between China's special rights and China's special duties that come with its status as one of the permanent five on the Security Council.

Consider Chinese financial contributions to the UN system. As if to add credibility to China's much touted national identity as the only third world country that gave but never received any bilateral or multilateral aid during the postentry Maoist period (1971–1976), Beijing, in a move unprecedented in the history of UN budgetary politics, requested in 1973 to have its UN assessment rate raised from 4.0 to 5.5 percent. This was a dramatic way of demonstrating China's self-ascribed preeminent status in the global community during the Maoist period, a period that saw China's leaders show an impressive capacity to wield influence in global politics without the full trappings generally associated with a great power.

In sharp contrast, Deng's China made a U-turn, pursuing a Realpolitik of reaping maximum benefits with minimal financial responsibility.

In a dramatic if not unprecedented move, China in late 1978 abandoned its policy of self-reliance by requesting aid from the United Nations Development Program, the largest multilateral technical aid organization. A year later China asked the UN to decrease its assessment rate (based on its own "complete national income statistics"). Despite the controversy surrounding the accuracy of the Chinese statistics, China's assessment rate was reduced from 5.50 percent to 0.79 percent; it now stands at 0.72 percent. This has decisively changed the cost-benefit calculus for Chinese participation not only in the UN proper but also in the UN system as a whole, since all the specialized agencies follow the scales of assessment determined by the General Assembly.

Currently, China is the largest recipient of World Bank multilateral aid (about $3 billion per year), even though the World Bank ranks it as the world's second-largest economy. As one of the permanent members of the Security Council, China should be contributing a significant percentage of the peacekeeping budget, certainly more than 0.978 percent. The United Kingdom, with the second-lowest assessment rate (6.372 percent) among the five permanent members, contributes nearly seven times as much as China. At the regular budget assessment rate of 0.72 percent, China's contributions to the UN regular budget are surpassed by other third world member states such as Brazil (1.62 percent), South Korea (0.80 percent), Saudi Arabia (0.80 percent), and Mexico (0.78 percent). In short, China today is a UN financial regime taker, not shaper, because what it gains from the UN in multilateral financial and technical assistance far exceeds what it contributes to the UN's regular and peacekeeping budgets.

Normative power can also be defined as the ability to define, control, and transform the agenda of global politics and to legitimate a new international order. Not surprisingly, few of the UN conventions and agreements on a wide range of global issues and problems—and few of the many UN reform proposals currently afloat—bear Chinese initiative or sponsorship. As China's economy began to boom in 1991, Beijing adopted a more assertive strategy in the quintessentially normative domain of global human rights politics. In the wake of the publication of its first white paper on human rights in October 1991—which acknowledged that the best defense is a good offense—China assumed a more offensive posture by positioning itself as the third world's most vociferous champion of cultural relativist human rights.

The allure of China's cultural relativist line—that protecting human rights should be keyed to and decided by each individual state in the light of its own history, tradition, and level of cultural and economic development—is obvious for any authoritarian or repressive state. But cultural relativism in both theory and practice is deeply flawed. It proceeds from the dubious premise that what is done in various countries in varying cultural and developmental conditions should be accepted as international norms and standards. To accept varying human rights conditions and practices in a multicultural world as empirical reality is one thing, but to accept multiple, culture-specific government practices as normative reality is something else—namely, to have no international standards.

In practice, China adopted a regional approach as part of a divide and conquer strategy in the UN, the logic of which was to slice up the concept of universal human rights little by little, region by region, until there was scarcely anything left of the UN human rights regime. Yet the UN Development Program's 1991 human freedom index, which measured eighty-eight countries against forty indicators of human freedom (for example, the right to travel, the right to use an ethnic language, freedom from capital punishment, freedom to express political opposition and maintain an independent press, the right to free legal aid and to an open trial), put China near the bottom—it was ranked eighty-fourth—with only two of the forty key human freedoms enjoyed by the Chinese people.

Thus, despite the prominence accorded human rights internationally in the 1990s, China seems to be doing more and more to achieve less and less. Lacking cooptive soft power and ideological appeal in a post-Communist era, Beijing instinctively invokes the pre-Holocaust and pre-Nuremberg principle of state sovereignty as a kind of sword with which to ward off external human rights pressures.

China As a Responsible Great Power?

By conventional measurements of the rise and fall of great powers (in terms of shifts in the international military and economic power balances), China is a rising great power. Yet it remains an incomplete great power in a rapidly changing world where transnational nonmilitary challenges to and soft sources of power are becoming increasingly important. Thus, China's future as a complete great power remains indeterminate, if not foreclosed.

Paradoxically, China is at once a growing and assertive regional military power in its near abroad and a weak state at home pretending to be a strong state. Despite its remarkable foreign policy achievements during the post-Mao reform era, China does not seem to be a fully satisfied status quo power. Its assertive unilateral Realpolitik may be seen as a function of a regime with weak legitimacy trying hard to bring about national reunification and restore what Chinese of every political coloration believe to be China's natural and inalienable right to great power status. Herein lies the logic of Chinese "exemptionalism": China-specific exemption in the global human rights regime and China-specific entitlement in global security and economic institutions, all in the service of restoring China's great power status.

While post-Mao leaders succeeded to a remarkable degree in making their country materially rich and militarily strong, gaps remain between actual and perceived power and between hard and soft power. Moreover, post-Mao leaders have left their country largely unprepared for dealing with the changing sources of power and with the challenges of globalization from above and localization from below. Indeed, one of the central challenges—perhaps *the* challenge—confronting post-Deng leaders is how to manage the tensions emanating from substate ethnonational fragmentation and localization, East Asian regionalization, and globalization. Encouraging China's constructive and positive participation in the shaping of a more just, humane, and peaceful world order is a clear and continuing challenge confronting the world community today, and will remain so in the coming years.

Ultimately, the critical question in assessing China as a great power is behavior. What matters most is not so much the growth of Chinese power but how and for what purposes a rising China will actually wield its putative or actual power in the conduct of its international relations. Despite Realpolitik in global institutions, a policy of multilateral integration coupled with multilateral containment is a more feasible and desirable option than a policy of bilateral engagement. Enmeshing China more fully in a global network of mutually interactive and beneficial multilateral regimes could more easily contain and even possibly transform from within China's unilateral free-riding or defective behavior. Here the United States has an important role to play in Chinese global learning: not by asking China to follow what it says, nor what it actually does, nor by endlessly debating how to engage or contain China, but by shifting its own post–Cold War foreign policy from a unilateral to a multilateral cooperative security approach—indeed, by acting like the responsible great power that it wants China to become.

Liu Huaqiu,
Strive for a Peaceful International Environment

How do Chinese leaders see their country's role in world affairs, and what does the Chinese government tell its people about its diplomacy? In this selection, one of China's top diplomats and foreign affairs strategists, Liu Huaqiu, outlines his country's assessment of the world in aftermath of the Cold War. Liu is generally optimistic about international relations and China's future role in global affairs, but he notes that hegemonism (China's code word for the United States) still threatens China's aspirations.

This selection was first published in the Shanghai newspaper Liberation Daily *(Jiefang Ribao), on November 3, 1997. At that time Liu was director of the Foreign Affairs Office of the State Council.*

In his report to the Fifteenth National Party Congress, Comrade Jiang Zemin pointed out: The five years since the Fourteenth National Party Congress are "a period in which China's international standing has risen notably in the midst of radical changes in the pattern of the world. We have unswervingly implemented the independent foreign policy of peace and continued to improve the external environment for China's reform, opening up, and modernization drive. China's influence in international affairs has continued to grow." In the face of a changeable and complicated international situation in the past five years, the Party Central Committee with Comrade Jiang Zemin as the core, under the guidance of Deng Xiaoping's thinking on diplomatic work, has displayed its outstanding ability in handling foreign and international affairs, thus bringing about a new situation in diplomatic work.

Our country's diplomatic activities are very dynamic. In the past five years, our Party and state leaders have made 124 visits to other countries and attended thirty-nine major international conferences and celebrations; they have visited 143 countries, or 525 countries if the number of their repeat visits to some of such countries are counted separately. In the past five years, we have received 188 heads of state and government during their visits to China. The exchange of such high-level visits has promoted the in-depth development of our country's friendships and cooperative relations with such countries. Our country's friendship and good-neighborly relations with surrounding countries have developed in an all-round way. New progress has been made in our country's solidarity and cooperation with the large numbers of developing countries. We have withstood the impact from the drastic changes in Eastern Europe and the disintegration of the Soviet Union, smashed Western sanctions, and developed our relations with developing countries. Our country has achieved remarkable results in multilateral diplomacy. In dealing with the disgusting acts of encroaching on our country's sovereignty and interfering in our internal affairs, we have upheld principles and waged a just struggle to our advantage and with restraint, thus effectively safeguarding our sovereignty, territorial integrity, and national dignity. On the basis of the four principles of "independence, complete equality, mutual respect, and noninterference in each other's internal affairs," the Chinese Communist Party has extensively developed its relations with the major political parties of most countries in the world. We have been opening wider and wider to the outside world, further expanding our economic and trade relations with other countries.

Such achievements are a result of earnest implementation of Deng Xiaoping's thinking on diplomatic work. China began to enter the new historical period of building socialism with Chinese characteristics following the Third Plenary Session of the Party's Eleventh Central Committee. In nearly twenty years previous to that, tremendous changes have taken place in the international situation. From the standpoint of dialectical and historical materialism and with great foresight, Comrade Deng Xiaoping soberly assessed the international situation; proceeding from the highest interests of the Chinese nation and the overall interests of world peace and development, he made a series of major readjustments in our country's foreign policy, forming his thinking on diplomatic work with the distinctive features of the times as follows: It inherits and develops the independent foreign policy of peace laid down by Comrades Mao Zedong and Zhou Enlai, changes the old view that "the low-flying swallows and the rising wind forebode a coming storm" and that a world war is inevitable and imminent, and makes the scientific judgment that the forces of peace are growing and that war is avoidable; we have readjusted our relations with major countries and changed the "one-front" strategy; the independence, security, sovereignty, and territorial integrity of our country and our national dignity are unswervingly safeguarded; it is pointed out that peace and development are the two themes of the contemporary world; it is made clear that the foreign policy of our country is independent, with peace as its purpose, and combines independence closely with peace; stress is put on opposing hegemonism and maintaining world peace; our diplomatic work is to serve the drive for socialist modernization; efforts are to be made to secure a peaceful international environment for a fairly long time to come; it is essential to develop friendship and good-neighborly relations with other countries; China will always belong to the third world, and it is necessary to protect the rights and interests of third world countries; state-to-state relations should not be handled in terms of social system and ideology; the policy of opening to the outside world in all directions is to be implemented and the relationship between independence and opening up to be handled properly; friendly relations are to be developed with all countries in the world on the basis of the five principles of peaceful coexistence; it is necessary to engage in extensive mutually beneficial cooperation to promote common development; efforts are to be made to advance the establishment of a peaceful, stable, just, and rational international political and economic order; the scientific concept of "one country, two systems" is put forward; and the strategic principles of observing things soberly, holding our ground, dealing with matters calmly, hiding our capacities and biding our time, and getting things done and making achievements are laid down. Deng Xiaoping's thinking on diplomatic work is a major component of Deng Xiaoping theory, a magic weapon for our country to achieve success in diplomatic work in the new period. It has become the guide to our country's diplomatic work and will continue to radiate brilliance and strong vitality.

Now our country is faced with opportunities in diplomacy that have seldom been seen since the founding of the People's Republic of China. As Comrade Jiang Zemin pointed out in his report to the Fifteenth National Party Congress: "For a fairly long period of time to come, it will be possible to avert a new world war and secure a favorable, peaceful international environment and maintain good relations with our surrounding countries." This is a scientific judgment made according to Deng Xiaoping's thinking on diplomatic work and on the basis of a profound analysis of the developing trend of the current international situation; with good grounds, this judgment is completely correct.

First, people of all countries in the world have learned a profound historical lesson that the two world wars of this century brought grave suffering to mankind. So, maintaining peace and opposing war have become the common understanding and action of people the world over.

Second, in the past only the United States and the Soviet Union were capable of fighting a world war. Now one country has disintegrated, and the other, tied up by many things, cannot act rashly and blindly. Third, the trend toward multipolarity is developing rapidly, which is conducive to world peace, security, stability, and prosperity. As the only superpower in the world today, the United States is still very strong overall, but its actual strength is relatively declining as it is continuously faced with competition and challenges from various quarters. The days when a very small number of major powers or groups of major powers monopolize world affairs and dominate the destinies of other countries are gone. Western Europe, Japan, Russia, China, and other new power centers are taking shape, and large numbers of developing countries are also continuously growing in strength. In the economic field, North America, Western Europe, and East Asia stand like the legs of a tripod. The forming of the European Currency Unit will pose a grave challenge to the position of the U.S. dollar. Regional and subregional cooperation organizations have sprung up like mushrooms in Asia, Africa, and Latin America, and they are developing rapidly. Politically, the United Nations is playing an increasingly important role, and the positive influence and role of the developing nations of the Group of 15 and Group of 77, the Nonaligned Movement, the Association of Southeast Asian Nations, and other groups and organizations are increasing. Intercontinent organizations are also very active. In the military field, the confrontation between the Warsaw Treaty Organization and the North Atlantic Treaty Organization, the two major military blocs, no longer exists. The European Union is striving to restructure the North Atlantic Treaty Organization, to build independent European defense, and to challenge the United States as the leader of the alliance. The development of the trend toward multipolarity has increased the checks and balances of various countries and regions on each other, which is conducive to preventing a new world war.

Fourth [sic], the most profound postwar readjustments have been made in the relations between various major countries, and they have increased their dialogues, their reliance on others for support, as well as their interdependence and cooperation. Although there are contradictions, frictions, and problems of various kinds among major developed countries, coordination and cooperation are still the main aspect in their relations. Major countries have established strategic partnerships one after another. It has become a major tendency that heads of state or government are actively engaged in diplomacy to seek dialogue and cooperation, instead of confrontation and dispute.

Fifth, economic factors are playing an ever more important role in international relations. Most countries in the world are making economic development their task of primary importance, and they all need a peaceful international environment to develop their economies and improve their people's living standards for a long time to come; they do not want any chaos caused by war or any other factors interfering with or disrupting the process of economic development. The rapid development of science and technology in the world has continuously deepened the interdependence of various countries and regions, which is bringing about a new situation in which there is something of each in the other.

Sixth, looking around the world, we find that the voice of the people in all regions who want peace, seek stability, promote cooperation, and strive for development is getting louder and louder. The status and influence of large numbers of third world countries in international politics are rising, and they are becoming an important force for maintaining peace and stability. Despite the occurrence from time to time of local conflicts, which are caused by racial, religious, or territorial factors, such conflicts are unlikely to be out of control or to develop into a new world war because restraining mechanisms exist in various regions and the whole world.

The current international situation is generally favorable to us, but it should be soberly noted that there are still many uncertain and destabilizing factors and the world is still not tranquil. In the process of change in the international pattern, new and old contradictions are intertwined. Hot spots in some regions have yet to be removed, and new ones have appeared; there is turmoil in some countries and regions. The Cold War mentality still exists, and hegemonism and power politics remain the main sources of threat to world peace and stability. There still exist such phenomena as having no regard for other countries' conditions and interfering in their internal affairs. A very small number of countries have expanded their military blocs and strengthened their military alliances, and they have not renounced the use of military means to maintain their strategic interests. Quite a few countries are readjusting their military strategies and stepping up research and development of high-tech weapons. Contradictions continue between different values and patterns of development, and the struggle between infiltration and counterinfiltration in the cultural and ideological spheres is intense. With no respect for developing countries' right to choose their own road of development, some Western countries take advantage of issues such as "human rights" to interfere in other countries' internal affairs in an attempt to impose their own social system, ideology, and values on the latter. The world's wealth has increased sharply in this century, but its distribution is very unfair. So the gap between the rich and the poor continues to widen, and poverty and hunger are far from being eliminated. The unjust and irrational old international economic order has not yet been radically changed. The environment is worsening throughout the world. The proliferation of weapons, international crime, drug trafficking, illegal immigration, terrorism, and other transnational problems are endangering world and regional peace and stability. We must not take those problems lightly but keep giving warnings in these regards and conscientiously perform our work well in various fields.

The fundamental task of our country's diplomatic work is to serve the purpose of its reform, opening up, and socialist modernization; to secure a peaceful international environment for a fairly long time to come; and to maintain good relations with our surrounding countries. Comrade Deng Xiaoping clearly pointed out that the main objectives of our country's diplomacy are (1) to oppose hegemonism and maintain world peace, and (2) to promote international cooperation and advance common development. The burden is heavy and the road is long in our efforts to achieve these objectives. The next five years are of the utmost importance for the development of our country. In diplomatic work our country will also be faced with various opportunities and challenges. How we should deal with such challenges and seize such opportunities to better serve the socialist modernization of our country is a question we must answer in diplomatic work. In his report to the Fifteenth National Party Congress, Comrade Jiang Zemin comprehensively put forward ten principles for our country's diplomatic work, which we must implement to the letter.

First, we should maintain independence. Comrade Deng Xiaoping repeatedly stressed: If developing countries in the third world have no national dignity and do not treasure their national independence, they will not be able to establish themselves; first priority must always be given to the sovereignty and security of the country. China's international standing is continuously rising, and its prestige and influence are constantly increasing. This is because we uphold independence, persist in proceeding from the interests of the people in China and the world, and realistically handle international affairs according to the requirements of international law and the merits of different cases; we are not frightened by evil, fear no pressure, and independently decide on our position and policies. Comrade Deng Xiaoping also pointed out: Safeguarding the unification of the motherland is our supreme task. The matter of sovereignty brooks no discussion. From now on we should continue to resolutely oppose splittism, "Taiwan independence," and the creation of "two Chinas" or "one China, one Taiwan"; we should continue to oppose foreign interference, and under no circumstances must any forces be allowed to change the status of Taiwan as part of China in any way. We should strive to realize the complete reunification of the motherland at an early date.

Second, opposing hegemonism and safeguarding world peace are our consistent stand and a long-term task facing the progressive forces in the world. After the end of the Cold War, hegemonism and power politics still threaten world peace and stability. The phenomena of the big bullying the small, the strong dominating the weak, and the rich oppressing the poor are nothing new, and such phenomena even become very serious sometimes. The superpower still makes indiscreet criticisms of others everywhere and willfully interferes with other countries' internal affairs, further complicating turmoil and conflict in some countries and regions. We maintain that all countries, big or small, rich or poor, strong or weak, are equal. We persistently oppose hegemonism and power politics and safeguard and promote the lofty cause of world peace and development. As a permanent member of the UN Security Council, our country will, as always, continue to play its positive role in realizing this lofty cause. The world is rich and varied, and this is an objective reality.

Mankind can make progress and the world can develop only when this reality is recognized and fully respected and the people of various countries with different social systems, values, and ways of life coexist peacefully. If one country has no regard for this objective reality, considers a given model superior to others, and attempts to impose its own social system, values, and way of life on other countries, it not only cannot be done but, on the contrary, will give rise to disgust and resistance from the latter.

Third, we should strive to bring about a just and rational new international political and economic order. Doing away with the old international order and building a new one is a just, strong, and long-cherished desire of the people of various countries in the world. China has always taken a clear-cut stand on this matter. We advocate that the new order should be built on the basis of the five principles of peaceful coexistence and in conformity with the purpose and principles of the UN Charter. Its main content should be as follows: all countries are entitled to choose their own road of development according to their conditions, and other countries have no right to interfere in this; all countries, big or small, strong or weak, rich or poor, are equal members of the international community, and no country should seek hegemonism or practice power politics; all differences and disputes between countries should be settled by peaceful means, and no one should resort to force or the threat of force; it is necessary to strengthen or expand economic, scientific, technological, and cultural exchanges and cooperation on the basis of equality and mutual benefit, to promote common development and prosperity, and to oppose inequality and discriminating policies and practices in economic and trade relations, and much less should economic sanctions against other countries at every turn be allowed. Now economic interrelations in the world are getting closer and closer, and the economic interdependence between North and South is continuously deepening. Developed countries should create a favorable external environment for developing countries; doing so is also beneficial to their own economic development.

Fourth, we should continue to improve and develop our relations with all countries in the world on the basis of the five principles of peaceful coexistence.

It is a basic position of our country in foreign affairs to strengthen its solidarity and cooperation with large numbers of developing countries. This is determined by our country's historical experiences and future development. Our country shares bitter historical experiences with a large number of developing countries, and we all are now faced with the common tasks of safeguarding our national independence and sovereignty and pursuing economic development. For years our country and large numbers of developing countries have shared a common fate, helped one another, and been closely united, effectively safeguarding our political and economic interests. Although tremendous changes have taken place in the international situation, our policy of strengthening solidarity and cooperation with developing countries cannot and will not be changed; China always belongs to the third world. If there were any doubt about this policy, it would fundamentally shake the foundation for our country's diplomatic work and cause tremendous damage to our country's economic development and international image.

China is different from Western countries in social system and ideology, and there are also historical and cultural differences; but there are wide-ranging common interests between the two sides, and the prospects for mutually beneficial cooperation are broad. We consistently hold: It is normal that there are some issues and differences between countries, and what is important is to put stress on long-term interests, respect each other, uphold the principles of equality and mutual benefit, refrain from interfering in each other's internal affairs, live together in amity, and work for common development. Facts show that the practice of imposing sanctions against other countries or threatening to do so or unilaterally pressuring other countries at every turn not only is not conducive to settling issues but aggravates or intensifies contradictions, which will harm the interests of both sides. Sino-U.S. relations have a bearing on the fundamental interests of the Chinese and American peoples and also on peace and development in the Asia-Pacific region and the world as well. As long as the two countries always take the overall situation into consideration, have their eyes on the future, earnestly comply with the three Sino-U.S. joint communiqués, and properly handle the Taiwan issue, they can certainly bring a relatively stable Sino-U.S. relationship into the twenty-first century. Japan is a close neighbor of China. China and Japan should use history as a mirror, adhere to the Sino-Japanese Joint Statement and the Sino-Japanese Treaty of Peace and Friendship, and work for the fundamental interests of the peoples of the two countries and for peace and development in Asia. China and West European countries should work together to build a new type of relationship oriented to the twenty-first century on the basis of mutual respect, seeking common ground while reserving differences, equality, and mutual benefit. We should continue to improve and develop friendly relations with Canada, Australia, and other developed countries.

In his report to the Fifteenth National Party Congress, Comrade Jiang Zemin emphatically pointed out: "We should uphold the good-neighbor policy. This has been our consistent stand and will never change." It was a very solemn policy statement. In the past five years we have strived to develop all-around friendly, mutually beneficial, and cooperative relations with our neighboring countries and maintained a favorable and peaceful environment with them. This is very gratifying. For historical and other reasons, however, there exist differences of one kind or another and even disputes between our country and some neighboring countries. This is not strange, and what is crucial is how to deal with those issues. We advocate peacefully settling such issues through friendly consultation and negotiation and maintaining the overall situation of peace and stability. It does not matter if some issues cannot be settled for the time being, we can put them aside for the moment and seek common ground while reserving differences. Now we are concentrating on economic construction, and maintaining peace and stability with our surrounding countries is all the more important for the smooth development of the modernization drive in our country. For this reason, our relations with our surrounding countries will certainly get better and better.

Fifth, to achieve our objectives of economic development, we must extensively conduct economic, trade, and technological cooperation and exchanges with various countries and regions in the world on the basis of equality and mutual benefit. It is a national policy of our country to open to the outside world in all directions. In the face of the new situation resulting from intense economic competition and rapid scientific and technological advances, we should take a brand-new stance in the world by improving the pattern of opening up in all directions, at all levels, and in a wide range, more effectively using the domestic and international markets and resources, striving to open international markets, and taking an active part in regional economic cooperation and world multilateral trade systems. In diplomatic work, we should continue to make unremitting efforts to achieve such purposes.

The Chinese Communist Party has consistently attached great importance to the development of foreign relations and made vigorous efforts in this regard, and it regards our Party's development of normal relations with other countries as an important part of the country's foreign relations. The CCP has always paid close attention to people-to-people diplomacy and to the positive role played by such mass organizations as trade unions and youth and women's organizations in enhancing mutual understanding, friendship, and cooperation with the people of other countries.

Political disturbances occurred at home and abroad in the late 1980s and early 1990s. Some people in Western countries predicted that the socialist system in China would "collapse," creating "the theory of China's collapse." But the cause of socialism with Chinese characteristics is thriving in China and full of vigor and vitality. So the theory of China's collapse has itself collapsed. Internationally, some people are now spreading the word that the development of China will "pose a threat" to the world, creating "the theory of China posing a threat." This is entirely groundless. (1) Historically, China long suffered from aggression, oppression, bullying, and humiliation from the great powers, fully understanding the true meaning of "do not do to others what you do not wish for yourself." (2) China has a large population and a poor foundation to start with, and it will take decades of arduous effort by China to achieve modernization and to reach the level of a moderately developed country; in addition, China needs a peaceful international environment, especially good relations with our surrounding countries, for a long time to come. (3) China has always implemented the military strategic principle of active defense, and its military spending is small; China's military spending in 1997 is only $9.71 billion, accounting for about 3.6 percent of U.S. military expenditures. In his report to the Fifteenth National Party Congress, General Secretary Jiang Zemin announced: In addition to the army reduction by one million men in the 1980s, we shall reduce the armed forces by another 500,000 in the next three years. China will never pose a threat to any country. (4) China persistently pursues its independent foreign policy of peace, and all its actions are aimed at maintaining peace. As early as in the period of the Western Han dynasty, Marquis of Huaiyin Han Xin made this famous remark: "Whoever dominates others even only in name will actually lose the popular support of the world." So, since more than 2,000 years ago, the Chinese people have warned themselves against seeking hegemony. General Secretary Jiang Zemin pointed out: "China will never seek hegemonism, even in the future when it becomes developed." Facts are stronger than rhetoric. With the passage of time, the so-called theory of China posing a threat will declare its own bankruptcy.

Mankind will soon stride into the twenty-first century. The world wants peace, countries want stability, economies need to be developed, and mankind wants progress—all these have become the mainstream of the present time. Peace and development are still the two outstanding themes of the world. Despite the facts that the international situation and international relations are complex and that the road ahead is still tortuous, as General Secretary Jiang Zemin pointed out, "The future of the world is bright." We should unswervingly implement our independent foreign policy of peace, proceed from the interests of peace and development and from the overall interests of our country's reform, opening up, and socialist modernization, and strive to secure a peaceful international environment for a fairly long period of time to come.

David Shambaugh,
The United States and China: Cooperation or Confrontation?

No international relationship is more central to China's foreign affairs or domestic development than that with the United States. Sino-American relations have historically been very unsteady, often even hostile. A stable and productive equilibrium has been elusive. In this selection coeditor David Shambaugh explores the reasons for this volatility in recent years and offers an assessment of the state of the relationship on the eve of the 1997 and 1998 summit meetings between Presidents Clinton and Jiang.

This selection was originally published in Current History, September *1997.*

A year ago Sino-American relations were tense. Both countries demonstrated military might in the Taiwan Strait, Beijing recalled its ambassador from Washington, and the two sides hurled invective at each other. A new cold war seemed in the offing. Since those strained times the relationship has stabilized. Military tensions have diminished, the aircraft carriers have returned to port, and the diplomats have resumed their postings. The two governments have made substantial efforts to arrest the downward spiral and rebuild ties.

While more stable and interactive, relations between the United States and China still exhibit considerable fragility and uncertainty. Some mutual interests mandate that the two continental giants should cooperate positively, and a complex web of commercial and cultural exchanges binds the two societies together. However, many other important issues divide them. Accordingly, in each country bureaucracies and interest groups work both to promote and to undermine the relationship. A tug and pull over the direction of the relationship exists not only between the two countries but within each. Distorted images and misperceptions exist on both sides, with the mass media reinforcing negative stereotypes and many opinion shapers in each country perceiving and portraying the other in adversarial terms. These suspicions restrict collaboration. Mutual trust and the political will to push the relationship forward positively are lacking.

Thus, the United States and China cooperate in some spheres and clash in others. Elements of cooperation and competition—and occasionally confrontation—coexist. A complex, multifaceted relationship has emerged in which each knows it must cooperate where possible but has real difficulties in doing so. Both countries recognize that the costs of a completely adversarial relationship would be high, and that it therefore behooves them to establish a workable equilibrium, but neither really trusts the other.

The Missionary Complex

More broadly, the impediments to establishing a mutually productive and cooperative relationship lie not only in the specific issues and constituencies of the moment but also in deeper historical and social forces. It is not just a matter of America adjusting to China as a rising power; national identity is also a key source of friction. The United States prides itself on being the world's only superpower; its president speaks often of providing "global leadership," and its foreign policy contains many universal principles that it seeks to impart to others. But the identity and mission of the Chinese Communist regime rest precisely on countering what it describes as "hegemony" and the "superpower mentality" while steadfastly refusing to adopt such universal principles as human rights and democracy. China's entire modern history since the midnineteenth century, and hence its core national identity, is one of resisting foreign dictates and building up national power to do so. Today, as China grows strong, Chinese nationalism grows stronger. And America's power and global agenda are butting up against it. America's superpower status and liberal internationalism are thus the antitheses of China's (official) national identity.

Americans, on the other hand, remain imbued with a long-standing "missionary complex" to transform China in their image. For the United States, it seems that the issue is never whether to change China but how. Over the years the American missionary complex toward China has stemmed from several impulses: a commercial impulse to modernize China, a political impulse to democratize China, a religious impulse to convert China to Christianity, an educational impulse to mold China's universities and research institutions, a cultural impulse to impart American values, and a strategic impulse to affect China's behavior in world affairs. These impulses have been apparent in American approaches to China for more than a century and remain present today. In each realm the American approach has been paternalistic, guided by a belief in the universal applicability of the American national experience. Sometimes American missionaries have found willing students and converts in China, but more often such paternalism has encountered staunch Chinese nationalism, pride, and resistance.

These missionary impulses—and the resistance they encounter—have never been more apparent than they are today in Sino-American relations. The United States continues to try to change China, while China insists on defining its own path of development. The stronger China becomes, the more resistant it is to American pressure and paternalism. Not only does China resist, but it now has its own agenda for changing American foreign policy and behavior. With these countervailing national identities and agendas, it is little wonder that the two powers distrust and often clash with each other.

In 1996 the distrust and difficulties reached a crescendo, with the "crisis" that arose out of Taiwanese President Lee Teng-hui's private visit to the United States, the first direct presidential elections in Taiwan, Beijing's belligerent military exercises in the Taiwan Strait, and Washington's dispatch of two aircraft carrier battle groups off Taiwan. Since the crisis tempers have cooled and tensions have relaxed. This moderation has allowed the Clinton administration to begin implementing its policy of "comprehensive engagement" with China.

Resuming the Dialogue

Comprehensive engagement with China evolved out of the need to repair the deteriorated relations that had existed since 1989, and to provide an overarching framework to guide America's ties with China. Since the Beijing massacre of that year, America's China policy had been captured by a host of special interest groups, with the result that the Clinton administration found itself pursuing a fragmented policy that was largely reactive to independent domestic interests. Competitive and contentious elements came to dominate the relationship, restricting cooperation in important areas where national interests converged. The new policy was thus driven by the need to stabilize the deteriorating relationship and to work together where possible. The strategy underlying this new American policy had three main components.

First, Washington sought to reinstitutionalize the relationship. Since

1989 the web of intergovernmental exchanges established during the previous decade had unraveled. Contact was minimal, often terse, and generally restricted to the foreign and trade ministerial channels. High-level dialogue was suspended, various sanctions were applied, and normal bureaucratic interaction atrophied. Thus the first step in the new policy of comprehensive engagement was to reestablish regular channels of communication at both high and working levels. Secretary of State Warren Christopher and his successor, Madeleine Albright, intensified the frequency of their meetings with Chinese Foreign Minister Qian Qichen. There were more regular working-level interactions between the Department of State and its Chinese counterpart, particularly on arms control issues. Many other U.S. government agencies and departments—including Commerce, Treasury, Immigration and Naturalization, the FBI, and the Drug Enforcement Agency—sent representatives to China to reestablish functional cooperation.

One of the key parts in the reinstitutionalization process was to restart military exchanges. After two postponements Chinese Defense Minister Chi Haotian paid an official visit to the United States in December 1996. General Chi toured a variety of military facilities and held talks with outgoing Secretary of Defense William Perry. Although several members of Congress refused to meet with Chi, President Bill Clinton received him. This visit triggered a series of military exchanges, including an exchange between Chairman of the Joint Chiefs of Staff John Shalikashvili and Chief of People's Liberation Army (PLA) General Staff Fu Quanyou; the sending of PLA personnel to universities in the United States as visiting scholars; exchanges between weapons laboratories; and ship visits. (The two sides also agreed that the United States Navy could continue to make port calls to Hong Kong after its reversion to Chinese sovereignty, which have been running at between sixty and eighty calls annually in recent years.)

The military-to-military exchanges have developed quickly, but they have not been entirely satisfactory. While the American military has willingly shown many bases and installations to visiting Chinese delegations, access to Chinese military bases and installations remain severely limited. Moreover, efforts to make the PLA more transparent in publicly reporting real defense budget allocations, troop deployments, defense doctrine, and strategic outlook have met with little progress. China continues to claim that its defense expenditure is but a fraction of Western estimates. In 1997 this amounted to $9.7 billion, although most credible Western estimates place it at four or five times this figure. It is hardly believable that the PLA could maintain a force of 2.9 million under arms (and a nearly 1.0 million strong paramilitary People's Armed Police and a 1.2 million reserve force) while financing an across-the-board modernization program (including expensive arms purchases from Russia and other countries) on $9.7 billion.

Problems of transparency and reciprocity will predictably begin to place limits on the further development of bilateral military relations. China's recent criticisms of the United States–Japan security treaty and the deployment of 100,000 American troops in the Asia-Pacific region have also not been well received at the Department of Defense. Nonetheless, the reestablishment of mutual military exchanges between the United States and China is an important component of the overall bilateral relationship and serves as a stabilizing force in the Asia Pacific and for global security.

High-level meetings at the presidential and vice presidential level have also taken place. President Clinton has met several times with President Jiang Zemin in Seattle, New York, and Asian capitals, and in late October Jiang is slated to pay a formal state visit to the United States. This will be followed, presumably, by a reciprocal visit by Clinton to China in 1998—the first by an American president in a decade. Vice President Al Gore also paid an official visit to China in February 1997.

These visits at the high and working levels have facilitated direct communication between the two governments over a number of issues of mutual concern, such as human rights, trade, arms control and proliferation, environmental protection, crime prevention, Taiwan, and regional security. Where the two sides disagree—and these areas are numerous—the reestablished channels permit discussion to narrow and resolve differences. Thus the first component of comprehensive engagement—reinstitutionalization of relations—has produced forward movement in the relationship and has served to maintain some normalcy of ties at a time when domestic interest groups in both countries have put the relationship under tremendous strain.

The second component of the new Clinton China policy was to reestablish a strategic dialogue with the Chinese leadership, military, and security establishment. To begin the dialogue, National Security Adviser Anthony Lake invited his counterpart, Liu Huaqiu, the director of the State Council Office of Foreign Affairs, to the United States in March 1996 for wide-ranging discussions. Lake reportedly told Liu that the nations of the world today have a choice in how they interact: as sovereign or interdependent units. Lake identified the United States as pursuing a foreign policy of interdependent multilateralism and implied that China needed to move in that direction. This channel of strategic dialogue is being continued by Lake's successor, Samuel Berger, but has been supplemented with interactions between military and civilian officials.

The third objective of comprehensive engagement was to integrate China into the international institutional order. The rationale for this policy goal is that it will be easier to deal with China in multilateral institutions, and that these will help constrain Chinese behavior that deviates from international law and norms, as well as from American foreign policy interests. Progress has been made in this regard with China's recent accession to a series of multilateral security regimes: the nuclear Nonproliferation Treaty, the Comprehensive Test Ban Treaty, the Chemical Weapons Convention, and the Biological Weapons Convention. While not a member, China has also essentially adhered to the Missile Technology Control Regime.

China's eventual accession to the World Trade Organization (WTO) will also be a major step forward in the strategy of giving it a stake in the rules and norms of the global system. Negotiations between China, the United States, and other industrialized nations over the terms of China's entry into the WTO have moved more quickly in the past year. Nearly sixty categories of issues have been agreed on in the China-WTO working party in Geneva, but a number of key issues remain unresolved, such as financial services, regulatory transparency, and hidden subsidies.

These three elements of comprehensive engagement—reinstitutionalization, strategic dialogue, and multilateral integration—are intended to stabilize and deepen a wide range of bilateral relations while further integrating China into the international order and thereby constraining its potentially disruptive behavior. The numerous domestic critics of this policy in the United States do not accept its premises and, during the spring of 1997, launched a frontal assault on it.

The Great China Policy Debate of 1997

The upsurge of criticism of China and the Clinton administration's China policy erupted earlier this year in the United States. It started in newspaper columns but quickly spread to newsmagazines, radio, television, and Congress. The new anti-China polemic was notable for crossing the political spectrum, from the liberal *New Republic* to the conservative *Weekly Standard*. Some respected analysts published best-selling books that sketched scenarios for eventual war between the United States and China. Many in this broad-based coalition, dubbed the "anti-China wave" (*fan Hua langchao*) by China's America watchers, sharply criticize President Clinton's policy of comprehensive engagement and call for a more confrontational policy toward Beijing. What is different about the groundswell of anti-China sentiment in 1997 is that it reached beyond the Washington beltway and foreign policy elite well into the country. The Christian Coalition and AFL-CIO labor union mobilized many in the middle and working classes against China. This development has tended to politicize China policy in a way not seen since the McCarthy period of the 1950s (indeed, some of the polemics and attacks on China specialists in this year's debate are eerily reminiscent of that dark period in American political history).

The critics portray the Chinese Communist regime as a strategic threat, commercial danger, political pariah, and morally repugnant dictatorship. They see the Clinton administration's policy as naive, appeasing, and having failed to bring about cooperative behavior on China's part.

Administration opponents have no shortage of complaints about the Chinese regime's behavior: its abysmal human rights record (a point conceded in the annual 1997 State Department human rights report) and treatment of dissidents; its repression of religious rights; its harsh birth control policies; its large bilateral trade surplus of $40 billion; its export of medium-range ballistic missiles to Pakistan and naval cruise missiles to Iran; its military bullying of Taiwan; its military modernization program; its territorial claims in the South China Sea; its suppression of Tibetan culture and religious life; its abuse of internationally recognized labor standards; its harsh prison conditions and export of goods made by prison labor; and its rollback of Hong Kong's democratic freedoms. China is also accused of surreptitiously channeling millions of dollars illegally to American congressional and presidential political campaign coffers during the 1996 election ("donorgate") and trying to recruit intelligence agents in the U.S. government. China's military is further known to have numerous affiliated companies doing business in the United States, conducting industrial and technological espionage, and even smuggling light assault weapons into the country.

All these perceptions and accusations fueled the "anti-China wave" during the spring of 1997. It was not enough, however, to undermine the annual extension of China's most favored nation (MFN) trading status. Despite intense debate, the extension passed the House of Representatives by a vote of 259 to 173. Characteristic of the mixed beliefs on the issue were the words of House Majority Leader Dick Armey (R-TX): "In my heart I would like to oppose most favored nation status for China as a way of expressing the deep repugnance I feel toward the tyranny of Beijing. But, intellectually, I believe that continued normal trade relations are best for the people of China." What Armey did not mention was the intense lobbying effort brought to bear on Congress by the American business community, as well as by Hong Kong and Taiwan (whose economic interests would be directly threatened by revocation).

Despite MFN's renewal, critics of China will remain sharply critical of the Clinton administration's policy. They will also continue to make China policy a partisan political issue within and between both parties. Representative Richard Gephardt (D-MO), a presidential aspirant, has already clearly identified China as a sensitive issue on which to attack his potential rival, Vice President Gore. Continued domestic criticism will limit the administration's freedom of maneuver and make it difficult to show that tangible gains are being made through the policy of engagement.

The critics call for a more robust and confrontational policy toward China but fail to spell out what such a policy would look like. Even Richard Bernstein and Ross Munro, the authors of *The Coming Conflict with China*, conclude their book with policy recommendations that bear close resemblance to the Clinton administration's policy of engagement. It is difficult to imagine that a policy of containment could be implemented effectively, even if it were thought desirable. Containment would necessarily entail a trade embargo, a wide range of sanctions, political isolation, and the deployment of military resources against China. These elements require extensive multilateral cooperation, which is precisely why containment would never work. Not a single Asian or European country would join the United States in such efforts to isolate China. It is doubtful that even Taiwan would join in. And a policy of confrontation, as opposed to containment, would entail harsh government criticism of China, an array of targeted sanctions, attempts to condemn China in international forums, the curtailment of government and nongovernment interactions, less support for trade and investment in China, more open support for Taiwan, and the deployment of U.S. military forces against China.

While a confrontational policy might satisfy domestic constituencies

in the United States, it would be counterproductive in eliciting cooperation from China. It would likely stimulate a wide range of Chinese
behavior that would work directly against American national interests.
China could, for example, increase its sales of missiles and other arms
to Iran, Iraq, North Korea, Burma, and other rogue regimes. It could
stop its behind-the-scenes help with implementing the North Korean
nuclear accord and could become less cooperative on regional and
international security agreements. Beijing could step up political and
military pressure against Taiwan and could further restrict the autonomy and freedoms guaranteed to Hong Kong. The PLA could accelerate purchases of advanced weapons from Russia and other countries and
place a much higher priority on developing a blue-water navy and other
elements of a power projection capability that could potentially threaten
the sea-lanes of East Asia—and United States interests. Neither a policy
of confrontation nor containment would make China conform to the
concerns of the United States—quite to the contrary.

Making Engagement Work

There is no real alternative to engaging China. But engagement should
be a means rather than an end. A policy of engagement should be
straightforward and defendable to the American public and United
States allies. Its goals should be threefold: (1) to elicit cooperation from
China on a broad range of issues of concern to the United States and
the international community; (2) to fashion policies toward, and an
American presence in, China that move it inexorably toward political
pluralism and a market economy consistent with international trade
standards; and (3) to integrate China into the international strategic
order as a status quo power that threatens neither its neighbors (including Taiwan) nor global security interests.

Such a policy must also be fully aware of China's history, pride, and
nationalism, as well as its century-long quest for territorial unity and economic modernization. Any American policy that is insensitive to these
aspirations will encounter substantial resistance. China must be treated
with respect. This does not mean that the United States or the international community should automatically acquiesce to China's claims
over the South China Sea, Tibet, Taiwan, or other occupied territories,
or countenance coercive behavior toward its neighbors, but it should
recognize that issues concerning territorial unification occupy a hyper-
sensitive place in Chinese diplomacy.

China and the United States are likely to be the two dominant world powers during the twenty-first century. It is imperative that these two continental giants learn to live and work together productively and cooperatively. For this to happen, issues larger than those that crowd the agendas of diplomats in Beijing and Washington—human rights, trade, and arms control, for example—must be resolved. The nub of the problems between the United States and China concerns the Chinese regime's internal, and America's external, behavior. The United States wants fundamental change in the former, while Beijing wants equally basic change in the latter. How these two elements interact will greatly affect the degree to which the two powers can coexist cooperatively and peacefully.

WILLIAM JEFFERSON CLINTON, CHINA AND THE NATIONAL INTEREST

In October 1997 Chinese President Jiang Zemin paid a state visit to the United States. This was the first state visit by a Chinese leader in twelve years, reflecting the abnormal status of bilateral relations between the two countries. Before the summit U.S. President Bill Clinton gave a speech outlining the importance of China to the United States and the rationale for his administration's policies toward the People's Republic.

This selection was excerpted from a presidential address made at the Voice of America in October 1997.

Next week, when President Jiang Zemin comes to Washington, it will be the first state visit by a Chinese leader to the United States for more than a decade. The visit gives us the opportunity and the responsibility to chart a course for the future that is more positive and more stable and, hopefully, more productive than our relations have been for the last few years.

China is a great country with a rich and proud history and a strong future. It will, for good or ill, play a very large role in shaping the twenty-first century, in which the children in this audience today, children all across our country, all across China, and indeed all across the world will live.

At the dawn of the new century, China stands at a crossroads. The direction China takes toward cooperation or conflict will profoundly affect Asia, America, and the world for decades. The emergence of China as a power that is stable, open, and nonagressive; that embraces free markets, political pluralism, and the rule of law; that works with us to build a secure international order—that kind of China, rather than a China turned inward and confrontational, is deeply in the interests of the American people.

Of course, China will choose its own destiny. Yet by working with China and expanding areas of cooperation, dealing forthrightly with our differences, we can advance fundamental American interests and values.

First, the United States has a profound interest in promoting a peaceful, prosperous, and stable world. Our task will be much easier if China is a part of that process—not only playing by the rules of international behavior but helping to write and enforce them.

China is a permanent member of the United Nations Security Council. Its support was crucial for peacekeeping efforts in Cambodia and building international mandates to reverse Iraq's aggression against Kuwait and restore democracy to Haiti. As a neighbor of India and Pakistan, China will influence whether these great democracies move toward responsible cooperation both with each other and with China.

From the Persian Gulf to the Caspian Sea, China's need for a reliable and efficient supply of energy to fuel its growth can make it a force for stability in these strategically critical regions. Next week President Jiang and I will discuss our visions of the future and the kind of strategic relationship we must have to promote cooperation, not conflict.

Second, the United States has a profound interest in peace and stability in Asia. Three times this century Americans have fought and died in Asian wars—37,000 Americans still patrol the Cold War's last frontier, on the Korean demilitarized zone. Territorial disputes that could flare into crises affecting America require it to maintain a strong American security presence in Asia. We want China to be a powerful force for security and cooperation there.

China has helped us convince North Korea to freeze and ultimately end its dangerous nuclear program. Just imagine how much more dangerous that volatile peninsula would be today if North Korea, reeling from food shortages, with a million soldiers encamped twenty-seven miles from Seoul, had continued this nuclear program.

China also agreed to take part in the four-party peace talks that President Kim and I proposed with North Korea, the only realistic avenue to a lasting peace. And China is playing an increasingly constructive role in Southeast Asia by working with us and the members of ASEAN to advance our shared interests in economic and political security.

Next week I'll discuss with President Jiang the steps we can take together to advance the peace process in Korea. We'll look at ways to strengthen our military-to-military contacts, decreasing the chances of miscalculation and broadening America's contacts with the next generation of China's military leaders. And I will reiterate to President Jiang America's continuing support for our one China policy, which has allowed democracy to flourish in Taiwan and Taiwan's relationship with the People's Republic to grow more stable and prosper. The Taiwan question can only be settled by the Chinese themselves peacefully.

Third, the United States has a profound interest in keeping weapons of mass destruction and other sophisticated weapons out of unstable regions and away from rogue states and terrorists. In the twenty-first century many of the threats to our security will come not from great power conflict but from states that defy the international community and violent groups seeking to undermine peace, stability, and democracy. China is already a nuclear power with increasingly sophisticated industrial and technological capabilities. We need its help to prevent dangerous weapons from falling into the wrong hands.

For years China stood outside the major international arms control regime. Over the past decade it has made important and welcome decisions to join the Nuclear Nonproliferation Treaty, the Chemical Weapons Convention, the Biological Weapons Convention, and to respect key provisions of the Missile Technology Control Regime. Last year at the United Nations, I was proud to be the first world leader to sign the Comprehensive Test Ban Treaty. China's foreign minister was the second leader to do so.

China has lived up to its pledge not to assist unsafeguarded nuclear facilities in third countries, and it is developing a system of export controls to prevent the transfer or sale of technology for weapons of mass destruction.

But China still maintains some troubling weapons supply relationships. At the summit I will discuss with President Jiang further steps we hope China will take to end or limit some of these supply relationships and to strengthen and broaden its export control system. And I will make the case to him that these steps are, first and foremost, in China's interest, because the spread of dangerous weapons and technology would increase instability near China's own borders.

Fourth, the United States has a profound interest in fighting drug trafficking and international organized crime. Increasingly, smugglers and criminals are taking advantage of China's vast territory and its borders with fifteen nations to move drugs and weapons, aliens, and the proceeds of illegal activities from one point in Asia to another, or from Asia to Europe.

China and the United States already are cooperating closely on alien smuggling, and China has taken a tough line against narco trafficking, a threat to its children as well as our own. Next week I will propose to President Jiang that our law enforcement communities intensify their efforts together.

Fifth, the United States has a profound interest in making global trade and investment as free, fair, and open as possible. Over the past five years, trade has produced more than one-third of America's economic growth. If we are to continue generating good jobs and higher incomes in our country, when we are just 4 percent of the world's population, we must continue to sell more to the other 96 percent. One of the best ways to do that is to bring China more fully into the world's trading system. With a quarter of the world's population and its fastest growing economy, China could and should be a magnet for our goods and services.

Even though American exports to China now are at an all-time high, so, too, is our trade deficit. In part, this is due to the strength of the American economy, and to the fact that many products we used to buy in other Asian countries now are manufactured in China. But clearly an important part of the problem remains lack of access to China's markets.

We strongly support China's admission into the World Trade Organization. But in turn China must dramatically improve access for foreign goods and services. We should be able to compete fully and fairly in China's marketplace, just as China competes in our own.

Tearing down trade barriers also is good for China, and for the growth of China's neighbors and, therefore, for the stability and future of Asia. Next week President Jiang and I will discuss steps China must take to join the WTO and assume its rightful place in the world economy.

Finally, the United States has a profound interest in ensuring that today's progress does not come at tomorrow's expense. Greenhouse gas emissions are leading to climate change. China is the fastest growing contributor to greenhouse gas emissions, and we are the biggest greenhouse gas emitter. Soon, however, China will overtake the United States and become the largest contributor. Already pollution has made respiratory disease the number one health problem for China's people. Last

March, when he visited China, Vice President Al Gore launched a joint forum with the Chinese on the environment and development so that we can work with China to pursue growth and protect the environment at the same time.

China has taken some important steps to deal with its need for more energy and cleaner air. Next week President Jiang and I will talk about the next steps China can take to combat climate change. It is a global problem that must have a global solution that cannot come without China's participation as well. We also will talk about what American companies and technology can do to support China in its efforts to reduce air pollution and increase clean energy production.

Progress in each of these areas will draw China into the institutions and arrangements that are setting the ground rules for the twenty-first century—the security partnerships, the open trade arrangements, the arms control regime, the multinational coalitions against terrorism, crime, and drugs, the commitments to preserve the environment and to uphold human rights. This is our best hope, to secure our own interests and values and to advance China's in the historic transformation that began twenty-five years ago, when China reopened to the world.

As we all know, the transformation already has produced truly impressive results. Twenty-five years ago China stood apart from and closed to the international community. Now China is a member of more than 1,000 international organizations—from the International Civil Aviation Organization to the International Fund for Agricultural Development. It has moved from the twenty-second largest trading nation to the eleventh. It is projected to become the second largest trader, after the United States, by 2020. And today 40,000 Chinese are studying here in the United States, with hundreds of thousands more living and learning in Europe, Asia, Africa, and Latin America.

China's economic transformation has been even more radical. Market reforms have spurred more than two decades of unprecedented growth, and the decision at the recently ended Fifteenth Party Congress to sell off most all of China's big, state-owned industries promises to keep China moving toward a market economy.

The number of people living in poverty has dropped from 250 million to 58 million, even as China's population has increased by nearly 350 million. Per capita income in the cities has jumped 550 percent in just the past decade.

As China has opened its economy, its people have enjoyed greater freedom of movement and choice of employment, better schools and housing. Today most Chinese enjoy a higher standard of living than at any time in China's modern history. But as China has opened economically, political reform has lagged behind.

Frustration in the West turned into condemnation after the terrible events in Tiananmen Square. Now, nearly a decade later, one of the great questions before the community of democracies is how to pursue the broad and complex range of our interests with China while urging and supporting China to move politically as well as economically into the twenty-first century. The great question for China is how to preserve stability, promote growth, and increase its influence in the world while making room for the debate and the dissent that are a part of the fabric of all truly free and vibrant societies. The answer to those questions must begin with an understanding of the crossroads China has reached.

As China discards its old economic order, the scope and sweep of change has rekindled historic fears of chaos and disintegration. In return, Chinese leaders have worked hard to mobilize support, legitimize power, and hold the country together, which they see is essential to restoring the greatness of their nation and its rightful influence in the world. In the process, however, they have stifled political dissent to a degree and in ways that we believe are fundamentally wrong, even as freedom from want, freedom of movement, and local elections have increased.

This approach has caused problems within China and in its relationship to the United States. Chinese leaders believe it is necessary to hold the nation together, to keep it growing, to keep moving toward its destiny. But it will become increasingly difficult to maintain the closed political system in an ever more open economy and society.

China's economic growth has made it more and more dependent on the outside world for investment, markets, and energy. Last year it was the second largest recipient of foreign direct investment in the world. These linkages bring with them powerful forces for change. Computers and the Internet, fax machines and photocopiers, modems and satellites all increase the exposure to people, ideas, and the world beyond China's borders. The effect is only just beginning to be felt.

Today more than a billion Chinese have access to television, up from just 10 million two decades ago. Satellite dishes dot the landscape. They receive dozens of outside channels, including English-language services of CNN, Star TV, and Worldnet. Talk radio is increasingly popular and relatively unregulated in China's 1,000 radio stations. And 70 percent of China's students regularly listen to the Voice of America.

China's 2,200 newspapers, up from just 42 three decades ago, and more than 7,000 magazines and journals are more open in content. A decade ago there were 50,000 mobile phones in China; now there are more than 7 million. The Internet already has 150,000 accounts in China, with more than a million expected to be on-line by the year 2000. The more ideas and information spread, the more people will expect to think for themselves, express their own opinions, and participate. And the more that happens, the harder it will be for their government to stand in their way.

Indeed, greater openness is profoundly in China's own interest. If welcomed, it will speed economic growth, enhance the world influence of China, and stabilize society. Without the full freedom to think, to question, to create, China will be at a distinct disadvantage, competing with fully open societies in the Information Age where the greatest source of national wealth is what resides in the human mind.

China's creative potential is truly staggering. The largest population in the world is not yet among its top fifteen patent powers. In an era where these human resources are what really matters, a country that holds its people back cannot achieve its full potential.

Our belief that, over time, growing interdependence would have a liberalizing effect in China does not mean in the meantime we should or we can ignore abuses in China of human rights or religious freedom. Nor does it mean that there is nothing we can do to speed the process of liberalization.

Americans share a fundamental conviction that people everywhere have the right to be treated with dignity, to give voice to their opinions, to choose their own leaders, to worship as they please. From Poland to South Africa, from Haiti to the Philippines, the democratic saga of the last decade proves that these are not American rights or Western rights or developed world rights, they are the birthrights of every human being enshrined in the Universal Declaration of Human Rights.

Those who fight for human rights and against religious persecution, at the risk of their jobs, their freedom, even their lives, find strength through knowledge that they are not alone, that the community of democracies stands with them. The United States, therefore, must and will continue to stand up for human rights, to speak out against their abuse in China or anywhere else in the world. To do otherwise would run counter to everything we stand for as Americans. (Applause.)

Over the past year our State Department's annual human rights report again pulled no punches on China. We cosponsored a resolution critical of China's human rights record in Geneva, even though many of our allies had abandoned the effort. We continue to speak against the arrest of dissidents, and for a resumed dialogue with the Dalai Lama, on behalf of the people and the distinct culture and unique identity of the people of Tibet—not their political independence but their uniqueness.

We established Radio Free Asia. We are working with Congress to expand its broadcast and to support civil society and the rule of law programs in China. We continue to pursue the problem of prison labor, and we regularly raise human rights in all our high-level meetings with the Chinese.

We do this in the hope of a dialogue. And in dialogue we must also admit that we in America are not blameless in our social fabric—our crime rate is too high, too many of our children are still killed with guns, too many of our streets are still riddled with drugs. We have things to learn from other societies as well, and problems we have to solve. And if we expect other people to listen to us about the problems they have, we must be prepared to listen to them about the problems we have.

This pragmatic policy of engagement, of expanding our areas of cooperation with China while confronting our differences openly and respectfully—this is the best way to advance our fundamental interests and our values and to promote a more open and free China.

I know there are those who disagree. They insist that China's interests and America's are inexorably in conflict. They do not believe the Chinese system will continue to evolve in a way that elevates not only human material conditions but the human spirit. They, therefore, believe we should be working harder to contain or even to confront China before it becomes even stronger.

I believe this view is wrong. Isolation of China is unworkable, counterproductive, and potentially dangerous. Military, political, and economic measures to do such a thing would find little support among our allies around the world and, more important, even among Chinese themselves working for greater liberty. Isolation would encourage the Chinese to become hostile and to adopt policies of conflict with our own interests and values. It would eliminate, not facilitate, cooperation on weapons proliferation. It would hinder, not help, our efforts to foster stability in Asia. It would exacerbate, not ameliorate, the plight of dissidents. It would close off, not open up, one of the world's most important markets. It would make China less, not more, likely to play by the rules of international conduct and to be a part of an emerging international consensus.

As always America must be prepared to live and flourish in a world in which we are at odds with China. But that is not the world we want. Our objective is not containment and conflict; it is cooperation. We will far better serve our interests and our principles if we work with a China that shares that objective with us. (Applause.)

Thirty years ago President Richard Nixon, then a citizen campaigning for the job I now hold, called for a strategic change in our policy toward China. Taking the long view, he said, we simply cannot afford to leave China forever outside the family of nations. There is no place on this small planet for a billion of its potentially most able people to live in angry isolation.

Almost two decades ago President Carter normalized relations with China, recognizing the wisdom of that statement. And over the past two and a half decades, as China has emerged from isolation, tensions with the West have decreased, cooperation has increased, prosperity has spread to more of China's people. The progress was a result of China's decision to play a more constructive role in the world and to open its economy. It was supported by a farsighted American policy that made clear to China we welcome its emergence as a great nation.

Now America must stay on that course of engagement. By working with China and making our differences clear where necessary, we can advance our interests and our values and China's historic transformation into a nation whose greatness is defined as much by its future as by its past.

Change may not come as quickly as we would like, but, as our interests are long term, so must our policies be. We have an opportunity to build a new century in which China takes its rightful place as a full and strong partner in the community of nations, working with the United States to advance peace and prosperity, freedom and security for both our people and all the world. We have to take that chance.

Thank you very much. (Applause.)

XI. GREATER CHINA

One of the most important goals of each new Chinese dynasty has been to reunify China territorially. When it came to power, the Chinese Communist Party was no different in aspiration. Although Mao's reunification efforts were largely successful, five places resisted complete reintegration. Tibet and Xinjiang—both of which were culturally, ethnically, geographically, and linguistically separate—were ultimately subdued by the People's Liberation Army but have remained in tension with Beijing ever since. Hong Kong, which was a British colony, was "reunited with the motherland" in 1997. The Portuguese colony of Macao was scheduled to be returned in 1999. Taiwan, which was occupied at the end of the Chinese Civil War in 1949 by Chiang Kai-shek and his Nationalist government, remains in a state of de facto independence and continues to be one of China's most troublesome and unresolvable problems. It is a measure of the importance Beijing's leaders attach to the issue of reunification that they have been implacably resistant to any formula that would compromise their claim to sovereignty over these five lands.

If there is any flash point capable of triggering a major confrontation between China and the United States, it is Taiwan. Indeed, a serious incident did develop in March 1996, when the PLA began firing missiles in the direction of Taiwan and the United States sent two carrier groups into the area as a warning.

THE DALAI LAMA ON CHINA, HATRED, AND OPTIMISM

The Fourteenth Dalai Lama, once the spiritual and temporal leader of all Tibetans, fled into exile in 1959 after Chinese troops occupied Lhasa. From Dharmsala, India, he has waged a four-decades-long global campaign to win new autonomy, if not independence, for Tibet from China.

This selection was excerpted from a conversation between His Holiness and Robert Thurman, a longtime supporter of the Tibetan government in exile and professor of Indo-European Studies at Columbia University, published in Mother Jones Magazine, November–December 1997.

ROBERT THURMAN: Your Holiness has said that in the future, when Tibet is free, you would cease to be the head of the government of Tibet. Is this because you would like to introduce the democratic principle of the separation of church and state to your nation?

DALAI LAMA: I firmly believe democratic institutions are necessary and very important, and if I remained at the head of government, it could be an obstacle to democratic practice. Also, if I were to remain, then I would have to join one of the parties. If the Dalai Lama joins one party, then that makes it hard for the system to work.

Up to now my involvement in the Tibetan freedom struggle has been part of my spiritual practice, because the issues of the survival of the Buddha Teaching and the freedom of Tibet are very much related. In this particular struggle, there is no problem with many monks and nuns, including myself, joining. But when it comes to democratic political parties, I prefer that monks and nuns not join them—in order to ensure proper democratic practice. The Dalai Lama should not be partisan either, should remain above.

Finally, personally, I really do not want to carry some kind of party function. I do not want to carry any public position.

THURMAN: But how about serving like the king of Sweden or the queen of England—as a constitutional Dalai Lama? As a ritual head, serving a unifying role? Would you consider this, if the people requested it?

DALAI LAMA: [*Laughs heartily*] I don't think so. I don't want to be a prisoner in a palace, living in such a constricted way—too tight! Of course, if there were really serious consequences if I did not accept, then of course I would do whatever was necessary. But in general I really prefer some freedom. Maybe, just maybe, I would like to become a real spiritual teacher, a working lama!

THURMAN: You've said you have a "comparatively better heart now" due to your exile. What has exile done for you?

DALAI LAMA: When we meet real tragedy in life, we can react in two ways—either by losing hope and falling into self-destructive habits or by using the challenge to find our inner strength. Thanks to the teachings of Buddha, I have been able to take this second way. I have found a much greater appreciation of Buddhism because I couldn't take it for granted here in exile. We have made a great effort to maintain all levels of Buddhist education; it has helped us have a kind of renaissance, really.

THURMAN: The loss of your own nation to China has been used as an example of the futility of nonviolence and tolerance. When is something worth fighting for?

DALAI LAMA: This is hard to explain. In our own case, we don't consider the loss of a monastery or a monument the end of our entire way of life. If one monastery is destroyed, sometimes it happens. Therefore, we don't need to respond with desperate violence. Although under particular circumstances the violence method—any method—can be justified, nevertheless once you commit violence, then counterviolence will be returned. Also, if you resort to violent methods because the other side has destroyed your monastery, for example, you then have lost not only your monastery but also your special Buddhist practices of detachment, love, and compassion.

However, if the situation was such that there was only one learned lama or genuine practitioner alive, a person whose death would cause the whole of Tibet to lose all hope of keeping its Buddhist way of life, then it is conceivable that in order to protect that one person it might be justified for one or ten enemies to be eliminated—if there was no other way. I could justify violence only in this extreme case, to save the last living knowledge of Buddhism itself.

For Tibetans, the real strength of our struggle is truth—not size, money, or expertise. China is much bigger, richer, more powerful militarily, and has much better skill in diplomacy. They outdo us in every field. But they have no justice. We have placed our whole faith in truth and in justice. We have nothing else, in principle and in practice.

We have always been a nation different from the Chinese. Long ago we fought wars with them. Since we became Buddhist, we have lived in peace with them. We did not invade them. We did not want them to invade us. We have never declared war on China. We have only asked them to leave us in peace, to let us have our natural freedom. We have always maintained that our policy is nonviolence, no matter what they do. I only escaped from Tibet because I feared my people would resort to desperate violence if the Chinese took me as their prisoner.

THURMAN: How does one counteract violence without hatred or anger?

DALAI LAMA: The antidote to hatred in the heart, the source of violence, is tolerance. Tolerance is an important virtue of bodhisattvas [enlightened heroes and heroines]—it enables you to refrain from reacting angrily to the harm inflicted on you by others. You could call this practice "inner disarmament," in that a well-developed tolerance makes you free from the compulsion to counterattack. For the same reason, we also call tolerance the "best armor," since it protects you from being conquered by hatred itself.

It may seem unrealistic to think we can ever become free from hatred, but Buddhists have systematic methods for gradually developing a tolerance powerful enough to give such freedom. Without mutual tolerance emerging as the foundation, terrible situations like those of Tibet and Sri Lanka, Bosnia and Rwanda, can never be effectively improved.

THURMAN: You use the term "cultural genocide" to describe what China is doing in Tibet but have suggested that Tibet could live with self-rule within China. How do you define self-rule, and what are its advantages over independence?

DALAI LAMA: Today, due to the massive Chinese population transfer, the nation of Tibet truly faces the threat of extinction, along with its unique cultural heritage of Buddhist spirituality. Time is very short. My responsibility is to save Tibet, to protect its ancient cultural heritage. To do that I must have dialogue with the Chinese government, and dialogue requires compromise. Therefore, I'm speaking for genuine self-rule, not for independence.

Self-rule means that China must stop its intensive effort to colonize Tibet with Chinese settlers and must allow Tibetans to hold responsible positions in the government of Tibet. China can keep her troops on the external frontiers of Tibet, and Tibetans will pledge to accept the appropriate form of union with China.

Because my main concern is the Tibetan Buddhist culture, not just political independence, I cannot seek self-rule for central Tibet and exclude the 4 million Tibetans in our two eastern provinces of Amdo and Kham. [Once part of an independent Tibet, Amdo is now known to the Chinese as Qinghai; Kham has been apportioned to the Chinese provinces of Gansu, Sichuan, and Yunnan.]

I have been clear in my position for quite a while, but the Chinese have not responded. Therefore, we are now in the process of holding a referendum on our policy among all the Tibetan community in exile and even inside Tibet, to check whether the majority thinks we are on the right track. I am a firm believer in the importance of democracy, not only as the ultimate goal but also as an essential part of the process.

THURMAN: To your mind, once self-rule is achieved, who should be in charge of the economic development of Tibet—the Chinese or Tibetans?

DALAI LAMA: Tibetans must take full authority and responsibility for developing industry, looking from all different perspectives, taking care of the environment, conserving resources for long-term economic health, and safeguarding the interests of Tibetan workers, nomads, and farmers. The Chinese have shown interest only in quick profits, regardless of the effect on the environment, and with no consideration of whether a particular industry benefits the local Tibetans or not.

THURMAN: What do you think it will take for China to change its policy toward Tibet?

DALAI LAMA: It will take two things: first, a Chinese leadership that looks forward instead of backward, that looks toward integration with the world and cares about both world opinion and the will of [China's] own democracy movement; second, a group of world leaders that listens to the concerns of their own people with regard to Tibet and speaks firmly to the Chinese about the urgent need of working out a solution based on truth and justice. We do not have these two things today, and so the process of bringing peace to Tibet is stalled.

But we must not lose our trust in the power of truth. Everything is always changing in the world. Look at South Africa, the former Soviet Union, and the Middle East. They still have many problems, setbacks as well as breakthroughs, but basically changes have happened that were considered unthinkable a decade ago.

THE JOINT DECLARATION OF THE GOVERNMENT OF THE UNITED KINGDOM AND THE GOVERNMENT OF THE PEOPLE'S REPUBLIC OF CHINA ON THE QUESTION OF HONG KONG

Because much of the territory that constituted the Crown Colony of Hong Kong was leased from China and because that lease was to end on July 1, 1997, Great Britain decided to return to Chinese sovereignty even that portion of the colony that had been ceded to it in perpetuity after the first Opium War. The terms for the colony's return were drafted in the early 1980s during protracted discussions between London and Beijing. Although observers feared that China would never grant Hong Kong real autonomy, after the Chinese government compromised the special autonomous region's new Legislative Council—so that only one-third of its members would be directly elected—things settled down. Indeed, many people living in Hong Kong were relieved by the restraint with which Party leaders on the mainland conducted their relations with the former colony.

This selection is the joint declaration signed by Britain and China in 1984.

The Government of the United Kingdom of Great Britain and Northern Ireland and the Government of the People's Republic of China have reviewed with satisfaction the friendly relations existing between the two Governments and peoples in recent years and agreed that a proper negotiated settlement of the question of Hong Kong, which is left over from the past, is conducive to the maintenance of the prosperity and stability of Hong Kong and to the further strengthening and development of the relations between the two countries on a new basis. To this end, they have, after talks between the delegations of the two Governments, agreed to declare as follows:

1. The Government of the People's Republic of China declares that to recover the Hong Kong area (including Hong Kong Island, Kowloon, and the New Territories, hereinafter referred to as Hong Kong) is the common aspiration of the entire Chinese people, and that it has decided to resume the exercise of sovereignty over Hong Kong with effect from July 1, 1997.

2. The Government of the United Kingdom declares that it will restore Hong Kong to the People's Republic of China with effect from July 1, 1997.

3. The Government of the People's Republic of China declares that the basic policies of the People's Republic of China regarding Hong Kong are as follows:

(1) Upholding national unity and territorial integrity and taking account of the history of Hong Kong and its realities, the People's Republic of China has decided to establish, in accordance with the provisions of Article 31 of the Constitution of the People's Republic of China, a Hong Kong Special Administrative Region upon resuming the exercise of sovereignty over Hong Kong.

(2) The Hong Kong Special Administrative Region will be directly under the authority of the Central People's Government of the People's Republic of China. The Hong Kong Special Administrative Region will enjoy a high degree of autonomy, except in foreign and defense affairs, which are the responsibilities of the Central People's Government.

(3) The Hong Kong Special Administrative Region will be vested with executive, legislative, and independent judicial power, including that of final adjudication. The laws currently in force in Hong Kong will remain basically unchanged.

(4) The Government of the Hong Kong Special Administrative Region will be composed of local inhabitants. The chief executive will be appointed by the Central People's Government on the basis of the results of elections or consultations to be held locally. Principal officials will be nominated by the chief executive of the Hong Kong Special Administrative Region for appointment by the Central People's Government. Chinese and foreign nationals previously working in the public and police services in the government departments of Hong Kong may remain in employment. British and other foreign nationals may also be employed to serve as advisers or hold certain public posts in government departments of the Hong Kong Special Administrative Region.

(5) The current social and economic systems in Hong Kong will remain unchanged, and so will the lifestyle. Rights and freedoms, including those of the person, of speech, of the press, of assembly, of association, of travel, of movement, of correspondence, of strike, of choice of occupation, of academic research, and of religious belief will be ensured by law in the Hong Kong Special Administrative Region. Private property, ownership of enterprises, legitimate right of inheritance, and foreign investment will be protected by law.

(6) The Hong Kong Special Administrative Region will retain the status of a free port and a separate customs territory.

(7) The Hong Kong Special Administrative Region will retain the status of international financial center, and its markets for foreign exchange, gold, securities, and futures will continue. There will be free flow of capital. The Hong Kong dollar will continue to circulate and remain freely convertible.

(8) The Hong Kong Special Administrative Region will have independent finances. The Central People's Government will not levy taxes on the Hong Kong Special Administrative Region.

(9) The Hong Kong Special Administrative Region may establish mutually beneficial economic relations with the United Kingdom and other countries, whose economic interests in Hong Kong will be given due regard.

(10) Using the name of "Hong Kong, China," the Hong Kong Special Administrative Region may on its own maintain and develop economic and cultural relations and conclude relevant agreements with states, regions, and relevant international organizations.

The Government of the Hong Kong Special Administrative Region may on its own issue travel documents for entry into and exit from Hong Kong.

(11) The maintenance of public order in the Hong Kong Special Administrative Region will be the responsibility of the Government of the Hong Kong Special Administrative Region.

(12) The above-stated basic policies of the People's Republic of China regarding Hong Kong and the elaboration of them in Annex I to this Joint Declaration will be stipulated, in a Basic Law of the Hong Kong Special Administrative Region of the People's Republic of China, by the National People's Congress of the People's Republic of China, and they will remain unchanged for fifty years.

4. The Government of the United Kingdom and the Government of the People's Republic of China declare that, during the transitional period between the date of the entry into force of this Joint Declaration and June 30, 1997, the Government of the United Kingdom will be responsible for the administration of Hong Kong with the object of maintaining and preserving its economic prosperity and social stability; and that the Government of the People's Republic of China will gives its cooperation in this connection.

5. The Government of the United Kingdom and the Government of the People's Republic of China declare that, in order to ensure a smooth transfer of government in 1997, and with a view to the effective implementation of this Joint Declaration, a Sino-British Joint Liaison Group will be set up

when this Joint Declaration enters into force; and that it will be established and will function in accordance with the provisions of Annex II to this Joint Declaration.

6. The Government of the United Kingdom and the Government of the People's Republic of China declare that land leases in Hong Kong and other related matters will be dealt with in accordance with the provisions of Annex III to this Joint Declaration.

7. The Government of the United Kingdom and the Government of the People's Republic of China agree to implement the preceding declarations and the Annexes to this Joint Declaration.

8. This Joint Declaration is subject to ratification and shall enter into force on the date of the exchange of instruments of ratification, which shall take place in Beijing before June 30, 1985. This Joint Declaration and its Annexes shall be equally binding.

Done in duplicate at Beijing on December 19, 1984, in the English and Chinese languages, both texts being equally authentic.

Prime Minister Margaret Thatcher
For the
Government of the United Kingdom
of Great Britain and Northern Ireland

Premier Zhao Ziyang
For the
Government of the
People's Republic of China

JIANG ZEMIN, CONTINUE TO PROMOTE THE REUNIFICATION OF CHINA

On January 30, 1995, Communist Party General Secretary and President Jiang Zemin gave a speech outlining "eight points" that were acceptable to Beijing leaders for the "peaceful reunification" of Taiwan and Mainland China.

This selection was excerpted from Jiang's speech.

Taiwan is an integral part of China. A hundred years ago, on April 17, 1895, the Japanese imperialists, by waging a war against the corrupt government of the Qing Dynasty, forced it to sign the Shimonoseki Treaty of national betrayal and humiliation. Under the treaty, Japan seized Taiwan and the Penghu Islands, subjecting the people of Taiwan to its colonial rule for half a century. The Chinese people will never forget this humiliating chapter of our history. Fifty years ago, together with the people of other countries, the Chinese people defeated the Japanese imperialists. October 15, 1945, saw the return of Taiwan and the Penghu Islands to China and marked the end of Japan's colonial rule over our compatriots in Taiwan. However, for reasons known to all, Taiwan has been severed from the Chinese mainland since 1949. It remains the inviolable mission and lofty goal of the Chinese people to achieve the reunification of their motherland and promote an all-around revitalization of the nation.

Comrade Deng Xiaoping has pointed out that the core of the issue is the reunification of the motherland. All descendants of the Chinese nation wish to see China reunified. It is against the will of the nation to see it divided. There is only one China, and Taiwan is a part of China. We will never allow there to be "two Chinas" or "one China, one Taiwan." We firmly oppose the "independence of Taiwan." There are only two ways to settle the Taiwan question: one is by peaceful means and the other is by nonpeaceful means. The way the Taiwan question is to be settled is China's internal affair and brooks no foreign interference. We consistently stand for achieving reunification by peaceful means and through negotiations. But we will not undertake not to use force. Such commitment would only make it impossible to achieve a peaceful reunification and could only lead to the eventual settlement of the question by the use of force.

After Taiwan is reunified with the mainland, China will pursue the policy of "one country, two systems." The main part of the country will adhere to the socialist system, while Taiwan will retain its current system. "Reunification does not mean that the mainland will swallow up Taiwan, nor does it mean that Taiwan will swallow up the mainland." After Taiwan's reunification with the mainland, its social and economic systems will not change, nor will its ways of life and its nongovernmental relations with foreign countries. This means that foreign investments in Taiwan and nongovernmental exchanges between Taiwan and other countries will not be affected.

As a special administrative region, Taiwan will exercise a high degree of autonomy and enjoy legislative and independent judicial power, including that of final adjudication. It may also retain its armed forces and administer its party, governmental, and military systems by itself. The central government will not station troops or send administrative personnel there. What is more, a number of posts in the central government will be made available to Taiwan.

The past decade and more have witnessed a vigorous expansion in cross-strait visits by individuals and exchanges in science, technology, culture, academic affairs, sports, and other fields under the guidance of the basic principle of peaceful reunification and "one country, two systems," and through the concerted efforts of compatriots on both sides of the Taiwan Strait and in Hong Kong and Macao and Chinese residing abroad.

A situation in which the economies of the two sides promote, complement, and benefit each other is taking shape. Establishment of direct links between the two sides for postal, air, and shipping services at an early date not only represents the strong desire of vast numbers of compatriots in Taiwan, particularly industrialists and businessmen, but also has become an actual requirement for future economic development in Taiwan. Progress has been registered in negotiations on specific issues, and the "Wang Daohan–Koo Chenfu talks" represent an important historic step forward in relations between the two sides.

However, what the Chinese people should watch out for is the growing separatist tendency and the increasingly rampant activities of forces on the island working for the "independence of Taiwan" in recent years. Certain foreign forces have further meddled in the issue of Taiwan, interfering in China's internal affairs. All this not only impedes the process of China's peaceful reunification but also threatens peace, stability, and development in the Asia-Pacific region.

The Chinese nation has experienced many vicissitudes and hardships, and now is high time to accomplish reunification of the motherland and revitalize the nation. This means an opportunity for Taiwan; it also means an opportunity for the entire Chinese nation. Here, I would like to state the following views and propositions on a number of important questions that have a bearing on the development of relations between the two sides and the promotion of a peaceful reunification of the motherland:

1. Adherence to the principle of one China is the basis and premise for peaceful reunification. China's sovereignty and territory must never be allowed to suffer division. We must firmly oppose any words or actions aimed at creating the "independence of Taiwan" and propositions that run counter to the principle of one China such as "two split sides with separate administrations," "two Chinas over a period of time," and so on.

2. We do not challenge development of nongovernmental economic and cultural ties by Taiwan with other countries. Under the principle of

one China and in accordance with the charters of relevant international organizations, Taiwan has become a member of the Asian Development Bank, the Asia-Pacific Economic Cooperation Forum, and other international economic organizations in the name of "Chinese Taipei." However, we oppose Taiwan's activities in "expanding" its "international living space" which aim to create "two Chinas" or "one China, one Taiwan." All patriotic compatriots in Taiwan and other people of insight understand that, instead of solving problems, such activities can only help forces working for the "independence of Taiwan" undermine the process of peaceful reunification. Only after peaceful reunification is accomplished can Taiwan compatriots truly and fully share the international dignity and honor attained by our great motherland with other Chinese.

3. It has been our consistent stand to hold negotiations with the Taiwan authorities on the peaceful reunification of the motherland. Representatives from various political parties and mass organizations on both sides of the Taiwan Strait can be invited to participate in such talks. I said in my report at the Fourteenth National Congress of the Communist Party of China held in October 1992 , "On the premise that there is only one China, we are prepared to talk with the Taiwan authorities about any matter, including the form that official negotiations should take, a form that would be acceptable to both sides." By "on the premise that there is only one China, we are prepared to talk with the Taiwan authorities about any matter," we mean, naturally, that all matters of concern to the Taiwan authorities are included. We have proposed time and again that negotiations should be held on officially ending the state of hostility between the two sides and accomplishing peaceful reunification in a step-by-step way. Here again I solemnly promise that such negotiations be held. I suggest that, as the first step, negotiations should be held and an agreement reached on officially ending the state of hostility between the two sides in accordance with the principle that there is only one China. On this basis, the two sides should undertake jointly to safeguard China's sovereignty and territorial integrity and map out plans for the future development of their relations. As for the name, place, and form of such political talks, a solution acceptable to both sides can certainly be found so long as consultations on an equal footing can be held at an early date.

4. We should strive for a peaceful reunification of the motherland since Chinese should not fight Chinese. Our not undertaking to give up the use of force is directed not against our compatriots in Taiwan but

against the schemes of foreign forces to interfere with China's reunification and to bring about the "independence of Taiwan." We are fully confident that our compatriots in Taiwan, Hong Kong, and Macao and all Chinese residing overseas would understand this principled position of ours.

5. In face of the development of the world economy in the twenty-first century, great efforts should be made to expand economic exchanges and cooperation between the two sides so as to achieve prosperity for both to the benefit of the entire nation. We maintain that political differences should not affect or interfere with economic cooperation between the two sides. We will continue to implement over a long period of time the policy of encouraging industrialists and businessmen from Taiwan to invest in the mainland and enforce Law of the People's Republic of China for Protecting Investments of Taiwan Compatriots. We will safeguard the legitimate rights and interests of industrialists and businessmen from Taiwan under whatever circumstances. We should continue to expand contacts and exchanges between our compatriots on both sides so as to increase mutual understanding and trust. Since direct links for postal, air, and shipping services and trade between the two sides are an objective requirement for their economic development and contacts in various fields, and since such links serve the interests of people on both sides, it is absolutely necessary to adopt practical measures to speed up the establishment of such direct links. Efforts should be made to promote negotiations on specific issues between the two sides. We are in favor of conducting these kinds of negotiations on the basis of reciprocity and mutual benefit and signing nongovernmental agreements on the protection of the rights and interests of industrialists and businessmen from Taiwan.

6. The splendid culture of 5,000 years created by the sons and daughters of all ethnic groups of China has become a tie that keeps the entire Chinese people close at heart. It constitutes an important basis for a peaceful reunification of the motherland. People on both sides of the Taiwan Strait should jointly inherit and carry forward the fine traditions of Chinese culture.

7. The 21 million compatriots in Taiwan, whether born there or from other provinces, are all Chinese. They are our own flesh and blood. We should fully respect their lifestyle and their wish to be the masters of their own destiny and protect all their legitimate rights and interests. Relevant departments of our government, including agencies stationed abroad, should strengthen contacts with compatriots from Taiwan, listen to their views and wishes, care for and look after their interests, and

make every effort to help them solve their problems. We hope Taiwan Island enjoys social stability, economic growth, and a high living standard. We also hope all political parties in Taiwan will adopt a sensible, forward-looking, and constructive attitude and promote the expansion of relations between the two sides. All parties and personages of all circles in Taiwan are welcome to exchange views with us on relations between the two sides and on peaceful reunification. They are also welcome to visit and tour the mainland. History will remember the deeds of all personages from various circles who contribute to the reunification of China.

8. Leaders of the Taiwan authorities are welcome to visit the mainland in appropriate capacities. We are also ready to accept invitations to visit Taiwan. The two sides can discuss state affairs or exchange ideas on some questions first. Even a simple visit to the other side will be useful. The affairs of the Chinese people should be handled by Chinese themselves, something that does not take an international occasion to accomplish. The Taiwan Strait is narrow, and people on both sides eagerly look forward to meeting each other. They should exchange visits instead of being kept from seeing each other all their lives.

Reunification of the motherland is the common aspiration of the Chinese people. All patriotic compatriots do not wish to see reunification delayed indefinitely. Dr. Sun Yat-sen, the great revolutionary forerunner of the Chinese nation, once said, "Reunification is the hope of all people of the Chinese nation. Reunification, and all people of the country will enjoy a happy life; failure to accomplish reunification, and they will suffer." We appeal to all Chinese to unite and hold high the great banner of patriotism, uphold reunification, oppose secession, spare no effort in promoting the expansion of relations between the two sides, and work for the accomplishment of China's reunification. The glorious day of reunification is sure to arrive in the course of modern development of the Chinese nation.

WHITHER CHINA?

XII. CHINA FACES THE TWENTY-FIRST CENTURY

One of the great imponderables of the next millennium is the future of China. The global environment, the world economy, international security, and the welfare of much of the human race rests on China's evolution. History has never witnessed such rapid economic progress for so many years as has been seen in China over the last quarter century. Much of this development has been positive—but as many of the selections in this volume illustrate, there have also been significant costs, and if the economic recession that has gripped Asia in 1998 continues, development in China itself could well be affected. In this final chapter, we take stock of several of the key variables that will shape China's—and the world's—future.

MICHEL C. OKSENBERG, MICHAEL D. SWAINE, AND DANIEL C. LYNCH, THE CHINESE FUTURE

Few studies have contemplated as carefully and judiciously the complexities facing China today, or the variables that will condition its future, as this one. In this selection, published in 1998, three prominent China specialists summarize the findings of a yearlong study group convened by the RAND Center for Asia-Pacific Policy and the Pacific Council on International Policy. This selection appears almost in its entirety to provide readers with both the breadth of analysis and the depth of insights offered.

Histtory teaches a hard lesson: "Getting China right" is a deadly serious matter. Overestimating the threats that China poses to American
interests, underestimating China's willingness to defend its interests,
and harboring illusions about China's readiness to accept American
goods and values: all can lead to disaster for both the United States and
China. Ambitious American politicians should place China off-limits as
a subject of demagoguery. The United States suffers severely when it
fails accurately to understand China and its domestic condition.

To be sure, accurate estimates of China do not guarantee a wise
China policy. Many other considerations come into play. The Chinese,
after all, must also "get the United States right," and their propensity for
failures in understanding is at least as great as ours. For example, Beijing
has tended to underestimate the American commitment to Taiwan and
to neglect the role of Congress in the making of American foreign
policy.

The Study Group on the Future of China

To get China right, during the past year a group of thoughtful observers
from different sectors—business and finance, the media and professions, academia and "think tanks"—have met regularly at the invitation
of the Pacific Council on International Policy and RAND's Center for
Asia-Pacific Policy to analyze the emerging and complex Chinese
domestic scene. The group was remarkably varied in its political orien-
tations, experiences in China, and methods of analysis. It invited leading specialists from throughout the United States and abroad to lead
seminars on different dimensions of China: the economy, the military,
the political succession, social conditions, and China's regional and
global roles. By the end of the series, to our surprise, the diverse group
had reached a consensus in assessing Chinese domestic conditions and
their general implications for American policy.

Consensus Views

The group rejected a pessimistic opinion about China that is being
expressed with increasing frequency in Washington and the American
media. Namely, although China has experienced economic reform and
rapid growth in the Deng Xiaoping era, its political system has changed

little; China remains a totalitarian system, with the world's worst human rights record; its people are oppressed and march to the commands of its top leaders. Moreover, China is said inevitably to be evolving not just into a major global power but into one with interests that will conflict deeply and extensively with those of the United States. It is asserted that China's leaders clearly intend to become the dominant power of Asia and possibly the world, and that they have a coherent strategy for attaining their objectives. Indeed, their foreign policy objectives are said to prevail over their domestic concerns, because their primary and immediate purpose is to remain in power, and the major threat of this quest comes from abroad—hence, the leaders' need, desire, and effort to accrue military might rapidly. In short, China has replaced the Soviet Union as the evil rising empire which will rival the United States in the decades ahead. According to this view, the United States should prepare itself for the coming conflicts with China.

The group also did not join another widely held view: China—far from inevitably rising—is headed for a collapse similar to that of the former Soviet Union or its Eastern European satellites. Marxism-Leninism, the ideology on which the Chinese Communists claim their right to rule, is bankrupt. Communist governments simply cannot endure; communist parties are inherently unable to reform themselves in a peaceful and orderly fashion. The process of disintegration in China has already begun, and the people yearn for democracy, as revealed in the spring of 1989. How and when a sudden collapse will occur is uncertain, but these observers claim that China's Communist regime surely is headed for the dustbin of history. Adherents of this view believe that the United States should distance itself from or even hasten the coming calamity.

Nor did the group accept the optimistic forecast of the Chinese future that some analysts offer. Namely, China's now inevitable economic development and integration into the international economy will necessarily propel it toward political liberalization and ultimately democratization. Proponents of this view state that the United States should be confident that China is headed in America's direction and facilitate its favorable evolution, especially by assisting its economic growth.

Rejecting all these views, our group stressed the uncertainties, openness, and complexities of the Chinese future. The country is in the midst of four major transformations that have carried China into uncharted waters. Its future will be determined by the decisions and behaviors of active, influential people, largely within China but also abroad, affecting and responding to these transformations. Remaining mindful that its influence is limited, the United States should cooperate with China to shape the future in beneficial ways while undertaking insurance measures in case of failure.

First, China is changing from an overwhelmingly agricultural to an industrial economy and thus from a rural to an urban society. Never in history has this large a nation developed this extensively, this fast. For nearly twenty years the economy of a nation of nearly 1.3 billion people has been growing at roughly 10 percent per year. Every year roughly 1 percent of the population—about 12 to 13 million people—has shifted from primarily agricultural to nonagricultural employment. The full ramifications of such a transformation are yet unknown.

Second, China is shifting from a planned, command economy to a heavily state-regulated market economy, and from a Leninist political system to some form of authoritarian or eventually possibly even democratic system. The experience of the former Soviet bloc demonstrates the enormous difficulty and uncertainty of these transformations.

Third, rapid economic growth facilitates the development of a large and growing middle class, historically unprecedented in China. The rising disposable income of this class suggests obvious implications for the world economy: China could become, in relatively short order, a major engine of global growth. Politically, if the new Chinese middle class mimics the middle classes of other countries, it will demand participation in political decision making and stability to protect its gains. Already the new middle class is increasingly armed with information and the communication tools to analyze the political scene and organize political action. What might finally cause it to spring into action?

Finally, China is completing a generational succession. A generation of Communist revolutionaries, reared in the early part of this century, ruled China from 1949 to the early 1990s. The successor generation, educated as engineers and technicians and steeped in the mores of Chinese bureaucracy, has now ascended to power. But it is not clear what vision, if any, they have brought with them to power.

Our group also cautioned that modesty was an essential attribute for students of contemporary China. The country is so big, complex, varied, rapidly changing, and with such a long history that it defies understanding. Analysts must offer their judgments with tentativeness. The only consolation available to the China specialist is the realization that participants in the game of Chinese politics—China's leaders, resident intellectuals, or dissidents residing abroad—find it equally difficult to foresee their country's future.

A Daunting List of Problems

China's leaders are preoccupied with a daunting list of domestic concerns and issues, many of which arise from the sheer size and complexity of their country. National security and foreign policy concerns are subordinated to these domestic issues; indeed, foreign policy choices are evaluated primarily in terms of their domestic implications.

Consider these basic imperatives in the governance of China:

- The leaders of China cannot take the unity of their country for granted. The huge nation is geographically and culturally diverse, and disunity and civil war have plagued China through much of its history.
- Never in history has a single government attempted to rule so many people within a single political system. China consists of 31 provinces, 160 prefectures, 2,500 counties and cities, nearly 100,000 townships and urban wards, and over a million rural villages. Seven layers of government separate the rulers at the top from the populace. Bureaucracy is inevitably enormous in such a vast setting, and the loss of information is considerable as data passes through the several layers of government.
- The leaders of China must ultimately bear responsibility for feeding nearly five times the population of the United States on roughly 60 percent of America's cultivated acreage. And the population is growing, though at substantially slower rates than many other developing countries. Fifteen million additional laborers enter the urban and rural workforce annually. Since 1972 and Nixon's opening to China, the country's population has increased by over 400 million people—more than the entire population of North America, or South America, or Africa south of the Sahara, or the Middle East, or the former Soviet bloc. As this number was absorbed into the economy, the absolute number of people living in poverty fell dramatically and employment opportunities for rural dwellers expanded rapidly.
- The leaders must respond to rising expectations for an improved standard of living, greater geographic and social mobility, and increased opportunity to participate in the decisions that affect people's lives. Meanwhile, income disparities are increasing both within and among

regions in China, as some benefit more swiftly from the country's growing involvement in the international economy than others.

- Severe environmental problems press upon the populace. Water and air pollution, soil erosion, and inadequate water supply north of the Yangzi are beginning to pose serious health problems and to constrain growth rates.

- Additional problems are posed by an aging population, by the need to import technology, equipment, petroleum, and agricultural commodities in order to sustain high growth rates and meet popular aspirations, and by the inefficiencies resulting from the many legacies of the previous command, state-controlled and -planned economic system.

- The leaders of China deserve empathy and some respect as they attempt to cope with this complex agenda. Both their accomplishments and their deficiencies merit acknowledgment.

Political Change

Conventional wisdom holds that, during the Deng Xiaoping era (1978–1997), China reformed economically but not politically. Foreign observers frequently contrast Deng's approach to reform with the Gorbachev-Yeltsin model, which gave pride of place to political reform over economic reform. This "wisdom" is actually incorrect. In fact, China's political system today differs considerably from that of the late Mao era. To be sure, the rate of political change is slower than the rate of economic change, and the instruments of totalitarian control—the public security apparatus, labor camps, severe limits on the freedom of assembly—remain in place, ready to be activated in case of need. Indeed, since the brutal suppression of the spring 1989 demonstrations, a whole new apparatus of internal control—the People's Armed Police—has been expanded to quell domestic unrest.

Nonetheless, the change is significant. People are no longer mobilized in an endless series of political campaigns. They need not affirm their adherence to Maoist ideological precepts on a daily basis. They enjoy the right of geographic and occupational mobility—freedoms denied in the Mao era. Individuals can withdraw from political life and pursue private interests—as long as these do not challenge the right of the leaders to rule.

Perhaps even more significant has been the enormous extent of administrative decentralization. Previously, the entire nation had to respond to the dictates of a single individual: Mao Zedong. He literally set the national agenda. And, on most issues, the lower levels of government responded with alacrity to Beijing's commands. Indeed, many of the nation's key industries were directly controlled by ministries in Beijing—even if they were located in the far-off Guangdong or Sichuan Provinces.

Today all that has changed. Authority is dispersed. Provinces, counties, and even townships control significant portions of government revenue. Personnel appointments now reside in the main either within the administrative level or one level above; in the past all key appointments were made two levels above. Almost every Party, government, or military unit runs its own enterprises and has its own sources of income. Agencies at every level have a sense of entitlement to their revenue, the land under their control, and even the activities for which they are responsible. Authority is fragmented.

This means higher levels have a tough time getting lower levels to obey their orders. Higher levels cajole, bargain, and entice lower levels to obey the directives that emanate from above. Admittedly, some hierarchies—such as the public security system—are more centralized than others. And the top leaders unquestionably retain the capacity to direct lower levels to achieve a limited number of objectives (such as implementation of the family planning program). But in other areas—for example, collecting central government revenue—higher-level leaders must exert great effort to secure the compliance they seek. The system is not as efficient and disciplined as communist countries are often imagined to be.

Contradictory Social Trends

Chinese society today is characterized by a bewildering array of contradictions. Its people exist in a spiritual vacuum and succumb to crass materialism but simultaneously demonstrate a growing interest in Buddhism, Christianity, and Taoism. They both yearn for an involvement with the outside world and are repelled by the foreign influence upon China. Cosmopolitanism and nativism, internationalism and nationalism, and regionalism or localism are all increasingly evident and coexist in an uneasy tension, even within most individuals. The populace is increasingly diverse in lifestyles, avocations, and aspirations, yet elements of a new national popular culture are being shaped by television, advertising, and increased geographic mobility.

Society clearly enjoys more autonomy vis-à-vis the state than in the past. In many respects the people keep the "tiger world" of Chinese politics at arm's length as they seek to earn a living. Increased geographic mobility means that tens of millions of Chinese citizens are no longer enmeshed in the control mechanisms that had been perfected for a stationary populace. Chinese people seek to evade the predatory behavior of police, market regulators, and other officials in the collection of endless fees, fines, and taxes. On balance, the domain of the state is shrinking and that of society is expanding. Voluntary associations are forming, many of them (such as unofficial churches or trade unions) illegal and subject to repression. While the state retains its tight control over the organization of religion and other nongovernmental institutions, the populace enjoys an increased capacity to worship in the officially sanctioned churches, mosques, and temples. And the number of licensed nongovernmental organizations is increasing rapidly. But at the same time local governments—urban wards, neighborhood committees, villages, townships, and counties—have grown considerably in the past two decades, with local budgets (and personnel ranks) swollen as a result of revenues earned from the enterprises they have spawned and the bank credit at their command.

Leaders at all levels of the hierarchy recognize that the Chinese people seek greater participation in the making of decisions that affect their lives. There is a clear yearning for greater political freedom. But at the same time the people demand order and security. There is little desire to risk the many gains of the past twenty years. The populace particularly resents the corruption, nepotism, and unaccountability of their leaders. They seek the rule of law, but not necessarily a rapid transition to democracy if the transition were to be accompanied by chaos and economic recession.

These contradictory trends both increase and decrease stability. The benefits that so many people have derived from the rapid growth of the past twenty years mean that they have much more to lose from political experimentation, and most people still remember the chaos, fear, and poverty of the recent past. Yet at the same time aspirations, income disparities, and discontent with the rapaciousness of high officials are all growing—fueling the demand for political reform.

The Improved Human Condition

The horrors of June 1989—when the leaders ordered the People's Liberation Army to occupy Tiananmen Square by force—remain indelibly imprinted in the minds of many Americans, for whom the brave soul who defied the column of invading tanks captured the moment of a regime crushing its own people. With that searing image still so fresh, many Americans are naturally inclined to believe the worst about the Chinese regime and its treatment of the Chinese people.

Yet the fact is that since that tragic moment, the human condition of most Chinese has continued to improve, as it had done from the end of the Mao era in 1976 until 1989. And we are not speaking just about improvements in per capita income and the availability of consumer goods. China's leaders have undertaken a number of measures to expand the political rights of citizens:

• They are attempting to introduce the rule of law. The leaders have instructed local governments to inform the populace about the laws that the national government has enacted and that local agencies are responsible for implementing. When local agencies disregard, exceed, or violate these laws, citizens in some locales are now able to request the local court to annul the action. Lawyers are being trained in modest numbers, and law offices are being established to assist plaintiffs to bring suit against the state. However, the courts do not have the right of judicial review to examine whether laws and administrative regulations are in compliance with the Constitution. And introduction of the rule of law will be hampered by the wide administrative discretion that local officials enjoy and the dependence of the courts on these officials for funding and personnel appointments.

• Village elections have been introduced and monitored to enable villagers to participate in the selection of their leaders. Many non-Communists have been elected. To be sure, the electoral process in most areas remains firmly under the control of the Communist Party, and the village Party organization still plays a major role in running village affairs. But the idea of democracy is being introduced at the grassroots level.

• Citizens have the right temporarily to migrate without first securing permission of their superiors. Peasants can lease out land that the village has assigned to them and that they choose not to farm themselves.

• The populace clearly enjoys a wider range of choice in the cultural domain. The number of magazines, newspapers, and books being published is increasing dramatically. Even in rural areas, videocassettes of Hong Kong and Taiwan movies, contemporary and classical foreign novels in translation, and traditional Chinese novels are widely available.

Arguably, most Chinese enjoy a greater degree of freedom than at any time in the past century. And yet most Americans would find the human rights situation in China intolerable. Freedom of speech and assembly do not exist. The government's treatment of Tibetan Buddhism is undoubtedly oppressive. Torture, arbitrary arrest, and indiscriminate application of the death penalty are widespread. The state interferes in the most cherished moments of life's passages—birth, marriage, and death—dictating the number of children a couple may have, the age of marriage, and burial practices. High-level officials whom the government-controlled media have identified as guilty of corruption go untried in court, their misdeeds not clearly explained to the public, while lower-level officials convicted of seemingly lesser crimes are sentenced to death. Although in private Chinese are quite willing to express their political views to close friends or foreigners whose discretion they trust, individuals who publish views or undertake actions that oppose the regime or denigrate specific leaders are arrested. The regime does not tolerate organized political dissent.

In short, although China's human rights record is improving, it still is unsatisfactory by most standards, including those held by most Chinese. To improve the human condition and to create a social setting that will truly sustain a regime committed to human rights require the strengthening of such norms as respect for the rule of law, trust in and a sense of obligation toward people outside one's own circle of family and friends, and tolerance of diversity. These will take many years, perhaps decades, to inculcate.

Moreover, the weakness of these norms should not be attributed solely to Communist rule, though the past forty years greatly eroded them. While precedents can be found in the pre-Communist past for the rule of law, tolerance, individualism, or a widespread social consciousness, these attributes were not dominant aspects of traditional culture. Certain practices that many foreigners find odious—such as widespread use of the death penalty—are deeply ingrained in Chinese culture. As pre-Communist Chinese novels, short stories, and anthropological studies make clear, life for the vast majority of Chinese has long been brutish. As a result, although arbitrary rule and constraints on freedom undoubtedly generate discontent, cynicism, and political apathy, they do not immediately lead to political opposition and rebellion. Rather the human condition produces widespread grievances toward the regime that people seem willing to endure—unless an opportunity or desperate need arises to act upon them.

The Political Quandary

To varying degrees, top officials realize that their political system is antiquated and lacks broad-based popular support. Their speeches in fact openly discuss the difficulties they face in recruiting and retaining high-quality, active Party members. They know the ideology on which the Party is based lacks popular appeal. They are well aware that the trend in the Asia-Pacific region is toward democracy, and they believe that their populace desires increased opportunity to participate in the decisions that affect their fate. And in private conversations several of the highest leaders—though with differing degrees of explicitness—acknowledge the many virtues of democratic rule. From the highest levels to the lowest, many officials appear to recognize that their regime can only regain popular support through sweeping political reform: strengthening parliamentary bodies, placing the military and police more firmly under civilian control, relaxing controls over formation of nongovernmental organizations, strengthening the judiciary, improving the civil service system, and granting the populace more meaningful avenues of political participation.

But the leaders fear political reform even as, increasingly, they recognize its necessity. They worry that the loosening of control will unleash a sequence of events even worse than what occurred with the dissolution of the Soviet Union or Yugoslavia. If the current structure of authority in China were suddenly to collapse, independent national governments at the current provincial levels would not be the result. Nothing in Chinese history would sustain such a notion. Rather, the likely result would be anarchy, chaos, and civil war to determine who would be China's next unifying ruler. All the leaders fear this chaos. None wishes to put at risk rule by the Communist Party, without which they believe China would cease to be unified. Recognizing the need for political change, they are deeply divided over the speed and manner in which political reform should be undertaken. Given the consensual decision-making process that exists among the top decision makers, they have only been able to agree on the circumscribed political reforms just listed.

In short, if the leaders could acquire a map charting a safe path for a peaceful transition to an openly competitive political system with the Communist Party remaining the dominant or ruling party at the end of the journey, some would probably choose to embark on that path. But no such map exists. And in its absence, the leaders cultivate popular support in other ways: maintaining high economic growth rates and unleashing popular nationalistic aspirations.

The Challenges to Economic Growth

Conventional wisdom now holds that the Chinese economy is on a trajectory of rapid growth likely to last for many more years, perhaps decades. Expectations of continued rapid growth undergird the predictions of China as a looming world power and rival to the United States. And, indeed, many underlying factors are likely to continue to propel the Chinese economy forward in robust fashion: a high savings rate; an industrious and entrepreneurial population; a demographic profile conducive to growth; the spread of science and technology that enable the populace to become more productive; the financial, managerial, and technological assistance provided by ethnic Chinese from Hong Kong, Taiwan, Southeast Asia, and North America; a generally propitious external setting that at least tolerates rapidly growing Chinese exports, invests capital, provides technology, and poses no military threat; and a leadership that has repeatedly demonstrated more acumen than the leaders of many other developing countries in guiding the economy well. Lending further credibility to optimistic assessments of China's economic strength has been its extraordinary export performance, its accumulation of over $140 billion in foreign currency reserves, the low level of domestic government indebtedness, and the maintenance of a foreign debt level (approximately $120 billion) that can adequately be sustained in light of China's export performance.

Yet China's economy is still only half-reformed: The state-owned banking system dominates the financial sector. Other state-owned enterprises (SOEs) dominate capital-intensive industrial production, and they employ the vast majority of urban workers. The government relies on SOEs to keep the urban peace by providing workers with social benefits such as housing, health care, and pensions because the fiscal system at present is far too inefficient to allow the government itself to fund a large-scale social welfare system. What is needed is a simultaneous reform of China's capital markets, industrial ownership structure, social welfare system, and fiscal system, since each constitutes an integral component of the total political-economic system.

Consider first the reform of the inefficient SOEs. These industrial behemoths employ two-thirds of the urban workforce and consume two-thirds of China's investment resources but produce only one-third of total societal output. It is, to be sure, an important one-third, consisting of the bulk of capital-intensive production. State-owned enterprises thus massively waste China's scarce societal resources. Their liabilities to banks as a percentage of assets increased from 11 percent in 1978 to 95 percent in 1995; many thus technically are insolvent, but are kept afloat by a politicized banking system forced to use the savings of China's hardworking population to fund the low interest rates—because stock and bond markets are underdeveloped. Yet until recently the government has permitted only a minuscule number of SOEs to cease their operations and go bankrupt. The leaders cannot abide the thought of tens of millions of urban workers suddenly being tossed out onto the street.

Because SOEs and the banks that prop them up need not face the threat of bankruptcy, they ultimately have very little incentive to use the factors of production efficiently, with the result that, as long as the current system remains in place, scarce societal resources will continue to be wasted on a grand scale. They will be siphoned away from their socially optimal uses, which in China typically means the uses to which they are put by the private, collective, and foreign-funded sectors. Moreover, partly because the state has historically depended on SOEs to supply it with most of its revenue, the rise of the non-SOE sector and SOEs' great inefficiency have produced a sharp drop in government revenue as a percentage of gross domestic product, from 31 percent in 1978 to 11 percent in 1995. The resulting political-economic profile is highly inconsistent with the pattern of the typical developing country and implies that the Chinese government will face a serious shortage of both funds and political support as it tries not only to reform SOEs and the financial system but also to tackle a set of severe ecological problems.

ENVIRONMENT

China's rapid rate of industrialization has involved a thoroughgoing assault on the environment—air, water, and soil. The Chinese people now live in a dangerously polluted milieu. Their health is at risk on a daily basis. Air quality in most rural areas does not meet minimum World Health Organization standards, for example, and over 80 percent of rivers are seriously polluted. The population is suffering from alarming increases in respiratory ailments in both the big cities and the rapidly industrializing countryside. Governments at all levels of the political system are now beginning to address this problem, but the primacy of economic development inevitably renders offices charged with environmental protection weak and hamstrung in bureaucratic competition with the more powerful industrial ministries. The result is exceedingly slow progress in cleaning up the environment or, in many cases, no progress at all.

ENERGY

China's energy supply exacerbates its environmental problems. China's thirst for petroleum exceeds its domestic supply; its dependency on petroleum imports—largely from the Middle East—is growing rapidly. Its hydroelectric potential is primarily located in the western regions of the country, far from population centers. Its natural gas reserves are modest. Its nuclear power industry is still in its infancy and still dependent on foreign technology, which is, however, quite accessible from Russian and European suppliers. Alternative energy sources are not available in large quantities. That leaves coal as the main resource to meet China's rapidly growing energy needs, and coal reserves are available in abundant supply. At present coal supplies roughly 75 percent of China's energy needs; roughly 80 percent of its electricity comes from coal-fired power plants. These figures will persist long into the future.

China's coal, however, is not high grade. Most has high sulfur content and contains other impurities. The net result is the emission of sulfur dioxide and acid rain affecting many areas of China and its neighbors. Moreover, China's increasing use of energy, its reliance on coal, and the inefficiencies in Chinese energy use result in rapid increases in emissions of greenhouse gases. Within a decade or two China will join the United States as the largest source of carbon dioxide emission. To alleviate these problems will require billions of dollars to increase energy efficiency and reduce emission of pollutants.

EDUCATION

China's economic growth also will be constrained by inadequate human resources. In fact, China has become a major importer of human talent. According to some estimates, as many as 50,000 Hong Kong citizens and 200,000 from Taiwan are serving in managerial, professional, and technical positions on the mainland. In part, this situation reflects Beijing's inability to attract over 150,000 Chinese graduate students sent abroad who have yet to return home. But China also is now plagued by years of neglect of education at all levels. For decades China's per capita expenditures on primary schools have ranked among the lowest in the world, and the dissolution of the communes has inadvertently led to an erosion in school financing and attendance in substantial numbers of villages. Meanwhile, universities have still not fully recovered from the battering their faculty suffered during the Mao years, and as is true of other agencies dependent on government funding, they are now expected to launch their own enterprises and secure foreign support to sustain their educational offerings.

The result is an inadequate supply of technically proficient men and women to serve the nation's managerial, engineering, and scientific needs. The shortages are particularly evident in the brain drain from rural and impoverished areas, where skilled labor is especially needed but wages and working conditions are not competitive, and in the difficulty urban firms have in retaining skilled personnel. Eventually, a free labor market and expanded higher education will overcome these difficulties, but for the foreseeable future China's growth rate will be adversely affected.

All of this suggests that the Chinese economy has many vulnerabilities. Recent economic difficulties in Japan, Korea, Malaysia, and Thailand are reminders that the Asian strategies for rapid growth—strong states guiding the economy, pursuing export-led growth, and encouraging high rates of capital investment—have their vulnerabilities. Straight-line projections that China will continue to grow at nearly 10 percent a year are unwarranted. Yet the factors stimulating growth are probably sufficiently powerful to sustain it at rates substantially higher than those prevailing in most other developing countries. An annual growth rate of 6 to 8 percent seems attainable to most experts for the foreseeable future if the leaders can implement their plans to reform the SOE and financial sectors. (On the other hand, failure to implement these reforms could cut the growth rate in half.) If China could sustain a growth rate of 6 to 8 percent for three or four decades, the country would emerge with one of the world's largest economies, although per capita income would still be well below the average in developed countries. But a 6 to 8 percent growth rate is substantially less than that achieved in the last two decades and may not be sufficient to meet the aspirations of the populace for employment opportunities and a rapidly improving standard of living. And the leaders have generated support for their rule by fulfilling these expectations.

Popular Nationalism

China's opening to the outside world, along with the telecommunications and transportation revolutions, has enabled "public opinions" to form outside state control. The leaders must struggle both to manage and to satisfy these opinions as they seek to maintain political stability and effective governance. Satisfying popular demands is one reason that the government encourages the proliferation of radio and television "hotline" programs, letters to editors in newspapers, and public opinion polling.

Nationalistic sentiments also rally the people behind the rulers. Popular nationalism has been evident in antiforeign demonstrations following victories over foreign sports teams, the resentment over not being awarded the Olympic Games, and the popularity of the anti-American diatribe *China Can Say "No."* Chinese attribute China's current predicaments and poverty to its century of invasion and exploitation by the Western powers and Japan. Many still harbor bitter memories toward Japan as a result of the atrocities it committed during its brutal occupation of Manchuria and large parts of core China from 1931 to 1945. All this contributes to a sense of grievance toward the outside world.

The leaders have clearly decided to appeal to these nationalistic sentiments in the absence of a convincing ideology. Nor is the use of nationalism simply an exercise in cynical manipulation of popular opinion. Most of the leaders clearly share these sentiments themselves. The deliberate use of the return of Hong Kong as an occasion for a national celebration exemplified this somewhat contrived but genuinely felt national pride and patriotism. Clearly, a nation that had been humiliated and scorned seems to be regaining its rightful place in the world. But the leaders can overplay their hand, arousing or unleashing anti-Japanese or anti-American sentiment that could engender a backlash in Tokyo or Washington. After all, in the final analysis, China needs Japan and the United States to fulfill its developmental plans.

Nowhere are the dilemmas posed by a resurgent Chinese nationalism more evident than in Beijing's policies toward Taiwan, Tibet, and Hong Kong. The essence of the leaders' nationalistic—some would say patriotic—appeal at home is that they are restoring China's greatness. And in the minds of most Chinese, the moments of greatness coincide with the moments of maximum unity, strength and national territorial integrity. The great leaders in Chinese history are those who brought all the rightful parts of the domain back into the fold. The despised rulers are those who contributed to China's fragmentation and penetration by foreign powers.

From Beijing taxicab drivers to Shandong farmers to Sichuan intellectuals, the refrain is the same: Taiwan, Tibet, and Hong Kong are all parts of China. They can enjoy considerable autonomy within a Chinese framework, but the residents of those places cannot deny their heritage any more than a family member can deny his ancestors. As one Shandong county official explained his sentiment: "If Taiwan tries to deny it is part of China, we will have to kick their butt." And as a Beijing taxicab driver put it, after expressing deep disenchantment with China's top rulers: "Look how incompetent they are! Over forty years have passed, and still they haven't gotten that little island of Taiwan back. Why do they deserve all the money they are getting?" This is not official rhetoric artificially implanted in the minds of the populace. It is popular opinion with which the leaders must reckon now that their other tools for managing the populace—the household registration system, total control over the media, and a high level of bureaucratic discipline—are breaking down.

In short, public opinion somewhat constrains China's leaders in their approaches toward Taiwan, Tibet, and Hong Kong. The leaders believe they would be condemned in some fashion if they were seen as surrendering Chinese territory. But it is by no means clear that the Chinese public demands the sometimes hard-line policies that the rulers have adopted toward these locales. For example, it is doubtful that popular nationalistic sentiments demanded the 1995–96 outcry over Taiwan President Lee Teng-hui's foreign travels, the opposition to the Dalai Lama's involvement in 1994–95 in identifying the reincarnation of the Panchen Lama, or the strict limits Beijing placed upon the number of Hong Kong's Legislative Council members to be democratically elected.

In these and other instances, it appears that China's leaders deliberately sought to convey a nationalistic message. Through rhetoric and public posturing, China's leaders have stimulated emotions among their people in their dispute with Taiwan, their handling of their territorial claims in the East and South China Seas, and their policies toward Tibet. They have castigated the Dalai Lama, President Lee Teng-hui of Taiwan, and the leader of Hong Kong democratic forces, Martin Lee, for allegedly seeking to "split" China and serving the interests of foreign powers. This rhetorical nationalism is a two-edged sword. The use of nationalistic appeals appears to rally the populace behind the leaders. But it makes the leaders captives of the sentiments they have cultivated, probably reduces their own flexibility on these issues, and surely alienates the objects of their wrath.

The net effect is to reduce the prospects for resolution of these issues in ways that accommodate the desires of the local populace.

The Military

Eight years ago, before the People's Liberation Army's quashing of the Beijing demonstrations, the United States was in the midst of selling military equipment to China: an advanced avionics package to the air force for its jet fighters, improved artillery shells to the army, and advanced turbine engines to the navy for its destroyers. Following the Tiananmen tragedy, the United States halted those sales, and ever since America's contacts with the PLA have been sporadic at best and always viewed skeptically by the U.S. Congress. Many Americans view the PLA as a prop for the dying Communist regime; the source of China's disturbing supply of advanced weaponry and technology to Pakistan and Iran; a prime source of corruption through its economic activities at home and abroad; and the prime force behind China's muscular behavior in the South China Sea and Taiwan Strait. According to this negative view of the PLA, the military has successfully pressured the civilian leaders to pursue an assertive foreign policy and rapidly to increase defense expenditures. In short, adherents of this view consider the PLA to be malevolent and increasingly important in Chinese domestic politics, with the inevitable consequence that China will pose a military threat to the United States in a relatively short period of time.

This view cannot be dismissed, but it is misleading:

• The PLA was not the instigator of the June 1989 suppression. Civilian leaders, including several Party elders, were the chief architects of the debacle. Substantial evidence exists that many retired PLA marshals and generals opposed the dispatch of the PLA into the streets of Beijing, and many of those who obeyed the commands of their Party chieftains initially did so without enthusiasm.

• The PLA as a whole is not the source of Chinese xenophobia. Elements of the officer corps have been at the forefront in seeking increased contact with the outside world, in part to secure the technology necessary for military modernization.

• Chinese military expenditures, although growing, have not been skyrocketing. The Chinese defense budget is one of the most opaque aspects of the Chinese scene, but even the highest of the well-founded estimates of Chinese defense expenditures judge the defense budget to be about equal to Japan's defense spending. Indeed, China's military expenditures as a percentage of total defense expenditures by all Asian countries have been decreasing steadily since the mid-1970s.

• The United States possesses overwhelming military superiority over China and will do so for decades into the future, providing the United States retains the will to keep its own defense budget at current levels. China remains vulnerable to devastating attack from American forward-deployed forces in the western Pacific.

• The Chinese military is complex and should not be treated as a coherent and integrated whole. There is a core of professional military, consisting of strategic forces, army (with central, regional, and local units), air force, and navy—with their own internecine bureaucratic battles; a military-industrial complex that is converting to production of civilian commodities; and a portion that is engaged in politics.

Retired high-ranking officers and the children of the deceased founding generation of the PLA are, in a sense, considered part of the military family, and, as civilians, they trade upon their military connections for personal gain. Part of the revenue of the PLA comes from government appropriations, but part is earned from enterprises under PLA control, many only loosely directed (if at all) from the PLA center. However, these enterprises do not pass all their profits to the PLA; most profits, in fact, are reinvested into the enterprises.

Generalizations are not easy to make about an institution as complicated as the PLA. Portions are corrupt, and others honest; portions are nationalistic, and others seek PLA participation in international peace-keeping efforts; portions are intellectually ill-equipped for the modern world, while others are extremely sophisticated and among the most enlightened people in China; portions are resistant to change, and others progressive.

Thus, as with other aspects of the China scene, a balanced appraisal is required, and historical perspective is needed. The PLA is neither evil incarnate nor a knight in shining armor. The foreign invasions and the massive peasant uprisings that affected China from the mid-1800s to the mid-1900s led to the militarization of the polity and society. The military became an important avenue of social mobility and a crucial actor on the political stage. And in many ways Communist rule has not fundamentally demilitarized the polity and society. The military remains an important part of the Chinese state; no person can emerge as the paramount leader against the concerted opposition of the military, and leaders must enjoy support from at least a portion of the military. A substantial segment of China's heavy industry has intimate links with the military. A major effort was made in the 1950s to demilitarize the polity, to establish a professional military, and to keep them in the barracks, but the military once more assumed civilian roles during the chaos of the Cultural Revolution. The Deng era again saw an effort to create a professional military and to delineate a clear boundary between it and the civilian sector, but that process is far from complete. Further, the PLA is an instrument of the Party; one of its stated tasks is to keep the Party in power, and its chain of command is from the military chiefs of staff to the Party's Central Military Commission and, ultimately, to the Party Politburo. Under these circumstances, with this historical background, it is difficult to disentangle the military from the rest of the Chinese state, and this condition is likely to persist for the foreseeable future.

However, the influence of the military does not explain China's commitment to military modernization. Modern Chinese history is the relevant factor: China's military weakness invited foreign aggression; its ineffective and fragmented internal security forces yielded disorder and civil wars. And since 1949, partly as a result of their own menacing and seemingly unpredictable behavior, China's leaders have experienced threats of nuclear attack and amassing of awesome might deployed against them. Against this background, the acquisition of military might has been a central objective of China's rulers not only in the Communist era but ever since the Opium War. China's leaders—no matter who they are—will surely seek to build a modern navy, air force, and army as their technology and economic resources permit. The differences among the leaders both in the military and outside it have involved, and will continue to involve, issues of priority and sequence: whether to postpone weapons research and acquisition in favor of constructing a firm, broad-based economic infrastructure; what are the most dangerous threats confronting China; what technologies are most important for acquiring strength; what strategies are appropriate to modern warfare and therefore what the force structure and weapons should be.

Thus, there can be no doubt that as China's economy grows, its technological and scientific resources will expand, and its government budget will increase. And although it is unlikely that the rate of increase will enable China to pose a greatly expanded direct threat to the United States (it currently can strike at U.S. territory with only a small number of intercontinental ballistic missiles), almost assuredly China will accrue greater military strength. But there is considerable doubt as to how rapidly this will occur. And, almost assuredly, China will obtain increasing capability to affect the military balance on its periphery, especially vis-à-vis Taiwan. Indeed, in recent years, as a result of markedly greater tensions over the Taiwan issue, many areas of China's military modernization have become focused precisely on improving the credibility of Beijing's long-standing threat to use force against Taiwan. This new development poses the most serious near-term threat to U.S. regional interests deriving from China's military modernization program.

Deep Versus Shallow Integration into World Affairs

Put succinctly, the key question confronting China's leaders is: Do they believe their national interests will be served by a deeper integration into the international and regional security, economic, and value systems? Or do they believe China's interests require limiting the nation's involvement to the relatively shallow extent that has been attained thus far? Certainly they have publicly proclaimed a commitment to deep integration, but will they implement these promises? In no small measure the answer to these questions will determine whether China emerges as a threat or a partner in the region and globally in the years ahead.

In the security realm, on the whole, China has yet to enter into agreements that significantly narrow its foreign policy choices. It has yet to make commitments in the arms control and weapons development areas that constrain its future military development. China's leaders demonstrate particular ambivalence over the existing security arrangements in East Asia that are undergirded by America's alliances with Japan and Korea and its forward military deployments. China's leaders recognize that the U.S.-Japan Security Treaty in some respects contributes to stability in the region by anchoring Japan in an alliance system, but they do not acknowledge that an American military presence in the western Pacific would continue to contribute to regional stability after tensions on the Korean peninsula have ended. In fact, its assertive claims in the South China Sea and its posture toward Taiwan have provoked regional security concerns that, over the long run, China is going to be a troublesome neighbor.

In the economic realm, China has yet to commit itself fully to the opening of its markets and to its full integration into the international financial and commercial systems, though it has applied for admission to the World Trade Organization and committed itself to making at least some important adjustments to its domestic economy as a price of membership. The current negotiations over China's entry into the organization concern precisely what sorts of adjustments will be made. Is China prepared to restructure its domestic economy to the deep extent necessary to make it congruent with an increasingly open international economic system?

And in the realm of culture and values, will the leaders of China continue to assert that, because of China's distinctiveness, certain internationally acceptable standards of governance are not applicable to it? Clearly, the issues at stake concern human rights, democratization, and the rule of law. Are China's leaders prepared to accept the notion that their performance should be judged by the same standards that are applied to other countries, particularly when China has pledged to adhere to certain international treaties and agreements? Do China's leaders somehow intend to wall their people off from international cultural currents? Is this even possible, given rapid advances in communications technologies and their dissemination throughout China?

In all of these areas—security, economy, and culture—both the leaders and the citizens of China are deeply divided. Some vigorously advocate a deeper integration into world affairs, arguing that unless China participates fully in the global system it will be unable to develop economically and attain for its people the benefits of modernity. Others believe further integration risks loss of China's cultural heritage and threatens the country's unity. Localities that are successfully incorporated into global and regional affairs will drift apart from those less integrated. Thus, deep integration risks the primary achievement of the Communist revolution—the reknitting of China. The vigor of this debate demonstrates the extent to which China's future orientation toward the Asia-Pacific region and the world as a whole has yet to be determined.

Policy Implications

American policy toward China cannot be solely a response to China's domestic scene. The policy must grow out of American interests toward China and must be integrated into a broader strategy in its foreign policy for the region as a whole. Moreover, American policy must take into account the China policies of U.S. allies and other actors in the region. Our survey of China's domestic condition does not, therefore, provide an adequate foundation on which to base China policy. Yet at the same time the Chinese condition does establish a set of parameters within which the United States must work. It suggest as much about what the United States should not do and what is not possible as it does about what should be done. To summarize our findings:

• The Chinese future is open and uncertain. China should not be seen as either an inevitable enemy with which the United States is certain to come into conflict or a sure partner that will pose no threat in the future.

• China's future path will be determined largely by its own internal considerations; American leverage is important but still limited. Certainly at the margins the United States can influence China's trajectory, and over the long run the cumulative impact can be considerable. But in the short run China's leaders respond primarily to domestic political and economic imperatives.

• The United States should not, therefore, develop an exaggerated sense of its own importance in Chinese eyes. And when Chinese leaders do not respond to American demands and urgings, or when they appear to slight American interests, the slight may not be deliberate. China's leaders may simply have more important considerations in mind that are hidden from American view.

• Because of China's uncertainty, American China policy must be flexible and nimble. Policy must not become tied to the fate of any particular Chinese leaders. Setbacks and reversals to American policy are to be expected. But when these occur one of the truisms about China must be kept in mind: China is never as good as it appears in its best moments, and never as bad as it appears in its worst moments.

• American policy should not be rooted in the expectation that China can or will soon become a democracy. Although a swift transition to democracy should not be dismissed as a possibility, a commitment by China's leaders to instituting a gradual process of democratization is perhaps the best the United States can realistically expect, and even that commitment has yet to be credibly voiced. And even in the unlikely case that China experiences a rapid political transformation, the resulting democracy would lack the underpinnings necessary to remain stable and function smoothly: the rule of law, a competitive party system, and a political culture of tolerance and trust.

• One of China's biggest impediments to sustained economic growth is its inadequate institutions: weak banking and revenue systems; overlapping, ill-defined jurisdictions among the central, provincial, and local governments; a weak legal system; a weak civil service system; and so on. Both China and the United States face the challenges of governance in a new era characterized by rapid technological and demographic change. These challenges offer some of the potentially most fruitful areas of cooperation between China and the United States.

• The United States must remain aware of the Chinese government's deep and enduring resolve not to permit Taiwanese or Tibetan independence. The majority of the Chinese populace appears to support Beijing's position on these matters and seems willing to accept the risks involved in using force to prevent either entity from attaining independence. The United States should harbor no illusion: The Taiwan issue is potentially explosive and involves risks of war.

• The Chinese government is not fully in control of the society; the central government is not fully in control of the national-level ministries. The U.S. government should understand that many actions occur contrary to the leaders' instructions. At the same time, the leaders are strong enough to intervene and enforce their will upon recalcitrant agencies on a limited number of matters of importance of them. Thus, the United States can legitimately expect them to enforce discipline when lower-level officials violate the leaders' prior commitments—once these violations have been brought to the leaders' attention. And the United States can elicit cooperation from the leaders on the limited number of carefully selected issues of highest priority to the United States, provided the United States is consistent, clear, persistent, and genuinely willing to "go to the mat."

• China's economy is likely to continue to grow rapidly but does possess major vulnerabilities. Hence, the China market presents considerable opportunities but also substantial risks. The U.S. government should not arouse unwarranted expectations among the American business community, nor should the business community approach the China market with romantic illusions. Hardheaded assessments must be made all around.

If the Chinese economy continues to grow for many more years at a rate of 6 to 8 percent annually, partly on the basis of increased exposure to the outside world through trade and investment, then inevitably China's "interests" in the global system will expand—especially its interests in the Asia-Pacific region and its capability to defend those interests by both military and nonmilitary means. China today thus constitutes a nascent "rising power" that the still-dominant power today—the United States—must find a way to integrate into the global order, to avoid growing Sino-U.S. tensions or even military conflict.

The British peacefully adjusted to the rise of American power during the first half of the twentieth century, but neither the British nor the Americans were able peacefully to manage the rise of first German and then Japanese power in the decades prior to World War II. In each of these cases, actions taken by both sides determined whether the appearance of a new major power would be accomplished harmoniously or antagonistically, and the same holds true for the Sino-U.S. relationship today.

Although China's ultimate emergence as a major regional and global military power is far from a foregone conclusion—environmental disasters or energy shortages could choke off economic growth, for example, or reform of state-owned enterprises could destabilize the political system—the United States and other interested parties cannot afford to adopt an ostrich strategy and simply ignore or reject the possibility that China might become a military competitor, perhaps even a hostile competitor. The wiser course would be to assume that China will continue to grow economically and militarily but not necessarily become hostile. The key would then be to devote serious intellectual and diplomatic efforts toward adjusting to the rise of China in a way that minimizes the likelihood of conflict. We have already argued that the first step in this effort would involve declaring China absolutely "off-limits" as a "football" in domestic American politics. But it would also involve diplomatic efforts to achieve a durable strategic understanding with China on critical features of the Asian and global security environments, including the major contours of the international and regional security, growth, and value systems. This, in turn, would require a primary emphasis by both sides on the strategic dimension of Sino-U.S. relations, and a recognition by both countries of the need for compromise.

Not everyone in the United States and China is equally convinced of this logic, however. Occasional displays of (especially) American and Japanese insensitivity to Chinese interests and pride serve to remind both China's leaders and people of the imperialistic depredations of previous generations of Westerners and Japanese. Chinese perceptions of their security threats and interests are rooted in this history and cannot easily be influenced by even the best-intentioned foreign initiatives. Alternatively, we as Americans need to determine to what extent and in what areas we are willing to compromise with an emerging China in order to reach a durable strategic understanding. For some, such compromise might require a greater level of "equal treatment" toward China than is tolerable. But some level of genuine accommodation of interests will likely be necessary if China's relative capabilities expand significantly over the decades ahead.

Nevertheless, precisely how China's leaders will perceive their interests and wield their increasing power will depend to a great extent on the policies adopted by the United States and other parties, especially Japan. If these countries greet China's rise with hostility, it surely will respond in kind. Of course, it would be unreasonable and unfair of China's leaders to assume, for example, that a U.S. commitment to maintain or even enhance its military position in the Asia-Pacific region would be inherently hostile, and in this respect China's leaders must themselves take responsibility for carefully analyzing American and Japanese motives and not automatically assume the worst. Nor should China's leaders automatically assume that when the United States takes a tough line where American interests (including human rights) are at stake such moves are inherently hostile or "anti-China." All countries enjoy the right vigorously to pursue their interests, and China will have to adjust its rise to the interests of the United States and Japan, just as Washington and Tokyo must learn to accommodate China.

On balance, China's neighbors and the international community should welcome China into their midst and work with China to strengthen and support the features of the international system. Then not only will Beijing's range of choice be constrained but also it will gradually develop an active interest and a greater stake in upholding the stability of the system. It bears repeating, however, that how the outside world treats China is not the only factor of importance. Probably most important will be the perceptions of China's leaders, which are rooted deep in a troubled history and not easily influenced by outside parties.

Conclusion

The Legacy of Reform

As China was poised on the precipice of the twenty-first century, it was in a state of high-speed and uncertain change. With the death of Deng Xiaoping, China appeared to have come to an end of the kind of "big leaders" culture that had marked its passage through the twentieth century. While the era of reform that this volume chronicles took place during Deng's tenure and was certainly animated by his leadership, it was also a period in which a host of new forces in China began to gather their own momentum.

Deng left a legacy that was every bit as revolutionary—or perhaps it would be more accurate to say counterrevolutionary—as that of Mao himself. During Deng's decade and a half as China's paramount leader, economic reform transformed life for one-fifth of the world's population. Yet even with such epic accomplishments, Deng's legacy as a reformer remains incomplete. He was a confusing paradox of flexibility and stubbornness. Mao Zedong once aptly described him as "a rare talent" who was like "a needle wrapped in cotton." While he succeeded in radically liberalizing Maoist economics, he allowed China's political structure to remain largely intact.

Deng's new reformism did not mean that he was about to tear down the edifice of the Maoist revolution. Although he did not rely on coercion against political opposition as much as Mao had, he repeatedly showed a willingness to crack down when he felt stability was under threat. As he said with chilling pragmatism when student demonstrations swept across the country in 1986, "When necessary we must deal severely with those who defy orders, and we can afford to shed some blood. Just try as much as possible not to kill anyone." On the question of democratizing China, he was unambiguous. "Democracy can develop only gradually, and we cannot copy Western systems," he warned. "If we did, that would only make a mess of everything."

While Deng disagreed with Mao on many issues, he was never completely willing to dethrone him. "We will not do to Chairman Mao what Khrushchev did to Stalin," he told Oriana Fallaci. "In evaluating his merits and mistakes, we hold that his mistakes were only secondary."

This ambivalence about Mao and contradictory penchants for liberal economic policies and conservative political policies came to characterize the reforms of the 1980s and '90s. Despite the enormity of the Party structure, the People's Republic still had no codified and established political system. In the absence of formal procedures for electing leaders or even for setting policy, stability depended on the adroitness of a paramount leader and his cronies in mediating between opposing political factions. Unlike Mao, who exaggerated differences, Deng had long experience in intra-Party affairs that taught him how to propitiate hardliners and reformers alike and thus maintain a fragile equilibrium. As described by the China specialist Lucian Pye, Deng's leadership style, which involved manipulating factions through his *guanxi* network, was "not unlike a Mafia godfather ruling from behind the scenes."

While Deng could be opportunistic, he was also remarkably constant in his beliefs and predictable in his actions, especially when it came to economic reform. He rarely agonized over difficult decisions or allowed himself to be plagued afterwards by qualms of conscience. Zhou Enlai was reported to have said that, when making decisions, Deng's old mentor Liu Bocheng gave the appearance of "lifting something that is light as if it were heavy" while Deng always gave the appearance of "lifting something heavy as if it were light."

Seemingly unaffected by ambiguity, Deng was ideally suited by temperament to be an autocrat. "The greatest advantage of the socialist system is that when the central leadership makes a decision, it is promptly implemented without interference from any other quarters," he candidly told one visitor. "We don't have to go through a lot of repetitive discussion and consultation with one branch of government holding up another and decisions being made, not carried out."

His self-confidence allowed Deng to take enormous gambles. First, he dissolved Mao's communes and leased the land back to private households, thereby transforming the face of Chinese agriculture. Then he turned to reform industry by encouraging private business, upgrading antiquated management and technology techniques, implementing price reforms, and encouraging foreign investment and trade. "We regard the reform as a revolution, which is totally different from a cultural revolution," he explained. Using the new engine of private profit as encouragement, Chinese private-sector workers made production figures skyrocket. It did not seem to matter to Deng that there was no clear plan for China's development. It was enough to try new things out, to "cross the river by feeling the way from stone to stone," as he often said.

Sometimes Deng's economic boldness made it seem as if he understood people's urge to improve their own private lives far better than the basic tenets of Marxism. Yet he eschewed any insinuation that he was making China "capitalist." "I have explained time and time again that our modernization program is a socialist one," he insisted in 1986. "Our decision to apply the open door policy and assimilate useful things from capitalist societies was made only to supplement the development of our socialist productive force."

When it came to maintaining the hegemony of the Party, Deng could be as stubbornly reactionary as those conservatives who looked askance at his economic reforms. While he sometimes called for "political reform," what he meant was not democratization in the Western sense but administrative reforms that would make the Leninist state more efficient. His goal was to make China strong, not democratic. It was one thing to jump-start China's economy by unleashing private entrepreneurs to compete against the state sector, quite another to unleash political dissidents to vie with the Party.

Yet few major societies in recent history have succeeded in undergoing such a significant and largely peaceful transformation as China during these years of reform. By reintegrating China into the world community, decollectivizing agriculture, privatizing much of industry and commerce, restoring the notion of ownership, creating financial markets—in short, allowing market forces to enter into almost every aspect of economic life—China's leadership brought their country into a new era. At the same time, by leaving the underpinnings of Mao's old political system essentially intact, they kept a large part of China in the past. China is still a Leninist state ruled by a single party according to the imperatives of personal power relationships; it is still propped up by a secret police and military answerable to the Party; it has no truly independent judiciary; and it maintains a vast prison system all too often used to silence political opponents.

Deng's idealized political model was a form of "Asian authoritarianism," a combination of a dynamic laissez-faire market cloned to a static system of authoritarian politics pioneered by the "Four Dragons" of Asia: Taiwan, South Korea, Hong Kong, and Singapore. As the Party-controlled *Beijing Review* noted just before his death, "With many problems facing China, stability is overwhelmingly important. . . . If we attempt to realize only democracy, it will turn out to be no democracy at all. Even worse is that the economy would not develop and the country would fall into chaos."

Given China's history, fears about "chaos" were not irrational. But Deng's fear of instability had a tendency to prevent him and his coterie from comprehending another reality that Marx understood only too well, namely, that ultimately economics and politics are insolubly connected. Deng seemed to imagine that China could radically change its economic stripes while politically remaining unreformed and that China's standard of living could be improved with infusions of economic freedom while their yearnings for more political freedom could be ignored. June 4, 1989, was a bitter reminder of the perils of such imbalanced reform, and it left wounds that even the subsequent economic boom could not heal.

The culture of materialism offered by China's new engagement in the marketplace certainly helped preoccupy people's attention during this period, but it was hardly able to answer other more subtle but urgent questions about national identity, which had a profound impact not only on how Chinese saw themselves and how they worked with each other but on how they as a nation would relate to the world at large.

The schizophrenia of the reform era—which saw Deng finally turn on his more liberal, self-appointed successors, Hu Yaobang and Zhao Ziyang—left Chinese wealthier and more hopeful about the future but deeply confused about who they were and how they might realize a stable future. What sort of leadership ought they to admire? Should they look to traditional political culture, Maoist revolutionary culture, or Western democracy for models of governance? To what core system of values should they turn to give coherence to everyday life and interpersonal relations? In short, What did it now mean to be Chinese? Given the way Deng's reforms had canceled so many of the precepts of Mao's revolution—which had earlier canceled many of the fundamentals of traditional culture—for most Chinese it was hard to know what stars to steer by.

There are those who believe the unbalanced regimen of reform that characterized this period may yet prove to be China's salvation. They argue that by maintaining political stability until a new middle class, more receptive to democratic values, arises and a "civil society" comes naturally into being, China might become the first Marxist country to segue out of Communism into the modern world without major upheaval. But others argue that Deng's lopsided approach ended up creating new and increasingly insurmountable contradictions—many of which are described in this volume—that will inevitably disrupt the gradualist process and plunge China back into the very state of chaos that everyone fears.

What makes it so hard to predict China's future is not only that there is no real precedent for such an evolutionary transition under a Communist Party but that Deng's successors—revolving around "the core leadership" of Jiang Zemin—seemed to have so little clear sense of where they intend to take their country. Still others feared what would happen if the legitimacy of the post-Deng leadership, which rested largely on its success encouraging high economic growth rates, was undermined by a downturn in the economy.

As China entered the twenty-first century, it was a paradox. While it could rightfully boast enormous economic accomplishments, its successes masked a host of potentially crippling problems that arose as a result of the economic reforms. And whether a political system that was so unresolved and so perennially caught between major transitions would be able to cope with these problems was far from certain.

Whether the most populous nation on earth would be able to make a final escape from Maoism without the kind of precipitous discontinuities that interrupted most other Communist regimes around the world could only become clear with time. The key question was, Where was China going? All that one could say with any certainty at the end of the twentieth century was that as unclear as that vision of China's future was, its people were going there with an incredible, and even frightening, speed.

Index

Accompany You Till Dawn (radio), 253

Agricultural Bank of China, 327

Agriculture: consumption, 335; cropping patterns, 7; decentralization of, 366–67; development, 23, 300; grain production, 48, 336–44; inputs/outputs, 302; modernization of, 22, 24, 55, 366; production, 7, 16, 49, 335–44; reform, 304; subsidies, 335, 338, 340

Albright, Madeleine, 473

Ali Wong, 399

All-China Federation of Industry and Commerce, 232

All-China Federation of Trade Unions, 130

Amnesty International, 403

Anarchism, 26

An Ji, 210

Anti-Bourgeois Liberalization Campaign, 234

Anti-Spiritual Pollution Campaign, 230, 233

Armey, Dick, 477

Asia-Pacific Economic Times (newspaper), 235

Authoritarianism, 8, 17, 19, 78, 103, 155, 272, 508

Autoculpabilization, 267

"Back to Reality" program, 167

Bai Hua, 17

Bamboo Gang triad, 398, 399

Banking system, 110; auditing procedures, 320; capital market development, 319; credit allocation in, 305; enhancement of, 311; monetary policy, 316; policy banks in, 320; private, 327; state-owned, 305

Baoding, 10

Baogao Wenxue (journal), 246–47

Bao Tong, 409

Becker, Jasper, 380

Beijing Association of Young Economists, 88

Beijing Bastards (film), 289–90

Beijing Daily (newspaper), 163

Beijing Federation of Autonomous Students' Unions of Universities and Colleges, 91

Beijing Institute of Socioeconomic Science, 82

Beijing Machinery Industry Research Institute, 208

Beijing Magazine and Book Wholesale Trade Mart, 251, 256

Beijing Massacre. *See* Tiananmen Square

Beijing Normal University, 188, 190, 197

Beijing Spring, 3, 79–102

Beijing Teachers' University, 84

Beijing University, 81, 84, 129, 188, 190, 197, 199, 208, 366

Beijing Youth News (newspaper), 237

Berger, Samuel, 475

Biological Weapons Convention, 475, 481

Book kings, 249, 250, 251, 252

Botteller, Pieter, 368

Boycotts, 84

Bo Yibo, 10, 25

Buddhism, 409

Bull, Hedley, 417

Bureaucracy, 198; competition in, 107–8; diffusion of interests in, 108–9; factionalism in, 11; fragmentation in, 107–8; immobility in, 107; inertia in, 103; military, 10; overcoming, 26; personnel system, 10; power clusters in, 10; propaganda network, 10; public security, 10; strength of, 19

Cai Lun, 293

Cai Shaoqing, 404

Capital: accumulation, 6; allocation, 315, 320; construction, 23, 48; flows, 330; foreign, 35, 111, 120, 121, 184, 313, 330; growth, 120; inflows, 111, 330; international monopoly, 80; investment, 313; local, 324; stock, 323

Capitalism, 13, 53, 55, 56, 80, 82, 125, 184; averting, 31; defining, 35; fear of, 17; labor productivity in, 217

Carter, Jimmy, 487

Central China Peasants Publishing House, 252

Central Discipline Inspection Commission, 143

Central Military Commission, 431

Certificate of Household in Extreme Poverty, 355

Chairman Mao Memorial Hall, 34, 195

Chan, Tommi, 399, 400

Changsha, 85

Changzhang Jingli Ribao (newspaper), 121

Chemical Weapons Convention, 475, 481

Chen Duxiu, 421

Chen Qi, 382

Chen Xitong, 79–95, 425

Chen Yi, 44

Chen Yun, 10, 16, 17, 45

Chen Ziming, 82, 235, 409

Chiang Kai-shek, 148, 186–87, 224, 488

Chi Haotian, 473

Children's Corps, 218

China Central Television, 244

China Cereals, Oils, and Foodstuffs Import and Export Corp., 339

China Daily (newspaper), 253, 369

China Press & Publishing Journal, 251–52

China's Worker Union, 368

China Through the Third Eye, 364

China Times (newspaper), 282

China Tourism Publishers of Audio-Visual Materials, 286

China Youth News (newspaper), 237

Chinese Academy of Sciences, 208, 293, 360

Chinese Academy of Social Sciences, 368; Institute of Journalism, 235

Chinese Buddhist Association, 270

Chinese Christian Church, 271

Chinese Communist Party Central Committee, 35, 37–49, 39, 43, 50, 52, 57, 76, 87, 150, 198, 361; Lushan Meeting (1959), 39, 226; Military Commission, 44–45, 46, 68; Organization Department, 158; Political Bureau, 47, 48, 57, 71, 83, 86; Propaganda Department, 90, 230, 232, 247; responsibilities of, 26; Secretariat, 48, 71; Standing Committee, 48, 71, 86, 101; Third Plenum, 15, 16, 21–29, 56, 99, 160; United Front Work Department, 270

Chinese People's Political Consultative Conference, 65, 121, 187

Chinese Writers' Association, 247

Christopher, Warren, 422, 473

Chu Anping, 225

Chun Yun, 39

Civil service, 63, 64

Class: bourgeois, 123; contradictions, 134; exploitation, 75, 76, 218; labels, 7; middle, 508; nongovernmental bourgeois, 121; and production, 36; relations, 120–24; social, 133; struggle, 12, 15, 22, 39, 52, 55, 134, 165, 200, 202, 233; working, 66, 74, 121, 130, 131, 217

Clinton, Bill, xvi, 165, 472, 473, 474, 475, 479–87

Coastal Development Strategy, 303

Commercialism, xv

Communes, 24, 38, 230, 324, 329, 348, 366

Communications, bottlenecks in, 19

Communist Party: changes in, 128–35; consolidation of, 72–73; corruption in, 131–32; erosion of authority, 105–7; founding, 29; "Great Wall of Iron," 225; maintenance of power, xviii; media in, 228; membership issues, 50, 73–74, 129, 145; opposition to, 95–102; organizational weakening, 128–29; organizations, 43; relations with masses, 129–31, 145–48; strengthening, 69–75; survival of, 143–45; ties with masses, 72

Communist Youth League, 66, 122, 218, 219, 232

Comprehensive Test Ban Treaty, 442, 475

Computers: access to, xvi; insects, 291; Internet, 256–59, 291, 485; software pirating, 291–96

Consumer: durables, 20; goods, 52; production, 20

Corruption, xv, xvii, 98, 100, 103, 112, 131–32, 142, 143, 191, 301, 314, 359–60, 378, 404, 514

Crime, xvii, 73, 394–405; and drugs, 284, 396, 402; economic, 17, 131–32; kidnapping, 402; money laundering, 396–97; organized, 394, 395; rise in, 103, 354, 401–5; Strike Hard Crackdown, 403; triads, 396, 398, 399, 400

Criminal justice system reform, 16

Criticize Confucius–Criticize Lin
    Biao campaign, 15
Cui Jian, 280–91
Cults of personality, 33, 138, 198
Cultural Revolution, 5, 6, 8, 11, 30,
    34, 40, 146; attacks on, 15; defining,
    42; incorrectness of, 30, 31, 41–49;
    and opposition of revisionism, 28;
    rationale for, 19; stages of, 44–47;
    values of, 13
Culture, 260–96; choices in, 513;
    cyberculture, 291–96; drugs in, 284,
    396; "gray," 283, 287, 289; high,
    261–79; liumang in, 284; low,
    280–96; popular music, 280–91;
    and private life, 261–79; under-
    ground, 290

Dai Qing, 225, 226, 227
Dalai Lama, 271, 409, 486, 489–92,
    521
Debt, foreign, xvi, 450, 516
Decadence, 127–28
*Deep Structure of Chinese Culture,
    The* (Sun), 263
Democracy: and centralism, 26, 28,
    32, 58, 155; development of, 172–74,
    184; "empty," 203; extending, 179;
    "false," 180; institutionalization of,
    66; necessity of, 168–70; socialist,
    16, 57, 58, 62, 65–67, 162; state-led,
    xviii; systemization of, 26
"Democracy: The Fifth Moderniza-
    tion" (poster), 161, 165
Democracy Wall movement, 6, 16,
    157–65
Deng Liqun, 116, 230
Deng Xiaoping, xv; on bourgeois
    liberalism, 182–85; dissent during

reforms of, 157–82; economic
    reforms, 299; on education, 215–23;
    effect on media, 246–56; and Gang
    of Four, 25; interviews with, 29–37;
    personal authority of, 138; political
    style, 138; purging of, 10, 47;
    reforms of, 3; rehabilitation of, 13,
    16, 39, 42, 46, 48; relations with
    military, 150, 151; and Tiananmen
    Square incidents, 79–102, 182–85; in
    transition after Mao Zedong, 5–49
Development: agricultural, 300;
    economic, xvi, 6, 23, 35, 51, 52, 56,
    137, 220, 221, 313; and education,
    220; Marxist, 75–77; policy, 330;
    private sector, 118; rapid, 23; rural,
    331; simultaneous, 23–24; socialist,
    76; strategies, 6, 309–10; sustain-
    able, 378; zones, 133
Development Institute of the China
    Rural Development Research
    Center, 88
Dictatorship, 184, 198; democratic,
    53, 56, 57; proletarian, 42, 126, 132,
    162, 187
Ding Zilin, 207–12, 422
Discipline: breaches of, 73; Central
    Discipline Inspection Commis-
    sion, 143; inspection, 60; labor, 26
Domesticization, 9
Dongfang 110 (television), 253
Drugs, 284, 396, 402, 481–82
Duan Changlong, 209
Du Yuesheng, 396

East Radio, 252, 253
East Turkestan, 271
Economic: austerity, 78, 104, 310;
    challenges, 516–19; competition,

113; controls, 111; crimes, 17, 131–32; decentralization, 148–50, 312, 314–15; decisionmaking, 112, 300, 312, 314; development, xvi, 6, 23, 35, 51, 52, 56, 137, 220, 221, 313; disparities, 357; expansion, xv, 3, 5, 6, 15, 118, 146–47, 312, 313, 349, 450, 451, 508; goals, 13; joint ventures, 369; laissez-faire, 355; laws, 16; liberalization, 16, 328; localism, 107; modernization, 68, 105; monopolies, 113; openness, 313; organizations, 58–59; planning, 103; policy, 16, 23, 50, 104; primitive, 12; reform, 21, 104, 270; retrenchment, 16
Economics Weekly (newspaper), 235
Economy, 299–344; command, 319, 508; commodity, 54, 55, 56, 57, 62, 68, 70; coordinated development in, 52; export-oriented, 303; hybrid, 109; individual, 121; informal networks in, 111–13; macroeconomic stabilization in, 309–10; marketization of, xv, 125, 145, 146–47, 235, 250, 301, 306, 310, 313, 315, 317, 349, 508; natural, 54, 55; open, 78; ownership structure, 117–20; planned, 306; private, 129; protected, 302; socialist, 53, 55, 62, 70, 119; supply-demand gaps in, 324; township, village, and private enterprises, 321–34
Education, 215–27, 518–19; access to, xvi; and economic development, 220; effects of *fang/shou* on, 215–23; enrollments, xvi; ideological, 69; liberalization, 15; literacy rates, 54; media in, 221; patriotic, 270; policy, 50; political, 218; primary, 217, 219; reform, 13, 215–23; right to, 178;

secondary, 217, 219; socialist, 215–23; teacher status, 221–23; technical, 221; underfunding of, 315; vocational, 221
Elections, 66, 179, 199, 513; laws, 320
Elitism, 82
Emergency Room Hotline (radio), 253
Employment: full, 310; opportunities, 52; rural, 52; urban, 52
Energy, 518; bottlenecks in, 19; investment, 306–7; production, xvi; shortages, xvi, 104
Enterprise responsibility system, 112, 113
Entrepreneurship, 120, 121, 144, 291, 324
Environment, 517; acid rain, xvii, 377, 379, 390; air/water pollution, 377, 379, 385–87, 390; degradation of, 142, 376–93, 510; greenhouse effect, 377, 387–88, 482, 518; investment in, 390–93; underfunding of, 315
Europe, Eastern, 3, 104, 117, 129, 271, 306, 507
European Currency Unit, 462
European Union, 462
Exchange: foreign, 110, 303, 311, 319; labor, 326; rates, 303, 304, 315, 319
Explorations (journal), 161, 162
Export(s), 111; growth in, xvi; incentives, 303; processing, 303; promotion, 315; volume, 120

Factionalism, 9, 10; bourgeois, 26; bureaucratic, 11; military, 103, 113–15; political, 3, 5–21
Fallaci, Oriana, 29–37
Family planning, xvi, 372, 382–83

Fang Lizhi, 175–82, 183, 234, 238, 418, 426

Farmers' Daily (newspaper), 237

Federation of Autonomous Workers' Unions, 91

Federation of China's Workers, 371

Fei Xiaotong, 331

Feudalism, 26, 33, 35, 53, 57, 67, 178, 198

Financial system: debts in, 311; liberalization in, 313, 316; reform of, 319–20; rural, 327

First Asian Popular Music Awards, 287

Five Principles of Peaceful Coexistence, 419, 466

Flying knights, 251

Four Cardinal Principles, 124, 126, 162, 183, 184

Four Heavenly Kings of Hacking, 293

Four Modernizations, 15, 22, 33, 35, 161, 166, 221, 223

Four Seas triad, 398

Frankenstein, John, 398

Freedoms: assembly, 195; demonstration, 158; expression, 188, 224; press, 157, 195, 229–56; religious, 269; speech, 163, 195; travel, 195

Friends of Nature, 387

Fu Changlu, 403

Fujian, 121

Fu Quanyou, 473

Gang of Four, 5–21, 22, 23, 25, 26, 29, 30, 33, 34, 36, 47, 165, 166, 216, 432

Gao Gao, 226

Garside, Roger, 163

Gender: rights, xvii; and unemployment, 352–54

Gephardt, Richard, 477

Ge Yang, 82

Goldstone, Jack, 363

Gong Xueping, 252

Gorbachev, Mikhail, xviii, 188, 189, 191, 242, 243

Gore, Al, 474, 477, 483

Grain bag policy, 336–44

Great Hall of the People, 84, 90, 190, 195

Great Leap Forward, 19, 30–31, 38, 39, 137, 138, 146, 167, 335, 380

Gross domestic product, xvi, 314, 450

Gross national product, 51, 53, 111, 120, 184, 306, 367

Group of 15/Group of 77, 462

Guangming Daily (newspaper), 242–43, 252

Gu Shengzu, 363

Gu Siren, 398

Hang-sheng Cheng, 311–21

Hao Zhijing, 208

Health care, xvi, xvii, xvii*n*, 315

Hedonism, xv

He Long, 48

He Xin, 224

He Yong, 288

Hong Kong, 85, 126, 128, 224, 235, 292, 303, 330, 488, 493–96, 520, 521

Hong Yang, 413

Hong Ying, 271–79

Hou Dejian, 199–200

Household Contract Responsibility System, 366–67

Housing, 318; construction, 20

Hua Guofeng, 6, 10, 15, 18, 22, 29, 35, 47, 50, 140, 166

Hu Angang, 360

Huang Kecheng, 39

Hu Baishou, 402

Hu Jiquan, 378, 379

Hu Jiwei, 229–31, 235

Hu Qiaomu, 227

Hu Qili, 242

Hu Yaobang, 6, 50, 78, 82, 83, 84, 85, 158, 187, 188, 234, 235, 238

Ideology: communist, 69; Left, 52; of Mao Zedong Thought, 30; Marxist, 53, 144; political, 202; reschooling in, 11; single, 12

Imperialism, 26, 53, 92

Import(s): duty-free, 303; grain, 338*tab*; protection, 315; quotas, 319; tariffs, 319; volume, 120

Income: annual, 130; differentials, 20, 129, 349–61; disposable, 508; distribution, 329; family, 130; gaps, 329; "gray," 296; household, 310; national, 110; peasant, 16, 111, 324; per capita, xvi, 130; rational, 127; real, 20; rising, 508; rural, 51, 130–31, 323; urban, 51

Individualism, 263, 264, 284

Industrialization, 53, 300; forced-draft, 15; rural, 328

Industry: balance in, 6–7; capital-intensive, 305; growth of, 111; heavy, 16; inefficiency of, 19; investment companies, 109; management of, 7; modernization of, 22, 53, 55; offshore, 330; output value, 117; rural, 302, 303; scale-intensive, 305; state-owned, 303, 305

Infant mortality, xvi

Inflation, 78, 103, 110, 142, 304, 316, 337

Infrastructure: investment, 307; market, 311, 317

Institutions: building, 5, 13, 304; changes in, 13; continuity of, 8; destabilizing, 19; educational, 220; financial, 113, 319; peasant, 7; political, 19; reform of, 13, 16, 50; restructuring, 33; transitional, 306

Intenational Monetary Fund, 319

International Civil Aviation Organization, 483

International Covenant on Civil and Political Rights, 418

International Covenant on Economic, Social, and Cultural Rights, 418

International Fund for Agricultural Development, 483

International Labor Organization, 407, 410

Internet, 256–59, 291, 485; access, xvi

Investment: agricultural, 340; capital, 313; energy, 306–7; financing, 313, 316; foreign, xv, 7, 146–47, 149, 302, 304, 305, 312, 313, 315, 331, 369, 484; increases in, 311; industry companies, 109; infrastructure, 307; peasant, 324; policy, 16; private, 35; rural, 323; state, 323

Islam, 271, 409

Japan, 330, 449, 462, 496, 519

Jia Lusheng, 246, 247, 248, 252

Jiang Jielian, 207, 208

Jiang Peikun, 422

Jiang Ping, 405

Jiang Qing, 6, 10, 13, 29, 37, 40, 42, 43, 45, 46, 47

Jiang Zemin, 117, 139, 140, 141, 143, 146, 152, 238, 240, 241, 361, 378, 432, 433, 459, 464, 469, 474, 481, 482, 483, 496–501
Ji Dengkui, 10
Journalism, 229–56; second-channel, 246–56; "yellow," 247
Judges Law (1995), 409
Judicial system, 67

Kafka, Franz, 265, 266
Kaituo (magazine), 234
Kang Sheng, 40, 44, 45
Khrushchev, Nikita, 8, 29, 32
Kissinger, Henry, 411
Korea, 40, 271, 292, 433, 480, 519
Kundera, Milan, 265–66, 267
Kuomintang, 82, 89, 92

Labor: agricultural, 315, 324, 366; construction, 368–69; demand for, 324; discipline, 26; division of, 12, 326; exchange, 326; family, 326; flows, 330; lay-offs, 350–52; local, 324; markets, 304, 326, 370, 519; migrant, 364, 371; mobility, 315, 326; peaks, 372; productivity, 55, 217, 220, 221; rural, 340, 362–73; shortages, 355; specialization, 326; strikes, 130; surplus, 326, 362–73; urban, 370
Labor Disputes Arbitration Commission, 130
Lake, Anthony, 474, 475
Land: acquisition, 329; allocation, 133; arable, 365–66; improper use, 365–66; leases, 315, 366; ownership, 24, 302, 315; private, xv

Laws: banking, 320; bankruptcy, 350; citizen awareness of, 67; civil, xvi; copyright, 315, 317; corporate, 317; criminal, xvi; economic, 16; election, 320; enforcement of, 67, 412–13; environmental, 317, 320, 378; liberalization, 16; media, 66; patent, 315, 317; on religion, 269–70; rule of, 513; tax, xvi; trade, 317; trademark, 317; violation of, 73
Leadership: central, 150; centralized, 26; collective, 32, 40, 71; communist, 56, 58; divided, 105; generational layering in, 35, 70; political, 59; politics, 137–42; regional, 141; renewal of, 35; systemic defects, 57; unity, 137, 138
Lee, Martin, 521
Lee Teng-hui, 521
Legal system, 317; inadequacies in, 311; socialist, 16, 26, 67–69; strengthening, 67–69
Liang Conjie, 387
Liao Yongxiong, 401, 402, 403
Liberalism, bourgeois, 17, 56, 82, 83, 100, 124, 125, 126, 182–85, 234, 243
Liberalization: cultural, 15; economic, 16, 328; educational, 15; financial, 311, 313; laws, 16; opposition to, 82; political, 16, 105–6; scientific, 15
Liberation Daily (newspaper), 232
Life and Death in Shanghai (Nien), 265
Life expectancy, xvi
Li Fuchun, 44
Lin Biao, 5, 13, 21, 22, 23, 26, 30, 40, 42, 43, 45, 46, 224
Lin Yifu, 366
Li Peiyao, 404

Li Peng, 81, 83, 84, 86, 139, 146, 189, 190, 194, 196, 201, 211, 243, 244, 245, 257, 378, 390, 412

Li Ruihuan, 268

Literacy, 54

Literature, 271–79

"Literature of the wounded," 158

Li Tieying, 83

Liu, Alan, 363

Liu Binyan, 233, 234, 235, 264–65

Liu Gang, 409, 422–28

Liu Huaqiu, 459–70, 474

Liu Ruishao, 82

Liu Shaoqi, 5, 16, 30, 31, 36, 39, 42, 43, 48

Liu Xiaobo, 88, 200, 409

Li Wei, 129

Li Xiannian, 47

Li Yining, 379

Love for the Republic (television), 227

Lu Chunlin, 209

Lu Dingyi, 44

Luo Ruiqing, 44

Lushan Meeting (1959), 39, 226

Macao, 330, 488, 498

Mao Zedong, 460; attacks on, 15; contributions and errors of, 30, 31, 32, 36, 37–49; and Cultural Revolution, 12, 30–31, 41–49; demise of, 18, 34; on education, 216, 219, 220; founding of People's Republic of China, 186–87; interventionist style, 9; polarities of, 13; reassessments of, 6, 29; relations with military, 150, 151

Mao Zedong Thought, 26, 28, 30, 32, 36, 42, 56, 219, 222

Market(s): black, 307; commodity, 326; competition, 301, 302–5, 306, 355; domestic, 54, 304, 322; economy, xv, 125, 145, 146–47, 235, 250, 301, 306, 317, 349; enhancement, 300; external, 322; factor, 326; financial, 327; free, 12; infrastructure, 311, 317; interbank fund, 320; labor, 304, 326, 370, 519; mechanisms, 16; niche, 302; performance, 301; prices, 303, 307, 308; regulation, 101; supplies, 52; urban, 329

Marxism-Leninism, 30, 35, 36, 41, 42, 53, 54, 56, 69, 75–77, 125, 129, 134, 144, 270, 507

Media, 228–60; access to, xvi, 7; censorship in, 231, 232, 233, 237, 242, 247, 253; commerce-driven, 246–256; cycles of repression in, 233–34; dissent in, 229–56; in education, 221, 222; laws governing, 66; literary reportage, 246; magazines/journals, xvi, 234, 235; newspapers, xvi; talk radio, xvi, 484; television, xvi; during Tiananmen Square incidents, 236–45; *See also* specific areas

Migration: internal, 363, 364, 365, 372; interregional, 304; mass, 142; push/pull factors, 365–70; right to, 513

Military, 78, 431–47; air force, 438, 440, 452; bureaucracy, 10; Central Military Commission, 431; doctrine, 437–43; expenditures, 434–37, 452, 473; factionalism in, 103, 113–15; future role, 521–25; generational changes in, 152–53; hierarchy, 153; internal crises, 105; modernization of, 114, 152, 432–47; navy, 440–42, 452; policy, 50;

Military (*cont.*)
    reform, 68; relations with civil
    society, 20, 150–54; weaponry,
    437–43, 452
Military Affairs Commission, 139
Ministry of Agriculture, 340
Ministry of Culture, 232
Ministry of Education, 221, 222
Ministry of Electronics, 254
Ministry of Finance, 110
Ministry of Internal Trade, 336, 339
Ministry of Public Security, 435
Ministry of Radio, Film, and Televi-
    sion, 90, 231, 289–90
Ministry of State Security, 435
Minying Qiyejia Bao (newspaper), 121
Missile Technology Control Regime,
    433, 475, 481
Modernization: agricultural, 22, 24,
    55, 366; defense, 22, 55; economic,
    68, 105; industrial, 22, 55; military,
    114, 152; political, 68; of produc-
    tion, 54; socialist, 16, 21, 22, 23, 26,
    28, 55, 77; technological, 22, 55
Mongolia, 3, 451
Monument to the People's Heroes, 93
Multilateralism, 413; interdependent,
    475
Music: popular, 280–91; punk rock,
    288

Nanjing University, 404
Nathan, Andrew, 164
National Environmental Protection
    Agency, 381, 387
Nationalism, 140, 149–50, 413, 471,
    472, 511, 519–21
National People's Congress, 16, 23,
    38, 40, 41, 48, 79, 99, 179, 198, 199,

230, 404; Environmental Protec-
    tion Committee, 383; Standing
    Committee, 26, 65
Neo-Maoism, 15, 16
New Observer (newspaper), 82
News Front (journal), 235
Newspapers, xvi, 229–56; Com-
    munist Party, 231–32; of govern-
    ment agencies, 232; internal
    reference, 232; *See also* specific
    newspapers
Nien Cheng, 265
Nie Rongzhen, 44
Nixon, Richard, 411, 487, 509
Ni Yuxian, 233
Nonaligned Movement, 462
North Atlantic Treaty Organization,
    462
Novak, Robert, 160
Nuclear Nonproliferation Treaty, 433,
    442, 446, 475, 481

One Hit, Three Anti's campaign, 11
"On the Reform of the System of
    Party and State Leadership" (Deng
    Xiaoping), 57
On the Road (television), 226–27
Opium Suppression Bureau, 396
Opposition: Democracy Wall move-
    ment, 157–65; nontoleration of, 8;
    student protests (1987), 165–212;
    Tiananmen Square, 50–102, 175–82
Organizations: bureaucratic, 107–8;
    Communist Party, 43; cultural,
    58–59; economic, 58–59; grass-
    roots, 75; illegal, 83; judicial, 26;
    mass, 58, 61–62, 149; news, 232;
    nongovernmental, 123, 512; patri-
    otic, 65; private enterprise, 121;

procuratorial, 26; religious, 270;
student, 82, 83, 202, 203
Oriental Television, 252, 253, 257

Panchen Lama, 409, 521
Patriarchy, 33, 67, 198
Peng, James, 413
Peng Dehuai, 16, 25, 39, 48
Peng Zhen, 16, 44
People's Armed Police, 80, 404, 434,
435, 474
People's Daily (newspaper), 97, 157,
160, 164, 188, 189, 229, 230, 232, 233,
234, 237, 238, 240, 241, 243, 244, 245,
257, 404
People's Liberation Army, 47–48, 49,
78, 80, 89, 187, 224, 293, 431–47,
452; combat effectiveness, 114–15;
factionalism in, 113–15; General
Staff Department, 254; pro-democracy participation, 114; professionalization of, 114; in publishing, 232;
in Tiananmen Square, 85–95, 262;
See also Military
People's Republic of China: Constitution, 58, 86, 89, 157, 163, 269;
crime in, 394–405; culture in,
260–96; Democracy Wall movement, 157–65; early nineties period,
103–35; economic reforms,
299–346; education and research
in, 215–27; environmental issues,
376–93; foreign policy, 59; founding, 187; future issues, 505–30;
generational changes in, 508; grain
production, 336–44; "great power"
aspirations, 448–58; health issues,
384–85; human rights in, 407–28;
internal affairs, 59; international

relations, 448–87; "lebensraum"
for, 451–53; Mao Zedong to Deng
Xiaoping transitional period, 5–49;
media in, 228–60; military in,
431–47; Most-Favored Nation
status, 412, 477; new transformations in, 507–8; post-Deng era,
136–55; private life in, 261–79;
radical reform period, 50–79;
regional economic interdependence, 12; relations with United
States, 470–87; return of Hong
Kong, 493–96; social effects of reform, 347–405; student demonstrations in, 165–212; territorial
reunification goals, 488–501;
Tiananmen Square crisis, 50–102;
United States policy debate on,
475–78; views on Taiwan, 496–501;
Zhao Ziyang period, 50–77
People's Republic of China Computer Information Network Protection Regulations, 257
People's University, 207, 208, 209, 210
Perry, William, 473
Personnel: civil service, 63; management, 63; reform, 62–64
Planning: central, 103, 304, 313; economic, 101, 103, 221; mandatory, 68;
production, 313; state, 304
Policy, 157; consensus, 137; debates,
108; decisionmaking, 51, 59; development, 330; domestic, 10–11;
economic, 16, 23, 50, 104; education, 50; errors, 6; foreign, 137;
formulation, 107; implementation,
12, 59, 107, 110; international, 137;
investment, 16; mercantilist, 315;
military, 50; monetary, 316, 319;
national, 137, 149; open, 69, 70;

Policy (*cont.*)
　opposition to, 149; political,
　104; reassessing, 37–49; science,
　50
Politburo, 137, 150, 190, 371; purges of,
　6; Standing Committee, 16
Political: capacity to rule, 137–55;
　change, 510–11; consciousness, 43,
　217; consultation, 58; control, 137;
　correctness, 217; criticism, 40;
　decisionmaking, 508; democ-
　ratization, 124; education, 218;
　evolution, 5–21, 18*tab*; factional-
　ism, 5–21; ideology, 202; infiltra-
　tion, 271; institutions, 19;
　leadership, 59; liberalization, 16,
　105–6; modernization, 68; open-
　ness, 6, 51, 70; oppression, 75, 76;
　pluralism, xv, 197; policy, 104;
　power, xviii; reform, 5, 21, 57–69,
　104, 188, 190; restrictions, xvii;
　rights, 201; stability, 33, 68, 104, 228;
　suppression, 158; system, 142–45;
　transition, 136; underground, 247;
　unification, 148
Political Consultative Conference,
　100
Politics: Deng-Chen system, 18–21;
　early nineties period, 103–35;
　factionalism in, 3; fang-shou
　cycles, 3; generational layering, 20,
　70; leadership, 137–42; Mao
　Zedong to Deng Xiaoping transi-
　tional period, 5–49; outer-party,
　155–212; post-Deng era, 136–55;
　radical reform period, 50–77;
　separation of Party and govern-
　ment, 58–61; Tiananmen Square
　crisis, 50–102; Zhao Ziyang period,
　50–77

Population: control, 357; "floating,"
　362–75; forced abortions, 409;
　peaks, 372; planning, 372, 382–83;
　rural, 367
Poverty, 126, 380, 408, 451; allevia-
　tion, 355, 359; management of,
　354–56; rural, 357–61; urban, 349,
　352–54
Power: abuse of, 72, 233; administra-
　tive, 65; centralization of, 55; dele-
　gation of, 61–62; expansion of, 62;
　grassroots, 61–62; hegemonic,
　454–57; hierarchical, 12; local,
　111–13; monopoly, 302; overconcen-
　tration of, 57, 61, 63; political, xviii;
　state, 58, 134; struggles, 104
Price(s): agricultural, 313; consumer,
　313; controls, 78, 304; flexible, 308;
　market, 303, 307, 308; stabilization,
　319, 337; subsidies, 111; two-tier
　system, 113
"Principle of Three Nots," 26
Prison Law (1994), 409
Privatization, 119, 129, 305; resistance
　to, 106
Production: agricultural, 7, 16, 19, 23,
　335–44; consumer, 20; costs, 326;
　energy, xvi; growth of, 51; means of,
　24, 77, 125; modernization of, 53,
　54; ownership of, 125; planning,
　313; relations of, 54, 55; social, 54,
　118; socialist, 35, 36
Project Hope, 281
Propaganda network, 10, 12
Prostitution, 354, 395, 396
Protestantism, 271
Public Security Bureau, 280, 290,
　354, 395
Publishing, 223–27; second-channel,
　246–56

Qian Liren, 243, 244
Qian Qichen, 473
Qin Benli, 238–41
Qinghua University, 81, 209, 291
Qiushi (journal), 270–71
Qiyejia Bao (newspaper), 121

Radio, xvi; East Radio, 252, 253; in
    education, 221, 222; shadow institu-
    tions in, 252–53; talk shows, 253,
    484
Radio Free Asia, 486
Railroads, 48
Rather, Dan, 192
Red Guards, 193
Reform: agricultural, 304; criminal
    justice, 16; dual-track system of,
    306–7; economic, 21, 104, 270,
    299–346; educational, 13, 215–23;
    financial, 319–20; first wave, 302,
    303; government, 62; gradualist,
    305–6; institutional, 13, 16, 50, 327;
    journalism, 229–56; limitation of,
    3; managerial, 308–9; military, 68;
    obstacles to, 56, 300–11; opposition
    to, 50; organizational, 108–9; per-
    sonnel, 62–64; political, 5, 21,
    57–69, 104, 188, 190; radical, 3, 15;
    rationalizing, 305; repercussions of,
    17; resistance to, 13, 304; rural, 106,
    302, 303; second wave, 303, 304;
    social effects, 347–405; structural,
    62; tax, 301; third wave, 304; trade,
    303
Regionalism, 20, 113, 136, 148–50
Regulations on the Security and
    Management of Computer
    Information Networks,
    256–59

Religion, xvii, 21, 267–71; adaptation
    to socialist society, 269–71; and
    danger of destabilization, 270–71;
    lawful management of, 269–70;
    repression of, 409
Religious Affairs Bureau, 268
Renmin Ribao (newspaper), 236
Research, historical, 223–27
Research Institute for Restructuring
    Economic System, 88
Revisionism, 28, 42
Rights: abstract, 415–19; abuse of, 67,
    408–13; citizen, 65, 201; civil, xvii;
    cultural, 407; economic, 407;
    educational, 178; ethnic, xvii; to
    existence, 208, 209; gender, xvii; to
    history, 226; human, xvii, 178, 212,
    407–28, 514; individual, 179; intel-
    lectual property, 415; managerial,
    303; migration, 513; political, 201;
    property, 118, 123, 417; religious,
    xvii; social, 407; to strike, 409
Rui Xingwen, 242

Satellites, 49
Savings, 310–11
Science and Technology Daily (news-
    paper), 237
Sector, collective, 117, 118
Sector, financial, 305
Sector, household, 310
Sector, informal, 350–52
Sector, planned, 302
Sector, private, 118, 119, 121, 304, 327,
    354, 355, 369–70
Sector, public, 119
Sector, service, xv, 355
Sector, state, xv
Sector, tertiary, 326

Shalikashvili, John, 473

Shanghai, 10, 85, 108, 139, 141, 146, 226, 329, 394–401

Shanghai Academy of Social Sciences, 370

Shanghai Bureau of Radio and Television, 252

Shanghai Cable Television, 257

Shareholding system, 118

Shimonoseki Treaty, 496

Singapore, 292

Smil, Vaclav, 379

Smuggling, 73, 402

Snow, Edgar, 395

Social: alienation, 287; awareness, 124–28; change, 5, 8, 124–28; class, 133; deterioration, 400–1; dislocation, xvi, 270; disruptions, 104; engineering, 299; expectations, xvi; inequality, 103; mobility, 20; production, 118; reality, 128; revolution, 137, 380, 381; rights, 407; stability, 58, 67, 140, 146, 315, 350; trends, 511–12; welfare, 311, 318, 371, 451

Socialism: building, 54; with Chinese character, 52, 54, 75, 184; primary stage, 52–57; scientific, 75, 76, 77, 125, 134; transformation, 133; utopian, 75

Socialist: consciousness, 218, 220, 221; construction, 51, 220, 221; democracy, 16, 57, 58, 62, 65–67, 162; development, 76; economy, 53, 55, 62, 70, 119; education, 216–23; feudalism, 112; legal system, 16, 26; modernization, 16, 21, 22, 23, 26, 28, 51, 77; principles, 54; production, 35, 36; realism, 246; society, 52; transformation, 68

Socialist spiritual campaign, 270

Solinger, Dorothy, 363

Song Jian, 381

Southern Daily (newspaper), 232

Soviet Union, 3, 8, 39, 40, 117, 380, 441, 449, 462, 507

Special economic zones, 7, 68, 100, 303, 309, 348, 364

Spirit of China (television), 227

Stalin, Josef, 8, 29, 32, 35

Standard of living, xv, 20, 23, 51, 52, 100, 121, 509–10

StarTV, 254, 257, 484

State: asset drain, 119; cadres, 63, 70; employment by, xv, 348–56; fragmentation, 105, 107–8; goals, 109; industry, 303; investment, 323; loss of resources, 109–11; managerial reform in, 308–9; monopolies, 305, 308, 310; ownership, 305, 317–18, 322, 348, 350, 371, 517; planning, 304; power, 58, 134; publishing activities, 246–56; rebuilding, 13; retail sales volume, 118; revenues, 51, 103, 314; role in education, 216–23; secrets, 86; security, 117; separate from Party, 58–61

State Administration for Grain Reserves, 336–44

State Bureau of Statistics, 367

State Council, 23, 47, 48, 87, 91, 132, 199, 269–70, 319, 336–44, 339; Office of Foreign Affairs, 474; Research Office, 120; Science and Technology Commission, 232

State Education Commission, 83

State General Press and Publications Administration, 247, 251–52

State General Publishing Administration, 247

State Planning Commission, 221, 336–44; Energy Research Institute, 388

Struggle, Criticism, and Transformation campaign, 11

Subsidies, 111, 335, 338, 340

Su Leting, 402

Summer of Betrayal (Hong), 271–79

Sun Longji, 263, 264

Sun That Never Sets, The (Jia), 252

Sun Yat-sen, 421, 501

Sun Yee On triad, 396, 398, 399, 400

Su Shaozhi, 82, 238

Su Xiaokang, 226, 227

Taiwan, 85, 89, 126, 128, 152, 162, 224, 271, 292, 330, 433, 444, 465, 470, 488, 496–501, 520, 521

Taiwan Relations Act, 444

"Talks at the Yan'an Forum on Art and Literature" (Mao), 260

Tan Wenrui, 236, 237, 242, 243, 244

Tan Zhenlin, 44

Tao Siju, 400

Tao Zhu, 16, 25, 48

Tax: business, 318; concessions, 314; evasion, 73, 319; export, 319; laws, xvi; reform, 301; state, 111; system, 318–19; value-added, 318

Technology: acquisition of, 15, 36, 313; foreign, 15, 35; modernization of, 22, 55; standards, 53–54

Television, xvi; access to, 484; in education, 221, 222; growth of, 254–56; *Love for the Republic*, 227; Oriental Television, 252, 253, 257; *On the Road*, 226–27; satellite dishes, 254–56, 484; shadow institutions in, 252–53; *Spirit of China*, 227; StarTV, 254, 257, 484

Ten-Thousand-Character Manifesto, 116–35

Thatcher, Margaret, 496

Their Struggle — From Marx to Hitler, 226

Tiananmen Square, xvii, 3, 50–102, 139, 146, 152, 175–212, 262; Beijiing Spring, 3, 78–102; Goddess of Democracy, 88; hunger strikes in, 88, 199–204; incident of 1976, 25, 33, 46, 47; martial law declared, 85–95, 262; media during, 236–45; "villages of freedom," 88

Tianfeng (magazine), 271

Tibet, 271, 451, 486, 488, 489–92, 520, 521

Torture, 409, 422–28, 514

Township, village, and private enterprises, 321–34

Trade: bilateral, 450–51; compensation, 331; dependence, 450; expansion, 326; external, 450; foreign, 111, 149, 302, 313, 317, 319, 330, 450–51; monopolized, 123; reform, 303; restrictions, 315, 482

Transportation: bottlenecks in, 19; shortages, 104; underfunding of, 315

Twelfth Congress of the Chinese Communist Party, 6

Unemployment, xvii, 19, 112, 142, 329, 348–56, 362–73

United Kingdom, 493–96

United Nations, 462; Arms Register, 446; Development Programme, 359, 456; Earth Summit, 378;

United Nations (*cont.*)
  General Assembly, 407, 456; International Covenant on Civil and Political Rights, 418; International Covenant on Economic, Social, and Cultural Rights, 418; Security Council, 413, 455, 456, 465, 480; Universal Declaration of Human Rights, 407, 417, 420, 485
United States: agricultural opportunities in China, 343–44; Christian Coalition, 476; Department of Agriculture, 341; impact of China's military modernization on, 443–45; missionary complex of, 471–72; normalization of relations with, 21; policy debate on China, 475–78; reaction to Tiananmen Square incident, 85; relations with China, 6, 470–87; Taiwan Relations Act, 444; trade with China, 450–51; views on China's future, 505–30
Universal Declaration of Human Rights, 407, 417, 420, 485
"Unrequited Love" (film), 17
Urbanization, 328, 370
Utopianism, 75, 76, 125

Vietnam, 21, 431
Voice of America, 85, 93, 484

Wall posters, 157–65; bans on, 16; big-character, 197–99
Wang Chao, 208
Wang Dan, 82, 190, 243, 408
Wang Dongxing, 10
Wang Hongwen, 45
Wang Juntao, 235

Wang Ruoshui, 235
Wang Ruowang, 234
Wang Shiwei, 225
Wang Yu, 422–28
Wang Zhaoguo, 270, 271
Wan Runnan, 123, 132
Warlordism, 148
Warsaw Treaty Organization, 462
Weapons: military, 437–43; nuclear, 433; testing, 49
Wei Hua, 288
Wei Jingsheng, 161, 162, 163, 164, 165–74, 183, 409, 413
Wen Wei Po (newspaper), 82, 212
White Snow, Red Blood (Zhang), 224–27
Women's Federation, 66, 122, 353–54, 355
Workers' Daily (newspaper), 237
World Bank, xvii, 359, 368, 389–93, 408, 450, 456
World Conference on Human Rights (1993), 207
World Economic Herald (newspaper), 82, 83, 235, 238, 239, 240, 241, 256
World Health Organization, 384–85, 389–90, 517
World Trade Organization, 319, 344, 415, 433, 475, 482, 525
Wu Chaoyang, 253, 254, 257
Wu'er Kaixi, 190, 243, 244
Wu Guofeng, 209
Wu Guoguang, 234
Wu Mingyu, 238

Xiao Bo, 208
Xinhua Book Distribution Company, 247, 250, 251, 252
Xiu Yichun, 413

Xu Liangying, 419–22
Xu Wenli, 409
Xu Xiangqian, 44

Yang, Tom, 399
Yang Jianli, 204–7
Yang Liu, 427
Yang Shangkun, 25, 44, 206
Yan Jiaqi, 82, 226, 238
Yao Wenyuan, 45
Ye Jianying, 44, 47
Ye Requi, 381
Ye Weihang, 209
Ye Xiaowen, 268
Ye Zhikang, 257
Yi Ding, 415–19
Young Pioneers, 218
Yuan Li, 208
Yu Xiaosong, 212
Yu Yuefeng, 383

Zhang Chunqiao, 12, 44, 45, 47
Zhang Jin, 209
Zhang Kunmin, 388
Zhang Qing, 395
Zhang Weiguo, 256
Zhang Wentian, 39
Zhang Xianghong, 209–10
Zhang Yuan, 289
Zhang Zhenglong, 223–27
Zhao Puchu, 270
Zhao Ziyang, 6, 35, 50–79, 78, 80, 83,
    86, 87, 106, 139, 189, 190, 235, 242,
    243, 244, 496
Zhou Dadi, 388
Zhou Enlai, 10, 13, 21, 25, 32, 33, 36,
    39, 45, 46, 48, 460
Zhou Feng, 427
Zhou Xiaozhou, 39
Zhu De, 36, 45
Zhu Houze, 234
Zhu Rongji, 371